ALSO BY ALEXANDER ROSE

Washington's Spies: The Story of America's First Spy Ring
American Rifle: A Biography
The Kings of the North: The House of Percy in British History

MEN OF WAR

The American Soldier
in Combat at Bunker Hill,
Gettysburg, and Iwo Jima

MEN
OF
WAR

ALEXANDER ROSE

RANDOM HOUSE

NEW YORK

Published in the United States by Random House, an imprint and division of
Penguin Random House LLC, New York.

RANDOM HOUSE and the HOUSE colophon are registered
trademarks of Penguin Random House LLC.

LIBRARY OF CONGRESS CATALOGING-IN-PUBLICATION DATA
Rose, Alexander.
Men of war: the American soldier in combat at Bunker Hill,
Gettysburg, and Iwo Jima. / by Alexander Rose.
pages cm.
Includes bibliographical references and index.
ISBN 978-0-553-80518-5—ISBN 978-0-8129-9686-9 (eBook)
1. Battles—United States. 2. Combat—Psychological aspects—History.
3. Soldiers—United States—History. 4. United States—History,
Military—Case studies. I. Title.
E181.R77 2015
355.00973—dc23
2014030958

Printed in the United States of America on acid-free paper

www.atrandom.com

2 4 6 8 9 7 5 3 1

FIRST EDITION

Title page image: © iStock.com / LifeJourneys
Bunker Hill image: © iStock.com / Duncan Walker
Gettysburg image: © iStock.com / Constance McGuire
Iwo Jima photo by Lt. James T. Dockery, 4TH MAR. DIV.

To Rebecca, without whom this book could not have been written, and to Edmund (aged five), without whom it might have been written faster.

Contents

MEN OF WAR

Introduction

"The Lord is a man of war."
—Exodus 15:3

A single question lies at the heart of this book: What's it like being in a battle?

It's one I've been asking myself since I was an undergraduate, when I discovered, in the university bookstore, a copy of John Keegan's *The Face of Battle*, a book published just a few years after I was born. I still have it, nearly a quarter of a century later. Cheaply bound and badly printed, the old paperback sits on a shelf in my study, but such are the times that I now also own a digital version that is duplicated on a variety of electronic devices as well as a Folio Society limited edition. I can legitimately say that, as priests and Puritans once did their Bibles, I carry my Keegan with me everywhere.

To those unfamiliar with *The Face of Battle*, let me explain. Keegan, who died in 2012, investigated the experience of the common British soldier—what he felt, heard, and saw—in three epic battles: Agincourt in 1415, Waterloo in 1815, and the Somme in 1916. Keegan also discussed the mechanics of fighting—for instance, the means by which King Henry V's longbowmen demolished the French cavalry—as well as the historiography of warfare (how we write about battles over time). His book can justly lay claim to being one of the finest works of history, military or otherwise, of the twentieth century.

Keegan was an inspiration to me as a historian, and *The Face of Battle* is the inspiration for this book. While Keegan restricted himself to English/British battles, I found that there was no American version based on American battles fought by American soldiers.

Writing one was easier said than done. The great majority of military books focus not on the combat experience of the regular soldier but on history from the bird's-eye perspective.[1] Popular historians still tend to accord top billing to what quaintly used to be called the Great Captains—the Caesars, the Pattons, the Lees and Grants, the Hannibals of history. Napoleon, like many an Immortal a monster of conceit, himself believed that "it was not the Roman army which conquered Gaul, but Caesar; it was not the Carthaginian army which, at the gates of Rome, made the Eternal City tremble, but Hannibal; it was not the Macedonian army which marched as far as the Indus, but Alexander."[2] To which he did not feel the need to add, it was not the million men of the *Grande Armée* that shook Europe, but myself.

Consequently, innumerable volumes have been written about the generalship of various commanders, their leadership skills, and how they won (or lost) their battles at the operational level, but relatively few about the lowly soldiers who served under them. Bertolt Brecht, the German playwright, alluded to this curious blind spot when he asked—*contra* Napoleon:

> The young Alexander conquered India.
> Was he alone?
> Caesar beat the Gauls.
> Did he not have even a cook with him?
> Philip of Spain wept when his armada
> Went down. Was he the only one to weep?
> Frederick [the Great] won the Seven Years' War. Who
> Else won it?[3]

To be sure, commanders are important in their own right, but I was more intrigued by the overlooked and the ordinary, the men whose names are catalogued in muster rolls and inscribed on gravestones, the men who are otherwise forgotten. We know what the general on his horse thought, but what of the corporal and private at the sharp end?

What was combat like for them? I was certainly not the first to wonder. As Tolstoy once put it, "War always interested me: not war in the sense of maneuvers devised by great generals—my imagination refused to follow such immense movements, I did not understand them—but the reality of war, the actual killing."[4]

Unlike that Russian novelist, who served in the artillery during the Crimean War, I could not seek answers within the realm of my own experience. I have never heard a shot fired in anger. Like Keegan, I am not a "flesh-witness" to war.

Instead, I—following Keegan's lead—exploited my status as an impartial observer to listen to, read about, and report on what veterans thought, felt, and did. There is a surprisingly large trove of raw information available if one, say, excavates the now-forgotten volumes of regimental histories published after the Civil War. These books were written by soldiers for soldiers and in them they speak with surprising frankness of their shared experiences. Then there is the Niagara of letters, memoirs, diaries, interviews, and newspaper accounts of various soldiers over the centuries; these often contain the unvarnished sentiments of vanished ages.

Selecting three properly representative battles from the legions of firsthand sources available was critical. So allow me to explain the thinking behind my decisions to include Bunker Hill in 1775, Gettysburg in 1863, and Iwo Jima in 1945. First, this trio is not supposed to represent necessarily the most *important* clashes; none of them, for example, were, to use a dated Victorian expression, "decisive battles."[5] Instead, I settled on finding the most *iconic* battles in American history, the major battles that everyone has heard of. Even so, of course, some readers may query my choices. Why Iwo Jima, for example, and not the Battle of the Bulge? To which I can only reply, well, I thought the European theater has already been treated more comprehensively than its Pacific counterpart. That's really all there was to it. All right, then, if that's the case and we restrict ourselves to the Pacific, why Iwo and not Okinawa or Peleliu? In this instance, I would argue that I am interested in a *typical* soldier's *typical* combat experience, not the details of a particular person's response to a specific battle. In other words, the experiences of a Marine at Iwo Jima are generally applicable to, or illustrative of, those of comrades fighting on other islands. In some respects, the battles, I guess you could say, don't matter that much. I felt that Bunker Hill, Gettysburg, and Iwo Jima presented fascinating case studies of combat up close, and the fact that copious primary and secondary resources were available for each clash was an additional, and most valuable, advantage.

Certainly, a few other factors swung the final decisions one way or another. For instance, I weighted the scale in favor of actions that involved American troops within a limited area in order to exclude the additional complications engendered by the presence of allies and the sister arms of land forces. Thus, Yorktown in 1783 was rejected owing to the significant contribution of the French navy to victory over the British. This is not to diminish French valor or to bang the jingoistic drum, but *Men of War* is a book about *American* soldiers. From this perspective, then, Bunker Hill seems more optimal: It took place on a small peninsula, lasted less than a day, and involved only American militiamen and British regulars; furthermore, naval participation was peripheral. Additionally, I attempt to remain as close to the killing ground as possible. Hence, for Gettysburg I devote little space to the cavalry actions since the overwhelming brunt of combat fell on the poor bloody infantry, and in the Iwo Jima chapter you will look in vain for material on airpower, important as it was.

You may notice, as well, that by starting with the Revolutionary War and jumping to the Civil War and thence to World War II, I've omitted several rather major conflicts: the War of 1812, for example, and World War I. But this is neither an exhaustive history of American warfare nor a general overview of U.S. military history. *Men of War* is instead a collection of snapshots of American soldiers in combat, one that draws hard distinctions and highlights continuities between the evolving forms and varieties of fighting over time.

So this is, you might have gathered, an unconventional book. It is a book about battles that is not about battles. As I am concerned almost exclusively with the combat experience of soldiers, I allocate only the minimum time necessary to discussing the *course* of the battles I've chosen. I have instead included summaries of what happened and other pertinent details at the beginning of each chapter so that you can follow the action, but my focus is on what the soldiers went through. For precisely the same reason, I devote much more space to wounds, their treatment, and the psychological effects of combat than on strategy, logistics, and politics.

The battles are distinct, and each chapter has a particular structure and essential theme. That of Bunker Hill takes perhaps the most traditional approach, but its intention is more radical: It argues that, notwithstanding the zealous attempts of historians to impose an orderly interpretation on the course of Bunker Hill (dividing it into phases, stages, and so forth), this is an intellectual artifice that would be wholly unintelligible to the actual participants. There is, in other words, no single authoritative sequence of events or narrative for the battle. Even for so seemingly basic a fact as the location of many units, there are multiple possibilities.

Bunker Hill is not unique in that respect: Combat, in any battle, is inherently chaotic, and most of the time the soldiers fighting on the ground have little or no idea what is happening even fifty yards away. On Iwo Jima, to take one example, very few Marines knew what time it was, let alone the day or where they were. (Many of their watches had broken by the fourth or fifth day, and the lack of sleep confused them still further.) To take another, at Gettysburg, the ambit of one's knowledge of the battlefield extended to the men on either side, a few ahead of you, the color-bearer, and, if you were lucky, the officer on his horse behind. No one knew what was going on, and much of the time battles are decided not by clever war games or brilliant generalship but by accident, initiative, chance, and such other intangibles as morale, background, culture, ideology, and experience.

For the Gettysburg section, my intention was to reconstruct for modern readers how a Civil War infantry action worked—the ways in which the defenders and the attackers acted and felt during a typical episode. How was a charge organized? What was the best way to defeat an assault? Why did officers wear swords and soldiers wield bayonets when they inflicted hardly any casualties? How did men withstand a preliminary artillery bombardment? What did the first few minutes of a fight feel like?

To most of us, upon learning the mechanics and ethos of nineteenth-century infantry tactics, they seem quite bizarre, even rather stupid. Why did soldiers line up, advance shoulder-to-shoulder toward the enemy, and then tolerate their own slaughter? It makes no *sense*. The chapter argues that while combat on the personal level is chaotic, in fact there is a logic, grammar, and vocabulary to it that shifts over time. In the case of the Civil War, massing troops together and using their combined momentum to advance was the key to victory, not a cause of failure. To that end, the defenders would try to atomize the attacking force into its component parts and thus retard its momentum. Today, in contrast, soldiers keep their distance from each other and move forward as they think fit.

Neither should we omit the nineteenth century's emphasis on *enduring* casualties to achieve battlefield objectives. Casualty aversion, in other words, is a more modern yardstick of effectiveness, often wrongly retrofitted to past eras. Indeed, a willingness to suffer, rather than inflict, high casualties was, at that time, considered evidence of a proudly masculine and divinely suffused will to win, not a worrying signal of lunacy or incompetence. Central, then, to the Gettysburg chapter is the principle that there exists no "universal soldier," in the sense that the internal motivations and beliefs—and the external culture enveloping them—of a past generation of soldiers are not necessarily applicable to a future one.[6] That is, a warrior of ancient Greece will have a profoundly different worldview, outlook, or mentality from one of the American Civil War. Military affairs and organizations are not, therefore, static and unchanging but typified instead by diversity, variety, and evolution (hopefully forward, but sometimes backward; often random, but occasionally punctuated). Battles, it should be obvious, need to be examined in their rightful context, and their participants, too, in order to understand why and how they fought, as well as to grasp what they experienced.

As for Iwo Jima, this chapter demonstrates the ways in which soldiers learn through combat how both to survive and to become more lethal as they intersect with the enemy, who also adapts his behavior in response. The conduct of warfare, then, is always dynamic, even—perhaps especially—at the level of the private soldier. This section of the book is structured in such a way as to delineate the kind of learning curves that any army must climb to reach maximum productivity and effectiveness, the awful irony being that acquiring such knowledge entails, as the poet Auden averred, the "necessary murder" of friendly troops—the very ones who would most profit from that knowledge. This is the true pity, and tragedy, of war, which is why a good number of military historians and professional soldiers tend to be more cautious and pacific than one might perhaps expect.

It is fitting that Iwo took place at the end of a long war, by which time Americans had gained bitter experience of the Japanese and had developed new techniques to combat them, whereas Gettysburg occurs at the Civil War's midpoint and Bunker Hill at the very outset of the War of Independence. At Bunker Hill, the Americans relied on their own older, culturally specific methods; at Gettysburg, Union and Confederate forces alike employed the same contemporary tactics; but at Iwo, U.S. Marines forged new ways to defeat the defenders, even in the midst of battle.

Their willingness to adapt to circumstances so rapidly was governed by practicality: Marines found that their traditional countermeasures against the Japanese did not work on Iwo owing to the singular nature of the island's geography and their discovery that the Japanese had updated their own defensive tactics. For that matter, American perceptions of the Japanese soldier's fighting abilities had also shifted drastically since Pearl Harbor. It would have been a very foolish Marine who landed on the beach still believing that the Japanese were a verminous race of miniature, bespectacled cowards, as contemporary racist propaganda suggested. In short, despite modern assertions to the contrary, American (and Japanese) racism played little role in how the battle of Iwo Jima was fought. Culture, in this case, came a very distant second to common sense. Marines quickly learned to treat combat as a job, admittedly foul, but one that had to be executed with grim efficiency. There was nothing romantic or cinematic about their task, no glorious uniforms or glittering medals, but instead there prevailed merely the imperative to process live humans into dead ones. Yet, so affected are we by Joe Rosenthal's emotionally evocative photograph of the Marines raising the American flag atop Mount Suribachi that we tend to overlook the industrialized nature of this Pacific battle and the toll it exacted.

Terrible as it may be, it seems war has its attractions. That flag fluttering high above Iwo marks a proud patriotic achievement, and there must, after all, be other reasons for war's historically universal presence and continuing global popularity. Notwithstanding the philosophical and abstract objections to the contrary, for a significant proportion of the young, war can be fantastic fun, at least in the beginning and before disillusionment sets in. It was George Washington, fresh from his first firefight during the French and Indian War, who excitedly related to his brother that "I heard the bullets whistle, and, believe me, there is something charming in the sound."[7] (Upon hearing of this upstart's braggadocio, King George II, a more bloodied old warhorse, wryly commented, "He would not say so, if he had been used to hear many.")[8]

Quite apart from the whiff of danger acting as a stimulant, combat can be narcotically attractive in other ways. For those away from home for the first time, war is a unique chance to see exotic, astonishing, and extraordinary things beyond imagination. Not only can the sight of fine uniforms, dressed lines, and blades glinting in the sun be beautiful, the titanic destructiveness of weaponry is also spectacular.[9] Participants can easily lose themselves in the enthralling majesty of it all. General John Burgoyne, who watched the battle of Bunker Hill from Boston, rapturously captured the sensory bounty unveiled before him in a letter to his nephew:

> And now ensued one of the greatest scenes of war that can be conceived; if we look to the height, Howe's corps, ascending the hill in the face of entrenchments, and in a very disadvantageous ground, was much engaged; to the left the enemy pouring in fresh troops by the thousands, over the land; and in the arm of the sea our ships and floating batteries cannonading them; straight before us a large

and noble town in one great blaze—the church steeples, being timber, were great pyramids of fire above the rest; . . . The roar of cannon, mortars and musketry; the crash of churches, ships upon stocks, and whole streets falling together, to fill the ear; the storm of the redoubts, with the objects above described, to fill the eye; and the reflection that, perhaps, a defeat was a final loss to the British Empire in America, to fill the mind.[10]

War, then, is vile, but experiencing combat is not necessarily all to the bad—even if we may not envy those given (voluntarily or not) the opportunity to fight—for no other activity allows individuals to sample the extremes of what it means to be human. Combat encompasses unadulterated terror and grinding boredom, unstinting comradeship and man being wolf to man, callous randomness and coolly calculated risk, barbarism and unexpected virtue.

If we can take anything from this book, it would be that there is not one "Face of Battle" but many, and therein lies the root of my, and perhaps your, fascination with the experience of combat.

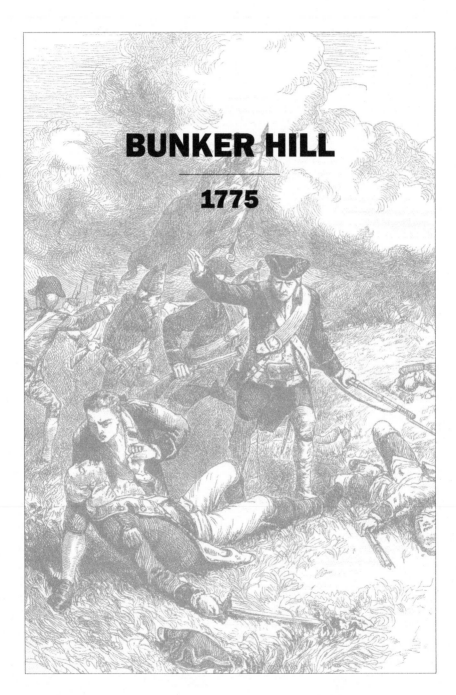

BUNKER HILL

1775

1. Introduction

The most curious thing about Bunker Hill is that, despite its iconic status in American history, it was in some respects quite a minor affair. Anywhere between 1,500 and 3,500 American militiamen—their strength varied over the course of the day, as men left and reinforcements arrived—fought roughly 2,400 to 3,000 British soldiers over the course of a few hours one pleasant afternoon on June 17, 1775, on a small peninsula across from Boston. By way of contrast, a more typical conflict of the era was the War of the Bavarian Succession between Austria and Prussia. In 1778—contemporaneous with the struggle in the American colonies—Prussia, the least populous and the poorest of the European powers, fielded no fewer than 160,000 troops.[1]

Yet these dry statistics belie Bunker Hill's consequence. As the *Annual Register* would briskly conclude near the end of the Revolution, "Most of these actions would in other wars be considered but as skirmishes of little account [though] it is by such skirmishes that the fate of America must be necessarily decided. They are therefore as important as battles in which an hundred thousand men are drawn up on each side."[2]

To its participants the battle certainly did not feel like a "skirmish": Bunker Hill holds the wretched distinction of being the bloodiest clash of the War of Independence. "I can only say from the oldest soldiers here," wrote the newly arrived Lieutenant William Feilding, "that it was the hottest fire they ever saw."[3] By day's end, almost half the British troops engaged would be dead or wounded. "Tho' Masters of the Field of Battle," one contemporary grimly judged, "the King's Troops are much the greatest Sufferers."[4] Another determined that the British army could now be divided into three: "The first company is under ground; the second is above ground; the third is in the hospital."[5] American losses were relatively small.

Before Bunker Hill, few believed that part-time militiamen could stand, face, and fight a professional army. Yet they did, and by acquitting themselves so magnificently demonstrated that the American cause was a viable and worthy enterprise. Which means we must ask: Who were they? How did they do it? And what was it like to fight at Bunker Hill?

2. The Battle

First, a summary of what happened. Late at night on June 16, 1775, a detachment of American militiamen commanded by General Israel Putnam sneakily took possession of Bunker Hill, a modest rise on the Charlestown peninsula. This triangular piece of land was attached to the Massachusetts mainland by a narrow strip called Charlestown Neck, and it jutted out between the Mystic and Charles Rivers to face Boston, where the British were holed up. Early the next morning, the British realized that these Americans were so close to Boston that they could bombard the city with cannon, but far worse, that Colonel William Prescott's men were now building an earthen "Redoubt" (a type of small fort) atop *Breed's* Hill, which was nearer even than Bunker. Once their work was done, the Americans would be so securely ensconced that it would be exceedingly difficult to dislodge them. Accordingly, British troops under General Sir William Howe were transported across the bay to the peninsula, where they prepared to assault the enemy before time ran out. Additionally, after the Americans had been put to the sword, Howe intended to advance on Cambridge, where the main American forces under General Artemas Ward were stationed. If all went well, the rebellion would be over by close of play, either that day or the next.

Meanwhile, fresh American militia units under Colonel John Stark had arrived to support Prescott, now grievously exposed at Breed's Hill. Instead of reinforcing him directly, however, they marched to *Bunker*

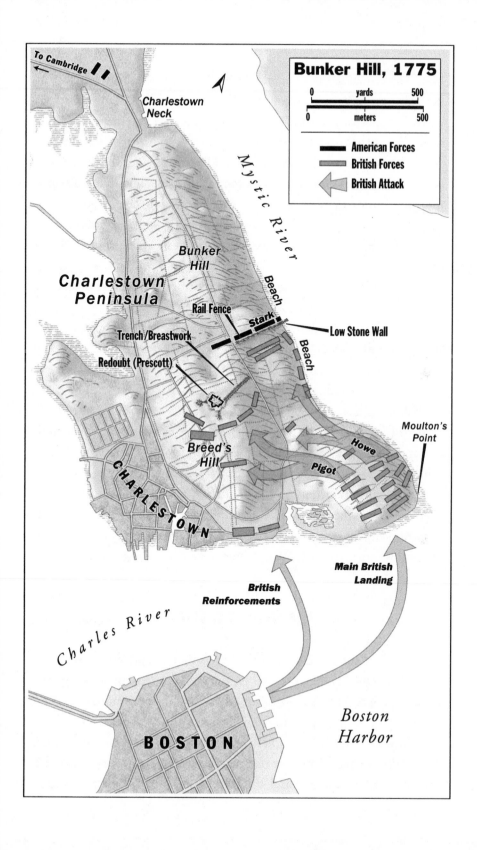

Bunker Hill, 1775

| 0 | yards | 500 |
| 0 | meters | 500 |

American Forces
British Forces
British Attack

To Cambridge

Charlestown Neck

Mystic River

Bunker Hill

Charlestown Peninsula

Beach

Rail Fence

Stark

Low Stone Wall

Trench/Breastwork

Beach

Redoubt (Prescott)

Moulton's Point

Howe

Breed's Hill

Pigot

CHARLESTOWN

British Reinforcements

Main British Landing

Charles River

BOSTON

Boston Harbor

Hill, which guarded the vulnerable Neck against a British attack from the rear. At the foot of Bunker Hill they hurriedly assembled a long defensive structure termed the "Rail Fence," which faced the spot where the British were assembling in preparation for the imminent clash. On the "Beach" directly below and perpendicular to his position, Stark built a low stone wall to prevent a surprise flank attack. Despite these precautions, Prescott had by this time realized the danger he was in and ordered his men to dig a trench, or breastwork, extending from the redoubt's walls to cover a weak spot between his position and that of Stark.

The British were now confronted by firmly entrenched defenders, making nonsense of their original plan. Even so, come what may, the Americans had to be destroyed. Howe divided his force into two divisions, the right under him, the left under Robert Pigot. Howe would attack the rail fence and the beach while Pigot assaulted Prescott's redoubt at Breed's Hill.

Following a series of bloody attacks, Howe's wing stalled but Pigot's managed to break through Prescott's defenses. A vicious bout of hand-to-hand combat sent the militiamen fleeing for the safety of Bunker Hill. Their positions lost, the Americans retreated across the Neck and set up defensive positions on the mainland. Some of the British gamely tried to pursue the enemy, but physical exhaustion and the sheer scale of Howe's losses convinced him to halt for the night. The battle of Bunker Hill was over, but the War of Independence had only just begun.

3. The Redoubt, Part One

The militiamen came garbed for battle as they did for work—as farmers and artisans.[1] Some even had on the same leather aprons they wore in their shops.[2] For the most part, the New England militia units reflected their respectable rural environments. In Captain Hutchins's company, two-thirds listed their occupations as "husbandmen"—that is, farmers—with most of the rest making a decent living as carpenters, cobblers, tailors, millers, and the like.[3] Many outfits also had within their ranks former slaves, maybe a couple of itinerants, the odd Native American perhaps, but the militiamen who fought at Bunker Hill for the most part owned property of some sort—an average-sized farm, say—and most of those who did not were the sons of men who did.

Many wore homespun shirts, sometimes made of canvas but of linen or flax in the summer, that were "a kind of loose frock, reaching half way down the thighs, with large sleeves, open before, and so wide as to lap over a foot or more when belted."[4] Their gaiters or stockings were tanned a dead-leaf color in vats, and their feet were clad in "cowhide shoes ornamented by large buckles, while not a pair of boots graced the company," as one octogenarian recollected decades later. Many had on weatherbeaten broad-brimmed hats often turned up on three sides to form a sloppy tricorne, sometimes complemented by a sprig of green or a homemade cockade; around their necks they tied an off-colored neckerchief or stock.[5]

It was hard, perhaps impossible, to distinguish the men sartorially from their officers—a profound difference to European military custom. Of the ten richest men in Lexington, for example, no fewer than eight were content to sign on as privates, and they dressed accordingly; rare indeed was the officer who took pains to get "above himself" and stand out from the crowd.

Typical was Experience Storrs of Mansfield, Connecticut, a prosperous farmer "portly in figure" who, when not tending his sick wife ("troubled with Histeruk Colluk Pains"), hewed wood, attended church, cleaned drains, worried about his colds, and mended stone walls—all while serving as his regiment's lieutenant colonel (an almost regal rank far beyond a man of Storrs's socioeconomic background in Europe). In March 1775 he agreed, with his friends Colonel Jedediah Elderkin and Major Thomas Brown, "to dress in a plain manner."[6] Similarly, at the redoubt Colonel Prescott wore a simple linen coat: British soldiers were later convinced that their foe was commanded by a "farmer dressed in his frock."[7] Even starchy Colonel John Stark, a man "always mindful of his rank," as his biographer had it, was "never a stickler for dress," restricting the peacockery to a waistcoat and some kind of "insignia."[8]

If the militiamen's outfits added up to a drab uniformity, their assortment of weapons was motley, to say the least. One veteran of the battle remembered, "Here an old soldier carried a heavy Queen's arm, with which he had done service at the conquest of Canada twenty years previous, while by his side walked a stripling boy, with a Spanish fuzee not half its weight or calibre, which his grandfather may have taken at the Havana [1762], while not a few had old French pieces, that dated back to the reduction of Louisburg [1758]."[9] Ezekiel Worthen of Kensington, New Hampshire, shouldered a French musket, made in 1752, that had been taken from the enemy, taken again by Indians, and retaken by Worthen during a skirmish. He also brought along a newer accessory: a cartridge box engraved with "Liberty or Death."[10] (Some weapons were newer acquisitions: Nathaniel Rice of East Sudbury proudly carried "a musket I took from the British at Concord.")[11]

The antiquity of most of the militiamen's pieces should not obscure their lethality. These were working, effective firearms. In an era when guns were expensive and manufacturing them was a painstaking business, it was common for even regular soldiers to use hand-me-downs. The British, for instance, were using Brown Bess muskets—still perfectly serviceable—purchased as far back as 1730.[12] By that standard, the Americans' arms, most of which dated from the French and Indian War, were relatively new and almost certainly better maintained.

Virtually every man at Bunker Hill brought his own firearm. Ascertaining exact figures for gun ownership in 1775 is extremely difficult. However, an analysis of the returns of thirty New England militia companies finds that the overall rate of private ownership was at least 75 percent and probably much higher. A keen company commander, such as Timothy Pickering of Salem, Massachusetts, ensured that 100 percent of his men were armed. Likewise, at the end of May 1775 all of the 509 men in Colonel Moses Little's Ipswich, Massachusetts, regiment were, boasted a Provincial Congress report, "armed with good effective firelocks." Meanwhile, "only" two-thirds of the fishermen from maritime Cape Cod owned their own weapons, no doubt because there was less call for them in their line of work.[13] Ultimately, those who fought at Bunker Hill would either bring their own musket, use ones illicitly stockpiled by their local militias, or, in a pinch, borrow them from stay-at-home neighbors.[14]

Like Colonel Abijah Pierce, who touted a fearsome walking cane at Lexington, the militias also lugged along a formidable, if ragged, collection of hand and edged weapons.[15] Many were repurposed from agricultural uses: At least one man was seen bearing a grain flail, numerous others with pitchforks, and a few with shillelaghs (wooden cudgels or clubs).[16]

Some armed themselves more traditionally. Cutlasses—short, machete-like hacking swords—could be wielded handily by beginners. Before he left for Boston, Israel Litchfield took the precaution of buying one, despite his complete lack of training.[17] During the battle his compatriot Israel Potter thought himself fortunate to be armed so: "Although without an edge and much rust-eaten, I found [the cutlass] of infinite more service to me than my musket" when a British officer swiped at his head with a sword. "With one well-directed stroke I deprived him of the power of very soon again measuring swords with 'a Yankee rebel.'"[18]

Nearly every American sword "had been made by our Province blacksmiths, perhaps from some farming utensil; they looked serviceable, but heavy and uncouth," remembered one veteran.[19] The country metalworkers had tried their best, but in style these weapons looked decidedly dated, as if they had been excavated from some century-old time capsule buried during the English Civil War (1642–1651). Aside from the cutlasses, American swords tended to be simple-hilted straight rapiers for thrusting.[20] For their part, recent immigrants fighting alongside the colonials tended to wield weapons from the Old Country: On the night before Bunker Hill the militant cleric John Martin girded himself with his trusty "Irish long sword," with which he soon slew one unfortunate Briton "by letting out his bowels" and another "by a stroke on the neck."[21]

What the Americans lacked and the British enjoyed in abundance were bayonets, but this would not prove a critical omission. While Captain Henry Dearborn alleged that among all the Americans there were only fifty bayonets available—and in his company just one—

bayonets were in fact rarely used in combat, their effect being primarily psychological rather than practical.[22] The bayonet, it was thought, made soldiers *feel* more aggressive when assaulting an already nervous enemy, who was liable to panic and run before a well-officered attack actually connected. But if the two sides came to blows at close quarters, a grain flail, cutlass, or pitchfork was almost certainly as dangerous as a bayonet, and probably more so. At Bunker Hill, it was only near the end, by which time the redoubt's defenders had been severely weakened by casualties and were out of ammunition, that bayonets—wielded by reinvigorated and reinforced British troops surging forward—helped to provoke flight.

For now, though—the night of June 16—the militiamen were bearing shovels, axes, and any other tools they could scrounge that could be used for entrenching.[23] Said fourteen-year-old Isaac Glynney, who was substituting for his sick father on militia duty, "I was firnishd with A Shuvel & orderd to March[.] I was Marchd on to Bunker hill [and] here I was Orderd to go to Useing [the shovel] to throw up A Brest work."[24]

Like many other participants, Glynney got Bunker and Breed's Hills confused. It was at Breed's Hill—a rise closer to Boston—that Glynney and the rest of Colonel Prescott's detachment stacked their muskets and began digging sometime between 11 P.M. and midnight. Accompanying them was Colonel Richard Gridley, a military engineer whose experience extended back to even before the French and Indian War.[25]

Gridley staked out an outline of what was to be called the "redoubt." This small fort was roughly 132 feet square, or rather, slightly rectangular, oriented northeastward.[26] Because Prescott insisted that the redoubt's walls be as complete and as high as possible, each man was detailed to labor for a one-hour shift, then to stand on watch for the next to rest, alternating through the night.[27] Gridley and Prescott both knew that when the British began shelling their position, the men, if they weren't protected, would break. The colonels agreed on six-foot-high earthen walls with a wooden and dirt platform running along the inner perimeter for the militiamen to stand on. Then, only their heads (and muskets) would be visible from outside.[28] Given the time constraints, it is unlikely that the walls to the rear were as lofty or as sturdy as those in front, but they would nevertheless afford a measure of protection. A break in the rear wall would serve as a passage for reinforcements and supplies—or a retreat.

The existing literature on the battle pays no attention to the design of this fort atop Breed's Hill, a consequence of assuming that Gridley improvised the fortifications and that they were nothing more than a few dirt walls, hastily dug. That the fort was quickly constructed—and left unfinished—is certainly true, but haste should not obscure the degree of knowledge and skill that Gridley applied to the task. Prescott's fort was in fact a scaled-down version of a European-style fortification. Indeed, at the time the name "redoubt" had a specific meaning: "a detached work, enclosed on all sides."[29] It was no ordinary rectangle, either, for as contemporary maps highlight, from the center of its southeastern wall (known as the *enceinte,* or main perimeter) jutted, prow-like, a hybrid of a ravelin and a bastion. Technically speaking, ravelins—a triangular structure described by the Marquis de Vauban (1633–1707), the French master of the lethal geometry of fortifications whose works were undoubtedly familiar to Gridley, as "beyond all doubt the best and most excellent of all outworks"—were freestanding, while bastions were four-sided edifices (two angled faces with two flanks) that looked like sharpened, angular spearheads and were attached to a wall.[30]

Ravelins and bastions enabled the defenders of a fortress to fire backward to either side to thwart attacks on the main wall while promoting greater depth of defense. Gridley's dirt-and-wood redoubt would not hold out for long against a concentrated artillery barrage or a sustained siege, but we should remember that he had had but a night to build it, that it was intended as a temporary defense, and above all that, thanks to its ravelin/bastion protrusion, inner platform, and good sightlines, it presented a formidable obstacle to British assaults.[31]

It would not be the only one. Later in the morning, Prescott would realize that he had left his northern, Mystic River–facing flank exposed, and so directed his men to dig a sixty-foot-long, four-foot-wide trench with a rudimentary breastwork made out of the excavated dirt. Connected to the redoubt, the breastwork was not much, but it would have to do.[32]

At about 4 A.M., when a lookout awoke him with news that the Americans seemed to be building a fort on the peninsula, Captain Thomas Bishop of HMS *Lively*, a twenty-gun sloop patrolling the bay, wasted no time beating to quarters and opening fire on the redoubt.[33] His guns soon began to take their toll, psychologically as well as physically.

No other class of weaponry inspired as much trepidation and fear in infantry as artillery. "A young soldier is much more alarmed at a nine-pounder shot passing within four yards of his head than he is of a bullet at a distance of as many inches," the British officer George Hennell later observed, "although one would settle him as effectively as the other."[34] Understandably so, for the feeling of powerlessness that came of being under fire from afar was then and still is among soldiering's greatest terrors. "The standing to be cannonaded, and having nothing else to do, is about the most unpleasant thing that can happen to soldiers in an engagement," said one veteran.[35] "To be exposed to fire without being able to return it," wrote another, was like "receiving a personal insult, and not having the power to resent it."[36] Unlike frontier fighting or close-quarters combat, where one's judgment, experience, and initiative could reduce the physical dangers, artillery fire rendered all such virtues irrelevant. A cannonball knew no distinction between veterans and rookies, but killed seemingly indiscriminately, randomly, instantly.

The good news was that once they accepted that their lives were in the hands of blind Fate, divine Providence, or dumb Luck (and had survived intact a fusillade or two), most soldiers tamed their instinct to panic. At Bunker Hill, Captain John Chester said, only his "new recruits" were "terribly frightened" by the cannon shot "buzz[ing] around us like hail."[37] In these moments, to calm their fears, officers made sure to inform them that relatively few fatalities were actually caused by cannon fire. "It frightens more than it hurts," as one French marshal used to assure his understandably skeptical troops.[38]

He was right, up to a point: In the eighteenth century, artillery accounted for just over 20 percent of all casualties.[39] A great deal, however, hinged upon whether the incoming fire was concentrated and aimed—which was more lethal—or merely an occasional barrage—which was much less so, owing to its random distribution.[40] Whether the defending troops were formed up in the open or scattered around under cover also made a great difference. At Bunker Hill in both cases, the latter form at this stage was typical, leading to relatively low American casualties.

Those who grasped the principle that a cannon's bark was worse than its bite often proceeded on their merry way, even as shells fell around them. Dr. James Thacher later saw American troops attending church who manifested "little or no fear of the consequences" and kept singing when a few cannonballs crashed through a wall or the roof.[41] In every case, officers were expected to affect a languid manner no matter how "hot" the shot. Near the redoubt, old General Putnam—who had seen it all before—"appeared unintimidated, as if they had not fired a gun," according to John Dexter, who watched him stride back and forth.[42] William Low thought that "Putnam was as cool as ever a man was."[43] Another veteran who remained unfazed was a man named Hill, a British deserter, who, said a grateful Amos Foster, "watched [the] British [guns], and, when they were about to fire, [he warned us and] we all laid down."[44] Having a few such men around to assuage the worries of others made an enormous difference.

Nevertheless, when artillery bit, its bite hurt. Direct hits were invariably fatal. At Bunker Hill, Major Andrew McClary, a New Hampshire tavernkeeper, would be torn apart when "a random shot . . . passed directly through his body."[45] And the head of a Dr. Dole outside Boston would be carried off by a cannonball with such force that a passing sergeant saw nothing but "a piece of the skin of his head with the hair on it, which was of a light brown beginning to be sprinkled with white hairs."[46]

Cannon fire, though, often affected more than just a single individual. A solid, round iron ball, launched into the side of a rank of men—known as "firing in enfilade"—would kill the first few and might grievously wound the next several.[47] During the battle, Private Peter Brown saw a British cannonball fired in enfilade that "cut off three men in two"—in other words, sever them in half.[48] Sergeant Elisha Bostwick described another that "first took the head of Smith, a stout heavy man & dash't it open, then it took off Chilson's arm which was amputated & he recovered it, then took Taylor [through] the bowels, it then struck Sergt. Garret of our company on the hip [and] took off the point of the hip bone." (Smith, Taylor, and Garret died.)[49]

Even so, shot that hit troops directly was not as panic-inducing as that which landed a distance off and bounced toward them at thigh height—perfect for crippling.[50] Though less immediately lethal than a direct hit, these balls that "grazed" the ground were particularly effective against dense formations. One contemporary soldier noticed that "balls which the troops perceive striking the ground about 100 or more paces in front of them, and approaching them with short bounds, cause much unsteadiness, waving, pressing, and confusion in the ranks, as everyone endeavours to get out of their way." Perhaps worse, whereas a soldier could sometimes see the dark sphere of a cannonball looming larger in the sky as it descended and plan to be elsewhere when it landed, one caroming off rough ground could be deflected in almost any direction. Nowhere was safe.[51]

Wounds caused by artillery were more terrible than ones inflicted by musket balls. Cannonballs, when they collided at full speed with an abdomen or chest, tore a hole corresponding to their size—a 12-pound round had about a 4.5-inch diameter—and splattered viscera outward. Hitting a leg or arm resulted in a stump left behind with a nearly smooth, darkly bruised layer of pulpified tissue with the bone sticking out.[52] A round, by way of comparison, might require a surgical amputation but never could remove an entire limb at a stroke.

Injuries to other parts of the body amply demonstrated the difference between the two types of ammunition. While the American surgeon Dr. Thacher tended one young soldier who had "received a musket ball through his cheeks, cutting its way through the teeth on each side, and the substance of his tongue," the victim later began "to articulate tolerably well." Another of his patients, however, "had the whole side of his face torn off by a cannon ball, laying his mouth and throat open to view."[53] He would have died soon afterward.

From relatively short ranges, mysteriously, a cannonball could kill or wound without even making contact. Captain Ebenezer Bancroft was standing near the redoubt when "a ball from the *Somerset* passed within a few inches of my head, which seriously affected my left eye so that it finally became totally blind."[54] Later, John Martin felt a cannonball hurtling past his chest "without touching." He was knocked briefly unconscious and upon wakening "vomited or raised much blood." Alive but "still in pain at his breast" and concussed, Martin could fight no more that day.[55]

Owing to the kinetic violence of an artillery hit, surgeons occasionally found parts of other men lodged in a comrade. One discovered a piece of jaw wedged in another man's palate, the item belonging to a friend whose head had disintegrated. Eyes, owing to their gelatinousness, made a prime site for foreign objects: There was a soldier whose eyeball contained someone else's tooth and another with a skull fragment lodged underneath his eyelid. In one wounded soldier's thigh, a doctor found three coins, none of which had originally belonged to the fellow in question.[56]

More common, at least among those new to war, were dreadful wounds to the feet and ankles caused by expended balls rolling sluggishly along. Asa Prince, for instance, had his ankle dislocated by one such as he crossed the Neck on his way to Bunker Hill. Luckily, he had only to crack it back into its socket and continue onward.[57] Others, not so fortunate, "lost their feet" when they "were crushed by the weight of the rolling shot" as they tried to stop them. After that, the more experienced men cautioned youngsters "against touching a ball, until it was entirely at rest," according to John Trumbull.[58]

At the redoubt, Private Asa Pollard of Billerica, a scout during the French and Indian War, knew enough to refrain from trying to stop cannonballs but became the battle of Bunker Hill's first victim when he sat down on the dirt embankment to devour a few leftover scraps of food.[59] Working nearby, Amos Foster saw how the fatal ball "struck the ground and hopped along before it struck him," evidently from behind. The cannon shot tore off Pollard's head.[60] Now that the *Lively's* guns had found their range, casualties began to mount. Soon, Aaron Barr of Captain Maxwell's company was struck by another cannonball that sheared off his leg. He was trundled back to Cambridge but died later in the day.[61]

Pollard's death and Barr's hideous cries scared the rest of the men, especially the younger ones. Colonel Prescott urgently needed to put a stop to the murmurings and reinspire confidence before their fears led them to put down their tools and retreat, or desert, back across the Neck. As it was, said a witness, "a number of the men [had already gone] and never returned."[62] William French of Dunstable, more bluntly, said that "some slunk off" at this time.[63]

Thus, when a subaltern asked what to do about Pollard, the colonel curtly ordered, "Bury him." "What? Without prayers!" replied the shocked lieutenant. Prescott conceded that a service could be held later. Unmollified, the men continued to congregate around the corpse, prompting Prescott's demand that Pollard's body be thrown into a trench and immediately covered with soil. The sooner Pollard disappeared, the sooner his troops would forget their fears. The colonel only reluctantly consented to a quick service then and there when a minister noisily insisted on a Christian burial, which was attended, under fire, by Pollard's company. After that, Prescott told them to get back to digging.

In ordering Pollard's funeral and distracting the men's minds with work, Prescott hoped to prevent them becoming maudlin about the loss of their comrade, but they clearly needed an additional dose of encouragement. Leaping onto the parapet, he leisurely walked back and forth, here encouraging the men, there entertaining them with a joke. He neither ducked nor flinched as the cannonballs flew over. Every man could see him, and Prescott was soon joined by other captains. By dint of such leadership, "the men soon became indifferent to the fire of the artillery" even after several more of them were killed— and just as rapidly removed from sight. (After the battle, the British found near the redoubt a mass grave, about two feet deep, containing a number of corpses, probably including Pollard's, of men killed in the artillery barrage.)[64]

For the moment, Prescott's actions successfully calmed the urge to run. As the sun rose and the day proceeded, however, the instinct for self-preservation would grow more pronounced. By late morning, his men could witness for themselves the forces gathering for the coming assault—as well as discover how vulnerable they were in their half-finished dirt fort. "We saw our danger being against ships of the line and all Boston fortified against us," wrote Peter Brown. "The danger we were in made us think there was treachery, and that we were brought there to be all slain."[65]

Brown was right to be alarmed. The militiamen had to sustain themselves on only a bite of bread and a nip of rum (the British had landed a lucky shot that blew up their two hogsheads of water). Having labored since midnight, they were exhausted. There were no reinforcements expected, no rescue anticipated. The arrival of three or four heavily armed boats—floating batteries—allowed the British to continue their bombardment. Joined by the *Lively*—and later the *Falcon* and the *Somerset* as well as the *Glasgow* and the *Symmetry*—they made any further work on the entrenchments too dangerous, even for the jaunty Colonel Prescott.[66] Now the redoubt's sole line of communication and retreat lay across the Neck, easily swept by naval fire. Prescott's Last Stand beckoned.

As the militiamen hunkered down, they could see the British forming their attack units on the Boston wharves.[67] British regiments at the time generally had attached two elite, or "flank," companies—one Grenadier, the other Light—which could be split off from the ordinary battalion, or line, companies for special operations. Grenadiers, chosen from their regiment's beefiest, tallest, and most aggressive men, represented brute force and served as heavy shock troops. The average height of the Grenadiers in the 4th Regiment, for instance, was five feet eleven inches—counted as gigantic at the time—while that of the hatmen (normal battalion troops) was five feet eight inches.[68]

The Lights were a recent innovation, one dating from the French

and Indian War and a particular specialty of General Howe, commanding the nascent expeditionary force. In rocky, hilly, or forested terrain,
a regiment's most agile and sure-footed soldiers were used as scouts and
sweeping flankers. They traveled fast, too, jogging several miles at a
time to catch the enemy unawares. Howe believed his Lights would
play a critical role in the battle to come, for, as a British military writer
of the time judged, they were especially useful for "seiz[ing] upon elevated positions and important posts, with a rapidity peculiar to themselves."[69]

At this early stage, the British plan appears to have been to land the
main Grenadier/Light formation plus two regiments (the 5th and the
38th) at Moulton's Point. Once ashore, the Grenadiers, supported by
the battalion companies, would assault the redoubt while the Lights
nosed toward the Neck. The latter's tasks would be to reconnoiter
ahead for American positions, to harry and trap soldiers fleeing the redoubt, and to shield the Neck and Bunker Hill from enemy counterattack. Meanwhile, the transports would return to Boston and convey a
second wave of regiments—the 43rd and the 52nd—to the peninsula.
Once Prescott had surrendered, the 1st Marines and the 47th Regiment would land, after which the remaining British forces in Boston
would be ferried over. That night, or perhaps the next morning, the
main army would move on Cambridge to destroy whatever was left of
the Americans.

Given the commotion on the Boston shorefront, it is not surprising
that when General Putnam arrived after midday and asked Prescott to
send a party back to Cambridge with the tools, the colonel retorted
that "not one of them would return." Nonsense, cried Putnam patri-
otically, "They shall every man return."[70] Prescott, knowing that the
tools were more valuable than the men, let his people go. Captain Bancroft, who witnessed the exchange, discreetly remarked that "an order
was never obeyed with more readiness." A group of volunteers enthusiastically picked up a shovel or two and "hurried over the hills." Few
would return.[71]

With the British assault imminent, it was again critical to buttress
the faltering confidence of those left behind at the redoubt. Prescott

and Putnam rallied the men with one of the most vivid and memorable exhortations in American history: "Don't fire until you see the whites of their eyes." What is less well known is that that cry was not conceived in 1775, but some time before, during Frederick the Great's wars in Europe. The first recorded instance of its use occurred on May 22, 1745, when Prince Charles Alexander directed his Austrians awaiting Prussia's strike to be "silent, till you see the whites of their eyes."[72] The phrase seems to have taken off, and by 1757, at the battle of Prague, it was sufficiently familiar to be included in the General Orders to the Prussian infantry: "By push of bayonets; no firing till you see the whites of their eyes."[73]

In America, older soldiers had picked up the catchphrase in the intervening decades. At Bunker Hill, it seems to have been not Prescott but General Putnam who first used it. Israel Potter in the redoubt wrote that at about noon the general "charged us to be cool and to reserve our fire until the enemy approached so near as to enable us to see the whites of their eyes."[74]

Yet there were more men who did *not* hear Putnam at all but were nevertheless familiar with the rally. For instance, Elijah Jordan recalled that "while we were waiting . . . orders were given to us not to fire till we could see the whites of their eyes; and this order, I was then told, came from Gen. Putnam; but I did not hear it from him."[75]

So, who said what when? The confusion highlights the problem of the mechanics of what is technically known as a "harangue": brief pep talks intended to buttress and burnish the confidence of soldiers.[76] Generally speaking, the shorter, more informal, and less complicated a harangue, the more effective it is, particularly when the commander is trusted and respected by his men. The Duke of Wellington, for one, never bothered with long speeches, high-minded sentiment, or impressive grammar. What was the point, he asked, "since you cannot conveniently make it heard by more than a thousand men standing about you?"[77]

To spread the word as far and as rapidly as possible, there were two methods of delivery. First, the commander paced up and down the line successively addressing units with a selection of rousing apothegms until all had heard at least one.[78] Second, he could declaim once, and his subordinates would pass the message down to their respective units.

What probably happened in the American lines, then, is that Putnam visited the redoubt before the fighting began. He did not give just one speech to everyone at once but toured the defenses bucking up the men here and there with the catchy exhortation not to shoot until they could see the whites of the enemy's eyes. Once the general had left, the mantra was repeated and emphasized by Prescott and his subordinates. The colonel, for instance, was remembered as imploring his paladins to "wait till you see the whites of their eyes"—but added, as a soundly thrifty New England militia chief would, "waste no powder."[79]

By 1 P.M., Prescott had also sent a 200-strong Connecticut detachment under Captain Thomas Knowlton to stake out Moulton's Point and give the British a warm welcome as they landed. But on his way there Knowlton was likely prevailed upon by General Putnam—who may, despite his brave words, have been having second thoughts as to the wisdom of a knockdown fight at the redoubt—to withdraw to Bunker Hill and establish a strong defense there to forestall a British rush for the Neck and keep an escape route open for Prescott's men. Once the British attack began in earnest, the Connecticuters could fire off a few volleys at the enemy before themselves wriggling free from Howe's noose and withdrawing. There would be neither a "battle of Bunker Hill" nor a capitulation, merely another Lexington writ larger.

Meanwhile, on the coast, as his scarlet-clad soldiers formed into three orderly lines, Howe paused. There in the distance, toward Bunker Hill, he could see thickening clouds of men where there were supposed to be none—as well as a defended position, also not there just an hour or two before. Suddenly, his first wave of 1,550 redcoats—a force he had assumed would be more than sufficient to cow Prescott or, if need be, take the redoubt and race ahead to the Neck—looked too few for the job.

What Howe was witnessing were Colonels John Stark and James Reed's New Hampshire regiments taking their place alongside Knowlton at a place commonly dubbed the "rail fence." Soon, even more men would arrive in response to the alarms being sounded throughout the

American camps. "Turn out! The enemy's all landed at Charlestown," Stephen Jenkins of Captain John Noyes's company remembered crying.[80] What had happened was that General Ward, informed of Howe's arrival, had finally decided that he must hold the British at the peninsula rather than passively wait for them in Cambridge and had directed every available man to speed to Charlestown. There was going to be a battle, after all.

Reacting to the American change of plan, Howe improvised. It was now critical to amputate the peninsula from the Neck without delay. As it was, Americans were already streaming over Bunker Hill.[81] No longer could the redoubt be the primary objective and seizing the Neck the secondary; now, rail fence and redoubt were of equal importance. *Both* needed to fall in order to conquer the peninsula. To that end, once the second wave of troops arrived, Howe split his forces more or less in half.

He would command the right division, comprising the nippy Light infantry (about 350 men), the ponderous Grenadier spearhead (about the same), and 500 to 600 line troops of the 5th and 52nd Regiments. He assigned the left division to Brigadier General Robert Pigot. That wing, of 600 to 750 line troops drawn mostly from the 38th and 43rd Regiments, would eventually be joined by the 47th Regiment and the 1st Marines under Major Thomas Pitcairn, adding another 600 to its number. Remaining behind in Boston as reserve but already preparing to leave were 140 men of the Light and Grenadier companies of the 63rd Regiment and the 2nd Marines.[82]

Howe's men were entrusted with the task of breaking the rail fence and thence rushing to block Charlestown Neck. In the meantime, Pigot's men would assault the redoubt and then swing rearward to flank the rail fence, should it still be standing. It was a tall order, but Howe expected a quick victory thanks to his excellent land artillery. After all, no fewer than six 6-pounders, two 12-pounders, and two 5.5-inch howitzers would soften up the defenders before the attacks even began.[83] Probably begged by Pigot for extra support, Howe shifted several of his guns to the center to help enfilade the breastwork shoring up Prescott's redoubt. This would ultimately prove to be a wise decision.

Howe's artillery alone might have been sufficient to cleanse the peninsula of militiamen but for a disastrous problem with his ammunition supply. Possibly due to the incompetence, or inattention, of his colonel of artillery, Samuel Cleaveland, who, it was widely rumored, "spends his whole time in dallying with the schoolmaster's daughters," Howe brought over crates of twelve-pound balls but no six-pounders, rendering most of his guns useless.[84] Perhaps, but it is also possible that the soldiers detailed to lug the ammunition simply brought the larger ones by mistake. Alternatively, young Benjamin Lovell, the clerk of artillery stores, *might* have been prevailed upon by his brother, James Lovell—a future member of the Continental Congress—to send the wrong ammunition deliberately. (The "schoolmaster" referred to above, perhaps not uncoincidentally, was their father, a Loyalist later judged to be insane.)[85] Whatever the reason for the mix-up, it meant that Howe would have to rely much more on his infantry than he had originally intended.

For maximum effect, the dual attacks on redoubt and rail fence were to take place simultaneously—a tough proposition owing to the hilly terrain between Howe and Pigot that obscured their sightlines and left them unable to communicate in a timely manner. The upshot was that the two wings would have to work autonomously, each commander hoping that his counterpart was keeping both pace and to the plan.

Within minutes at the beach, this optimistic scheme would come to grief.

4. The Beach

As ten companies of Howe's Grenadiers, backed up by the 5th and 52nd Regiments, splayed across the field, eleven companies of Light infantry formed below in a narrow but long column on the peninsula's "beach"—in actuality a muddy, stony shelf several yards wide at low tide. The intention was to launch a sneak flank attack while the heavy and regular troops diverted the attention of the rail-fence defenders with a frontal advance.

Within minutes of arriving at the rail fence, Colonel Stark, however, had perceived the danger and sent one of his best companies under Captain John Moore—a wily veteran of the French and Indian War—to clamber down the bank and build a low stone wall, behind which they were now crouched in a triple row. Owing to the curvature of the shoreline, the Lights and the Americans could not see each other.[1]

The British had not thought to scout ahead, and the leading company of the Lights—that of the 23rd Regiment, better known as the Royal Welch Fusiliers—advanced confidently to its doom, four men abreast in eight rows.[2] Not until they were 100 to 150 yards away from the stone wall did it begin to dawn on the Lights that the Americans had anticipated their move. When they finally saw Moore and his militiamen, the British probably halted around the curve to consult urgently with Howe via messenger.

Howe ordered forward the Lights. It was the worst possible plan of attack, but he desperately needed to coordinate their advance with that of his Grenadiers against the rail fence. The 23rd Regiment's Lights began to pick up speed; once they were between 50 and 80 yards from the American position, Moore's Yankee accent could be heard bawling for his men to open fire. When the first volley smashed into the 23rd, the front rows immediately toppled over, and the men behind them, suddenly stopping short, began tripping over their fallen comrades as those farther back collided with those in front of them. The slippery mud, the ankle-twisting rocks, and the tide's lapping waves only compounded the confusion. The officers desperately tried to rally their men into some sort of order as incessant sheets of fire roiled the ranks. It did no good. Within a minute, at least a third of the company was down. Miraculously, not a single man was killed instantly—testament to the Americans' lack of murderous accuracy, which had been sacrificed for rapidity—though over the coming months two corporals, a drummer, and six privates would die of their injuries; a sergeant and four privates remained disabled, probably permanently.[3] To the Americans, no other battle action "exhibit[ed] equal scenes of blood in so short a time from so few men engaged."[4] Abigail Adams informed her husband, John, two days later that "our enemies were cut down like grass before the scythe."[5]

The remaining men of the 23rd naturally recoiled backward to escape the furious slaughter. As they could not run sideways, there was nowhere for them to go but to barge, pushing and brawling, into the ranks of the unit behind them—the Lights of the 4th Regiment—instigating further derangement as companies successively collapsed under continuing American fusillades.

This phenomenon of panic rippling through the ranks is a relatively common one. A Prussian named Küster who fought at the battle of Hochkirch in 1758 recalled what it felt like to be unexpectedly gripped by panic: "All of a sudden I was overtaken by a fear which deprived me of all my courage, and a terror which set my limbs a-trembling. A little child could have pushed me over."[6] Then came the relentlessly insistent urge to run.

Panic rarely breaks out simultaneously among an entire group. Instead, flight involves at first only a few individuals—like the survivors of the 23rd or Küster—whose behavior then adversely influences those nearby. Once it begins, the effect of "panic upon a multitude," said an officer who saw troops fall to pieces in 1780, is "like sympathy, it is irresistible where it touches."[7] The astounding rapidity with which the cantagion spreads "can only be fully realized by those who have witnessed a false alarm on a dark night with an army in the field," warned Viscount Wolseley, a nineteenth-century general. "When under the influence of panic, men for the moment are mad, and act without reason. Whilst the fit lasts, they are capable of the most idiotic actions [and] nothing but some violent shock . . . or some chance and often trifling occurrence brings them back to the grave realities of their position."[8]

At the bloody beach, there was no such "violent shock" to bring the Lights back to their senses. Instead, the situation only worsened when the rear units—which had suffered no casualties—took fright as the forward companies came scrambling pell-mell around the curve. The men at the back had not yet seen what was happening up front. They had heard the cries of pain and the crash of muskets, they smelled the smoke, they felt the anxiety wafting in the air, but this excess of sensory stimuli went unmatched by hard information. In the absence of data on what lay around the fatal bend—ultimately, just a company of militiamen, greatly outnumbered—they could not make rational assessments of risks and probabilities. So they imagined instead the fearful and awful things awaiting them: a battery of artillery, perhaps, or American cavalry, or thousands of reinforcements. Dread of the unknown turned these otherwise disciplined infantrymen into a stampeding horde, proving the old military rule of thumb that it is always the troops in the least immediate danger who turn and run first.[9]

According to Peter Thacher, who was watching the debacle from across the Mystic River, the entire column of Lights "retreated in very great disorder down to the point where they [had] landed, and there some of them even [scrambled] into their boats." Their officers, chasing them, used "the most passionate gestures and even push[ed] forward the men with their swords." After a time, they successfully managed to prod some of the men back onto the beach, but when they suffered another of Moore's broadsides, the remnant of the Lights again fled to Moulton's Point and the safety of their landing craft.[10] Howe's flanking gambit had failed disastrously.

Worse, some of the shaken and shuddering remnants of the Lights scrambled up to the field above, where the Grenadiers had started their advance toward the rail fence, and opened fire. They were, in the words of an officer writing in the *Edinburgh Advertiser,* "in such consternation that they fired at random, and unfortunately killed several of [the Grenadier] officers." For a more precise account of what happened, we must rely on a private letter written by Lieutenant Colonel James Abercrombie, who was commanding the Grenadier companies. The Lights, said Abercrombie, "gave me a plumper [army slang for volley] and killed two officers and three privates." Perhaps another twenty men were wounded. Abercrombie himself was shot in the middle of his right thigh and would die of an infection five days later, but not before understatedly mentioning that the Lights "must be drilled before they are carried to action again."[11]

Abercrombie's comment highlights a deeper truth regarding the beach assault. The real cause of the collapse on the beach was not the tactical situation—had the British surged ahead, Moore's defenders would have been overrun—but the Lights' unreadiness for combat. They were, in other words, susceptible to disintegration even before Moore unleashed his volleys. Historically, when a unit with a large proportion of battle-seasoned veterans panics, the underlying reason is often administrative incompetence: excessive demands on already combat-stressed men or retention at the battlefront past their peak effectiveness.[12] Raw or inexperienced soldiers, in contrast, tend to run when unpleasantly shocked by enemy action or the novelty of combat. Lacking the bonds of unit pride and loyalty to comrades, which require substantial spells of training and service to develop, individuals have little to lose if they forbear sacrificing themselves for the greater good of the outfit or their friends.[13] Even so, the presence of a respected leader can often induce them to return to their positions either by appeals to remember their duty or by a violent act (such as shooting "cowards").[14]

On that beach, not only were there few such respected leaders, either because they were dead or too new to their positions (Captain Thomas Mecan had taken over the 23rd Lights only that morning) to have earned sufficient trust, but British morale, experience, and training were also quite poor to begin with.

There is a long-standing idea that the British army was at the time the finest in the world.[15] Perhaps it was, but even so, the regiments stationed in Boston in 1775 could not be said to be the cream of the crop. Too often forgotten is that before the running skirmish at Lexington and excepting a minor war against the Caribs, the British had not seen real combat since the battles of Minden and the Plains of Abraham (both times against the French) in 1759. Back then, more than half of British soldiers had been older than thirty, with a fair deal of fighting under their belts. By Bunker Hill, that cohort of now-gray-haired veterans had mostly retired. Though there were still a few "Old Soldiers" around—such as John Henderson, a veteran of Culloden in 1746 and a soldier under Wolfe at Quebec—who could keep order among the younger men when the lead started flying, they had their work cut out for them.[16] The army as a whole in Boston contained a significant proportion of soldiers who had served several years in uniform, but very few had any combat experience at all; they were accustomed only to peacetime duty.[17]

Junior officers tended to be unblooded, green, often new to the army. On June 9—not even ten days before Bunker Hill—General Thomas Gage ordered that because "there are many young officers who have lately joined their Corps, [their superiors] will take care that they are instructed in their duty, and not put on out-guards or posts of consequences till they are well informed, and have a knowledge of what they are to do." He was not amused to discover a week later that these selfsame young officers had been sending their troops out on exercises while they luxuriated in their quarters.[18]

In a telling indication that the raw officers and soldiers ignorant of battle conditions at the Boston garrison desperately needed practice, on June 14—only three days before the battle—Gage urgently directed that every regiment "will drill the recruits and drafts without a day's delay . . . beginning with the platoon exercise, and teaching them to fire ball. Proper marksmen to instruct them in taking aim and the position in which they ought to stand in firing. And to do this man by man before they are offered to fire together."[19]

To understand the import of Gage's words, it is crucial to know that five stages of drill were taught. Following a course in the fundamentals of marching, the first was the "manual exercise," in which the recruit learned the tedious sequence of movements allowing him to load and fire his musket and to use a bayonet. The second was the "platoon exercise," a step that showed soldiers how to fire in volley as quickly as possible. After this came the advanced exercises, such as "evolutions" (about-turns, left-turns, closing files, and the like), "firings" (an elaborate system designed to perfect firing when advancing, retreating, and standing by section), and, finally, "manoeuvres" (a fiendishly complex repertoire of battlefield deployments).[20] Gage's *specific* instruction to begin training with the "platoon exercise" indicates that many of his Boston regiments had completed only the most basic training. Their lack of fire control and tactical coordination would exact a dreadful toll during the coming battle.

Gage also mentioned the men known as "drafts," a reference to the custom wherein soldiers serving in various regiments at home and abroad could be transferred away from their friends and family to fill slots where needed. In early 1775, America was clearly the next battleground, and drafts were dispatched as reinforcements. The official size of each regiment in or bound for the Colonies was increased from 380 privates to 560, though in actuality their strengths varied.[21] To take a more specific example, roughly a quarter of the men in the Grenadier companies of the 4th, 52nd, and 59th Regiments were fresh drafts. These newcomers lacked the opportunity to meld and assimilate with the old-timers, to learn their rhythms and habits, and it was perhaps no coincidence that these units would suffer among the highest casualties on June 17.[22]

As late as June 12, the Grenadiers were still bringing in unfamiliar men who had never trained for a heavy-infantry, first-strike role. The Grenadiers were capable soldiers individually, but at the company level they sorely needed more time to integrate their disparate elements and increase their military effectiveness and esprit de corps.[23] More broadly, the various Grenadier companies were unaccustomed to working jointly, and there had been virtually no collective training. Indeed, they had formed together for exercises just once (on June 4) after Lexington.

The baleful state of a significant portion of British regiments at the time can be quantified using the example of the three companies of the 18th Regiment, which were sent to Boston in October 1774 and spliced together with two companies of the 65th. It's possible that this composite battalion stood out to contemporaries as a particular handful—we have no explicit data either way for any other regiment in Boston at the time—but what is certain is that immediately afterward, the number of disciplinary problems rocketed. Between October 1774 and May 1775, no fewer than a third of the composite battalion's strength of 218 men were punished, one third of those multiple times. Drunkenness was cited most of the time, as well as the kind of disorderly behavior (insolence, fighting, and causing disturbances) that was no doubt often exacerbated by booze. About four in ten men had been sentenced to receive one hundred lashes.[24]

Gage's measures before Bunker Hill were too little, too late. Bad habits among the regulars could be broken only by proper training, purges of troublesome officers and men, the evolution of cohesion, and the annealment of combat, which is why Lieutenant Richard Williams concluded that "it requires one campaign at least, to make a good soldier."[25] Some musketry practice here and there, in other words, could not compensate for the hard hand of war, competent leadership, and unit pride.

Unfortunately for the British, age, experience, cohesion, and perhaps even training were all on the American side. During the French and Indian War, the provincial militias had been much younger than their British-regular counterparts. In 1756, volunteers from Massachusetts had a mean average age of twenty-six, with more than half aged between fourteen and twenty-four years old.[26] At the war's beginning, unlike the older British, these youths were mostly unblooded, but over its course they acquired an enormous amount of combat experience. That experience, moreover, was not restricted to a small band of veterans, but encompassed an entire, exceedingly martial society. The population of Massachusetts, for instance, would grow from about 205,000 to 255,000 between 1755 and 1763, during which period there were approximately 34,000 males who fell within the prime age range of sixteen to twenty-nine years. Of that group, between 15,000 and 20,000 would serve in the provincials at some point (or multiple times) during the French and Indian War. Thus, *an absolute minimum of 30 percent and probably closer to 40 percent* of all Massachusetts males aged between sixteen and twenty-nine enlisted for military service.[27] In some towns, the proportion was still higher: In Lexington, up to 60 percent of eligible men went to war.[28] Perhaps it was little wonder that everybody, it seemed, had a relative away with the militias at one time or another. Nathaniel Hawthorne was not exaggerating when he later wrote that during the war "every man was a soldier, or the father or brother of a soldier; and the whole land literally echoed with the roll of the drum, either beating up for recruits among the towns and villages, or striking the march towards the frontiers. . . . The country has never known a period of such excitement and warlike life, except during the Revolution."[29]

Flitting forward twenty years, to 1775, we find that those relatively young males had matured into men in the thirty-to-forty-nine age bracket. Nearly 40 percent of the militiamen Peterborough, New Hampshire, dispatched to Boston that summer were in that band. This pattern is found elsewhere. The youngest Lexington militiaman was aged sixteen, the oldest sixty-six. Half were between thirty and forty-nine, and about a quarter were in their twenties, giving a mean and median age average of thirty-two years—about the same as for Peterborough.[30] And in Captain Hutchins's company of sixty-three Derryfield men, just nine were not yet nineteen.[31] Judging by these statistics, we can safely assert that there were more older brothers than younger, more fathers than sons, more uncles than nephews fighting in 1775.

Indeed, the character of these militia units resembled nothing less than a family enterprise. A representative case at Bunker Hill was Captain "Short Bill" Scott's Peterborough company, consisting of twenty-six men.[32]

Capt. William "Short Bill" Scott
Lieutenant William "Long Bill" Scott
Sergeant Randall McAlister
Corporal Charles White
George McLeod
James Hockley
John Graham
David Scott
James Scott
Thomas Scott
David Robbe
John Taggart
Samuel Mitchell
Thomas Morison
David Alld
Thomas Greene
Joseph Henderson
Richard Gilchrist

William Scott
Joseph Greene
Dudley (or James) Taggart
William Gilchrist
William White
James McKean
Joseph Taylor
William Graham

A not overly interesting catalogue of names, it may seem at first, but if you run your eye down the list, certain surnames recur. Among these twenty-six individuals there are six Scotts, for instance, along with two Whites, two Grahams, two Taggarts, two Greenes, and two Gilchrists. In other companies throughout the region, we see the same incidence. Thus, in Captain John Parker's Lexington militia there were sixteen Munroes, thirteen Harringtons, eleven Smiths, eight Reeds, four Hadleys, four Muzzys, four Hastings, four Tidds, three Simonds, three Wellingtons, three Winships, and many pairs. Out of 141 names on the total roster, only 27 had a unique surname. More than a quarter of his men were directly related to Parker himself.[33] In New Salem, Connecticut, Captain William Meacham was killed at Bunker Hill, but in his fifty-three-man company, three of his brothers (all privates) and his brother-in-law served alongside no fewer than seventeen of his kinsmen.[34] In Captain Benjamin Ames's Andover company, his deputy, Lieutenant David Chandler, was aided by Sergeant William Chandler and marched off to war to the beat of drummer James Chandler alongside a further five relatives, privates all.[35]

Generally, the senior men of a local dynasty—the older fellows, the better established, the veterans of the French and Indian War—occupied a company's top slots (captain, lieutenant, sergeant, and corporal) while their younger relatives served as privates or drummers. So in Concord, Massachusetts, Colonel Thomas Barrett's son and son-in-law were both captains under his command, and they in turn relied on two more of the colonel's sons serving as ensigns, who in turn passed orders down to yet another of the colonel's sons and a nephew acting as corporals, and they in turn told still more nephews in the ranks what to do.[36] War as a family business was not, in short, anything out of the ordinary.

As rural America was a close-knit society—two-thirds of marriages were between partners born in the same small town and half of all families were "re-related" to each other via wedded cousins or siblings—even unrelated individuals would nevertheless be connected to their militia brethren through local business relationships, childhood friendships, political affiliations, and religious ties. The bonds between the militiamen magnified their fighting power, particularly when the chips were down and the enemy threatened to break them. In battle, the reluctance to appear a coward in front of one's comrades is an age-old phenomenon, one only intensified by the men's familiarity with one another. The shame of running away would be terrible and result in disinheritance or loss of commercial, property, and marriage opportunities while forming an inextinguishable source of malicious town gossip for a lifetime. In an era when personal mobility was limited, gaining such a reputation would be devastating, as the afflicted could rarely move away to start their lives afresh.[37]

Often forgotten is the relatively high degree to which blacks were integrated within the militia companies—not until after World War II would so many again serve alongside whites in the military. None, of course, were officers—tolerance went only so far—but at least thirty-three blacks would fight at Bunker Hill. Fifteen of these were free, the balance enslaved.[38]

This number might not sound very high, but there were relatively few blacks living in rural New England in the eighteenth century. Boston's population in 1760 was 15,631, of whom 14,390 were white and 1,241 black, or about 8 percent, but as one traveled farther inland, away from the coastal fisheries, ports, and trading vessels that employed large numbers of seafaring blacks, it became increasingly rare to see African-Americans. In Concord, according to the 1754 census, there were just fifteen; in Lexington, twenty-four. Even by 1790 the total black population of the five New England states would amount to a mere 16,822, or 1.5 percent of the more than a million people living there.[39]

The number of blacks who fought at Bunker Hill was broadly proportionate to their presence in the white population.[40] That slaves participated in combat at all was a quirk of the Puritan outlook. Those in, for instance, Massachusetts, were treated differently than in the South. Slaves were considered not quite property—though they were—but as "servants for life"; they sat at the family's table, worked alongside their masters, and wore similar clothes. Blacks could also testify in court, even against their owners. On the other hand, as "servants for life," their children were considered, as one observer remarked in 1795, "an incumbrance in a family; and when weaned, were given away like puppies."

Reflecting this ambiguous status, blacks were forbidden to participate in militia training but, in spite of the fear of a slave insurrection on the part of whites, there was no prohibition on their using firearms. This loophole was a relic of the days when Indian raids and French attacks were distinct dangers and every man was needed in an emergency. Consequently, on May 20, 1775, the Massachusetts Committee of Safety banned slaves, but not free blacks, from serving in the militia forces outside Boston. The Provincial Congress, however, ignored the resolution, so there were both slaves and freemen at Bunker Hill. Even so, there was no obligation for a slave to fight; indeed, one reason for them to volunteer was the possibility of earning their freedom.[41]

Blacks' familiarity with weapons, if not militia drill, helps explain the presence of one carrying a musket in John Trumbull's famous 1786 picture *The Death of General Warren at the Battle of Bunker's Hill, June 17, 1775*. There is every evidence, too, that blacks were not relegated to auxiliary or support roles but participated fully in the fighting. Salem Poor of Andover, for instance, had purchased his freedom in 1769 and was enlisted in Colonel James Frye's regiment. He helped dig the redoubt's defenses on the night of June 16. Six months after the battle, on December 5, Poor received an extraordinary, perhaps unique, accolade: No fewer than two colonels (including Prescott), one lieutenant colonel, and three lieutenants testified to the General Court of Massachusetts that he had "behaved like an experienced officer as well as an excellent soldier" during the battle.[42]

The family and community bonds that connected the militiamen meant that the Americans could generally trust their leaders to an extent that the British regiments at Bunker Hill could never match. Those in charge of the militia units had neither purchased their commissions nor risen thanks to backroom politicking. They were, after all, elected. What counted among the militiamen was experience, which is why when they voted for their officers they generally chose men who had learned their business in the French and Indian War. For instance, in 1755, one Lieutenant William Prescott of Massachusetts enlisted twenty-five men to fight the French in Nova Scotia. In 1775, more than half his original company joined him—now a colonel—at Bunker Hill, to live or die alongside their clan chief at the redoubt.[43] Similarly, Captain Isaac Baldwin of Hillsborough, New Hampshire, could bring to bear the experience garnered from participating in fully twenty firefights alongside John Stark—now also a colonel, but holding the rail fence—during the French and Indian War. So attractive was his résumé that of Hillsborough's forty-three eligible residents, nearly half signed on to his company, and many more living in nearby towns rushed to volunteer.[44]

Militiamen refused to serve under officers who had not proven their credentials. Just before Bunker Hill, four Massachusetts companies decided that they disliked their commanding officer, Colonel Samuel Gerrish, so they ousted him and elected Captain Moses Little in his place. Having raised 509 men, nearly all armed with good muskets, Captain Little had, after all, more amply demonstrated his abilities as a warrior than his hapless superior. Meanwhile, another three companies voted to depart from Colonel John Nixon's regiment and align themselves with ones more to their liking.[45] The administrative havoc these changes caused within the American high command was offset by an increase in unit morale and cohesion as men picked which of their kinsmen and comrades they wished to fight alongside.

Despite not having been to war for two decades, the militias were not out of practice. More than half a year before Bunker Hill, many militia companies had secretly begun to train together. As a result, not only did the French and Indian War veterans become accustomed to working with the younger, greener men but the latter also learned to heed their elders.

In the winter of 1774, the Provincial Congress strongly recommended that since "the improvement of the militias in general in the art military has been therefore thought necessary," each town should provide drill and target practice "three times a week, and oftener as opportunity may offer."[46] Now, thrice may have been somewhat ambitious, but twice was common. To that end, Captain Isaac Davis, a gunsmith and farmer from Acton, set up a firing range that his men used at least two days a week between November 1774 and April 1775.[47]

Israel Litchfield, a twenty-two-year-old shoemaker from Scituate, Massachusetts, left a record of what it was like to be a militiaman in those heady days.[48] One afternoon, he and his friends went to Foster's tavern, where his new company had arranged to meet for their first training session. More than sixty local men turned up.[49] Between November 1774 and April 1775, they followed the Provincial Congress's drill recommendations, no matter how harsh the weather. Unlike the British in Boston, they made sure to exercise with other local militia companies to improve their coordination. On April 13, 1775, with that in mind, the Scituate outfit congregated with Captain Turner's "company of Rangers" and Captain John Clapp's "company of minute men" at a Liberty Tree, after which "the three companies drew up in battalion and were exercised by Major Jacobs."[50]

They, like most others, used the Norfolk Exercise, a system of training developed in England in 1757 specifically for militias and helpfully reprinted in abridged cut-out-and-keep form in the *Massachusetts Gazette* of October 6, 1774 (and thereafter given wide circulation).[51] The authors of the quick-to-learn Norfolk Exercise boasted that it would teach an officer the essentials of drill and turn citizens into "half soldiers" within a week.[52] Perfect, then, for your average militiaman, like Israel Litchfield, who knew his way around a rifle but less so a parade ground.

At the time the British army was using the official 1764 manual for its drill, but the Provincial Congress considered it too perplexing for militiamen to use.[53] The main objection was not that militiamen were too ignorant to be able to follow its rules but that the manual obsessed over minor ceremonial details and added dozens of superfluous steps and exercises. Just as their sartorial philosophy went back to basics, so did the militia leadership insist on a simpler way of fighting, one more fluid and more flexible than that generally taught to redcoats. While the European tactics of the day required officers to maneuver large bodies of men in column and line precisely around the battlefield—a process requiring intense drill practice and harsh punishments for errors—Americans had little need for such iron discipline, given how loosely organized their militia companies were.

In this respect, the British enjoyed, in their own eyes, the significant advantages of a clear hierarchy, a robust organizational structure, and a sound system of discipline—the hallmarks of a professional army. They were right. At Bunker Hill, American operations would be hampered by personal dislikes and local rivalries. From the beginning, no one was quite sure who was in command of the peninsula and who was to take orders from whom. General Israel Putnam of Connecticut claimed paramountcy, but Prescott at the redoubt was a Massachusetts colonel who owed no fealty to him and could, if he wished, ignore his directives. As John Adams later wrote, because "Massachusetts had her army, Connecticut her army, New Hampshire her army, and Rhode Island her army," in practice this meant that despite their differences in rank Putnam and Prescott regarded each other as equals and (usually) worked by consensus while retaining their own authority.[54]

At least Putnam and Prescott managed to get along. Colonel John Stark at the rail fence, on the other hand, loathed Putnam, a dislike, according to a Dr. Snow, apparently stemming from "Putnam's [earlier] interference with the irregularities of the N.[ew] H.[ampshire] troops, particularly some violence committed by Stark and his regiment against

Col. Hobart, the [New Hampshire] paymaster." The "violence," provoked by Hobart's reluctance to issue pay or supplies, probably involved
some roughhousing and hurtful remarks about his parentage. Whatever the issue was, the court-martial subsequently pursued by Putnam
had "reported unfavorably" concerning Stark, a man in whom it is said
that New England cantankerousness combined with Scots-Irish con-
tentiousness. He was never easy to get along with, and there was also
much "rivalry and jealousy" between him and his fellow New Hampshireman at the rail fence, Colonel James Reed.[55] One of the reasons
that Stark did not join Prescott in defending the redoubt may lie in the
official list drawn up of each regiment's seniority within the American
forces—a ranking that depended on a number of factors including
when the regiment was raised and its commander promoted. In it,
Stark's was ranked seventh and Prescott's tenth, and the prideful Stark
might have bristled at subsuming himself under Prescott, so he plumped
for the rail fence and stayed out of Prescott's ambit. In the end, this
proved the correct decision, but we can speculate that it was more spite
than brilliance that prompted it.[56]

The *amour propre* of the various militia commanders and their reluctance to recognize anyone's authority but their own added substance
to the spreading suspicion in Congress that the militia was an obsolete
institution, one that had once been useful for combating Indian raids
but was no match for a professional force like the British army. Challenged by the redcoats, the members of Congress predicted, the militiamen would break and run. Their revolutionary enthusiasm might be
commendable, but the harsh reality was that when militias were "opposed to troops regularly trained, disciplined, and appointed, superior
in knowledge, and superior in arms," as George Washington declared,
they turned "timid, and ready to fly from their own shadow."[57]

To that end, Nathanael Greene, who would rise to become one of
Washington's finest commanders, was so exasperated with the motley
collection of militia companies at Cambridge that he asserted that "we
have no occasion for them. We have here as many of the Province militia as we know what to do with." He—as did Washington—preferred
establishing a *real* army, based on British lines, to fight the coming

war.[58] Indeed, only three days before the battle, the Continental Congress authorized just such a thing, the Continental Army, and placed Washington in charge.

Putnam was aware that Bunker Hill looked to be the militias' last, defiant gasp before the business of war was handed over to the experts. It was absolutely true that no militia could withstand an aggressive assault by the British across an open field, but Putnam understood a key distinction the critics had overlooked: Militia units were immensely robust if wielded properly in battle yet brittle and easily cracked if not. Wise commanders were aware of this characteristic, wiser ones took it into account in their campaign planning, and the wisest did not place militias in untenable positions in the first place.

The heart of the matter was that a militia's weaknesses emerged only if its members were expected to behave and perform as regulars: American militias were short-term citizen soldiers, not long-service professional troops, and had to be treated as such. This entailed insisting, first, that battles had to be fought on American terms, not British ones, to benefit fully from the militias' strengths; second, that they were best at manning defensible positions, not overcoming them; and, third, that their task was to stave off an enemy's easy triumph, not to defeat him.

His militiamen "were not afraid of their heads," the general shrewdly remarked, "though very much afraid of their legs; if you cover these, they will fight forever."[59] And so they were. By providing protection for their men's legs behind wall and fence, Putnam and the other commanders at Bunker Hill ensured that they would stand and fight. Moreover, the defensive posture played to their strengths, for, as the militia officer Timothy Pickering believed, the provincial companies needed "no other discipline" than "being good marksmen and dexterous in skulking behind trees and bushes."[60] In other words, to Americans "discipline" meant *self*-discipline based on experience, prudence, and independence. It was not a synonym for authority imposed from above.

This was a critical distinction between the worldviews of American militiamen and their British antagonists. To outsiders, the militias circa 1775 did look "undisciplined"—as indeed they were, judged by conventional European yardsticks—but to derive, as the British did, from that uncomplimentary description the idea that they accordingly lacked combat effectiveness was an ultimately fatal category error. At the rail fence, where Stark's men were waiting for the Grenadiers to come at them after the debacle on the beach, this harsh lesson would soon be driven home.

5. The Rail Fence

With their flank on the beach secured, the militiamen behind the rail fence at Bunker Hill watched the orderly lines of Grenadiers and regulars begin their frontal assault. For the Americans, the choice of ground was inspired. When the Connecticut detachment under Captain Knowlton had first arrived there, they had found "a fence half of stone and two rails of wood. Here nature had formed something of a breastwork, or else there had been a ditch many years gone. [The Connecticut detachment] grounded arms, and went to a neighboring parallel fence, and brought [its] rails" back.[1] The original fence had demarcated the boundary of a farmer's land; now it was fortified by the extra wood, and any gaps between the rails were packed with hay, grass, earth, and bushes.[2] Opinions vary on the extent of protection it provided: The American Captain Chester believed the barrier "made a slight fortification against musket-ball," but General Howe—who attacked it—felt that it "effectually secured those behind it from musketry," and still another soldier, that it was "ball-proof."[3] Another militia officer discreetly remarked that it didn't really matter, "for if it did not stop the balls, the men would think that it would, and that would give them confidence."[4]

Despite its admirable location, the rail fence was severely undermanned until Colonels Stark and Reed reinforced Knowlton's Nutmeggers. That captain had too few troops to protect the length of the fence, leaving its left-hand side (which ran north to the Charles River) almost undefended. Since British practice was to place the most elite troops on the right—a place of honor since the Middle Ages—when the attack came, it was certain that the defenders' left would come under heavy pressure. With Knowlton graciously acknowledging his help, Stark accordingly strung out his regiment along that section, with Colonel Reed's men taking their place between Stark and Knowlton.

Ahead of them stretched roughly 700 yards of open fields. At that range, one soldier could see only another's head as a small "round ball" and the rest of him, very hazily, only if he was wearing bright white cross-belts and breeches. Not until 600 yards would our soldier be able to see "upper and lower parts of the body," while at 500 yards "the face may be observed as a light coloured spot; the head, body, arms, and their movements, as well as the uniform, and the firelocks (when bright barrels) can be made out." Only when the British reached a distance of between 200 and 250 yards would "all parts of the body [become] clearly visible, the details of the uniform . . . tolerably clear, and the officers . . . distinguished from the men."[5]

In short, not for some time would there have been any visible target worth pointing a musket at, let alone being able to see the whites of their eyes—especially since those waiting behind the rail fence were amazed at the enemy's "very slow march" and their "slow step."[6] Their lethargy was considered quite curious. After all, the British army was taught to move at three different speeds: the "ordinary" or common step of 75 paces per minute, each pace measuring 30 inches (covering roughly 60 yards of ground per minute); the "quick" step of 108 30-inch paces per minute to seize ground rapidly (90 yards); and a still quicker rate for wheeling motions.[7]

By the standards of the day, the British generally marched at a smart clip.[8] During the coming war, for instance, whenever German mercenaries (whose cadence topped out at 72 paces per minute) served alongside British soldiers, they would complain—in between deep gulps of air—whenever the drums began beating the quick step. Captain Georg Pausch grumbled that such rapidity was appropriate only in the winter "in the chase, with fast horses and good dogs!"[9] The American militias advanced more slowly still. Their common step, the default march in the field, was to a 24-inch pace at a rate of 60 per minute.[10] From the American point of view, then, when they recalled that the British were approaching with a "very slow march," we can assume that the redcoats' pace was less than between 60 and 75 paces per minute.

The question is why. The usual reason given for their nonchalance is that the British were weighed down by heavy packs and equipment. According to Charles Stedman, who in 1794 wrote one of the first narratives of the battle—and in so doing created one of its enduring myths—the Grenadiers were "encumbered with three days' provisions, their knapsacks on their backs, which, together with cartouche-box, ammunition, and firelock, may be estimated at one hundred and twenty-five pounds weight."[11]

A more careful measurement, however, finds that a redcoat bearing this load would in fact be carrying about fifty, perhaps up to sixty pounds—less than a French Foreign Legionnaire of the 1830s (100 pounds) or a British Chindit guerrilla of World War II (86 pounds), but about the same as a modern American soldier's kit in urban combat.[12] It doesn't really matter, though, because the Grenadiers were not lugging much more than their muskets, some ammunition, and their bayonets. The rest of their baggage and packs had been left in Boston, whence they would be ferried to Moulton's Point following their inevitable victory.[13]

Heavy knapsacks were not, therefore, the reason for the languid pace. At bottom, Howe was faced at Bunker Hill with a terrible and irreconcilable dilemma. It is often forgotten that Howe, despite his later reputation as a ditherer, had long been in the progressive vanguard of British tacticians, his particular specialty being the then-innovative Light troops and their fast, flexible formations (known as "open order").[14] Howe recognized more than anyone that speed and suppleness were of the essence, then, if one wanted to attack a fixed entrenchment like the rail fence. But Howe had wasted his skilled Lights at the beach, and the rest of his line troops lacked their abilities, leaving him in the unenviable position of having to march his forces slowly toward Stark's expectant guns.

Tactically speaking, conventional eighteenth-century armies relied on long, straight lines marching steadily forward to gain momentum and menace as they methodically, remorselessly, imperturbably rolled toward wavering defenders, who would often break and flee before the mass onslaught. There was no better way to lose battles than for soldiers to become higgledy-piggledy. Tacticians therefore devoted much thought to the deceptively complex task of keeping lines uniform and even. The key to success was for every man to march in precise lockstep, "without tottering, and with perfect steadiness," according to one British manual.[15]

For well-drilled troops, this ideal could be realized, but at Bunker Hill the redcoats' lack of training and coordination bedeviled them from the outset. Howe was accordingly forced to rely on rather dated, if relatively simple, tactics to chivy the various regiments' troops into a straight line and get them marching toward the rail fence—if at a slow place, to maintain their cohesion. Twenty years earlier, during the Seven Years' War in Europe, marching three ranks in "close order" had been the accepted standard. Such a formation crammed as much firepower into as compact a space as possible, intensifying the damage inflicted by each volley. Yet a slimmer two-rank system in which the men were relatively spread out had temporarily gained a toehold during the French and Indian War in North America, a land where free-ranging forest firefights were common.[16]

Through the start of June, however, in Boston the British units were *still* drilling in three ranks, in close order. Only on June 3, just two weeks before Bunker Hill and probably prompted by Howe, did Gage order his troops to start "draw[ing] up two deep on their regimental parades as well as on the general parade."[17] Such a change caused much confusion among men and officers alike, requiring as it did major alterations in marching order and firing procedures. Sergeants, corporals, lieutenants, and captains all had to stand in different places, unlearn their memorized training, and try to accustom themselves to maneuvering these much longer, but only slightly thinner, formations. Now, just wheeling the line to reorient which direction it faced required immense concentration from everyone involved.

A turning movement resembled the hub and spoke of a wagon wheel. The men on the hub had only to swivel at a relatively slow pace to turn, say, forty-five degrees, while those on the outer end of the spoke would have to march with sufficient speed to ensure that they arrived at the same time. If the varying speeds were not precisely timed and carved into the men's muscle memory, the once-rigid line would end up looking like a tangled piece of string. Another eternal problem was, as a French specialist remarked in 1772, "once the battalion begins to move at any speed, the second and third ranks fall into inevitable disorder, the formation wavers on the march, the files get in each others' way, and the direction of fire loses its proper alignment."[18]

It would not have been possible for the Boston regiments to hone these skills in a fortnight. As it was, none, apart from the Lights, appeared to have even attempted to practice expanding their files—an advanced technique that would have caused untold chaos without first having perfected the basic two-rank formation. So it was that at Bunker Hill Howe was encumbered with troops who could neither be reliably maneuvered nor permitted to spread themselves out. In his mind, then, it was imperative to get them lined up nice and straight at Moulton's Point and then, as he ordered, to start "moving slowly and frequently halting" so that the Grenadiers and the regulars could shuffle back into place.[19] The result, as his colleague General Henry Clinton observed, was "one long straggling line two deep."[20] Hence the bemusing sight of the British troops advancing far more slowly than expected.

Making matters worse was the topography. As a Prussian soldier of the time cautioned, "a ploughed field or a churned up meadow" would inevitably reduce "harmony to dissonance."[21] Since the hay growing in the fields between Moulton's Point and the rail fence had not been cut in some time, it was now waist-high. Worse, the hay hid the deep furrows left behind by plowing the rocky dirt. Twisted ankles and stumbles were a certainty. The crop also obscured the ten or twelve fences of "strong posts and close railing, very high, and which could not be broken readily" (as Howe admitted), that divided one field from another.[22] Over each of these "great obstruction[s]," remarked Lieutenant Williams, the Grenadiers would have to clamber, not only further throwing off their pace but turning them into targets as they scaled the top and were backdropped by the sky behind.[23] Captain Thomas Stanley, who visited the site a few months later, heard that "the men were obliged to ground their arms to get over them."[24] Once on the other side, they had to waste still more time hauling the muskets over.

It's important to realize that these problems did not affect every British soldier in the same way at the same time, just as not every company in the army was overwhelmed by raw recruits and unable to fire effectively. Otherwise, none of Howe's regiments could have conjured themselves up out of bed that morning, let alone begun to mount an assault. These liabilities, in other words, were less cumulative than piecemeal, in the sense that each bore an impact on individual units differently and to a greater or lesser extent. A Grenadier company, for instance, comprising men with five to fifteen years' experience would not have found advancing in two lines onerous—unless it was also confronted by disadvantageous terrain or held up by a green and poorly officered unit nearby. Taken together, however, the various challenges severely depreciated the entire army's combat effectiveness.

This was before taking into account the pitiful vulnerability of the British to the defensive advantages enjoyed by their opponents. Chief among the latter was the volume of fire emanating from the rail fence, which was, according to Lieutenant Thomas Page (who mapped the battlefield), 900 feet long.[25] Records suggest roughly 1,595 militiamen (1,395 New Hampshiremen and 200 Connecticuters) awaited the British behind the fence—or one man for every half a foot.[26]

This, clearly, is an impossible figure, even if they stood sideways rather than frontally. British manuals generally allocated 22 inches—1.83 feet—to each man when calculating ranks (as the Marine Corps does today), but they needed more space to reload and fire.[27] The Americans, more loosely organized, probably required more elbow room, so let us say they were allotted 2.5 feet (or 30 inches) per man.

Simple arithmetic indicates that there must have been *four* ranks of men along the greater part of the fence. Even assuming (because the right-hand side was farther from the heaviest fighting) that each of the men in the Connecticut detachment occupied just two feet and was "double-parked" (so covering 200 instead of 400 feet of fence if standing in single line), that would still leave only 700 feet available for the

1,395 New Hampshiremen. Using the 2.5-foot measure, 700 feet would fit just 280 men in a single rank, or 560 in two, 1,120 in three, and 1,400—almost exactly our 1,395 calculation—in four.

How, then, did they all shoot? The most probable explanation is that during the battle the front row fired, then stepped back several feet so that the man behind him could take his place while he reloaded. This was done repeatedly so that all four men waiting their turn had a chance to shoot. Owing to the strong familial structure of New England companies, most militiamen would have chosen their trio of "teammates," so while there no doubt would have been some jostling, ribbing, and elbowing if someone took his own sweet time to fire, the cycle probably worked quite smoothly and allowed plenty of opportunity for each man to load and prime his firearm carefully. With three other men eager to take their shots, those needing a few minutes to clean their barrels, measure their powder, or change the flint had ample time to do so. In contrast, a leading complaint among professional soldiers was that the synchronized volleys common in Europe forced men to prepare their muskets for the next round with excessive haste, thereby causing innumerable misfires and wasted shots.

At the rail fence, after Stark "harangued his regiment in a short but animated address; then directed them to give three cheers" (according to Henry Dearborn), he encouraged his militiamen to take their shots as they wished and at whatever range they judged effective.[28] This was a slap in the face of General Putnam, who had earlier visited the position. Then, recalled Reuben Kemp (of Stark's regiment), Putnam had "charged the men not to fire till the enemy came close to the works; and then to take good aim, and make every shot kill a man. But there were a few pieces discharged before the order was given to fire. General Putnam appeared very angry and passed along the lines quickly, with his sword drawn, and threatened to stab any man that fired without order."[29]

That the New Hampshire colonel and his men ignored Putnam so defiantly illustrates the division between the old-school officers like him and such stiff-necked soldiers as Stark, who preferred to do things their own way, the French and Indian way. Putnam's whites-of-the-eyes insistence on the troops withholding their fire until they could unleash at close range a synchronized blast was based on European practice. But for Stark, the British made an attractive target *now,* his men were keen as mustard, and some three or four ranks impatiently wanted their turn. He understood, as well, the folly of trying to keep the boys reined in. Any "attempt to control them by uniformity and system," according to the rail-fence veteran Henry Dearborn, was doomed to failure, because "each [man had] his peculiar manner of loading and firing, which had been practised upon for years, with the same gun."[30]

The importance of knowing every inch of a weapon to maximize combat effectiveness cannot be overestimated. The advent of machined, interchangeable parts and standardized production lay far in the future, and this was an age when every single piece of a firearm was hand-made.[31] The quality of construction, the type of wood and robustness of the iron, the length of the barrel, the placement of the sights, the tightness of the screws, the strength of the firing mechanism, the pull of the trigger, the weight of the weapon, all varied widely from weapon to weapon. Neither should we forget the idiosyncrasies introduced by deviations in the ammunition itself, such as the ball being unsymmetrical through faulty casting (air pockets in the lead, for instance), improper measuring, mixed granulation, dampness, and indifferent ramming of the gunpowder.

As hunters and farmers, the militiamen relied on their guns to sustain and defend themselves, and since they had generally used the same firearms for much of their lives, they knew exactly what their peculiar tics were and compensated accordingly. For instance, Israel Litchfield, from Scituate, was quite typical in devoting a great deal of time to maintaining his weapon and its accoutrements in the lead-up to Bunker Hill. According to his diary, on November 16, 1774, he "worked upon [his] gun." In February 1775 he "made [. . .] a cartridge-box, [. . .] covered it with a coltskin. It will carry 19 rounds." Then he helped his captain, Samuel Stockbridge, make some cartridge-boxes for the other men in the company. On March 10, he "scoured up [his] gun" to clear away the fouling in the barrel caused by unburned gunpowder residue before taking it the following day to Hezekiah Hutson, the gunsmith, to "put in a new main-spring into [his] lock."[32]

On March 20—about a month before the fight at Lexington—Litchfield (now a sergeant) proudly brandished his refurbished firearm at target practice, where "we fired three volleys. Capt. Stockbridge shot at a mark about 12 or 14 rods [70 yards or so] and hit it exactly within an inch."[33] The next day, Litchfield busily fine-tuned his musket and, more specifically, made sure that he was using exactly the right amount of gunpowder to guarantee a successful firing with sufficient energy propelling the ball to kill at a hundred yards:

> I spent the whole day a-scouring her and cleaning the lock and fixing her. After I had cleaned and oiled the lock I put in a good flint and tried her to burn three corns [grains] of powder. I cocked her and snapped and she burned them. I told out just three corns and tried her again and she burned it so I tried her eleven times successfully and she burnt three corns of powder every time and did not miss. The 12th time she missed them but I overhauled and cocked her and she burnt them the next time. Then I tried her to burn a single corn of powder and she catched a single corn four time successively after that: the fifth time she missed a single corn, but I overhauled her again and she burnt it the next time.[34]

It is unknown at precisely what range Stark's men began firing in earnest: The cross-straps marking white Xs on the Grenadiers' chests certainly made an attractive target at 200 to 250 yards, though some of the defenders (as Reuben Kemp mentioned) loosed a few rounds before they reached that point. The latter would have inflicted little or no physical effect, for, owing to their ballistic and aerodynamic inefficiencies, lead balls decelerate quickly as they travel toward the target. On flat ground, a .69-caliber ball (a common one at the time) powered by a normal load of 482 grains of gunpowder will exit the muzzle at about 1,500 feet per second; at 100 yards that velocity will have dropped by nearly a third, to 1,029 fps.[35] Thereafter, it will fall at a still greater rate and drag its kinetic energy down with it, meaning that if a soldier was a few hundred yards away a bullet striking him would essentially bounce off him as if he were Superman. Many accordingly ended up with such splendid war souvenirs as dented watches and snuff boxes that had deflected bullets. Dick Mather was especially fortunate. A musket ball that hit him directly in the forehead was "flattened . . . like a bullet of clay when it has been thrown against a stone wall." A friend suggested he donate both his head and the squashed ball to the Royal Society in London as Wonders of Science.[36]

At about 200 yards, the Grenadiers and regulars would have started suffering casualties, though few outright fatalities. While the great majority of shots would have missed, a steadily increasing proportion would have told—and that number would only rise as the British narrowed the distance. "The generality of the Americans were good marksmen," later judged Sergeant Roger Lamb of the Fusiliers, a talent he attributed to their fondness for "hunting, and the ordinary amusements of sportsmen. The dexterity which by long habit they had acquired in hitting beasts, birds, and marks, was fatally applied."[37] Stark also markedly enhanced his men's aim by ordering them to rest their muskets on the fence rather than shoot from the shoulder.[38]

Such precision was not particularly important at this stage, in any case, since the volume of fire emanating from Stark's position offset any missed shots, especially when the enemy paused to negotiate fences. The morning after the battle, ominously reported the *London Chronicle*, their wooden rails "were found studded with bullets, not a hand's breadth from each other."[39]

The moment when the British reached a range of around 100 yards would help decide the engagement. Among professional military men, that was judged the optimal distance to balance accuracy against hitting power. At that range, a standard musket firing a nearly one-ounce ball would leave a bloody cavity in a man's flesh measuring 9.5 cubic inches—more than enough to take him out of action and probably necessitating a limb's amputation if the bullet hit a bone.[40] From there, the extent of trauma rose sharply. At 75 yards, a typical round created an entry wound nearly two inches in diameter, then tunneled through the flesh and juiced tissue to leave an exit wound more than three inches wide.[41] A range of between 25 and 60 yards seems to have been the ideal killing distance, as musket balls had not yet lost most of their kinetic energy, and neither had they sheared too far off their intended vectors, thus almost allowing the defending musketman to count on hitting what he was aiming at.[42] The militiaman Needham Maynard, describing the "thundering noise" of the fusillade along the length of the rail fence, estimated that at a range of 55 yards (or thereabouts) the British "fell in heaps—actually in heaps. They kept falling. . . . The bodies lay there very thick."[43] Generally, the last chance a defending soldier would have to fire a round at the enemy would occur between ten and twenty yards. If it hit, the bullet would scoop out nearly 23 cubic inches of tissue, muscle, and flesh, but if it did not, the enemy would be imminently within bayonet's reach and the defending line seconds away from collapse and panic.[44]

The object of any attacking force was obviously to reach that crucial stage in as whole a condition as possible and with the greatest possible momentum, while that of the defenders was to break the oncoming mass down into small pieces and slow its advance. Accordingly, the first step was to destroy the enemy leaders and those accomplices who helped keep the formations together. "Our men were intent on cutting down every officer they could distinguish in the British line," said Dearborn. "When any of them discovered one he would instantly exclaim, 'there,' 'see that officer,' 'let us have a shot at him,' when two or three would fire at the same moment; and as our soldiers were excellent marksmen and rested their muskets over the fence, they were sure of their object."[45] After the battle, it was noticed by the British that among their hit officers "few had less than three or four wounds," indicating that they were the unfortunate objects of several Americans' interest.[46]

General Howe, who led from the front, naturally received special attention. He was, to put it mildly, conspicuous on the battlefield, not only for his fine uniform and a servant named Evans, who showed the proper feudal spirit under fire by valiantly bearing a bottle of wine "for refreshment," but for the twelve staff officers accompanying him. The group attracted such intense fire that of that dozen, eleven were seriously wounded and the twelfth killed in action.[47] Howe, either through the grace of God or because his escorts painfully shielded him from the bullets, escaped from the carnage with little more than a bruised ankle caused by a ricocheting ball, though his uniform was soggy with his aides' splashed, spurting blood. (The faithful Evans was shot in the arm but was more upset about the demise of the wine bottle.)[48]

In Europe, officers were generally ruled out of bounds for such targeting, for they were the social superiors of those they commanded, and to the British a pungent whiff of dishonor surrounded the baleful colonial practice of remaining hidden and aiming at one's betters. The American way of fighting would later reduce the British to purplish, sputtering rage as the full horror sank in of Bunker Hill's butcher's bill. One typical rant went, "Dastardly, hypocritical cowards, who . . . do not feel bold enough to dare to look a soldier in the face!" They were nothing better than "skulking assassins, who can only fire at a distance, from behind stone-walls and hedges!"[49]

This American trick was particularly unsettling for Enlightenment-era officers because it challenged their rational interpretation of war. In the words of Captain Robert Donkin, "The cowardliness of the rebels [makes them] delight more in murdering from woods, walls, and houses, than in showing any genius or science in the art military."[50] Smart shooting, in other words, was proof of an inability to fight well. An odd position to take, at least to our modern sensibilities, but one that helps us glean the essentially alien nature of eighteenth-century warfare.

On the heels of the attritional losses of officers, the attacking companies began to falter but kept plowing onward. It is here that one Lieutenant James Dana enters the story. An officer serving with Knowlton's Connecticut contingent, he claimed to have fired the shot that finally provoked the British into throwing away their remaining ace in the hole: the "First Fire."[51]

As muskets were charged with a single ball and reloading was time-consuming, conventional eighteenth-century actions were based on the principle of "first fire," according to which the attackers reserved their precious musket blast until they were well within point-blank range, after which they could finish off the job with a rapid bayonet assault. It was "a received maxim," according to the foremost military writer of the day, "that those who preserve their fire the longest, will be sure to conquer."[52]

Forbearance was key. The attacking troops were expected to absorb the enemy's first fire and march indomitably on until they could shock the empty-musketed defenders with their counter-volley. Against undertrained or unprepared troops, the technique was often devastatingly effective. Lord Percy bragged to a friend that during the battle of New York—a fiasco for General Washington—the redcoats were ordered to "receive the rebels' first fire, and then rush on them before they had recovered their arms, with their bayonets." The tactic "threw the [Americans] into the utmost disorder and confusion, they being unacquainted with such a manoeuvre."[53]

At Bunker Hill, it was expected that the Grenadiers and regulars would keep forging ahead after the Americans had loosed their first fire. Howe's plan, therefore, hinged on maintaining strict fire control among his troops, but Stark's militiamen obliterated such assumptions. For one thing, they were not guided by the same military manuals. In other words, they ignored the traditional stress on first fire and indulged instead in free fire—from relatively long range and with sufficient accuracy to test the redcoats' patience to the breaking point. Further, owing to the four ranks of militiamen cyclically laying down fire, there was no "first" volley to endure. The incoming shots were incessant.

And the relative greenness of the British troops played, yet again, an adverse role in the battle. Even at Lexington, their lack of forbearance had been noticed. One report concluded that when the soldiers returned the rebels' fire, they did so "with too much eagerness, so that at first most of it was thrown away for want of that coolness and steadiness which distinguishes troops who have been inured to service." After criticizing the lieutenants and captains who had not prevented this "improper conduct," the report conceded that "most of them were young soldiers who had never been in action, and had been taught that every thing was to be effected by a quick firing. This ineffectual fire gave the rebels more confidence [as] they suffered but little from it."[54] There is little reason to believe that matters had greatly improved in the two-month interval between Lexington and Bunker Hill. Lieutenant Frederick Mackenzie of the 23rd complained after the first fight that "our men threw away their fire very inconsiderately . . . and without being certain of its effect."[55] Of their performance at Bunker Hill another officer of the same regiment, Lieutenant Richard Williams, would write privately that the men "foolishly imagine[d] that when danger is feared they [should] secure themselves by discharging their muskets, with or without aim."[56]

Now under, in Howe's words to a confidant, "a heavy fire, well kept up by the rebels" and checked by yet another of the infernal fences, a good number of aggrieved Grenadiers paused to exchange shots. They had hitherto executed the advance, continued he, "with a laudable perseverance, but not with the greatest share of discipline" and now Howe's line became jumbled by some raising their muskets to their shoulders while others continued to march forward. More and more shots rang out as the rest of the Grenadiers stopped to fire, "and by crowding fell into disorder, and in this state the 2nd line mixed with them."[57]

Hardly a round went unwasted. The British could point their muskets only at the Americans' exposed heads—a difficult shot at the best of times, and particularly treacherous when under pressure—and nearly all of their fire sailed skyward. "I should presume that forty-nine balls out of fifty passed from one to six feet over our head," recalled Henry Dearborn, "for I noticed an apple tree, some paces in the rear, which had scarcely a ball in it from the . . . ground as high as a man's head, while the trunk and branches above were literally cut to pieces."[58] Needham Maynard added, "there was hardly one of us hit [even while] their officers were shot down; there seemed to be nobody to command 'em."[59]

Among the militias on the receiving end, the sound of bullets, even if flying harmlessly overhead, was at first alarming—especially if one was new to battle. But warriors often steadied the worriers, said Roger Lamb, by assuring them that "there is no danger if you hear the sound of the bullet which is fired against you, you are safe."[60] This was something of a comforting fib, or perhaps an old soldier's tale, because at any distance immediately beyond the muzzle from which they exited, projectiles traveled at less than the speed of sound, meaning that their subsonic approach, passage, and departure could be easily heard from several feet away. They made a kind of distinctive "whistling noise not very agreeable to the ear," in the words of one man, to which another added that it sounded like "hissing" and "whining."[61] Amos Farnsworth, soon to fight at Bunker Hill, wrote in his diary on May 27 that during a recent skirmish "the bauls sung like bees round our heds."[62] Indeed, soldiers of the era might remark at the relative quietness of today's firefights, wherein bullets fly as fast as 4,000 feet per second. The loud, sharp "whip-crack" noise characteristic of a modern round is owed to its breaking of the sound barrier. As the bullet is traveling faster than the shock wave it generates, a person downrange cannot hear a supersonic bullet approaching—only after it has passed, as indicated by the "crack" left in its wake. In that case, it is certainly good news, because it means that you are not dead, so Lamb was prematurely right after all.[63]

Still worse than being left with empty barrels and nothing to show for it was the "disorder," as Howe put it, into which the British companies had descended. Once a unified formation atomized into small, scared groups scurrying for cover, it marked the death knell of any assault. It was now, Howe confided to a friend, that he experienced "a moment that I never felt before."[64] For an officer of proven valiance, one raised in the most tightly coiled, tight-lipped eighteenth-century martial tradition, to admit to even a tincture of alarm or a scintilla of doubt is remarkable, and one of only a few such instances extant.[65] Honor was virtually synonymous with displaying courage and maintaining one's reputation for steadiness under fire.[66] For that reason, Monsieur de Lamont, a leading French military intellectual whose works were popular in America, advised every officer that he "must never turn his back, [no matter] how great soever the loss is on his side; for if a man is once suspected of cowardice, he is past all hopes."[67] (It was no shame to lack natural courage if one wasn't an officer, he conceded with a slight but detectible sniff, but those sorts of people became churchmen and lawyers.)[68]

No matter his inclination and notwithstanding his losses, Howe had little choice therefore but to continue the attack. It was almost immaterial now whether he failed, but it was critical that he do so honorably. Fortunately for the general, his career, and his reputation, the surviving officers managed to chivy the Grenadiers back into a rough line, but not before, in the words of the militiaman Captain Chester, they had "partly brok[e and re]treated."[69]

Collecting his wits, Howe made two decisions. He sent a message back to Boston urgently ordering the reserves, still waiting on the wharf, to sail for the peninsula. These reserves comprised the 47th Regiment and the 1st Battalion of Marines. Second, he instructed the Light infantry to salvage their honor by attacking the rail fence directly and immediately on the right. With the reserves still some time away, Howe needed to keep up the pressure on the enemy by using his Lights as regular infantry.

What happened next is bitterly described by an anonymous British officer:

> As we approached, an incessant stream of fire poured from the rebel lines: it seemed a continued sheet of fire for near thirty minutes. Our light infantry were served up in companies against the grass [i.e., rail] fence, without being able to penetrate; indeed, how could we penetrate? Most of our Grenadiers and Light Infantry, the moment of presenting themselves lost three-fourths, and many nine-tenths, of their men. Some had only eight or nine men a company left; some only three, four, and five.

"I have lost some of those I most valued," he continued. "This madness or ignorance nothing can excuse. The brave men's lives were wantonly thrown away. Our conductor [Howe] as much murdered them as if he had cut their throats himself on Boston common. Had he fallen, ought we have to have regretted him?"[70]

The folly of continuing an assault with disrupted soldiers against a fixed entrenchment was borne out by the devastating casualties sustained by the Grenadiers, the Lights, and the regulars at this stage of the action. Truly, as Stark remarked a year later when he toured the battlefield, before his rail fence the British "dead lay as thick as sheep in a f800."[71] The devastating results can be gleaned from the British muster rolls compiled after the battle. Take the Light company of the 35th. At breakfast that morning of June 17, the company consisted of one captain (Drewe), two lieutenants (Bard and Massey), one volunteer gentleman (Madden), two sergeants (Knowles and Poulton), one corporal (Nodder), one drummer (Russ), and thirty privates—making a total of 38. By dinner, just three privates were left unharmed. *Everybody* else was dead, dying, or wounded. Ten were killed in the field, and they were joined within the next two weeks by five others, followed by still more dying of their injuries and infection over the coming months.[72] In sum, when Captain Drewe (himself hit several times) compiled his report at month's end, nearly 40 percent of his command was dead, about 53 percent wounded, and 7 percent left unhit—a casualty rate of 93 percent incurred within just a few minutes.

Losses among the Grenadiers were equally terrible. A day after the battle, Captain Walter Sloan Laurie of the 43rd's Light infantry was detailed to bury the dead, now lying where they fell. Laurie had missed the action, being relegated to Boston duty, so as one of the few of his regiment's officers still in one piece, he sailed to the peninsula to supervise the grisly task. His party buried no fewer than ninety comrades (ten sergeants, seven corporals, and seventy-three privates) belonging to thirteen regiments. Of the total, one sergeant and eleven privates were shown to have been Grenadiers of the 43rd. Over the next few days, five more Grenadier corpses were discovered. If we assume that the 43rd's Grenadier company numbered, as did the others, between thirty-eight and forty men, then on June 17 alone it lost nearly half its strength. By August, another four privates and a sergeant would die of their wounds.[73] And of course the line troops also suffered grievously. Even marching behind the Grenadier vanguard, by day's end the battalions of the 5th and 52nd had lost (killed and wounded) a major, eight captains, five lieutenants, four ensigns, seventeen sergeants, and 225 privates.[74]

Imagine the scene. Before the militiamen lie hundreds of contorted British corpses. Hundreds more are desperately crawling toward a fence, a rock, or a ditch to find shelter before dying. The rounds that kill instantly elicit a loud shrill cry on impact, noticed soldiers of the time, while those that will eventually be fatal cause rapid unconsciousness. With the others, the wounded soldiers will experience pain, shock, and primary hemorrhage.

The degree of pain hinged on where and in what context he was hit. If the soldier was passionately engaged in fighting at the time, he may not even have realized he had been shot until dizziness, tiredness, and nausea (from loss of blood) overcame him—or if a concerned comrade pointed to the wound. More commonly, of course, the victim was aware that he was wounded. Survivors described the pain on being struck by a musket ball as being "like a flash of fire," "the sharp stinging pain from a sudden smart stroke of a cane," or the "shock of a heavy, intense blow." The latter sensation appeared most often in connection with a bullet hitting flesh or muscle but avoiding bone. That was a good thing, for the shattering of bone nearly always meant amputation. Because spherical bullets, universal at the time, entered relatively cleanly but tore flesh and tissue as they left at reduced velocities, generally little pain was felt at the entrance wound but much more at the exit—which is why there are several instances of soldiers shot through the outer neck or the thigh who turned around angrily to the rank behind to berate the poor man there of being careless with his bayonet.[75]

The intensity of the pain was not a reliable indicator of wound severity. A very serious injury could well be less agonizing than a minor one owing to loss of sensation and function as well as the advent of shocked stupefaction. The agony, in most cases, soon faded and was replaced by numbness. Then came, as John Malcolm recalled, the "burning thirst, universally felt after gunshot wounds."[76] On a hot June day, the desire to drink would have become maddeningly intense.

Dr. Grant, a surgeon in Boston who tended the injured after the battle, bitterly wrote, "Many of the wounded are daily dying, and many must have both legs amputated," adding that most of the casualties he had seen had been shot in the lower extremities.[77] Relatively few could have saved themselves by walking away from the combat zone, then, but would have had to wait until after the Americans had left to be transported to the hospital. Many would not last so long; they died where they had fallen before the rail fence.

Dr. Grant's remark also sheds additional light on the lethal mechanics of Stark's defense. Whereas the British had shot over the Americans' heads, the militiamen had "under-elevated" their muskets by aiming at the enemy's abdomens (in the redoubt, for instance, Prescott was heard shouting, "aim as low as the waistband" and "aim at their hips") to benefit from their shots ricocheting upward even if they fell short and hit the ground ahead of the enemy.[78] Such a bullet, thanks to the shallow angle at which it hit, would theoretically deflect at a similar or slightly more acute one, thus placing the groin, thighs, knees, shins, ankles, and feet at risk. A crippling hit in those places would render a man *hors de combat*—almost as good as a kill.[79] Hence Putnam's insistence that if you protected their legs, the militias would hold.

Dr. Grant, however, also mentioned that he had never seen such severe trauma caused by musket balls and accused the Americans of charging their guns with "old nails and angular pieces of iron" to enhance their deadliness. If true, then at close range these makeshift projectiles would have exacted injuries far more horrific than those meted out by the more ballistically efficient regular bullets. Their irregular shapes, propensity to fragment, and erratic yawing would have shredded more tissue and flesh, as well as have left larger, more jagged entry and exit holes, than regulation round balls.

But what were these "angular pieces of iron" and "iron nails"? A musket was a highly adaptable weapon in the sense that any object, so long as there was gunpowder in the chamber, could be blasted from its muzzle. It was not uncommon, for instance, to see ramrods—left inside the barrel by forgetful soldiers—flying out, and neither was it unheard of to load small bits of scrap metal along with the ball to make a primitive shotgun. Alternatively, a few individuals might have scored a deep cross into the lead balls, turning them into rudimentary dumdum bullets, which burst or mushroomed and shredded meat rather as "angular pieces of iron" would. Just as likely, perhaps, is that a number of defenders, having run low on ammunition, borrowed rounds from their neighbors that were too large a caliber to fit their barrels and improvised hammers to bash them into a usable size. Hitting a round ball naturally contorts it into a cylindrical shape; such an object tumbles rather than spins, causing greater damage to flesh, tissue, and organs. And lastly, it is not altogether improbable that some militiamen had customized their rounds by molding the lead around a broken-off piece of nail or thick wire. It was a nasty, if lethal, trick akin to inserting a stone into a snowball; later in the war, commanders on both sides stamped it out whenever it was detected. Howe, for instance, complained to Washington in September 1777 that his soldiers had found bullets "cut and fixed to the end of a nail" in an "encampment quitted by your troops." Washington replied that though this was "the first of the kind I ever saw or heard of[,] you may depend the contrivance is highly abhorred by me" and assured his counterpart that this "wicked and infamous" practice would cease.[80]

But that effort to humanize combat would come later; for now, over at the redoubt, the savagery was about to peak.

6. The Redoubt, Part Two

There are two contemporary maps of the battle of Bunker Hill, one drawn by Lieutenant Henry de Berniere and the other by Lieutenant Page, British officers both. On them, one notices rigidly straight lines of advance and retreat, symmetrically precise formations, neatly dotted vectors of artillery fire. Just as a highway map cannot convey the actual feeling of driving, their sketches are an abstraction of the battle. In a manner typical of Enlightenment military science—not art—they depict an idealized and rational vision of what happened, not the gritty, addled reality. During battle itself, similarly, soldiers are rarely sure what happened. Blurriness, scattered memories, tunnel vision, and fuzziness are almost universal among veterans. That both Berniere and Page mistakenly transposed Breed's Hill with Bunker Hill—and that no one noticed—is only further evidence of their maps' illusory qualities.

Superimposing ex post facto a neat, easily comprehensible pattern on the tumult and bedlam of battle, any battle, is ultimately an exercise in futility, albeit a necessary one—for how else could we construct a coherent account of their course? In this respect Bunker Hill suffers from a defect common to every clash in history: No man was everywhere at once. Each individual present had his own restricted view of how the fighting progressed. Those in the redoubt, for instance, could barely see their comrades behind the rail fence, and vice versa. For that reason, in his account Colonel Prescott vaguely mentions "a party of Hampshire, in conjunction with some other forces, lined a fence at the distance of three score rods [330 yards] back of the Fort"—the redoubt—and never again refers to the events that happened there.[1] Mirroring Prescott's confined perspective, Captain Charles Stuart, who watched the battle from Boston with his brother-in-law, Lord Percy, talks only of an attack on the "Fort" and had no idea what was happening at the rail fence, which he could not see from his position.[2] Likewise, Colonel Stark would have been as cut off from the redoubt as Howe, who could not have known in any timely manner how Pigot was faring against Prescott's defenses. Consequently, envisaging the battle, as traditional narratives do, as a sequence of coordinated, planned actions and reactions is wrongheaded from the outset. Each commander instead worked autonomously and tried to make sense of what was happening only in his immediate area.

Within the lower ranks, similarly, every memoir, diary, account, and letter tends to capture only a snippet of the broader battle; their takes are microscopic and subjective, not panoramic and objective. In scientific terms, combat is anisotropic, in the sense that its properties and characteristics vary according to the changing perspectives of observers and participants.

There are, in other words, *many* Bunker Hills, or rather, multiple facets of the same battle. Every soldier, in short, focused solely on what was happening directly before his eyes to the exclusion of all else. He could not help but do otherwise. When engaged in a battle, soldiers pay virtually no heed to the precise topographical names or characteristics of where they are: They classify terrain not as map coordinates but as, say, a useful hill from which to hold off the enemy or a bit of woodland with good cover or a difficult field to traverse. It is only afterward, sometimes long afterward, when they consult maps and photos or talk to former comrades or read a history of the battle that they begin to work out, piece by piece, where they were and what happened. By that time, "official" names have been bestowed upon various geographical features or famous episodes, and the old soldiers naturally adopt them to help make sense of their experiences.[3]

Even then, owing to the cunning of memory, their recollections of what happened are inevitably jerky and disordered. Of combat, vivid details seem real yet may be false, uncontestable facts become uncertain, and the conventional linear progression from past to present to future dissolves into a half-remembered sludge periodically interrupted by disturbing flashbacks, out-of-order sequences, and fragmented recollections. These disconcerting effects are not a product of passing time and increasing age but set in immediately after combat.

At Bunker Hill, for that reason, nobody seems even able to give a universally accepted answer to the basic question of how long the fighting lasted. Participants and spectators variously estimated the time between the first exchanges of musketry and the militias' withdrawal at "ten or fifteen minutes," "about an hour," "battle began about 3, and retreat about 5," "thirty-five minutes," "above an hour," "three quarters of an hour," "about three hours," "four hours," "an hour and a half," and "half an hour," to list just a few.[4] The disparities are partly owing to the companies' different arrival times and the subjective reliance on tracking the sun's passage across the sky to estimate the time of day, as well as the extent of their heavy combat involvement, but the faulty memories that attend combat are generally caused, or at least exacerbated, by underlying psychological and physiological factors.

Under conditions of high stress and extreme excitement, such as during a gunfight, the way in which individuals process incoming sensory information alters. They think less rationally, their deliberative and analytical skills rapidly deteriorating as their cortexes filter or tune out stimuli unessential to survival. Actions become automatic, instinctive—a type of cognition known as "experiential." A common symptom of operating in such mode is that sensory perceptions undergo severe distortion.

Studies have found at least half of participants will experience the event in slow motion, a fifth in faster-than-normal time; two-thirds will hear at "diminished volume," meaning that the sound of nearby gunshots is greatly muffled, and a fifth at amplified levels; about half will see what is happening with tunnel vision and black out everything not directly ahead and the other half with amazingly heightened clarity. Most individuals will suffer memory loss, while others will "remember" events that never occurred. These symptoms nearly always overlap. So someone with tunnel vision may see objects in startling, swollen detail—such as shell casings apparently the size of beer cans—swimming within their narrow field of vision while being oblivious to all else.[5]

Weirdly, too, combat can turn men into supermen, or so they think. More than half of respondents to a detailed questionnaire on their physical changes during shooting events said they experienced a sense of increased strength or a potent adrenaline rush.[6] Some, as a result, become impervious to pain. At Bunker Hill, the British captain Edward Drewe was so enraged by fighting that he was shot three times (thigh, foot, and shoulder), dislocated his shoulder, and received two serious contusions before he finally fell—but he survived.[7] Others may not even realize they've been wounded. Abel Potter, for instance, was bayoneted in the leg but was shocked to discover later that his "boot was filled with blood."[8] David Holbrook of Massachusetts was not only bayoneted (also in the leg) but "thump[ed] on the head" by a musket and yet felt fine until he almost lost consciousness through loss of blood.[9] Interestingly, it was only some time after they had left combat that these men noticed the flow of their own blood. In high-stress environments, the body restricts the blood supply to the extremities in order to ensure the core functionality of the heart, lungs, and other major organs. Owing to vasoconstriction, then, a soldier may be wounded in the arm or leg without bleeding much; ironically, once the external danger recedes, the risk to life increases as the wound reopens.[10]

Even when they remain unscathed, soldiers experience a host of powerful physiological effects in combat. Whereas a normal resting heart rate is between 60 and 80 beats per minute, hormonal or fear-induced pulse spikes allow individuals to reach their optimal combat-performance level—complex motor skills, visual reaction times, and cognitive reaction times hit their peak, though fine motor skills have deteriorated—between 115 and 145 bpm. They may feel as if they are gods.

Nevertheless, if stress levels continue to rise, so do heart rates. Between about 150 and 175 bpm, mental and physical abilities begin to deteriorate and their ability to process cognitive information and to use logical reasoning to act quickly, effectively, and decisively on that data plummets. Researchers have found that the deficits on performance at this stage are greater than for major alcohol intoxication, drug sedation, or clinical hypoglycemia (low blood glucose). Understandably, for many soldiers the heady combination of elevated heart rates, adrenaline surges, and a euphoric sense of invulnerability makes war feel great. For some, the experience becomes narcotically addictive, as any hallucinogenic, dreamlike state would be.

Above 175 bpm, however, individuals regress to infantilism or animal instinct. Soldiers engage in submissive behavior and lose control over their bowels or bladders. They will tend to freeze, torn between the desires to fight and flee. Headlong, unstoppable, unthinking flight frequently results but if they plunge ahead, their gross motor skills—used in charging or running—are at their zenith and may cause them to carry a position, though this condition renders soldiers useless for any task other than overwhelming an enemy.[11]

The ambiguity, fragmentation, and distortion that come with combat should raise suspicions about the "official version" of what happened during any given battle. It certainly does for Bunker Hill, where accounts continue to insist that at the redoubt, the British were repulsed twice by the Americans before launching a third successful assault that swept away the defenders.[12] We first read of this interpretation in a missive from the Massachusetts Provincial Congress to the Continental Congress dated June 20—just three days after the battle.[13] Accordingly, the Committee of Safety's official report—the one communicated to His Majesty's Government in London five weeks later, on July 25—observed that there were two failed assaults followed by a third, triumphant attack.[14] In Britain, the press followed this line in their reports of the battle—a remarkable instance of newspapers printing a story essentially dictated by the enemy, one that has proved amazingly resilient over the centuries. Small wonder, perhaps: The battle of Bunker Hill, seen this way, appears to have been a rationally organized, straightforward affair with discernible lines, precise movements, and three meticulous attacks.

Yet it was not nearly so clear and easily comprehensible to those who participated in it. Militiamen and soldiers alike were much vaguer on what happened. Said Sergeant Thomas Boynton, who was in the redoubt, after the enemy "came within gun shot we fired, and then ensued a very hot engagement. After a number of shots passed, the enemy retreated, and we ceased our fire for a few minutes. They advanced again, and we began a hot fire for a short time."[15] His chief, Prescott, told John Adams that "the enemy advanced and fired very hotly on the fort, and meeting with a warm reception, there was a very smart firing on both sides. After a considerable time, finding our ammunition was almost spent, I commanded a cessation till the enemy advanced within thirty yards, when we gave them such a hot fire that they were obliged to retire nearly one hundred and fifty yards before they could rally and come again to the attack."[16] On the other side, Captain Charles Stuart observed that "our men, astonished at the heat of their fire, retreated from the Fort, but were rallied by the courage and intrepidity of their officers, and renewed the charge *again and again* till they conquered."[17]

These recollections all describe intervals of waiting interrupted sporadically by "hot" or "smart" bouts of firing comprising "a number" of shots back and forth. Prescott at one point managed to orchestrate a volley when the British were thirty yards away, but aside from an initial organized line advance, there does not appear to be a succession of distinct attacks and retreats in formation, only multiple bursts of piecemeal rallies and advances in, as we shall see, various locations.

The "charges" alluded to by Captain Stuart were made in fact by small knots of men gamely attempting to keep the line but failing. Some took cover, others opportunistically rushed ahead ten yards while the defenders were reloading, and still more stumbled backward before recovering and moving forward again. The soldiers did not uniformly move as one but followed a ragged, ad hoc combination of keeping up, keeping down, keeping back, and above all, keeping moving. This is the reality of close combat with small arms, then as now.

The nitty-gritty details of Pigot's assault emerge more clearly if we ignore the official version and focus instead on the random snippets of what participants saw and experienced. Thus, once the British landed and began forming up for the initial attack, Prescott—a more conventional commander than Stark—followed Putnam's directions and ordered his defenders to reserve their first fire. He even became "indignant" when a few miscreants did not toe the line. Prescott "threatened to shoot any man who disobeyed; his lieutenant-colonel, Robinson, sprang upon the top of the works and knocked up the leveled muskets."[18]

In the meantime, the 1st Marines and the 47th, 38th, and 43rd Regiments had found that the upwardly sloping ground before them, like that stretching ahead of Howe's Grenadiers, was covered with "rails, hedges, and stone walls," according to Lieutenant John Waller. Here, however, they were at least told to "shelter ourselves by laying on the grass" as they waited to climb the obstacles.[19] Still, once they surmounted them they persisted in marching "rather slowly, but with a confident, imposing air."[20]

This attitude did not last long. The problem of fire control yet again proved the Achilles heel of the British. According to Isaac Glynney, the British first formed up and "marchd on towards us [and] as soon as they Came within gun Shot they Begun to fire upon us." We should assume that "within gun shot" range means roughly 100 yards away—way too far to have inflicted any significant hits on the protected militiamen. In some places, conversely, Prescott's threats held true. Referring to his company commanders, "our officers," said Glynney, "thinking it more Proper to Reserve our fire we with Held till they Came within four or five Rods [between 22 and 27.5 yards, or 66–82 feet] of us[. T]hen we were Orderd to fire which we Did."[21] But in many other spots along the wall, the militiamen opened up as they wished, as Prescott acknowledged in his letter to Adams. He was not altogether happy about it, noting archly that "after a considerable time . . . our ammunition was almost spent," thanks to all the enthusiastic free firing.

Part of the problem, of course, was that Prescott could not be everywhere at once, especially as the attacks occurred at unpredictable times and varying speeds on opposite sides of the redoubt. To the south, the 1st Marines and the three battered regular regiments were already struggling, but to the north, Howe inadvertently came to Pigot's rescue when elements of the Grenadiers, the 5th, and the 52nd swerved to avoid the rail-fence fire and ran toward the rough breastwork that was connected to the redoubt. Prescott was now under attack on two flanks.[22]

Only now, belatedly, did the British artillery come into its own. Mired in mud, too distant to threaten the rail fence, and low on suitable ammunition, these cannon were coincidentally close to the outlying American defenses. Dragged at great cost into position—two captains, one lieutenant, a sergeant, and eight privates were wounded in the process—the guns raked the breastwork with grapeshot to open a path for the beleaguered Grenadiers and their support.[23] The Americans stationed outside the redoubt's walls now began to incur heavy losses as they fled the breastwork. Of Lieutenant Thomas Grosvenor's "own immediate command of thirty men and one subaltern, there were eleven killed and wounded; among the latter was myself, though not so severely as to prevent my retiring."[24]

It was the first British success of the day. Seizing upon it, Howe adapted his plan. No longer was the rail fence his primary objective. Instead, he ordered the Lights to continue to hold their ground there as a feint to draw off militia fire while the Grenadiers, 5th, and 52nd exploited their position. According to a rather surprised Henry Dearborn, who had been expecting a renewed assault at the fence, "only a few small detached parties again advanced, which kept up a distant, ineffectual, scattering fire."[25] All the action now switched to the redoubt.

Howe was also optimistic that reinforcements from Boston would soon arrive. General Clinton, who had been impatiently cooling his heels in the city, had taken the opportunity to "embark 2 marines [2nd Marines] and another batt[alio]n"—the 63rd—and ordered them to sail to the peninsula as quickly as possible. Clinton himself did not wait for the 63rd and the 2nd Marines to finish boarding; he raced for the battlefield in his own boat and "landed under fire" on the beach near the redoubt. Once there, Clinton roused "all the guards and such wounded men as could follow which to their honour were many and advanced in column."[26]

As best we can make out, to the south the British were creeping forward and had made it to around 30 yards from the redoubt. As Clinton indicates, the redcoats were no longer in a hidebound line formation but had organized into much more mobile columns that were surging closer and closer. Prescott husbanded his men on the wall and urged them to hold fire. When he gave the word, as Isaac Glynney wrote, "we Shoed [showed] them yankey Play & Drove them Back again[.]"[27] There was probably another volley of sorts a little later, when the British reached a distance of ten yards. By now, wrote Prescott, "the ground in front of the [redoubt was] covered with dead and wounded, some lying within a few yards."[28] A man inside the redoubt noted that "it was surprising how they would step over their dead bodies, as though they had been logs of wood."[29] As losses mounted, the British columns naturally dissolved into small groups of men spread out and taking cover where they could.

It was becoming evident that this was the beginning of the end. Prescott was now so short of ammunition that he ordered any remaining shells for his cannon broken open and their precious grains of powder distributed.[30] More alarmingly still, his little army was shriveling, not through death or dismemberment but by desertion. Scores of militiamen had made themselves discreetly scarce by means of the gap, or exit, at the northwestern side of the redoubt. Prescott's force by now may have amounted to just 150 men.[31]

The only good news was that the reinforcements General Ward had sent from Cambridge had by now arrived at the Neck or were standing atop Bunker Hill. Yet some were balking from entering the fray. Amos Farnsworth in the redoubt was annoyed to see "a great body of men near by" who were doing nothing to help.[32] Others, noticed Captain Chester, were being *too* helpful: "Frequently twenty men round a wounded man, retreating, when not more than three or four could touch him to advantage."[33] Colonel Gerrish's regiment, for instance, was not budging from its safe spot, but his deputy, a Dane named Christian Febiger, roused enough men to form a useful detachment and led them into battle.[34] While heading toward the redoubt with his unit, Chester met "with a considerable company, who was going off rank and file"; he "ordered my men to make ready. They immediately cocked, and declared that if I ordered would fire. Upon that [the other company] stopped short, tried to excuse themselves," and complied with Chester's instruction to follow him to the redoubt.[35] Thanks to the influx of fresh men (and the not entirely voluntary additions commandeered by Chester), Prescott's outpost was able to hold out for some time longer.

Inside, nevertheless, the situation was growing ever more precarious. The British, too, had received reinforcements and were obviously girding themselves for a renewed attack. The militiamen were each grappling with the dilemma of staying or going. Wrote Captain Bancroft, "Our men turned their heads every minute to look on the one side for their fellow soldiers . . . and on the other to see a sight to most of them new, a veteran enemy marching on firmly to the attack, *directly in their front*. It was an awful moment."[36]

Their spirits remained halfheartedly hearty ("We are ready for the redcoats again!" they cheered, with one eye on the exit). In preparation for the final struggle, Prescott "directed the few [of his men] who had bayonets to be stationed at the points most likely to be scaled" around the redoubt.[37] Then came, remembered Bancroft, "the very crisis of the day, the moment on which every thing depended." As more and more of the men decided to sneak toward the rear, he accompanied Prescott to harangue them. Prescott's unflappable assurance and his towering reputation momentarily held them in check. He did not *order* the defenders to stay—that was no way to motivate a militiaman—but he earnestly pleaded with them to hold fast the line for a short time, if only for the sake of honor, before promising to allow the faithful to go in peace.

Bancroft, who was convinced nothing could be done to stem the rising panic, was so amazed by the speech he claimed to recall it verbatim nearly half a century later. Prescott entreated his listeners "that they must *not go off*, that if *they* did *all* would go; that it would disgrace us to leave at the bare *sight* of the enemy the work we had been all night throwing up, that we had no expectation of being able to hold our ground, but we wanted to give them *a warm reception, and retreat*."[38]

Reassured that they were not expected to sacrifice themselves as a futile gesture to salvage American honor, the men returned to their posts—Amos Farnsworth proudly recorded that subsequently "I did not leave the intrenchment until the enemy got in"—after which Prescott told all to hoard their ammunition and prepare for one last point-blank broadside before they could escape to the rear.[39]

In the meantime, according to Abel Parker, the colonel "ordered the men from one side to the other, in order to defend that part which was pressed hardest by the enemy," while bellowing (added Bancroft) that they were "to take particular notice of the fine coats and to aim as low as the waistband, and not to fire till ordered."[40]

Given the contradictions in the various accounts, which side of the redoubt was being "pressed hardest" at that moment is hard to say. What is incontrovertible is that the British now had the bit between their teeth and were pressing hard on both flanks.

To the south and under "a very heavy and severe fire," Lieutenant John Waller of the 1st Marines and his men were "checked . . . but did not retreat an inch" as they approached the redoubt's walls.[41] Nearby, however, the situation was fast unraveling. The Marine commander, Major John Pitcairn, was shot and severely wounded while "rallying the dispersed British troops" (according to the Rev. Dr. Jeremy Belknap in 1787), who were, in Waller's words, "jumbled" and "in confusion" and "half mad" near the foot of the redoubt's earthen walls.[42] Since Pitcairn (claimed the Rev. Dr. John Eliot) "received four balls in his body," his shooting was a collective one by diverse hands.[43] Pitcairn, no doubt wearing a "fine coat," would certainly have made a tempting target for any of the militiamen guarding the walls, but the number of wounds he suffered gives some indication of the ferocity of the fighting taking place.[44] (Major John Tupper of the 2nd Marines would report to the Admiralty that Pitcairn "died about two or three hours later," after being transported to Boston.)[45]

With Pitcairn incapacitated, Captain Stephen Ellis assumed command of the remnants of the 1st Marines near the wall. It was do or die. "Had we stopped there much longer, the enemy would have picked us all off," Lieutenant Waller told his brother, so he rushed to form "the two companies on our right" while begging "Colonel Nesbitt, of the 47th, to form on our left, in order that we might advance with our bayonets to the parapet. I ran from right to left, and stopped our men from firing; while this was doing, and when we had got in tolerable order, we rushed on, leaped the ditch, and climbed the parapet, under a most sore and heavy fire."[46]

On the opposite side, the Grenadiers, the 5th, and the 52nd were mounting their own push toward the redoubt wall and were also making headway despite heavy losses among their officers. Among them was Major Williams of the 52nd, who after being wounded was left to lie there bleeding out because his juniors, said Ensign Martin Hunter, refused to leave cover for fear of being shot. Perhaps he might still have done the right thing, Hunter admitted, but Williams "was not a very great favorite [with me], as he had obliged me to sell a pony that I had bought for seven and sixpence." (The major would die in a Boston hospital of his wound.)[47]

Captain George Harris was more fortunate. Upon his being shot in the head, Lieutenant Francis Rawdon ordered four men to rush Harris to safety despite the captain's murmuring, "For God's sake, let me die in peace." So hot was the American fire—perhaps the sight of a killable officer attracted it—that two of his escorts were wounded and a third killed (thus bearing out Hunter's reluctance to lend aid).[48] Meanwhile, as his men roared, "Push on, push on," Rawdon was impressed that the Americans kept up their shooting until "we were within ten yards of them." Indeed, "there are few instances of regular troops defending a redoubt till the enemy were in the very ditch of it," but Rawdon saw "several [Americans] pop their heads up [over the wall] and fire even after some of our men were upon them."[49]

The British paused at the foot of the walls, fearful that the defenders were reserving their main broadside for a point-blank massacre. But then, said one American, "one of our people imprudently spoke aloud that their powder was all gone, which being heard by some of the regular officers, they encouraged their men to march up [the parapet] with fixed bayonets."[50]

It may have been a sergeant of the 63rd's Grenadiers, or perhaps a Lieutenant Richardson, who was the first to mount the parapet and shout "Victory!"[51] Elsewhere, Lieutenant Waller clambered to the top while a captain and lieutenant fell next to him. It was now, he mourned to a friend, that "poor Ellis," "Archy Campbell," and "Shea" were killed and "Chudleigh, Ragg, and Dyer" wounded. Across from him, he saw that "three captains of the 52nd"—Nicholas Addison, William Davison, and George Smith—"were killed on the parapet," as well as "others I knew nothing of."[52]

Even as their chances of turning back the assault were inexorably declining, the Americans were giving as good as they got. When "a British officer mounted the embankment, and cried out to his soldiers to 'rush on, as the fort was their own,'" Phinehas Whitney shouted "'let him have it,' and he fell into the entrenchment."[53] Ensign Studholme Brownrigg of the 38th was so astounded by the tenacity of the defenders that he thought there were 3,000 of them.[54] Another officer told his friend in England that at this point he honestly believed that he and his men would end up as nothing more than "food for gunpowder."[55] "They advanced towards us in order to swallow us up," the redoubt's young Peter Brown later proudly told his mother, "but they found a choaky mouthful of us."[56]

Finally, noticing that the British were placing their muskets on top of the wall as they scrambled on top, Prescott bawled, "Take their guns away—twitch 'em away! And you that can handle stones, seize 'em and knock about!" Isaac Glynney picked up a few and pelted the invaders while others fired at whoever was in front of them. Ebenezer Bancroft "was loading my gun the last time, just withdrawing the ramrod," when "an officer sprang over the breastwork in front of me and presented his piece. I threw away the rammer which was in my hand, and instantly placed the muzzle of my gun against his right shoulder, a little below the collar-bone, and fired, and he fell into the trench."[57]

Prescott later maintained that he could have held the position "with the handful of men under his command, if he had been supplied with ammunition." He believed the enemy "would not have rallied, if they had been again repulsed" by a good couple of volleys.[58] Perhaps so, but this is immaterial, given that by now the militiamen were almost out of ammunition. Though the conventional narrative of the battle, in order to magnify for patriotic and cultural reasons the disparity between the modest yeomen-militia and the superior, tyrannical foe they faced, has emphasized that the Americans had been short from the very start, in fact most men were initially more than adequately equipped.[59] Or more precisely, they had sufficient ammunition for an *ordinary* firefight, but they exhausted their supplies when Bunker Hill proved an *extra*ordinary one.[60]

"Each individual was furnished with one quarter of a pound of powder in a horn, one flint, and lead sufficient to make fifteen charges either of ball or buck shot," attested James Wilkinson.[61] It has naturally been assumed that these officially distributed fifteen rounds were all that was obtainable, yet in fact the amount of available ammunition was highly variable by province. Thus, the troops in some Connecticut regiments received eighteen rounds apiece even as Lieutenant Thomas Grosvenor's company enjoyed no less than "one pound of gunpowder and forty-eight balls" per man.[62] On the other hand, Colonel Brewer's Massachusetts regiment initially had to make do with just five rounds.[63]

Moreover, the ammunition supply was not static. The walking wounded were employed to hurriedly pare and scrape dead men's ammunition down to roughly compatible sizes for the varying barrel calibers and hand them out so that none went to waste.[64] And ammunition could be pooled: Aaron Smith later said that "a man at his side, a negro, [was] so crippled by a shot in the leg that he could not rise up to discharge his gun, but could load and re-load, which he continued to do, both Smith's and his own, and then hand them to Smith to fire, until their ammunition was expended."[65]

Even so, let us assume that on average each militiaman arrived on the field with fifteen rounds. Few before Bunker Hill had imagined that men could blaze through so much ammunition in a single brief encounter: That number was judged by American commanders as more than sufficient and at the time was counted as a needlessly lavish distribution. George Washington, for his part, believed that between twelve and fifteen rounds per man could last for an entire months-long *campaign,* while the British, less parsimonious, regarded sixty as enough for a season of several battles—but they expected a lot to be left over for the following year.[66]

In the event, Jesse Lukens reckoned that at Bunker Hill alone he and his comrades had each fired about *sixty rounds,* and Josiah Cleaveland remembered that he "fired 40 cartridges; borrowed 3 more." Another Bunker Hill soldier boasted that "he discharged his piece more than thirty times," while Nathaniel Rice of East Sudbury claimed that he fired his musket twenty-six times and another militiaman "seventeen times at our unnatural enemies."[67] Still others "fired at the enemy twenty times, some thirty, and some till their guns were so heated, that they dared not to charge them any more."[68] Even accounting for the men's exaggerations and erroneous recollections, judging by the amount of ammunition used relative to the smallness of the battlefield, the brevity of the battle, and the limited number of participants, Bunker Hill featured perhaps the heaviest, fiercest combat of the eighteenth century.

But finally run out of rounds the militias did—heralding the inevitable collapse of the redoubt. Throughout the battle, the Americans had wisely avoided close-quarters combat in favor of shooting from afar, but during the struggles for fixed defenses bayonets came into their own.[69] This was a British specialty, and the opportunity they had panged for all day. As General Burgoyne advised, against enemies who placed "their whole dependence in intrenchments and [firearms,] it will be our glory, and our preservation to storm when possible."[70] When confronted by such obstacles as walls and breastworks, he was implying, it was more sensible to risk one's life charging them than to lose it waiting to be picked off by distant musketry.

After the battle, angry participants would allege that it was "barbarous to let men be obliged to oppose bayonets with only gun barrels."[71] In an enclosed area, like the redoubt, soldiers thrusting bayonets forward would herd defenders toward a wall or corner by impaling or pricking them with the steel points. The writhing and flailing bodies could then be used as a kind of bulldozer to push deeper into the crowd of other defenders and cram them into a still more constricted space for easier killing.

For their part, the militiamen "began to knock the guns [with bayonets] aside—to spring on 'em with stones—to give 'em heavy punches, feeling that they must sell their lives there," said Maynard. The Americans tore muskets away from their British owners and "for a moment we had a pretty good time: We hit 'em . . . with their own guns. We took about 30 of their guns, I should think."[72] One of Lieutenant Webb's militiamen, Edward Brown, "sprang, seized a regular's gun, took it from him and killed him on the spot."[73]

Nevertheless, the weight of the British had the advantage, and the Americans fell back. For Waller, "nothing could be more shocking than the carnage that followed the storming of this work. We tumbled over the dead to get at the living, who were crowding out of the gorge of the redoubt."[74] The "gorge" to which he referred was the exit that Prescott had prudently left clear. Acknowledging that his militiamen had done all they could, he sounded a general retreat. Most gratefully took up the offer. There was nothing dishonorable in their decision; these men were exhausted. Unlike the British, who had enjoyed a sound night's sleep and a hot breakfast, Prescott's defenders had been awake since early Friday morning, nearly thirty-six hours before. After a busy day in camp, they had marched to the peninsula and spent the night building the redoubt with barely a morsel or gulp to sustain them. In the morning they had been under prolonged artillery fire and, of course, for most of Saturday afternoon, they were fighting for their lives. Ravenous, thirsty, disoriented, scared, dusty, outnumbered, the Americans could hold out no longer.

For his part, Peter Brown "jumped over the walls and ran half a mile, where balls flew like hailstones and cannon roared like thunder," while David How remembered that after his friend was shot right next to him, he grabbed his musket, "let fly" at a looming redcoat, and fled for the rear.[75] Meanwhile, to cover them, Prescott and a band of die-hards heroically defended the gateway to Bunker Hill, the Neck, and safety.

The scene became one heaving, bloody bedlam amid the swirling dust and smoke—so thick and dark that men had to feel their way to an exit.[76] With bayonets bent and muzzles dipped in gore, the British thrust ahead, delayed only by Prescott's paladins, who swung their cutlasses and employed muskets as makeshift poles to parry the enemy's bayonets. Another particularly effective method was to "club" a musket: holding it by the muzzle and swinging it with force at a head or face, often shivering to pieces their wooden stocks.[77] In general during such melees, men do not tackle each other individually but instead lunge or swing at, hit or cut anyone nearby not instantly recognizable as an ally. When two men do come to blows, the resulting fight is rarely a thing of choreographed beauty; it is all flailing fists and clumsy rebuffs and desperate slashes.

Understandably, then, for this stage in an infantry action, that of hand-to-hand combat, it is rare to find coherent or authoritative accounts of what happened. As it is probably the most exhilarating, terrifying, animalistic, anarchic, primitive experience of all, this mode of fighting is more prone to memory blackouts, disjointed recollections, and sensory kaleidoscoping than even conventional combat. Descriptions of what happened are accordingly sparse, but we are fortunate in possessing a few vivid snapshots of what the final moments in the redoubt were like.

Israel Potter and some comrades had "to fight our way through a very considerable body of the enemy, with clubbed muskets," in order to escape. Fortunately, Potter had brought a cutlass, with which he parried a sword slash at his head by an officer. The point of the latter's blade cut his right arm near the elbow, but Potter managed to make "one well-directed stroke" that almost severed the other's arm.[78] Captain Bancroft, meanwhile, had "a severe struggle to escape out of the fort." Holding "my gun broadwise before my face," he "rushed upon" the redcoats in the way "and at first bore some of them down, but I soon lost my gun." Now disarmed, he "leaped upon the heads of the throng in the gateway and fortunately struck my head upon the head of a soldier, who settled down under me, so that I came with my feet to the ground." Immediately, "a blow was aimed at me, with the butt of a gun, which missed my head but gave me a severe contusion on the right shoulder. Numbers were trying to seize me by the arms but I broke from them, and with my elbows and knees cleared the way so that at length I got through the crowd." There was now just one man standing between Bancroft and life, "and the thought struck me that he might kill me after I had passed him." So, "as I ran by him I struck him a blow across the throat with the side of my hand. I saw his mouth open, and I have not seen him since."[79]

Once the majority of militiamen had fled, the ground, said Lieutenant Waller of the Marines, was "streaming with blood and strewed with dead and dying men." At least thirty Americans had been bayoneted or killed in the fort during the fighting, but now "the soldiers [were] stabbing some and dashing out the brains of others." It "was a sight too dreadful for me to dwell any longer on."[80]

As many of the wounded as possible had been borne away by their friends, but some thirty-six or thirty-seven were left behind, including Colonel Parker and two or three other officers.[81] Some of these, if we rely on Waller, were later murdered in the redoubt. We can be quite sure, as well, that all the victims were Americans, for killing takes time and possession of the field, and the fleeing militiamen had neither.

Such is the savagery of hand-to-hand combat that it is hard to leash one's intense emotions, particularly in the immediate aftermath of the fighting. It is then that the overwhelming majority of slayings occur of prisoners and the wounded, not days or even hours later, when passions have cooled. At Bunker Hill, the British repeatedly bashed in the skulls of the wounded—or the already dead—with the butts of the muskets and ran them through multiple times with bayonets. We see this kind of frenzied "overkill" erupting among victors in any number of past battles. To take one example, in England, at Towton in 1461, there was a fierce clash between the Lancastrian and Yorkist forces during the Wars of the Roses. Recently excavated skeletons reveal that out of twenty-eight skulls, fully twenty-seven bore multiple wounds—nearly all inflicted *after* the killing stroke on the first or second blow. Some men had been hit up to thirteen times. One typical victim received five strokes from a bladed weapon to the left front side of his head, followed by another powerful down-to-up slash from behind that left a wide horizontal gash. With the corpse lying face up, one of the soldiers then delivered a massive blow with a heavy sword that cleaved open his face diagonally from the left eye to the right jaw, severing most of his throat at the same time. As at Bunker Hill, not only did these manic attacks occur once the victim was already dead but also after the main fighting was over and the perpetrators were no longer in danger.[82]

Had the British found Prescott among the wounded, there can be little doubt of his awful fate. However, quite astoundingly—almost as much so as Howe's miraculous survival—the colonel escaped from the maelstrom with nothing worse than a coat rent by several bayonet slashes and a ripped waistcoat. One of his men remembered that Prescott "did not run, but stepped long, with his sword up" throughout.[83] One can only speculate that the British did not focus all their energies upon killing him because Prescott was dressed as an ordinary farmer and did not stand out.

The refugees from the redoubt had exchanged one hell for another. As they ran toward Bunker Hill, the British followed and shot at them from behind. A large number of men who had escaped relatively unscathed from the melee now fell, more severely wounded. Israel Potter, for instance, who had so far received only that "slight cut" from an officer's sword, now suffered two hits, one in the hip and the other in his left ankle.[84]

The retreat could easily have turned into a rout had a mixed bag of companies and a few packets of militiamen not rapidly set up a rough line to cover those men streaming their way. Captain Chester's Nutmeggers, as well as the units headed by James Clark and William Coit, plus a hodgepodge of companies from Colonel Moses Little's and Colonel Thomas Gardner's regiments banded together on the south slope of Bunker Hill, looking toward Breed's. They took positions "just by a poor stone fence, two or three feet high, and very thin, so that the bullets came through." "Here we lost our regularity," wrote Chester, with "every man loading and firing as fast as he could. As near as I could guess, we fought standing about six minutes." His lieutenant affirmed that that they held back the British with "a brisk fire from our small-arms."[85]

General Clinton appealed to Howe, who was still shaken by the debacle at the rail fence, to let him chase and catch the militiamen before they could exit the peninsula. He would have only minutes to regain the initiative. "All was in confusion," Clinton noted. "Officers told me that they could not command their men and I never saw so great a want of order."[86] Howe allowed him to take whatever troops he could round up and try to flank the troops on Bunker Hill—a plan that held out the possibility of severing the disrupted Americans from the Neck. Clinton ran with his men to the abandoned fort, ordered Lieutenant Colonel John Gunning to "remain in the redoubt with 100 with positive orders to keep it, and took with me all the rest" toward the thin American line.[87]

Clinton's boldness might have paid off had the militias utterly collapsed in panic, but on Bunker Hill the initial chaos was instead subsiding into an orderly withdrawal across the Neck. Small groups of militiamen paused to shoot at Clinton's troops to cover others moving to the rear, until they in turn were relieved and fell back. Lieutenant Rawdon acknowledged that the Americans maintained "a running fight from one fence, or wall, to another, till we entirely drove them off the peninsula."[88] General Burgoyne agreed, saying "the retreat was no flight; it was even covered with bravery and military skill."[89]

It was a hard fight. Colonel Gardner was mortally wounded and, according to a neighbor, Colonel Little "narrowly escaped with his life, as two men were killed one on each side of him, and he came to the camp all bespattered with blood." And of Captain Nathaniel Warner's twenty-three-man company, no fewer than seventeen were killed and wounded.[90] Robert Steele, a drummer boy, was told to go fetch two quarts of rum and a pail of water to succor the twice-hit Major Willard Moore and other injured militiamen. The beverages, perhaps unsurprisingly, "went very quick," he wrote.[91]

The British could see wounded men being carried from the field under fire. Among those who made it across the Neck was a Peterborough, New Hampshire, sergeant named McAlister—a Scotsman who had deserted the British army some years before; he had been shot "in the face and side of the neck, the ball having entered the mouth, and coming out one-half in the back of the neck and the other half in the mouth." He was rescued by a comrade who, knowing his fate as a deserter should he be captured, threw him across his back and brought him to safety.[92] Another man, John Barker, saw his friend Captain Benjamin Farnum fall wounded. Ignoring the oncoming British, Barker hauled Farnum across his shoulders, told him to hold on for dear life, and ran to safety, mumbling to himself, "The Regulars sha'n't have Ben."[93] In 1829, aged eighty-three, Farnum had the honor of becoming the last captain at Bunker Hill still alive, though he was somewhat lamed by the two musket balls in his thigh.[94]

Thanks to the American refusal to abandon their comrades, only thirty-one prisoners were eventually taken by the British, many of whom were severely injured. Most lay in the redoubt, but others would have fallen along the line of retreat. None were treated with much gentleness. Hit in the hip, a Mr. Frost had "crept in among the British wounded," presumably for warmth, companionship, or in hopes that someone would take pity on him and help him. Unfortunately, when he was found, the soldiers threatened to run him through if he did not get up. "But I was too stiff to move," so "they hauled me about till I became more limber," and he was taken to Boston.[95] Bill Scott suffered a fractured leg early in the fighting and would be shot another four times over the next few hours. Waking from unconsciousness and bleeding from "nine orifices" (entry and exit wounds, presumably), he discovered a British soldier looming over him. The redcoat demanded to know why he should not execute him, to which Bill, now beyond caring, replied, "I am in your power and you can do with me as you please." The soldier was pleased to but a passing officer stopped him and took Scott prisoner. Left out overnight, the militiaman was trundled onto a wagon and transported to Boston for treatment the following day. Like Frost, he was later evacuated to Halifax in Canada (and, like Frost, escaped a year later).[96] They were the lucky ones: By September, just ten of the wounded prisoners were still alive.[97]

There were even some uninjured Americans trapped on the peninsula, who hid as best they could, but by the early evening they were emerging—armed, scared, and dangerous, as Lieutenant John Dutton of the 38th would find out. Suffering from gout, he had left his company to change his stockings and was warned by his orderly that two men were approaching. The orderly thought it prudent to fall back, but Dutton laughed off the suggestion, supposing that "they were coming to surrender and give up their arms." But "his incredulity proved fatal to him [when] they lodged the contents of their muskets in the bodies of the hard-fated lieutenant and servant, notwithstanding that the King's Troops were within fifty yards of him when he lost his life, and some of the Light Infantry quite close to him." The Americans were killed a few minutes later.[98] Dutton and his luckless servant were the last British casualties of the bloody day.

Meanwhile, noticing that knots of militiamen were holed up in some houses on the Neck, Clinton urgently requested Howe to permit him to take some game Light and Grenadier companies to pursue them once they were flushed out by artillery. "I knew it would be a complete finishing to a great though *dear bought victory*"—another such, he admitted, "would have ruined us"—but, he sadly noted, "my scheme was not approved."[99]

Howe was probably right. There was no point in continuing the battle. It was getting dark, and his soldiers would have found it impossible to force their way across the Neck, let alone to continue on to face Ward's forces in Cambridge. It would have been hard attritional fighting every step of the way, for, as Burgoyne reported, all the Americans had done was proceed "no farther than to the next hill [Winter Hill], where a new post was taken, new intrenchments instantly begun."[100]

The British troops, also, were exhausted, a result of the typical crash after a lengthy bout of combat. The burn-off of adrenaline causes soldiers intense fatigue and helps explain why even victorious commanders can find it difficult to execute a knockout blow against a weakened opponent in the closing moments of an engagement. At Bunker Hill, officers often spoke of their men, even in victory and no matter how high their spirits before the battle, to be "weak and outdone," "very dull," "confused," and "discouraged and beat out" immediately follow-ing it.[101]

Soldiers who have not yet fully purged adrenaline from their system tend to suffer from jitters—a hallmark of insomnia.[102] As the sky dark-ened over the peninsula, any number of men found themselves unable to sleep. One such was Martin Hunter of the 52nd, who never could forget "the night of the 17th of June" as he vainly sought restfulness. "The cries of the wounded of the enemy . . . and the recollection of the loss of so many friends was a very trying scene for so young a soldier."[103] On the other side, John Trumbull felt "that night was a fearful breaking in for [the] young soldiers" surrounded by such a scene "of military magnificence and ruin."[104]

For most of those present that day, the battle of Bunker Hill was over. For the wounded, it was as if it had never ended.

7. The Wounded and the Dead

Those militiamen borne by their comrades to safety were, by the stan-dards of the day, well cared for. Losses had not been overwhelming, and among the American forces there was a laudable number of doctors—a general rubric that at the time included barbers, apothecaries, butchers, and enterprising clergymen turning their hand to succoring the travails of the body rather than of the soul.[1] At Bunker Hill alone, twenty-nine physicians fought, and Americans as a whole were looked after by a young and credentialed lot. Of the forty-three doctors who attended during the siege of Boston, about 85 percent were in their twenties and thirties, half had attended college, all had been trained as medical apprentices—a rarity—and two even possessed medical degrees.[2]

Though they were short of medical supplies and new to battlefield surgery, many of these local and country practitioners were accustomed to dealing with gunshot wounds incurred during hunting as well as deep cuts—agricultural tools caused many injuries. Nevertheless, as in any war, the variety and severity of wounds inflicted by weaponry were really quite remarkable: Men could be hacked, shot, fractured, bludgeoned, pierced, exploded.

Sword slashes, for instance, which would have occurred in the redoubt, were particularly damaging to the face and head. At the battle of Waxhaws (May 29, 1780), the American lieutenant Pearson's "nose and lip were bisected obliquely, several of his teeth were broken out in the upper jaw, and the under completely divided on each side" after he was attacked with one.[3] Another time, Jonathan Nickerson was "struck down to the ground, his skull fractured, and cut through the bone for four inches or more and, while lying on the ground, was . . . struck four strokes to the head and several in the body with a cutlass."[4] Curiously, such injuries were not usually fatal, and many similar victims lived without major surgical intervention.[5]

Bayonet wounds, unless they were in the abdomen, were usually quite simple to treat, the weapon itself being a sharp instrument that penetrated without introducing foreign objects that would infect the wound. Abdominal injuries, which could lead to peritonitis—caused by food leaking through a perforated intestine—would not kill instantly, but often surely. A surgeon would poke inside the gut with a probe tipped with lint. If it came out dirty and smelly, the patient was fated to die. Otherwise, he did the best he could to suture the wound while pushing an escaping intestine back into place with two forefingers.

Gunshot cases were more troublesome, as there were any number of places a soldier could be hit. Lieutenant Mackenzie compiled a list of wounded officers at Lexington while usefully noting the locations of most of their injuries. On that baleful day, Lieutenants Gould, Baker, and Hawkstone ("said to be the greatest beauty of the British army") were hit in, respectively, the foot, hand, and cheeks, while Lieutenants Cox and Kelly and Ensign Lister were wounded in the arm, Lieutenant Colonels Smith and Bernard and Captain Souter in the leg, Lieutenants Sutherland and McLeod in the breast, and Lieutenant Baldwin in the throat. Lieutenants Knight and Hull died of serious trauma. Hull was hit at least three times but survived until May 2, while Knight, who died the next day, was likely the victim of a head shot.[6] Worse, bullets inflicted a wide variety of wounds, ranging from compound fractures and loss of soft tissue to injured ligaments, burst vessels, and joint trauma.

Nor was there a concept of triage—of separating the less severely wounded from those with greater need and then focusing on the cases with a higher possibility of survival.[7] (For those with obviously inoperable wounds, wrote a doctor, "a few words of consolation, or perhaps a little opium, was all that could be done or recommended . . . for prudence equally forbids the rash interposition of unavailing art, and the useless indulgence of delusive hope.")[8] Officers on both sides received premium treatment, of course—but everyone nonetheless suffered from a lack of litters and ambulancemen in an era before the advent of an institutionalized system of hospitals and a professional body of military surgeons—so the regular ranks waited their turn, notwithstanding the extent of their injuries.

Accordingly, especially when confronted by hundreds of casualties, doctors simplified their techniques to a few one-size-fits-all basics in order to expedite treatment for the most men possible.

Amputation was the accepted method of treatment for bullet wounds, and few doctors devoted much time to debating alternative avenues of treatment. Medical textbooks were firm on the issue, stating forthrightly that "if the bone is smashed, the limb has to be removed" or "if the joint is injured, the appendage has to be amputated."[9] Given a sharp blade and a steady hand, most skilled surgeons could whip off a leg in twenty minutes—a handful could do it in fewer than five.[10] The good news for the wounded was that the first cut and dealing with the loose arteries hurt by far the most—"all thought that [a] red-hot iron was applied to them when the arteries were taken up," said one observer—while the rest of the operation passed indifferently and apparently (almost) painlessly, thanks to opium, alcohol, and general stupefaction.[11]

Contemporary surgeons were brisk and businesslike. Dr. Thacher, after describing the "mutilated bodies, mangled limbs, and bleeding, incurable wounds . . . covered with putrefied blood [and] filled with maggots," nonchalantly remarked that "amputating limbs, trepanning fractured skulls, and dressing the most formidable wounds, have familiarized my mind to scenes of woe."[12] To their minds, the more rapid and decisive an action, the greater the easing of pain and suffering. The calculus was very simple: Forgoing surgery would lead to septicemia and gangrene, while even waiting to see if the body healed itself often led to secondary hemorrhaging and tetanus. In either case, death was certain. If, on the other hand, the surgeon operated immediately to excise traumatized flesh, at least the patient would enjoy a modest chance of survival. The aggressive policy to amputate as soon as possible stemmed not from callousness but from the humanistic, if utilitarian, conviction that severing the injured limb would aid the greater good of the body.[13]

Speed was of the essence. The official necrology reported to London a week after the battle by a chastened General Gage were 226 British killed and 828 wounded.[14] At first glance, the battlefield ratio of killed to wounded—one fatality for every 3.6 men wounded—appears quite "good" by eighteenth-century standards in the sense that there were relatively few deaths. At four major European battles of that era (Blenheim, Ramillies, Belgrade, and Kunnersdorf), by way of comparison, the average ratio was 1:2.[15]

Read another way, however, the figures from Bunker Hill reveal a staggeringly high number of wounded. As noted earlier, the Americans had aimed "below the waistbands" of the British at fairly close range, a practice that resulted in severe injuries to the legs. Many redcoats, as Dr. Grant observed, needed to have *both* amputated; it is worth bearing in mind that about half to two-thirds of soldiers whose legs were removed at mid-thigh died soon afterward, mostly owing to traumatic hemorrhaging.[16] Indeed, the volume of severe lower-limb wounds and the concomitant rise in deaths sparked a rumor in Boston that the militiamen had played a dirty trick. Dr. Jackson Hall, an American physician, was outraged to hear from a Boston customs collector named George Messerve "that all the balls fired by our people were poisoned, they were (he said) first dipped in some glutinous matter then rolled in white arsenic and dried, that he himself saw a box containing 60 pounds weight thus poisoned taken from off Bunker's Hill" as the militiamen retreated. It was, of course, an "infamous and damnable false representation," reported Hall, but "this story is believed here by the Government party." (For their part, the Americans would charge that when the British eventually evacuated Boston, they mixed arsenic in with bottles of medicine to kill *their* unwitting wounded.)[17]

The myth that one side was poisoning its rounds stretched back to the sixteenth century, when firearms were first making their appearance on the battlefield and physicians struggled to explain their frighteningly high fatality rate. After William Clowes, the finest surgeon of the Elizabethan era, suggested that musket balls secretly coated with poison were the reason, there was a spate of executions of prisoners by captors outraged that their dead comrades had been murdered by means most foul. (Not for another century after Bunker Hill would the actual cause of so many deaths be shown to be simple infection.)[18]

Ultimately, many of the wounded would die over the coming weeks and months—a fact cunningly omitted from Gage's report, which had an interest in obfuscating the figures he sent to London so as to avoid ignominy. Judged Dr. Ezra Stiles, the future president of Yale who took it upon himself to investigate Gage's fudged numbers, the British commanders were indulging in "designed concealment" of the facts by means of "insidious stratagems and delusions" to confuse outsiders.[19] Take the 23rd's Grenadier company, originally of thirty privates plus noncommissioned officers. On June 17 itself, not a single of its members was killed in action—which would have "improved" Gage's totals—yet between that date and September 24, no fewer than two sergeants, two corporals, a drummer, and five privates died of their injuries, and another nine privates were still listed as "wounded." Given the time span, we can assume that those wounds were permanently debilitating.[20]

Similar attrition, covered up, can also be detected among General Howe's staff of twelve aides-de-camp who accompanied him during the attack on the rail fence. Of this dozen, just one (Captain Sherwin) was killed in action that day, but all the rest were wounded. Gage's report noted this, but it would not be until January 1776—when interest and fury had long since subsided—that the dire truth about these "wounded" officers emerged. That month, the *London Chronicle* noted in passing that "a few days ago arrived in town, from Boston, Lieutenant Page, of His Majesty's Corps of Engineers, on account of the wounds he received the 17th of June, in the action at Charlestown. This gentleman is the only one now living of those who acted as aides-de-camp to General Howe." Over the intervening months, it seems, all but he had died. (Page had lost his leg.)[21]

Regarding American casualties, George Washington, the incoming commander of the Continental Army, told his brother on July 27 that there were 138 killed, 276 wounded, and 36 missing (really, captured, perhaps including a few who took the opportunity to "disappear" to escape creditors or wives), or 414 killed and wounded.[22] This makes for a killed-to-wounded ratio of 1:2—the typical rate, as already noted, for a contemporary battle.

Unfortunately, it is quite impossible to deduce the American wound-lethality rate. All I can say is that in all the documents I have consulted, I cannot recall citations of large numbers of men subsequently dying, and there are grounds to believe that that figure was significantly lower than that of the British.

First, there might have been a qualitative difference between British and American wounds. The most fearsome British injuries were sustained at fairly close range in the lower limbs, increasing the likelihood of damaging arteries and rapid blood loss, whereas relatively few Americans were shot at that distance. During the retreat from the redoubt, when many Americans were hit, they were some distance away from the advancing British, thereby lessening the bullets' potency. American anecdotes suggest that men were either killed outright or they limped away. Israel Potter, sprinting for Bunker Hill, was hit in the hip and the left ankle but made his way to safety "without any assistance." Though in much pain from his leg injury—"the bone was badly fractured and several pieces were extracted by the surgeon"—he rejoined his regiment six weeks later.[23] Amos Farnsworth was between 55 and 80 yards away from the redoubt when he was shot in the right arm, "the bawl gowing through a little below my elbow breaking the little shel bone." He was also hit by a ball in the back, "taking off a piece of skin about as big as a penny but I got to Cambridge that night." Considering that a British silver penny of the time measured .47 inches in diameter and the standard British musket caliber was .75, Farnsworth's entry wound was a small one, probably the consequence of a ricochet or grazing shot. Not overly serious, in short.[24]

Second, Farnsworth's elbow injury raises the possibility that American doctors treated their wounded patients differently than did British doctors. The British were following established custom, and they had no time, as we've seen, for pausing to allow wounds to heal themselves. Had Farnsworth been wearing a red coat, his arm would have been off in short order, increasing the chances of infection and death. American doctors, on the other hand, enjoyed a measure of discretion. On the frontier or in rural areas, where most of them practiced, patients with gunshot wounds were brought home for treatment, not consigned to a rough hospital where disease ran rampant. Since the loss of a limb in an agricultural society would adversely affect a family's sustenance and means of survival, amputation would not be the immediate, unquestioning first resort of a doctor rushing to get to the next victim. He would instead treat and dress the wound with traditional poultices and ointments and wait to see what happened. If, after a few days, the patient's condition appeared to be worsening, he would perform the necessary operation; if, conversely, the patient seemed stable, he would postpone the surgery, perhaps forever. Thomas Greene, for instance, received "a bad wound from the enemy by a musket ball which passed quite through the shoulder, thereby making a compound fracture of the scapula and socket of the humerus." He, "in a fainting and almost expiring state, was saved by his friend [Richard] Gilchrist, who transported him on his back from Bunker Hill to Medford." In Boston, such a wound would have naturally resulted in an amputation, but as it was, the doctor decided to keep him whole. Greene survived the war, though he was painfully troubled by his shoulder wound for many years afterward and eventually received a pension for being "unsound and unable to do but little" work.[25]

Third, and lastly, unlike the British the Americans were not over-whelmed with casualties, which meant that there was not an intermi-nable line of patients needing treatment by exhausted, shorthanded doctors. Each of the distressed could be given more time and attention by one of the no fewer than eight physicians plus associated staff avail-able in the hospitals—the governor's house and a minister's home, quite hygienic places both—set up for them.[26] (By way of comparison, the British could initially call on three surgeons, with a few support staff, and casualties were crammed onto the docks, the almshouse, and the poorhouse—whose occupants were expelled.)[27] The militiaman Is-rael Potter certainly did not complain about the quality of care. He was "conveyed to the hospital in Cambridge, where my wounds were dressed and the bullet extracted from my hip by one of the surgeons. The house was nearly filled with the poor fellows who, like myself, had received wounds in the late engagement, and presented a melancholy spectacle."[28] Melancholy it might have been, but it is probable that far fewer wounded militiamen subsequently died than their British coun-terparts. (The ones who did were interred in the garden.)

British officers who died were buried in Boston "in a private man-ner, in the different churches and churchyards there." Bunker Hill was an anomaly in this respect. Because Boston was so close, the corpses could be properly entombed. More commonly, battles were fought well away from cities, and officers were laid to rest in individual, though anonymous, graves on the field. Enlisted men were deposited in com-munal pits, and on Sunday, the day after the battle, burial parties ar-rived on the peninsula to begin that grisly chore.

So it was that Captain Walter Sloan Laurie, supervising one such burial party, put Prescott's breastwork to good use by dragging at least ninety bodies into it and ordering his men to shovel the excavated earth on top.[29] At least then he could be sure that the grave was sufficiently deep so that if there was a heavy rain, the "heads, legs, and arms" of the dead would not, as often happened elsewhere, emerge from the ground, causing, in the words of one veteran, "a most dreadful smell."[30]

Laurie additionally interred sixty-eight corpses described as "reb-els." (They included the former president of Congress, Joseph Warren, who had joined Prescott in the redoubt. As Laurie boasted, "I found [him] among the slain, and stuffed the scoundrel with another rebel, into one hole, and there he, and his seditious principles may remain.")[31] Clearly, whether the militiamen were due the honors of war was not among his foremost concerns. Hygiene, however, was. In the words of General Howe, "a pestilence from the infection of the putrified bodies might reach the Camp," and so they had to be properly buried whether Laurie liked it or not.[32]

Another officer assigned to burial duty, Lieutenant Robert Dupont, discreetly alluded to a historically endemic problem of war: the looting of corpses. On Monday, June 19, his detail buried sixty-nine privates from "regiments not distinguishable being stript of uniforms." By that not only did he mean such regimental insignia as metal buttons, epaulettes, and decorations but indeed, anything portable. Some of the dead would have been stripped of their shoes, shirt, coat, gaiters, belt, and hat. There being no militiamen present and the peninsula clear of local residents, who often were responsible for such desecration, the culprits were certainly British troops. In many cases, cash was, of course, the object. William Crawford of the 20th forthrightly bragged that during his time in the army he retained a prayer book (despite possessing "no religion in my heart") because he "found [it] a safe depositary for my money, which I won in battle by rifling the dead and wounded."[33] In mid-July, so many off-duty soldiers were "opening the tombs or graves in the burying ground in Charlestown" that Howe announced that anyone caught doing so would be "severely punished."[34]

For their part, soldiers felt that plundering the dead helped make up for the privations they suffered and the risks they ran for distinctly modest wages. What harm was there, as one wrote, in taking an officer's good shoes? Another declared that "exchange is no robbery" when he swapped his old equipment for better kit belonging to a dead comrade. On the other hand, Sergeant Cooper was not ashamed to admit that there was once a soldier whose belt he coveted, and "though he was not quite dead I stripped him of it."[35] The sergeant did not bother to help him—he was beyond help—but it was certainly not unheard of to kill even a moderately wounded man for his belongings. Since Dupont was working on Monday, the initial round of looting would have taken place over the course of Saturday night or the Sabbath, and we can be quite sure that at least a few of those sixty-nine privates had survived the battle only to be murdered by their own side when it was over.

There was generally very little ceremony, respect, or solemnness allotted to the task of burial and memory. "The frequency of danger made us regard death as one of the most common occurrences of life," wrote one British officer, who clarified that if a man was wounded he received every commiseration, but if he died, his fellows showed an "indifference . . . which manifested in them a stoical disregard of existence." Another attested that "there was no real grief for any [officer] beyond a week or two—all a shadow that passed away. Their effects were sold by auction. We bought their clothes and wore them, and they were sold again perhaps in a month, being once more part of the kit of deceased officers killed in action." Even over their graves, there was rarely a funeral oration; instead, as happened with the late Major Jervoise, visitors "cut indecent jokes, laughing and jeering at the memory of a man whose heart was good and whose soul was brave."[36] Junior officers tended to be the most jovial, for the death of a luckless superior meant preferment.[37] Lieutenant William Gordon of the 52nd excitedly wrote home that thanks to the battle "I got five steps, which brings me within three of being the eldest lieutenant: I am in great spirits, and expectations, of getting a company [i.e., reach the rank of captain] before matters [in America] can possibly be concluded."[38]

Though the number of physically wounded was simple to tabulate, the extent and degree of mental trauma incurred by Bunker Hill veterans is more of a challenge. It is likely that profound psychological problems were, relative to their modern incidence, somewhat uncommon. For one, militia and civilian life existed along a continuum; among the Americans, "tours of duty" lasted only a few months, so there was no perceived need for men to readjust to home life as the stressful absences from home were relatively brief. Within the militia companies, moreover, many men worked alongside their kinsmen and friends, further reducing the incidences of isolation, depression, alienation, or anxiety upon their return home.

Just as important, there was no inkling of combat stress, shell shock, or what would later be called post-traumatic stress disorder (PTSD), since eighteenth-century soldiers lacked much of what we might term psychiatric self-awareness. Sigmund Freud would not be born for another three-quarters of a century, and such familiar (to us) mental concepts as the unconscious and neuroses were unheard of. Though the word *psychology* had been coined in the sixteenth century, it had long been the province not of doctors but of Protestant theologians concerned with the mysterious origins of the soul, or more precisely, whether its attributes were created by God or transmitted by parents. By the time of the War of Independence, philosophers had begun applying the notion to the great questions of free will and responsibility, but it was very far from being understood in the modern sense or being applied to ordinary people, let alone soldiers and their experience of combat.[39]

In other words, troops simply did not understand what happened to them in war in the same way as those born in later centuries. Though they might have behaved oddly and suffered from psychological problems after a battle like Bunker Hill, it was difficult to express their inner thoughts and emotions in terms meaningful to us—even if they had wished to. Unable to comprehend that future generations might find his memoirs fascinating, for instance, Amos Foster, a veteran of Bunker Hill, instead tantalizingly wrote, "I saw a good deal, and remember a good deal, but it is not worth writing that I know of."[40] We know of just eleven autobiographical accounts left behind by British common soldiers who were stationed in America between 1770 and 1783, yet nearly fifty thousand men served in the infantry during the War of Independence. Of the British redcoat or the American militiaman—as a thinking, feeling individual—we know very little, to put it mildly.[41]

Much of what we can gather from their diaries and letters, British and American alike, is an uncomplaining acceptance of death, hardship, and scarcity—not surprising given their routine experiences of cold, hunger, pain, sickness, and cruelty even during peacetime. Jarring to today's sensibilities is the soldiers' propensity to list in the most matter-of-fact way the whereabouts and number of their wounds while remaining silent as to the suffering that accompanied them. The pension applications that they submitted many decades later accordingly restrict themselves to citing, say, an elbow or knee that has been "troublesome" since the battle or a shoulder injury that has prevented them from working. There is never a hint of self-pity, only a surfeit of understatement masking the physical and psychic pain many must have experienced. For those accustomed to the graphic, introspective modern version of the genre, accordingly, the writings of those who fought at Bunker Hill come across as sparse, unfeeling, and chilly, strangely obsessed by the names of regimental colonels, the time they went to church, and the weather. Occasionally, a classical allusion to a hero of Troy, Athens, or Rome enlivens the text.

Of paramount importance to them, then, was not inner experience but external behavior. It was critical that one's actions be seen by peers, superiors, and kin as honorable, noble, and valiant, and that meant remaining mum even in the face of terror and hurt. Hence artists of the era avoided depicting soldiers in contemporary uniforms, preferring instead the robes and togas of the ancients—for they represented the timeless aristocratic virtues of heroism, honor, and sacrifice. King George III dismissed Benjamin West's 1770 painting of the 1759 death of General Wolfe at the Plains of Abraham specifically because he had portrayed some redcoats "in coats, breeches, and cock'd hats."[42] By the time of Bunker Hill there was a movement toward greater historical realism—West was eventually encouraged to depict the late Wolfe in what he actually wore—but the painter nevertheless continued to insist that in his picture "Wolfe must not die like a common soldier under a bush."[43] Wolfe could not be shown to be suffering or to be acting dishonorably, for fear of being "common"—and no one at Bunker Hill, be he humble farmer or modest artisan, desired to be tarred with that form of indignity.

Even so, there can be no doubt that some Bunker Hill veterans had fitful dreams, reacted to certain triggers, or experienced violent episodes, even if—for the reasons given above—we can glean only sparse hints, not absolute proof, of the phenomenon. One comes from a diary kept by the British lieutenant John Barker. In his entry for September 13, 1775, he wrote that "Captn. [Charles] Chandless of the Marines cut his throat." Three weeks later, another officer clarified to Lord Denbigh that Chandless had "in a violent fever cut his own throat."[44] General Gage's casualty report to London does not cite Chandless as having been wounded in action, so an injury was not the instigating factor. The reason for his suicide therefore remains a mystery. It is possible he was simply delusional owing to sickness or that he suffered from preexisting mental problems—but it might be that he was scarred by what he had seen during the battle and could not stand to live any longer. There may have been more sufferers among the relatively high number of officers who sold their commissions and resigned from the army in the weeks and months following the battle.[45]

More anecdotal evidence of disturbance may be found in the American painter John Trumbull's memoirs, where he says that on June 18 he met:

> my favorite sister, the wife of Colonel, afterwards General Huntington, whose regiment was on its march to join the army. The novelty of military scenes excited great curiosity through the country, and my sister was one of a party of young friends who were attracted to visit the army before Boston. She was a woman of deep and affectionate sensibility, and the moment of her visit was most unfortunate. She found herself surrounded, not by the "pomp and circumstance of glorious war," but in the midst of all its horrible realities. She saw too clearly the life of danger and hardship upon which her husband and her favorite brother had entered, and it overcame her strong, but too sensitive mind. She became deranged, and died the following November, in Dedham.[46]

Then there is the Rev. David Osgood, once the brimstone-spewing chaplain of a New Hampshire regiment, who was long tormented by what he saw and experienced that sunny June 17. Years later he could not forget, "nor can I ever forget while consciousness abides with me, my own mental sufferings" caused by battle. His heart "sickened with pain and anguish, [which] seemed without end, a burden lay upon my spirits, by day and by night, almost too heavy for frail mortality." When he tried to sleep, "visions of horror rose in my imagination." Nothing, not "the delightful vicissitudes of day and night, the cheery rotation of the seasons," could bring him the "accustomed pleasure" they once had.[47] Yet he retained his unshakeable faith that "on our part it was necessary" to fight for liberty in this needful hell, and he eventually emerged into the light and found peace.

8. Aftermath

In this period, generally speaking, the side that enjoyed numerical superiority on the field beat its opponent. At Bunker Hill, the Americans outnumbered their foes at most points during the battle, yet they quit the battleground, and in this conventional sense may be said to have lost. British victory hinged not on numbers, then, but on applying, accidentally, the most force at the critical point. When the Americans at the redoubt were weak, the British managed to storm the works, thereby sparking the retreat. Many of the latter were under no illusions how close a call it was. "Had we been defeated on the 17th of June," Lieutenant Rawdon wrote to his powerful uncle, the Earl of Huntingdon, "it was over with the British empire in America, and I can assure you at one time the chance was against us."[1]

But could their possession of the peninsula at sunset really be declared a victory? Howe had established his paramountcy there, but that was cold comfort while General Frederick Haldimand, who had served as Gage's second-in-command until he departed Boston the day before the battle, could comment in his diary that the British commanders had, he hoped, learned enough to never again try to "buy another hill at the same price."[2]

The terrible losses the British incurred certainly cast some doubt on their triumph, mostly because winners at this time tended to suffer fewer casualties (expressed as a percentage of total forces engaged) than did losers. Let us compare Bunker Hill with other battles of the era in Europe and America. There had been little fighting since the Seven

Years' War/French and Indian War, and so all of our examples date between 1756 and 1760, well within living memory. The average percentage of casualties among winners was 15 percent; among losers, 24 percent.[3] At Bunker Hill, conversely, British casualties amounted to 44 percent; American casualties 16.5 percent (assuming an elastic average of 2,500 men present—and 414 casualties). The American figure, clearly, approximates the general average among the winners, whereas the British was almost twice that of the usual *losers'* percentage.

On a more abstract level, we should also take into account the impact on morale and strategy caused by the fight at Bunker Hill. A week later, a shaken General Gage confidentially informed the Earl of Dartmouth that "the trials we have had show that the rebels are not the despicable rabble too many have supposed them to be, and I find it owing to a military spirit . . . joined with an uncommon degree of zeal and enthusiasm."[4] The body blow inflicted by a seeming hodgepodge of militiamen to its prestige and hubris was felt throughout the British army. One officer conceded to a friend that "the Americans are not those poltroons I myself was once taught to believe them to be; they are men of liberal and noble sentiments; their very characteristic is the love of liberty; and though I am an officer under the King of Great Britain, I tacitly admire their resolution and perserverance, against the present oppressive measures of the British Government."[5] Another ruefully confessed the day after the battle that "we have indeed learnt one melancholy truth, which is, that the Americans, if they are equally well commanded, are full as good soldiers as ours."[6]

By yardsticks such as these, the Americans were the victors, despite an inconsequential and temporary loss of territory that would be regained nine months later to the day, when, as a consequence of George Washington continuing the siege of Boston, the British evacuated that untenable city and left for Canada. In the summer of 1776, they would return, not to Boston—forever lost—but to a new base, New York, and continue the war from there.

The militiamen would not fight that war, but they made it possible. Whereas their mutinous stand at Lexington and Concord two months before on April 19, 1775, could have been otherwise dismissed as a one-off incident, a single act of cheeky defiance before inevitable submission, an annoying little gunfight in some country village, the sheer effrontery and stiff-necked stubbornness of the militias at Bunker Hill bloodily demonstrated that the rebellion was a potent, viable threat to His Majesty's interests—and one that would not be so easily vanquished as expected.

That June 17, the militias guaranteed their place in history while exiting from it. Militiamen there would still be, but even before the battle Congress had decided to establish a professional Continental Army to fight the protracted war rendered likely by their valor. Bunker Hill was thus both the last silver-trumpeted blast of the old colonial order and the herald of a new age of independence.

And so, when speaking of these obstreperous clan-like companies, these little platoons raised in the backwoods and the farmlands, we should reflect upon the pithy words of the Revolutionary soldier Colonel William Grayson (paraphrasing the poet Matthew Prior): "In short, at this time of day, we must say of them, as [of the] price of a wife: Be to their faults a little blind, And to their virtues very kind."[7]

GETTYSBURG

1863

1. Introduction

In early July 1938, some 1,800 veterans of the Civil War gathered for the last time at Gettysburg. Their average age was ninety-four, and each passing year was thinning their spindly ranks. To the other 75,000 visitors to the battlefield on that seventy-fifth anniversary of the great clash, the old men were the last remaining representatives of an America long vanished. Their accents, their clothes, their manners, everything about them bespoke an era fast receding from living memory. Since their youth, the country had transformed from a sleepy rural society where no one could travel faster than a horse into a gleamingly modern superpower of cities and corporations, movies and electricity, machines and factories.

The old men, many with empty trouser legs pinned up or sleeves tucked neatly into coat pockets, sat sheltered from the sultry heat under canvas tents set up on the field where Pickett had launched his terrible Charge, arguably the most glorious, and the most misbegotten, episode in American military history. Some reminisced fondly of the cannon fire and rifle volleys; others mutely remembered the carnage. Then, from above, a strange hum was heard, growing louder by the second. Looking up into the beautiful blue sky, the soldiers saw eighteen fighter planes soaring overhead that suddenly spiraled down like angry hornets to escort six new B-17 Flying Fortress bombers—the same aircraft that would soon desolate and incinerate Nazi Germany. If that sight was not astounding enough, a billowing cloud of yellow dust heralded the approach of thirty-one tanks that in turn performed maneuvers in the very same field where 12,500 doughty Confederates had once marched forward in flawless lines for nearly a mile under heavy Union fire.[1]

The clank of armor and the buzz of propellers aweing and alarming the wizened survivors of the Civil War vividly demonstrated to all the gulf between the old nineteenth-century warfare of glinting bayonets and unfurled banners and the new, mechanized, industrialized version. Nevertheless, the Civil War is today too often counted as the first of a trilogy of great *modern* and *total* wars of annihilation, the mighty clash from which would spring the demonic struggle of the First World War and its still more incarnadined successor two decades later.[2]

Popular as it is, this view of the Civil War is wrongheaded. To begin with, to describe the fighting from 1861 to 1865 as a "total war" is to retrofit a French term only confected in 1917. Adopted and adapted by the Nazis in the 1930s, it was cleansed of its dubious antecedents after 1945 by American military writers, who likened the recent bombing campaigns against Germany and Japan to Sherman's March to the Sea.[3] Total war, in other words, was a singularly twentieth-century form of warfare that considered the enemy population, industry, and infrastructure as legitimate and as important a military target as combatants in the field—a concept and means of warfare quite alien to those living in the nineteenth century, when generals thought almost exclusively in terms of defeating the enemy in a decisive battle, at least at the interstate level of army versus army.

If it was not total, neither was the Civil War "modern," though it can appear more contemporary than it actually was because some of its technology bears a distinct family resemblance to that of a later era.[4] The Civil War witnessed the use of railroad transport, rapid-firing guns, electric-telegraph wires, mortars, barbed wire, land mines, hand grenades, submarines, torpedoes, ironclad warships, gas shells, explosive bullets, telescopic-sighted sniper rifles—all put to bloody work in the next century and in some cases still used today. But very few of these technological marvels exerted a meaningful impact on the war's conduct or outcome, and virtually all of them had already been used in European wars.

If anything, the Civil War was characterized not by its gleamingly advanced technology but by a reliance on traditional tools, methods, and aesthetics. Nearly all movement was conducted on foot and by beast, and the vast majority of soldiers used guns similar to those owned by their grandfathers. As had long been the case, for much of the Civil War battlefields were compact, engagements generally lasted a few days rather than months or years, and senior commanders led personally from the front. Even the dress affected by generals and colonels alike recalled an earlier era. Their formal uniforms drooping under the weight of colossal, tasseled epaulettes and groaning with gold buttons, their swords proudly clattering in their scabbards and their boots polished to a gleam, American officers still followed the fashion dictates of Napoleon's marshals.

For much of its duration, the Civil War was thus a standard-issue late-nineteenth-century conflict with more in common with the Crimean War, the Napoleonic Wars, and even the War of Independence than World Wars I and II. If the Civil War was typical of its era, then so, too, was Gettysburg. Despite the attention it has subsequently attracted from historians, filmmakers, and the public, Gettysburg was neither extraordinary nor even that "important" in the grand scheme of the Civil War (the fall of Vicksburg on July 4, for instance, was of far greater import). It is Gettysburg's *conventionality*, not its uniqueness, that makes it such an interesting case study in the American soldier's experience of combat.

2. Combat in the Civil War

The style of fighting at Gettysburg was reminiscent of, if not identical to, that of Bunker Hill nearly a century earlier. The typical infantry engagement involved three crisis points. The first was located at the hundred-yard mark, the median range for Civil War firefights.[1] There are reports of shots being taken at 220 yards and upward, but most soldiers soon realized that long-distance fire was pointless: One rarely hit anything.[2] Instead, in order to improve its lethality, defending officers often tried to avoid firing the first volley until the enemy was fifty yards away—the second crisis point, for it was here that the attacking side collectively decided whether to continue on or to retreat. The final crisis point was at around thirty yards, when it was the defenders' turn to weigh whether to hold the line or to withdraw.[3] If they stood their ground, hand-to-hand combat would soon ensue.

The default tactic of Civil War combat was the straightforward frontal assault. To modern observers, these blunt force attacks and their colossal casualty lists seem astoundingly bloody, and, not to mince words, astonishingly stupid. Over time, their repeated use burned through manpower to a remarkable degree. For instance, a fairly typical unit that fought at Gettysburg, Company E of the 20th North Carolina, began its war on April 16, 1861, with 107 men. Over the next four years, twenty-six of these would die in battle and fourteen of disease, leaving sixty-seven living at war's end. Of the survivors, fifteen were permanently disabled with wounds, and sixteen had been wounded but recovered fully (at least physically, if perhaps not psychologically), thus leaving thirty-six unharmed (or one-third of the original recruits). Nineteen of these, however, had never been in combat, as they were detailed for other duties, so really only seventeen (16 percent of combat veterans) emerged from the war unscathed.[4] Another example is provided by the 137th New York regiment, which mustered 1,007 men on September 27, 1862. Of these, a third—323—would be killed and wounded during the war, and another 171 would perish of disease, accidents, and other noncombat causes.[5]

Despite these unencouraging figures, to those living at the time assaults made sense and few complained about them. To understand why, one must bear in mind two factors. First, the widespread acceptance of high losses was partly due to the belief that the primary intent of battle was not to kill the enemy while minimizing your own casualties—this is a byproduct of a very twentieth-century reliance on kill ratios, body counts, and casualty aversion as yardsticks of military effectiveness—but to *endure* startling (to us) casualties in order to achieve victory. A willingness to suffer, rather than inflict, high casualties was considered evidence of a muscularly Christian and heroically masculine will to win, not of lamentably poor command, bad planning, flawed execution, and idiotic decision-making, as we might assume today. In our eyes, attacking an entrenched position manned by thrice one's number might be regarded as insane and criminally wasteful rather than as bold and brave, but to Civil War contemporaries a man's internal "moral" power could conquer any such "physical" obstacles as fieldworks, artillery, and rifle fire.

Soldiers of the era were fascinated by the mysteries of this intangible inner spirit. There was a religious aspect to it, undoubtedly, but they were also profoundly influenced by the Romantic movement, originally an artistic and philosophical endeavor that exalted the dramatic, celebrated the intense, cheered the wondrous, and venerated the sublime. Since armed forces are as swayed by trends and fashions as any other sector of society, it is also important to factor in what might be called militarily correct thinking when it comes to organizing for war. For instance, in line with the Enlightenment fascination with mechanisms, tidiness, and rules, the characteristic metaphor of conventional eighteenth-century warfare had been that of the clock: a system of cogs, springs, and shafts precisely calibrated, eminently predictable, and dutifully subject to known principles that ticked in perfect time. Generals played the role of lordly watchmakers, elegantly maneuvering their magnificently drilled units across a given space and occupying such recommended terrain features and power centers as hills, bridges, and cities to gain the advantage of a positional fait accompli over the enemy. Theoretically, once realizing he had lost freedom of movement or action, the enemy would honorably capitulate without a fight. Thereafter, the victor would extract from him a duchy or two, purely as compensation for time and trouble. If he played the game well, said Maurice de Saxe (1696–1750), who gloried in the title of Marshal General of All the Armies of France, a truly successful commander might end his career without a battle honor to his name.[6] (As we've seen, reality was much messier; at Bunker Hill the American militias did not follow the rules.)

By the early nineteenth century, the martial world's orderly "clock" had been smashed by Napoleon, hero of the Romantics and guiding light for generations of commanders. American generals in particular enthusiastically succumbed to the Napoleonic fantasia.[7] Thomas Jackson, soon to be famed as "Stonewall," spent several days touring Waterloo in 1856. "In listening to Jackson talking of Napoleon Bonaparte, as I often did," recalled Dr. Hunter McGuire, "I was struck with the fact that he regarded him as the greatest general that ever lived."[8]

What the new breed of soldier thought of eighteenth-century generalship was perfectly captured by Napoleon in his dismissive notes, scribbled in the margins of the *Military Memoirs* of Henry Lloyd (c.1718–1783), once the echt and ur of Enlightenment military intellectuals who wanted to learn how to war. In response to the ousted master's impeccably Enlightened precepts, he wrote: "Ignorance," "Ignorance," "Ignorance," "Absurde," "Absurde," "Absurde," "Impossible," "Impossible," "Faux." This was all just in the first four pages.[9]

The clock was replaced by the steam engine—a new invention that generated its own motion.[10] Its thermodynamic process *transformed* energy from one source into another, unlike a clock, which merely transmitted it. As the engine converted lumpen coal into power, a lumpen man in combat, animated by his impulses, imagination, and ideology, could achieve the impossible.

No more was the heady blood-red wine of battle to be avoided; it, not skillful choreography, was to be embraced instead as the supreme test. A standard textbook studied by West Pointers just before the Civil War emphasized that whereas the fuddy-duddy Enlightenment style of warfare "looked only to the capture of one or two places, or to the occupation of a petty adjacent province," the secret of Napoleon's exciting success was "to burst, with the rapidity of lightning, upon the centre of this [enemy] army [or] to outflank it, to cut it off, to break it up, to pursue it to the utmost, forcing it in divergent directions; finally, quitting it only after having annihilated or dispersed it."[11] Indeed, a few days before Gettysburg, Robert E. Lee echoed the sentiment: "I shall throw an overwhelming force on their advance, crush it, follow up the success, drive one corps back upon another, and by successive repulses and surprises, before they can concentrate, create a panic and virtually destroy the army."[12] Later, Ulysses Grant would agree, albeit in typically blunter terms, that "the art of war is simple enough. Find out where your enemy is. Get at him as soon as you can. Strike at him as hard as you can, and keep moving on."[13]

In this light—the quest for decisive battle to demonstrate vigor and virility—losses in the tens of thousands were obviously peripheral. "Troops are made to let themselves be killed," Napoleon averred, proving his point by losing fully 863,000 of them.[14] It mattered not, because soldiers were nothing but coals to be cast into the furnace of war, their cindered remains testament to the energy their bodies had supplied for victory.

As Lee, Grant, and a host of other generals would find, the "spirit of the offensive" did not, nevertheless, radiate naturally from the souls of most men, especially at the outset of a real-world assault. "There is no romance in making one of these charges," as John Dooley of the 1st Virginia put it, for "when you rise to your feet . . . I tell you the enthusiasm of ardent breasts in many cases *ain't there,* and instead of burning to avenge the insults to our country, families and altars and firesides, the thought is most frequently, *Oh,* if I could just come out of this charge safely how thankful *would I be!*"[15] That was not quite the right attitude, needless to say, and hence the reliance on morale-boosting bayonets to inspire men during attacks.

Bayonets are perhaps the most misunderstood weapon of them all. They were virtually useless in combat, except in very specific circumstances—as at the redoubt at Bunker Hill, when the British could poke and prod the exhausted militiamen into flight. Subsequent generations have laughed them off as ridiculously quaint, as passé as the halberd, the lance, and the crossbow.[16] As evidence of their archaism, critics point to the manifold uses to which Civil War soldiers put them: skewers, tent stakes, and, in the memorable case of the chaplain of the Irish Brigade, a candelabrum, to hold the burning taper while he read his daily office.[17] So impotent were they that between May 8 and May 21, 1864—a period encompassing the battle of Spotsylvania, which featured some of the most intense combat of the war—the Army of the Potomac recorded a mere 14 bayonet wounds, compared to 749 caused by artillery fire and 8,218 by bullets.[18] Indeed, when someone actually died of a bayonet wound, it excited comment: Ignoring the other 185 casualties suffered by his regiment, Oscar Ladley of the 75th Ohio marveled to his family that a man "was killed by a rebel bayonet thrust in the groin."[19]

Yet soldiers of the time considered the weapon indispensable. The Union commander General George B. McClellan—in a sentiment echoed by his Confederate counterparts—instructed the troops in 1862 to "above all things rely upon the bayonet."[20] *Scientific American,* a publication never hesitant to rap the knuckles of what it regarded as reactionary military types, commented approvingly that, at least when it came to bayonets, McClellan "understands his business."[21] Stonewall Jackson, meanwhile, demanded a super-sized version for his men that was "six or more inches longer than the musket with the bayonet on, so that when we teach our troops to rely upon the bayonet they may feel that they have the superiority of arm resulting from its length." He wanted more cold steel, in other words, not more hot lead. General Lee, it should be added, approved the request.[22]

Leading soldiers understood that bayonets, when employed during an assault, symbolized for their bearers the aggressive necessity of coming to grips with the enemy—even if they were not used to kill. As Ambrose Bierce, the writer who fought at Shiloh (and several other battles), pointed out, while the bayonet was "a useless weapon for slaughter," this was irrelevant since "its purpose is a moral one."[23] Civilians like Sidney Fisher, who mentioned to a veteran "that a confused melee of furious men armed with [bayonets], stabbing each other & fighting hand to hand in a mass of hundreds, was something shocking even to think of," were invariably surprised when old soldiers clarified that while they had participated in many bayonet *assaults,* they had never been involved in any bayonet *fights.*[24] The Confederate officer Heros von Borcke went so far as to dismiss any accounts of bayonet-fighting as "exist[ing] only in the imagination."[25] By the time soldiers reached the enemy position, either the other side had run away or there was the usual melee of clubbed muskets, stones, and fists.

Thanks to their bayonets, their faith in the spirit of the offensive, and the detonation of their internal dynamos, soldiers spoke of becoming possessed by a "great magnificent passion" that "sublime[d] every sense and faculty" as they charged.[26] A man of the 19th Maine inexplicably "found myself rushing with all our crowd upon the enemy with an impetuosity that was irresistible."[27] By the time they reached the objective, said Benjamin Urban of the 30th Pennsylvania, troops typically "screamed in the mad delirium of battle, the fury of hell seemed to have entered into every breast, and the insane desire to kill dominated every other passion."[28] Achieving such an exalted state was the pinnacle of Civil War combat.

The second factor contributing to the enduring popularity of the frontal assault becomes clearer when we consider the real-world dilemmas facing a captain or colonel needing to make an urgent tactical decision about how to tackle a nearby enemy. He could choose from only a limited menu of options.

He could deploy in a defensive line and await the attack. This was the safest response, but would gain him neither ground nor glory. If his men did fend off the enemy, they would still be expected to mount a rapid counterattack.

Alternatively, he could order an immediate, full-throated, bayonets-fixed frontal assault. Many would die in the attack, but if successful it would break the enemy line and put them to flight.

Third, he could request a neighboring unit to create a diversion to one side while he organized an attack on the enemy front. On a smoky battlefield where communications were poor, however, coordinating and synchronizing such a complex plan was beyond the abilities of many officers. Again, too, success still required a frontal attack.

The final option was to mount a flank attack of his own. This high-status maneuver was a potentially decisive stroke, but the associated risks were enormous. Thus, Colonel Wheelock G. Veazey, commanding 16th Vermont, "moved [his forces] about 15 rods by marching by the left flank and filing to the left, so as to gain upon the enemy and bring my front facing obliquely to his left flank. When this position was gained I received permission to charge. The result of this charge was a very large number of prisoners, and, in the two movements, three stand of colors, the colors being stripped from one standard."[29] Veazey's gamble succeeded, but more often a commander had to split his force, with one smaller section holding the enemy's attention from the front as the larger discreetly circled to the side, which left his weakened center vulnerable to an enemy charge if the flankers were spotted, as they usually were. Even if the enemy did not take the opportunity to charge, they could swiftly change direction to face the oncoming flank attack—thereby unexpectedly turning it into a frontal attack, but now one where our luckless commander was outnumbered.[30]

Given the unappetizing choices available and the painful costs of failure, it becomes obvious why Civil War officers often relied on a conventional frontal attack in line formation. The most realistic option, as well as the easiest to arrange and the fastest to execute, it was also, paradoxically, far likelier to succeed than more creative tactics. And tempting as they may have been, these "cleverer" tactics were generally beyond the abilities of Union and Confederate officers. Few of these men, after all, were professional soldiers, and the majority had been civilians just a short time before. They were urged to keep it simple, not least by Henry Halleck, the general-in-chief of the Union armies at the time of Gettysburg, whose manual *Elements of Military Art and Science* was first printed in 1846 and republished each year until the end of the war. In it, he prescribed twelve fundamental "orders of battle" for units on the battlefield. Of these, fully eleven recommended plain linear deployments.[31] Similarly, Southerners, said General P. T. Beauregard, "always attack in *line* of battle" to get the job done.[32]

3. The Machine Breaks Down: The Reality of Combat

The stress on basic frontal line assaults stands in stark contrast to what a first-class commander aided by trusted subordinates and equipped with an excellent army could achieve. The acknowledged master in this respect had been, of course, Napoleon. The late emperor had instilled within his marshals an appreciation of the fluid concepts of versatility, surprise, and swiftness, and his corps and divisions maneuvered along multiple axes to exploit an opponent's weakness, phased their attacks to place him under unrelenting pressure, mixed infantry with cavalry to form rudimentary combined-operations arms, switched rapidly between columns and lines as needed, and swiveled freely to seize unexpected opportunities. Even a regular line was broken into components capable of autonomous articulation: One section could turn to face an oncoming threat while the others kept still or advanced.[1]

These were exceedingly difficult tricks to pull off. Which is why Civil War officers stuck to the basic rules they had learned from their manuals. As a result, when they tried to maneuver bodies of enthusiastic but often semi-trained volunteers to the right place at the right time, their attacks were generally clumsy, ill coordinated, asynchronous, and unimaginative, almost invariably following a binary structure of either holding position or advancing along a single axis directly at the enemy.

This absence of martial dexterity played a major, if unacknowledged, role at Gettysburg and during the war as a whole. One can easily see why frontal attacks took so many casualties when we consider that, for instance, just four of the 124th New York's thirty-nine field, staff, and company officers had any military experience whatsoever, and yet they were expected to handle a raw regiment in battle.[2] More alarmingly, during XI Corps's approach to Gettysburg on July 1, news arrived of Major General John Reynolds's death. Its senior officers were thus instantly promoted a notch to positions for which they lacked any training or background. And so, in one historian's words, "minutes before engaging the enemy, the oncoming troops would be thrust into mortal combat led by a general who had never before commanded a corps in action, another who had never before commanded a division in combat, a colonel who had never maneuvered a brigade in action, and a lieutenant colonel who had never led a regiment in combat."[3] Such challenges have humbled even history's greatest soldiers, let alone those recently drawn from the towns and farms of New England and the Mississippi Valley.

We should also bear in mind the rotten state of field communications. Superiors habitually issued unclear, contradictory, confusing, or taskless orders to their subordinates: V Corps was once directed to advance in four different directions at the same time.[4] Perhaps worse, field officers would receive orders long after they were pertinent or necessary—unsurprising, as it required nearly two hours for a message to wend its way from army headquarters down to even a brigade commander.[5] Subordinates, for their part, could cause chaos by issuing foolish or foolhardy commands without referring to their superiors. On the cusp of taking a battery of Union guns, for instance, South Carolinian regiments immediately obeyed an abstruse instruction (one participant, Private John Coxe of the 2nd South Carolina, called it "an insane order") to "'move by the right flank,' by some unauthorized person," allowing the fleeing Union gunners to return to their guns and unleash close-range fire upon the hapless attackers. General Joseph B. Kershaw later lamented that "hundreds of the bravest and best men of Carolina fell, victims of this fatal blunder."[6]

Meanwhile, brigade and regimental commanders, let alone company officers like captains and lieutenants, rarely enjoyed knowledge of broader goals, the purpose of their unit's movements, what was happening elsewhere—or even where they were.[7] For that reason, Brigadier General John Geary of XII Corps was left to stumble around in the dark at Gettysburg, wondering what to do and never knowing what was expected. He reported that when his 2nd Division was ordered to leave its entrenchments, "I received no specific instructions as to the object of the move, the direction to be taken, or the point to be reached, beyond the order to move, by the right flank and to follow the First Division."[8] Likewise, Brigadier General Alpheus Williams, commanding the XII's 1st Division, confessed that he too was "wholly ignorant of the topography of the country, I had seen no map of the localities around Gettysburg."[9]

Civil War battlefields were therefore often haphazard affairs, with regiments bumping into one another, waiting impotently while under heavy fire, wandering aimlessly to and fro, or attacking the nearest enemy who came to hand with no support and a complete lack of co-ordination. John Dooley, 1st Virginia, complained mightily of some North Carolinian regiments, which "should have charged simultaneously or immediately following us, thus overlapping our flank (right), and preventing our force from being surrounded in that direction. Unfortunately, owing to bad management . . . they were of no assistance to us in the charge; and, advancing either in the wrong direction or when too late, two thousand of them fell into the enemy's hands."[10]

When they were not directly engaged in the chaos, soldiers often lingered around uselessly before moving somewhere else and lingering there instead. Captain William Danforth told his wife that after arriving at Gettysburg on July 2 "we lay under a cross fire for three or four hours. It was hard. Then we marched under fire to another position. We marched by the flank 4 men abreast, for more than ½ mile then we changed to the front & marched in line of battle about a 100 rods [a third of a mile] and then lay behind a wall some time. We could not do much with our muskets, but lay in 3d line of battle until about dark. Then we went into the front line and lay in line until morning."[11] At no point did Danforth have any idea where he was, whether he could be helping an ailing unit, or what he was otherwise supposed to be doing.

Too much opprobrium should not be heaped on participants' heads; most officers tried the best they could but soon realized that the tactical movements so cleanly delineated in their manuals bore little resemblance to the messy reality unfolding before them. "The idea almost everyone forms of a battle is something like a vast chessboard," warned Thomas Evans of the 12th U.S. Infantry, "on which the masses of infantry are pawns, the cavalry, light artillery, and commanding officers the pieces, and the commanding generals the players," but naïfs were quickly disabused of that notion.[12] "To the book-soldier all order seems destroyed, months of drill apparently going for nothing in a few minutes" once the guns started firing, wrote D. L. Thompson of the 9th New York.[13]

War was entropy, they learned. Under battle conditions, the structure of even a well-trained company or regiment, perfectly formed up and pointed in the correct direction at a clear objective, would begin to disintegrate the minute it began moving forward. Frontal assaults relied on a combination of mass and momentum to sweep them forward swiftly enough to retain a semblance of cohesion. And so any attack that dissolved into scattered groups of men was almost certainly doomed to costly failure. Some scared soldiers would instinctually fire their weapons, prompting their comrades to stop, seek cover, and take their individual shots. The enemy thus gained time to recharge his artillery pieces and fire extra rifle volleys. Withdrawal—a euphemism for flight—accompanied by heavy casualties was inevitable unless officers could get their men back into line and moving again at a rapid clip, a highly rare occurrence.[14]

If the engine driving Civil War combat was the frontal assault, then in order to understand how one worked in practice, we need to disassemble it and study each piece. So, following a brief interlude to outline the background and main events of the battle, I'll examine what happened and what soldiers experienced by breaking down a generic infantry action in which one side is attacking the other's defending position. By such means, the genuine face of Gettysburg can be revealed in all its glory—or horror.

4. The Battle

In late June 1863, during his invasion of the North, General Robert E. Lee ordered his Army of Northern Virginia to converge near the Pennsylvania town of Gettysburg, as did the recently appointed chief of the Army of the Potomac, Major General George G. Meade. Both expected a major clash sometime in the first week of July, yet both were surprised when it actually occurred. On June 30, Confederate advance troops under Brigadier General J. Johnston Pettigrew were approaching Gettysburg when they witnessed a body of Union cavalry commanded by Brigadier General John Buford closing in from the south. Without engaging, Pettigrew returned to headquarters and reported his discovery. Early the next morning, his superior, division commander Major General Henry Heth, sent two brigades to reconnaissance in force. . . .

July 1. Day One, *Morning:* The heavily outnumbered Buford, in the meantime, had deployed defensively across three successive ridges to the west of Gettysburg: Herr Ridge (the most westerly), McPherson Ridge, and Seminary Ridge (the most easterly). His intention was to delay the Confederate advance long enough to permit the main Union forces to establish a position on the heights—Cemetery Hill, Cemetery

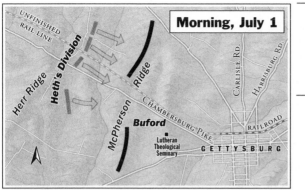

Morning, July 1

UNFINISHED RAIL LINE

Herr Ridge

Heth's Division

McPherson Ridge

CHAMBERSBURG PIKE

Buford

Lutheran Theological Seminary

RAILROAD

CARLISLE RD.

HARRISBURG RD.

G E T T Y S B U R G

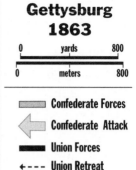

Gettysburg 1863

| 0 | yards | 800 |
| 0 | meters | 800 |

Confederate Forces

Confederate Attack

Union Forces

Union Retreat

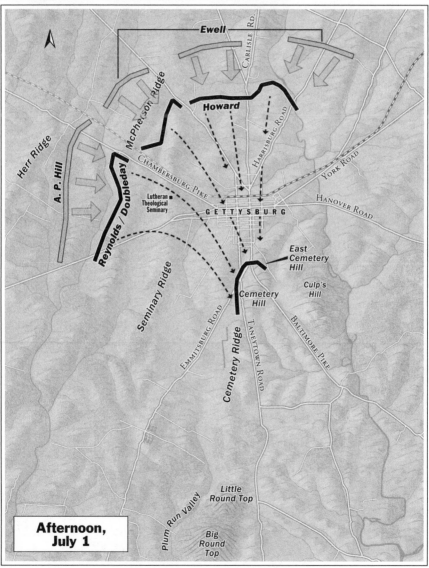

Ewell

CARLISLE RD.

McPherson Ridge

Howard

HARRISBURG ROAD

Herr Ridge

A. P. Hill

CHAMBERSBURG PIKE

Lutheran Theological Seminary

Reynolds / Doubleday

G E T T Y S B U R G

YORK ROAD

HANOVER ROAD

East Cemetery Hill

Culp's Hill

Seminary Ridge

Cemetery Hill

EMMITSBURG ROAD

Cemetery Ridge

TANEYTOWN ROAD

BALTIMORE PIKE

Plum Run Valley

Little Round Top

Big Round Top

Afternoon, July 1

Ridge, and Culp's Hill—south of Gettysburg. At about 7:30 A.M., the two Southern brigades marching eastward along the Chambersburg Pike encountered Buford's forward outposts. It was here that the first shots were fired. By 10:30, the Confederate brigades had pushed Buford's men back to McPherson Ridge. Fortunately for the Union Forces, the vanguard of Major General John Reynolds's I Corps had arrived (Union corps are designated with Roman numerals, Confederate with Arabic) and would soon be followed by reinforcements. Reynolds was killed early in the fighting, with Major General Abner Doubleday assuming command of his corps. The Southern brigades, meanwhile, were heavily engaged with mixed success until midday, when they paused to await the other two brigades of Heth's division and another division to arrive.

July 1. Day One, *Afternoon:* The fighting recommenced, this time more advantageously for the Confederates as their Union opponents fell back to Seminary Ridge, thence to the Lutheran Theological Seminary and subsequently to Cemetery Hill to the east. To the north, meanwhile, Lieutenant General Richard Ewell's 2nd Corps had proceeded along the Harrisburg and Carlisle roads as Major General Oliver Howard's XI Corps hastened to block it by setting up a semicircular defensive line arcing from west of Gettysburg to the northeast. Howard, however, had tried to cover too much ground with too few troops. At about 2 P.M., two full Confederate divisions crashed into the Union positions, which quickly disintegrated. Howard retreated south past Gettysburg to Cemetery Hill, an immensely strong position. Grasping that Union forces would be difficult to dislodge if they were given an opportunity to entrench, Lee ordered Ewell to take the Hill "if practicable"—a dangerous caveat—while the Northern troops were still reeling from the onslaught. Ewell eventually decided against an all-out assault, giving his foe critical time to recover.

July 2. Day Two, *Morning:* By mid-morning, the rest of the two armies had arrived. Overnight, the Union soldiers had worked hard to solidify their position. Most of XII Corps had been sent to Culp's Hill, and the

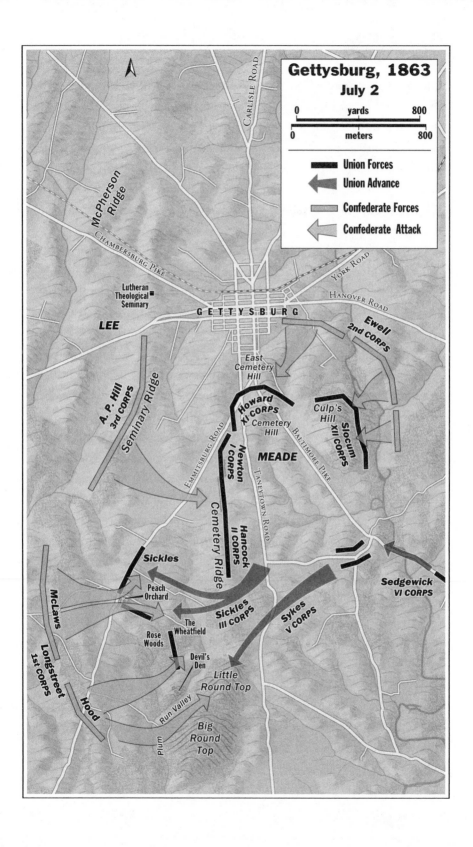

Gettysburg, 1863
July 2

0   yards   800

0   meters   800

Union Forces

Union Advance

Confederate Forces

Confederate Attack

CARLISLE ROAD

McPherson Ridge

CHAMBERSBURG PIKE

YORK ROAD

HANOVER ROAD

Lutheran
Theological
Seminary

GETTYSBURG

LEE

Ewell
2nd CORPS

A. P. Hill
3rd CORPS

Seminary Ridge

East
Cemetery
Hill

Howard
XI CORPS

Cemetery
Hill

Culp's
Hill

Slocum
XII CORPS

EMMITSBURG ROAD

Newton
I CORPS

MEADE

BALTIMORE PIKE

TANEYTOWN ROAD

Cemetery Ridge

Hancock
II CORPS

Sickles

Sedgewick
VI CORPS

Peach
Orchard

McLaws

Sickles
III CORPS

Sykes
V CORPS

The
Wheatfield

Rose
Woods

Longstreet
1st CORPS

Hood

Devil's
Den

Little
Round Top

Plum

Run Valley

Big
Round
Top

line from there circled northwest to Cemetery Hill (I and XI Corps), then straight south, spine-like, for nearly two miles along Cemetery Ridge (II and III Corps), ending just north of a prominence named Little Round Top. From above, the Union defenses resembled an upside-down fishhook. The Confederate 3rd Corps was centered on Seminary Ridge, about a mile west of Cemetery Ridge, while more soldiers occupied Gettysburg and staked out a curved line mirroring that of their opponents, terminating opposite Culp's Hill. The Confederate line was considerably longer than the Union's, and worse, there were fewer men to hold it. The Union commanders, on the other hand, could easily shuttle units back and forth if a weak spot developed. Lee's trump card was Lieutenant General James Longstreet's 1st Corps, which had stealthily moved south along the Emmitsburg Road, beyond the Union's farthermost flank. Lee planned for his 2nd Corps divisions to mount a diversionary expedition against Culp's Hill as the 3rd Corps attacked Cemetery Hill. At the same time, Longstreet's two divisions (under Major Generals John Bell Hood and Lafayette McLaws) would hit the Union left. If all went well, Meade's advantage of interior lines would be negated as his troops were pinned down and flanked, but success hinged on a rapid and well-coordinated general attack taking place. Unbeknownst to Lee, however, Major General Daniel Sickles's III Corps had left its original position at the southern end of Cemetery Ridge to move forward to the Emmitsburg Road. The Union line now ran from the boulder-strewn Devil's Den northwest to the Peach Orchard and then northeast along Emmitsburg Road. The position, which Sickles had selected without bothering to wait for Meade's approval, was fundamentally untenable in the face of superior Confederate numbers, but instead of Longstreet being able to outflank the Union left, McLaws's division, much to its surprise, would now need to undertake a direct frontal assault.

July 2. Day Two, *Afternoon:* Worse, owing to delays, Longstreet's attack did not begin until 4 P.M. Meade immediately sent in his reserves, comprising V Corps, most of XII Corps, a division of II Corps, and a portion of VI Corps. Meanwhile, Hood's division had deviated east from

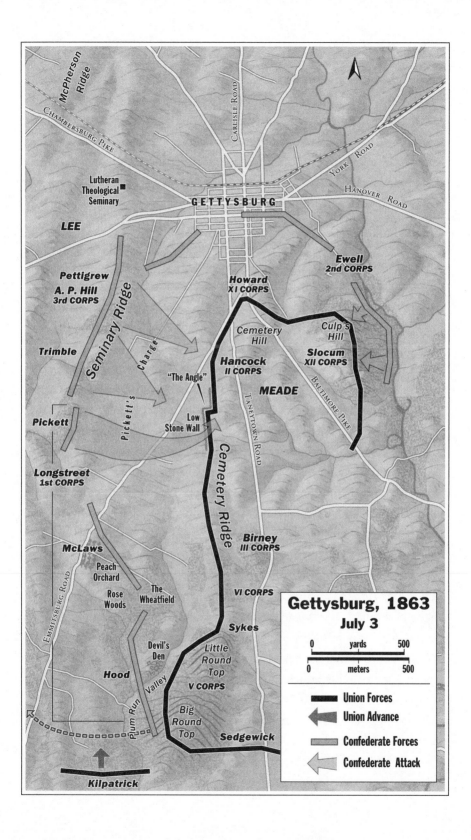

Gettysburg, 1863
July 3

its assigned course and was engaged in heavy fighting at Devil's Den, Plum Run Valley, and Little Round Top as it swung north. At the latter, a key strategic point, a small brigade held out against multiple Confederate assaults by men of Hood's division, culminating in a famous bayonet charge against the disheartened Southerners. McLaws had been held back during Hood's action, and only at 5 P.M. could he unleash his brigades at III Corps. His initial target was the twenty-acre Wheatfield and Rose Woods, and it was here that some of the bloodiest combat occurred as Union and Confederate forces mounted a welter of attacks and counterattacks. To their northwest, two Confederate brigades eventually pushed through the Peach Orchard as Sickles's men broke. By that point, III Corps was essentially destroyed. To the northeast, however, a Confederate attack under Major General Richard Anderson that began at 6 P.M. against the remnants of III Corps initially won some success but eventually petered out. Despite enormous losses, the Union left still stood. On Meade's right, the Confederate 2nd Corps did not begin its attack on Culp's Hill until 7 P.M. Owing to the failure to synchronize Confederate movements, Meade had benefited from being able to shunt most of his XII Corps from Culp's Hill to the left, leaving but a single New York brigade and some reinforcements to defend his right. The New Yorkers, however, were strongly entrenched, and the Confederate attack was fended off. The XI Corps troops on East Cemetery Hill likewise held out against a determined, if unsupported, assault that evening.

July 3. Day Three, *Morning:* The piecemeal attacks on the Union left and right had failed, but Meade's center remained relatively unscathed. It was toward this position on Cemetery Ridge—defended primarily by the II Corps—that Lee now directed his attention. He intended to coordinate a major attack there with a smaller one at Culp's Hill. A breakthrough in the center would provoke a Union collapse as Meade's left and right lost contact with one another, leaving them prey to Confederate flank attacks. To soften up the Union defenders, there would be a colossal artillery bombardment before the infantry advanced. Meade, however, did not permit Lee the luxury of completing his dispositions. At dawn, the Union batteries on Culp's Hill fired on the Confederate brigades below, prompting a futile succession of three Southern infantry assaults on the hill, each ending in failure and ultimately disrupting Lee's plan to harmonize the twin attacks.

July 3. Day Three, *Afternoon:* Despite the setback, at approximately 1 P.M. the Confederate guns thunderously opened up against Cemetery Ridge. A quarter of an hour later, their Union counterparts returned fire. Low on ammunition and poorly coordinated, the South's artillery did not inflict significant damage on the defenders—though gunners mistakenly believed otherwise—and at about 3 P.M. firing virtually ceased and 12,500 soldiers began their advance across three-quarters of a mile of mostly open ground. This mile-wide grand infantry assault would come to be known as Pickett's Charge after Major General George Pickett. Casualties quickly mounted as flanking artillery fire raked their ranks, followed by shells and canister from the guns in the Union center. The Confederates marched indomitably on. There was a near-breakthrough at a salient in a low stone wall called the Angle, but inrushing reinforcements repulsed the attackers, and they were unable to exploit the temporary breach. The Confederates fell back to their own lines in disarray, but half never returned. The battle was over.

Aftermath: That night, Lee established a strong defensive position on Seminary Ridge, vainly hoping that Meade would take the bait and attack. After collecting as many of the dead and wounded as he could on July 4, Lee evacuated and began the long and difficult retreat to Virginia. Meade would shadowbox with his opponent along the way but failed to exterminate the Army of Northern Virginia, leaving Lee free to fight another day.

5. Marching to Gettysburg

Every single soldier at Gettysburg was tired, thirsty, and hot. Regiments, bundled into brigades, had been ordered to rush to the area once it was known that a major battle was in the offing. Even for troops accustomed to long marches along dusty or muddy roads, the hurried advance to Gettysburg was reckoned especially onerous.

"They marched us like dogs," complained Private Daniel Handy of the 2nd Rhode Island. A companion, Charles Nichols, told his sister that by the end his "feet [were] all blistered, and every bone [was] aching. As for me I could scarcely move a foot" when he actually arrived at the battlefield. Their regiment had tramped thirty-five miles overnight and for much of the following day with just three five-minute halts.[1] Blisters the size of quarters were the least of it. After the 5th Wisconsin marched twenty-six miles in a day, Richard Carter's right leg was as "swollen as full as the skin can hold + so full that the skin is discolored."[2]

Sheer exhaustion would affect performance during the battle. Despite having tramped twenty-eight miles in eleven hours, Law's Alabama Brigade was upon its arrival almost immediately ordered forward to storm Devil's Den and Little Round Top—an assignment difficult even for fresh troops and close to impossible for tired ones.[3] During the colossal artillery duel on the third day, Colonel Wheelock Veazey saw "the most astonishing thing I ever witnessed in any battle" along his section of the Union line. Most of the men of his 16th Vermont, having lain down to take cover from the shell and shot screaming overhead, actually "fell asleep, and it was with the greatest effort only that I could keep awake myself."[4]

The Alabamians' failure to take Little Round Top was also caused partly, said one, by parchedness: Lack of water combined with fatigue rendered men helpless when the Union counterattacked.[5] In suffering from dehydration, the Alabamians were not alone. Few soldiers in either army had consumed much more than the barest amount of water required to function. While there was plenty available, the liquid was believed harmful to drink straight on hot days thanks in part to a well-known *New York Times* letter to the editor—much clipped out and sent on by parents and spouses eager to help their favorite recruit as he marched off to war—that had advised soldiers to consume as little as possible.[6]

Sunstroke, exacerbated by dehydration, predictably afflicted both armies on the way to Gettysburg. Artilleryman Robert Carter said that Colonel Gleason of the 25th New York and seventeen men in his division all died of it within a day.[7] The Texas Brigade recorded no fewer than two hundred cases of fainting, severe muscle cramps, body-temperature spikes, and blinding headaches in a single day.[8]

Not every unit suffered equally. In regiments whose officers ignored conventional wisdom and told their men to drink freely when they were thirsty, sunstroke was a minor problem. Just four men of the 5th Maine's 340 troops, for instance, went down with it, a rate of 1.2 percent. The officers of the 124th New York and the 17th U.S. Regulars, on the other hand, actively prevented their men from refilling their canteens at roadside wells and pumps—and suffered grievously as a result. More than half the New Yorkers were rendered useless, while a third of the Regulars were too weak to stand by the time they were needed to launch an important attack at the Wheatfield.[9]

Since there was little contemporary comprehension of the link between adequate hydration and heat-related illness, there was generally little sympathy expended on sufferers, for "sunstroke" was an excuse commonly offered by malingerers. If the afflicted were lucky, as was Captain McKee of the 155th Pennsylvania when he fainted near Gettysburg, they could rest and return to their regiment once they recovered.[10] More often, they were ordered to march until they dropped; even then, officers would sometimes beat the semiconscious with the flat of their swords as punishment for their cowardice.[11]

But the oppressive heat was most often cited by soldiers as their abiding memory of those July days. Michael Jacobs, a resident of Gettysburg, kept meticulous observations of the weather conditions during the battle. The first day was cloudy, with a barely discernible breeze—smoke sometimes rose vertically—and temperatures in the mid-seventies by 2 P.M. July 2 was just as calm and cloudy, but the sun emerged after lunch and the temperature hit 81 degrees in the early afternoon. The final day was much brighter by 2 P.M., though a "massive thunder-cloud of summer" threateningly rolled in that afternoon. Wind speed was again very gentle, but the mercury had risen to 87 degrees by the time of Pickett's Charge.[12] Despite the otherwise tolerable temperatures, exceptionally high humidity made wool-clad, parched soldiers feel as if it was in the high nineties at least. Even on the morning of July 1, when it was a very pleasant 72 degrees, the humidity was so pervasive that thirty men of the 150th Pennsylvania simply passed out or stopped marching.[13]

For much of the battle, the sun looked, fittingly, like Mars—both the god of war and his planet: Suspended high in the heavens and glowering down upon these mortals, it resembled nothing less than "a big ball of blood," in the words of Thomas Day of the 3rd Indiana Cavalry.[14]

As soldiers neared the field, they forgot their woes as the "deep-toned booming" of the artillery grew louder. The sound, wrote a captain, was easily mistaken by raw troops for fireworks or drums.[15] The young lieutenant Lloyd Harris assumed that the silly residents of Gettysburg were celebrating July 4 early. His veterans, who had run the gauntlet at Antietam, Fredericksburg, and Chancellorsville, knew better.[16] As they marched closer, they would begin to feel the ground trembling and quaking beneath their feet. Billy Bayly, who lived near Gettysburg, heard the Union batteries firing in unison and likened the barrage to "the roar of a continuous thunderstorm and the sharp angry crashes of the thunderbolt." The "reverberation from [the] discharges shook the windows in the house," which itself shuddered.[17]

The first sight soldiers would have of the field were the black and gray clouds of smoke the artillery was belching out. It was hard to see what lay ahead. Sometimes emerging from the enshrouding fug were the panicked and blackened figures of their fellow soldiers, lately bested by the enemy. The spectacle threatened to unman them. George Squier of Indiana confessed that the sight of ragged troops streaming back missing fingers or hands "rather daunted my fervor and for the first time I doubted my courage."[18] It certainly did not help that as the survivors passed, they cried, " 'Don't go out there' 'You'll catch hell' 'We are all cut to pieces' 'We are whipped.' "[19]

Benjamin Thompson soon found it "difficult to keep a line in the face of these squads of flying men" pushing through his brigade's ranks and between its files.[20] Some soldiers tried their best to help by grabbing hold of these broken and maddened men, said Alfred Carpenter of 1st Minnesota, but "at last gave it up entirely, believing they were more injury than help to us."[21] A few tried more direct means, such as a Corporal Plunkett who swore "like a pirate," seized "a big tin coffee pot," and "smash[ed] it over the head of one of the frightened boys. . . . The blow broke in the bottom but the fellow kept running."[22]

It would soon be their turn to enter the maelstrom. They kept on marching.

6. Skirmishing

As the regiments reached their positions and settled in to prepare for an action, a number of men were selected for skirmish work. Skirmishing was a relatively new development, dating from the Napoleonic Wars. Because so many aristocrats had been executed or exiled in the early years of the French Revolution, the new republic's generals had been hard-pressed to find sufficient officers to lead and train their enthusiastic but inexperienced armies. Until they reconstituted their officer corps, French commanders adapted an eighteenth-century practice of sending small numbers of *piquets* ("pickets" in English) forward to guard outlying approaches. They also released swarms of men ahead of the main body to harass the enemy. The British, meanwhile, were relying ever more heavily on their highly trained Light units to snipe at and scout the foe. In short order, the once-distinct roles of *piquets*, harassers, and Light troops had merged into a single form of fighting known as skirmishing.

American military manuals from 1812 onward attached increasing importance to skirmishing, and by the Civil War it was standard practice to send detachments forward to anywhere between fifty and four hundred yards of the enemy's positions. There, they would perform the same role as an insect's antennae: to feel out the foe's whereabouts and numbers, to sense when dangerous movement was afoot, and to brush against over-territorial rivals. The heavy work of combat, meanwhile, would be left to the jaws and pincers of the line troops and artillery waiting behind.

A company or two per regiment would be assigned skirmishing duty whenever the enemy was in the vicinity. More were ordered when hostile forces were close enough at hand to launch an attack—either surprise or counter. For that reason, the worried commander of the 16th Vermont sent up three companies (about a third of the regiment) on the night of July 2; that of the 47th Alabama did the same before the assault on Big Round Top; but fully four companies of the 19th Maine (almost half the regiment) were dispatched on July 3.[1] When Davis's Brigade came under fire early on July 1 by Buford's cavalrymen, for instance, the former immediately threw forward three lines of skirmishers to keep the Northerners busy while the rest of his troops readied themselves.[2] The folly of neglecting one's skirmish line was borne out disastrously by Brigadier General Alfred Iverson, commanding the 5th, 12th, 20th, and 23rd North Carolina, when he sent his brigade across a field without an advance screen. It walked straight into a Union line that had been crouching behind a wall and instantly opened up with a devastating volley, killing and wounding hundreds.[3]

Having been selected, each skirmisher would slither forward a few hundred yards, seek out a modicum of cover to wait out his time, and keep an adequate distance from his comrades.[4] It was lonely work, especially for soldiers accustomed to the main battle line's elbow-to-elbow familiarity, and when it wasn't boring it was exceedingly dangerous. Since a skirmisher was expected to shoot at his counterpart whenever possible, he was constantly under threat of assassination by an unseen foe. The 25th Ohio lost fourteen men by such means in a twenty-hour stint on the skirmish line, while the 136th New York suffered 106 casualties over two days.[5] During the bitter tussle over the Bliss Farm, a key tactical point, twenty-eight skirmishers of the 39th New York were killed and wounded in four hours.[6]

During a charge, of course, such high casualties would be incurred within minutes, but the slow attrition and the constant stress of skirmishing ground agonizingly on men's nerves. Small wonder that soldiers almost universally hated it.[7] For Benjamin Thompson, "line fighting is barbarous, but skirmishing is savage—nay, devilish. To juke and hide and skulk for men and deliberately aim at and murder them one by one is far too bloodthirsty for Christian men."[8] George Yost of the 126th New York told his father that "I would do anything rather than skirmish with those fellows. I never want to do it again. I will charge and repel charges but don't put me in that place again."[9]

It was the silence, not just the solitude, that was unsettling. In regular combat, the pervasive, encompassing cacophony of noise allowed a soldier to reassure, or delude, himself that the enemy had not noticed him in particular; out skirmishing, however, it was painfully obvious when he was being specifically targeted. An incoming bullet was disconcertingly distinct amid the quiet of the skirmish line: The sound of one passing nearby was described as a "sharp *zip*—p-i-n-g-g-g," while another soldier likened it to "a very small circular saw cutting through thin strips of wood." One musician's ear was so finely attuned that he could define the noise as "a swell from E flat to F, and as it retrograded in the distance receded to D—a very pretty change."[10]

Even if one was hidden, merely firing one's rifle immediately attracted unwelcome attention when its revealing puff of smoke floated upward. An enemy bullet or two often followed, catnip for daredevils but heart-stoppingly terrifying for ordinary men.[11] Understandably, many skirmishers ignored their orders to shoot the enemy whenever possible in order to keep themselves safely hidden until they could be relieved. They hoped the favor would be returned, but not everyone played by the unwritten rules. Corporal Samuel Huxham of Company B, 14th Connecticut, was out on the skirmish line on July 3 in front of Cemetery Ridge. His company had crawled two hundred yards through a wheat field before arriving at a rail fence where they could secrete themselves among its posts and lower rails. After some time lying prone and motionless, Huxham needed to stretch and began to kneel. Several minutes later, Private Hiram Fox quietly called to him but received no answer. Wriggling his way over, Fox found Huxham dead with a bullet hole in his head.[12]

Poor Huxham was evidently the victim of a marksman prowling the dangerous no-man's-land of the skirmish lines. Some of these were simply regular soldiers with a hunting background who happened to be on skirmishing duty, but there were other fine shots formally designated as sharpshooters and often collated into specialist units. A scattered few were renowned as the elite of the elite: former national or state shooting champions, or those capable of competing at that level, who owned a customized target rifle equipped with advanced optical sights and a tripod.[13]

Sharpshooters were an effective defense against skirmishers. Soldiers often spoke of snipers "annoying" or "galling" them, and they were truly a nuisance. For the most part, sharpshooters served to hold up forward movements, as happened when several hidden marksmen pinned down Louisiana Brigade skirmishers below Cemetery Ridge on July 2. "We had to remain there—more than five hundred yards in advance of Ewell's main line of battle—hugging the ground behind a very low ridge," wrote Captain William Seymour. "It was almost certain death for a man to stand upright and we lost during the day forty-five men in killed and wounded from the fire of the enemy's sharpshooters, who were armed with long-ranged Whitworth rifles."[14]

In difficult terrain, sharpshooters came into their own. At Gettysburg the boulder-strewn, crevice-filled landscape of Devil's Den was a marksman's paradise. Eight men of Company E of 3rd Arkansas were found shot precisely in the head, while, as A. P. Case of the 146th New York noted, "behind one short low ridge of rock lay a row of eighteen dead who had been tallied out one by one by our sharpshooters."[15] As Captain R. K. Beechan explained, Confederate sharpshooters exacted their own heavy toll against Union soldiers standing backlit against the setting sun.[16] They lost so many men that, according to the 30th Pennsyvania's Benjamin Urban, "strict orders were given to keep down."[17]

Sharpshooters, being detested for their trade, were not taken prisoner. Said the 2nd Pennsylvania's E. M. Woodward, "the boys never showed [them] any mercy" if they surrendered.[18] When some Union soldiers charged into Devil's Den and captured twenty Confederate snipers, "they were much alarmed at being caught, because as sharp-shooters they expected no quarter, and begged lustily for their lives." When Sergeant Richard Tyler assured them that they would be treated fairly, they refused to believe him until they discovered that their captors were members of a sharpshooter company themselves. Only then did their "dejected spirit" suddenly transform to "one of undisguised happiness."[19]

Since there was no need to capture sharpshooters alive, soldiers invented several invariably lethal ways to flush out an irritant. One effective method was to flank him. A few men of Urban's regiment "crept out through the grass as far as possible without being seen," circling to the left and right of the tree branches where they suspected their tormentor was hiding. "Then several men in the center deliberately stood up . . . to draw his fire and compel him to reveal his exact location, which he promptly did, and as promptly was he riddled by the deadly fire of the concealed Bucktails. It was afterwards seen that he had tied himself to the tree so that he could not fall down."[20]

Alternatively, overwhelming firepower could accomplish wonders. When the 40th Virginia was being harassed by sharpshooters "concealed in a large wooden building on our left," Captain Wayland Dunaway ordered his entire company to stand up and "fire a volley into the house and that put a stop to the murderous villainy."[21] In standing up en masse like that, however, the company had to be wary of being suckered into exposing an entire unit to deadly counterfire from other marksmen hidden nearby. The 22nd Massachusetts fell hook, line, and sinker when they rose up and poured a lively broadside into what they thought was a nest of sharpshooters from the 3rd Arkansas. Remembered one of those fooled, "we soon learned that our fire had been drawn by the old, well-known Yankee trick of displaying hats upon sticks or ramrods."[22] A related gambit was the bait-and-switch. While on skirmish duty, Private Charles Comstock of the 13th Massachusetts was plagued by a Confederate directly ahead of him who sent a shot whizzing past whenever Comstock fired. He loaded a gun left behind by some wounded unfortunate, set it alongside his own, and pulled its trigger. The rebel's head popped up and Comstock removed it with a follow-up shot from his own gun.[23]

Finally, if all else failed, one could set a thief to catch a thief. Bedeviled by Confederate sharpshooters firing "from two openings in the second [story]" of a barn, Richard Thompson of the 12th New Jersey called upon a detachment of Captain William Plumer's Massachusetts snipers who carried their own "very heavy, long-range telescope rifles, with a sort of tripod rest." After Plumer's men hit a few of them, the Confederates understandably turned more cautious. Now, whenever they saw a muzzle flash they vanished from the openings until the bullet hit wood, then returned fire and ducked back down.

The frustrated Union snipers countered by forming "themselves into squads or partnerships of three." The first man would fire, the rebels would vanish, then the two others would count to three, see the Confederates reappear at the pair of openings, and each would fire at his appointed target. The trouble from these miscreants soon ceased. "Alas! How little we thought human life was the stake for which this game was being played," exclaimed Thompson, who was nonetheless relieved at their being put out of his misery.[24]

While sharpshooters roamed in the daylight, night possessed its own terrors for skirmishers. Push too far forward into the unrelenting darkness and a skirmish line would run smack into one coming the other way or even the main force itself, provoking a firefight at close quarters.[25] Lieutenant Milton Daniels, Sergeant Patrick Wade, and ten privates of the 17th Connecticut had a fearfully close call when, before dawn, they unwittingly crept into a field whose "trampled grass" and scattered "bits of cracker and bread" meant only one thing: A brigade at the very least had recently camped there. In the end, it turned out well, for this was the morn of July 4, and Lee's army had retreated an hour before.[26]

Being kidnapped was also a danger. Four men of the 14th Connecticut vanished one night, snatched by Confederates when they accidentally ventured too far beyond their lines. Thomas Galwey, of the

8th Ohio, had been stalking an orderly searching for General Stephen Ramseur's brigade and was just about to pounce when a comrade named Private "Bucktown" Brown cocked his gun and "alarmed our bird, and he turned and fled."[27]

That orderly was remarkably lucky: Out on the forward lines, the wounded often died alone. There were times, however, when someone took pity on an ailing man and tried to help. Thomas Galwey, the Ohioan, was skirmishing on July 3 when "about the middle of the forenoon, a cry of, 'Don't fire, Yanks!' rang out [and] a [Confederate emerged from hiding behind a tree to] give a drink to one of our wounded who lay there beyond us. Of course we cheered the Reb, and someone shouted, 'Bully for you Johnny!'" After Union and Confederate alike stood to cheer, the sharpshooter turned around and went back to the tree, and then at the top of his voice shouted, 'Down Yanks, we're going to fire.' And down we lay again."[28] Such admirable demonstrations of chivalry were few and far between, despite mawkish tales told after the war in the spirit of brotherly reconciliation. Less edifying were instances of outright sadism, such as that witnessed by a 14th Connecticut soldier named Stevens. He watched a Union sharpshooter entertain himself by hunting a wounded skirmisher "unable to stand, who was trying, by a series of flops, to drag his body up the slope to the shelter of his own lines." Said Stevens, the unsporting gentleman "fired at him for several minutes as frequently as he could load and take aim; but we confess[ed] to a feeling of relief and gladness . . . when the man let up on the poor fellow and had failed to hit him."[29]

A skirmisher was not safe even at the end of his shift. The palpable relief gained from repairing rearward was tempered by the "lively popping all along the line of their opponents as long as a man was in sight," remembered one with a shudder.[30] Those returning were only too keen to see the enemy paid back in kind. Some men of Battery D, 5th U.S. Artillery were preparing their guns for the next phase of combat when a skirmisher of III Corps limped toward them holding his eyeball, still attached to its cord. The victim of a sharpshooter, he told the artillerists, "See what they gave me. Give them [Hell] and I will support you."[31]

7. Artillery Versus Artillery

As skirmishers and sharpshooters hunted each other, the men in the main line were preparing either to advance or to dig in. For them, the period before an imminent action contained its own terror, one that those assigned forward duty were thankful to escape: coming under artillery fire.

The primary task of artillery was, depending on the side, either to hinder an infantry attack or to ease its path. Before turning its unwelcome attention to the waiting soldiery, however, the enemy artillery would seek first to suppress any nearby guns. Neutralizing the opposing batteries was counted, said Captain James Smith, as the supreme "trial of skill between artillerists."[1] Indeed, Colonel Benjamin Scribner of the 38th Indiana noticed of artillerymen that "cannon against cannon they appear to delight in; they seem to feel complimented when the enemy turns his guns upon them."[2] One Vermont soldier likened the sight of rival batteries menacing each other to "grim bulldogs" facing off before a fight.[3]

It was best, if possible, to fire on batteries still trundling into position, when they were most vulnerable—as well as most visible, since smoke had yet to obscure their whereabouts. It was likely, too, that the guns' limbers and caissons—two-wheeled wagons that bore the battery's ammunition chests, spare parts, and tools—would be close at hand, increasing the chances of destroying something vital with each shot.[4]

If such an opportunity did not arise, an artillery commander would try to situate his guns at an oblique angle to those opposite. While the enemy lost valuable time reorienting his cannons to face the new threat directly, the other's guns would be firing at the lengthy profiles of the wheels and carriage rather than the slimmer silhouette presented by their muzzles. Both sides always sought a slight hill to hide behind. A rise of even just two feet meant that low-trajectory cannonballs would hit the ridge and bounce over their heads. Additionally, because artillerists watched for a puff of dust and dirt to see where their shot had landed, a reverse slope obscured those telltale signs and made it harder for the enemy to adjust his aim.[5]

It was tempting to allow each crew to select its own target, but experienced commanders ordered their battery to concentrate all fire on a single gun.[6] Converging upon one target from multiple angles increased the likelihood of destroying it, and a completely wrecked gun was not only worth more than several lightly damaged, and quickly repaired, ones, but often unnerved neighboring gunners and reduced their accuracy.[7] "The moral effect produced by such a result [is] still more terrible than the physical," advised one of the leading American artillery experts, John Gibbon, for all knew then that the enemy had found his range and would be searching for a new victim.[8]

Even at the best of times, artillerymen were rarely sure whether their shots were causing damage. During a duel between the 9th and 5th Massachusetts batteries and Captain James Reilly's and Captain A. C. Latham's North Carolina guns southeast of Seminary Ridge, Sergeant Baker of the 9th admitted that "what effect our firing had on them we do not know; but their fire seemed to slacken somewhat."[9] His captain claimed that two rebel limbers were destroyed, whereas none were—but since Latham and Reilly did lose a howitzer and a six-pounder gun, the Bay Staters' fire was actually more effective than they thought.[10]

That uncertainty could be exploited. As one colonel warned his general, "I will only be able to judge the effect of our fire on the enemy by his return fire," so to deceive an aggressor into believing that he had inflicted more damage than he had, defending guns might play dead amid the darkening smoke.[11] When Colonel H. C. Cabell's Confederate position fell suddenly silent, for instance, his opponent reported that he had either silenced the Southerners or compelled them to withdraw.[12] When the unwitting attacker turned his guns toward another target, he would be left prey to accurate counterfire from the "destroyed" cannons.

Adding to the problem, too, was that artillery fire could be virtually impotent—even when accurate. Shoddy manufacturing, incompatible fuses, and defective primers sabotaged a surprisingly large amount of ammunition. Owing to production problems and diminishing resources, Confederate shells malfunctioned more frequently than that of the Union. One Northern newspaper reported in August 1863 that "the ground occupied by our forces is literally strewn with unexploded rebel shells, while along the Confederate fortifications very few can be found," adding, "not one-sixth of the shells thrown by the rebels exploded."[13] This was probably an exaggeration but, even so, artillerists low on ammunition made do with whatever they could scrounge, even failed shells. On July 3, William Jenvey of Hill's battery (1st West Virginia Artillery) "fired back a few of the Rebel shells, hot as they were, literally paying them back in their own coin."[14]

Part of the inherent confusion and wastage of artillery battle was owed to distance—ranges of 1,200 to 1,600 yards were not uncommon, making targets difficult to see and leading to unreliable damage assessments—but the lion's share may be attributed to the sheer volume of smoke that rapidly accumulated. A 1st Rhode Island battery was enveloped so murkily, said a witness, that "objects could not be seen at a distance of four rods [66 feet]."[15] Artillerymen therefore sought to find and destroy their target in the short window between commencing firing and total blackout.

There were various ad hoc methods of acquiring a bead quickly. Augustus Hesse, manning the 9th Massachusetts's rightmost gun, would drop flat to the ground after each shot so that he could see its effect beneath the billowing curtain of smoke. Meanwhile, Captain James Smith would run out beyond the smoke cloud, peer into the distance, and observe "the position and proximity of the enemy," then "rush back, seize the trail of a gun, slew it around for the purpose of directing the fire a little to the right or left."[16] Inevitably, however, the deepening fug left gunners working blind. Captain John Bigelow said that Confederate firing (as did his own, presumably) eventually became "so wild, that not one of their shots was conspicuously effective."[17]

Unsurprisingly, given the speed with which gunners had to work and the randomness of the shells and shot landing hither and yon, artillery duels were most unpleasant for not only anyone involved but also those close by. The thudding, shaking, and din caused by a heavy or direct cannonade, for instance, disoriented gunners and those around them. In the midst of one such bombardment, said Sergeant Frederick Fuger of the 4th U.S. Artillery, "the hills and woods [around him] seemed to reel like a drunken man."[18] Another soldier noticed that as the enemy shot hurtled overhead, he and his comrades' "nerves were strung to the highest pitch; water ran from every pore in the skin like squeezing a wet sponge, and our clothes were wringing wet. It was nature's provision for our safety, as it prevented a total collapse of the nervous system, and the mind from going out in darkness."[19]

The harm was not just psychological. Artillerists, especially those assigned spots near the muzzle, frequently ruptured their tympana, which caused blood to stream out of their ears; severe hearing loss would be the bane of many gunners' lives. Thomas Fisher, who was sixteen and attached to the 9th Massachusetts, for instance, lived to eighty-eight, but for him the world would be permanently silent.[20] After battles, men were so hard of hearing that they often had to shout at one another for a week or more. And one could always recognize the postwar reunions of artillerymen by all the shouting into ear trumpets.[21]

Among infantrymen, one of the least desired duties was guarding the batteries from a surprise attack by cavalry. Detachments were usually placed either to the side or just behind the guns but sometimes were told to stay in front and keep their heads down. Wherever they were, however, it was awful. Lieutenant L. A. Smith, 136th New York, recalled that "if you laid down on the ground and put your fingers in your ears you got, in addition to the crash in the air, the full effect of the earth's tremor and its additional force as a conductor. One of our men found afterwards that his teeth were loose and within a few days nearly all of them dropped out."[22]

Above, he continued, the sky was "fairly black with missiles exploding continually and sending their broken fragments in every direction" and when, if one dared to glance around, "you saw long fiery tongues leaping toward you, thick clouds of sulphurous smoke settle down around you, blackening the countenance almost beyond recognition."[23] The effect was nauseating, said the 14th Connecticut's Sergeant Hincks:

With every discharge, a gun directly behind him "threw the gravel over me, and I could not only see and smell the thick cloud of burning powder but could *taste* it also."[24]

Perhaps the worst part of guard duty was its danger, much grumbled about by unprotected soldiers, who became collateral damage as they passively endured a bombardment. The 108th New York was obliged, for instance, to lose around 50 percent of its engaged strength to enemy cannon fire while stoically protecting the 1st U.S. Artillery.[25] Artillerymen were not wholly sympathetic to their complaints. For gunners, the duel with their opposites was extraordinarily hazardous, and they were sacrificing themselves for the good of the infantry. However, being in the artillery was generally less risky than infantry service—in the Army of Northern Virginia, four in ten foot soldiers were killed and wounded in the war, compared to one in five gunners, and at Gettysburg the Union and Confederate artillery suffered an average of 11.5 percent casualties as against a general infantry loss of 30 percent—up to 80 percent of all artillery casualties were incurred during these intense shoot-outs.[26]

This was because while most artillery shots missed, when they did hit they were truly devastating. Surveying the aftermath of the duel between the Confederate batteries and the Union artillery massed on Cemetery Hill and Culp's Hill, Robert Stiles of the Richmond Howitzers wrote that "never, before or after, did I see fifteen or twenty guns in such a condition of wreck and destruction as this battalion was. It had been hurled backward, as it were, by the very weight and impact of the metal from the position it had occupied on the crest of a little ridge into the saucer-shaped depression behind it." All around he could see nothing but "guns dismounted and disabled, carriages splintered and crushed, ammunition chests exploded, [and] limbers upset."[27]

Exploding ammunition-laden caissons or limbers, each bearing hundreds of pounds of shot, shell, and canister, were the most impressive sights to onlookers. When a shot struck home, it provoked "a thundering report" (in the words of a Vermont veteran) and, wrote Alanson Nelson of the 57th Pennsylvania, made "the ground tremble something like an earthquake." Then came a swirling pillar of smoke that ascended several hundred feet "carrying fragments of timber, wheels, clothing and bodies high in the air," as one sergeant described it.[28] Sometimes one could see "frightened horses, one or two missing a leg," dashing wildly from the smoke as the enemy's cheers rang out.[29]

There was usually nothing left of those who manned the wagons. After a limber belonging to Battery B, 4th U.S. Artillery, was blown up, a gunner held up a blackened piece of jacket to Captain James Stewart and said, "Sir, this is all I can find of Smith, the driver." (In this very rare instance, there was an agreeably happy ending. Stewart discovered a month later that Smith was actually in a Detroit hospital, having lost nothing more than his eyes and limbs.)[30] Passing infantry, unless warned away, were blissfully ignorant of the risks they ran by marching too closely to the ammunition stockpile. One such explosion on July 3 killed several sergeants and corporals of the 14th Vermont.[31]

The artillerists actually operating the guns may rarely have fallen victim to exploding limbers and caissons, which were stationed well away from the battery once the fighting started, but they were still vulnerable to incoming shell and shot. The key to keeping casualties low was to keep the crews some distance apart. For this reason, it was optimal to spread out one's guns a minimum of twelve yards from each other—thirty was better, advised Colonel Charles Wainwright.[32] Responsible siting explained why, according to an analysis of eighteen documented solid-shot hits, only one man was killed or wounded in fully fourteen of them, with two men killed in the other four.[33]

In an understandable if misdirected instinct, the men sometimes gathered around a stricken friend to try to help. Not only did their well-meant intentions hinder the gun's firing, but their clustering exposed everyone to grave risk. Captain Bigelow, wondering why a gun had gone silent, pushed his way through a small crowd of new recruits and saw Henry Fenn lying on the ground with much of his skull torn off by a shell fragment. The artillerymen "asked me, seemingly regardless of the shells exploding about themselves, if they could not take him to the rear. The poor fellow, however, was unconscious and dying; I saw there was no hope and answered them 'No! but back to your guns and give as good as you have received.'" The men did so but were "horrified at my heartlessness."[34]

Veterans, on the other hand, knew only too well what could happen if they clumped together. Private Cyrus Boyd was alerted to the dangers when he came across "five dead Confederates all killed by one [small] six pound solid shot." They had been sitting in a row when the shot raked them from the side. "One of them had his head taken off. One had been struck at the right shoulder and his chest lay open. One had been cut in two at the bowels and nothing held his carcass together but the spine. One had been hit at the thighs and the legs were torn from the body. The fifth and last one was piled up into a mass of skull, arms, some toes, and the remains of a [uniform]. Just a few feet from where they lay the cannon ball had struck a large tree and lodged."[35]

From this interesting description we can reconstruct the path of the lethal object. Fired from some distance away, the shot descended along its parabolic arc—it sequentially hit a head, a shoulder, an abdomen, and the pelvis or thighs—but such was its kinetic force that it did not, despite the many bony obstacles, deviate from its trajectory. The odd man out is the final victim, who ended up as a "mass" of gore. It is likely that the cannonball hit him in the feet as he crouched, ricocheted off the ground directly upward through the groin and abdomen, and violently exited through his upper torso, thereby separating his arms and shattering his head.

As the official medical history of the war would equally remark, cannonballs "virtually encounter no resistance from a single human body."[36] Being hit by one generally entailed death. The Mississippian private Jeremiah Gage lost only his left arm, but when the hospital surgeon encouragingly remarked that he looked likely to survive, he replied, "'Why, Doctor, that is nothing; here is where I am really hurt,' and he laid back the blanket and exposed the lower abdomen torn from left to right by a cannon shot, largely carrying away the bladder, much intestine, and a third of the right half of the pelvis; but in both wounds so grinding and twisting the tissues that there was no hemorrhage."[37]

There was usually no need for a hospital. On one occasion Edward

Ripley was standing behind a gun when he was suddenly "dashed in the face with a hot steaming mass of something horrible" that spattered shut his eyes and seeped into his mouth and nose. Thinking, perhaps irrationally, that his own head had exploded, Ripley was grateful for the attentions of a nearby officer who cleaned away the "mass of brains, skull, hair, and blood" from his face and chest. "As I opened my eyes the headless trunk of the artillery man lay between my feet with the blood gurgling out."[38] Though mercifully quick, decapitation by cannonball was extremely violent. Corpses did not slowly fall to their knees and fall over, as one tends to see in movies; rather, as Lieutenant Frederick Hitchcock observed upon seeing a Confederate major die, "his poor body went down as though some giant had picked it up and furiously slammed it on the ground."[39]

Solid shot's dire effects on animals disturbed even hardened soldiers. One witness saw dead horses littering the field—Cushing's battery alone lost sixty-three of its eighty-four horses on July 3—"some torn almost asunder by cannon balls, some pierced in the side . . . and others with their legs completely shot away."[40] A stricken artillery horse, meanwhile, was a dangerous beast—Robert Stiles of the Richmond Howitzers saw not a few "plunging and kicking, dashing out the brains of men tangled in the harness"—but these at least could be put down, as happened when "cannoneers with pistols [crawled] through the wreck shooting the struggling horses to save the lives of the wounded men."[41]

More unnerving were the horses that cried. The Pennsylvanian Benjamin Urban noticed that while nearly all horses perished silently, there was an occasional exception. After being "struck fairly in the back by a cannon ball, and his spine shattered and broken," there was one who kept "rising on his front feet and trying to drag his paralyzed body, and when he could not, he gave that awful cry which I pray I may never hear again. It was the most dreadful thing I ever heard, and sent the cold chills down every man's back that heard it. One of the men quickly crept up, and pressing a revolver against his head, sent a merciful bullet crashing through his brain."[42]

There were wickeder things in the offing, not least of which was the surviving artillery's imminent bombardment of the hitherto untouched infantry. It was when the guns went conspicuously silent that everyone knew their crews were loading them with shell in preparation for the storm to come.

8. Artillery Versus Infantry

Shell was a hollow projectile of cast iron containing a bursting charge. This was intended either to explode some way above troops' heads, sending spinning, sharp metal fragments downward, or to plunge into the ground and burst upward. A related weapon was spherical case-shot, whose interior was packed with small iron or lead balls suspended in a sulfur or tar-pitch mixture that would detonate outward in a cone-shaped pattern.

There was an unnervingly diabolical aspect to shellfire. One soldier wrote that as shells flew over and detonated, "such a shrieking, hissing, seething I never dreamed was imaginable, it seemed as though it must be the work of the very devil himself."[1] The 136th New York's J. W. Hand employed similar Miltonic language when recalling how the shards hurtling through the air gave "forth the whole infernal gamut of unmusical high notes, the key depending on the velocity."[2] Most horrid to Benjamin Thompson, meanwhile, were "the stifling fumes of burning sulphur from exploding shrapnel"—a sign, surely, of Lucifer's malevolent presence.[3]

Shells, unlike solid shot, were designedly anti-personnel forms of ammunition and as such were feared and detested more fervently. To give some idea of the disparity in effectiveness, between May and July 1864 the Army of the Potomac recorded 88 wounds caused by cannonballs—but 2,112 by shells.[4] Before Pickett's Charge, Major Thomas Osborn of the Union XI Corps artillery on Cemetery Hill could see the enemy formation in plain view. While each of his solid shot "which struck either line cut out two men," when "a shell exploded immediately in front of either line it cut out four, six, eight, or even more men, making a wide open gap in their line."[5]

Those on the receiving end of shellfire bitterly understood Major Osborn's point. When one found its mark it exacted a heavy toll. Franklin Sawyer of the 8th Ohio watched as a Virginian brigade came under accurate Union fire: "They were at once enveloped in a dense cloud of smoke and dust. Arms, heads, blankets, guns, and knapsacks were thrown and tossed into the clear air."[6] A South Carolinian named W. A. Johnson was with Kershaw's Brigade in the Peach Orchard as "shells were cutting off the arms, legs and heads of our men, cutting them in two and exploding in their bodies, tearing them into mincemeat."[7] Similarly, when a Confederate shell hit Company C, 150th Pennsylvania, six men were killed—it alone was responsible for 11 percent of the regiment's deaths at Gettysburg.[8] The men of 2nd North Carolina were on the edge of the woods crowning Oak Hill when a shell burst among them, killing and wounding nine.[9] George Benedict was hurrying past the 13th Vermont when a shell killed a private and sergeant outright, halved another man (a leg, "bared of all but the shoe and stocking [was] thrown several feet from the body"), and knocked out the lieutenant colonel.[10]

William Peel of the 11th Mississippi "heard a shell strike in the right of the reg't, &, turning over, as I lay on my back, I looked just in time to witness the most appalling scene that perhaps ever greeted the human eye. Lt. Daniel Featherston, of Co. F, from Noxubee County, was the unfortunate victim. He was a large man—would have weighed perhaps two hundred pounds. He was lying on his face, when the shell struck the ground near his head, &, in the ricochet, entered his breast, exploding about the same time & knocking him at least ten feet high, & not less than twenty feet from where he was lying."[11] Even when they failed to explode, they were dangerous: What was apparently a twenty-pound Parrott shell, wrote Colonel Wainwright in his diary, "struck in the center of a line of infantry who were lying down behind the wall. Taking the line lengthwise, it literally ploughed up two or three yards of men, killing and wounding a dozen men or more. Fortunately, it did not burst."[12]

The single deadliest shell fired at Gettysburg seems to have been the one that inflicted twenty-seven casualties on the 55th Ohio, but we should bear in mind Colonel Goode Bryan of the 16th Georgia's claim of thirty killed and wounded among a company that was left with just seven men and an officer.[13]

It was one thing to be shelled by the enemy, quite another by one's own side, as could happen when artillerymen carelessly shortened their fuses so that shells exploded either too soon or too low.[14] At Culp's Hill, where about half XII Corps's casualties were caused by friendly fire, the 123rd New York's Robert Cruikshanks explained to his wife that "the battery had to throw their shells close to our heads and for some cause some of [them exploded behind] us which killed and wounded some of the men in the 46th Penn. Vols."[15]

As artillerists plainly could not see what they were hitting, shouting and gesticulating did little good. Lieutenant John Callis "raised my sabre above my head waving it, and at the top of my voice ordering the Capt. of the battery to cease firing. But amid the roar of musketry, and screeching of shot and shell through the air, he seemed not to hear me."[16] The only sure way of telling errant guns to cease fire was to send a runner (as did the 145th New York, only to be told "not to fret," right before three further casualties), or, better still, for a livid commander to go back and chew out the miscreant himself.[17] After one such incident, said Robert Cruikshanks, "there were no more shell exploded behind us after the Colonel had seen the officer."[18]

The best protection, such as it was, against shell, no matter from which side it originated, was to lie down and not move. Understandably, every soldier was desperate to present the smallest possible target. Winfield Scott of 126th New York "wished to be made thin, thinner than hard-tack, yea as thin as a wafer," and the 15th Massachusetts's Private Roland Bowen "thinned myself down to an old five-cent piece, crowding my nose into the sand, out of sight." Meanwhile, William Johnson, 2nd South Carolina hunkered down in a depression and watched Union artillerists preparing to pull the lanyard that would discharge the gun. When they did, he instinctively "stopped still and turned my thin edge to the fire."[19]

Whereas solid shot was often instantaneously fatal, shell fragments ripped off extremities, snapped bones, punctured organs, pulped tissue, and gashed flesh, leaving many alive but in urgent need of aid, which they rarely received. At Antietam, Dr. G. J. Fischer calculated that of fifty-seven amputations he had performed, only about 10 percent were due to shell fragments whereas three-quarters stemmed from bullets.[20] The relatively low number of the former was due not to the ineffectiveness of artillery but to the unlikelihood of the victims' reaching a hospital in time.

Survivors of shell attack, even if they did not lose limbs, suffered from a variety of mental and physical symptoms, some of which would later come to be associated with combat stress disorders. Intrigued by the phenomenon, the Union's medical authorities compiled records on such cases during the war, eventually providing an analysis of 130 such nonfatal casualties. Of these, seventy-one returned to duty a short time later after suffering from temporary deafness, blindness, muteness, or grinding headaches. More than thirty also returned to their units following a bombardment, but their symptoms could not be ascertained. Some twenty-three, however, were discharged from the army for a variety or combination of often euphemistic reasons, including permanent deafness, meningitis, paralysis, optical nerve palsy, insanity, and "spinal affliction and nervous prostration"—that is, they cringed, shook, and whimpered almost incessantly.[21]

There were some extraordinary instances of survival against the odds. Luther White, 20th Massachusetts, was unconscious for three days after being struck by a shell fragment that tore away much of his jaw, throat, and one of his ears, awakening only when he was about to be buried.[22] A man named Hubbard, 7th Indiana, saw a member of the 66th Ohio hit in the face by a fragment and "thought it the ugliest sight I witnessed during my three years of service. As he was led along it seemed to me that his face would clap together, and the blood would gush out, making a sickening sight. I have learned that man got well and lived after the war."[23] And on July 3 Abe Goldstein of the 6th Carolina witnessed a Georgia sergeant nearby "tumble headlong to the earth." The man eventually rose and curious observers could see where "a fragment of a shell . . . had taken his right ear off close to his head, as clean as though it had been cut off with a Surgeon's knife." Asked what the sensations were, the sergeant "said he felt as though he had been overtaken by a cyclone and that a six-storey building had fallen upon him. The noise of the passing fragment of a shell on the drum of his ear sounded like the sudden explosion of a thunderbolt." He then coolly bit off the end of a cartridge and prepared to charge with Pickett.[24]

The sergeant had it right. Since, as Captain Edward Bowen of the 114th Pennsylvania advised, no duty called "for such bravery and endurance, as . . . remaining passive under an enemy's artillery fire that has got an accurate range, and from which there is no protection," there really was just one viable defense against the torment.[25] And that was to attack as soon as possible.

9. Infantry Versus Infantry—The Attack

The longer a unit dawdled at its start line, the higher its casualties as artillerists improved their aim. Time was blood. Whereas the 2nd South Carolina, which was kept waiting, incurred two-thirds of its casualties from artillery fire and the rest from musketry, the 13th Mississippi, which promptly left its position and mounted a shock assault, suffered just two casualties (of 62 known wounded, or 3.2 percent) from shellfire and the balance (96.8 percent) from infantry fire.[1]

Soldiers were keen to go, for the "howling, shrieking story of shot and shell was more trying to the nerves than to be engaged in close action with the enemy," wrote E. C. Strouss of the 57th Pennsylvania, which waited in a field as a Confederate cannonade rained down upon them.[2] Officers knew they had only a limited window to order an assault before a unit began to disintegrate and the men's courage to flag. As it was, in the minutes leading up to a charge, soldiers turned uncharacteristically silent, a sure sign that they were brooding on what was to come. Captain William Seymour of the Louisiana Brigade, whose men were about to storm Cemetery Hill on July 2, looked around and saw, not fear, but only their "quiet, solemn mien" that (he rather subtly added) "fully appreciated the desperate character of the undertaking."[3]

Some men softly murmured prayers, some gazed on photographs of their loved ones, others read letters from them, a few composed suitably heroic last words in their heads.[4] Anyone who did, smoked—vigorously.[5] Those who did not tore the tough brown paper from a cartridge and chewed it mixed with a few grains of gunpowder.[6]

The pervasive quiet masked a knot of tension growing within each soldier. Illinoisan Lucius Barber recalled that he, and every man, experienced a creeping sense of "involuntary awe and dread" in the lead-up to action.[7] As it spread, said the Confederate Edmund Patterson, this sense turned into "a painful nervous anxiety" that, in him at least, manifested itself as "a dull feeling about the chest that made breathing painful."[8] No one, no matter how tried and tested in battle, ever escaped this gnawing unease before a fight. The 1st Virginia's John Dooley concluded that "soldiers generally do not fear death less because of their repeated escape from its jaws," for in each battle they saw so many frightful and novel forms of mutilation and death, and were so thankful for their deliverance from those fates, that they dreaded for their lives anew every time.[9]

Yet surprisingly, few men actually broke and fled to the rear. Several factors probably account for their remarkable fortitude. First, they understood that according to contemporary opinion, combat itself was not the only test of manhood—so was waiting for it. Abner Small, who fought in many of the war's major battles, believed that what counted was how men coped with "dread" when their unit was on the cusp of a fight, where they were "near enough to feel its fierce pulsations and get an occasional shock of its power."[10] If they could just control their mounting fear and hold fast, this would all soon be over.

The most common way of staying put was to look side to side at one's friends and be reassured that they, too, were intent on keeping the line. No man wanted to be the coward, hereafter reviled and shunned in equal measure. Officers, too, played an important role in stiffening sinews. In a citizen army soldiers were impressed by raw charismatic courage, not necessarily competency—an attribute stressed more by modern professionals—and leaders were expected to exhibit absolute coolness and unyielding fearlessness under fire. At Seminary Ridge on

July 3, the 2nd Vermont came under, in George Benedict's words, heavy artillery bombardment "from direct point-blank" and then "an enfilading fire, from a battery of Whitworth guns far to the right, which sent their six-sided bolts screaming by, parallel to our lines." But, never minding the deadly maelstrom, "the general, staff, and field officers alone, *as their duties required,*" stood erect even as everyone else kept their heads down.[11] Sergeant Isaac Barnes told a friend that seeing his higher-ups so calm "cured my fears in a great measure."[12]

Sometimes, the desire to demonstrate an almost preternatural imperturbability to those around them reached comic levels of one-upmanship, such as the time Captain Wadsworth rode up to Major Thomas Osborn at the height of an incoming bombardment. Both men sat astride beautiful horses which they deliberately stood broadside to the enemy fire to increase their vulnerability. "While we were talking," recalled Osborn, "a percussion shell struck the ground directly under the horses and exploded. The momentum of the shell carried the fragments along so that neither horse was struck nor did either horse move. When the shell exploded, I was in complete control of my nerves and did not move a muscle of my body or my face. Neither did Wadsworth, but I dropped my eyes to the ground where the shell exploded, and Wadsworth did not. I never quite forgave myself for looking down to the ground when that shell exploded under us."[13]

Officers' conspicuous heedlessness of danger steadied the line and buttressed morale—but at great cost to their own lives. In the Army of Northern Virginia, for instance, officers were 2.25 times more likely to be killed in action than enlisted men. At Gettysburg, more than a quarter of Union officers were killed and wounded, compared to a fifth of enlisted men; fully a third of Lee's generals became casualties.[14] In some hard-fighting units, the proportion was higher still: After the battle, Lieutenant Oscar Ladley of the 75th Ohio informed his mother and sisters that "15 out of 18 [officers] are gone."[15] And on July 2, in less than a quarter of an hour the 11th New Jersey lost no fewer than five commanding officers, some of them in charge for a minute or two at most.[16]

To further ease tension as the minutes ticked by, officers encouraged their men to make noise—and lots of it. Northerners awaiting an onslaught were often disquieted to hear "jerky, canine cries" issuing from the Confederate lines.[17] This psychologically intimidating sound, redolent of the war cries of Indian tribes or the booming yelps of Scottish Highlanders, was the infamous Rebel Yell—a frightful thing to hear, even for veterans. The men of Company A, 6th Wisconsin, had first encountered it at Gainesville, but at Gettysburg they still shuddered whenever it echoed toward them. "There is nothing like it this side of the infernal region," they said, recalling with horror "the peculiar corkscrew sensation that it sends down your backbone."[18]

According to an enthusiastic practitioner, W. H. Morgan, the yell was "one continuous shout of mingled voices, without any intermission, unisonance or time. Each man just opened his mouth as wide as he could, strained his voice to the highest pitch and yelled as long as his breath lasted, then refilling the lungs, repeated it again and again. It was a commingling of shrill, loud sounds, that rent the air and could be heard for a distance of two miles or more, often carrying terror to the enemy."[19]

To counter its effects, Union officers encouraged their men to remain composed by crying, as Morgan remembered, "hip, hip, huzza, huzza, huzza" in "unison and in time." To him, it may have sounded "coarse and harsh to the ear," but to Yankees the clipped syllables and indomitable rhythm betokened masculine control over themselves and their environment in the final moments before all hell broke loose. For the men of the 22nd Massachusetts and others, "our solid, defiant cheers" (in contrapuntal reply to the "discordant screeches" and "womanlike scream[s]" of the rebels) did more than anything else to steady the nerves.[20]

At this point, it was best for the attacking side to get their men up and out—even if such a move appeared to make little obvious sense. Hence the colonel, lieutenant colonel, and major of the 7th New Jersey, which was pinned down by Confederate guns, recognized that soon "it would be impossible to hold the men together inactive" and ordered them to "Fix bayonets; forward, double-quick, charge!" toward the Southern lines, which they could not even see. Over a third of the regiment became casualties within a few minutes—including its colonel and lieutenant colonel.[21] Despite these fiascos, it was rarely hard to persuade soldiers to begin to advance at a good clip. If anything, as Private Boland, 13th Alabama, admitted, "we moved somewhat faster, attempting to run from under the shells, which were just falling behind us."[22]

Once they began to move, soldiers felt the violent release of their pent-up tensions. Rice Bull, a soldier of the 123rd New York, wrote in his diary that until jumping off, one's "nerves are almost at the breaking point," but "then the strain relaxes and the fear and nervousness passes away."[23] W. L. Goss had been suffering from a "sickening feeling and a cold perspiration" and "a sort of faintness and lack of strength in the joints of my legs, as if they would sink from under me," but as soon as he began marching forward, "my knees recovered from their unpleasant limpness, and my mind gradually regained its balance and composure."[24]

Initially, they exulted in the feeling of liberation. Andrew Humphreys "felt like a young girl of sixteen at her first ball; I felt more like a god than a man; I now understand what Charles XII meant when he said, 'Let the whistling of the bullets hereafter be my music.'"[25] For his part, Sam Watkins from Tennessee "had been feeling mean all the morning as if I had stolen a sheep, but [now] I felt happier than a fellow does when he professes religion at a big Methodist camp-meeting. I shouted. It was fun then. Everybody looked happy."[26]

That palpable sense of joy was soon followed by the unpleasant realization that one was participating in a very serious pastime. Watkins said that for a time "it all seemed to me a dream" and that "I seemed to be in a sort of haze," but he was brought abruptly short when "siz, siz, siz, the minnie balls from the Yankee line began to whistle around our ears," and he surmised (correctly) that "sure enough, those fellows are shooting bullets!"[27] Henry Stanley, the future explorer of Africa, served in the 6th Arkansas and remembered that while at first "my ears tingled, my pulses beat double-quick, my heart throbbed loudly," he began to look around and saw that his comrades were shedding their excitability and turning "pale, solemn, and absorbed."[28]

As well they might. Within the first minute or two of an advance the attackers would begin taking casualties, as would the defenders (at a much slower rate and depending on whether shell was still falling or there was enfilading fire). For the men on both sides, it became critical to maintain, as one Lieutenant Wheeler advised, "a perfect indifference to circumstances" to avoid falling prey to paralyzing fear and shock at seeing one's comrades come to grief.[29] For the sake of personal survival, then, Charles Benton of the 150th New York quickly hardened himself to seeing "men killed in numbers . . . without any . . . emotions of dread or horror" so that his mind was able to "[devote] itself to whatever work it may have [had] at hand."[30] Charles Wainwright, in his first battle, immediately grasped this harsh but vital truth, confiding that to his surprise "I had no feeling but one of perfect indifference" to "seeing men shot, dead or dying." Indeed, "when Lieutenant Eakin fell against me, and cried out that he was 'a dead man,' I had no more feeling for him, than if he had tripped over a stump and fallen; nor do I think it would have been different had he been my brother."[31] Many soldiers followed Wainwright's example in suppressing their normal "civilian" emotions, like that of empathy. John Campbell, 5th Iowa, conceded that despite the dead and dying strewn around "there was a strange, unaccountable lack of *feeling* with me." He clarified why: "Out of battle and in a battle, I find myself two different beings."[32]

As these men understood, the best way to get an unpleasant and dangerous job over with was to switch off, keep plugging forward, and look nowhere but straight ahead—to treat the bloody affair, as Benton said, strictly as "work." When on July 2 eight companies of the 1st Minnesota formed up and marched on the double through concentrated fire toward the Alabama Brigade—they were outnumbered five to one and the charge was regarded as suicidal—Matthew Marvin remembered that "it seemed as if every step was over some fallen comrade. Yet no man wavers, every gap is closed up. . . . Bringing down their bayonets, the boys press forward in unbroken line. Men stumbled and fell. Some stayed down but others got up and continued." Another Minnesotan, Alfred Carpenter, added, "Bullets whistled past us; shells screeched over us; canister . . . fell among us; comrade after comrade dropped from the ranks; but on the line went. No one took a second look at his fallen companion. We had no time to weep."[33] Of the 262 men who took part in the assault, 215 became casualties within five minutes. Despite losses of 82 percent, the Minnesotans achieved their objective of protecting Cemetery Ridge.

The example of the 1st Minnesota was perhaps a statistical outlier, but a constant in every infantry advance was maintaining command and control over formations whose neatness began to decay from the moment they set off. Holding a straight line through rough terrain, over uneven ground, up and down even moderate slopes, past fences and around hedges was almost always harder than anticipated. A clump of trees in the path of the oncoming line, for instance, would force some sections to skew around it and then rush to catch up to the others. Negotiating the side of a shallow ditch would cause some to lag while others jumped across; when all reached the other side they would have to risk pausing to re-form the line, often under fire. On broken terrain, like that of Devil's Den, where "the ground [was] covered with large boulders, from the size of a wash pot to that of a wagon bed," preserving "anything like line of battle [was] impossible" but, as 5th Texas's Private John Stevens pledged, "we do the best we can."[34]

To understand the scale of the problem, consider that a company at full strength occupied a 27-yard-long front, a regiment of ten similarly endowed companies needed 300 yards (with three yards between each company), and a brigade of four regiments spread out over 1,300 yards, or nearly three-quarters of a mile.[35] At the beginning of its advance, a formation, rifles nursed against right shoulders, would march at the "double"—140 steps per minute, or 109 yards every sixty seconds, for up to 300 yards—meaning that any butterfly effect precipitated by an obstacle would ripple through the ranks.[36] And ripple quickly: Private Coxe, 2nd South Carolina, was charging at Union guns in a hitherto successful assault when a foolish order halted the advance, causing havoc where there had been none. "In a few moments," Coxe annoyedly wrote, "the whole brigade was jumbled up in a space less than a regiment behind a rocky, heavily wooded bluff. . . . We were truly 'in a box,' liable to be captured or annihilated at any moment."[37]

It was a badge of pride when officers, aided by sergeants and corporals, succeeded in maintaining their troops' orderliness. When Kershaw's Brigade attacked the Union positions it was, for instance, universally regarded as fine work, prompting a colonel to boast, "For four hundred yards our line moved forward not wavering nor hesitating in the slightest degree."[38] During Pickett's Charge, the gray waves were so immaculate that General Lewis Armistead took the time to ask General James Kemper, "Did you ever see a more perfect line than that on dress parade?"[39]

One textbook method of promoting good line formations was borrowed from seventeenth- and eighteenth-century European practice. In order of battle a regiment's companies were arranged in a specific configuration based on the seniority of their captains. Thus, from right to left the order was generally 1st, 6th, 4th, 9th, 3rd, 8th, 5th, 7th, and 2nd companies. (In American regiments, companies were named alphabetically, but the principle was the same.) The most experienced captain led the extreme right, the second most senior the extreme left, the third-most in the center, and so forth. By interspersing veteran commanders with raw ones a colonel could keep his lines long, strong, and hopefully disentangled by not placing too many newly commissioned officers at one end.[40]

Music had once helped regulate the rhythm of the march, but those days were long gone, even if the romantic visions remained. The young Charles Benton, for instance, was disappointed not to find "bands and drum corps march[ing] ahead of the soldiers and play[ing] sweet music to drown the groans of the dying and cheer the living on to victory and glory. Had I not seen more than one brave picture of our revered ancestral patriots being led to the fray in that poetic manner? But in real service I never heard a note of music [apart from an occasional bugle] during a battle."[41] This was partly because musicians were seconded as medical orderlies to fetch and carry the wounded from the battlefield, and in any case, the roar of artillery and crackle of musketry would have drowned out their drums and fifes.[42]

In the absence of instruments, officers fell back on their swords to maintain formation and pace. Major Edward Pye, 95th New York, employed his to lead the regiment forward by waving it above his head while crying, "Guide Right! Forward, Charge!"[43] They occasionally came in handy, too, for thwacking recalcitrant men across the shoulders or rear. Lieutenant Oscar D. Ladley boasted to his family that when a few soldiers of his regiment faltered, "my sword was out and if I didn't welt them with it my name ain't O.D.L. It was the only good service it has done me yet."[44]

The widespread ownership of swords can bemuse modern audiences. To be sure, they were worthless in combat. In desperate firefights, wrote Lieutenant Colonel Philip Work of the 1st Texas at Houck's Ridge and Devil's Den, "many of the officers threw aside their swords, seized a rifle, and, going into the ranks, fought bravely and nobly."[45]

Yet these mostly ceremonial implements were treated reverently by contemporary soldiers, for being useless did not make them pointless. At the outset of the Civil War, high birth bought high rank—despite lacking any military qualifications, Philippe Regis Denis de Keredern de Trobriand, who inherited a French title, was appointed colonel of the 55th New York, while Captain Joseph Davis (nephew of CSA President Jefferson Davis) made general in about a year. But by Gettysburg, any man's neighbor, no matter how mean or modest, could, either through merit, attrition, luck, conniving, or favoritism, be promoted and outrank him.[46] An increasing number of humble men had been raised from the dust to positions once reserved for the American nobility. The recent immigrants and lowly artisans who joined as privates and later received commissions to lieutenant or captain could not expect, as if by *dieu et mon droit,* to be followed by their former peers, especially those who in civilian life had been their social or economic superiors. A sword—ancient token of rightful command—therefore served as a marker of traditional authority for men who lacked it. Even if they did not acknowledge an officer's hereditary legitimacy to lead them, enlisted men were obliged to respect the emblem of his power. This realization dawned on one young officer when he noticed that the Pennsylvanians were breaking under the Confederate onslaught at the

Angle. Drawing his sword and successfully ordering them to "halt" and "face about," it was only then that he understood that this implement, which "had always hung idle by my side, the sign of rank only," had transformed, when wielded "bright and gleaming" at the critical moment, into "the symbol of command."[47]

Swords were undoubtedly handy for rousing the men to follow their appointed, if not anointed, leader, as well as for directing soldiers back into line, but they were hard to see once the assault began in earnest. Troops were accordingly told to keep their eye on the regimental and state colors—large flags, descended from heraldic and Napoleonic banners, borne aloft in the center of the line and easily discernible against a smoke-darkened background. Amid the coming tumult, any man, no matter how disoriented or scared or alone, could count on finding his regiment (or what was left of it) wheresoever were its colors. The colors were life, a sign that its heart pulsated and throbbed still.

On a broader level, colors represented group pride and identification, the implication being that even if a soldier was reluctant to acknowledge "swordly" authority, he would nevertheless strive to maintain the high regard and favorable opinion of his friends by marching forward together. More practically, officers used the colors as a mobile rallying point, a center of alignment, and a directional indicator. During the 6th Wisconsin's advance it soon devolved into a V-shaped wedge, with the colors "moving firmly and hurriedly forward," according to Colonel Rufus Dawes, "while the whole field behind [began] streaming with men who had been shot, and who [were] struggling to the rear or sinking in death upon the ground." Dawes bawled, "Align on the colors! Close up on that color! Close up on that color!" arresting the regiment's dissolution and "hold[ing] the body together."[48] On the Confederate side, when the colors belonging to the 42nd Mississippi drooped during an attack on the 147th New York, J. V. Pierce on the Union side watched as "an officer in front of the [42nd's] centre corrected the alignment as if passing in review. It was the finest exhibition of discipline and drill I ever saw, before or since, on a battlefield."[49]

10. Infantry Versus Infantry—The Defense

Across the swath of deadly ground separating the antagonists, the defenders were steeling themselves for the onslaught. Whenever possible, they would line up behind a low stone wall, a wooden fence, some hastily erected breastworks, a slight ridge, even a hedge—anything that might serve to shield their bodies. There were times when soldiers had to fight in the open, but once they had enjoyed the benefits of digging in, few preferred it otherwise. Said Harry Dean of the 7th Ohio, which fought for the first time "behind breastworks or fortifications" at Culp's Hill, "all agree that it is a pretty good way to fight."[1]

Once ensconced, their eyes focused most immediately on the faraway flutterings and snappings of the various flags calling their flocks to congregate, but they kept their ears pitched for the jangling and rattling of metal equipment—the most telltale sign of movement en masse. Officers and NCOs kept a particularly beady eye open for men who looked less preoccupied than unoccupied. To keep them busy, they would stalk back and forth ordering soldiers to double- and triple-check their weapons or repeatedly run through the manual of arms—the series of motions by which soldiers loaded, fired, and recharged their rifles. The 18th Massachusetts performed precisely this exercise over and over again as they awaited the Confederates during Pickett's Charge.[2] Among the several benefits of the practice, its sheer mindlessness took the men's thoughts off the imminent melee.

Some soldiers were also dispatched to harvest as many guns as they could find. Fortunately, there were usually plenty lying around, especially if the ground had already been fought over. Once they were brought back, they too were cleaned and loaded and, as the 1st Delaware did when the grand Confederate assault began to coalesce on July 3, were "distributed along the line . . . thus forming an embryo arsenal," according to J. L. Brady.[3] "Some of the men were so energetic as to have four loaded muskets, it was very common for men to have two," wrote Captain David Shields.[4]

They would need them. Each time a soldier fired, unburnt powder residue was blasted down the barrel; after heavy use the accumulated fouling made the gun prone to malfunction and increasingly difficult to reload. That was why George Bowen, 12th New Jersey, in the process of firing thirty or forty shots over the course of a day, had to use "several guns to do it as they got so full [with residue] that [I] could not get a load down them."[5] At one critical moment during a firefight, the gun belonging to Private Valerius Giles of the 5th Texas became so clogged that his ramrod got stuck midway in the barrel and he had to bang it on a rock to drive it down.[6] Once the weapons had been divvied up, defenders methodically inventoried their ammunition. As cartridges and the percussion caps needed to ignite the gunpowder were fiddly things at the best of times, it was only sensible, as the 12th New Jersey did while awaiting a Confederate attack, to empty their cartridge boxes and arrange the ammunition on top of a wall or, as Private Robert Carter of the 22nd Massachusetts noticed, to make a little pile on the ground.[7]

Only then did they have a chance to watch the spectacle unfolding before them. The first sight of approaching troops was one of initial grandeur tinctured with mounting horror. The New Yorker Winfield Scott enjoyed a close-up view of Pickett's Charge, waxing that "the movement of such a force over such a field, in such perfect order, to such a destiny, was grand beyond expression"; Scott's "heart was thrilled at the sight. I was so absorbed with the beauty and grandeur of the scene that I became oblivious to the shells that were bursting about us. This passage of scripture came to my mind, and I repeated it aloud: 'Fair as the moon, bright as the sun, and terrible as an army with banners.'" (He was referencing the Song of Solomon 6:10.)[8] Edwin Southard of the 119th New York was similarly mesmerized by the first appearance of Early's Division on July 1—until he realized that the "beautiful" long gray line rolling forward "in excellent array, the sunlight flashing from their fixed bayonets and unsheathed swords" was in fact an "appalling spectacle, for it rendered our line untenable and defenseless."[9] According to Oscar Jackson, the scariest sight of all was a mass of men advancing "with a firm, slow, steady step"; he later "stood a bayonet charge when the enemy came at us on the double-quick with a yell and it was not so trying on the nerves as that steady, solemn advance."[10]

The attacking side only marched that slowly when it was out of effective rifle range—as the more excitable defenders soon learned. Warren Olney's regiment could see the enemy forming up about four hundred yards away and so "without word of command," took some potshots at them. "After three or four rounds, the absurdity of firing at the enemy at that distance with our guns dawned upon us, and we stopped. As the smoke cleared up we saw the enemy still there, not having budged or fired a shot in return."[11]

When the enemy approached the two-hundred-yard mark and began to pick up the pace, defending officers would cry, "Up men! They are coming! Fall in—fall in!" as Private David Ballinger, 12th New Jersey, recalled, and pace up and down the line, issuing a reassuring word here and adjusting a poorly placed rifle there.[12] Alonzo Hill, 8th Pennsylvania, saw his friend Jake Archibald raise his rifle to a 45-degree angle, only for an officer to bellow, "Not so high! You're not firing a salute," as he used his sword to press the offending piece down horizontally.[13]

As the enemy colors hove nearer and one could become hopeful or crestfallen by counting the number of battle honors stitched into the flags—the more there were, the more hardboiled the regiment—the defenders took beads on the most prominent targets. Officers, of course, were always eminently selectable, but others were equally popular. Distinctively tall or stout men, for instance, would attract unwelcome attention. Worried that he might otherwise miss, the 116th Pennsylvania's Daniel Chisholm jotted down in his notebook that he "picked out the very largest man I could see & took sight."[14] Color-bearers always came in for more than their fair share of bullets, as demonstrated by the ragged state of their flags at the end of a hard fight: that of the 149th New York was perforated by eighty-one bullet holes at Gettysburg.[15] Private John Vautier, 88th Pennsylvania, was behind a wall with his friends when Iverson's Brigade (5th, 12th, 20th, and 23rd North Carolina) appeared. "A color-bearer making himself very conspicuous by defiantly flaunting his flag in plain view [caused Sergeant

Evans to remark], as he brought his piece to his shoulder, . . . 'I will give those colors a whack.' "[16]

Then they waited. And waited. And waited.

The officers' most important task was to remind the men not to jump the gun and start firing willy-nilly. They must await the command to pull the trigger in order to maximize the devastation inflicted by a synchronized first volley. Over at the 14th Connecticut's position, "Major Ellis emphasized this order, Adjutant Doten went forth and back along the line repeating it, and Sergeant Major Hincks and the line officers reiterated it—and so our men, with aim well taken and finger on trigger, submissively waited."[17]

Finally, the order would come to fire: "Give it to them!" would shout the colonel, and the men (in this case, the 19th Maine) "sent a sudden volley into the teeth of the advancing enemy."[18] The first broadside, as a correspondent for *Scientific American* described it, was "a rattle and roll, which sounds like a falling of a building, just as some of you have heard the bricks tumble at a great fire."[19] Leander Stillwell, a country boy like so many others, employed more rural imagery in likening the roar down the line to "the sweep of a thunder-storm in summer-time over the hard ground of a stubble-field"—only, he added, "a million times louder."[20]

The efficacy of this initial volley varied proportionally to the distance between defenders and attackers, and accounting for that differential was part, but just one part, of the dismal mathematics of Civil War combat. It was widely reckoned that a unified force approaching at the double-quick traversed a hundred yards per minute.[21] Another rule of thumb was that a defending unit could fire in combat an average of once per minute (estimates range from once every two minutes to twice a minute).[22] Therefore, if the enemy had reached the hundred-yard mark, the defenders had time for only a single volley before its line was breached. But these were merely theoretical averages, not real-world ones. Skill and judgment were needed to adjust one's particular circumstances to fit the developing situation. For instance, marching one hundred yards under fire and over hard terrain would slow down any attacking force, leaving it vulnerable to extra shots from the defenders. On the other hand, not only did the terrain—hillocks, barns, and ditches, for example—reduce incoming fire by obscuring the defenders' sightlines but the attackers also naturally accelerated into a run upon reaching the thirty-yard mark, thereby leaving the defenders with even less time to get off another shot. Another example: Some units fired more often than others. Thus, one of the fastest times recorded was a round every thirty seconds (at Antietam, by the 52nd New York) and the slowest every 4.6 minutes (at Stones River, by the 3rd Kentucky).[23] And, as we've seen, many soldiers stockpiled between two and four guns before a fight; not having to reload between each shot, or at least being able to switch rifles when their barrels began to foul or overheat, multiplied the number of times they could fire. Jeremiah Hoffman, 142nd Pennsylvania, said that during one clash he and the others simply dropped their guns when they became too hot to handle and grabbed the ones waiting next to them.[24] Even when they ran out of spares, a New Yorker recalled, a man could throw away his gun and bid "those beside him to be careful where they fired, rush forward and pick up, in place of it, one that had fallen from the hands [of] a dead or wounded comrade."[25] When all these factors are taken into consideration, it becomes more evident how at Gettysburg the 154th New York, facing two Confederate brigades (Louisianans and North Carolinians) managed to expend between six and nine shots per man in the limited time available. Even if that figure was a statistical outlier, it is perfectly reasonable to presume that the defending side could fire between two and four shots if they began the cycle when the enemy began its assault at the hundred-yard point.

As at Bunker Hill, that range was used as the benchmark because it balanced hitting power against accuracy. In 1775, the militiamen had been good shots but the technological limitations of their weapons and ammunition had restricted their lethality at more than one hundred yards. By Gettysburg, conversely, bullets and firearms alike had greatly improved but marksmanship had declined so precipitously that one hundred yards, more or less, was still the point where defenders could begin to inflict any damage.[26]

In the 1850s, the U.S. Army had given shooting practice short shrift. Given the compressed training of Civil War regiments, little better could be expected. When Captain George Wingate first tested his New York company, for example, he found that hardly anyone could hit a barrel lid at a hundred yards.[27] Then there was the 5th Connecticut, a prestigious unit that held a shooting contest to entertain its members in August 1861. Forty men lined up and took aim at the side of a barn twenty feet long and fifteen feet high. Less entertainingly, at a range of one hundred yards, just one of the forty rounds hit the wood lower than the average height of a soldier. Put another way, had this result been replicated in battle, 97.5 percent of the shots unleashed by this fearsome, company-strong volley would have missed the approaching enemy. "And these soldiers were probably a fair average of New England troops in this respect," commented an embarrassed Captain Edwin Marvin.[28]

Troops new to war were often surprised by how few of them were hit even at such a moderate range. Leander Stillwell, for instance, was puzzled to hear "an incessant humming sound away up above our heads, like the flight of a swarm of bees." He and his comrades eventually surmised that the sound was caused by bullets sailing harmlessly anywhere from twenty to a hundred feet overhead.[29] Private Robert Carter observed that "the green leaves and twigs overhead fell in a constant shower, as they were clipped by the singing bullets."[30] As he and his fellows advanced in the face of a Union broadside, George Neese assumed that they would all die, yet "the regiments appeared as complete as they were before the fight."[31] Of this phenomenon, the authoritative *Army and Navy Journal* concluded that "the escape of so large a majority of the men, amid such storms sweeping and yelling around their ears, has always been the greatest mystery."[32]

Since one hundred yards was something of a crapshoot, it was generally preferable, if more nerve-racking, to reserve the first fire until the enemy was fifty yards away (some excellent regiments, such as the 19th Maine, sometimes held their volley until as little as thirty-five yards separated the two sides).[33] At that range, hits were almost guaranteed. Sergeant John Freer was at Brinkerhoff's Ridge when "twenty-five or thirty rebs came almost straight for the place we occupied [behind a rail fence]" as "another party, of about the same number, [headed] toward the cross-fence to our left. The boys were restless and wanted to open the ball, but I ordered them to hold their fire. When the rebs were within eight or ten rods [about fifty yards] I gave the order to . . . Give 'em hell!"[34]

At this crisis point, without any room for error if the defenders blew their opportunity to devastate the enemy, officers and sergeants prowled up and down the line, repeating the admonition, as George Grant of the 88th Pennsylvania recorded, "to await command and aim low" when the Confederates reached the fifty-yard mark.[35] At the Angle on July 3, the Union troops could see Pickett's Confederates moving forward and their fingers instinctively tightened on the triggers. "Do not hurry, men, and fire too fast," their own Brigadier General John Gibbon reassuringly counseled as he rode to and fro. "Let them come up close before you fire, and then aim low, and steadily."[36]

"Low" was defined as the knees or shins.[37] As at Bunker Hill, aiming low helped counteract soldiers' fatal tendency to over-elevate their rifles while exploiting the principle that a leg wound neutralized a combatant almost as effectively as a head shot. Crippling attackers en masse was the surest means of slowing a formation's momentum and atomizing its mass. Another advantage was that as the smoke rose, the enemy's lower limbs became the first visible target. At Devil's Den, for instance, when Benjamin Urban heard someone cry, "Look under the smoke, boys!" he and the others "depressed our pieces and sent a volley into the mass of 'men in grey' struggling up the hill, some on their hands and knees, sending them flying down the slope broken and demoralized."[38]

If performed correctly at close range, the first volley or two would mow down the oncoming tide of men. Private John Vautier was a member of the 88th Pennsylvania, part of a group of regiments determined to fend off Iverson's Brigade of Tar Heels: He described seeing "the field in front . . . swarming with Confederates, who came sweeping on in magnificent order, with perfect alignment, guns at right shoulder and colors to the front." At the word, there was a simultaneous crash of rifles, and a sheet of flame and smoke "flar[ed] full in the faces of the advancing troops, the ground being quickly covered with their killed and wounded as the balls hissed and cut through the exposed line."[39]

A Confederate artilleryman named Robin Berkeley walked the same contested ground that night and counted "79 North Carolinians laying dead in a straight line. I stood on their right and looked down their line. It was perfectly dressed. Three had fallen to the front, the rest had fallen backward; yet the feet of all these dead men were in a perfectly straight line" thanks to a single "volley of musketry."[40]

Generally speaking, however, the aftermath of an infantry charge was messier than that: One broadside rarely ended the action. It was hard to stop troops when their blood was up. Edmund Patterson, 9th Alabama, described how his regiment "met such a perfect storm of lead right in our faces that the whole brigade literally *staggered* backward several paces as though pushed by a tornado," and yet after the officers cried "Forward, Alabamians,—Forward!" the remaining men "swept forward with wild cheers."[41] According to Private Roland Bowen (15th Massachusetts), infantry formations that had received a blow would momentarily seem "to be suspicious or in doubt as if they had lost their confidence. They hesitated, they reeled, they staggered, and wavered slightly, yet there was no panic."[42] The gored attacking line—even when "gappy, hesitating, incoherent, and sensitive," according to Henry Stanley—would pull itself together as officers urgently began "waving their swords and telling them to stand fast and not break or run," as Chauncey Harris of the 108th New York related to his father.[43]

After successive charges on a position, one could sometimes tell just by looking at the ebb and flow of corpses where the line had been dammed, fallen back, and renewed the attack.[44] The Pennsylvanian Amos Judson recounted of the Confederate assault on his position at Little Round Top that, following the initial volley, "which made the enemy reel and stagger, and fall back in confusion," the Southerners rallied and advanced, hundreds approaching "even within fifteen yards of our line, but they approached only to be shot down or hurled back covered with gaping wounds." Later, Judson counted "over forty dead bodies within a circle of fifty feet in circumference. They laid in every conceivable position among the rocks in that low swampy ground, some crouched behind rocks as if about to fire, some lying upon their faces, and some stretched upon their backs."[45] A circle with a fifty-foot circumference has a diameter of nearly sixteen feet and an area of just under two hundred square feet. Fitting more than forty bodies in such a space implies that a significant number overlapped or were entangled— telltale evidence that multiple fusillades had been fired at troops who had refused to cede the day to the defenders.

Once soldiers began firing, they did not cease. At first, depending on how they had been trained, either every rifleman fired a single volley simultaneously, or the soldiers would cycle through front and rear ranks to create an almost continuous hail, or they fired serially either by file or company to create a ripple effect from right to left.[46] The simplest and most reliable method of keeping control for the longest possible time was the second option: shooting by rank. At Culp's Hill, said S. R. Norris of the 7th Ohio, they reserved "our fire until the first line of battle was well up the slope and in easy range, when the command, 'Front rank—Ready—Aim low—Fire!' was given and executed, and immediately the rear rank the same, and kept up as long as the line remained unbroken."[47] A common, if minor, complaint among de-fenders was that the frontmost rank was often deafened or scorched by the one behind. Tactical manuals may have emphasized that the rear men should always jut their muzzles to "reach as much beyond the front rank as possible," but even when George Bowen, 12th New Jersey, carefully followed this instruction, every time he fired those ahead of him "looked back and told me I would shoot them, swearing about it."[48]

There was always a lot of swearing in a defensive line, especially once fire synchronization began to disintegrate after a few volleys. As the need for self-control evaporated, loud cursing spread through the ranks from top to bottom. Captain John DeForest remembered that "the swearing mania [became] irrepressible."[49] Hitherto genteel officers and docile privates suddenly erupted into every "extremity of lan-guage." Remembered Theodore Dodge, there were unending cries of "Give 'em ____, boys!" and "Rake ____ out of 'em, boys!" while Private Henry Meyer (148th Pennsylvania) found it peculiar that "some of the boys swore energetically, who never before were heard to utter an oath."[50] Benjamin Winger said that the men liked it when their officers burst into "a lot of good, hard swearing" because "they thought if the officers could swear till a blue streak went up, they [too] could afford to be brave."[51] As Victorian curse words were less sexual or scatological than blasphemous (as Dodge clarified, the "familiar synonym for heat"—Hell—was incessant), a captain's willingness to utter ungodly oaths was a confident and heartening sign that he did not expect to be justifying himself before Saint Peter anytime soon.

11. The Attack Continues

The defense often concentrated its fire on the color company (the unit entrusted with the regimental standards or flags), which accordingly incurred higher losses than any other.[1] But it was the color-bearer and color-guard themselves, rather than the whole company, who were the true loci of attention. Aiming at them was not mere sport; if the colors fell, the entire attacking force could collapse as its command structure unraveled, lines stopped moving, and units became ensnarled. The object, then, was to eliminate bearer and guards as rapidly as possible. For that reason, every guard escorting William Murphy, who carried the colors of the 2nd Mississippi, was "killed and wounded in less than five minutes."[2]

Murphy was extraordinarily lucky to survive; more often, when assaults went wrong, color-bearers were massacred. The record number of losses at Gettysburg was set by the 26th North Carolina, with seventeen color-bearers killed and wounded. The hideous comedy of the 26th began with color-bearer Sergeant J. B. Mansfield, who was stationed with his guards six paces ahead of the regimental line. As the North Carolinians advanced toward the 24th Michigan, Mansfield was shot in the foot (no doubt by a Union man aiming low) and then handed the colors to Sergeant Hiram Johnson. Less than a dozen yards later, he, too, was shot, and the banner was taken by Private John

Stamper. The line remained dressed until the 26th reached a ravine covered in reeds and underbrush. The formation began to break up as the men scrambled to cross the stream. Stamper was shot at that point. Private George Washington Kelly next took the flag but was hit in the ankle within a minute by another low-flying round. His successor, Private Larkin Thomas, was hit before he could take more than a few steps. The flag then fell to Private John Vinson, who fared still worse than Thomas, he being shot but a second or two later. Two more, Privates John Marley and William Ingram, grabbed it but both were killed within a few minutes. Thankfully, Captain W. W. McCreery took the banner and waved it aloft to encourage the men, some of whose spirits may have been sagging by this point. For his pains, he was shot through the heart and fell on top of the flag. Next, Lieutenant George Wilcox pulled it out from under McCreery, but within two steps he was shot twice in the chest. Now Colonel Henry Burgwyn himself seized the flag, bawling "Dress on the colors" and handing them to Private Frank Honeycutt just before he was shot through both lungs. Honeycutt, as he reached over, was shot through the head. Lieutenant Colonel John Lane cried, "It is my time to take them now! Twenty-sixth, follow me." But he was shot in the neck, jaw, and mouth about thirty paces from the enemy line. Lane nevertheless managed to entrust the colors to Captain W. S. Brewer, who carried them to victory. By the end of the battle, four more men (including Brewer) would become casualties. Unfortunately, when the last, wounded bearer, Private Daniel Thomas, finally reached the enemy's works, he was obliged to surrender because hardly anyone from his regiment was left to help him fight. (The 26th suffered 89 percent casualties, or 743 men out of 839.)[3]

The sometimes suicidal requirements of the color-bearer's task may prompt us to ask why anyone would volunteer for the job. For the sake of regimental honor is the traditional reason given, but while this factor may have influenced some men's decisions to abide by the flag come what may, it is too general, romantic, and convenient a motivation to explain the phenomenon fully.

There were several other competing reasons why soldiers undertook color service. First and foremost, surprisingly, much of the time noth-

ing happened to you. As the new color-bearer of the 28th Massachusetts, Sergeant Peter Welsh, assured his worried wife before Gettysburg,
"this regiment has been in seven battles and has had but one color
bearer killed [and] two men wounded."[4] It certainly helped that the
other soldiers "swarmed around [the color-bearer] as bees cover their
queen" during an advance, wrote another veteran, further reducing the
likelihood of getting hit.[5]

But the chances of survival improved still more because color units
often included the more experienced soldiers, were supervised by senior
commanders, and were the least likely to be lethally enfiladed thanks to
their central position in the line. There were also sound personal mo-
tives for accepting an ostensibly higher level of risk. As color-bearer,
crowed Sergeant Welsh, he was excused general picket and guard duty,
did not have to carry a musket or ammunition when marching, nor
would he be ordered to skirmish, for the colors always remained safely
behind the forward screen. Bravely bearing the colors, too, brought a
man to the attention of his major and colonel, and it was upon their
good offices that a sergeant could be commissioned. The best part of
becoming a lieutenant, Welsh brightly reminded his wife, was that one
could then resign and return home. (Though he survived Gettysburg,
Welsh would be mortally wounded carrying the colors in May 1864 at
Spotsylvania.)[6] Then, too, for men with a checkered service record, vol-
unteering offered the possibility of redemption: Private Vinson of the
26th North Carolina, who, as noted, was shot after (briefly) seizing the
colors, had been tried for desertion a month before the battle, and on
June 30 was given the choice of color duty or execution.[7]

No matter where men were in the line, however, for every yard they
gained, comrades on either side, in front and behind, were shot in increasing numbers. Oddly, the sounds rather than the sights stuck more
in their memories. The 74th Pennsylvania's Louis Fischer long remembered the "dull thud" of bullets striking his nearby friend, Lieutenant
Roth.[8] Roth had evidently been hit in a soft spot: Soldiers like Thomas
Evans, 12th U.S. Infantry, soon learned to distinguish between "the
grating sound a ball makes when it hits a bone" and "the heavy thud
when it strikes flesh."[9] John DeForest knew that the man next to him

was as good as dead when he heard "a sharp crack of broken bone, followed by a loud 'Oh' of pain and horror." Looking around for confirmation, he saw the victim "fall slowly backward, with blood spurting from his mouth and a stare of woeful amazement in his eyes. A bullet had shattered his front teeth and come out behind his left jaw."[10]

Almost every old soldier could later tell a story of his or a friend's astounding escape from the jaws of death thanks to a lucky object that stopped an otherwise fatal bullet. Salmon Beardsley, 154th New York, recalled "a ball [that] went through my canteen and bruised my hip a little . . . but [I] soon found that I was only scared by the water running down from my *wounded* canteen instead of blood from my body."[11] John Roberts of the 17th Maine, said Private John Haley, was "wounded in the Testament which had stopped the bullet on the way to his heart," though for others "packs of cards had played the same part several times."[12]

The vast majority of bullet wounds, however, *were* serious. The sensation of being shot varied with the distance between muzzle and flesh as well as the location and nature of the wound, but generally there was little prolonged agony. Soldiers described a brief pang of pain when first hit—Alfred Lee, 82nd Ohio, "felt the sting of a bullet"—and spoke of a dull feeling of "shock, without discomfort" (A. B. Isham, 7th Michigan Cavalry) or of being struck by "something blunt" (Vincent Osborne, 2nd Kansas), similar to a "blow as from a stone" (Confederate Major Henry Kyd Douglas).

Shortly afterward came "slight dizziness" (Osborne) and "a peculiar tingling as though a slight electrical current was playing about the site of injury" (Isham) or extending down the affected limb, on the heels of which numbness and paralysis quickly set in. One's breathing would then turn "hard and labored, with a croup-like sound" (Ebenezer Hannaford), and the victim would feel as if the wind "had been thumped out" of him (Douglas).

By this stage, the soldier would be experiencing a "metamorphosis from strength and vigor to utter helplessness" (Lee) and a spreading "powerlessness" that forced him to drop his gun (Hannaford), presaging "a sinking sensation to the earth; and, falling, all things growing dark" (Private Ward, 4th Alabama).[13] Observers would see the wounded man, said Alonzo Hill of 8th Pennsylvania, "convulsively clasp his hand to his breast—perhaps brow—a moment stand, then stagger, reel, and fall to the earth gasping for breath—the hot blood gushing from his wound."[14]

Breathless and fading from shock, when soldiers tried to cry out for help, often nothing but pathetic groans or hoarse pleas would emerge. As Samuel Wing of the 3rd Maine explained, "The first effect of a [serious] wound is numbness, and the wounded seldom speak above a whisper."[15] If the soldier was dying, even a whisper was beyond his abilities. When a comrade was shot in the head, all that Robert Carter of the 22nd Massachusetts could hear was him "gasping in that peculiar, almost indescribable way that a mortally wounded man has. I shall never forget the pleading expression, speechless, yet imploring."[16] In either case, we can dispense with the usual sentimental tales of soldiers' clearly enunciated last words and worthy declarations of how fortunate they were to die doing their duty. Most just blubbered incomprehensibly for their mothers or tormentedly contemplated their final moments.

A few men who were surprised to survive their wounds left behind vivid accounts of what it felt like to die. Temporarily blinded and paralyzed, Sam Emerson of the 3rd Arkansas had been left lying at Devil's Den, where "occasionally the rattle of musketry and the roar of cannon came rushing over my lacerated brain like traces of fire. In vain did I attempt to calm my feelings. . . . I doubted the reality of all around me, and strove to shake it off as a horrible dream. . . . I was mad with terror and anguish. . . . By and by the storm of battle passed away. The distant mutterings of the cannons soon ceased to fall upon my ear. Then again all was dark. . . . I felt as if eternity had begun its reign. . . . Oblivion had stretched her pall over me."[17]

12. The Critical Moment

During every assault there arrived a moment—generally around the fifty-yard crisis point—when soldiers either fought or fled. An attacking force that had sustained overwhelming casualties, experienced a drastic loss of momentum, or received an unexpected enfilade was by far the most liable to retreat. In these circumstances, a false alarm, the death of a beloved commander, or a misheard order could produce immediate panic. The slightest equivocation could result in collapse. On the other hand, advised Colonel Scribner, "victory is often achieved by the troops that hold out even for a moment after both sides have become impressed with the idea that they all will be killed and must fly to safety."[1] At this stage, as Charles Benton (150th New York) observed, the relationship between attackers and defenders was liable to turn into "a resolute test of endurance; a grim determination to fight to a finish; a primordial test of blood and nerve; a trying of which [side] could longest bear being killed. It was a death grapple."[2]

There was no universally applicable determination of when or if an attack would fail. The timing and outcome of the matter hinged on several varying factors, such as the rate and severity of the attackers' losses, the experience of the unit involved, the quality of leadership, and the distance to their objective. Thus, when the 6th Wisconsin rushed the Confederates in the railway cut on July 1, it started with 420 men but ended with 240. Normally, such rapid casualty accumulation might induce retreat, but the 6th was a first-class regiment under sound and able command that knew it had to cross the deadly zone or be annihilated.[3]

At this tipping point, the bravest, or most reckless, men of the unit played an important role. Even as their comrades were contemplating withdrawal, some soldiers would propel themselves forward to the "dead-line"—an imaginary frontier beyond which no man could survive unless his fellows followed en masse. If they hesitated, he was doomed. At Pickett's Mill in May 1864, for instance, Ambrose Bierce noticed a "well-defined edge of corpses" at the dead-line, with not a single man managing to get closer to the Confederate position. Behind them, "man by man, the survivors withdrew at will."[4]

Once a retreat was in the offing, it tended to take one of three forms. First, as Bierce noted, individuals would peel off and scurry away "man by man" until hardly anyone was left. A few would fire their weapons before taking cover or going mysteriously "missing" in some nearby woods. Soldiers who had stayed on the field then became targets for the defenders, who now had time to reload at leisure.

Alternatively, there might be a steady and dignified withdrawal as the attack petered out. As an Indianan colonel pointed out, veteran soldiers would yield ground but "keep together as if attracted to each other by a sort of moral gravitation." He likened the sight of old troops "unconsciously reform[ing] their ranks" as they retreated to that of cavalry horses, which instinctively closed up in formation when their riders were absent.[5] Even under pressure, said Berry Benson of South Carolina, veterans "dressed upon the colors in some rough fashion."[6] Order and bulk were to be found wheresoever the flag was—command and mass being the most critical factors in making it out alive. No matter the devastation, a regiment needed to stay together to dissuade a counter-charge and pursuit by the defenders, an act that invariably ended in an easy slaughter. An excellent example of grace under fire was the withdrawal of the 2nd Division of III Corps on July 2. Watching the drama, Alfred Carpenter wrote that "back over the plain they came, slowly, not faster than a walk, loading as they came and every now and then turning and pouring a deadly volley into the pursuing foe. The Rebs came in two splendid lines, firing as they advanced," but were hesitant to risk coming in closer for the kill.[7]

More often, however, a check during an assault rapidly descended into collective headlong flight. In these cases, the fastest runners, said Corporal George Mason of the 154th New York, would be the lucky ones who got away.[8] To lighten the load, those fleeing "threw away everything—cartridge boxes, waistbelts, and haversacks—in their stampede," wrote the 8th Ohio's Thomas Galwey of a Virginia brigade's retreat after Pickett's Charge. "The ground was covered with flying Confederates. They all seemed to extend their arms in their flight, as if to assist their speed."[9]

The slow were soon left behind. When the 143rd Pennsylvania hurriedly departed the Seminary, said Avery Harris of Company B, there was no "semblance of military order with every man for himself and the Rebs take the hindmost."[10] George Bowen of the 12th New Jersey cheerfully admitted to competing against the rest of his company to return to safety. "Seeing the men all running for the rear I took after them, soon catching up with Lieut. Col. Harris of the 1st Del. who was getting to the rear as fast as he could, he swung his sword around, called me a hard name, telling me to go back, this I did not do but made a detour around him and got across that three-quarters of a mile in record time to the rear."[11]

The wounded and the lame were also abandoned. The 8th Florida's William Penn Pigman was retreating from the Wheatfield and Peach Orchard on July 2 and confessed that "there is no time to stop for friends who are hurt during the heat of an engagement." Others were more circumspect but equally clear-eyed. William Warren, 17th Connecticut, heard a dear friend cry, "O Dear, Help me, Help me" when he was shot, but "it was not time for me to stop," he confided to his journal, "so I kept on."[12] Those forsaken may have given "beseeching looks"—as Captain James Stewart remembered—but received only, in the words of the 143rd Pennsylvania's John Musser, "a parting glance of sympathy" from those who remained mobile.[13] Decades later, J. V. Pierce could still hear the mortally wounded Edwin Aylesworth's piteous appeal, "Don't leave me, boys," though they had.[14]

All knew their fates. Following a fight in the Wheatfield, W. H. Sanderson (2nd U.S. Infantry) recalled many years later, "out of that squad of 17 we left seven of our comrades in the wheat. All were wounded, and I think one or two killed. We never saw any of them again, and so concluded they all died of their wounds in some Southern prison-pen, as they fell into the hands of the rebels."[15] He was probably right: The fatality rate among POWs on both sides was astonishingly high. To take a typical instance, the 154th New York went to Gettysburg with 265 officers and men, of whom 173 were taken prisoner. More than a third (63) would die in captivity. At least another eight would die soon after coming home, and many more would suffer terribly in later years as the scarring left behind by dietary deficiencies, disease, and stress exacted its price in the form of poor mental and physical health.[16]

13. Holding the Line

Assuming that the attacking infantry absorbed the blow at the fifty-yard mark and plowed on, the defending side would soon face the choice of whether to stay or run. Unless they were greatly outnumbered or out of ammunition, it was generally better for defenders to try to hold their position, for while the attackers were in the midst of a furious, unthinking rage that spurred them to suicidal extremes, the defenders now found their most intense focus. During the fighting at Culp's Hill, "I was struck by the cool and matter-of-fact way in which our men were loading and firing," said Charles Benton of the 150th New York. "And yet it was but yesterday the same men had paled at the sight of a wounded man."[1] In a fierce firefight near the Lutheran Seminary, Nathan Cooper of the 151st Pennsylvania, meanwhile, was amazed to find himself "just as cool and composed as I ever was butchering hogs."[2]

If they could muster themselves into a volley line, the defenders might even unleash one final broadside that would put paid to the attack once and for all. During their advance on the seminary, the men of Company K, 14th South Carolina, came so close that they heard the enemy's lieutenants "distinctly encouraging their men to hold their fire, until the command to fire was given. They obeyed their command implicitly, and rose to their feet and took deliberate aim as if they were on dress parade, and to show you how accurate their aim was, 34 out of our 39 men fell."[3]

The defenders also had one lethal trick left up their sleeve: Artillery would blast canister to scythe down the attacking infantry. Canister essentially converted a cannon into a giant shotgun peppering dozens of iron balls at high speed into the approaching ranks at essentially point-blank range (less than fifty yards). Not only could a cannon fire roughly three times a minute and be aimed low to exploit ricochets, but crews would also double- or even triple-shot their piece for short periods to increase lethality.[4] During Pickett's Charge, for instance, Sergeant Fuger of Cushing's Battery opened up with overcharged canister, punching two fifty-foot-wide holes in the Confederate line.[5] If the enemy came still nearer, artillerists urgently set about "cutting the fuses . . . so that they would explode near the muzzles of [their] guns."[6]

Against a few rounds of well-directed canister, human beings were distressingly vulnerable.[7] A single gun blast against Lieutenant William Johnson's company in the 2nd South Carolina killed Captain George McDowell and Privates R. Elmore Chaney and William Lomax, mangled Private John Fooshe's leg (he died a few weeks later), ripped off Private James Casson's skull above the eye, and shoved Private George McKenzie's rifle across his chest with such force that he was almost killed. The rest of the 2nd South Carolina fared just as poorly. According to Lieutenant Colonel Gaillard, "I saw half a dozen at a time knocked up and flung to the ground like trifles. There were familiar forms and faces with parts of their heads shot away, legs shattered, arms tore off." Between a third and a half of the regiment would be recorded as dead or wounded. All Private John Coxe could or wished to recall of the experience was "the awful deathly surging sounds of those little black balls as they flew by."[8]

Those "little black balls" inflicted graver wounds than any bullet. Lewis Crandell of 125th New York told his parents that "my pants were stiff with dark clotted blood, one man by me [was] shot with grape [canister] in the head the hot blood flew in my face nearly blinding me."[9] After he was hit, South Carolinian J. R. Boyle of the 12th watched his shoe (with ankle and calf attached) soar away.[10] A day after the battle, Robert Carter found a man with "as many as twenty canister or case shots through different parts of his body, though none through a vital organ, and he was still gasping and twitching with a slight motion of the muscles and vibrations of the pulse, although utterly unconscious of approaching death."[11]

For those not yet hit, the single avenue of escape from death or disfigurement lay in reaching the defensive line and storming the artillery. If they had made it this far, attacking soldiers had overcome any desire to retreat and were in a state of combat narcosis—a combination of stoicism and fury that propelled them inexorably forward. According to a rattled Northern gunner during Pickett's Charge, the Confederates swarming toward him were aware of the muzzles of the guns pointing directly at them but did not care: "The poor wretches knew what it meant—it meant death within the next three seconds to many of them, and they knew it. I remember distinctly that they pulled their caps down over their eyes and bowed their heads as men do in walking against a hail storm. They knew what was coming."[12] But they also knew that there was no stopping them now that their blood was up. "We were mad and fully determined to take and silence those batteries at once," wrote Coxe.[13]

14. At Close Quarters

Once the attackers reached the thirty-yard crisis point *and* showed no sign of slowing down, then the tactical advantage shifted to the aggressors. By this time, defensive fire was beginning to slacken and sputter out: Adrenaline surges could only spur on attackers and hurt defenders because they complicated coordination, degraded dexterity, and reduced fine motor control—precisely the skills needed to load and fire a weapon with any accuracy.

"It is not an uncommon thing for a soldier amidst the excitement of battle, to load his gun, shut his eyes and fire in the air straight over his head," complained Adjutant John Schoonover of the 11th New Jersey.[1] Much of the time, actually, these panicking defenders were not, despite repeatedly pulling the trigger, even firing at all. After the battle Union officials collected twenty-four thousand loaded guns that had been left abandoned on the field. Now, some of these had been discarded in favor of better rifles—every man of the 15th New Jersey was ordered to leave behind his Enfield and pick up an "excellent Springfield musket"—but at least half of them were charged with two loads, and another quarter with between three and ten. One specimen was packed with no fewer than twenty-three charges. In most cases, soldiers under pressure had either crammed down the cartridge without first breaking it or had inserted it the wrong way up (so that ball preceded powder).[2] A German military expert named Hohenlohe confirmed in 1866 that during his tours of various European battlefields he too had "found muzzle-loading rifles loaded with ten successive cartridges, of which the first was put in hind before (a proof that the soldier had not noticed that the first shot had missed fire, and had therefore kept putting in fresh cartridges one over the other)."[3]

Anyone, no matter how green or veteran, could overcharge his firearm as the attackers rapidly narrowed the gap. Scared and new to battle, Josiah Wolf of the 143rd Pennsylvania thought he had rammed home two cartridges by mistake and was loath to fire his gun during a firefight with the 2nd North Carolina. Corporal Simon Hubler took it upon himself to do it for him and painfully discovered that "the recoil was terrific. . . . I am of the opinion that he had five or six charges in instead of two."[4] Leander Stillwell, conversely, was a highly experienced and competent soldier, accustomed to guns since his boyhood days of squirrel-hunting, and yet the pervasive "confusion and uproar" around him caused even him to unwittingly double-load and fire, suffering for his error "a deafening explosion, and a kick that sent me a-sprawling on my back!"[5]

While this was all happening, the attack wave would be breaking into a run and readying a vengeful blast to stagger the defenders and give them time to storm the entrenchments before the defenders recovered. The 1st Minnesota did just that when, after a purposeful march forward in perfect alignment, they loosed a volley at thirty yards before their colonel shouted "Charge" and the regiment surged forward with leveled bayonets.[6]

The defenders now had roughly twenty seconds, if that, to react before the wave hit. Sometimes they evacuated. An orderly withdrawal would force the attackers to pay a heavy price for the ground gained, as when the 1st Texas assaulted the 124th New York at Houck's Ridge. "The enemy stood their ground bravely, until we were close on them, but did not await the bayonet," recalled Private James Bradfield. "They broke away from the rock fence as we closed in with a rush and a wild rebel yell, and fell back to the top of the ridge, where they halted and formed on their second line. Having passed the rock fence, and as we were moving on up the hill, an order came to halt." No doubt some diligent officers of the 1st Texas wanted to re-form their lines for a final push, but "it cost us dearly, for as we lay in close range of their now double lines, the enemy poured a hail of bullets on us, and in a few minutes a number of our men were killed and wounded."[7] A panicked retreat, on the other hand, led inevitably to disaster. As Sam Watkins fondly remembered, when the enemy ahead of him wavered and fled "we were jubilant; we were triumphant. Officers could not curb the men to keep in line. Discharge after discharge was poured into the re-treating line. The Federal dead and wounded covered the ground."[8]

When the defenders stayed put, however, the fighting instantly reached its ferocious climax. "If men ever became devils," wrote William Harmon, it was when they finally collided. "We were crazy with the excitement of the fight. We just rushed in like beasts. Men swore and cussed and struggled and fought, grappled in hand-to-hand fight, threw stones, clubbed their muskets, kicked, yelled, and hurrahed."[9] Similarly, when the 19th Maine was thrown into the melee, according to John Smith, "for ten or fifteen minutes the contending forces, in some places within rifle length of each other and in other places hopelessly mingled, fought with desperation. Those in front used the butt ends of their rifles, and those in the rear of the crowd of Union soldiers fired over the heads of those in front, and some of them hurled stones at the heads of the Confederates."[10] But Edward Hill put it most vividly when he characterized the 16th Michigan's struggle at Little Round Top as follows: "guns clubbed, stones hurled with barbaric strength, death welcomed in a teeth-a-set and hand to throat embrace, mercy vainly asked."[11]

Seizing the enemy colors was the primary objective; once they had fallen, it was the end. Men were promised the most wonderful reward—a trip home—if they managed to take them. Spurred on by that prospect, a Confederate of the Phillips Legion, having shot one man and bludgeoned five others, "was in the act of reaching for the flag when a fellow named Smith jumped in ahead of me and grabbed it. I came very near clubbing him, but he put up such a pitiful mouth about having a family of small children that he wanted to see so bad, I let him have it so he could get a furlough."[12]

Owing to the value of the big guns, both as trophies and as assets, storming them was of almost equal importance, but artillerymen were notorious for being tough hand-to-hand fighters. They were well equipped with tools that could be turned smartly into dangerous weapons. Sergeant Frederick Fuger of Cushing's Battery, for instance, told his men to fight off the oncoming Confederates with their trail handspikes. These were heavy metal or wooden poles about four and a half feet long originally intended to lever the cannon left and right, but they made, explained Fuger, "the finest weapons for close contact."[13] They did, indeed. One Sergeant Darveau of Pettit's Battery, confronted by a Confederate officer, "seized a trail hand-spike, and struck him full across the forehead, killing him on the spot."[14] Another favored option was the rammer, a lengthy wooden staff that pushed powder and ammunition down the barrel. When their battery was overrun by the 21st Mississippi, for instance, Corporal Adams watched the 9th Massachusetts's Private John Ligal "[save] himself by braining a Confederate with his rammer head."[15]

If they managed to hold off the attackers, the artillerymen would hasten to disable their guns.[16] They could break the wheels, shove several cannonballs down the muzzle, dent the barrel by smashing it with sledgehammers, or spike it—anything to prevent the victors from turning the guns around and firing them at retreating troops.[17] Alternatively, they could try to limber up their guns to horses to haul them to a safer place. To stop their escaping, attackers slew the animals, as happened when the 2nd Mississippi overran Captain James Hall's 2nd Maine battery. First, they shot the horses and only then, said W. B. Murphy, did they stop to pour "such a deadly fire into [the hapless gunners] that they left their [last] piece and ran for life."[18]

The most popular method of claiming a gun was to jump on it. Colonel Humphrey of the 21st Mississippi remembered how "Lt. George Kempton [straddled] a gun [of the 9th Massachusetts] waving his sword and exclaiming, 'Colonel, I claim this gun for Company I.'

Lieutenant W. P. McNeily was astraddle of another, claiming it for Company E."[19] One had to perform this ritual in a sober and sensible way to avoid misfortune. Mounting a gun, for instance, promptly turned a man into the foremost target of everyone around him. When the Louisiana Brigade broke through the Union lines at East Cemetery Hill, Major Harry Gilmor "saw one of our color-bearers jump on a gun and display his flag. He was instantly killed. But the flag was seized by an Irishman, who, with a wild shout, sprang upon the gun, and he too was shot down. Then a little bit of a fellow, a captain, seized the staff and mounted the same gun; but, as he raised the flag, a ball broke the arm which held it. He dropped his sword, and caught the staff with his right before it fell, waved it over his head with a cheer, indifferent to the pain of his shattered limb and the whizzing balls around him. His third cheer was just heard, when he tottered and fell, pierced through the lungs." (The captain survived.)[20]

15. Surrender

Once the guns were taken and the colors lowered, surrender was nigh. There were few instances in the Civil War of massacres after an action, so long as the act of capitulation was performed properly. By and large, officers would not throw away the lives of their men on useless last stands but instead surrender on their behalf once it was evident that the opposing side had the advantage, either in position, numbers, or initiative. In return for throwing in the towel early and behaving in a knightly manner, an officer was accorded due dignity, not least of which included the right to surrender his sword to another. During the struggle at the railway cut, for instance, Colonel Rufus Dawes sensibly adhered to protocol by addressing only Major J. R. Blair, 2nd Mississippi, who "replied not a word, but promptly handed me his sword, and his men . . . threw down their muskets."[1]

If no officers were present, men began "wav[ing] hats, handkerchiefs, newspaper or whatever they had to surrender," according to a Union soldier accepting the submissions of Confederates when Pickett's Charge collapsed.[2] V. A. Tapscott, 56th Virginia, saw those around him surrendering "some with hands up, some with feet up, some with black clothes, some one color and some another, most of them shedding hats and caps."[3]

Soldiers could be shot out of hand, however, if they abused their privileges. The 30th Pennsylvania, after an uphill charge, received the surrenders of twenty Confederates, among whom was, said Benjamin Urban, "one big fellow [who thought] he could kill one Yankee yet, raised his gun again and fired it in the faces of the men not ten feet in front of him, and then threw it down. A fatal mistake for him, for one of the Bucktails, who had just barely dodged the bullet, with a 'No you don't; you _____,' shot him through the body."[4]

In movies, soldiers are frequently shown cheering after a hard-fought victory. There was little of that in reality. Instead, recalled Major John D. Musser, 143rd Pennsylvania, "officers and men shook hands in silence, great tear drops standing in their undaunted eyes."[5] Inside, as the wrath and rage of the assault burned out as rapidly as once they had flared, soldiers, according to Abner Small of the 16th Maine, "felt a strange exaltation" because they were "horribly glad to be alive and unhurt."[6]

In any case, the survivors were in no fit state for celebration. The immediate physical toll exacted by combat is often overlooked, but it would help explain the oddly pacific aftermath to the bloody, broken *mise en scène* surrounding them. Soldiers had, wrote Colonel Włodzimierz Krzyżanowski, "bloodshot eyes" and "were sweaty, blackened by the gunpowder, and they looked more like animals than human beings [with an] animal-like eagerness for blood."[7] The 9th Alabama's Edmund Patterson "was almost too weak to stand, and my cheeks as hollow as though emaciated by a long spell of sickness."[8] "Think you of a gang of coal-heavers who have just finished putting in a winter's supply ordered by some provident householder in midsummer, and you get a fair impression of troops at the end of a day's fighting," attested Allen Redwood, 55th Virginia, while a veteran told *Scientific American* that "at the end of a battle I always found that I had perspired so profusely as to wet through all my clothes. I was as sore as if I had been beaten all over with a club."[9] Frank Haskell claimed that he too was "drenched with sweat," but his skin had turned a "burning red" color, and he resembled nothing less than a "boiled man."[10]

16. The Return to Normal

The sun and lack of water at Gettysburg would have compounded the soldiers' exhaustion significantly; it was a wise officer who sought billets for his men in the hours following a clash. Every soldier longed for sleep, though some, like Thomas Evans of the 12th U.S. Infantry, could not get even that. "After the heat and excitement of the day were over I lay down and tried to sleep," he said. "But the din of the engagement was still in my ears, and kept up a perpetual buzzing that I could not drive away. I had a bad headache, my throat was parched, my eyes were aching. I could not sleep."[1]

As they eventually drifted off one by one, false alarms remained a menace. At around 1 A.M., reported Colonel Dawes of the 6th Wisconsin, "a man in the Seventh Indiana Regiment, next on our right, cried so loudly in his sleep that he aroused all the troops in the vicinity. Springing up, half bewildered, I ordered my regiment to 'fall in,' and a heavy fire of musketry broke out from along the whole line of fire."[2]

But when soldiers did drift away, it was wonderful. The Confederate artilleryman E. P. Alexander ruminated that "in ten seconds I was . . . sounder asleep than I had ever been before, or ever before even realized it was possible to be. For there is a sort of higher power of sleep, with qualities as entirely different from the ordinary as light is from heat. . . . I have never been able to obtain it except in connection with the excitement attendant on a battle & not more than three or four times even then." It felt as if he had let himself "sink under a dense fluid which penetrated alike eyes & ears & pores until it pervaded the very bones bringing with it, instantly, everywhere a trance of delicious rest & freedom even from dreams."[3]

By the following day and night, soldiers were returning to their normal selves. "Sad as were the memories of the previous evening, as much as we missed the comrades who fell in that desperate charge," recalled one New Yorker, "yet soldiers and officers sat and chatted and joked, even as if nothing had happened."[4] David Hunter Strother witnessed, sitting amidst the carrion of 300 slain Confederates at Antietam, Union troops "cooking, eating, jabbering, and smoking," even sleeping among the corpses, with nary a second thought.[5]

Strother's account affirms that following the massive adrenaline surge-and-dump of combat and a good night's sleep, the extraordinary became the ordinary. Thus, when Benjamin Urban saw men "playing a quiet game of cards on the bloody stretchers they had been carrying" he was briefly irritated but "soon began to think differently, for I saw that behind the simple act there was absolutely no sense of its incongruity."[6] A Union soldier accordingly thought it entirely unexceptional to eat his dinner

within six paces of a rebel in four pieces. Both legs were blown off. His pelvis was the third piece, and his head and chest were the fourth piece. Those four pieces occupied a space of twelve feet square. I saw five dead rebels in a row, with their heads knocked off by a round shot. Myself and other amateur anatomists, when the regiment was resting temporarily on arms, would leave to examine the internal structure of man. We would examine brains, heart, stomach, layers of muscles, structure of bones, &c., for there was every form of mutilation. At home I used to wince at the sight of a wound or of a corpse; but here, in one day, I learned to be among the scenes I am describing without emotion.[7]

A protective sense of imperturbability seemingly radiated from participants, as if nothing remarkable had recently occurred. Rufus Dawes told his wife that just a few days after he had lost half his regiment, the entire "terrible ordeal" seemed "more like a fearful, horrible dream than reality."[8] When George Bowen of the 12th New Jersey settled down for a well-earned dinner, a stray cannonball flew over and, glancing off a nearby tree, narrowly missed him but smashed into the chest of the man sitting alongside. Bowen was coated with his neighbor's blood, flesh, and shattered bones, but he barely noticed; he just slowly shook the residue from his hand, wiped the stuff from his face, and scraped off his rations before tucking in.[9]

Veterans like Cyrus Boyd, however, were less convinced that Bowen and those like him could keep their minds and emotions switched off after combat so easily. He had seen "pieces of clothing and strings of flesh hang on the limbs of trees," and he believed that something untoward did change within men who experienced intense combat. "War is *hell* broke *loose* and benumbs all the tender feelings of men and makes of them *brutes*," he confided in his diary. The pity of war was not that killing happened but that indifference to killing became normal. Still, combat retained its attractions, even for Boyd, partly explaining why soldiers kept soldiering: "I do not want to see any more such scenes and yet I would not have missed this for any consideration."[10]

17. Sights, Sounds, Smells

What first struck soldiers as they emerged from their post-combat fog was the mess war leaves behind. Robert Carter, 22nd Massachusetts, described the "debris of battle" as comprising "haversacks, canteens, hats, caps, sombreros, blankets of every shade and hue, bayonets, cartridge boxes—every conceivable part of the equipment of a soldier."[1] A nurse witnessed a landscape of "artillery wagons crushed, broken muskets scattered in every direction, unused cartridges in immense numbers, balls of all kinds, ramrods and bayonets, bits of clothing, belts, gloves, knapsacks, letters in great quantities, all lying promiscuously on the field."[2]

Then the bodies—dead and still alive—swam into focus. They were everywhere.[3] At Gettysburg, both armies lost around twenty-three thousand men (including killed, wounded, missing, and captured), with Lee expending a third of his force and Meade a comparatively impressive quarter. The ten worst-hit Confederate regiments lost an average of three-quarters of their troops, which alone accounted for 2,651 of Lee's casualties.[4] On the Union side, the once-two-hundred strong 141st Pennsylvania suffered so many losses that for three months afterward the regiment could muster no more than forty men at any one time.[5] Private William Smith of the 116th Pennsylvania told his family a week after Gettysburg that there were just nine men left in his company, 108 in the entire regiment.[6] The 116th, which was weak to begin with, was not even one of the hardest-hit regiments, losing merely a third of its strength.[7] In comparison, some fifty-four Union and thirty-four Confederate regiments—between them, an average of one in five infantry regiments engaged—suffered losses of greater than 50 percent.[8]

These dry statistics euphemistically disguise what "casualties" and "losses" actually looked like. Robert Carter saw how Kershaw's and Wofford's brigades had marched right up to the muzzles of the Union artillery at the Rose Farm. The guns, double-shotted with one-second fuses, had left behind "arms, legs, heads, and parts of dismembered bodies . . . scattered all about, and sticking among the rocks, and against the trunks of trees, hair, brains, entrails, and shreds of human flesh still hung, a disgusting, sickening, heartrending spectacle."[9] Try as he might, John Haley from Maine could not adequately depict the carnage or make it seem real to outsiders; all he could see before him was a wasteland of "men's heads blown off or split open; horrible gashes cut; some split from the top of the head to the extremities, as butchers split beef."[10] Walking around Culp's Hill, Nurse Sophronia Bucklin saw "boots, with a foot and leg putrifying within, l[ying] beside the pathway, and ghastly heads, too—over the exposed skulls of which insects crawled—while great worms bored through the rotting eyeballs. Astride a tree sat a bloody horror, with head and limbs severed by shells, the birds having banqueted on it."[11] Another man saw a pair of "booted and stockinged feet, still standing in their place." Their owner had crawled away, leaving behind a sloppy red stain, as from a snail.[12]

Robert Stiles happened across "several human or unhuman corpses s[itting] upright against a fence, with arms extended in the air and faces hideous with something very much like a fixed leer."[13] Private Robin Berkeley of the Confederate artillery "saw the body of a Yankee, which had been cut in two. The head, arms, and about one-half of his ribs had been thrown against a fence, and remained with his heart and entrails sticking to the top rail, while some 10 feet off the lower part of the body had been thrown into a mud hole in the road."[14] Over at Culp's Hill, Philo Buckingham saw "some [soldiers] sitting up against trees or rocks stark dead with their eyes wide open staring at you as if they were still alive—others with their heads blown off with shell or round shot[,] others shot through the head with musket bullets. Some struck by a shell in the breast or abdomen and blown almost to pieces, others with their hands up as if to fend of[f] the bullets we fired upon them, others laying against a stump or stone with a testament in their hand or a likeness of a friend, as if wounded and had lived for some time."[15]

As Buckingham inferred, not everyone had enjoyed the good fortune of dying quickly. In the days following the battle, untold numbers of wounded were left in the field, a great many expiring before they could be found or rescued. One of the casualties, George Metcalf of the 136th New York, recalled that at first the air around him "was filled with groans, moans, shrieks, and yells. Prayers were offered and curses pronounced. Piteous appeals were made for water, for help, for death." But as time went on, this cacophony slowly grew "fainter and more indistinct until lost in one constant low, faraway moaning sound." Over the next night or so, even the moans evaporated, and you would only occasionally see "a dark form rise from the ground as some poor wretch by a superhuman effort would attempt to rise, and then it would disappear."[16]

For those left behind who survived, the experience was, to put it mildly, a memorable one. Decades later, Metcalf could still see the afflicted "when my eyes are shut, and hear the sounds I cannot describe whenever I let my mind dwell upon that night of all nights, as I lay among the dead and dying on the night of July 3rd on the battlefield of Gettysburg."[17] Elsewhere, a wounded Lieutenant Inman, 118th Pennsylvania, was abandoned behind enemy lines and left alone among the dead. "That night a number of stray hogs came to where I lay and commenced rooting and tearing at the dead men around me," he wrote. "Finally one fellow that in the darkness looked of enormous size approached and attempted to poke me—grunting loudly the while. Several others also came up, when, waiting my chance, I jammed my sword into his belly, which made him set up a prolonged, sharp cry. By constant vigilance and keeping from sleeping I contrived to fight the monsters off till daylight."[18] The New Hampshireman Charles Drake was not so fortunate: His right leg had been mangled by canister, and he could only watch helplessly as the hogs gnawed the flesh from its bones.[19]

Man was wolf to man, of course. Sergeant J. A. Bosworth of the 141st Pennsylvania was lying with a leg wound behind Confederate lines and had hid himself behind a stone wall. A group of Southerners came along in time, and "I asked one of them for a drink of water; he gave it to me, but while I was drinking he was loading his gun. He said he hated our men, then went off about eight rods [44 yards] and shot at me." Bosworth managed to plunge deeper into the bushes, and after several rounds the sadist got bored and left.[20]

Fortunately, soldiers essayed out each night to scout for their wounded friends. A group from the 6th New Jersey was picking its way through some woods when a man tripped and tumbled over. One of his hands landed on a cold, dead head, while "my feet rested on another body, and my lantern was out. I felt for a match. I had none. But presently some of the men came up; the lantern was relighted, and the glare revealed a sight which I pray God my eyes may never look upon again. The body upon which my hand had fallen was that of a corporal; both legs were blown completely off. That over which I had stumbled was the body of a private with one arm severed, not entirely off, at the shoulder." With the lantern illuminating a circle of twenty feet, the soldiers glanced around and slowly realized that surrounding them lay seventeen slaughtered bodies.[21]

As early as July 4, said Sergeant Thomas Meyer, "the dead were already in a terrific state of putrefaction. Faces black as charcoal and bloated out of all human semblance; eyes, cheeks, forehead, and nose all one general level of putrid swelling, twice the normal size . . . while the bodies were bloated to the full capacity of the uniforms that enclosed them."[22] George Benedict of the 12th Vermont specified that the dead's faces exhibited "a deep bluish *black,* giving to a corpse with black hair the appearance of a negro, and to one with light or red hair and whiskers a strange and revolting aspect."[23] Staring into their faces, one could see, said Edmund Brown of the 27th Indiana, "their lips as thick as one's hand, their eyes wide open with glossy, glaring eyeballs, unspeakably hideous and revolting."[24]

Robert Stiles, a Confederate artilleryman, observed corpses that had "burst asunder with the pressure of foul gases and vapors."[25] The horses were worse, wrote Alanson Haines, 15th New Jersey, because they "swelled to elephantine proportions."[26] A chaplain added the curious detail that as horses bloated, their "uppermost hind leg[s] lifted into the air."[27]

There were even worse ways to die than by shot and shell. A soldier of the 77th New York visited Sherfy's barn, used as a hospital before shellfire set it ablaze with the wounded trapped inside. "The crisped and blackened limbs, heads and other portions of bodies lying half consumed among the heaps of ruins and ashes" were among the "most ghastly pictures" he ever witnessed.[28] There were, as on any battlefield, the remains of those who died in strange and tantalizing circumstances. William Livermore and his comrades in the 20th Maine entered a house near the Peach Orchard on July 6 and found "some [dead] Rebels with there [*sic*] hands tied but did not know what it was for unless they tried to desert. One we found with a handkerchief tied over his mouth. He was wound[ed] mortally and they did it to keep him from hollaring."[29]

If the sights were awful, worse perhaps, and certainly more lingering, was the smell. "The stench on the battlefield was something indescribable, it would come up as if in waves and when at its worst the breath would stop in the throat; the lungs could not take it in, and a sense of suffocation would be experienced. We would cover our faces tightly with our hands and turn the back towards the breeze and retch and gasp for breath," was how Sergeant Meyer put it afterward.[30] Late into the night, "the fearful odors I had inhaled," wrote Stiles, the Confederate gunner, "remained with me and made me loathe myself as if an already rotting corpse."[31]

18. The Dead

For the still-living, being found by their friends did not necessarily entail rescue. Soldiers followed an ad hoc system of triage: Men suffering from serious abdominal, head, or chest wounds were left where they were in order to concentrate on bringing those with a chance of surviving to the hospital.[1] Shooting the mortally wounded to put them out of their misery does not seem to have occurred regularly, and there were too many people looking to bayonet them discreetly, but suicides did happen with some frequency. After the Confederate charge at Culp's Hill, the 147th Pennsylvania's A. M. Eby saw a Confederate soldier of the 1st Maryland Battalion with a stomach wound flopping about in agony. He and his fellows watched as the man diligently loaded his musket, placed the muzzle under his chin, and pulled the trigger with the ramrod.[2] When Private Arsenal Griffin, an artilleryman, was disemboweled by an exploding shell, he cried out for this comrades to finish him. When none did it, he drew his revolver, said "Goodbye, boys," and blew his brains out.[3]

For those unable or unwilling to kill themselves, soldiers instead waited respectfully for the inevitable before burying their remains. Thus, on Sunday, two days after the battle ended, George Bowen (12th New Jersey) watched a Confederate, "who had been wounded in a dozen places, still breathing, one shot had gone clean through his head, striking the temple on one side and coming out at the other temple, he laid there just breathing, he would gradually stretch out his hand, feel around till he got something between his fingers, whether grass or dirt it did not matter, then he would gradually raise his hand to his head and try to poke the stuff into the wound." Bowen and his friends assumed he would "die at any moment, so dug a grave for him," but were summoned away before he expired.[4]

It was normal practice to loot dead men. Sergeant Thomas Meyer of 148th Pennsylvania observed that "it was a rare occurrence to find one [a corpse] who not been robbed by the battlefield bandit or robber of the dead. Generally the pockets were cut open and rifled through the incision." The guilty "were well known by the large amounts of money they had, and the watches, pocketbooks, pocket knives, and other valuable trinkets they had for sale after the battle. All regiments had them."[5] A Vermont man noticed how many of the dead had their jackets and shirts torn or thrown open in the front, exposing their chests and stomachs, presumably by "human jackal[s] searching for money."[6]

The wounded were by no means inviolate, and it was always sensible to cooperate when your turn came for frisking for fear of being silenced. Private Robert Wadding of the 148th Pennsylvania, shot in the groin on July 1 and disabled for life, was lying stricken in a field but remained quiescent when a pair of looters searched his knapsack and belongings. They otherwise left him alone before moving on to their next victim.[7]

Union troops profited greatly from their victory. Left in possession of the field, they had ample opportunity to loot both Confederate *and* Union corpses. The pickings could be good. William Livermore of the 20th Maine found one Confederate carrying forty-three sheets of expensive writing paper (originally taken from a Union soldier) as well as "30 or 40 envelopes in the same, nice stockings & shirts that never was put on."[8] Others struck pay dirt when they came across Southerners who had not yet spent the cash from their last payday at the end of June, just a few days earlier. One such scavenger found $30.60 (nearly three months' wages) on a single corpse, which made for a most welcome surprise.[9] Dead officers of either side were highly sought after because they had more money and nicer things. The body of the late Captain Lucius Larrabee (44th New York) was recovered with $90 missing from his pockets, while Lieutenant Willis Babcock (64th New York) was stripped of his sword, watch, memorandum book, and purse.[10] Lieutenant Colonel Morgan recalled that by the morning of July 4, "our men" had plundered every dead Confederate who had participated in Pickett's Charge. "I saw a Federal trying unsuccessfully to pull a ring from the finger of one of the bodies. As I rode away I heard the Federal's companion say, 'Oh Damn it, cut the finger off.'"[11]

So comprehensively would the dead be liberated from their earthly possessions that when civilians sneaked onto the battlefield a few days later to see what they could steal, there was annoyingly little left but worthless love letters and such unsellable trash as locks of some child's hair.

After the civilians came, a small team of doctors arrived from Washington, D.C. Their mission was a sensitive one, one they preferred to keep secret. They were content to let witnesses assume that they were there to help set up the hospitals to take care of the long-term wounded.

In fact, they had been sent by Dr. John Brinton, chief of the army's new Medical Museum, to collect specimens. Resident Jenny Jacobs recollected seeing several "medical students . . . preparing skeletons, and in a cauldron [they were] boiling the remains of heroes." She could learn nothing more of this mysterious activity, but it is evident that the doctors were reducing the fleshy bits of corpses to bones for more efficient storage in the kegs they had brought with them. Private Phillip Pindell, 1st Maryland Battalion, (involuntarily) aided the interests of science by having his face and hair boiled away. Nevertheless, the haul—just thirty-eight—from Gettysburg would be surprisingly small considering the bounteous supply of possible specimens lying around, but that was mostly owed to the rapid work of the burial details.[12]

If the dead were lucky, their comrades took good care of their remains. Sergeant William Howe of the 134th New York wrote home that "all our men killed were buried where they fell, and in a nice place, too, by the fence in the pasture. . . . Our boys are all buried by one another."[13] When they could, they added headboards with their names, ranks, and regiments, but identification tags were rare (soldiers could buy their own from sutlers or stores in the cities if they wanted), so it was often difficult to recognize a man, even a familiar one, if he was dismembered or decomposed. Looting, too, had stripped many of belongings that might otherwise have helped identify them. Today, around 1,600 of the 3,512 Union troops buried at Soldiers' National Cemetery remain unknown.[14] Confederates fared still worse. Frank Haskell saw "patches of fresh earth, raised a foot or so above the surrounding ground," with signs nearby on which was scrawled in red chalk, "75 Rebils berid hear" or, next to an arrow, "54 Rebs there."[15] As often happens in war, the occasional bizarre anomaly provoked every man's curiosity, such as the discovery of a female dressed in a Confederate uniform who was buried by soldiers of II Corps.[16]

Most often, burial parties dug long, shallow trenches near concentrations of corpses and indiscriminately let them "[tumble] in just as they fell, with not a prayer, eulogy, or tear," wrote Robert Carter. Up to ninety would be squeezed into a single mass grave.[17] At other times, as the men of the 17th Maine did, they bent their bayonets into hooks to drag the dead to the pits, but this method was not always satisfactory.[18] When two gravediggers came across a soldier "all bloated up, seated leaning against a tree," they found it "impossible to handle the man to get him there [to the pit], he was so decayed like, and we hitched his belt to his legs and dragged him along, and no sooner did we start with him than his scalp slipped right off. We just turned him in on his side and covered him with earth" instead of taking him any farther.[19] Bodies that had been hit by shell fragments were particularly prone to falling to pieces. Better than dragging was to jerry-rig a stretcher out of two poles with a canvas strip attached between. Two men handled the stretcher while a third used another, shorter pole to roll the body onto it. Still, as Private John Parker of the 22nd Massachusetts said of his work on July 5, often the carcasses were so badly decomposed and flayed that they tended to "slide off" into the grave.[20]

Unfortunately, once they were in there, the corpses' limbs were all askew, wrote Cyrus Boyd, so soldiers would jump "on top of the dead straightening out their legs and arms and tramping them down so as to make the hole contain as many as possible."[21] The 12th New Jersey's George Bowen "saw one man who had died with his arm in such position that it stuck up when put in the hole," so "a man took his shovel struck it a blow breaking his arm so that it fell, this was done to save having so much dirt to throw."[22]

Horses were harder to bury than humans, and soldiers soon gave up trying. Instead, they either left them to rot or dragged them to a pyre for burning. John Foster, who was helping the wounded, saw "here and there great girdles of fire blazon[ing] the slopes, telling of slaughtered animals slowly consuming."[23] Since some 4,400 were killed at Gettysburg, it took a long time to burn them all.[24]

19. The Wounded

Given the limitations of care in the field, soldiers brought to a hospital had generally suffered only wounds optimistically considered survivable. It was usually the subsequent infection that killed them, for while it was understood that cleanliness was an important part of treatment, the way in which germs were transmitted was unknown. Decades later, Dr. W. W. Keen asked God to

forgive us our sins of ignorance. We operated in old blood-stained and often pus-stained coats, the veterans of a hundred fights. . . . We used undisinfected instruments from undisinfected plush-lined cases, and still worse, used marine sponges which had been used in prior pus cases and had been only washed in tap water. If a sponge or an instrument fell on the floor it was washed and squeezed in a basin of tap water and used as if it were clean. Our silk to tie blood vessels [and sew up wounds] was undisinfected. . . . If there was any difficulty in threading the needle we moistened it with (as we now know) bacteria-laden saliva, and rolled it between bacteria-infected fingers. We dressed the wounds with clean but undisinfected sheets, shirts, tablecloths, or other old soft linen rescued from the family ragbag. We had no sterilized gauze dressing, no gauze sponges.[1]

Keen's words should be borne in mind when, using modern standards as a yardstick, Civil War surgeons are belittled for their seeming incompetence and cruelty. Most former civilian physicians were in fact scrupulous and well-meaning but had to learn on the job owing to a lack of resources at the beginning of the war. In 1860, for example, the entire sixteen-thousand-man U.S. Army employed all of thirty surgeons and eighty-three assistant surgeons—of whom twenty-four joined the Confederacy—and the Medical Department's budget was $90,000. From there, military medicine made enormous strides, an achievement obscured by an emphasis on judging progress by anachronistic standards of care, training, and knowledge. Indeed, by 1865 more than 12,000 doctors had served with the Union armies and 3,236 in those of the Confederacy. The North's medical budget, meanwhile, had risen to $11,594,000 by around the time of Gettysburg—a 12,882 percent increase in three years.[2]

Though there were a few fools—such as a Dr. Bailey of the 12th South Carolina who was so drunk that he botched Lieutenant J. R. Boyle's leg amputation not just the first time, but also when he redid it—most doctors at Gettysburg were dedicated and hardworking men who had to perform untold numbers of operations under extraordinarily trying circumstances.[3] Dr. John Billings wrote to his wife on July 6 that he was "utterly exhausted mentally and physically, have been operating night and day and am still hard at work." Even three days later, he was "covered with blood and . . . tired out almost completely," the only good news being that he had "got the chief part of the butchering done in a satisfactory manner." It was only on July 10 that he managed to get someone to scrub "all the blood out of my hair with Castile soap and bay-rum and my scalp feels as though a steam plough had been passed through it."[4] Others were not so lucky: One surgeon complained that his feet were so swollen after working almost nonstop for four days and two nights that he could barely stand. Rest was out of the question because he had another hundred amputations scheduled.[5]

The onerousness of their task was magnified by the relative scarcity of ambulances, orderlies, and supplies caused by the unexpected number of casualties, Lee's desire to travel light (the Confederates had four hundred ambulances, to the Army of the Potomac's thousand), and Meade's decision to move his extra wagons (carrying tents, stretchers, blankets, and food) to the rear in case he needed to retreat. Additionally, when the Union general pursued Lee on July 6 and 7, he took with him most of the medical personnel, leaving just 106 medical officers to deal with some 21,000 wounded men. Granted, most of the required surgeries had already been performed, but post-operative care was often minimal.[6] Whereas his leg had been removed on July 3, Charles Fuller of the 61st New York had to wait another six days "before a doctor could be found to look at my stump."[7] Nevertheless, it is difficult to find many complaints about the quality of medical treatment by injured soldiers. That the experience was awful should be taken as a given, but as J. W. Hand of the 136th New York put it many years later, "the care of the wounded was all that could be desired."[8]

Even the enemy wounded were often given proper attention. The 4th Texas's splendidly named Captain Decimus et Ultimus Barziza (he was the tenth and, his parents presumably hoped, last child) was shot in the leg and taken to a hospital where he and his fellow wounded were placed "side by side with the enemy's."[9] Suffering from a serious lung wound, Lieutenant Samuel Davis was told by a "very diminutive surgeon of Teutonic persuasion" that "I dink the probability is you die," but he recovered after being taken to a fine hospital in Chester, Pennsylvania. (Indeed, he fared so well that on the night of August 16 he escaped back to Richmond.)[10] On the other hand, Barziza and Davis were officers. Enlisted Confederates and Union men were generally treated decently but received second-class care. Few seemed to regard this as beyond the pale: As H. S. Peltz, a nurse at one Union hospital pointed out, the Confederates were housed in a nearby barn, and "while the soldiers of the North were dying for lack of care it was not strange that these poor creatures were left in an even worse condition."[11]

Whosoever they were, doctors tended to ease the exits of those who stood little chance of making it. For euthanistic purposes, Dr. Joseph Holt always carried a handy "two ounce bottle of black drop—a concentrated solution of opium, much stronger than laudanum" that ensured the mortally wounded never woke up.[12] If any man had been hit in the abdomen, said one surgeon, "one need not amuse oneself by hunting" for any bullets lost in there; he was as good as dead, and it was best to put him out of his misery quickly.[13]

Those left over might be placed in temporarily converted schools, houses, barns, and churches but were often kept outdoors. An orderly urged readers to put out of their minds any "thoughts of a long room, with cots having white sheets" when they heard the word *hospital*.[14] Instead, as Lieutenant Beath of the 88th Pennsylvania saw at McPherson's Barn, there were rows of "helpless soldiers, torn and mangled, [whose] lacerated limbs were frightfully swollen and, turning black, had begun to decompose; the blood flowing from gaping wounds had glued some of the sufferers to the floor."[15] In another field hospital, according to J. W. Stuckenberg, the patients were "writhing in pain, and deeply moaning and groaning and calling for relief which cannot be afforded them. The finest forms are horribly disfigured & mutilated."[16]

Any number of soldiers went almost mad waiting their turn for treatment—little surprise considering the conditions. John Dooley, a Confederate taken in by a Union hospital, said of his first night that all he heard were "groans and shrieks and maniacal ravings; bitter sobs, and heavy sighs, piteous cries; horrid oaths; despair." One man of his regiment lapsed into delirium, shouting "frantically a hundred times at least the words, 'I'm proud I belong to the 1st Va. Regiment!' "[17]

When Charles Weygant visited III Corps hospital, "a man I was about stepping over, sprang to his feet, shook in front of me a bloody bandage he had just torn from a dreadful gaping wound in his breast, and uttered a hideous, laughing shriek which sent the hot blood spurting from his wound into my very face; at which he threw up his arms as if a bullet had just entered his heart, and fell heavily backward across a poor mangled fellow, whose piercing wails of anguish were heart-rending beyond description."[18] The screams emanating from one place were so distressing that, as Fannie Buehler remembered, "the Regimental Bands . . . came every afternoon and played patriotic airs in front of the hospital" to muffle their sound.[19]

In the days following the battle, the primary duty of hospitals was not to make patients comfortable but to amputate in order to save lives. A common sight was "the surgeons, with sleeves rolled up and bloody to the elbows, [who] were continually employed in amputating limbs. The red, human blood ran in streams from under the operating tables, and [there were] huge piles of arms and legs, withered and horrible to behold."[20] These discarded bits and pieces of people accumulated frighteningly quickly. J. W. Muffly of the 148th Pennsylvania saw a "pile of hands, arms, feet, and legs . . . which had now reached the window sill."[21] Nellie Aughinbaugh of Gettysburg remembered watching surgeons throwing "arms and legs out the windows into the yard to lay there in the sweltering sun of that hot July."[22] Corporal George Wilson of the 150th New York gained still more direct experience when, after being hit in the head with a spent bullet and knocked unconscious, he was taken to the hospital and then mistakenly laid outside among the dead. The next morning he "awoke to find himself partly covered with the arms and legs the surgeons had amputated and thrown near him."

But there was little doctors could do with severed limbs but get rid of them as quickly as possible. They were working not only against the unending procession of casualties but the clock as well. According to the best contemporary medical opinion, the optimum time for amputation—that is, the window in which mortality was lowest—was roughly within twenty-four hours of receiving the injury, though it was far better to operate within half a day, before inflammation or contamination set in as shock wore off. From that point on, the fatality rate rose to more than a third of patients if the surgeons delayed longer than forty-eight hours from time of injury. If they did not operate at all, however, half of all men would die, and half the remainder would be left forever unfit for civilian employment.[23]

In this respect, the very fact that there were so many amputees in, for instance, Mississippi in 1865 that the state was obliged to spend one fifth of its revenue on prosthetic limbs can be counted as a positive consequence of the belief that it was better to err and amputate unnecessarily than to be overly cautious. If an infection or gangrene developed because a surgeon had delayed, he would need to wield the knife higher up the limb than he otherwise would have—making an already risky operation markedly more so. A Confederate soldier in Lee's army at this time enjoyed a 97 percent survival rate if his foot was taken off in reasonable time, but only a 62 percent chance if his leg was severed at the thigh. With good reason, then, amputations were a surgeon's first choice, not his last resort.[24]

In any case, very few soldiers opted to postpone or avoid amputation in the hopes of recovering naturally. At least proceeding to the operating table promised a rapid relief from pain thanks to the recent introduction of the miracle drug chloroform. The first reported clinical use of it as a stupefacient was by the Scot James Simpson on January 19, 1847, at his obstetrical practice, after which its use in wartime rocketed.[25] We should bear in mind that chloroform was a new technology, and as such, some doctors resisted its application—also that given the choice, some soldiers preferred to grit their teeth rather than take the newfangled drug. Private C. L. F. Worley of 5th Alabama, for instance, said, "Cut off the leg, Doc, but leave off the chloroform; if you can stand it I can."[26]

Their behavior was motivated more by fear about their manliness than by any concern about safety. Death from a chloroform overdose or adverse reaction was very rare—there would be just thirty-seven such deaths during the Civil War—but a minority of physicians regarded anesthetic as appropriate only for women and children.[27] Virile, vigorous males, counseled one Dr. White, a Union surgeon with a Massachusetts regiment, should avoid the stuff. When White brusquely asked Private James Winchell whether he was going to have his arm taken off, or "are you going to lie here and let the maggots eat you up," Winchell opted for the chloroform, to which request White replied, " 'No, and I have no time to dillydally with you.' " Finally, a humiliated Winchell agreed to the operation, set his teeth together, and had his arm cut off, proudly relating that afterward "Surgeon White praised my spunk, as he called it, and treated me to a half gill of brandy."[28]

White was an aberration in this respect. More representative of the profession was Dr. John Chisolm of South Carolina, who rued the tendency of old-school sawbones to "moralize upon the duty of suffering," to laud "the lusty bawling of the wounded from the smart of the knife," and to "characterize the cries of the patient as music to the ear."[29] Like most other doctors, Chisolm saw the introduction of chloroform as a divine blessing, for, as F. E. Daniel, another Confederate surgeon, put it, the patient "slept all through the ordeal. A minute seems not to have elapsed since the first whiff of the chloroform; he felt nothing, knew nothing. He wakes to find his leg gone."[30]

For the soldier who chose chloroform, the process was swift and straightforward. When it was the 61st New York's Charles Fuller's turn to have a leg sawn off, he was lifted onto the table and "a napkin was formed into a tunnel shape, a liberal supply of chloroform poured into it, and the thing placed over my nose and mouth. I was told to take in long breaths. To me it seemed a long time before the effect came, probably it was a short time, but at last my head seemed to grow big and spin around." When he awoke, he was given morphine, which presently "produced a happy state of mind and body."[31]

That is not to say that chloroform could not lead to some frightening moments. After Sergeant Francis Strickland of the 154th New York was shot in the right elbow, Dr. Van Aernam administered the anesthetic but did not dose him sufficiently. Strickland awoke halfway through the procedure and blurrily watched with horror as the surgeon tied his slippery arteries and sewed his flapping skin over the stump to cover it. Then he saw an orderly throw his arm and clothes through an open window and onto a big, sloppy pile of severed limbs.[32]

There were cases, too, of Lovecraftian hallucinations under the drug's influence. Adoniram Warner "fancied that I was wafting at an inconceivable velocity over space through regions of every degree of darkness and of light now in one and now in another and whirled round and round at a rate so horrible that I shudder to think of it and still I thought there was no end to this and that these wild pangs that I felt would last forever." At one moment, "all would be light and glorious—the universe radiant all over with rainbow light and then in a moment, as it seemed to me, all was black and dark and the universe seemed filled with all loathsome things—serpents, lizards . . . crocodiles—monstrous beasts of all shapes mixing their slime in their gnashing for me and sounds that no letters will spell greeted my ears."[33]

But thankfully, these horrible instances were few and far between. They would, in any case, pale against the long-term aftereffects of battle. Most obviously, the wounded would continue to die for days, weeks, months afterward, sometimes even a year later. The 62nd Pennsylvanian offers a typical timeline. Private Cyrus Plummer was shot in the groin on July 2 and lasted a day before succumbing. That same day, Private Charles Gibbs was shot in the left lung but held on until July 6. Sergeant Jacob Myers, who was hit in the forehead, died on July 9, with Lieutenant Patrick Morrise dying two days later from a bullet taking off much of his skull. Corporal Joseph Sherran died on July 27 from two leg wounds, one in each. Captain James Brown died July 28 from injuries. Finally, Corporal Jacob Funk made it to a hospital in Philadelphia but died from his wounds on May 24, 1864.[34]

Then there were injuries that may have appeared minor or superficial but never healed. Private William Goodell was admitted to a hospital after a shell exploded a few feet behind him. He exhibited no physical wounds, but it was known at the time that shells or shot landing nearby could cause partial or complete paralysis, deafness, blindness, loss of voice, rupturing of blood vessels, and profound mental confusion—all without leaving a mark. Goodell was apparently struck deaf and dumb. He had electricity applied to his misbehaving tongue but still, within six months he was suffering paralysis in his left leg and the right-hand side of his face drooped. There were also occasional, half-hour-long convulsions and severe head pains. He undertook some "trifling mechanical work," in the words of his doctors, but by January 1876 his spine had curved severely rightward, his hands and feet had partially lost sensation, and he was totally incapacitated. An attendant was needed to tend to his daily wants and needs. By September 4, 1877, a doctor reported that Goodell was now "quite lame and gets about with difficulty." Unfortunately, the story ends there, but it is likely that he died soon afterward.[35]

The prevalence and virulence of long-term wounds contributed heavily to the explosion in morphine and opium use after the war. A large number of veterans became addicted to these painkillers during their hospital treatments. In 1868, Horace Day estimated that addicts numbered in the tens of thousands; by 1870, state officials were actively worrying about the profusion of homegrown opium, particularly in Vermont, New Hampshire, and Connecticut. There were also crops being raised in Florida, Louisiana, California, and Arizona. As late as 1902, investigators were still finding chronic drug abuse in old soldiers' homes.[36]

There was intense psychic scarring as well, but we should bear in mind that, as with the Bunker Hill veterans, confidently assigning diagnoses of PTSD to Civil War veterans is fraught with difficulty owing to changing standards and definitions based on historical and current samples.[37]

A common error is to elide temporary cases of acute stress disorder or combat stress reaction (immediate but usually recoverable reactions to trauma that include paralysis, weeping, muteness, curling fetally, and screaming) with deeper post-traumatic stress disorder (resulting from long-term exposure to extreme psychological pressure, with symptoms that may include irritability, anxiety, flashbacks, nausea, insomnia, paranoia, delusions, memory problems, violent behavior, and headaches). The gloom exhibited by Corporal Augustus Hesse of the 9th Massachusetts Battery is a case in point. At Gettysburg, his battery, which lost three of its four officers, six of eight sergeants, and nineteen enlisted men, was "cut up so terable[.] oh I feel so bad that I could cry."[38] He wrote this on July 7. But we cannot assume that he never recovered from the initial shock of losing so many comrades; it is possible that his was a temporary reaction. Indeed, Hesse (who was wounded in the arm) returned to the army and mustered out in June 1865 as a sergeant. His letters subsequent to the battle come across as quite cheery.[39] Another example is that of Lieutenant Colonel David Thomson of the 82nd Ohio, whose adjutant, Lieutenant Stowell Burnham, was mortally wounded on July 1. On July 16, Thomson wrote to his daughter saying, "Oh! How I miss Burnham," and on August 11 added, "How much I miss Burnham. Glorious good fellow was he, and most generously did he live." A little more than a week later, on August 19, Thomson wrote again: "I miss Burnham more and more. It was too bad that he was killed. Yet he died nobly and bravely. He and I were companions. I had none more so. Now I am alone." A close reading of the lines seems to indicate that Thomson was slowly coming to terms with his grief, had begun to console himself that his friend had lived well and had died "nobly and bravely," and was in the process of accepting that he must soldier on, even if it must be alone. It cannot be definitively proven, but it does seem likely that Thomson's incapacitating sorrow was not debilitatingly permanent.[40]

Similarly, many examples of men running away owing to "cowardice"—evidence, at the time, of low moral character—can be ascribed to simple combat stress reaction, while any number of men registered as "missing" were in fact soldiers who had succumbed to stress sometime during the fight and would make their way back to their units once they had recovered their composure. When Captain Francis Jones of the 149th Pennsylvania was wounded and lying in the McPherson Barn, he spotted a German of his company named Private Frederick Heiner "looking in the stable door. I called to him to inquire how he was wounded. He replied that he was not wounded at all, but he said, 'Captain, I was so terribly frightened on the first of July, I crawled under a hay stack as we passed it.'" His panic having subsided, Heiner redeemed himself by staying to help Jones.[41]

There were many others, like the wounded Jesse Morgan of the 7th New Jersey, who ran the gauntlet at Gettysburg and mused thereafter on the cruelty and waste of war, only to be back with their regiments within a few months.[42] Indeed, every Civil War army depended on the willingness of men to return to fight for their ideals (for union, for independence, for freedom, for slavery, for money, for pride, for fun), even if they suffered for them. Benjamin Thompson was a captain of the 111th New York at Gettysburg who in the immediate aftermath of Pickett's Charge "could not long endure the gory, ghastly spectacle." He "found my head reeling, the tears flowing and my stomach sick at the sight" of "the men [lying] in heaps, the wounded wriggling and groaning under the weight of the dead among whom they were entangled." For "months the spectre haunted my dreams, and even after forty seven years it comes back as the most horrible vision I have ever conceived."[43] Thompson was a troubled man, yet he continued with his regiment until March 1864, when he volunteered to transfer to the 32nd United States Colored Regiment—proof of his steadfast abolitionist beliefs—and stayed in harness until the end of the war, finishing it as lieutenant colonel. During Reconstruction he served at Fort Pulaski in Georgia as provost marshal and later moved to Minneapolis to become a successful tea merchant with a "large circle of friends" and an elder in the First Presbyterian Church.[44]

Thompson overcame his short-term combat stress and, while disturbed occasionally thereafter by nightmares, does not appear to have been actively disabled by full-blown PTSD over the subsequent decades. Compare his case with that of Colonel William Lee, beloved commander of the 20th Massachusetts at the battle of Antietam, where almost half his regiment was lost. A lieutenant, Henry Abbott, wrote to his father two months after the clash that Lee had come undone: "After the battle he was completely distraught. He didn't give any orders. He wouldn't do anything. The next morning he mounted his horse, and without any leave of absence, without letting any body [know] where he was going, he set out alone." He vanished for an entire month until Lieutenant George Macy, "who was bringing up some recruits, met him about ten miles away from the regt. Without a cent in his pocket, without any thing to eat or drink, without having changed his clothes for 4 weeks, during all which times he had this terrible diarrhea. . . . Macy gave him a drink and some money and got him into a house, put him to bed stark naked, and got his wits more settled, and then came on. When the poor old man came back to the regt. they thought he been on an awful [drinking] spree, he was so livid and shaky. Macy says he was just like a little child wandering away from home." Even now, he "is undoubtedly very much shaken in his intellects." Lee would resign his commission on December 17, though in actuality his duties had long been relinquished to subordinates.[45] He died thirty years later, forgotten and alone. The only people who remembered him at his funeral in a near-empty church, said one of his former officers, were some immediate relatives and "the few grey heads who stood for the men of the Twentieth."[46] It seems quite clear that Lee never recovered from his mental breakdown.

We also cannot know for certain the extent and depth of short-term stress and long-term PTSD in Civil War veterans, partly because so many likely cases were euphemized out of the record to preserve their subjects' dignity. In Colonel Lee's case, for instance, the official regimental history confined itself to stating delicately that after Antietam he "suffered a great deal from the various illnesses of camp brought on by exposure to wet and cold [and became] dangerously sick [and] left for Boston on [October] 29th on leave of absence for his health."[47]

Not least, too, given the rudimentary psychiatric knowledge of the era, it is often hard to distinguish between genuine PTSD symptoms and hereditary or genetic ailments. An ambiguous case was that of John Corns, who had shown no signs of disability before the war. Over the course of his service, however, he became pale, emaciated, and estranged from his relatives at home. After mustering out of his unit, he returned to Indiana but could not hold on to jobs and turned progressively more unstable. He would "look wild and excited and being evidently in great mental commotion," then shout "there is some one after me" and "do you see them coming over the hill, we will all be lost and destroyed." He said that his head hurt and would cover it with his hands and cry out. At other times, he would imagine that he was drilling troops or that he was an aide to a famous general. Corns was later sent to a poorhouse, where he was chained up. The question is whether these symptoms were manifestations of developing mental illness or part of a combat-induced disorder—or a combination of both.

Corns was not alone in this respect. A study of sixty-nine Union soldiers committed to the Indiana Hospital for the Insane between 1860 and 1871 reported the following symptoms: "raves—talks about the war and the Bible," "tears clothing," "was exposed in Army. Has not been well since," "has suffered great lack of sleep . . . Is troubled in sleep with persons [unintelligible] his life . . . and threatens to do these imaginary persons harm," "tried to stab his father and himself," "loses consciousness but does not fall down," "has had fear of being killed by [unintelligible] and others," and "became insane at Battle of Pea Ridge."[48]

As with Corns, these are all strongly positive indicators of delayed stress reactions, but at the time as many as a quarter of these cases were deemed hereditary and presumed to have relatively little to do with their Civil War service. Perhaps that is so, though only 14.5 percent of the patients had previously demonstrated signs of insanity, a hint that the physicians might have been conveniently classifying combat-related cases as "inherited" ones.

Even taking into account all these cautionary factors, we can say with some certitude that many Civil War soldiers were traumatized and afflicted, either in the immediate or the longer term, by their battle experiences. Thus, a sophisticated statistical analysis of the postwar medical records of 17,700 veterans found a very strong correlation between the percentage of regimental company killed and increased incidence of postwar gastrointestinal and cardiac problems, nervous disease, and depression. In this instance, the number of a man's friends killed stands as an index for such traumatic stressors as combat intensity, handling corpses, witnessing death and dismemberment, killing others, and realizing the imminence of one's death.[49]

The harder and more gallantly he struggled for cause, country, and comrades, then, the more likely that a soldier would be wretched with sickness and racked with pain, that he would be tormented by fears that he was neither useful nor ornamental to the world, when he attended those old men's reunions celebrating that great fight near the town of Gettysburg.

IWO JIMA

1945

1. Introduction

Of all the Pacific battles fought by the Marines—among them Guadalcanal, Peleliu, Saipan, Tarawa, Okinawa—Iwo Jima is the most iconic, the most famous. It is the Gettysburg of World War II. As the subject of bestselling books (*Flags of Our Fathers*) and popular movies (*Sands of Iwo Jima, Letters from Iwo Jima*), as well as the location of "The Photo"—Joe Rosenthal's immortal shot of five Marines and a U.S. Navy corpsman raising a flag atop Mount Suribachi—Iwo Jima overshadows any other amphibious Pacific battle in the American public's imagination, emotions, and memory.

In World War II, the Marine Corps was expressly designed for one thing: to hurl itself with the greatest possible violence toward a hostile beach, destroy the enemy at close quarters, and seize control of an island.[1] Part of the fascination with the battle on Iwo Jima stems from its legendary ferocity and annihilatory nature—the consequences of the American republic's bloodied sword arm meeting the Japanese empire's obstinate shield. Nearly two and a half times as many Marines would die at Iwo Jima—a speck just a third of the size of Manhattan—in five weeks as in the entirety of World War I (about eighteen months). Indeed, of all the Marines killed during the Second World War, a third would die at Iwo Jima. It is the only battle in which Marine casualties exceeded those of the Japanese.

Objectively and strategically speaking, however, Iwo neither formed a "turning point" in the war nor was "decisive" in the sense of deciding outcomes. By 1945, the Japanese Empire as a whole was doomed, and the Americans were everywhere triumphant. In Washington, the only issues were how long it would take to conquer Tokyo and how many corpses would there be along the way. Likewise, the Marines had won the battle of Iwo Jima from the moment they splashed ashore; it was just a matter of time, multiplied by force.

The battle, moreover, may not even have been so very important. The reasons for which it was ostensibly fought—to provide a base for bombing operations against Japan and an unsinkable aircraft carrier for damaged B-29s that would otherwise have ditched into the sea and drowned their crews—have lately been questioned as justifications *ex post facto* for the blood-price paid by the Marine Corps. Such assertions, understandably and predictably, remain extremely controversial among veterans as well as the public at large.[2]

Be that as it may, Iwo Jima is the focus of this chapter because it presents a case study in how armies solve problems and learn to fight. The Marines quickly invented new techniques and adapted their tactics after landing on Iwo Jima and discovering that their best-laid plans had come undone against unexpectedly dense Japanese defenses. Iwo Jima, then, *is* important, just perhaps not for the reasons traditionally suggested.

The Marines' rapid adaptation to circumstances undermines the popular suppositions that the war in the Pacific was racially based and that the "barbaric savagery" against the Japanese (and vice versa) was motivated by biological hatred. A close study of the actions of the Marines on Iwo Jima highlights instead that American responses to the Japanese were instrumentalist, not ideological, in nature. That is, Japanese were killed by the most effective methods and weaponry available because, in the face of unyielding resistance amid difficult terrain, this was the only way to win. This very practical aspect has been omitted from most accounts of Iwo Jima but will be discussed in detail here.

2. The Nature of the Battle

First, a brief account of the general course of the battle, which will, unavoidably, be vague. Unlike Bunker Hill or Gettysburg, where units' movements can be more or less tracked for the duration of the fighting, to the ordinary Marine on Iwo each day and night was just like the previous and the next. The battle was less one of structured stages than of dull, unvarying routines. Each and every day was consumed by advancing painfully slowly, taking cover, avoiding snipers, destroying pillboxes and bunkers, helping wounded comrades, killing Japanese, and killing more Japanese. Then trying, and failing, to get some sleep. The next day, it started all over again, and so on until there was literally no more island left to conquer. As their severely attrited squads, platoons, and companies dissolved and re-formed, Marines lost track of time, location, and unit. Their memories of what happened where and when and with whom are uniformly hazy, making it difficult to construct a solid timeline or map of their movements.

The structure of this chapter necessarily differs from the earlier two. Whereas for Bunker Hill, we could deduce a militiaman's experience of combat depending on his location (redoubt, beach, rail fence) and for Gettysburg we could do the same by deconstructing the era's formal templates (artillery bombardment, attack, defense), for Iwo Jima I'll mostly examine combat method—that is, how Marines first confronted obstacles and then surmounted them by watching, doing, adapting, and learning. The Marines on Iwo Jima would discover that by adhering to the method they could make sense out of madness, even vanquish it.

3. The Strategy

The Pacific War was predicated on the twin principles of acquiring advanced bases and island-hopping, both accomplished through amphibious assaults. Westward across the central Pacific the Marines would drive toward the Japanese home islands.[1]

To hold them up, the Japanese had established a defense-in-depth strategy of zones and rings, each tiny island chain supporting the others as a base of operations. The Marines, in turn, would assault a given stronghold, subdue it, and move out and onward to allow fresh troops room to garrison it. The island would thereafter be turned into a staging point for the next assault as Seabees—naval construction engineers —built airfields and harbors. Aircraft would begin to use the island as a secure base, supplies would be stockpiled in vast quantities, and the Navy could find safe anchorage for refitting and repair. An offshoot of island-hopping was leapfrogging, in which certain Japanese strongholds on an island chain would be bypassed and isolated from reinforcements using airpower and submarines. The Pacific strategy was an updating of Frederick the Great's eighteenth-century wars of geography, in which possession of certain fortresses, towns, and roads would eventually constrict the opponent's freedom of movement until he either surrendered or, alternately, fought at a disadvantage—and then surrendered. The major difference was that the Japanese were not princes and lords of the Enlightenment: They did not surrender but fought—to the very end.

Adhering to the set strategy, between November 1943 and November the following year the Marines successively seized advanced bases in the Gilbert, Marshall, Mariana, and Palau chains of islands and atolls, each hop bringing them closer to Japan. Guarding what Tokyo called its "Inner Vital Defense Zone" was Iwo Jima, described by one Japanese officer as the "doorkeeper to the Imperial capital" itself. Once Iwo Jima was taken, the next stop would be Okinawa (340 miles from mainland Japan), where the Marines advancing westward from the Central Pacific would join up with the Army divisions that had driven northward from the South Pacific. Together, they would invade Japan— but the dropping of the atomic bombs and the Soviet conquest of Manchuria ended the Pacific War before that inevitable cataclysm could take place.

From the Japanese perspective, Iwo Jima was admirably located to harass the B-29 Superfortress bombers raiding Nippon on their way both in and out. Iwo served also as a two-hour early warning system that could alert the mainland of incoming sorties while its complement of prowling fighters forced Allied bombers to fly more circuitous routes to their targets, making it necessary to carry extra fuel at the expense of their bomb payloads. On the way back, damaged planes were easy prey for the waiting fighters. In addition, Iwo's own complement of bombers had staged raids on U.S. bases at Saipan and Tinian. By the fall of 1944, more B-29s had been lost on the ground than in the sky.

Originally, the assault on Iwo Jima had been scheduled for October 1944, but unexpected delays caused by the Mariana and Palau invasions forced a postponement until the new year. The five-month wait proved expensive, as the Japanese, now commanded by the extraordinarily able Lieutenant General Tadamichi Kuribayashi, a fifth-generation soldier who would fight the Americans here for the first and last time, worked feverishly to reinforce the island's garrison (it ballooned from around fifteen hundred to roughly twenty thousand) and to strengthen its fortifications. The Marines would pay the price in blood.

The Americans themselves had done their utmost to frustrate the Japanese preparations in the hopes of making their assault easier. Beginning in August 1944, the Seventh Army Air Force dispatched regular bombing raids on Iwo. From December 8, as the Marines ramped up to invade, Iwo was subjected to daily attack. Near the end of January 1945, aircraft pummeled Iwo remorselessly, day and night, for two weeks. Heavy cruisers bombarded it five times in December and January alone. In total, the softening-up stage was the heaviest cumulative bombardment of the Pacific War, with 6,800 tons of bombs and 22,000 naval shells slamming into a piece of earth 5.5 miles long, 2.5 miles broad at its widest point, and comprising about eight square miles.

Three days before D-Day—the day of the invasion of Iwo Jima, February 19, 1945—the Navy hit Iwo with still more intense ferocity to blast away any remaining opposition before the Marines landed. The Japanese by then were too deeply entrenched, too hardened, for the bombardment to have any chance of succeeding. Waiting offshore, nonetheless, were the 3rd, 4th, and 5th Marine Divisions (together making up the V Amphibious Corps), the largest force of Marines ever committed to a single battle.

4. The Battle

At 0645 on February 19, the order went out: "Land the landing force." With the 3rd Division held in reserve, the 5th was to storm the 2.5-mile-long beach just north of 548-foot-high Mount Suribachi as the 4th landed on its right flank, overlooked by the Rock Quarry perched on the bluffs dominating the beach.

After the first wave of Marines landed at approximately 0900, they rapidly advanced inland, receiving fire from concealed Japanese machine-gun positions, pillboxes, and mortar teams. Shortly after 10 A.M., Kuribayashi unmasked his heavy guns, hidden in the interior, and attacked the assault troops now crowding the beachhead. Horizontal-firing anti-aircraft guns on either side of the bight supplemented the deadly crossfire. Barrages were expertly rolled up and down the beach, slaying Marines by the score. The assault came close to stalling as panicked Marines remained frozen on the beach, their only cover the craters left behind by Japanese artillery—which, of course, had now registered their locations. Over the next hour U.S. commanders on the ships received radio messages similar to the following one, sent at 1046 by a 28th Marines unit: "Taking heavy fire and forward movement stopped. Machine gun and artillery fire heaviest ever seen." Aircraft urgently swooped in to drop napalm while the naval guns blasted whatever they could see. Slowly the Japanese fire tailed off and, with the aid of tank and mobile-artillery support, the Marines managed to restore their momentum and get off the beach.

By the end of the day, the Marines had daringly hacked their way seven hundred yards across the neck of the island, severing Suribachi from reinforcement and establishing a line of control across to the western coast. Some thirty thousand Marines had landed (with another forty thousand or so to come as the battle ground on), along with artillery units and many tanks. At one point there would be sixty thousand men crammed into an area of 3.5 square miles—or 17,143 per square mile, about the same density as the crowded city of San Francisco.

On the right flank, the struggle for the Rock Quarry continued.

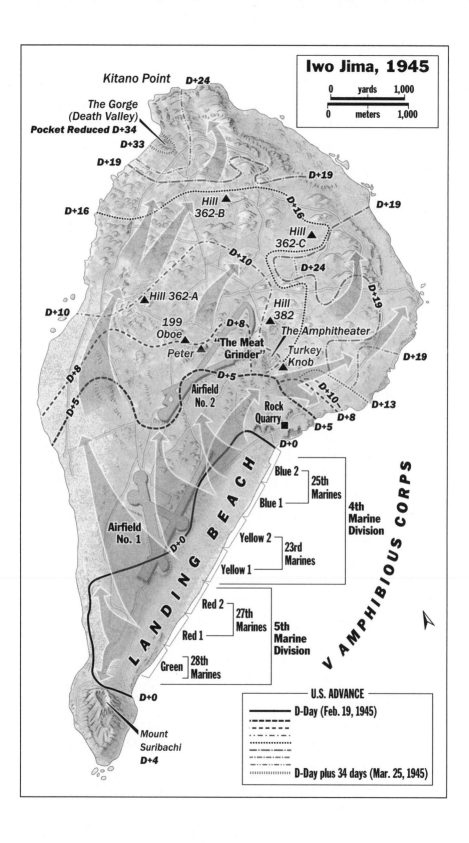

222 | MEN OF WAR

The 3rd Battalion, 25th Marines, would clamber the cliffs by nightfall, sacrificing five hundred men and twenty-two officers in the process. The Marines on the first day suffered total losses of 2,420 men, about 8 percent of their strength and a casualty rate impossible to sustain for more than a few days without general collapse.

That night, the Marines settled down and prepared for the expected mass banzai charge—but none came. Instead, there was just indirect fire from the island's interior and small probes by what Kuribayashi called "prowling wolves" (infiltrators and scouts). On the second day, Marines attacked Suribachi. Scores of concrete blockhouses guarded the approach and lower elevations. All of them would need to be destroyed. It took three more days, but on February 23 (D+4), they did it and famously raised the flags to flutter over Iwo Jima. Hard fighting continued, however, even past the Rock Quarry. There was no cover from enemy fire, and pillboxes exacted a heavy toll. Marines in that sector were able to advance perhaps a couple of hundred yards a day with disproportionate casualties.

Moreover, the Japanese defenses in the north of the island remained defiant and were, if anything, more thickly studded and deeply implanted than those in the south. On February 24 (D+5), the Marines turned their attention to pushing up the island and penetrating Kuribayashi's double-tiered main defensive belt. They were initially organized into a pleasingly straight (in terms of military aesthetics) line crossing the island east to west, but over the coming weeks the battle would degenerate into a random staccato of small-unit actions as the Marines struggled against the impregnable defenses. On the left (west) side, Hills 362-A and -B would prove particularly difficult, and on the right (east) side, Hill 382, Turkey Knob, and the Amphitheater—a complex collectively dubbed "the Meat Grinder"—would kill and maim thousands of Marines. Taking just two small hills (Peter and 199 Oboe) alone required three days of intense close-quarters combat.

The American advance continually bogged down amid the tortuous terrain and stubborn resistance. In nine days' fighting, for instance, V Amphibious Corps advanced four thousand yards in exchange for seven thousand casualties—a loss equivalent to a third of an entire division. Despite the severe losses, Marine prowess and mission effectiveness began to rise sharply about two weeks into the battle as they integrated the myriad of combat lessons acquired since D-Day. They had, in a very real sense, learned on the job. Soon afterward, Kuribayashi's main line was forced, and he moved back to a command blockhouse in the far north. The Marines plowed forward, proceeding ever farther into the northern badlands of narrow, twisting gorges and dark caves. On March 9 (D+18) a patrol finally reached the northern coast, its squad leader sending back to headquarters a canteen filled with seawater, accompanied by a note reading, "For inspection—not consumption."

On March 16 (D+25), Iwo Jima was officially declared "secured" (to much unofficial laughter) when the Americans controlled 90 percent of the island. The remaining 10 percent was the real trouble. Kuribayashi's stronghold at Kitano Point remained defiant, and scores of caves, spider traps, and pillboxes still had to be cleared. Fighting moved on to the Gorge (sometimes known as Death Valley), an eight-hundred-yard pocket honeycombed with man-made and natural defenses, followed by more than a week of relentless cave-by-cave, rock-by-rock assaults.

Kuribayashi died, perhaps leading a final banzai charge on the night of March 25. Or he may have committed suicide on March 23. His body has never been found. On the evening of March 25 (D+34), the Marines flushed out what was evidently the very last cave, and the next day the battle was declared over.

5. The Landing

Like lambs being fattened up for the kill, or so they joked, Marines always feasted on steak and eggs before landing on hostile shores.[1] As the traditional sacrament of D-Days, it made a nice change from the usual beans and coffee, even if the Navy's largesse turned out to be the last rite of many.[2] A few were too nervous to eat; their mates wolfed down their leavings.[3] Francis Cockrel, for his part, derived no little reassurance from the no-expenses-spared breakfast upgrade: The appearance of expensive steak and real eggs "made us feel the government was being pretty big about the thing."[4]

There certainly had been no stinting on the Iwo Jima operation. The task force assembled to assault Guadalcanal back in August 1942 had numbered fifty-one ships; for the task of wresting Iwo Jima from the grip of its Japanese occupants, the American armada grew to ten times that size.[5] No fewer than twelve aircraft carriers, six colossal battleships, nineteen cruisers, and forty-four destroyers were present, aided by hundreds of assorted patrol, escort, and support vessels.

Their holds contained the raw sinews of war: 4,100,000 barrels of black oil, 595,000 barrels of diesel oil, 33,775,000 gallons of aviation gasoline, 6,703,000 gallons of motor gas; 38 tons of clothing; 10,000 tons of fleet freight; 7,000 tons of ship supplies (rope, canvas, fenders, cleaning gear, hardware); 1,000 tons of candy; and 14,500 tons of fresh, frozen, and dry provisions. The 5th Division alone was accompanied by 100 million cigarettes.

Ammunition, the currency of combat, arrived in similarly stupendous quantities. In little over a month of fighting, the Navy and Marines would together expend 2,400 rounds of 16-inch shells; 5,700 rounds of 14-inch; 1,400 rounds of 12-inch; 11,700 rounds of 8-inch high-capacity; 8,400 rounds of 6-inch high-capacity; 17,700 rounds of 5-inch star; 12,000 rounds of 5-inch; 10,000 rounds of 4-inch; 70,000 rounds of 4.2-inch mortar; and some 28,000 tons of infantry cartridges—the combined weight of 237 Boeing 747s.[6] One can understand the necessity of amassing such stockpiles: During the recent battle for Peleliu (September–November 1944), the Marines had expended a statistical average of 1,590 rounds of heavy and light ammunition to kill each Japanese on the island. This figure included 1,330 standard rifle rounds and ten grenades.[7]

By way of comparison, the Japanese on Iwo had stockpiled 20 million rifle and machine-gun cartridges for their 20,000-odd small arms. At first glance, a thousand rounds per man seems sufficient, but since the Japanese had forecast that the battle would last two months (their prediction was more accurate than that of the Americans, who forecast a couple of weeks at most), it worked out to seventeen cartridges per day per man over sixty days—including machine guns, which guzzled ammunition at a prodigious rate. A Marine who fired just two eight-round magazines from his M1 Garand rifle—which he might every few minutes during a firefight—would have almost equaled his Japanese counterpart's entire allotment for the whole day.[8] Unlike the Marines, too, the Japanese could not resupply. With a single exception, they had to fight with what they had. (That exception: One time, a lone plane got through the American air screen and dropped a cargo of bamboo spears for the beleaguered garrison.)[9]

For three days the Navy had bombarded Iwo Jima to soften up its defenders for the amphibious assault to come. Even now, as H-Hour approached, pilots were assailing Japanese defenses and emplacements, swooping low to strafe targets with their machine guns. Now, while the Japanese had their heads down, it was time for the Marines to go. They formed up on deck in preparation for disembarking to the landing craft assigned to their units.

There was the usual rush for the lavatories. The line at one head, recalled Allen Matthews, "was as long as a beer line back in camp," and many of the men, like Dan Levin, had already urinated multiple times.[10] Others, among them Captain Bertram Yaffe, simply vomited over the side as often as they needed to.[11]

In a well-meaning effort to take the men's minds off what fates awaited them, the bandsmen of the 3rd Division struck up a selection of toe-tapping symphonic melodies, and (often unwilling) listeners had to guess what they were. Most were unfamiliar with both composer and work, but there were a few experts among the crowd. Alvin Josephy watched a burly Marine listen to a Tchaikovsky piece and exclaim jubilantly, "Christ! That's the *Moon Song*. Tommy Dorsey, ain't it?"[12]

As at Bunker Hill and Gettysburg, equipment checks were obsessively repeated to stave off attacks of nerves. Pfc. Robert Snodgrass busied himself reconfirming that every piece of the company's machine guns was locked into place and scrounged an impressive number of spare parts "so you can save your ass once the thing actually gets going."[13] Allen Matthews ran through his checklist over and over:

"Canteen tops tightly screwed, yes; grenade pins bent sufficiently to keep them from being pulled accidentally but not enough to hamper my pulling them when I needed to, yes; chamber and operating rod of my rifle free of dust, yes; oil and thong case and combination tool in my rifle butt." And, of course, "extra cigarettes were in the gas mask carrier."[14]

A gas mask was, perhaps surprisingly, considered absolutely necessary by Marine planners, for at this late stage in the war the Japanese were assumed to be sufficiently desperate to use chemical weapons. At Peleliu just a few short months earlier, small stockpiles of grenade-sized glass spheres filled with hydrocyanic acid, a volatile nerve agent, had been discovered.[15] (On Iwo, nothing similar would be found, though one day a thick green vapor wafted past Sergeant Ray Miller. The mysterious cloud turned out to be caused by the detonation of picric acid, used in some older Japanese artillery shells.)[16] While a few of the more nervous Marines, like Pfc. Fred Schribert, hurriedly slipped on masks as soon as they saw even a wisp of white smoke, others soon "repurposed" theirs. James Vedder, a battalion surgeon with the 27th Marines, used his to store six apples and oranges he'd liberated from the ship's mess that morning.[17] Most men, though, threw them away as soon as they landed.

Disposal of a mask barely lightened the considerable load Marines carried. Depending upon his specialty, each bore anywhere between 50 pounds (for a corpsman or surgeon) and 122 pounds (for mortarmen) of gear during the landing.[18] Because it was critical to get as much equipment ashore as rapidly as possible, the earlier waves of Marines were treated as temporary packhorses and had to lug an extra burden, such as a five-gallon can of water, a couple of mines, or a box of machine-gun ammunition. All these encumbrances were inevitably dumped the second their boots touched sand for the sake of reaching cover in short order.[19] Aside from their packs, which included a poncho, canteens, an entrenching tool, socks, rations, a first-aid kit, and the like, Marines made sure that they were adequately armed. Gerald Averill, for example, carried a .45 pistol, a Thompson submachine gun, two 30-round magazines taped end to end, and four more in canvas carriers on his belt.[20] Jay Rebstock hauled a Browning Automatic Rifle (known as a BAR, it was essentially a light-machine gun), a .45 pistol, 240 rounds of BAR ammunition, a bandolier containing even more ammo around his chest, and a bunch of grenades.[21] Allen Matthews was typical in bringing "a dangerously sharpened bayonet," his combat knife, four grenades, and a cartridge belt with no fewer than ten magazines.[22]

As time went on, Marines would ruthlessly dispense with any frippery. Within the week, Richard Wheeler was down to just his "helmet, rifle, bayonet, two fragmentation grenades, one thermite grenade, a cartridge belt, a knife, two canteens, and a first aid kit—still a good 25-pound load."[23] By the end of the battle, men often carried nothing but a spare bandage, a rifle, some ammo, a canteen, and a few grenades— not even a helmet, which they had discovered was better at deflecting shrapnel than rifle bullets, the only type of ammunition the Japanese had left by then. They preferred to wear soft hats, which were in any case "less trouble when you had to run," said Howard McLaughlin.[24]

For the moment, nevertheless, they were clean and eminently presentable in their fresh dungarees, which had been dunked in a soapy mixture and impregnated with insect repellent. The evening before, they had all shaved, not merely for cosmetic reasons but because doctors insisted that if you were shot in the face, at least your dirty whiskers could not infect the wound and complicate recovery. It was thoughtful advice considering that the campaign was expected to last less than a fortnight.[25] But it would be soon forgotten. While in Rosenthal's photograph, the flag-raisers' uniforms still look relatively clean, if lived-in, by the battle's dire finale, the Marines' clothes had disintegrated: There were deep rips in the knees and elbows, and most looked like hoboes. Nearly everyone wound up with athlete's foot and, from lack of washing, red, raw "creeping crud" or body fungus under the arms and in the crotch that required painful fungicidal treatment to eradicate.[26]

For the moment, those assigned to LVTs (Landing Vehicle Tracked, often called *amtracs,* short for "amphibious tractor") descended ladders into the dark, deep bowels of the Landing Ship, Tanks (LST, sometimes known scornfully as a "Large Slow Target"), where their conveyances awaited.[27] The noise of the engines was deafening, and the cavernous space was soon filled with noxious, thick exhaust fumes. Some men put on their gas masks, but these merely filtered, not freshened, the poisonous air. Nausea and dizziness spread quickly. Irritated men jostled each other in the crowded vehicles. They stood where they were for up to half an hour.[28]

Then, unexpectedly, the colossal jaws of the ship clanked open and the Marines craned their necks to see the emerald sea and azure sky that lay before them. Blessedly clean, 70-degree air rushed in. Ahead, the first of the tractors beetled forward, followed one by one by the rest. Then it was Allen Matthews's turn:

> The roar of the motors increased, the treads screeched against the steel deck, and we jerked forward a few feet, swerved awkwardly to the center of the tank deck and moved towards the bow doors and the fumes of the tanks preceding us brought tears to our eyes. . . . Each of us held to the side of the tractor for support . . . and the huge machine thrust its nose into the air suddenly, climbed laboriously, leveled off momentarily, and then plunged sickeningly into the water. . . . The spray flew back over us, but we did not know it until the tank righted in the water, rolled heavily, then gently, and our treads churned at the water and we too moved to the starboard.[29]

Those selected for boat transport avoided nausea but had their own troubles. They were expected to clamber down almost fifty feet on cargo nets into a moving, unstable, barge-like vessel—a Landing Craft, Vehicle, Personnel (LCVP), better known as a Higgins boat—while balancing their packs and loads.[30] One misstep, worried Corporal Hershel "Woody" Williams, and an equipment-laden Marine would tumble into the vasty deep, sinking instantly.[31] Their trainers had emphasized that good timing was key to a successful descent, for the most dangerous moment was when a Marine had to leap from the bottom of the cargo net into the boat below. If the gap between troop transport and landing craft was too wide, he might easily slip through into the water, but assuming the coxswain was keeping his craft sufficiently close, the soldier needed to make sure that he let go just as the boat reached the crest of a swell. Timed correctly, the Marine had to fall only a couple of feet. But if he jumped too early and the boat rose suddenly, shattered ankles, concussions, and fractured spines would be the result. Too late, and the poor Marine would plummet between five and twelve feet into a boat lurching downward.[32] Since a Marine often waited for three or four waves to time his leap of faith just right, disembarkations of thousands of men were prolonged affairs that annoyed those trapped in the amtracs paddling nearby.

The landing boats joined the packs of amtracs already formed into circles, endlessly trailing each other's wakes as they waited for the order to draw up in line abreast and pause at the "Line of Departure"—the invisible boundary two miles offshore running parallel to the beach—to prepare for the charge toward Iwo Jima. It was only now that Sergeant Henry Weaver noticed that his boat's coxswain had painted "TOO LATE TO WORRY" on the inside bow ramp.[33] It was.

Marines at least could take comfort from the massive barrage hitting the beach to ease their landing. A Japanese military report had estimated that a single American battleship possessed firepower equivalent to five full-strength Japanese infantry divisions.[34] At Iwo Jima, the Navy put on a show that impressed even the most jaded Marines. Corporal James "Salty" Hathaway was an amtrac crew chief circling his vessel below a battleship firing into the rock and sand of Iwo: "You could actually see a sixteen-inch shell come out of the muzzle of those ships." As it soared overhead, sounding like a freight train rushing by, the shock waves lifted the amtrac out of the water, and Hathaway heard its tracks speed up as they urgently sought purchase in the air. Meanwhile, as each thundering broadside was loosed, the battleship rocked back twelve feet to absorb the titanic recoil of her guns. It was as if the vessel had reared up like a horse.[35] A man on board likened the concussive feeling to having your chest "pushed by invisible hands" each time a gun went off.[36]

Surrounding the island like hunters warily circling a wounded, and still dangerous, animal, the *Tennessee, Nevada, New York,* and *California* had concentrated their fire on the coastal guns and beach defenses—blockhouses, pillboxes, and anti-aircraft batteries, mostly—picked out by low-flying aerial spotters. Intelligence analysts concluded, not entirely accurately, that 17 coastal guns, 16 out of 20 blockhouses, and 50 of 100 or so pillboxes—some of which turned out to be dummies—had already been destroyed in the landing zone. That left a significant number of mobile mortars, rocket launchers, mines, and artillery pieces as well as the remaining strongholds for the Marines to handle. To help, a screen of destroyers and assault vessels was currently engaged off the beach, laying down curtains of heavy suppressive fire on targets overlooked by their larger kin. In the half hour before the first wave began its run in, no fewer than eight thousand shells of various sizes slammed into Iwo Jima.[37] Like many others awed by the intensity and ferocity of the bombardment being inflicted on the island, Robert Sherrod could not help thinking, "Nobody can live through this." The landing would surely be a cakewalk, as the more optimistic souls were already predicting. But as a veteran of several harrowing amphibious assaults, Sherrod reminded himself privately, "I know better."[38]

In the meantime, the armada of landing craft formed up abreast at the Line of Departure. A control vessel was stationed at either end, and smaller ships placed along the Line marked a grid-like layout of lanes and rows. The more exalted ranks—brigadier generals and above—visited the Line to ensure that all was in order, sailing here and there, as Civil War commanders had once traveled on their horses, to exchange pleasantries with the officers and reassure the men. By 0815, the first three waves were ready. Flags snapped in the breeze. All was eerily still. The sky was bright and clear. Thanks to the unlimited visibility, Marines could see to their left the thick, wartlike, mustard-yellow volcano of Mount Suribachi and to their right the looming bluffs of the Motoyama Plateau. Iwo's "silhouette was like a sea monster with the little dead volcano for the head, and the beach area for the neck, and all the rest of it with its scrubby, brown cliffs for the body," wrote John Marquand, a *Harper's* correspondent.[39]

This sea monster seemed alive. There were menacing shrouds of grayish-black smoke clinging to its silhouette, left behind by the on-slaught of liquid fire and high explosives. Those around him, remembered Sergeant T. Grady Gallant, could see "that the island itself was strange, stripped bare and standing in the cold waters of the sea, its face ghostly and smeared with tans and yellows and grays and dull black."[40]

The Marines' sandy destination lay betwixt volcano and bluff, as per the preferred practice of landing midway on an island, advancing rapidly crosswise to sever it and its garrison in two, then mopping up the forces isolated at either end.[41]

At precisely 0830, the command vessel dipped its pennant. Nearly seventy armored LVTs gunned their engines and crossed the Line. As they plowed steadily through the waves, braving the whistling shells that suddenly emanated from the island, from the air they resembled water bugs trailing white-plumed wakes. Their job was to form the vanguard of the subsequent infantry waves by firing their powerful 75mm howitzers and machine guns at close range into the landing area as a *coup de grace* to the naval and air attacks that were tailing off. Then came the first infantry assault wave, transporting some 1,360 Marines. Every five minutes, so as to leave sufficient room between them, a successive wave would begin its journey. Within forty-five minutes, planners expected, nine thousand Marines would have landed in an expanding, unstoppable torrent upon the sands of Iwo Jima. Ultimately, there would be nearly a score of waves of flesh and steel, most carrying soldiers but others bringing heavy equipment, headquarters staff, and supplies. On their return journeys, they would ferry casualties.

Those involved might have been surprised to learn that, despite its modernity, Marine amphibious warfare bore distinct resemblances to nineteenth-century land tactics. The men at Iwo Jima were not so very different from their ancestors at Gettysburg, themselves similar to those who had fought at Bunker Hill. Off that tiny Pacific island in 1945, the artillery (naval gunfire and aerial strafing) softened up the enemy in preparation for the primary charge to come; then skirmishers (the first amtracs) were thrown forward to screen the main assault, probe the defenses, and disrupt the opposing line; and finally, the regiments (Marines in landing craft, organized into waves) advanced in orderly, inexorable fashion to achieve their objectives and break the enemy's will.

Marine Patrick Caruso "gazed at the others in the craft; their faces reflected the appearance of purpose, determination, seriousness, and an occasional smile. There was a definite air of exhilaration among the men. Morale was high and contagious. The feeling can best be described as that of an impatient football player sitting on the bench and eagerly waiting to be called by the coach to get into the game. Our anxiety to 'get into the game' supplanted any sense of fear. Yes, certainly there was apprehension about not knowing what to expect, but there definitely was not fear at this point—that came later."[42] There were some lighter moments to pass the time. George Wahlen and his friends watched the Corsair fighters swoop overhead and scored their pilots' prowess by how closely they approached Suribachi's slopes. When they dived daringly deeply to hit a camouflaged gun, they shouted out, "Single!" and if they pulled out gingerly to avoid counterfire, "Married!"[43]

On Dan Levin's boat, things were more muted. His "trip in was a thing of profound resignation, congealed thought, emotion searing and intense." Most enlisted men crouched, occasionally glancing over the side, while the sergeants preferred to stand up. One of the latter, Frank Krywicki, saw the craft next to theirs get hit by incoming fire but said nothing to his men.[44]

His discretion was probably for the best. When a Japanese gunner zeroed in a boat, there were rarely survivors. Sergeant John Thurman watched a landing craft to his right receive a direct hit. Blown upward, it splashed down, "taking its men with her as the amtrac disappeared below the water and leaving a whirlpool like effect. I saw what looked like a back pack and then a helmet liner spinning around in the bloody water. That's all that was left."[45] Machinist's Mate 3rd Class Albert D'Amico was horrified to see "a boat take a direct hit, thirty-six Marines plus two sailors. You didn't even see a toothpick [left] in the water." But, as at Gettysburg, there could be no stopping an advance once it started. "I kept going, and a shell would land here, a shell would land there, all around you, you didn't know where, you just kept going to the beach. You get hit, you got hit, that's all."[46]

On the Japanese side, their spirits had run high since the arrival of the fleet—despite the immense, dazing bombardment they had endured. At 0630 on February 19, antitank officer Lieutenant Sugihara Kinryu spotted American landing craft circling about two thousand yards offshore. "So, the real landing has come at last!" he exulted in his diary, with palpable relief. As part of a purification ritual to prepare for death, he changed into new underwear the army had thoughtfully provided, cleansed himself, and issued to his men the new socks and towels that had arrived the night before.[47] Other men donned the *senninbari,* a thousand-stitch cloth band that was wrapped around the stomach as a spiritual charm for good luck. Intended to ward off bullets, they did not always work.[48]

The first Marines ashore landed at 0903, three minutes past their scheduled arrival time. Nothing more than some sporadic small-arms fire and some light mortars greeted them. The Marines waiting their turn at the Line of Departure speculated that the Japanese had already evacuated, or, better still, had committed mass suicide. *This would be easy,* thought some. By 10 A.M., an entire assault battalion had landed. "On shipboard, listening to the optimistic reports, we relaxed," Alvin Josephy reported. "Then the Japs came to life."[49] They had initially held their fire to lure more troops onto the beach, which they intended to turn into a slaughterhouse. Machine guns, mortars, and artillery, everything they had, opened up mercilessly on the surprised Marines. It didn't matter: The attack must continue, come what may.

So, not long after Sugihara had steeled himself to meet death and Josephy had breathed a sigh of relief, Dan Levin "heard an abrupt violent howl and the boat lifted, then rammed forward grating and stopped with a shock. We were all hurled off our feet." They had hit the beach. Then the metal bow ramp cranked suddenly down. "A smell I imagined—but I smelled it!—of roasted and burning flesh swept into my nostrils. I leaped ashore on a new and fearful world."[50] Soon afterward, A. J. Benard, a Seabee in charge of a bulldozer being shipped in, realized that "there were so many dead men in front of the ship that there was no way for me to unload [the vehicle] without crushing their bodies. . . . I had no choice but to go over them."[51]

6. The Beach

Marines experienced the first minute or so of their time on Iwo Jima as a chaotic, vivid melee of images. Few were as fortunate as the last man out of Gerald Averill's boat, who "caught a mortar fragment in the calf of his leg before he reached the ramp. He tumbled backward into the boat, the ramp came up and was secured, the boat backed off and headed seaward. A Purple Heart, a battle star on the Asiatic-Pacific ribbon, and a free ride to the hospital ship without ever setting foot on Iwo." A million-dollar wound if ever there was one.[1]

The experience of the 27th Marines' Mike Vinich was more typical. "The ramp went down, and honest to God, the bullets came in. Many of the men were machine-gunned to death as they were exiting. I was pulling bodies of my men aside as I tried to make my way out. Blood was everywhere. It was very similar to the opening scene in *Saving Private Ryan,* but I think the fire was more concentrated at Iwo."[2]

When their amtrac disgorged, Corporal William McConnell saw the other squad leader, Corporal Paul Langford, break the rules by leading his men out to the left. Their training had emphasized alternating left and right for each man, precisely to avoid what happened next. A Japanese machine gunner merely traversed his barking weapon at chest level and every Marine but one was killed. But for this minor error, their military careers might have lasted longer than five seconds. McConnell's squad, which he had been forced to take right to avoid getting entangled with Langford's, lost no one.[3]

As they exited, Marines caught brief, brilliant flashes of extreme horror. Sergeant Gallant saw a Marine with blond, close-cropped hair who from the shoulder down had been severed precisely along his spine, leaving behind a kind of half-man. The left side was entirely gone, but its opposite was still dressed in dungarees with a complete head and neck, arm, and leg. Strung out from his remaining torso was a seemingly endless length of grayish-white intestine stretched out like a snake and coiling at Gallant's feet. When his eyes tracked its course, Gallant found the man's left chest, albeit lacking its arm and leg, lying several yards away. Marines were jumping over it as they exited their own craft.[4]

Dan Levin sought cover as rapidly as possible. He plunged through the ankle-deep water, found his footing in the sand, and "then fell forward into it, in a depression scooped out by some shell. I burrowed my body into the sand but kept glaring around, still startled and unbelieving." He realized, despite having urinated several times before leaving the troop transport, that he'd wet himself. Next to him, he was startled to discover, was a "Marine with a beautiful face and shoulders and all below the shoulders a viscous, red-shot, and dragging mess of rag." Nearby, his fellow Marines were wildly piling mangled legs and severed heads around them to use as barricades against the bullets.[5]

When Gallant looked to either side and behind him, all his overwhelmed mind could take in was a snapshot of "broken amphibious tractors, wrecked and riddled with holes, some overturned and smoking, others flooded and listing with waves breaking against them, splashing them and then running back into the deep. Out to sea were clusters of boats milling about in twos and threes, and mostly heading out to sea, though some craft were adrift, tossed by the waves and dead in the water. In these wallowing boats and amphibious tractors, sailors bailed with helmets or prepared to abandon ship as the crippled vessels shipped water and slowly sank in the swells."[6]

Despite the messy and unpleasant reality from the individual or personal perspective, on the grander scale all was proceeding according to plan. The Marine amphibious-warfare theorizing of the prewar years was being played out, almost to the minute, in what by any definition could be counted as a highly successful landing operation on a distinctly hostile shore.

Key to its continuing success was to move inland en masse to seize airfields and ground while the Japanese were still in disarray and reeling from the onslaught. Every man knew, and had been told repeatedly, to get off the beach as quickly as possible. The beach was death, to be sure, and they had to make room for the constant stream of new arrivals. Ultimately, a bare minimum of five hundred yards' depth would be required on the beachhead to squeeze in vehicle parking areas, roads, mess kitchens, supply centers, aid stations, evacuation areas, command and headquarters posts, anti-aircraft guns, reserves meeting zones, and ammunition dumps—everything needed to keep the Marines fighting elsewhere on the island.[7] In the words of one combat correspondent, "imagine a city the size of Sioux City, Iowa; Saginaw, Michigan; or Stockton, Calif., springing up in a few days and dependent for its food, water, clothing supplies (to say nothing of tons and tons of ammunition, which a city would not require) on sources entirely outside it."[8] Unfortunately, the beach itself ranged from just 150 to 500 feet deep, so it was clearly imperative that combat units move out while they still could.

Space would become a growing problem over the next few days. The more crowded the beach became, the more Marines would need to cluster together, leading to spiraling casualties as the enemy artillerymen found their marks. Allen Matthews found himself mentally repeating his trainer's warnings: *"Run run run get off the beach get off the beach don't ever hole up on the beach unless it's absolutely necessary because they are sighting on the beach and they'll get you sure as hell get off the beach."*[9]

Easier said than done. Two factors militated against "getting off the beach." The first was the terrain. The "sand" of Iwo Jima was not normal beach sand; instead it was soft, black volcanic ash into which men sunk up to their calves. They moved, seemingly in slow motion, amid the bone-dry cinders; it was like trying to plod through a shifting, slippery mountain of dry beans. But at least men could move. Vehicles quickly bogged down, rendering their crews vulnerable to artillery fire and leaving the infantry without support. Robert Neiman, commanding a company of tanks, was held until the fourth wave to allow a few scouts to check whether their planned landing place could bear the weight of the machines. Hearing nothing even as the fifth wave passed by, Neiman ordered the skipper of his landing craft to head in, telling him to beach very gently so that they could test the ground and retract the boat if necessary. Despite his best efforts, the craft became stuck, and Neiman drove his lead tank ("Ill Wind") down the ramp. Within seconds, it was trapped in the ash. He and Gunnery Sergeant Johnston got out and dug around the tracks while the driver vainly tried reversing. They had to abandon Ill Wind on the beach and reboard. After landing somewhere else, they again had to retract. Finally, one of the scouts, Corporal Charles Jewell, appeared and shouted that he had found a spot where the sand would hold firm. Only there, after much time and far from their assigned zone, could they and two other tank units finally land and blast a way past the beach.[10]

Further hampering the Marines' progress, ahead of them about forty feet from the surf line, lay the first of a succession of unusual wave-cut "terraces," each ranging from 10 to 15 feet high. These provided some cover from machine-gun fire but none whatsoever from trajectory projectiles like mortars. Worse, scaling them took the wind out of men, already lumbered down with their heavy loads. Francis Cockrel sprinted twenty yards off the boat to the first terrace, climbed it, and sank, spent. "I was exhausted. Not tired; just utterly limp and useless. It was that sand, as loose as sugar. I lay there five minutes before I had energy to run another twenty yards and hit the stuff again."[11]

Every second that a Marine stayed in the open catching his breath, he was under bombardment from the Japanese gunners. Sergeant Gallant likened this unenviable situation to standing on what was, in effect, a two-mile-wide street "bounded on the left by a height comparable to a 55-story building [Mount Suribachi], and on the right by a rise comparable to a 35-story building [Motoyama Plateau]."[12] Their residents fired almost nonstop on the pedestrians below. Many of the shots were not random: Allan Mortenson saw enigmatic "narrow boards with Japanese characters on them driven vertically into the ground" near him. It would later emerge that these were markers used by hidden forward observers to determine accurate ranges for the gunners above.[13]

The second factor hampering rapid transit from the beach inland was the natural temptation to stay prone, preferably in one of the hundreds of holes left behind by exploding shells and mortars. In moments of mortal danger, most people tend to freeze, their minds unable to encompass the magnitude of the existing risks; it requires a deliberate, cool decision to take quick action, in this case to leave cover and move forward under fire. Doing the latter was on the face of it the more dangerous option, which made staying put even more attractive—only, however, on the face of it.

Indeed, passively sheltering on the beach was by far the most lethal thing one could do. Hunkering down by yourself in a shell hole was bad enough; charitably allowing others to share it was worse, for then a well-placed shot would kill several occupants rather than just one. Japanese observers would wait for a hole to fill up before directing fire into it to maximize casualties. Thus, John McMahon made the mistake of clustering in a shell hole with twelve others. Inevitably, a shell arrived. McMahon was the sole survivor—escaping with only a broken ankle.[14]

The baleful results were everywhere evident. Jim Craig passed a shell hole six or seven yards across in which were scattered the torsos and limbs of eight Marines. A single mortar had landed directly on them.[15] Shortly afterward, Robert Sherrod walked along the beach tallying up the bodies that had died with hideous violence: "In one shell hole there were 12 dead, in another eight, in another seven. Four corpsmen, their stretcher beside them, had perished not far from the water line."[16]

Direct hits left little behind. When Colonel Chandler Johnson was killed, "the biggest piece we could find," said Rolla Perry, "was his rib cage." Art Stanton found his collar, weirdly bloodless. Another Marine found a hand and wrist with watch attached. The watch still worked.[17] Of a Marine Jim Craig stumbled across whose hole had been hit by a mortar, "all that was left was a shoe with a foot and part of a leg still in it. The [hole] was pink and white around the sides with blood and tissue mixed in with the black volcanic ash."[18]

Whatever pieces could be found were scattered far and wide. Sherrod saw plenty of "legs and arms [lying] fifty feet away from any body."[19] Likewise, while digging a hole, Frank Walker pulled up someone's leg. His friend Tom Nichols was four feet away doing the same and excavated much of the fellow's intestines.[20] There was a lieutenant who ducked as a mortar landed nearby. When he opened his eyes, a severed finger was lying placidly beside him. Immediately, "he looked at his own hands, then examined the hands of the two men crouched beside him. All were intact. The finger belonged to one of three men in the hole fifteen yards away, whom the mortar had struck and torn into three bloody rags."[21] Some strikes resulted in utter obliteration. Of the 5,931 Marine deaths at Iwo Jima, 117 remain unaccounted for. Some of these had left absolutely no trace of their existence after artillery or mortar hits.[22] Their coffins would later be shipped home empty, with grieving relatives sensitively left none the wiser.[23]

The shrapnel flung off by indirect hits was almost as devastating. One surgeon analyzed the composition of the shrapnel he was rapidly learning about: "The smaller fragments buzzed by like swarms of angry bees. The medium-sized pieces sounded like a flock of purple grackles moving from one clump of trees to another. Some of the largest chunks were the size of dinner plates and make a soft sighing sound as they passed by. They were also clearly visible as they floated close by overhead. These large fragments could readily cut a man in half if he were to get in their way."[24] They could certainly decapitate you. When Patrick Caruso jumped into a shell crater he found a headless Marine sitting there with "a cigarette still burning between two of his fingers and a rifle in his other hand."[25] Another Marine recalled that he had just given a man a cracker when he was killed. The fragment "cut the top of his head off right above the eyes, all the way to the back of his neck, and the piece was hanging from his collar like a bucket lid."[26]

A near-miss by an explosion or shrapnel was always a shaking occurrence. Howard McLaughlin vividly recorded his experience of the last few seconds before a shell landed inches from his left foot. Amid the cacophony of battle, "everything went totally silent and there was no sound but the air passing around the shell as it fell toward me. I didn't hear the explosion till long after it hit, but I could hear the shell breaking apart from the explosion as it hit the sand. There was total silence for what seemed like two or three minutes and then I heard the crash of thunder inside my helmet, along with the wave of air and heat of the concussion."[27] After taking cover on the beach, recalled Howard Baxter, "big hunks of shrapnel were falling all over the place. I had a piece . . . that landed along the side of my shell hole. It was molten red hot—just sizzling. It just missed the whole frame of my body by about six inches. It burned itself in the sand. It was steaming, and you could almost see through it, it was so hot."[28] Allen Matthews was nearly as lucky when he was thumped by a large piece of shrapnel that was completing the end of its arc. "I felt a blow on my back, my knees buckled and I sprawled forward." He later found it lying on the ground and kept it as a souvenir, this thing that "had struck me with the force of a hard-thrown baseball."[29]

When shrapnel did not kill immediately, it left injuries that at best rendered Marines unable to serve and at worst killed them later. Two quite typical casualties were treated by the surgeon James Vedder. The first was left with a shattered face and could barely suck in a breath. Vedder cleared his airway by plunging a rat-toothed forceps down what was left of his throat and pulling out a large piece of jawbone. He wondered "how our plastic surgeons would ever restore this man's identity." The second "was sprawled on his back in a deep coma with several square inches of bone missing from the side of his head, leaving the brain covered only by the dura membranes. Another piece of shrapnel had sliced off all the upper muscles of his left shoulder." The best Vedder could do was tend him with sterile dressings, infuse plasma, and get him ready for evacuation.[30] It is unlikely that he made it home alive.

Shrapnel was not the only danger: The Japanese interspersed phosphorus shells among their high-explosive barrages. According to Howard McLaughlin, the former, exploding two hundred feet above, admittedly "looked pretty from a distance" when they "went off like big multi-legged white spiders in a Fourth of July fireworks display."[31] But then hurtling down came the shards of bright-white phosphorus, burning at a temperature that ate through clothing, skin, flesh, even bone. Exposure to air accelerated oxidation and resulted in hideous burns. Water did nothing but exacerbate the trauma, a lesson well-meaning friends often learned too late. The only way of rescuing the victim was to brush off particles using dry gauze or cotton (or to dig them out using the point of a combat knife), then apply an oily oint-ment like Vaseline and bandages to prevent air from further inflaming the phosphorus.[32]

During an attack, luck determined whether one would vanish from the earth, lose several limbs, or emerge unscathed. When the hit came, survivors were momentarily confounded by what had just occurred. Glen Lougee, a corpsman, was tending to Leon Justice, whose leg had been blown off, helped by Gilman Horgan. A mortar round landed nearby. Lougee remembered "we both turned and looked. As I turned back, I stared into Horgan's eyes for just an instant. Then it happened. Another mortar shell exploded close to Horgan. He disappeared, just like that. Everything went black for me." When he returned to con-sciousness a few minutes later, Justice was still in a stupor but otherwise all right. "Pieces of meat were sticking to my uniform. It wasn't mine, nor was the blood which ran into my mouth. Leon started moaning. Part of Horgan's trunk, a section of his disintegrated body, lay across Leon's chest. I lifted my hands to remove it, and realized his entrails were lashed across my arms. Feces oozed from an open end of one of the pieces. A sharp piece of bone stuck outward from my belt. Very slowly it dawned on me that Horgan took a direct hit from the shell."[33]

The randomness of the hits disconcerted even veterans. John Thompson had landed at Saipan and Tinian, but the sustained mortar barrage on Iwo was unlike anything he had previously experienced: "It gave me the most helpless feeling in the world. The artillery shelling was bad enough, but at least you felt you could get a fix on their shells. Not those mortars. It was impossible to figure out where they were coming from or going to, simply impossible."[34] Was it better to stay where you were? Or scuttle to a new hole? Or find one that had already been hit? Which of these was the place of greatest safety?

Much of the time, despite their training, soldiers just stayed put, for the storm of steel and high explosives breaking over their heads on the beach was numbing. While the mortars "whistled like ghouls just over-head," recalled Dan Levin, beneath Alvin Josephy the ground literally shook: "It was as if a man were lying on a bouncing beach."[35] In just one minute, Robert Sherrod counted a furious tattoo of no fewer than twenty explosions within fifty yards of him.[36] Such was their elevated stress that men unconsciously ground their teeth, clamping down especially hard whenever a shell exploded. They were left to wonder hours later why their teeth hurt so much.[37] Adrenaline- and fear-triggered thirst afflicted everyone. Allen Matthews was possessed by a "compelling desire for a drink of water, for my mouth was so dry that gum which I had been chewing suddenly adhered to my teeth and to my gums and to my tongue and to my lips." Soon his blood was pumping so hard "that I could feel my temples expand and contract within the fatigue cap which I wore under my helmet."[38]

An overwhelming onslaught of potent sensory stimulants paralyzed men into inaction. "Surrounded by a crescendo of whistling mortars, artillery shells, and whirring rockets, all followed by thundering blasts," Bertram Yaffe simply froze. It took the screams that followed to startle him into motion.[39] Any number of others, however, remained stunned and subjugated into submission. Some men sat, said Yaffe, "with haunting, vacant stares—the hollow men, rigid in the benumbed silence of combat fatigue. They don't bother to dive for cover. I touch a shoulder, open a canteen, help light a cigarette, but I don't linger. I want to get on with my job. It's easier that way."[40] He knew that they were sitting ducks, but everyone had been ordered not to stop to help wounded or helpless men. Lending a hand slowed the assault's momentum, tied up riflemen of greater utility in the front lines, hampered the medics, and, as a practical matter, caused the kind of "bunching up" or clustering that Japanese observers were keeping a keen eye out for.[41] Helping a lost soul, in other words, could not help but lose more.

Others exhibited more extreme symptoms. Two hours after the first wave had landed, ships began receiving the first psychiatric casualties. Robert Sherrod saw one "screaming at the top of his voice and twisting violently in his stretcher."[42] A man, already lying wounded, was sent into hysteria when a shell burst nearby, observed Sergeant Gallant. "Then he opened his mouth as wide as he could. His eyes were staring and fixed upon the sky, his forehead deeply furrowed and his eyebrows lifted, pulling at his eyelids, almost. He sat this way—taut and stiff and straining every muscle of his body. He sat, his mouth wide open, stretched white at the sides . . . and screamed . . . and screamed . . . and screamed."[43]

The nightmarish quality of the beach in the initial hours was exacerbated by the unexpected number of wounded. Planners had forecast a high casualty rate, but not as steep as this. For the entire battle, planners had predicted an 18 percent casualty rate.[44] Yet on D-Day alone, *a single day,* fully 8 percent (2,420) of the thirty thousand men who landed would be killed or wounded. The potential implications of a *months*-long battle on the cumulative casualty total were horrifying.[45] As it was, the hospital ships and transports were overwhelmed. Len Maffioli was aboard the USS *Sanborn,* and there were "at least a dozen landing craft circling our ship and requesting that we take their wounded. We couldn't help them because our sick bay was already full. The tables in the officers' wardroom were being used as operating tables, and the wardroom and passageways were jammed with casualties on stretchers."[46]

On the beach, corpsmen hurriedly patched up wounded Marines as best they could and, if they could walk, directed them toward the water, hoping that someone would help them back to a ship. Otherwise, they were on their own. When Edward Jones came across a Marine with his right eye hanging from its socket, he pushed it back in as best he could, shot him with morphine, scrawled a large red M on his forehead (to prevent accidental overdoses), pointed out where he should go, and moved on to the next patient.[47]

Slowly, inexorably, nevertheless, the Marines inched forward. Hole by hole, they advanced closer and closer to and then over the terraces. Movement began for two related reasons. The first was that senior officers, as they had done at Bunker Hill and Gettysburg, visibly behaved as if everything was under control and remained resolutely imperturbable. When Greeley Wells landed, he followed everyone else in leaping into a shell hole and staying put. But then he saw Colonel Harry B. Liversedge and Lieutenant Colonel Robert H. Williams striding up the beach "as if they were in the middle of a parade." One had a riding crop, "which he was slapping on the side of his leg, and both of them were urging us on, saying, 'Get up! Get off the damn beach!' It was an amazing thing. They walked the length of that doggone beach yelling at the men, and the Marines just did it—they got right up and started to move. Of course it jarred me as well, and I got up, and we got over the high ground."[48] Francis Cockrel later saw Liversedge acting so coolly that "I thought that things couldn't be very bad. I guess the sight of him helped a lot of other guys too."[49]

The stirring sight of colonels and the like acting as if everything was proceeding precisely according to schedule convinced the worried, panicked Marines that the chaos was surmountable, that there was "a Plan," that if they followed orders, adhered to their training, and paid attention to their superiors, all would be well. There was a logic to the madness enveloping them, it seemed. As a result, the initial kinetic and sensory shock began to wear off, psychiatric stress decreased, and experience kicked in.[50]

Booze helped, too. Though alcohol was not widely available, medical personnel had access to extraordinarily potent medicinal brandy. One Marine, feeling increasingly nervous, downed a refreshing two-ounce bottle a friendly doctor had given him and felt much better.[51] Corpsman Edward Jones had been entrusted by a Dr. Collins with a duffel bag containing fifty such servings. While under shellfire he drank one. "It smoothed everything out for me. It calmed anxiety and restored reason."[52]

Critical to survival was learning how to sense when shelling was least likely and to move in tandem with its ebbs. Mortars were not quite so random as originally imagined. Like anyone else, their Japanese operators followed predictable rhythms and routines. John Lardner estimated that "it seems to take about twenty minutes under shellfire to adjust your nerves and evolve a working formula by which you can make progress and gauge, very roughly, the nearness of hits and the pattern of fire." Once you had mastered this trick, you realized the folly and danger of "wishful pinned-down thinking" (Lardner's term for staying in a hole and hoping you were safe).[53]

To that end, Bertram Yaffe had learned at Bougainville and Guam how to tell when "the whistling is headed in my direction. I dive under a disabled tank or hug a revetment. If the interval between bursts short-

ens, I move on quickly. It means they have zeroed in on that spot."[54]
Similarly, another Marine veteran knew that if a shell was low and
about to hit the earth, it made a "tearing sound"; if it was high but
descending quickly, it had a "rushing, ghostly cry"; and if "it is absolutely safe, very high and very fast, it [left] behind it a *whish-whish-
whishing* sound."[55] Ray Miller, a neophyte, was nevertheless fortunate
enough to land in the same shell hole as Gunnery Sergeant Joe Whalen,
who had survived several battles. He advised Miller to watch the planes
overhead. They would come in to strafe and when they dropped napalm on gun emplacements the firing would let up for between ten and
fifteen seconds. That was the cue to run to the next shell hole.[56]

When they finally surmounted the terraces, Marines were subjected
to withering fire from the myriad of blockhouses, bunkers, and pillboxes waiting for them. For Stanley Dobrowski, "everything fell apart.
It was just mass confusion. The thing I noticed immediately was the
tremendous amount of noise, concussion, small-arms fire, explosions
of artillery and mortar shells." "That's when the Japs opened up with
everything they had," recalled Ray Jacobs. "I mean everything. The din
of all those different-caliber weapons, the blasts of the shells, it was just
incredible."[57]

Once they got their bearings, though, the slog was easier than on
the beach. There was now little risk of being pushed back into the sea,
and the way forward to their objectives was clear. Taking an active role
in demolishing pillboxes and other Japanese emplacements, no matter
how dangerous, was better than waiting passively for a mortar round to
kill you. Whereas on the beach units had instantly atomized into individuals desperately scrabbling for a hole in the ground, once they were
over the terraces Marines began to find their comrades and crystallized
back into distinct squads and platoons reporting to a familiar chain of
command.

On the plains above the beach, even the artillery bombardments
seemed more "rational," if still terrifying. Marines could look up and
watch, as at a tennis match, the naval and Japanese gunners exchanging
fire. Both sides used coherent rolling artillery barrages, the kind recognized by Robert Leader, who had never experienced one before but was

sharing a crater with a sergeant who had, "as a work of devilish crafts-manship. It was so well executed that the sergeant could predict the arrival and impact point of each shell as the gunners moved the barrage back and forth and up and down over our position."[58] Rolling barrages were easily survivable—even enjoyable to an extent, because they re-stored a sense of predictability to the battlefield after the chaotic ran-domness of the beach—unless you happened to be directly underneath one. Lieutenant Jim Craig was in a hole with his men about 75 yards inland when he saw a telltale series of explosions 200 yards ahead. The next salvo came 100 yards closer. Then the third landed in front of them but hurt no one. The next was behind them. It was over.[59] They had nothing to fear from the American retort, which began its own "heavy steps inland, two hundred yards at a stride, crashing and thun-dering and tearing with burning, metallic hands" as it advanced toward the Japanese defenders.[60]

Very few Marines had actually seen a Japanese. There had been some expendable troops on the beach, lucklessly assigned to manning anti-aircraft guns, machine guns, and the like, who had been rapidly eliminated. Early on, for instance, Jay Rebstock had scrambled from his LVT to find, sited twenty feet directly in front of him, a fire pit. His comrades soon clubbed the occupants to death with their rifles.[61] Dan Levin even found one of the sacrificed enemy in an embrace of sorts with a dead Marine. "Each had been torn away except for the head and some entrails—the Japanese boy by our shelling, the American boy later by Japanese shell or mortar fire. The two helmeted heads lay fac-ing each other, with such pained and soulful expressions on the two faces that I could hardly bear to look. Their entrails curled around and their ends met, twining about each other."[62]

These doomed beach defenders would be the last Japanese most Marines would see for some time. Over the next while, for instance, Rebstock would encounter precisely one of the enemy, a lone soldier who suddenly charged him at full pelt from out of nowhere. He mowed him down with his trusty BAR.[63]

Frustration at this invisible enemy, the one hammering them with impunity, sometimes boiled over. When a Japanese soldier was briefly glimpsed in the distance, said Howard McLaughlin, men would "stand up, holler and shout like kids at a football game, with everybody firing at him as if he was a duck in the shooting gallery at a county fair."[64]

The most curious, if discomfiting, thing about the Japanese was not their invisibility during combat—their tactic of holing up in bunkers, pillboxes, and tunnels was well known—but the lack of dead bodies. It seemed to Marines that, despite their best efforts, the immense firepower at their command, and the liberal, even wanton, shedding of their own blood, hardly any Japanese were being killed. When Guy Rowe landed in the evening of D-Day and strode inland, he saw stacks of piled bodies. He was cheered that "we sure killed a lot of Japanese"— until he realized they were wearing Marine dungarees.[65] No enemy uniforms were to be seen. Richard Nummer, a corporal, estimated that "for every dead Jap, I seen twenty-five dead marines easy."[66]

On the larger scale, Jim Craig's battalion would suffer 20 percent casualties over the course of the first three days, for instance, but inflicted, *at least as it appeared,* none, since resistance remained unvacillating.[67] They felt as if they were fighting a phantom war. Indeed, by the third day, as a whole the Marines had suffered 5,300 casualties and yet could account for just 600 Japanese.[68] Air observers overhead reported the strange phenomenon of seeing thousands of moving figures in one half of the battlefield and none on the other.[69]

Understandably, morale among Marines fell quite precipitously in the days following the landing, particularly once they began noticing the Meat Wagons. Combat reporters did not send dispatches home about these gruesome vehicles for fear, as one put it, that relating "total battlefield truth could injure morale" among the civilian population.[70] But every Marine was familiar with them. Operated by Graves Registration units, these vehicles picked up the dead and transported them back to the collection points and cemeteries already sprouting up.

No one spoke when they were near. Frank Crowe watched as the Graves people, wearing heavy rubber gloves reaching to their armpits as well as black rubber aprons, stopped their trucks and carefully laid the slain on the flatbeds. "Of course, there was also a detached arm or leg here, a head there, and half a torso somewhere else. These, too, were gathered and placed in the truck."[71] Ernest Moreau noted that "this one dead Marine . . . was just like a baked potato. Two men went to pick him up, and the bones came right out of his arms. Just like a chicken that's overdone."[72] Stanley Bryan recalled the body fluids that were "oozing out and sometimes you'd see gorgeous blond hair on this black face of some 18-year-old kid—and millions of flies, billions of flies."[73] When Pfc. John Thurman saw a convoy of three trucks trundle slowly across the broken terrain, he could see "five layers of dead Marines laying crosswise over each other; it was hard to tell how many Marines there were. There were bodies that were badly torn up with legs and arms missing, or half of a body left and the smell was suffocating." The first two trucks bore bodies and the last "the legs and arms, but [they were] chunks of meat and flesh you could not make out and these parts were stacked and mixed in a pile not knowing who they belong to."[74]

Given the depressing one-sidedness of the casualty count, Marines naturally began to wonder whether Iwo Jima was a defeat in the making. The words of Tokyo Rose, broadcast to much mockery on the voyage out, came back to Ken Cosbey and now seemed more tragic than comic: "Good morning, 4th Division, I understand you are headed for Iwo Jima. The week after you land you can hold your roll call in a phone booth."[75]

The decline in morale proved short-lived, as the mystery of the absent bodies was soon solved. The Japanese, it emerged, had been venturing out, usually at night, and hauling their dead back to their bolt-holes. Investigating one site of a recent firefight, where he knew there would be corpses, John Thurman found only Japanese shoe prints and drag marks.[76] The mass dumping grounds would eventually be found once Marines, said Anthony Visconti, "got into the caves" pockmarking the island. "You've never smelled anything like it. There were hundreds of decaying corpses."[77] Soon after landing, for instance, Len Maffioli and his friend John "Hook" Grant noticed a cave entrance and decided, rather foolishly, to explore it. The cave opened up into a large room carved out of sandstone. In a corner a ramp led down to another room the same size, ten feet below. Then another ramp led down about fifty feet into another large space, this one packed with the bloated, stinking carcasses of Japanese soldiers. They left in a hurry after hearing voices wafting up from a still lower level.[78] Since the secret to the Japanese vanishing act was now known, there was no attempt to catalogue the dead or tote a body count. Instead, the cave was rapidly "sealed" with explosive, trapping all, alive and dead, within. The Japanese efforts to hide their dead lasted less than a week, for by that time they were on the run. From then on, corpses were simply left behind to rot in the sun.

Some of these "corpses" were not, however, dead. They were wounded men feigning death and holding grenades to kill unwary Marines or to blow up a vehicle. Saturo Omagari was one such, along with three or four comrades who sliced open their own slain, daubed themselves in the congealing blood, and stuffed their uniforms with unraveled intestines. Omagari, who miraculously survived the battle, hoped to gain glory by destroying a Sherman tank and had to try "hard to remain calm, clenching my teeth to avoid nausea" as he lay among the bodies.[79] Elsewhere, remembered Corporal Richard Nummer, when you were on burial duty you had "to watch out there wasn't a Jap among 'em waiting for us, with a rifle or grenade, whatever they could find."[80] (The trick sometimes backfired: Ray Crowder saw two dead Japanese dressed in Marine uniforms who had shot each other by accident.)[81]

Despite Kuribayashi's assurance to Imperial Headquarters that such sacrifices caused "great damage to American tanks and forces," the truth is that, like hiding bodies, this tactic succeeded only for a short time before Marines began taking effective countermeasures.[82] In this case, the solution was brutally straightforward: "Shoot their dead to be sure they were," as Robert Leader put it. While he "found this *coup de grace* repulsive," it had to be done.[83] Every time corpses were discovered, either in overrun pillboxes or simply lying around, what was known as a "possum patrol" would shoot each one several times. "It was cheap insurance—a bullet only costs a dime," as one Marine explained.[84]

In his entire time on Iwo, George Nations could recall seeing just one dead Japanese with but a single bullet hole in him.[85]

7. The Nights

The Marines' conquest of Iwo Jima was executed strictly by day; the night they yielded to the Japanese. Every dusk, then, the Marines ceased operations and hunkered down along the line in their foxholes.

Of central concern to American units was "tying in" to the ones on either side of them in order to form a straight line across their assigned area. This desire to close gaps in the defensive perimeter and to link up with neighbors began at the division level and continued down successively through the regiment, battalion, company, platoon, squad, and finally, individual foxhole level. There was nothing more dangerous than being left too far forward of the line at nightfall, if, or rather when, the Japanese attacked.

In previous operations, the Japanese had mounted mass banzai charges on the first night of an invasion, and on Iwo Marines accordingly prepared for one—only to be left bewildered when the enemy never appeared, as bewildered, indeed, as when the first wave to hit the beach had encountered paltry counterfire. The actions of the Japanese on Iwo Jima were becoming ever more enigmatic. On other islands, they had emphasized the banzai frontal assault to break through a weak spot on a nascent Marine line. Over the coming weeks on *this* island, such attacks would be exceptionally rare. Instead, Marines would cope with small-scale "cutting-in attacks," as the Japanese dubbed them, by infiltrators hoping to create a sense of insecurity behind the lines by sniping opportunistically at random soldiers and sabotaging arms dumps. One remarkably successful effort resulted in a huge explosion at a 4th Division dump as two boatloads of flamethrower fuel, gas, and ammunition went up.

The nocturnal spate of cutting-in attacks wore on Marines to a greater degree than a single, all-out banzai assault at the beginning of an operation. Although banzais were initially terrifying, any satisfactorily tied-in unit could deal with them easily enough: Coordinated machine guns squirting bullets at close range would leave hundreds of Japanese dead and wounded in short order. On Iwo, there were a few attempts to organize banzais, but these were minor piecemeal threats, quickly extinguished. Thus, when Howard Snyder and his squad were facing a trench containing a number of Japanese they could hear were becoming more excited, as if whipping themselves up into a fury before launching a final, diehard bid for glory, he and Harold Keller merely lobbed in grenade after grenade while James Robeson and Louie Adrian used their BARs to cut down anyone who emerged. Eventually, all went silent and that was the end of that.[1]

This is not to say that infiltration tactics were of much use, however. Kuribayashi was forced to report to Tokyo by the beginning of March that "the look-out American forces became very strict and it is difficult to pass through their guarded line. Don't overestimate the value of cutting-in attacks," he advised.[2] As Kuribayashi indicated, because Marines actively learned from experience and improved their defensive methods, over the course of the battle these stealth attacks dramatically declined in frequency, skill, and scale. A battalion of the 28th Marines, for instance, counted seventy-five bodies lying outside its perimeter very early on, but in coming weeks there would be just a handful.[3] The introduction of star shells, which brightly illuminated the deep Pacific dark, was particularly advantageous: One Marine, frustratedly trying to fight off invisible Japanese, was saved when a star shell went up and outlined a dozen of them running through a ravine. "They looked like little devils running through the gates of Hell," he said. "All they needed were pitchforks."[4] Another important factor was the sheer magnitude of Marine firepower that could be rapidly applied in an emergency. On March 9 (D+18), for instance, the Japanese launched a powerful attack on the joint tying in two regiments. A single company there lavishly burned through 500 grenades, 200 rounds of 60mm mortars, and 20,000 rifle and machine-gun rounds in exterminating the enemy. Within twenty-four hours, much of the ordnance had been replaced.[5]

Marine defensive proficiency reached such a pitch that some Americans, like Allen Matthews, began to prefer night actions to daylight operations. When the sun was up, he argued, the enemy vanished and Marines were "charged with routing him out of emplacements we seldom saw until we were fired on." When the moon was up, conversely, the Japanese had to come to them, and Marines quickly understood "that the enemy was not superhuman, that he possessed no special faculties for night vision, and that consequently when we were alert we almost always saw him before he saw us."[6]

As Matthews conceded, one had to stay frosty to keep winning. Despite their improving abilities, Marines did not, or could not, relax their guard, for, no matter how infrequent, when an infiltration was attempted, it happened without warning and could be very messy. For this reason, without fail the very first things Marines did when the sun began its descent was to check the immediate area for anyone, as Frank Caldwell put it, who might "give us some trouble at night." They would peer into holes and investigate suspicious terrain to make sure no one was hiding there. They took no chances—with good reason. When Caldwell and some others noticed a pile of rocks lying against a six-foot rise they threw a phosphorus grenade among them. "All of a sudden those rocks parted, and out comes a Japanese soldier just reeking with smoke. His uniform was on fire. Tears were coming out of his eyes. I could even see that, I was so close to him. He had one of those Japanese grenades in his hand. He was in the process of throwing that as a last resort right amongst us. He got it away, but we dodged it, and we proceeded to mow him down." Curious about him, Caldwell removed his helmet and found a family photo tucked inside featuring his wife and six "cute-looking little children." He was otherwise anonymous.[7]

Afterward, Marines dug a line of foxholes, each about ten yards from each other. A regulation foxhole was designed to accommodate two men—three at a pinch—and was six feet long, three deep, and four wide.[8] The dimensions varied depending on soil and laziness, but a foxhole either too deep or shallow was asking for trouble. Once done, the next step was to site the machine guns properly. Squads and platoons could call on a few water-cooled heavy machine guns and several lighter air-cooled ones that needed setting up to interlock their fields of fire "in a solid wall right down the line," according to Corporal Glenn Buzzard.[9]

Specialist machine gunners escorted the heavies, which weighed 98 pounds and were transported by Jeep but could fire their powerful .50-caliber ammunition almost ceaselessly thanks to a large water tank that prevented the mechanism and barrel from overheating. Regular Marines handled the .30-caliber lights and were ordered to hold their fire until they saw at least five Japanese attacking. Any fewer than that and riflemen could do the job. It was an order honored more in the breach than the observance, for every Marine detailed to man a light machine gun immediately inserted an ammo belt and cocked twice to ready it to fire at the touch of a finger.[10]

Nevertheless, all realized the importance of not wantonly revealing one's positions, so gunners assiduously devoted themselves to stripping out every tracer bullet from their freshly issued ammunition belts.[11] The Marine Corps had considerately made every fifth bullet in a belt a tracer that tore bright streaks in the night to allow men to see where they were firing. Unfortunately, the Japanese could then also see where they were firing from. In the event, the most useful weapon was not a gun at all but a grenade. Since a muzzle flash of any kind served as a homing beacon for the enemy directly to your foxhole, it was far better to toss grenades and avoid revealing their source.

Trip wires, noisemakers, and barbed wire were set up beyond the defensive line as early warning signals. Much of the time these did not work as well as a few dozen pairs of eyes and ears nervously scanning for anything out of the ordinary, as the Japanese were dab hands at crawling silently, avoiding silhouettes, and camouflaging themselves against blackened backdrops. Bayonets were wrapped in rags to prevent their glinting; likewise boot soles to muffle footfalls. Barbed wire, in any case, was easily dug under using a scoop, though in one instance some enterprising Marines neutralized the problem by sprinkling grenades around to "go off like booby traps" if the wire was disturbed. "Blew hell out of the Japs," grunted their sergeant.[12] Another relatively effective technique was to string a length of cord between the holes so that if a sentry saw a Japanese soldier, or even thought he saw one, he would "jerk it five times or more—just pull like hell—to let them know what's up" along the rest of the line while noiselessly safeguarding one's location.[13] It was, however, rather more common to start firing to let everyone know as unmistakably as possible that an attack was in the offing.

With these basics completed, the men settled down into their foxholes and started their nightly routine. First things first: Weapons needed cleaning. Iwo's powdery sand fouled and clogged guns at a frightening rate, a systematic problem that military planners had failed to predict. In Dave Davenport's platoon, rifles regularly misfired and machine guns often loosed just a single round before jamming. Before setting off on a mission, everyone would snap off a few shots to make sure their rifles were working.[14] A malfunctioning gun was, of course, no minor issue: Corporal Bill Faulkner described one action against a bunker that almost led to the deaths of several comrades. Led by Lieutenant Wesley Bates, the patrol had damaged the structure when "some wounded Japs came charging around the bunker. We tried to fire but our weapons were jammed with sand. I finally got off a round. The Japs turned and ran right into a machine gun we had set up to cover the attack. We moved around to the front of the bunker and found several Japs, all wounded but jabbering and trying to pull the pins of grenades. Bates tried his Japanese on them, asking them to surrender, but no luck. Five or six guys tried to shoot them, but all [their] rifles were jammed. Finally a rifle began to work, and the job was done."[15]

When they could, Marines prudently threw away useless weapons and picked up new ones as they came along. Corporal Frank Walker was probably quite typical in that in four days he went through ten carbines, five or six Garands, and several flamethrowers.[16] There were pickings galore if the troops were either in the field (where they could grab guns left behind by the dead and wounded) or visiting an arms collection area (where they were issued recycled ones collated from the same source). Marines preparing to spend the night in their foxholes, however, had to make do. A man's most valuable possession in that instance was a toothbrush—not for its intended use but for scouring sand out of his rifle.[17]

Personal care came next. Since Iwo lacked fresh water (as Japanese supplies diminished they became increasingly desperate to steal it), barrels were shipped from Hawaii, and it inevitably tasted metallic. Stale, too, as their initial supply had been canned seven weeks before, and there would be times when gasoline cans had been reused, lending the contents a distinctive taste. If they were lucky, Marines were given a packet of hot-chocolate powder that they could stir in using their combat knives (which served also as spoons and forks). More often, there was coffee powder, and Marines were justly envious of those in the demolitions squad or the combat engineers, as their perks included free access to C2 explosives. They would find three fist-sized rocks on which to balance an upturned helmet discarded by someone less fortunate, pour in a pint of water with the coffee, and place a golf-ball–sized chunk of C2 underneath. Burning at white heat, the C2 boiled the water in less than twenty seconds.[18] The king of beverages on Iwo Jima, however, was pineapple juice, a rare taste of the tropics that arrived in a four-gallon can issued at the behest of a quartermaster—sometimes with the aid of a bribe. It was invariably guzzled immediately.[19]

While the Japanese soldiery survived on occasional handfuls of rice, the Marine diet was sufficient to keep immediate hunger at bay and to provide scientifically determined minimums of nutrition, even if it was later found that there were not sufficient calories in each meal to sustain a combat soldier for more than five days (hence the dramatic weight loss among Marines on Iwo; William Hurza, for instance, weighed 180 pounds on D-Day and 145 a month later.)[20] There was just enough variety in the official K-ration to avoid complete monotony. Foxhole-bound Marines opening the waxed cardboard box would find two packages of hard biscuits, a small metal container holding one of three types of "spread" (some kind of repulsive eggy concoction, cheese, or minced meat), some sweets, coffee or powdered grape "juice," and a pack of four cigarettes. The rations were hardly luxurious, but they were better, as Sergeant Ray Miller pointed out, than what a lot of the men were used to at home, including himself. Sometimes "there was maybe enough time for a piece of candy, some coffee . . . , and a pleasant after-dinner cigarette," he enthused. "Boy, this was livin'!"[21]

Given their diet, Marines were constipated for most of their time on Iwo. Howard McLaughlin was typical in defecating just once a week or every ten days. Part of the popularity of the Marine Corps pineapple juice was that it acted as an instant, if quite violent, laxative. After weeks of K-rations, Ray Miller was ecstatic when a pal gave him some. "This was delicious," he exclaimed. "How good to taste fruit again; such refreshing sweetness." And very soon afterward, with an unfortunate degree of bad timing, his insides began to churn just as a Japanese barrage began. But he had no choice: He "pulled 'em down fast, and added my own contribution to the chorus of artillery. . . . I ate no pineapple again for forty years."[22]

Contributing to the endemic bowel blockage was that, once ensconced in their foxholes, Marines were loath to risk exiting them. If there was any daylight remaining, they could come under sniper fire as they squatted; if Japanese mortars were falling, leaving the safety of a foxhole was madness; and if one simply had to do one's business outside at night, the others did not say, "We'll see you" or "Take it easy," but "Keep a tight asshole."[23] At night, too, it was easy to get lost trying to find your way around. One Marine became disoriented in the pitch black and ended up walking in front of his own line; he was mistaken for an infiltrator and killed by an alert sentry.[24] Provided one's foxhole-mate was amenable, of course, it was preferable to dig a deep hole at one end and "cover [it] like a cat," remembered Gerald Averill.[25] But it would be you who had to sleep on top of it.[26] As for urinating, that, too, was dealt with by digging a sump hole and filling it with earth. But to avoid being shot in the head by a sniper, you never stood up to do it; you lay on your side and aimed as best you could.[27]

When night fell, the two-man teams in each foxhole divvied up sentry duty. Each Marine took one hour on, one hour off, and so on until the next morning. Until lights out, the men would chat back and forth, about mostly innocuous matters. If, as they say, there were no atheists in foxholes—though this cliché is quite inaccurate; on Iwo there were plenty—neither was there much deep philosophizing or many spiritual crises to overcome. A journalist, walking the line of foxholes, wrote down the snippets of conversation he overheard. They included: "Huh! I got seven letters today . . . and an ad from a roller-skating rink in L.A."; "Reckon they'll banzai tonight. 'Bout time for a big one"; "Had some coffee today. Feel like a million now"; "My wife's birthday comes this month . . . she's eighteen"; "You shoulda heard those Nips yelling last night. When they sealed up that cave, they hollered and squealed all night"; and "Let's hit the sack. It's seven o'clock."[28]

At about 7 o'clock, then, one man would bunk down as best he could at the far end of the foxhole. Because it was cold, he wrapped a poncho around himself (usually over his head, as well), which provided the additional benefit of creating a "tent" for having a cigarette. The exuded smoke was believed to keep you warm.[29] His rifle stood next to him—upright, of course, to reduce the risk of dirt entering the mechanism and barrel.[30] Grenades were always within easy reach, and often he grasped a combat knife. Many men kept a .45-caliber pistol handy as well. The rifle and grenades were for fending off a sneak attack; the knife and pistol were for hand-to-hand fighting in the foxhole.

As the one dozed, the other set up his position. Several grenades were lined up on a dug-out "shelf" below the parapet, each primed for instant use by pulling the safety pin halfway free. A knife was stuck into the sand. Several ammunition magazines were carefully lined up next to the grenades. And then came night.

Sentry duty was generally tedious. Smoking at least relieved the boredom and provided a way of keeping awake, even if officers issued severe reprimands if they saw or heard a cigarette being lit. Dave Davenport used to check whether the coast was clear of superiors, spread out his poncho, and wait for a flare or star shell to go up. Then he used a Zippo to light up underneath the poncho. "If the lighted cigarette is cupped carefully and the smoker bends below ground level to puff, using the light of a newly opened flare it is safe enough. Perhaps not safe and sound—but anyway safe." Everyone did it.[31]

Another method to keep one's eyes open until the end of the shift was to think about a succession of almost random things. Patrick Caruso, for instance, speculated about what his brothers were doing (both were fighting in other theaters) and how his sister was. He mused over how before Iwo going on dates, making the football team, and doing well in exams had been so important but now seemed merely quaint relics of a previous life. For those who found such reminders of home and peace too maudlin, a well-known trick was to "focus on a trivial thought or perform an exercise." In Caruso's case, he would compile a list of the various possible functions of his helmet: as a bucket to wash clothes, a pail to catch rainfall, a bowl for shaving, a basin for washing, a spade to dig a foxhole, a seat, a pot over a fire, and even protection from bullets.[32]

Generally through sheer fatigue, a sentry would sometimes fall asleep. This was the greatest crime conceivable on Iwo Jima, for the man who drifted off was placing not just his and his foxhole mate's lives but the lives of the entire line at risk. Sentries accordingly glanced to their left and right to make sure they could see a bobbing or moving helmet, indicating wakefulness, in the neighboring foxholes, but it was often difficult to tell in the dark.[33] Once, Corporal William McConnell was shaken by his friend Tipton, who told him that Malotte next door was asleep. McConnell looked over and said he wasn't. Both men checked several times, not quite able to decide. It eventually turned out that Malotte had fallen asleep kneeling against the wall with his head and torso perfectly upright.[34]

Such miscreants were roundly abused, humiliated, and insulted. When a foxhole pal of Allen Matthews passed the word along to the next hole along that a counterattack was imminent but received no acknowledgment, he rightly suspected that its occupants were asleep. He strode angrily across and bawled them out, brandishing the grenade that he swore he would throw in there the next time it happened.[35] Punishment was not restricted to harsh words and threats. No one wanted to share a foxhole with a man who had fallen asleep, and each night offenders from up and down the line were forced to hole in together until they had redeemed themselves.[36]

The primary role of the sentry was, of course, to watch for possible infiltrators and the warning signs of a banzai. Theoretically, anyone moving in front of the line was an enemy and must be shot immediately, but sentries enjoyed a little discretion, particularly if it was still a little light outside and the wounded still needed bringing in. Passwords were used without fail to weed out Japanese infiltrators. They changed nightly. Sometimes they were states and capitals; at other times, American automobile makers; and at still others, cities. The presumption was that the Japanese might conceivably know one or two examples offhand but certainly not five recited rapidly in a row. Thus, all along the line you would hear repeated cries of "Chicago, Louisville, Atlanta, New Orleans, San Diego" or "Buicks, Studebakers, Fords, Chevrolets, Chryslers" as corpsmen and litter-bearers came in from the cold.[37]

Depending on the unit, there were variations on the theme. In Richard Wheeler's, the sentry would challenge with one car make and expect to hear another in return.[38] In another, the sentry would cry "President" and the visitor had to reply with the name of one.[39] Being clever and answering with one of the more obscure occupants of the Oval Office was asking for trouble. Abe Levine of Brooklyn, evidently a man not overly conversant with antebellum history, nearly shot a Marine who supplied "Fillmore." Levine's rule of thumb was that "when you give me the password, you give me Roosevelt, Washington, or Lincoln. Them's the only presidents I remember."[40]

The Japanese soon learned most of these simple-to-guess passwords (or eavesdropped from close by), and some—much to the surprise of many Marines—were quite proficient in mimicking an American accent. Some overcame the shibbolethic inability to pronounce "r" and "l," though this was very rare, and failed attempts resulted in death. Marines like Pfc. Thomas Farkas adapted by demanding two car makes, for example, in quick demand-and-response succession (one of which had to be "Chevrolet," which usefully contained both an "r" and an "l") or resorted to passwords like "lemon," "lanolin," and "yellow."[41] After several corpsmen were murdered going to the aid of wounded men— who turned out to be Japanese ambushers—crying "Corpsman, corpsman," medics like Milton Gertz advised Marines to call for them using the code word "Tallulah."[42] More securely still, a Marine would shout "rotten" and want to hear "lemons" back. Only a natural English speaker could match the proper adjective-noun combination and pronounce it properly.[43]

As the Marines advanced up the island, the use of passwords on the front line would decline precipitously.[44] There, because no one was sufficiently mad to patrol too far ahead and risk being left isolated at night in the badlands, any moving object was assumed to be Japanese. Corporal Al Abbatiello laid out the simple principle: On the line, "nobody got out of that hole after dark. If there was anybody walking around, and it was dark, you shot him. That's the way it went."[45]

The pressures of sentry duty often caused one's sight and hearing to play tricks. One Marine recalled that there inevitably came a moment when you realized that all noise had ceased: "Suddenly you can hear movement and scraping sounds from every depression and rock pile around you. Nights like that can take hundreds of hours to end." Sometimes, simply to break the silence, a sentry would fire a few rounds or lob a grenade in order to spook others into action.[46]

More often, jittery sentries began firing at phantom infiltrators because their eyes told them that they were lurking amongst the shrubs, behind the rocks, and under the wire ahead of them. (They well could have been: Japanese soldiers were trained to scout to within thirty yards of enemy positions without being detected.)[47] Allen Matthews was absolutely convinced that an innocent bush concealed "the form of a squatting man" and that nearby tufts of grass were crawling with Japanese. The steam rising from the sulfurous rocks conjured up visions of murderous figures emerging from the penumbra. Abbatiello confided that "I shot more steam than I did anything else" at night on Iwo Jima.[48]

Adding to the confusion were the startling, blinding shifts from dark to light. The Marines' world was either an inky, impenetrable black or suddenly filled with eerie greenish or sickly yellow light when a star shell or flare burst. At first, it was as if a flashbulb had gone off directly in your eyes, and sentries had to adjust quickly. Suspended from parachutes, the shells rocked back and forth as they floated languidly to earth, "making the shadows around the rocks and debris ahead of you constantly change shape and size. Is that the silhouette of a man you see along the side of that pile of rocks? You look away to the side for a second to clear your vision and now that 'man' had moved." The only way to keep one's bearings was to not concentrate on a fixed spot as the light descended, but at the same time, not to allow the eyes to move too much. Otherwise, your imagination would run wild and convince you that the Japanese were sneaking forward to slit your throat. Better, instead, to rely on peripheral vision to detect movement.

The optimum method, Marines learned, was to "turn your whole head slowly from side to side to side, starting with the ground closest to you and working outward till the flare goes out."[49]

No matter who was asleep and who on guard, everyone was permanently on edge. Land crabs, one of the island's few native specimens of fauna, caused numerous false alarms. A dozing John Thurman jumped out of his skin when something heavy landed on his chest. Assuming that the enemy was about to bayonet him, he frantically grabbed for a weapon but saw only a large crab scuttling away. He stabbed it and threw it out of the foxhole.[50] When Bernard Dobbins did the same, he heard shouts of "Grenade!" and two Marines came rocketing out of the next hole over.[51]

Not every infiltrator was a phantom or impertinent crab, of course. The threat was very real. When a surprise attack did happen, it happened very quickly and at unsettlingly close range. Joe Simms was wide awake at 0130, finger on the trigger, ready to detect twigs snapping or a shadowy figure briefly glimpsed. Then "suddenly, in rapid succession," he heard cushioned footsteps, "blinked as a bright parachute flare flashed . . . and heard a rifle crack from the neighboring foxhole. He swung his BAR around as a second shot rang out." Just ten yards away from his foxhole lay sprawled two Japanese. They were perhaps dead—but only perhaps—so he fired his BAR into their bodies to make sure.[52]

As a last resort, there were always grenades. A Marine in the 3rd Battalion, 9th Marines, liked to simulate them by rolling stones down the slope outside his foxhole to worry any approaching Japanese.[53] But much of the time close-quarters grenade fights were a matter of timing and judgment, for there were critical differences between American and Japanese grenades. Japanese ones supplied a more powerful explosion than their American counterparts, but the latter were better designed and manufactured. Japanese grenades fragmented into metal shards much smaller and finer than the chunks flung off by American ones.[54] All things equal, fewer casualties on average were incurred by Americans than Japanese during grenade fights. There was no equivalent on the defenders' side, for instance, to a prolonged duel on the third day near Mount Suribachi in which apparently seventy-seven Japanese in one area were killed by American grenades.[55]

If a direct hit was scored by a Japanese grenade, the victim generally died. Thus, Allen Matthews observed several Japanese who had died tightly clutching grenades (owing either to faulty fuses or to suicidal impulses). One corpse he examined "lay on his back and his arms were flung wide. Both hands were gone and what had been his chest was now a gaping hole with small bits of ribs sticking out of the torn flesh"; another's "arms were mutilated and his hands missing but the cavity in his body from the blast of his grenade was lower—across his belly so that portions of his intestines hung over his legs."[56]

But if a Marine had dived to the ground, had taken even minimum cover, or was a few yards away, he had a decent chance of being left either lightly wounded or unscathed (if shaken).[57] John Thompson, for example, was lying in a shell hole when a Japanese grenade blew up behind him. "If it had been an American grenade I would have been killed, but as it was my pack absorbed a good deal of the blast."[58]

Jack Lucas was one of those who survived a Japanese grenade. During a grenade exchange, he leaped on one to save his comrades (an act for which he won the Medal of Honor) and described the experience when it exploded:

> The blast was deafening. One moment I was prostrate on the ground, and the next, I was floating upward. With eyes wide open, I watched as my body rose above the trench floor. . . . After the initial blast, silence filled my universe. The peace and tranquility was euphoric and calming. There was no noise, no pain, no battle, and no real time, only total and absolute peace. I never lost consciousness. The force propelled me into the air, rotating my body 180 degrees. When the momentum had spent itself, I dropped to the earth, landing on my back. My ears began to ring as though I had received a near-knockout punch. . . . My mind struggled to process the muffled noises but everything sounded as though I were underwater. . . . Except for an intense tingling sensation, I had no feeling. I was numb all over. I had suffered over 250 en-

trance wounds. . . . As feeling gradually returned to my body, the initial unpleasantness of pain made its presence known, and soon accelerated to an excruciating level finally enveloping me completely in an unrelenting grip of agony."[59]

Japanese grenades differed also in that whereas American ones could be prepared earlier by leaving the safety pin halfway out, the former was first armed by screwing the firing pin down and pulling the safety pin (a kind of fork attached to a short length of string, cord, or rope), and only then was the fuse ignited by a sharp blow to a hard object, such as a helmet or rock. That final step, that distinctive click of metal against stone or steel, served as the fatal giveaway in the silence of the night, said John Lyttle.[60] Once a Marine heard it, he knew he had between four and five seconds (the same delay as an American grenade) before it exploded. If that was not enough, he could also see the streak of its red arc as the grenade flew toward him.

The handful of seconds between ignition and detonation was, pointed out one Marine, "a surprisingly long time. It was possible to throw a grenade at a Jap, have him pick it up and throw it back at you, and still have enough time for you to scoop the grenade up and get it away from you before the explosion."[61] That was a dangerous game: Tibor Torok avoided playing it by each night filling with dirt an empty sandbag he always carried so that with it he could smother any grenade that fell in to his foxhole.[62]

If grenades and close-range fire failed to stop an attack, the infiltrators would jump into the nearest foxhole and attempt to slay the occupants. Nighttime hand-to-hand combat in such a confined space can probably be counted as the ne plus ultra of raw savagery on Iwo, pitting as it did men of equal skill and ruthlessness against each other in a lethal duel. There were no rules, no quarter, no surrender. Such melees were inevitably chaotic, with each participant's version differing slightly from the others, but the sequence of events (from his own perspective) were etched vividly in the memory.[63]

Corporal William Byrd and his foxhole mate fought off two Japanese in a "struggle [that] lasted an eternity. I had one of them in a viselike grip around the neck. I remember how he smelled. He probably didn't think I smelled very good either. My buddy . . . was cut on his hand and arm, but he was still fighting. I was hit with a rifle butt under my left eye. It was the hardest blow I ever received in my life. I still have the scar. I vaguely remember another Marine coming to help. One of the Japanese was stabbed to death, the other was shot. I remember blood running into my mouth."[64]

There was neither rhyme nor reason in foxhole fighting. There was no doctrine or approved method. One used whatever weapon came to hand—a pistol, a knife, a clubbed rifle, a grenade. Such apparently antiquated arms as swords and bayonets were surprisingly common. Near Mount Suribachi, a Japanese officer lunged with his sword at a Marine, who caught the blade in his hands, wrenched it away, and slew its owner.[65] Indeed, bayonets were used for actual *fighting* far more frequently than in the Civil or Revolutionary War. When Alfred Stone, for instance, was rushed by a soldier, "I raised my rifle up and watched him impale himself on my bayonet in the midsection of his body. He fell to his left, and I could not get the bayonet out of his body. I had to fire a round into his body to loosen the bayonet." He then shot another Japanese trying to work the bolt of his rifle.[66] The Japanese preference for bayonets—they were taught that it exemplified the "spirit" of the offensive—may have, paradoxically, saved Marines' lives. In the confines of a foxhole, their technique of the single "long thrust" was of little utility whereas Marines were taught to rely on short, violent movements with their bayonets.[67] Worse, their instructors had directed them never to club their rifles, an American tradition since at least the time of Bunker Hill, and one of which the Marines took full advantage.[68]

Still, Americans would experience a remarkable variety of attempts to kill them. Sergeant Bill Harrell and Pfc. Andrew Jackson Carter were sharing a foxhole when Harrell, asleep, heard Carter's M1 bark several times. Instantly alert, he saw four Japanese lying before them and heard a bubbly groan emanating from one of them. They shot at the lump a few times to guarantee he was dead before Carter's rifle jammed due to the sand and he headed back to the command post for a replacement.

In the meantime, a grenade landed next to Harrell from an overlooked infiltrator. Flung backward by the blast, Harrell was left with a numbed body but could feel a "peculiar" sensation, as if strange fingers were scratching at his left forearm. Wondering what it was, he looked down and saw his "left hand was off at the wrist and hung by shreds of tendon down along his forearm." Carter, luckily, returned and Harrell pulled out his .45 with his good right hand. Two Japanese scrambled from some nearby foliage, one swinging a sword. Carter fired his new rifle, which jammed (the damn sand, again), but grabbed an enemy one they had recently found lying around and were saving as a souvenir. As one Japanese piled into Carter, who ran him through with the souvenir gun's bayonet, the swordsman lunged, deeply slashing Carter's left wrist, but Harrell's .45 roared and killed him. Meanwhile, the bayoneted Japanese was gurgling and coughing his life out. After he was dealt with, Harrell ordered Carter to go get help. The sergeant had no illusions that he would die before Carter returned, but as he settled down and made his peace with the Lord, a panting figure landed next to him. Harrell stirred and swiveled his head only to meet the gaze of a Japanese next to him, their heads a foot apart as the enemy checked whether he was dead. His unwelcome new acquaintance chattered to someone else, crouching nearby. Then the first very deliberately and slowly took a grenade—making sure Harrell could see it—cracked it on his helmet, and shoved it under the Marine's chin. As he prepared to leap from the hole, Harrell shot him with his invaluable .45 and coaxed the grenade loose. At the opposite end of the foxhole, the other Japanese tried to scramble out in a panic as Harrell tossed the grenade, now a second or two from exploding, at him. Harrell would lose his other hand when it went off, but the Japanese lost his life. The next morning, even hardened Marines were astounded by what was being called Harrell's and Carter's "pocket Alamo" (they were Texan): No fewer than twelve Japanese lay dead in and around their foxhole. (Harrell became a rancher after the war.)[69]

Despite the heroics, the survivors of such deadly, adrenaline-powered encounters were left shaking and disturbed. Frequently, dead Japanese were shot, stabbed, and beaten by Marines exorcising their aggression in a frenzied manner reminiscent of the British following their conquest of the redoubt at Bunker Hill. When Ray Hansen frantically used his entrenching tool to hit a Japanese who had grabbed his leg and foot, he cried to Les Murrah to shoot him. Murrah did so by standing on the man's head and firing directly into it. Afterward, Hansen began to pummel the corpse and when Murrah asked why, he replied, "I'm killing him." "But I've already killed him," pointed out a quizzical Murrah. "I know it, Les," said Hansen, but "I'm killing him again before he kills one of us." When he had finished, there was little left of the Japanese apart from some flayed flesh and a red mess. Murrah found that his own hands would not stop shaking for a long time.[70] Quite a few Marines, understandably, were worse affected, though generally only temporarily. Russell Boydston, for instance, had to be evacuated to a ship to recover from hearing the screams and seeing what his friend Bill Terrill had done to the Japanese soldier who had tried to kill him.[71]

All that can be said is that if the nights were bad, the days were worse.

8. The Madness in the Method

During the day, every day, Iwo Jima was Pandemonium, the High Capital of Satan, its blasted plains, pyres of ruins, and cave-pocked ridges luring Marines ever closer to a City of Dis. Nothing, at least at first, made sense on Iwo: It was a Golgothic madhouse, a place where men did nothing but die. Fittingly, the place even looked, as someone quipped to Alvin Josephy, "like Hell with the fire out."[1]

But Iwo had never been pretty. In 1891, a naturalist named Henry Seebohm had received a "box of birds' skins and eggs from Sulphur Island," or Iwo Jima, sent by a Mr. Holst, a recent visitor. Seebohm would inform readers of *The Ibis,* an ornithological journal, that its "centre is very barren, principally black sand and grey clay, with a few dried-up tufts of grass, and an occasional hardy bush. Everywhere are scattered stones and rocks, especially to the north-east." There was also "a plain of what seemed to be pure sulphur, which was boiling furiously in three or four holes when visited by Mr. Holst. Close to the north shore are some hot springs. There are a few large trees on the island, and both in the north-east and in the south-east is dense low scrub, bound together with climbers."[2]

By the time the Marines were hurled headlong firing from the ethereal sea toward the damnable island, the terrain was more malefic still. Its twisted gullies, its narrow blind alleys and dark crevices, its jutting rocks and threatening boulders, its (few) gnarled trees and clumps of dead brown grass combined to bestow on the island a diabolical aspect. "Looking around" as he waited out a bombardment, John Lardner noted, "I had the leisure for the first time to think what a miserable piece of real estate Iwo Jima is. Later, when I had seen nearly all the island, I knew that there were no extenuating features." This fiendish place "has no water, few birds, no butterflies, no discernible animal life—nothing but sand and clay, humpbacked hills, stunted trees, knife-edged kuna grass in which mites who carry scrub typhus live, and a steady, dusty wind."[3] Dave Davenport, slogging it out across the barren landscape, was somewhat curter in his description: "This fucking bloody bastard of an island."[4]

Naval and artillery fire tore deeply into the heart and guts of the island, leaving behind a wasteland that lay, as Bertram Yaffe put it, "perforated by bomb craters and eerie geysers of sulfurous mist—an expanse broken by the silhouettes of derelict tanks and places and bodies half-rising as they stiffen grotesquely."[5] It was the sulfur, the reeking, Luciferian sulfur that made the ground hot to the touch, so hot you could warm rations in the dirt, that caused the bodies to "half-rise."[6]

When corpses lay on the earth for days, absorbing the gas, they puffed up, and Marines heard a mysterious sound "like letting the air out of a bicycle tire, loud at first, then gradually becoming softer, until it stopped." The culprits were dead soldiers whose bloated bodies had burst, releasing noxious effusions of sulfuric stench.[7] Whenever a stray bullet or piece of shrapnel rent a hole in one's torso, which was quite often, "the smell would become almost suffocating," recalled John

Thurman.[8] Bored Marines accordingly played pranks, according to George Gentile, by throwing stones at gassy Japanese corpses to "pop" them and annoy passersby.[9]

When a body expanded, *everything* did. John Lyttle noticed "one guy [who] looked like he was ready to float down the streets of New York in the Macy's Thanksgiving Day Parade. This bloating was not limited to the stomach, but every arm, leg and finger as well. Even his head was swollen." A Marine fetched out his wallet, and the men gawked at a photo of the man and his smiling bride on their wedding day.[10]

Lyttle was too delicate to mention one specific part of the anatomy that also grew. Howard McLaughlin saw a naked Japanese soldier whose "seemingly intact corpse saluted each passing Marine with an erection, swollen somehow by the violence of his death to monstrous size."[11] Finding another similarly affected, Ernest Moreau and his friends lay down and began "shooting at that thing for target practice."[12]

Some Marines began to indulge in extreme behavior. There was, as always, an enthusiasm for souvenirs, but, as the Japanese commonly booby-trapped corpses, it was generally tempered by an appreciation for the risks involved. Most booby traps consisted of eight ounces of explosives packed into a container the size of a large tuna can. In its center there was a small round plunger that, when ejected by a spring, would detonate the contents. A U-shaped safety clip held the spring in place, and after perching a bait object on top the operator would pull out the safety, arming the trap. If the bait was removed it would go off instantly.[13] When they came across a suspicious body, then, Marines would loop a length of rope around a hand or foot, retreat a safe distance, and tug hard enough to move the corpse some distance.[14] Not just bodies were booby-trapped: Anything known to attract Marines' magpieish attention could be wired. Helmets, saki bottles, pistols, and the pièce de résistance, officers' "samurai swords," were often found ready to harm unwary Marines. When the Japanese had time, even dead Marines were used as bait to kill those collecting them.[15]

Every Marine knew the dangers.[16] One time, John Thurman saw a dead Japanese officer lying twenty feet away in the entrance to a pillbox knocked out by artillery. There was a nice pistol in his holster, a lovely souvenir. He had obviously, however, been killed some time ago, which meant that he was almost certainly rigged to explode. And so he was: As Thurman peered more closely, he caught "the remaining sunlight reflecting off of a very fine hair wire that was tied to the pistol."[17]

Still, there were those willing to take a risk to pick up some prime souvenirs. Fred Schribert, who later conceded that what he and two friends had done was "stupid," once ducked into a cave and emerged with a valuable trove that included a flag, a sword, a pistol, a fountain pen, combat ribbons, and even some family photos, which they kept.[18] The trick, of course, was to scavenge only very recently killed Japanese; particularly popular were their wristwatches.[19] Flags, too, preferably bloodstained and bullet-holed. For those with more elevated tastes, such as James Vedder, an intact porcelain cup embossed with the symbol of the Imperial Japanese Army and a working phonograph provided much-missed elements of refinement.[20]

The Japanese, in contrast, did not loot as thoroughly as Marines. This was for several reasons, including a lack of opportunity. Neither did the Marines carry much that might interest a beleaguered garrison. On Iwo, Allen Matthews's worldly possessions consisted of two penknives, an empty wallet, eleven cents in change, a rifle-cleaning brush, a few photographs of his family, an inkless fountain pen, and a package of rifle-cleaning patches.[21] Tibor Torok, like many others, left behind on the ship his money, photos, letters, jewelry, and any identification save his dog tags, which were wrapped with tape so they did not clink or reflect the sun's rays.[22] The Japanese wanted only food and water, so if they were lucky, they might have managed to acquire from the slain a half-empty canteen and some crackers.[23]

These material objects aside, in some quarters there was a penchant for the removal of body parts. In a practice unheard of at Bunker Hill and Gettysburg, where the enemy was generally regarded as civilized (if wrong-headed) and combat was not zero-sum, one could see, said Jack Lucas, Marines severing the little fingers of the enemy dead, packing them in salt bags, and sending them home as good-luck charms.[24] Ears, too, were sometimes sliced off.[25] It is unlikely, simply because of the fear of booby traps, that collecting bodily bric-a-brac was inordinately widespread among Marines. More probably, the hobby was restricted to a very small number of Americans who actively amassed these treasures—and they, in turn, were seen as perverse by their peers, who were nonetheless reluctant to snitch on them.

A subtle distinction, perhaps, but a significant proportion of body souvenirs were acquired not for thrills but for immediate commercial gain. Gerald Copeland once found a group of Marines standing around a fifty-gallon oil drum in which they were boiling skulls, after having first "popped the eyes out." Copeland "thought that was interesting" and asked why they were doing it. They replied that "we make a lot of money at this" and related further that sailors aboard the ships were buying Japanese skulls in a frenzy.[26] Then there was the quartermaster back at the beach who offered Ernest Moreau and his clique a lavish supply of K-rations in exchange for a Japanese head. After acquiring one (details are patchy), they "boiled the skull to kill all the maggots, and knocked all the gold teeth out." It turned out that the quartermaster, a former dentist, was overjoyed at their otherwise toothful gift, so it worked out profitably for all concerned.[27] The instigators of skull-boiling were, it seems, rear-echelon and ship-based personnel, the ones who rarely got a chance to go up front and experience combat first-hand.[28]

Gold teeth were another matter, as Moreau indicated. The Japanese were famed for their fillings, and more than one Marine supplemented his assets with Nippon gold. George Nations and a friend were most annoyed when they searched near the front lines (getting sniped at for their pains) only to find nothing but heads with missing teeth.[29] Many decades after the war, a mild-mannered former teacher and school administrator named Warren Peters confided that he had been one of those who collected a "sackful" of gold teeth on Iwo Jima. "That's a gruesome thing," he explained, "but I think that's an indication of how ruthless you let yourself become and how you don't care, you don't really consider them as humans. It's a hard thing to explain. I couldn't do that, I don't think if I were a mortician I could do that at the present time."[30]

Taking body parts of any kind for fun or profit was officially frowned upon, and overly zealous indulgence in the practice was widely regarded as an incipient sign that a Marine was perhaps overdue for a rest. A clearly traumatized Peters, for instance, seems to have begun to descend into a moral haze after his best friend, Charles Chapman, was killed by a sniper while standing next to him. Similarly, George Gentile remembered one fellow who everyone knew had "started to go wacko, and he had a pouch hanging from his cartridge belt and a pair of pliers." He went "around extracting the teeth out of the Japs' mouths and put them in his pouch just as if it were an everyday thing."[31]

There were other warnings that Iwo Jima was getting to a Marine. The least serious affliction manifested itself as disorientation, temporary amnesia, deafness, vomiting, and headaches and was caused primarily by concussion blasts emanating from shells and mortars landing nearby. Their explosions created intense waves of compressed air that disrupted or blocked the brain's nervous electrotransmissions, inflicted blunt trauma damage, or caused severe internal injuries. A passing pressure wave could, for instance, rapidly inflate the victim's stomach with air before emptying it so violently that his intestines were torn apart, his lungs collapsed, and his brain knocked the inside of his skull. It was possible to die instantly if the round fell close, and many men remarked—as they also had at Bunker Hill and Gettysburg—on the placid, statuelike corpses they found, many with no obvious bleeding. The extent of the concussive effects varied upon the size of the round and the locations of the victims. Inside one concrete blockhouse, for instance, Captain Fred Haynes saw eight or ten corpses. Some of them, killed by concussive waves and evidently protected from the primary explosive blast by walls or doors, "looked almost peaceful," while the unluckier ones had their "intestines and arms and legs scattered around."[32] The power of a 16-inch naval shell was colossal, however, no matter where you were. Thomas Brown saw three motionless Japanese lying intact fifty feet away from a huge, fifty-foot-wide crater. Fifty feet from the opposite side—150 feet distant from the first group, in other words—lay another five.[33]

There were considerable numbers of temporarily shocked Marines, especially after a prolonged barrage, and their strange and befuddled behavior prompted many to believe that they had entered a surreal world. Most of the time, the symptoms evaporated shortly after, even if the headaches sometimes took weeks or even months to dissipate. One such was Corporal Glenn Buzzard, who was in a shell hole with Otis Boxx when a shell struck. Nothing remained of Boxx but his lower jaw, while Buzzard, miraculously, received only slight shrapnel wounds. "I was shocked, no question about it . . . my mind was gone," said Buzzard. He couldn't hear, and his vision was blurry. He passed out and came to later in a hospital ship; he later returned to his unit.[34]

More seriously, a man's comrades had to watch for subsequent indications of what was variously known as the Asiatic stare, the bulkhead stare, or, perhaps most famously, the thousand-yard stare (sometimes two-thousand-yard stare)—a phrase coined during the Peleliu campaign a few months earlier and popularized by *Life* magazine.[35] This affliction was caused neither by trauma nor by the fall of artillery, but by day after grinding day of bone-tiredness, nervous exhaustion, poor diet, and exposure to extreme danger. The most obvious symptom was, predictably enough, "a vacant, faraway stare," as James Vedder described the condition, characterized by wide-open, bloodshot eyes, whites showing all around the pupils, wrinkled forehead, and raised eyebrows. Irritability, extreme reaction to noise, and obsessive behavior about minor things usually went hand in hand.[36] Thereafter, victims would begin to act strangely and erratically. As a doctor explained, Marines' reflexes slowed considerably, and they were unable to make conscious decisions, ultimately entering a stupefied, dreamlike state. It was "a way the brain tried to keep you from going crazy," the doctor thought.[37]

The "stare" could infect not just individuals but also entire units, or whatever was left of them. At one point, Odell Arnold's thirteen-man squad had lost three killed and four wounded while the rest suffered from combat-fatigue symptoms.[38] When Alvin Josephy encountered two companies of combat-hardened Marines, they

> looked as if they had just come out of a hard-fought football game. They leaned against the sides of their foxholes, exhausted and

breathing heavily. Their eyes were wide open and staring, as if they could not forget the terrible sights they had seen. I recognized many friends and tried talking to them, but it was useless: They looked through me, their answers made no sense, their minds wandered. One man tried to ask me how the battle was going. He couldn't get his question out. He finished half the sentence, then repeated the last words, over and over, like a man falling asleep. But he wasn't drowsing; his mind just wouldn't function.[39]

Some men would cry and purge the condition temporarily from their system. After a bloody attack on a pillbox, Howard Baxter's platoon sergeant "pulled us back and broke down and cried. He lost one of his best friends. He reached a point and had a good bawl for about five minutes, and then he was all right."[40] Others, like Baxter himself, felt the same but predicted that "if I let myself go, I'd be gone. I just jammed it down inside. I think a lot of us did."[41] But as Raymond Mik warned, those who continued to stare "off into space, those were the ones who gave you a lot of trouble." They were perched precariously on a mental ledge. Keith Renstrom suspected that his lieutenant, hitherto "a solid officer," was entering dangerous territory when he ordered Renstrom to fetch barbed wire from the beach when none was needed. Speaking in an unsettling tone of voice, the lieutenant kept weirdly repeating, "Wire, wire, go get lots of wire." By the time Renstrom returned, he had cracked up—"who knows what pushed him over"—and was being evacuated.[42]

Renstrom had observed a phenomenon that commonly occurred during one of these states. Quite often men would snap, usually after a relatively minor incident. As Sergeant Gallant clarified, the "Gooney Bird Stare did not come all at once. A Marine did not suddenly have it. It came by slow, subtle changes over a period of time." At first, he became inattentive and unaware or uncaring of what was happening around him. Then he would fixate on something inconsequential but seemingly very important, such as fried eggs—how he missed them, how he liked them cooked, how outrageous it was that there were none—and slowly work himself up into a lather. Shortly after, his reddening eyes would grow ever wider and his movements increasingly robotic. It was still possible to return to a normal state from that point, but some men were too far gone.[43] They would plunge into a fit of madness and might begin to mutilate the dead, launch a suicidal one-man assault against a machine-gun nest, or see hordes of invisible Japanese trying to kill them. Corporal Willard Burroughs, for instance, stunned his friends on March 9 when, in the midst of intense sniper fire, he suddenly and inexplicably stood up in full view of the enemy, shouted insults at the Japanese soldiers nearby, and was shot in the heart.[44] Added Raymond Mik, "At night, if that happened in the line, you had to be sure that they got off the ones who were screaming. I never reached that point, but I was probably close to losing it."[45] Another man, witnessed by Robert Allen, did lose it when he "reached down and picked up an object protruding from the sand. The sight of a detached hand destroyed the last of his fragile sanity. . . . Screaming, he began to tear the clothing from his body, and he disappeared."[46]

The most alarming incidents occurred when the victim relived, amplified, or perhaps imagined the event that had provoked him. Dr. Vedder described one private who arrived at the aid station: "His eyes were rolling about wildly. His facial muscles ran through the gamut of contortions that alternately depicted fear, hate, and rage as he shouted incoherently. He was swinging a large samurai sword about indiscriminately. If anyone tried to approach him, he would make half-hearted lunges with his recently captured weapon. From his disjointed remarks, we learned that we were the enemy and he was surrounded. Before he died, he planned to kill as many Nips as possible." Generally, the only way to calm men in this condition was to knock them down and out; in this case, an assistant crept behind the private and decked him with a shovel between his shoulder blades. He was quickly disarmed, heavily sedated, and evacuated to a hospital ship.[47]

The good news was that a few days away after a breakdown was generally sufficient to restore normality. Ideally, though, officers would notice men "starting to crack, who'd had too much," said William Doran, and "let them go back and get supplies, get away from the front action."[48] Afterward, if there remained lingering doubts as to the soldier's mental stability, they would be assigned to a beachmaster like Sergeant James Boyle, who used them to carry equipment and ammunition until they could return to their units.[49] Even a minor respite from the immediate front line could be enough to restore a man. Frank Caldwell, a company commander, was asked by one of his Marines to send him back because he was liable to crack. Caldwell proposed letting him join the mortar section for a time. The mortarmen were located just twenty yards to the rear, but that was far enough away to bring the Marine back from the edge. He later rejoined his squad.[50]

George Wahlen, a corpsman, first noticed significant and rapidly escalating numbers of combat-fatigued troops on the fifth day of the campaign, or February 24 (D+5).[51] Another corpsman, Ray Crowder, who had just arrived, confirmed that on February 25 "the majority" of his patients were suffering from "shell shock, combat fatigue, and blast concussion."[52] There had been psychological casualties, of course, on the very first day, even the very first hour, but the quality of the trauma had shifted. At first, men psychologically more disposed to breakdown—owing to existing mental disturbance, family background, insufficient screening during recruitment, genetic factors, their particular experience upon landing, or a combination of these elements—had tended to collapse. Socioeconomic status, age, and education, too, were correlated with elevated anxiety and stress; by far the highest rates (77 percent) were seen among rural or poor urban soldiers over thirty years old with but a grade-school education (this was at a time when college attendance was a rarity and mostly confined to officers), and the lowest (40 percent) among high-school graduates aged under twenty-five, who were believed to be more adaptable to circumstances.[53]

From D+5 onward, however, combat fatigue began to afflict everyone, regardless of background, genes, and prior experience. No one could count himself immune. Aside from a lack of proper food and protracted exposure to fire, a prime cause was that by that time hardly any Marines had snatched more than a few hours' sleep on each of the preceding four nights. The random crash of nighttime artillery and the whirring of missiles and flares above denied men the luxury of deep sleep; all they could do was "doze." The clamor, said Alvin Josephy, invaded their "fitful dreams" so that it "sounded like someone banging doors in a house in which we were trying to sleep. The doors were all around us, upstairs and downstairs, in the same room and on the other side of the house."[54] That was only if they managed to nod off, of course. Most of the men digging in, he noticed, "seemed too groggy and dazed to sleep. It was as if they were afraid something else might happen to them if they relaxed their guard and closed their eyes."[55]

Sleep deprivation combined with stress was clearly exacting a severe toll by D+5. Indeed, by the end of that day, total Marine casualties amounted to 7,758, of which 558 were listed as cases of combat fatigue.[56] As the Marine Corps lagged behind the Army in acknowledging and treating neuropsychiatric casualties, instead choosing to classify them euphemistically as resulting from such external factors as "blast concussions" or "severe dehydration" (just as "sunstroke" had been used during the Civil War), the official figure of 558 is certainly a grave underestimate.[57] Alice Goudreau, a nurse at a naval hospital that treated Iwo Jima casualties, wrote soon afterward (in November 1945, before the issue could be hushed up) that "the majority of our ambulatory admissions" were men suffering from "war neuroses." They arrived, she said, "by the hundreds" and "were in such a severe state of shock that they had to be led by the hand from the planes and ambulances." An air-raid siren, a blackout, even "the sharp slam of a screen door" would "send them scurrying into corners and under their beds in quivering, stuttering huddles."[58] Many more men remained on the island, never diagnosed, staring listlessly and moving like zombies until either the end came or they were wounded.

It was on D+5, and this was no coincidence, that Marines first noticeably began losing track of time and place. George Nations wrote that after that date "events are no longer separated in my mind as to the day they happened. All the days and events seem to run together."[59] Tibor Torok suffered "about two weeks of memory loss" from about D+5 onward.[60] It did not help that their watches were easily lost or stopped working owing to sand, saltwater, and shock. Frank Walker misplaced his "watch early on" and that belonging to John Thurman broke on the fourth day.[61] Foxhole mates Ernest Moreau, who had lost his watch, and Tony Steltzer, whose broke, were forced to time their hour-long sentry shifts by using a rosary to recite a given number of Hail Marys.[62] The disorienting loss of chronology affected the Japanese as well. Seaman First Class Koizumi Tadayoshi stated that after the first few nights "I lost track of what the date was or even the day was."[63] Even when their watches still worked, Marines like Howard McLaughlin descended into a haze, their sense of continuity inexorably vanishing as time went on: He rued that he had "no guide posts, no references to tie remembered events to. Between running off one landing craft on D-Day and staggering aboard another one 36 days later, I am sure that there are many days that I have no recollection of at all."[64]

Unlike set-piece battles like Bunker Hill or Gettysburg, which were conducted over a limited time span, on Iwo Jima days and nights, mornings and afternoons elided. All became permanent penumbra, the grayish, shadowy place between light and darkness. The raising of the flag atop Mount Suribachi on the fourth day is quite often the last distinct memory men had of the battle's progress; after that, it descended into a series of repetitive, automatic small-unit and individual actions hardly distinguishable from one another. For one corporal, "each day and night was filled with points of contact with a determined enemy. Blockhouse after blockhouse contained Japanese soldiers determined to kill us."[65] Robert Maiden spent entire days "snooping and pooping and running and hitting the deck and running" between bunkers. He never had any idea where he was, nor was he interested.[66] For another Marine, Iwo Jima's problem was "that there are too many damned ridges. You take one ridge and then you got to take another. There's always another ridge."[67] The next was just like the last, and the one before, and the one after the next. That was all Iwo Jima was—a grinding, repetitive slog that had to be endured until it ended.

Later on, veterans could relate precisely *what* happened during particularly vivid events but not *when* or *where* they occurred. Gerald Averill described the jarring moment when normal continuity disappeared as resembling "when a smoothly moving film on the screen change[s] to a series of color slides, some of them painfully acute. Slide on. Slide off. Click. Click. Nothing in between."[68] In combat, which was near constant, one man recalled that "time seemed to take on a surrealistic quality. Everything happened in slow motion. Small sounds were amplified, and the din of battle was silence. Your eyes saw everything. Your mind noted and remembered it all in minute detail. Time will never dull these scenes, nor will I ever be able to erase them from my mind's eye."[69] And yet, as Liberato G. Riccio put it, "I still don't know for sure where I was at any point on the island, even when I read about it later and started retracing my steps. I sort of recognize certain locations, like when we were under a mortar attack."[70]

A sense of powerlessness, too, set in. Marines quickly realized that they stood very little chance of making it off Iwo in one piece, let alone alive. As far as they were concerned, no matter the fine doctrine and intricate planning of the Marine Corps, they had been sent there to die.

In the beginning, Marines were optimistic rationalists: Men calculated the odds of dying but "were convinced it wouldn't happen" to them, observed Corporal John Thompson.[71] Before every landing, Dave Davenport "always looked at the other guys. I never figured it would be me. I always kind of measured the thickness of a buddy, or buddies, near me during a shelling or a pin-down by small arms fire. Will their bodies stop shrapnel or a bullet and shield me? I knew others looked at me the same way. We talked about it. It was always the other guy not you."[72] Believers tempered their rationalism with a faith that God would see them through, but secular and religious alike always pictured themselves, said Allen Matthews, "as grieving over the loss of friends, for never could we picture our friends grieving over us. Thus does ignorance protect the sanity of the untutored mind."[73]

For most battles, such mental tactics were adequate preparation. But not on Iwo, where, "after a few days" of combat "a funny thing occurred," according to Thompson. "You started to realize the chances of not only your buddy getting hit but of you getting clobbered were extremely high. It became a matter of would you be killed or just wounded?"[74] Fred McDiarmid confidently began his time on Iwo by assuming, "They can't hurt me," but after seeing how many others were being hit, started saying to himself, "I hope they don't hurt me," until finally the best he could hold out for was, "I hope I don't get killed."[75]

His pessimism was fully merited by the remarkable attrition rates on Iwo Jima. Very, very few men lasted the entire battle unscathed. The casualty figures, moreover, are untainted by the incidence of disease, that historical bane of armies but almost nonexistent on Iwo Jima. (When "sickness" or "illness" was mentioned as a reason for evacuation, it really meant mental breakdown.)

The staggering churn of casualties began at the regimental level. The 26th Marines, for instance, began D-Day with 146 officers and 3,110 enlisted men. Even after receiving 882 replacements during the battle, its strength at the end was 80 officers and 1,388 men. At the battalion level, the figures turn starker still. The average battalion size at the beginning was 36 officers and 885 enlisted men, but by mid-March these had fallen to 16 and 300 (including hundreds of replacements)—not much larger than a peacetime company.[76] Frank Walker was a corporal in 2nd Battalion, 28th Marines, which happened to start with 1,680 men, of which 1,571 (including replacements) would be killed or wounded. Only 109 made it off Iwo safe and sound.[77] Perhaps most vividly, whereas a battalion's complement of sergeants on paper was 69, at the end one sergeant major sadly mused to an enquirer of his, "Well, I got six now."[78]

Lower down, company after company reported numbing losses. Just over a month after D-Day, the strength of the companies comprising the 2nd Battalion, 28th Marines, had plummeted from an average of 250 men each to between 45 and 85, over half of them replacements.[79] Gerald Averill's company in the 26th Marines landed with 242 men, and a week later half were gone; even after influxes of replacements, just 80 Marines from his outfit would leave Iwo at the end of the battle.[80] Other companies' losses were even severer: Company F, 1st Battalion, 26th Marines, was left with 45 men; Howard Baxter's company in 2nd Battalion, 27th Marines, declined from more than 200 to 27; Robert Maiden's Company D, 2nd Battalion, 26th Marines, dropped from 224 to 24; K Company, 3rd Battalion, 9th Marines landed a few days after D-Day, but of its 252 officers and enlisted plus replacements, only 12 would be left standing at battle's end.[81] The most rapid depletion appears to have been suffered by Company C, 1st Battalion, 21st Marines, which landed with 279 men two days after D-Day and could roll call, according to Corporal Woody Williams, just 17 Marines on March 5—not even two weeks later.[82] The skeletal nature of many companies by the end becomes more shockingly apparent when the replacement Marines are removed from consideration: Seventeen days into the battle, of the more than 200 in one company that had landed on D-Day, there were just three original members left.[83]

Losses among platoons and squads were accordingly horrendous: The 28th Marines' first platoon in C Company was diminished by 95.5 percent, with just one Marine (Pvt. Antoine Chiasson) remaining alive and unwounded among its original three squads, each of twelve or thirteen men.[84] If that was not extraordinary enough, a significant number of platoons and squads experienced a hitherto unthinkable casualty rate of greater than 100 percent. In these units, no original members remained, and even their replacements, and *their* replacements, had been burned through.

The turnover of junior officers and noncommissioned officers was so rapid that there was little point in introducing oneself. Pfc. Keith Neilson's company went through three commanders in two days, while Captain David Severance's new lieutenant was shot fifteen minutes after arriving.[85] That was, admittedly, an extreme case: The more usual life expectancy of a junior officer was roughly forty-eight to seventy-two hours—an ominous milestone considering that in World War II the rule of thumb was that if you could make it past the first seventy-two hours in the field, your chances of dying declined to 1 percent.[86] By that time, you could expect to have learned the necessary fundamentals of staying alive; on Iwo, officers died before they could learn how not to. Corporal Richard Lowe used to see Sergeant Vince Varzevicius showing their fresh-faced lieutenant around the platoon's lines and positions. Then he would do it again a couple of days later for the anonymous new guy, and then again.[87]

In Lieutenant Patrick Caruso's case, his fellow officers did not enjoy even those few days in harness. When he landed on February 23, of the company's seven officers he was sixth in seniority. By the following evening, he was informed by Sergeant Moore, "Lieutenant, you're in charge of K Company." (The seventh in seniority, due to be Caruso's replacement when it was his turn to die, himself died a day later. And all three sergeants who served under him would die, too. And every officer of I and L companies to boot.)[88]

The "official" toll exacted by the fighting on Iwo Jima is complicated by these sour facts. Whereas on paper, total Marine casualties amounted to roughly 35 percent (25,851 casualties of 75,000 Marine and Navy personnel)—itself an extremely high figure—a significant proportion of those were men from support units (motor transport, cooks, and so forth) roped in later on as hapless replacements. In certain units, as well, such as the heavy machine-gun detachments that were generally located just behind the front line to provide emergency backup, attrition was less severe. Corporal William McConnell's machine-gun squad saw major action and yet suffered just one man killed and several more lightly wounded (none were evacuated).[89] Among the frontline combat infantrymen, however, a more accurate overall casualty rate has been estimated at 80 percent.[90]

Worse, as they advanced up the island and Japanese resistance turned ever more ferocious, the risks increased for frontline Marines. In the later stages of the battle, the Marines' desire to end the fighting as quickly as possible, combined with their exhaustion, the influx of inexperienced replacements, and the harsh terrain's imposing a need for ruthless close-quarters engagements, resulted in many, perhaps preventable, casualties.

There were frequent cases of carelessness—in the twin senses of making errors and not caring—in the final weeks. According to Fred Haynes, by that point

many men fought in a murky half-awake state, too tired to remain attuned to their surroundings. This was a grave problem, because on Iwo Jima, vigilance could not guarantee survival, but its absence all but ensured death or serious wounding. Among the frontline veterans, one often saw men who had lost a great deal of weight. Their eye sockets appeared hollow, and there was a strange disjunction between the movement of the head and the eyes. Many very tough Marines were approaching the point where we officers could not expect them to continue fighting indefinitely.

Indeed, instances of falling asleep on sentry duty rose at this time, even when every Marine knew it jeopardized lives.[91]

We also begin to see an increasing incidence of acts of brave foolhardiness intended to win the battle faster and go home. In the northern cliffs, Patrick Caruso and his company became "cocky and brash . . . because we sensed the end was actually within reach." Caruso, who should have known better, took to running in open terrain to take a message rather than zigzagging and jumping between foxholes to avoid the snipers. (For his recklessness, he was soon shot in the leg and evacuated to Guam.)[92] Similarly, Captain Carl Bachman led an unnecessary raid of sixty volunteers, which was caught in the open and massacred by mortars and machine-gun fire. Among the few who returned was Bachman, who, said Fred Haynes, from then on "led his company with total disregard for his own life." He was soon killed.[93]

Only in the last days did Marine behavior become overtly, maybe sometimes overly, cautious—for the understandable reason that no one wanted to be the final casualty of Iwo Jima, the guy who died just hours before his unit returned to the ship. Jim Doyle almost became that guy when, after having come through the entire battle without a scratch, he lost two fingers to a grenade-armed infiltrator.[94] A typical reaction was recorded by Bernard Dobbins. He and his squad were actually heading to the beach to depart when an officer ordered them to pick up any unexploded shells they happened to come across. They refused, telling the lieutenant, "You want to pick up duds, you go do it," and kept walking.[95] Likewise, on Richard Lowe's last day, he "was extra careful walking back to the beach." As his company filed up the ship's ramp, "I could hear a machine gun rattling away in the distance [but] I didn't look back. I just kept walking."[96]

From the first few days onward, then, a sense of fatalistic randomness replaced that of optimistic rationalization among Marines. No longer did they believe the quaint notion, inculcated during their training, that they were monarchs of their own fates, never slaves to chance, and could rely on their Marine-taught skills, judgment, and prowess to control the future. Instead, as Howard McLaughlin put it, pretty soon everyone realized that the best outcome was to be wounded.[97] Mused McLaughlin, the men directly engaged with the Japanese were better off accepting what was coming. It was a revelation born of "realizing that [a soldier] has no control over whether he lives or dies, and relying on some higher authority to determine when it's his time."[98]

Whereas McLaughlin harked back to the conventional Calvinistic assumption that God determined a man's exit from life, drawing succor from its corollary that he could therefore fight unhindered by any sense of foreboding, its secular variant—increasingly popular in World War II—was the "your number on it" theory of being hit. It was a credo among the older, more experienced men, such as the sergeant sharing Jim Doyle's shell hole. Doyle was lugging a heavy radio set, and the sergeant pulled the long aerial over the top of the hole's rim, alarming Doyle, who feared being marked by the Japanese gunners. His mate just laughed, telling him to "take it easy on your first cruise, son. If you're going to get it, you're going to get it; that's all there is to it."[99]

In this respect these Marines echoed their Civil War ancestors, who were equally intrigued by the interplay of uncaring Fate, blind Chance, and divine protection in battle. Back then, after several actions William Ketcham of the 13th Indiana "knew perfectly well that if a cannon ball struck in the right place, it would kill or maim [and] I knew it was always liable to strike somebody and therefore liable to strike me, but I always went where I was ordered to go and the others went, and when I was ordered to run and the others ran, I ran."[100] As the more pious J. W. Hand of the 136th New York added, one should treat the "concentrated fire of a hundred cannons" as one did the "destructive forces of nature—the lightning, the tornado, the earthquake": Do your best to avoid them, but do not attempt to "resist." After all, who were you to resist the will of the Lord?[101]

On Iwo, likewise, William Doran saw men on either side of him in a foxhole blown up by a mortar, and others shot seconds after he had been talking to them, but he himself was never wounded. It was "a perfect example of how you have no control over what's going to happen" in war. "There's no rhyme or reason for it, just count your blessings."[102] Fred Haynes and Colonel Harry Liversedge were standing a couple of feet from Daniel McCarthy, the regimental surgeon, when a mortar round landed. "A small fragment of shrapnel killed him [McCarthy] instantly," said Haynes. "Neither the colonel nor I suffered even so much as a scratch. It was just plain luck. There is no way to explain who was hit and who wasn't."[103]

Belief and atheism alike left men equally mystified why they were saved. Glenn Buzzard confessed that "when I stop to think about it, I have no idea. I'm a Christian. I believe in God. I believe in the hereafter. But why me? I was no better or no worse than [his friends] Cooksey or Elmer Neff or Bowman or any of those guys. But yet they took it, you know what I mean? They're gone. Why, I don't know. I can't answer it. I didn't do anything any better than they did. I wasn't a better scholar, I wasn't a better . . . anything. . . . I have no idea. I cannot answer it."[104] Craig Leman, on the other hand, reasoned that "it's not going to make a damn difference if I pray or not. If it's going to hit me it's going to hit me. I'm not going to pray and see what happens. That's what I did and I never got hit." In fact, "I saw people get shot while they were praying."[105] To that end, Robin Barrett, who landed on five Pacific islands and yet was never wounded—his Civil War equivalent would have been one Private John Haley, who made it through twenty-eight battles and skirmishes from August 1862 until June 1865 and emerged without a scratch—concluded that the best way to handle the subject was not to "question why somebody else got killed or somebody else got injured or whatever it is, just be thankful that you didn't. And it's the only way you can survive. Otherwise, you'd go completely off your rocker." Ultimately, the best way to get by, then, was just not to think either too deeply or too hard about one's chances in a lethal environment. Private Haley, for example, was content to attribute his own remarkable record to having "achieved successful mediocrity" in all things.[106]

Despite assertions or convictions to the contrary, whether one was hit on Iwo was not entirely a matter of chance or destiny but was, in the end, partly conditioned by choices, skill, and experience. There were, in other words, ways to rig the game, if only slightly—as Marines would gradually realize over the course of the battle. Of course, it was still depressingly possible to do everything "right" and die, but the odds were slightly shortened in your favor if you learned some tricks.

Some were as simple as remembering never to walk fully upright or in a straight line. To present a slightly smaller target for shrapnel and sniper alike, the men on Iwo would crouch, hunch, or crawl, except when they ran, and then they made sure to zigzag and corkscrew as they jumped in and out of cover.[107] Allen Matthews described the method, mastered only through experience, by which one painstakingly moved forward: When shelling subsided, "I rose to my knees, looked quickly about to try to locate my squad [and] headed out toward my direct front. My eye glimpsed two holes either of which could serve as the next possible haven." He saw there was a dead Marine in one, which meant it had already been zeroed in by the enemy mortars. So "I veered immediately to the left and entered the second crater." After a few minutes, he "peered over the lip of the hole to determine the next avenue of advance. A small hole lay to the left about 20 yards away but I could see the helmets of other men already there. To my direct front was a large crater, and although it appeared about 50 yards away, an inordinately long distance, I decided to run for it."[108]

Another rule was that you never, ever repeated your movements. If you went right last time around a rock, go left next time. If you paused last time, don't wait this time, advised Howard McLaughlin.[109] Likewise, never pop your head up to look around more than once in the same place. Snipers were everywhere, and they searched for such behavioral predictability. Even when in their "own" territory, said Bertrand Yaffe, wise Marines kept to the rules and habitually took an hour to traverse less than a mile.[110]

Other tricks were practical in nature, allowing a Marine to get the best out of his equipment, regardless of what his training had taught him. Within a few days every Marine learned to undo the chinstrap on his helmet, despite having scrupulously tightened it during the landing. This counterintuitive act, which seemingly placed the wearer at greater risk of head injuries, actually helped prevent them. First, if you were shot in the head (as many were, by snipers), a fastened chinstrap hampered the corpsman from getting your helmet off. Second, it was better to let a concussion blast knock a helmet off and send it flying rather than let your head absorb the full impact—*and* have your neck snapped by the tight chinstrap for good measure.[111] When, for instance, Pfc. Fred Schribert was on watch at 0530 and a shell fell nearby, "my helmet took off and went about twenty-five yards. Lucky I didn't have it buttoned. That thing took off and I thought for sure my head was in it."[112] Hence the frequent and seemingly inexplicable sight of Marines running with one hand grasping a rifle while holding their helmets down with the other, their otherwise easily secured chinstraps flapping freely.

More important than anything else, though, was the ability of a new arrival to learn quickly and to adopt best practices by watching and listening to the "old men"—defined as Marines who had survived, miraculously, all of ten days on Iwo Jima, and who, as Alvin Josephy put it, "were bearded and hunched over. Their clothes were dirty and torn, their eyes watery and distant, their hair matted, their lips puffed and black; and their mouths were open as if they were having trouble breathing."[113] Perhaps so, but they were still alive.

Replacements, of which there were two types, were "cannon fodder, that was it," according to Frank Caldwell. "A lot of them didn't know what end the bullet came out of. We had to really get them up to speed [and did] the best we could."[114] Caldwell was not exaggerating: One replacement threw a dozen grenades at the Japanese, just as he had seen in the movies, before someone helpfully mentioned that he needed to pull the pin first.[115]

The first type of replacement, sometimes called "infantillery" because they were sent into whatever branch had the most urgent call, was drawn from clerks, stevedores, liaisons, cooks, and other rear-echelon units, who were often less than enthusiastic about their new assignment because they had seen and heard enough of the battle to want to avoid it.[116] Thus, when Captain Jack Downer was asked to raise fifty volunteers from a headquarters and service company, just ten men stepped forward. The other forty were chosen by lot.[117]

The second type, by far the more common, were young draftees who were intended as shipborne reserves to be fed into battle as required. Such was the Marines' insatiable need for manpower to offset losses that these received poor, almost useless training before being dispatched to the battlefield. One large draftee group at Iwo Jima had received just six weeks' training and another unit four.[118] This was perhaps enough time to break in their boots, but by any measure it was murderously inadequate preparation for combat. Line troops, in contrast, benefited from an extra six months of exercises to impart skills in weapons handling and field tactics.[119] The extra time and practice made a critical difference in surviving Iwo, as everyone but the replacements was aware. On March 8, when Marines were being ground up and minced into the ground at a prodigious rate, Major Robert Kreindler, a personnel officer of Third Division, commented sadly to a combat journalist that "so many of these casualty reports indicate what green troops we are having to use. They get killed the day they go into battle as brand-new replacements. Seventeen years old . . . and they are dead."[120] The only people worse off than replacement infantry were replacement litter-bearers, teenagers who on average enjoyed the shortest life expectancy of anyone on Iwo. Dr. James Vedder was once assigned sixteen of them: None knew anything about setting up perimeters or firing automatic weapons, but all had just turned eighteen and had surnames starting with B. For all the fine talk of valor, patriotism, and sacrifice, Vedder's assignees had been selected in a block and hurriedly sent to be killed. On Iwo, four litter-bearers were sent out to recover a wounded Marine, but typically only two or three came back. A replacement litter-bearer would embark on multiple runs each day until the inevitable happened.[121] Those sixteen would not last long.

Replacements of any kind were instantly recognizable by their appearance, among other things. Robert Donahoo, for instance, joined a company on his first day ashore. A veteran described him as clean-shaven and wearing "fresh, immaculate clothing." Before he had even reached the front line or unhitched his rifle from his shoulder he was dead, killed in a rocket attack before two hours had passed.[122] Apart from a lack of whiskers, the instant giveaway—to friend and foe alike—of a replacement was his uniform. The smarter ones quickly realized that the Japanese took an especial interest in their clean dungarees. Bernard Dobbins saw one new, and clearly astute, guy remove his helmet, pour water and sand into it to make mud, and then rub it all over his face and clothes.[123]

Key to staying alive on Iwo was camouflage: Never stand out from the crowd, as that enterprising replacement demonstrated. On the island, it was a kind of sartorial race to the bottom, with junior officers leading the effort to blend in with the men. They sometimes succeeded only too well, exceeding the enlisted Marines in slovenliness, bedraggledness, and general dirtiness in order to avoid being targeted by snipers. The first things lieutenants and captains did was tear off their bars and other identifying insignia, ditch their carbines and .45 pistols for Garands, and ban anyone from saluting them.[124] Soon, the only way to distinguish an officer from an enlisted man on Iwo was by checking a small stenciled number and rank marker on his jacket.[125] Sergeants and corporals, too, faded into the background as best they could. As Colonel Thomas Wornham pointed out, "The Japanese were just sitting back, and anybody who looked as though he was giving an order, why they'd pick him off."[126] Officers and NCOs alike curtailed non-urgent visits to their foxholes and ordered radiomen and messengers to stay away after it was realized that the activity attracted Japanese fire.[127] Any orders that had to be given were, according to Ted Salisbury, "whispered."[128] The same necessity to avoid sticking out applied to others, of course. Because the Japanese actively targeted physicians, battalion surgeons always traveled between aid stations by shouldering stretchers and dressing as regular litter-bearers.[129] They would still be shot at, but at least not singled out.

Replacements were easily killed because they unwittingly broke every rule until they wised up. As they walked they naturally clustered together, said Guy Rowe, whereas standard procedure was to move in single file, each man anywhere from fifteen to forty-five feet from the other in order to mitigate the risk of a mortar killing them all at once.[130] When carrying a box of grenades or rations, replacements had not yet learned to heave it, as the more grizzled men did, onto whichever shoulder was facing known sniper territory. The heavy wooden box performed a satisfactory job of protecting one's head from a bullet, recalled George Gentile, once a replacement himself.[131]

Worse, they had no idea how to act when the firing started. After four officers and ninety-nine enlisted men arrived as reinforcements and came under fire on March 1, the subsequent report drily observed that "from their actions and movements it was apparent that they had not been in the front lines before." As rockets landed "and the more experienced Marines scattered for foxholes, the replacements stood around wondering at the commotion."[132] Frederick Karch remembered the time when he and several other veterans sixth-sensed an incoming shell and hit the deck even as a newly arrived officer, Captain Jules Blaustein, "was still standing up when the round landed. He was carrying his carbine across his chest, and a piece of shrapnel went through the carbine's stock, and left him holding two pieces, and the shell burst impact was such that it knocked him backwards and he fell into a shell hole." (Now inducted into the mysterious ways of combat, he soon got "on with the war.")[133]

Whenever a replacement, like Blaustein, was standing when he should have been prone, or crawling when he should have been running, it was known as being "out of phase," and one unpleasant experience was usually enough to shock anyone into synchronizing with everyone else.[134] As Pfc. Gentile confirmed, "The first time you heard that whine [of mortars], you didn't know enough to move [but] after that first time, boy, you hit the ground faster before the mortar did or else you were dead." Replacements "started to learn survival techniques real early," or they didn't survive, and so they quickly became alert to what their senses were telling them.[135] The silence that descended after a heavy firefight, for instance, was interpreted by beginners to mean the coast was clear, whereas, said one Marine, "most times it meant a patient, well dug in, and hidden enemy was waiting. Waiting for the right moment for them. This, of course, meant it was the wrong moment for you. Too many times, this wrong moment became the last moment for some."[136]

The good news, according to another, was "the infantryman's basic trade, staying alive, is either learned or not learned in one day on the lines."[137] Survival, however, was not simply a matter of picking up practical tips and tricks; it was just as much reliant upon a profound mental adjustment to the demented environment.

9. Understanding Hearts and Minds

Despite the risk, the astounding casualties, and the knowledge that they were liable to die at any moment, Marines kept going. There are any number of possible reasons for this doggedly irrational behavior. A sense of comradeship with others in the unit, love of country, a desire to test one's mettle, of course, but on Iwo the grinding, lengthy nature of the battle argues against any of these as a primary cause. A more profitable avenue to explore is Marines' conquest of fear and their related discovery that, notwithstanding its hellish, thrilling, or grotesque aspects, war is best treated as a job, one that needs to get done to get home. Once a Marine grasped that war is work—unpleasant, unfair, and unwelcome work, but work nonetheless—he could begin to adapt, rather than succumb, to Iwo's idiosyncratic battlefield conditions and accept its necessarily harsh realities.

Everyone was always scared on Iwo, but fear subsisted for the most part as a constant, cumulative, corrosive feeling that bred a "bad memory, inability to concentrate, a demanding appetite for liquor, a short temper, a body that tires quickly, a weary, soul-deep resignation." Men learned to tamp it down and could outwardly appear calm, controlled, and mentally alert—yet the unceasing, low-grade sense of fear chewed "into your body and into your mind like a cancer beyond cure," as one Marine put it.[1]

There was no shame on Iwo at being scared. Indeed, as Francis Cockrel wrote, "It was a familiar, almost a friendly topic; it was the stuff guys bragged about to each other—how full of it they were, this time or that."[2] Everyone knew that a breakdown could happen to anyone. On Iwo, it was a "constant inner battle," said a Marine who had fought at Tarawa, Saipan, and Tinian, "to maintain some semblance of sanity, clarity of mind, and power of speech. Everyone tells me they felt as I did."[3]

But when fear finally hit full on, there was no mistaking it. Left beyond the lines and believing that he had been forgotten about, Allen Matthews "shivered violently and the shivering was different from anything I had ever experienced at night for I shook not only with the muscles in my legs and arms and fingers and neck but I trembled violently internally, too, and my stomach at the base of my ribs felt as if it were suffering from a great tic; it was caught first in a mighty hand which squeezed so violently that my breath caught and then the spasms eased off gradually, only to clutch me angrily again."[4]

The first time a soldier experienced this type of deep fear, he tended to freeze. There were several ways in which a soldier could break the paralysis. First, he could relax and then will himself into action. At one point, Jay Rebstock suddenly stopped and became unbearably thirsty. "Scared shitless," he "could not move, and I drank almost an entire canteen of water, and only then did my legs move forward."[5] To prevent freezing in the first place, when he detected the clammy claw of fear Bertrand Yaffe would repeat, "If I can just get though the next ten minutes, I'll be all right. Just a few minutes!" while Jim Craig confirmed every couple of seconds that "I'm still alive and okay."[6] On Iwo, as at Bunker Hill and Gettysburg, stopping meant death.

Alternately, a paralyzed man could be chivvied or embarrassed into action. When Gerald Averill found a sergeant prostrate in the sand, he managed to break fear's narcotic spell "with a little sweet talk, and some more with considerable sting to it."[7] This technique did not always work. When another sergeant visited Averill's foxhole and confided that he was liable to crack, he tried to console the man by telling him he "must do his duty," but the effect was only temporary. The ruined sergeant was evacuated two days later.[8]

Or third, he could think of home and his earnest desire to return to it. Matthews recovered his mental footing only after he "thought of my family and that was painful. I tried to put the thought aside but could not and they were with me as clearly as if they sat there in the flesh. I knew then more keenly than I'd ever felt before that I did not want to die."[9]

As their forebears had similarly discovered in 1775 and 1863, the best way to keep fear in its box was to keep yourself engaged in your immediate task. William Doran advised that when "you're so busy, and things are happening so fast, you're disconnected from the fear."[10] For Woody Williams, "I had a job to do, and I suppose I got so wrapped up in it I didn't have time to think."[11] Charles Chandler, a corpsman, controlled his nerves by "detach[ing] myself and focus[ing] on what I was doing and then when I was through with that something else would come up and I would pass on to that. Later you start thinking about it, but at the time you don't have the luxury of doing that."[12] Conversely, Francis Cockrel's worst moments on Iwo came when "I had to lie still for a time, and shells were landing not very far off. I had time to think then: 'Maybe the next one will come here.'" But he managed to fight off mounting apprehensions by occupying his mind trying to work out how to storm a nearby pillbox. Thinking through the problem, Cockrel said, ate up the "time to think about what might happen to you. When known risk is involved, you balance it against the . . . importance of the pillbox; but you don't paw it around with your emotions."[13]

It was best to focus solely on what needed to be done, not on what might happen. Thanks to his training, Wayne Bellamy already knew what was required to achieve his unit's objectives for the day, so he just "automatically" went ahead with his task.[14] It was often easier, or rather simpler, than even that. "Whatever they wanted you just did," remembered Domenick Tutalo, a replacement who was initially terrified but succeeding in controlling himself.[15] Likewise, Al Abbatiello was scared but "did what I was told to do, and I did it when I was told to do it."[16]

When everyone "did what they were told to do" or "did what they were trained to do," order arose from chaos, persuading scared waverers that events were under control, madness had not triumphed, and death not imminent. Fred Haynes observed that by mid-afternoon of the first day, for instance, even the beach landing zone had slowly begun to transform into a sane place. Marines "were adapting, finding ways to put together fire teams, taking care of the wounded and dead. . . . In general, we were sorting ourselves out and getting on with the business at hand. Somehow, amid the mayhem, little pockets of order and purpose emerged."[17]

Indeed, the key to taming fear, the solution to achieving victory, was to realize, individually and collectively, that fighting is a job. To keep your balance you cannot cast your mind back and wonder why you volunteered, complain that others get to stay at home, or question whether you should have left your family. "You see, you can't live in that world, at home," explained Joseph Kropf. "Don't ever live in that world. You've got to live in the world of 'This is my job.'"[18] A soldier should never confuse war with "heroics and dramatics, of dash and spectacle," advised Francis Cockrel. While there are "periods of urgency, certainly, demanding the right decision, made instantly, and split-second timing and desperate effort," they are but parts of a whole "and the whole is no more or less than dangerous drudgery—mean, exhausting work at which men get shot and blown apart."[19]

The "work" had to be executed as efficiently and as effectively as possible to reduce casualties and shorten the time needed to conquer the island. As David Severance put it, "We knew that as soon as we covered all the real estate, they were gonna pull us out. It was just a matter of pushing, trying to get up to the north end."[20] Marines quickly adapted to the necessity of fighting a ruthless battle of annihilation against an equally ruthless enemy. In short order, they waged a war where no quarter was given, asked, or expected.

No act was ruled out of bounds so long as it brought the Marine Corps closer to victory. William Doran, for instance, was amused when a raw lieutenant rebuked him for fashioning dum-dum bullets for his .45 pistol. They were forbidden by the Geneva Conventions, he admonished. Doran, a veteran of several Pacific landings, promised the officer that "we'll have a little discussion about the Geneva Convention[s] and what's right and what's wrong in a war. Well, we never had that discussion."[21]

Emotions were fatally tangential to achievement of the objective.

Like many others, Patrick Caruso occasionally came eye to eye with a Japanese trying to kill him, and "you [would] freeze for a brief moment, then the adrenaline flows and you quickly try to get him before he gets you. This soon becomes instinctive."[22] When Joseph Kropf found a wounded Japanese soldier, his lieutenant directed him to execute the man. "So I had to bayonet him. And that's not a nice feeling. You know how you have to bayonet. It's cruel, and you see the blood gushing out, and you see the eyes. That's when you say, That could be me."

In these situations, Marines distinguished between the code of "kill or be killed," which was eminently rational, and "the lust to kill," which was a dangerous sign of mental turmoil.[23] The relative lack of primeval emotion or outright hate or bloodthirsty desire for revenge on Iwo is striking. Marines spoke instead of "numbing" themselves in order to perform their job of taking the island. Luther Crabtree was surprised to find that "I didn't have any anger throughout that entire battle; I was numb. As I look back on that, I think I was so well trained that I just did my job." (Crabtree's calmness is all the more remarkable considering that on February 26 he came across the corpse of his brother, shot in the head by a sniper.)[24] Within only a few days of landing, Charles Lindberg discovered that "I didn't have any feelings. You'd burn them because they'd do it to us. . . . I was numb; just doing my job."[25] Howard Baxter, similarly, thought that the best way of staying alive was to "shut down your emotional system," quash any feelings you might have, and "get the job done."[26]

American behavior on Iwo, among other places, has nevertheless been attributed to individual and institutional racism against the Japanese: The Pacific enemy was treated far more barbarically than his Atlantic counterpart, because Germans (and Italians) were white and the Japanese were not.[27] Certainly, there was endemic and casual racism among American troops and society (particularly toward blacks), but one could say the same of virtually any country or nation at the time, at least by modern standards, and the American version of racism, despite its noxiousness, was a far cry from the annihilationist style practiced elsewhere. In any case, that one race or another was intellectually, physically, and aesthetically superior to others was an evident and universal "truth" taken for granted before 1945 among even the most enlightened citizens of the world. It was a vestige of the "scientific" racism of the nineteenth and early twentieth centuries, and we should not be surprised to find it subsisting among members of the United States Marine Corps. Wartime propaganda depicting the Japanese as termites, bats, rats, monkeys, and the like can be dismissed as just that; how seriously it was taken is open to question.

The free use of flamethrowers, the implacable liquidation of Japanese forces, the mass machine-gunnings, the burial of live men in caves—the exterminationist acts so frequently invoked to demonstrate that Pacific combat was allegedly motivated by a racist urge to rid the world of the Nipponese pestilence—were in fact arguably practical, or instrumental, reactions to the particular conditions pertaining on Iwo Jima. Flamethrowers were used because they were found to work spectacularly well, not because the Japanese were ideologically regarded as a lower race than the white Germans.

Indeed, in the 1930s, American military analysts had not treated the Imperial Japanese Army (IJA) as an "alien" menace whose personnel existed outside the conventional laws of war and thus could be exterminated like vermin. They instead assumed that the IJA was part of a shared, "civilized" military culture and so naturally dissected its capabilities along the same lines as they did its German and Italian equivalents. By those conventional measures, the IJA fell particularly short. It possessed few tanks, aircraft, artillery pieces, and heavy machine guns—then considered the weapons of the future—and lacked any discernible skill in combined air-sea-land operations—then considered the epitome of martial progress. It was a generation, if not more, behind and something of a joke force, much as the Habsburg Austrian army had existed in the nineteenth century only to be beaten.[28] Even Japan's soldiers were ridiculed as being better suited to some medieval peasant army. In the U.S. armed forces, beards were forbidden and shaving compulsory; boots were polished; uniforms starched. In the peacetime IJA, in contrast, except when they donned dress uniforms for ceremonial duties, men and officers alike went unshaven for days, had dull buttons, dirty boots, ill-fitting trousers, and patched elbows.[29] Any number of military analysts confused their relaxed slovenliness with lack of discipline and absence of ability.[30]

Where the IJA crucially erred, all agreed, was in relying so heavily on infantry, the stodgy combat arm effortlessly overshadowed by the silvery glamour of air forces and the globe-spanning might of navies. It was assumed that Japan, if it came to war, would quickly collapse once the Marines took the outlying Pacific islands and the U.S. Navy sunk its fleet. Any lingering apprehensions of the Japanese army were laid to rest in 1939 at the battle of Nomonhan (sometimes known as Khalkhin Gol).

Unlike Britain, the United States, France, and Germany, which had advanced along a steep learning curve on the Western Front between 1914 and 1918, Japan had never fought a first-rank power, only Tsarist Russia and Imperial China. At Nomonhan, that lack of experience became obvious when the IJA was crushed by the Soviet army, itself a force accorded little credit by Western military experts. Put bluntly, regarding Japan's performance at Nomonhan, it is difficult to think of a battle more incompetently fought, of operations more disastrously executed, of plans more obtusely pursued, of armies more ineptly commanded. Japanese generals displayed, for instance, a bizarre obsession with protecting their regimental colors, a necessity in the nineteenth century to ensure unit cohesion and coordination but an affectation in an era of camouflage, radio communication, and integrated armored, air, artillery, and logistics arms.[31] Worryingly, it was not as if Nomonhan was a fluke, a onetime failure by an otherwise sterling force. Throughout Japan's campaigns in China during the 1930s, foreign observers reported that despite winning in the end the IJA consistently struggled against its much weaker opponent.[32]

Informing many of these analyses, of course, was an implicit assumption that an Asian army could not possibly compete with a white Western one. One observer reassured readers that "Japanese officers are technically less sound than ours" and that while they possessed "magnificent 'nerve' and fighting ardor," there was little to worry about. After all, a Japanese's "weakness consists of his failing to remain master of combat," for "his courage and conception of honor are far more in-spired by . . . passion than by a real and realistic understanding of the necessities of the craft of arms." American and European officers, in contrast, were rational, masculine, and disciplined—making them more than a match, if it came down to it, for any Japanese soldier, whose "feminine and emotional quality" typically made them "lose control of their nerves."[33] One should not forget either the curious image many Americans had of the Japanese physique before the war. Bucktoothed, compact, and bespectacled—on top of being feminine and emotional—the Imperial Japanese Army simply was impossible to take seriously.

To reiterate, despite these patronizing remarks (typical of the time as regards foreigners of various creeds and hues), the role that outright rac-ism played in American and European evaluations of the IJA was never-theless minor. The dismissal of Japanese capabilities before the war was partly due to a more prosaic combination of a lack of analysts trained in Japanese—before 1941 there were at most a dozen U.S. Army and Navy intelligence officers capable of making informed evaluations—as well as to Tokyo's habitual secrecy and its impressively effective security police.[34] But the real reason Japan was judged, disastrously, not to be a potentially formidable antagonist in the Pacific is that in order to fill the gaps in their knowledge, American analysts had erred in assessing Japan on the basis of their *own* yardsticks of progress—a terrible blunder when Japan had already shed its once-shared military culture.

To Americans, Japan's unmodern reliance on infantry was *ipso facto* a deplorable weakness, but to the Japanese, it was a strength. Mass-producing modern armaments required a powerful industrial economy, which they lacked, whereas men would be trained along the mystical lines of such martial values as *bushidō*—the warrior's code emphasizing loyalty, duty, sacrifice, courage, and strength—to multiply their strik-ing force, aggression, and speed. If the entire Japanese economy could produce just 47,900 motor vehicles of all classes in 1941—its peak—and the United States that same year manufactured 3.5 million cars, well, then, the Japanese could excel in lightning-fast surprise infantry attacks executed at night with a suicidally "offensive spirit." The Americans might enjoy overwhelming logistical superiority, matchless heavy weaponry, and advanced technology, but the IJA played to its strengths by marching on a bowl of rice a day, traveling with nothing more burdensome than light machine guns, grenades, and portable mortars, and being second to none in unconventional hand-to-hand combat.[35]

Japanese propaganda trumpeted the superiority of the spiritual approach to warfare. Soldiers and the civilian population alike were taught that *bushidō* was an ancient tradition unique to Nippon, as was worship of the emperor and the glory of self-sacrifice for the greater good of the nation. But really none of this was true: *Bushidō* dated from the seventeenth century—hardly "ancient"—and in most respects was almost indistinguishable from traditional Western, even universal, military or chivalric ideals. In any case, the code had long been in abeyance and only in the mid-1920s was it revived, debased, and radicalized for nationalist and imperialist purposes. Conscripts and officers were brainwashed through harsh discipline and rigorous indoctrination into believing that surrender was disgraceful, that lesser breeds must be brutalized, and that fighting to the death was idyllic.

The sea change in cultural attitudes manifested itself most forcefully in the treatment of prisoners of war. In contrast to their despicable behavior in World War II, before the 1930s Japanese soldiers had treated the prisoners they had taken well. Indeed, they used to themselves surrender with nary a complaint, yet by the end of that decade we find nothing but adulation for a Major Kuga Nobura, who had been taken by the Chinese at Shanghai after being wounded. When he was released from captivity, he immediately returned to the battlefield site of his ignominious and unwilling surrender and committed suicide to erase the shame. For this act, all seven Japanese movie companies produced stirring films about his death.[36]

Just as Americans underestimated (or perhaps, "misestimated") Japanese skills before the war, in the months following the surprise walloping at Pearl Harbor in December 1941 they swung wildly to the opposite extreme as they watched a mere eleven Japanese divisions conquer Southeast Asia. Hong Kong, Malaya, Singapore, the Philippines, the Dutch East Indies, and Burma—all were subdued by their invincible armies. Allied troops, repeatedly surprised and outflanked by the nimble Japanese, conjured up for the public a pessimistic image of the enemy as fanatical "supermen" brilliantly adept at jungle and island warfare—and seemingly unstoppable, thanks to the very same intangible and "ancient" martial qualities once considered quaintly premodern.[37] Thankfully, the reverses at Guadalcanal and New Guinea by the start of 1943 tempered this depressing reaction, and a more realistic evaluation of the enemy ensued.

Analysts began taking a harder and closer look at the Imperial Army's inflated reputation for invincibility. As a February 1943 intelligence report reminded readers, "With more than a year of war behind us and with experience gained in fighting . . . we can begin to see how much we have misunderstood the [Japanese]."[38]

Before the war, the Japanese had been dismissed; after Pearl Harbor, feared. Now, arrogance and terror were replaced by a practical determination to understand this savage and curious foe properly. The acquisition of solid intelligence on IJA doctrine, tactics, and soldiers thus became of prime concern. Rather fortunately, as the Americans assaulted the outer rim of Japan's empire in 1943 they stumbled upon troves of material. Since every Marine and soldier was instructed to bring in any letter, diary, map, or order they found during the fighting (all of which was passed diligently to intelligence specialists), more than 350,000 documents would fall into American hands by the end of the war. Much of the material was invaluable, a result of Japanese High Command's blithe belief that the Americans still lacked translators combined with the IJA's obsession with recording everything in writing and officers' oddly optimistic reluctance to empty their pockets of sensitive memoranda before embarking on suicidal banzai missions.[39]

Over the course of 1943 and 1944, thanks to regular bulletins put out by various intelligence bodies summarizing the latest Japanese techniques and a wholesale reorientation of the training system to take account of these findings, American troops became remarkably familiar with Japanese tactics, habits, and tricks. It is important to remember that this transformation was happening at precisely the same time as "race war" rhetoric was heating up among the American public as once-classified news of Japanese atrocities (such as the execution of captured Doolittle Raid fliers, the Bataan Death March, and the famous photograph of an Australian, Leonard Siffleet, being beheaded by a Japanese officer) was released by Allied governments.[40] While the latter resulted in a lot of chest-puffing at home about mercilessly terminating the Japanese, soldiers—the ones who had actually been in combat—ignored all the brave talk in favor of practical, concrete, and efficient methods of killing the enemy.

Once so feared, Japanese jungle-warfare tactics, for instance, were revealed as being essentially the same as those printed in the U.S. Army's basic manual on the subject. Another crucial finding was that Japanese officers were instilled with a credo of blind obedience, remained inflexible, lacked initiative, and consistently underrated their American opponents. If they were killed, sergeants and corporals were reluctant to assume command, and their units tended to collapse into an unthinking mass defaulting to an all-out banzai charge to exhibit the appropriate degree of self-sacrificing spiritual firmness. The enemy, in other words, was discovered to be *predictable,* the Achilles heel of any armed force.[41]

In response, the Americans adapted their tactics to counter those of the Japanese. The purpose of many small-scale infiltration attacks, it was discovered, was actually to send individuals to probe the strength and location of American defenses before the main force attacked en masse. Whereas the Americans had been employing the traditional method of establishing isolated lookout posts far ahead to sound the alarm, these were always bypassed by the infiltrators. So the practice was soon abandoned in favor of a perimeter line of mutually supporting foxholes, which was much more resistant to both infiltration and banzai attacks (as the Marines on Iwo Jima would gratefully attest). Once tied-in foxholes became the norm, Japanese charges became, as a late 1944 intelligence report commented, "determined but unoriginal" and hence defeatable.[42]

American offensive tactics also evolved to offset the Japanese expertise in siting their defensive entrenchments to best exploit the terrain. Soldiers were actively encouraged to try new tactics and report the results.[43] As data accumulated, it would become standard practice to employ .30-caliber light machine guns for suppressive fire at a distance and to use BARs, once reserved as a support weapon for riflemen, as anti-personnel weapons in their own right. These reforms were originally not top-down instructions outlined in manuals but on-the-ground findings discovered through trial and error by ordinary enlisted men and young officers that were disseminated *because they worked.*

Another example, soon to be of great importance on Iwo, stemmed from soldiers encountering cave defenses at Biak in May/June 1944. Aerial attacks against these fortified rocks were of little avail, and they were situated in places that were hard for naval gunfire to hit. Troops began to clear them out by pouring gasoline into the entrances and igniting by grenade. Pacific-wide intelligence bulletins noted the method's success and suggested increasing the use of flamethrowers in subsequent island battles.[44]

These lessons translated into concrete changes in weaponry. In July 1942, for instance, a regular Marine division had no portable flamethrowers, but by May 1944, no fewer than 243 were standard issue (plus several terrifying flamethrower tanks). At Iwo Jima, a battalion commander would report that "the portable flame thrower was the one indispensable infantry weapon." In the same period, the number of BARs rose from 513 to 853 and rose from there almost every month until the end of the war. Reflecting the Japanese propensity for hand-to-hand combat, shotguns—which served admirably as close-range weapons—were also distributed; their number accordingly increased from zero to 306.[45]

It seems evident, then, that the use of flamethrowers was not predetermined by racial animosity but was instead a situational, instrumental response to the facts on the ground. Consider that flamethrowers, until very late in the war, had been regarded as, at best, marginal weapons. First used against the French by the Germans in 1915, they were but rarely employed afterward, and even then whatever limited success they enjoyed was psychological rather than practical. Firing a brief burst of flame (an igniter lit a mixture of light and heavy fuels, propelled by nitrogen) up to just twenty yards—a suicidal distance from the enemy line for any lone attacker—they were sometimes given to condemned criminals to operate. In 1921, General Amos Fries, the head of the U.S. Chemical Warfare Service, the very man charged with developing the weapon, publicly disparaged flamethrowers as virtually useless.

Only in 1940, when it was reported that German and Italian flamethrowers had been used, did the United States attempt to develop a one-man portable version. In mid-1944, following several unremarkable models, the M2-2 Portable Flame Thrower was belatedly approved. The two factors that rendered it a viable weapon that would quickly be adopted for Pacific use were its new type of fuel and the development of tactical doctrine governing its use.

The earlier, low-viscosity mixture of heavy and light fuels had produced a "bushy" billowing blast of flame accompanied by heavy black smoke—which was fine for the Army, interested as it was in burning away jungle vegetation from defensive emplacements and using the smoke to provide good cover for the follow-up attack. The Marines, however, had different needs. They had found that the prevailing mixture may have provided a roaring blaze outside of a concrete bunker but that it did not kill its occupants. Their preferred method to deal with the problem was to squirt the lit fuel as a stream inside a bunker's narrow openings from longer range.

Fastening on a new technique in which adding a substance dubbed napalm ("na" from aluminum napthenate and "palm" from the coconut fatty acids used to make it) thickened the fuel mixture, the Marines demanded almost three times as much napalm added to their flamethrowers as did the Army in order to create the desired stream effect at up to forty yards with relatively little smoke. It was this new, high-viscosity combination of gasoline, diesel fuel, and napalm that they took to Iwo.

At the same time, Marines were issued new instructions for the tactical employment of flamethrowers to maximize their effectiveness against Japanese combatants. In mid-December 1944, the Marines conceived specialist assault platoons of about twenty men trained in the use and maintenance of flamethrowers, demolitions, and rocket launchers. They would operate in conjunction with and under the protection of riflemen. Less than two months later on Iwo, as we shall see, these assault platoons would prove deadly against their adversaries.[46]

The new technology interacted dynamically with the improved methods, organizational changes, and the fresh insights into Japanese thinking to produce lethally effective tactical countermeasures and an *ahumanized* attitude toward their use. On Iwo Jima Americans approached their task with all the emotional investment of exterminators hired to kill some termites, or as a creditor views a debtor—as red numbers on a spreadsheet that need tidying up.[47] There was, after all, no existential threat to the continental United States by the Japanese Empire, nor was there significant historical enmity between the two countries, nor was there the ideological-racial witches' brew characteristic of the Eastern Front fighting between the Nazis and the Soviets.[48] Instead, beating the Japanese on Iwo was a job that just needed doing, and they used whatever tools worked most satisfactorily. By the end, the task of slaughtering Japanese was known unemotionally as "processing," as in a meat factory, and relied implicitly on machinery, engineers, and chemical products for its success.[49]

Finding the men who could do that job proved simple enough, for the men of the Marines of 1945 were not the same as those who had served earlier. Before the outbreak of war, the Marines had been highly selective, so selective that in 1939, 1940, and 1941 the Corps had accepted just 38,080 volunteers from 205,000 first-time applications—a percentage approaching that of an Ivy League college. Many of the successful inductees, most from poor rural or tough urban backgrounds, had signed up for financial reasons ($21 per month was a lot for a youth otherwise relegated to pumping gas or working in the mines), for adventure, for an escape from Depression-era unemployment, for evading the law after some indiscretions. That all changed on December 7, 1941—Pearl Harbor. What would become known as the "High School Class of '42" rushed to join the colors. Hordes of seniors, wrathful at Japanese perfidy and filled with righteous idealism, quit school and rushed to the recruitment office. According to Roger Doskocill, "we became Marines by choice, and nobody was going to mess around with us or our country." Bearing him out are the numbers: In November

1941, the month before Pearl Harbor, the Marines had inducted 1,978 men; in December 1941, that figure soared to 10,224; and in January 1942 alone, 22,686 men volunteered to fight.

Within a couple of years, a very large proportion of them would be dead or crippled, the result of unexpectedly heavy American losses. By the end of 1942, the Marine Corps was having trouble meeting its recruitment goals using increasingly less gung-ho volunteers. After lowering its physical and moral standards that April to make up numbers, it would soon come to rely on a third type of Marine recruit to fill the ranks. In January 1943, the government eradicated purely volunteer enlistments in one's chosen military service. Henceforth, Selective Service would assign draftees to whichever arm most urgently required manpower. There was one exception—the Marine Corps, which forcefully argued for its traditionally exclusive role—in the sense that a man who received his draft notification could opt to "prefer" the Corps over the Navy and the Army. If there was room in the quota and he passed the qualification procedures, he would become a Marine "enlistee" rather than a conscript. Additional numbers—desperately needed for the increasingly bloody Pacific campaigns—were acquired by targeting seventeen-year-olds (Selective Service covered only men aged 18–36), who would sign up and be activated for duty on their next birthdays. The Corps also, not entirely enthusiastically, took its first women and blacks after realizing that they could fill rear-area and support positions, thereby releasing young white males for frontline combat duty.[50]

Marines of the 1943–45 period, therefore, were not career Marines, nor were they naive—the bloom had come off that rose at Tarawa, Saipan, and Peleliu—let alone idealistic, though they were natively patriotic. A vivid example of their apathy at the time, as opposed to idealized postwar recollections, can be drawn from their knowledge of the Four Freedoms. In the January 1941 State of the Union address intended to serve as a rallying cry for public support of a possible, or likely, war against Germany and Japan, President Roosevelt had listed the "four freedoms" that everyone, everywhere ought to enjoy. These were Freedom of Speech, Freedom of Worship, Freedom from Want, and Freedom from Fear. After Pearl Harbor, the Four Freedoms became increasingly central to the war effort against fascism and imperialism. In February and March 1943, the most popular artist in the country, Norman Rockwell, contributed four paintings to the *Saturday Evening Post*, which were accompanied by widely publicized essays explaining their importance and meaning, while the Postal Service issued a special one-cent stamp. Yet in July 1943 a substantial survey of enlisted men found that *nearly half* had never heard of the Four Freedoms, that the same proportion had heard of them but could name only one or perhaps two (almost certainly the freedoms of speech and of worship, which were familiar from, and perhaps confused with, those enumerated in the Bill of Rights), and that just 13 percent could name at least three. More than 80 percent—four-fifths—of American soldiers, in other words, were unaware of, unclear on, or uninterested in what they were apparently fighting for midway through the war. That situation was unlikely to change: Two-thirds of the soldiers felt that even understanding what America's war aims were was of "medium, low, or no importance" and just 4 percent said that they would "like to know more about" the reasons "why we are fighting the war." Rather, as the researchers concluded, they "were satisfied to regard the war as an unavoidable fact—a fact because it was presented to them as fait accompli, and unavoidable because their love of country required that foreign aggression [e.g., at Pearl Harbor] be opposed."[51]

In the Pacific in 1945, few cared about a grand mission to win the war for democracy. They just wanted to do the job they had been handed as quickly as possible so they could go home. While they were young, highly aggressive, justly proud of the Corps, and aware of their elite status as shock troops, no air of romance suffused their task. On Iwo, there was no place for such inefficient martial virtues as valor or honor, marksmanship or sportsmanship. Those quaint relics had been left behind long ago at Bunker Hill and Gettysburg. These Marines were products of a machine age and trained specifically for industrialized slaughter.

The Japanese, for their part, only obliged the foe by their stubborn adherence to spiritual values as the key to overcoming doctrinal and material deficiencies. The mystical dominated the logistical at every stage. On the small-unit tactical level, *bushidō* could admittedly bring victory against unprepared enemies but not against properly trained and lavishly equipped forces. Individual heroics could achieve only so much (or so little) against an industrialized army, and it is sobering to be reminded that in 1945 alone the United States manufactured sixty-one times as much organic high explosive as Japan did even as (the late) First Lieutenant Sadakaji was still being lauded as a national hero for attacking a tank with a sword at Nomonhan.[52]

By hook or by crook, the Japanese were destined to lose at Iwo Jima. Like a drowning man cursing the sea, they could only rage impotently against the tremendous might of steel and iron, brass and oil, that pressed upon them as they shed their blood. Marines, meanwhile, sustained heavy casualties but whatever they lost numerically in combat effectiveness they more than made up for in improving their mission effectiveness—the ability to execute their tasks and objectives. The reason was that every hour, every day, they spent on Iwo permitted them to enhance their techniques and hone their skills at liquidation. The cost in blood was accordingly high, but despite initial impressions, all was not hopeless and crazy on Iwo: There were ways, it seems, to make Pandemonium more bearable, even beatable.

10. The Method in the Madness

In the lead-up to Iwo Jima, the Marines benefited immensely from sustained intelligence analysis of Japanese tactics, tics, procedures, and routines while avidly pursuing a course of military adaptation in response to their combat experience. As a result, the Corps had successfully evolved to suit the peculiar realities of the Pacific theater, and adversaries once regarded as fierce and strange had ceased to be either—even if they remained formidable and dangerous.

One manifestation of this trend was the development of a new structure of fire team–based rifle squads (each four-man fire team, led by a corporal, was centered on a BAR and supported by two riflemen). They moved in a diamond formation, with the corporal in front, the

BARman and a rifleman five yards behind, and the other rifleman five yards in the rear. There were three fire teams to a squad—twelve men plus a sergeant to command—and a squad in turn advanced in a triangular shape: two fire teams abreast in the front with the third centered in the rear to provide cover. Three squads comprised a platoon of about forty, which was led by a lieutenant. A basic company was made up of three platoons, which again formed into a triangle covering an area of 150 yards. Added in were special-weapons platoons, squads, and teams, all armed with a selection of heavy and light machine guns, mortars, bazookas, explosives, and flamethrowers.[1]

Unlike the traditional line-and-column formations of previous eras, which required precise coordination and experienced command to avoid entropy, the "rule of three" structure was designed for maximum dispersion, flexibility, and adaptability combined with heavy firepower on call. Whereas his forebears at Bunker Hill and Gettysburg had relied on direct sight and close proximity to comrades to maintain cohesion, on Iwo Jima Pfc. Joe Simms kept his eye on only one man, his squad leader, as a "reference point." His squad was usually spread out about thirty-five yards apart and up to twenty yards deep. "Some were down while others were up and running," and Simms "rarely saw all the other twelve men at the same time."[2] Had a Civil War soldier respawned on a battlefield of World War II, he would have been discomfited by its emptiness.

Nor was there any pretense to maintain strict order in combat to preserve forward momentum. When men were told to move out, said Pfc. Don Traub, you were expected to "run forward like hell in a zigzag pattern, then hit the deck while rolling away from the spot where you landed and find some sort of cover."[3] When a platoon as a whole advanced, each Marine "moved from hole to hole, rock to rock," taking turns to cover and be covered by his mates as he rushed forward in a tactic known as "snoopin' and poopin'."[4]

A critical development was the emphasis on cross-training; that is, a regular Marine rifleman was taught how to operate a broad variety of weapons and so, if necessity called, could serve in any capacity.[5] In combat, Marines switched jobs as casually as required. "Anybody who was close, that's who did the shooting [of the light machine gun] and then got out of the way," said Bernard Dobbins. He himself was a machine gunner, but he fetched ammunition, threw grenades, brought water, took point, or picked up a rifle without hesitation.[6] Weapons nonspecialization and a lack of territoriality allowed units to re-form and divide freely to recover from losses and absorb fresh arrivals. Following heavy casualties, the carcass of Dean Voight's platoon, for instance, was left with a mixture of machine gunners and raw replacements but was easily regenerated by an influx of mortar men to form a regular, capable unit.[7]

Marine vertical hierarchies were as fluid as their horizontal organization. If a platoon or squad leader was disabled, said Alfred Stone, everyone knew that "the next man in rank assumes leadership of the unit."[8] The burden of command was shouldered willingly, if with a degree of apprehension. When Dobbins was bumped to squad leader, he confided to his sergeant that he didn't know what to do. Never fear, came the helpful reply, "your first mistake will be your last." There would always be someone to take your place.[9]

For Dave Davenport such instant promotions were key to units remaining organized, self-sufficient, and on the move. "The attack goes on. The [original] plan is carried out or a new plan worked out," he explained. "The fallen leaders are replaced by a natural move up. When Ludvick was killed I was elevated to squad leader. Mueller and Carson became squad leaders the same way. If we fall someone will replace us."[10]

Hence the astonishing ability of American squads, platoons, and companies to continue functioning and fighting despite Iwo's staggering casualty rates. On Iwo, it was common to see junior lieutenants or sergeants in charge of companies and privates overseeing platoons and squads. Thus, Robert Maiden's company went through seven commanders, two of them NCOs.[11] One platoon in the 28th Marines remained viable even after its leadership changed no fewer than eleven times. (Its final commander was Private Dale Cassell, who lasted for three days before being killed on March 14, D+23.)[12]

The Japanese, in contrast, had emphasized officer-led command,

and it was often remarked that once one of their lieutenants or captains was incapacitated his unit collapsed. According to Dave Davenport, the men "milled around in total confusion if they were not in holes. They didn't have instant leadership come to the front. They didn't seem to have any contingency plan. No alternatives were put into effect by anyone. Their inability to adapt and adjust was woeful." So the Marine response was to target the officers. Rather like at Bunker Hill against the British, the Americans cried, "Pick off the leaders. . . . Drop that Nip waving his sword or his arms."[13]

On Iwo itself, the Marines modified equipment, exploited their unit structures, conceived new methods, and finessed existing techniques to enhance performance and to counter unexpected Japanese behavior. During the fighting itself, senior commanders demanded none of these ad hoc improvements, which were instead passed from man to man, squad to squad, by hearsay, observation, and experience at the ground level.

There were three types of self-guided military improvements. First, material changes. For instance, in Europe, whereas American tanks had to contend with powerful antitank guns, *Panzerfausts,* and heavy Tiger tanks, in the Pacific the Japanese relied on direct human attacks using satchel charges, magnetic mines, regular mines, and in many cases, explosives strapped directly to soldiers' bodies. Thus in the Pacific the Sherman tanks were adequate protection against individual Japanese attacks once some singular field modifications were added.[14]

A typical Japanese attack would involve one man blinding the tank with smoke grenades, the next forcing the crew to close the hatches by throwing fragmentation grenades, a third fixing a mine on a track to immobilize it, and a fourth to place a charge on the hull or turret to blow it apart. To "mod" the Shermans, therefore, sandbags were layered over engine covers to dull the explosions. Spare track blocks were wrapped around the turret side armor for the same reason. Sometimes, tankers welded long nails, pointed end up, to turrets and hatches to impale suicidal Japanese who insisted on holding on to their charges. More effective than nails were "birdcages," two-inch-high domes of heavy-duty wire mesh spanning the turret and hull hatches that prevented the enemy from placing explosives directly on top. Each side of a tank was protected by a thick curtain consisting of wooden planks that left four inches of open space between it and the metal skin. Into the void, the crews sometimes poured a secondary wall of reinforced concrete. The concrete diffused explosions; the wood defeated magnetic mines. As an additional measure, as tanks advanced they were surrounded by a screen of riflemen whose job it was to spot hidden threats and to kill suicide runners.[15]

Taken together, these countermeasures and field modifications drastically reduced tank losses in everyday combat.[16] Seaman First Class Koizumi Tadayoshi was a member of an attack team and later recorded his surprise that he was not able to destroy any tanks. After creeping behind enemy lines, for instance, he watched a Sherman for a time before realizing that there was simply no way to get to it. He found a tree branch and eventually pushed a mine toward one of its tracks but was spotted and shot at by the riflemen. They missed, but as he ran away the tank fired its flamethrower (another expedient improvement created by engineers, who added compressed-air cylinders to propel a stream of napalm over a hundred yards) and burned his legs.[17] His team was finished, as was he, but the tank remained as dangerous as ever. Indeed, on March 9 (D+18), when Saturo Omagari and a few others sliced open their own dead, stuffed their uniforms with the intestines they'd cut out, and then played dead intending to destroy a Sherman, they managed to attack "the tanks, but it was without avail."[18]

11. The Japanese Defensive System

On Iwo, much to their surprise, Marines were confronted by the deep, thick defensive system established by Kuribayashi in the final frantic months before they landed. Their planners had not adequately anticipated its scale. The lesson: If the Americans learned from experience and adapted to changing battlefield conditions, then so too did the Japanese, though at a slower pace. By Iwo they had shifted from an exclusively offensive orientation toward a defensive position designed to delay and frustrate the enemy with high casualties in the (vain) hopes of impeding a probable invasion of Japan.

In the early part of the war, Japanese anti-landing doctrine had directed commanders to destroy the enemy at the "water's edge"—the beach—when he was at his most vulnerable. A thin but potent strip of fortifications on the beach itself would decisively defeat enemy forces as they approached and attempted to disembark. When they landed on Tarawa in November 1943 during the Gilberts campaign, the Marines, as a result, were forced to contend with anti-personnel mines, antitank mines, concrete obstacles studded with iron rails, double-apron barbed-wire fencing, and a hearty coconut-log seawall, from behind which impervious gun emplacements made of reinforced concrete and coral sand blasted their tanks. By nightfall on the first day, twelve out of fourteen tanks had been knocked out, and the Marines were perched precariously on the beach. Had the Japanese vigorously counterattacked that night, when Marine commanders were tremulously reporting that the "issue remains in doubt," it is possible the landing would have been pushed back into the sea.[1]

By January/February 1944, when American forces landed in the Marshalls to conquer Roi-Namur and Eniwetok, Japanese defensive doctrine had not changed. The Marines, meanwhile, had learned to focus on heavier and more prolonged supporting naval gunfire to scour the beach fortifications, equipped themselves with armored vehicles and rocket craft, and were sending underwater demolition teams to reconnoiter beaches before the attack.[2]

In April of that year, Imperial General Headquarters in Tokyo issued a manual called *Explanation of the Combat Guidance for Garrison on Islands,* which continued to stipulate the increasingly discredited water's-edge strategy. Island defenders, headquarters staff insisted, were to fight and die on the beach.[3] When the Americans came to Saipan during the Marianas campaign in June/July 1944, however, the Japanese could not follow Tokyo's dictates because enemy submarines had prevented much of their defensive materiel from arriving. They had hardly any mines or obstacles, while concrete gun positions were unfinished, and there were dozens of artillery pieces left parked in the open awaiting emplacement when the Americans landed. The general in charge of the island was forced to ignore the manual's orders: He left just a third of his force to defend the beach and took the rest inland to prepare to counterattack. His forty-eight tanks were kept away from the landing zone and were poised to launch a major assault once the Americans broke past the waterline. In the end, the Japanese counterattacks were beaten back with heavy losses, and the island was taken, but the creation of a "mobile ground defense" located in the interior impressed a beleaguered Imperial Army staff with its ability to extract American blood while buying time.

A hastily revised manual, *Essentials of Island Defense,* that circulated in August 1944 stressed constant counterattacks supplemented by a series of resistance zones, delaying actions, and defense in depth to offset the advantage of the Americans' devastating naval gunnery. There would be no more efforts to mount a decisive engagement at the waterline during a landing. The new policy was dubbed *fukkaku*—an "endurance engagement" that would bleed the Americans white.[4] Over the coming battle at Peleliu between September and November 1944, Japanese commanders adopted and adapted the new manual's instructions. Following a failed counterattack, Colonel Kunio Nakagawa ended the practice of banzai attacks, instituted "passive infiltration" (defenders hid and attacked the Americans from the rear), and ordered his men to set up honeycombed, fortified positions in caves, ridges, hills, and tunnels.

It was at this point, as the Japanese had successfully transitioned from a beach-deployment doctrine to an inland-deployment one, that American strategists made a terrible error.[5] They had begun planning the Iwo Jima invasion in the summer of 1944, when Saipan-style "human wave" counterattacks on the first night and a "mobile ground defense" later on were au courant.

Had the landing occurred then, Iwo Jima would today be a lesser example of Pacific warfare—an easy victory. Thus, on April 6, 1944, General Hideyoshi Obata, the 31st Army commander, had inspected Iwo and determined that it required a then-recommended waterline defense. But on May 29 Kuribayashi arrived, when Japanese attention was shifting away from the water's edge. He stopped construction of beach defenses and started banking on a modish counterattack followed by defense in depth. But by February 1945, when the actual landing took place, Kuribayashi had updated his tactics, and a dangerous *fukkaku*-style defense instead awaited the Americans.

The United States, in short, had failed to keep up with their enemy. For this mistake, they can be forgiven: The virtually unknown Lieutenant General Tadamichi Kuribayashi was a starchy cavalryman with a solid combat record distinguished primarily by its conservatism. Unexpectedly handed command of Iwo Jima, he would in fact prove to be an innovative, imaginative foe, the one regarded after the war by his Marine antagonists as the most redoubtable and skilled of any Japanese general. Kuribayashi's risky decision to favor a variant of the *fukkaku* endurance engagement amply demonstrates the extent to which the Marines were tangling with a very canny unknown quantity. On Iwo, Kuribayashi created *Shukketsu-Jikyu* (or *Shukketsu and Jikyu Senjutsu—* "bloodletting and delay"), a passive-defense system based on interlinked fortifications inland designed to prolong the operation, reduce the will to fight, and impose maximum enemy casualties.[6]

Hence the Marines' surprise when they first landed on D-Day on Iwo and there was barely any resistance on the beach itself. The consensus among commanders was that Kuribayashi had, according to the journalist John Marquand, "clearly concluded to wait and take his punishment, to keep his men and weapons under cover, until our assault waves were on the beach. Then he would do his best to drive them off."[7] The consensus was wrong. Kuribayashi was all too pleased to let the assault waves land and *not* to drive them off.

What resistance there was had in fact been foisted upon Kuribayashi by his naval counterpart, who insisted on building gun emplacements and pillboxes there. Virtually all of these concrete extravagances were destroyed on the first day: twenty-three of twenty-four naval gun positions were knocked out before the first Marines even landed, as Kuribayashi had predicted, and the Marines overran every single pillbox, all 135 of them, within the first three hours. Nor, despite an intense effort to "button up" Marine positions before the expected banzai charges, were there organized counterattacks to speak of on the first few nights.[8] Very occasionally, one of his more zealous and desperate officers would disobey Kuribayashi's orders and mount a useless banzai charge, mostly for the sake of good form, but their rarity demonstrates only the general's commitment to passive defense. Indeed, the heavy shelling of the beach began only after the Marines had landed in numbers sufficient to justify winnowing them out.

12. Adapt or Die

Despite the initial success of the landing and the establishment of a beachhead, the first two weeks or so of the Iwo Jima operation were characterized by the Marines' desperate struggle to comprehend the newly altered nature of island combat. As a result, when they headed inland, Marines bogged down. Plans that should have worked, or that had worked before, simply did not, owing to the masterpiece of military defensive science that confronted them.

In the space of several short months and with a minimum of resources, Kuribayashi had created the alpha and omega of island strongholds. With the aid of military engineers imported from Japan, he had fortified his Pacific redoubt to near perfection. Later observers, it was noted, "who had inspected German fortified areas in both world wars testified that never had they seen a position so thoroughly defended as was Iwo Jima."[1]

Every square inch of land was exploited to matchless degree. Every position covered its neighbors with interlocking fields of crossfire. In some places they were clustered so thickly that a machine-gun nest would be sited just yards to the rear or flank of its neighbor—and there were tiers of such defenses stacked in the bluffs. In many places, Marines could not tell where bullets or mortars were coming from, or they received more incoming fire from behind and the sides than from the front. According to Sergeant Alfred Edwards, "One of our machine gunners got shot through the mouth. We thought we saw where the bullets came from. We looked over there, and another guy got shot from the opposite direction."[2] Colonel Thomas Wornham likened the situation to being "just like shooting fish in a barrel, and you were the fish."[3]

Worse, each position was connected by underground tunnels (one, for instance, was eight hundred yards long with 214 exits), so that the defenders of a destroyed post could emerge minutes later through an undetected one.[4] There were sixteen miles of tunnels on Iwo Jima. According to Thomas Williams, "The Japs weren't *on* Iwo Jima; they were *in* Iwo Jima," and Robert Leader likened their winding, branching subterranean fortifications "to the ant farms we had as children."[5] Each and every hidden position had to be found and demolished before an area could be secured.

It was not just the absolute number of positions that hindered progress but their sheer density. In one area 2,500 yards long and 1,000 wide, the 4th Marine Division had to contend with no fewer than ten reinforced-concrete blockhouses, seven covered artillery positions, and eighty pillboxes that together contained fourteen 120mm guns of various models, a 90mm dual-purpose gun, one 70mm battalion howitzer, six 47mm antitank/antiboat guns, three 37mm antitank/antiboat guns, nineteen 25mm twin-mount machine guns, and a 13mm machine gun. These were just the armaments and positions that were identified; many others were destroyed before they could be catalogued.[6] In a single map grid alone of 1,000 square yards—a miniature box about 32 yards by 32 yards—air observers spotted twenty-nine pillboxes, eleven machine-gun nests, and fifteen anti-aircraft guns interspersed with antitank traps, barbed wire, and fire trenches. And the defenses better camouflaged would have been missed.[7] Indeed, an otherwise detailed military map of the time notes ominously in its legend: "Thousands of caves used for defensive purposes, personnel, and storage have not been plotted."[8] Iwo, in short, was a place where, as a report of the time noted, a single company of combat engineers "knocked out more than 165 concrete pillboxes and blockhouses; they blasted 15 strong bunkers and naval gun positions, and dug up or exploded 1,000 mines and booby traps, filled in 200 caves with bulldozers, trapping more than 100 Japs in one cave alone. Some of the caves were three stories high and blocked by high reinforced steel doors."[9]

Such willpower and effort did not come cheaply. As casualties mounted, a disadvantage of the Marine credo of having the next man in line immediately take the place of the one above him became apparent. As junior-ranking officers unused to handling large formations were promoted to fill "vacated" spots, they resorted to dull, unimaginative, officially sanctioned tactics (the same thing had happened during the Civil War) as they sought to overcome the mare's nest of Japanese fortifications. For instance, when a company of the 23rd Marines lined up to storm an airfield two hundred yards away, Arthur Rodriguez could only think, as they got the order to "fix bayonets," that "this is crazy, just like the Civil War. But at least we won't be bunched up." When they set off, "we all started to charge and yell. To me this was like a Banzai charge, so that's what I was yelling. I heard some Rebel Yells."[10] Again, as at Gettysburg, "orders that came down usually w[ere] very elaborate," recalled Ted Salisbury, "but we'd end up going straight ahead as far ahead as you could go. Sometimes it was yards, sometimes it was more, until you [piled up] casualties so hard that you just had to stop. And then they'd reevaluate the situation."[11] Daily progress up the island slowed to increments of fifty or perhaps a hundred yards, every yard yielding a bloody harvest of Marine corpses, as each morning's attack predictably began after the inevitable artillery or naval barrage— following which the enemy, just as inevitably, emerged unfazed from their dugouts. Every attack defaulted to a boring frontal assault, and instead of concentrating their efforts on weak points to force a breakthrough or flank the enemy, commanders parceled out their assets equally and strove to advance in a single, steady line spanning the entire island to prevent Japanese infiltrators. According to Robert Hogaboom, the 3rd Division's chief of staff, at Iwo at first "the Corps appeared to wish to hold hands and to keep the lines dressed abreast, keep the Divisions abreast of each other. This meant that the Division on the left and the Divisions on the right had much more difficult terrain to pass than we did. They had to cross over the ravines and attack across the deep declivities that were across there and I personally believe it slowed up the operation."[12]

One can sympathize with commanders' apprehensions, but the extreme caution might have lost more lives than it saved, as Hogaboom implied. As a result, on many occasions a unit, after sustaining heavy casualties, would return to its original starting point, only to repeat the mistake twenty-four hours later. The official history of the battle noted drily of one such failed assault that the rebuffed unit "continued the attack [the next day] with no change in formation or plan."[13]

It took Marines between two and three weeks to reject what had worked in the past, climb the learning curve, rethink their tactics, and adjust their techniques. It was only then that enemy resistance truly began to collapse. Sometimes, even a minor change could shift the advantage to the American side.

March 5 and March 6 (D+14 and 15) were key dates in this respect. Until then, Marines had been attacking the center strongholds of the island to little avail. Each morning at 0730—the Japanese could set their watches by the bombardment ordered to precede the day's attack—they set out on their assault. And each morning they were halted after a few dozen yards by a "steel wall of Jap mortar and small-arms fire." On March 5, now exasperated and bleeding heavily from their losses, the Marines hoped to break the enemy by organizing "the greatest artillery barrage of the campaign. Three artillery regiments, massed with V Amphibious Corps artillery, fired approximately 45,000 rounds into the concentrated Jap positions among the rocks." No one could possibly have lived through such torment, yet by day's end the Marines had advanced, a report grimly noted, just one hundred yards.[14]

But then on March 6, one general, who was ordered to jump off the next morning at the usual time, instead surprised the enemy by forgoing any artillery and attacking at 0500. Hundreds of yards were gained at little cost.[15] Word of his success spread rapidly. The very next day, Ray Crowder and his company were ordered to launch a surprise attack at 0500 in order to take a ridge that had thus far defied every attempt. Again, there was to be no opening artillery barrage. No one knew whether it would succeed; some of the men grumbled that everyone would be massacred, but in the event they met little resistance. The second platoon encountered some Japanese, but they were asleep, while the first platoon reached its objective without firing a shot.[16] It would not always be so easy, especially once the Japanese adjusted their schedules, but still, the Marines had broken free of their straitjacket. As Corporal William McConnell remembered, he received "an unusual order" around this time: "Units that could advance were to do so even if it meant leaving the flanks open and unprotected. This was new to me." That day, they conquered three hundred yards, a "major" achievement.[17] From then on, it was difficult to go back to the old ways.

We can see adaptation in action by reading the official after-action reports of 2nd Battalion, 26th Marines. On February 21 (D+2), as per approved procedure, their patrols attacked active pillboxes and caves bypassed by preceding units. It took another five days (until February 26, D+7) to establish conclusively that rifles were of course useful in this respect, but only hand grenades and antitank guns could be counted as "indispensable weapons in attacking pillboxes and caves." Corporals Folsom and Trentham of Company F proved the point by using them to destroy five pillboxes. By March 2 and 3 (D+11, 12), grenades had become the weapon of choice against caves because Marines had learned that "flat trajectory weapons [e.g., rifles] were useless except for direct targets of opportunity." Two days later, as they reached the two-week point on Iwo, the battalion was employing tanks, personally directed by infantrymen, to blow apart pillboxes and seal caves. It was a method that "proved more satisfactory" even than relying on grenades. Unfortunately, by March 10 (D+19) the tanks were coming under heavy attack from Japanese artillery and were highly vulnerable in the craggy terrain. After two days of losses, on March 12 "it was decided that new tactics must be used. Artillery, mortar, and small-arms fire was ineffective, and the terrain unsuitable for air bombardment," so combat engineers were brought up to clear the tanks' path of mines while an armored bulldozer leveled a road "through the rocks to the front lines . . . and tanks were immediately brought up to fire to the front." Within a day (March 13, D+22), "the infantry-engineer-tank coordination proved to be the solution to breaking the unusual and particularly strong lines of resistance." As tanks blasted camouflaged positions, infantrymen spread out and "used sniper tactics, firing at all movement to the front." Then "the assault squad was combined with engineer personnel under Sgt. John Potter, of Co. D, and was used very effectively in close fighting, sealing caves and knocking out pillboxes" that the tanks had not quite finished off.

On March 14 (D+23), all the hard work and deadly schooling paid off. The battalion advanced no fewer than four hundred yards in difficult terrain "in spite of low morale, fatigue, and an average strength of 70 men per company." That night, a final infiltration attack was beaten back. It was an unmistakable sign that resistance had broken and that the Japanese were at their wits' end. Two days later the battalion was relieved and departed Iwo Jima on March 27.[18]

On the other side of the hill, we witness the gradual breakdown of the Japanese as the Marines battered them day by day. In the beginning, the Marines were not facing (despite superficial appearances and movie clichés) a ragtag bunch of fanatics scattered haphazardly about. There was, in fact, a professional, balanced, organized order of battle. Not only did Kuribayashi have such distinct elements as machine-gun battalions, engineer companies, infantry regiments, and military police, but he could also call on expert well-digger, disease prevention, and radar/communications components (plus a "special weather unit").[19]

Yet as early as February 23 Japanese organization was falling to pieces under the onslaught by Marines learning and adapting as they went. An official report stated that the plans to stop the enemy advance had "become hopeless," their fixed defenses "useless" against "the air-sea-land cooperation of the enemy." By that date, a third of the island was in U.S. hands.

Under incessant attack, units, or what was left of them, were rapidly cut off from communications and left by themselves to work out what to do. Telephone wires had been severed by artillery; since there was no way to repair them, messengers had to be sent—a time-consuming, unpredictable, and dangerous process. In order to deliver and receive a simple order from his command post just a couple of hundred yards away, a Lieutenant Sugihara had to take three runners with him in the hope that one of them at least would get through. The trip took nearly an hour and a half.[20] By March 10, according to First Lieutenant Musashino Kikuzo, "during the daytime we hid in caves, and at night we wandered in the battlefields, aimlessly, without hope."[21] Adding to the confusion, most of the defenders had no idea where they were on the island, were sealed off from any knowledge of the outside world (including the neighboring bunker), and were kept in the dark as to Kuribayashi's plans (aside from a vague admonition to die gloriously) or their degree of success.

A significant proportion of the "fanatical" fighting in the bunkers, blockhouses, pillboxes, and caves after the first few weeks but before the very end, then, we can ascribe to their defenders' not having an inkling of what was happening or who was winning. In their minds, it was perfectly possible that the Americans were being beaten, so it was rational to keep fighting. As early as dusk of D-Day, Lieutenant Sugihara could gain heart from his estimate that the Americans had failed to land more than two thousand men on Iwo—an easily defeatable force, but one, alas, that Sugihara had drastically undercounted. In fact, V Amphibious Force had brought ashore thirty thousand Marines.[22] He was not alone in his fictions. After all, among the defenders it was common knowledge that Japanese "Special Attack Units" had already sunk "six carriers, two battleships, two cruisers, possibl[y] four destroyers," a belief that, if accurate, would have meant that the U.S. Navy lost more materiel at Iwo Jima than at the battles of the Coral Sea, Midway, the Philippine Sea, and Leyte Gulf combined.[23] Senior commanders knew, of course, that the situation was hopeless—and told Tokyo so—but their subordinates' ignorance was bliss, for then there could be no surrender to the Americans.

13. Minefields and Antitank Weapons

From the bloodless official reports and scarce diary entries of Americans and Japanese alike, we cannot extract much impression of what the learning curve actually entailed, in terms of flesh, for Marines (or Japanese). There were four primary types of defenses the average Marine would encounter on Iwo Jima, so to rectify this we'll examine each of these in turn to discover how they were surmounted.

Of the quartet, minefields were the most easily dealt with, although, as John Thurman pointed out, because the Japanese did not deign to mark their presence, the first inkling of being in one came when somebody suddenly burst apart.[1] When that happened, everyone immediately halted but did not drop deckward (as they would if a mortar had landed). Corpsman Jerry Cunningham was with a squad under Sergeant Smallwood, who ordered the men to freeze one hundred feet along a path. "It seemed like hours, but it was probably a matter of several minutes that we stood there afraid to move," he remembered. Each Marine then precisely and painstakingly, and of course unhurriedly, retraced his footsteps to exit the minefield.[2]

If retreat was impossible, the alternative was to plug on and hope for no more casualties. Sharp eyesight and a light tread became critical. Cecil Downey, an assistant machine gunner lumbered down with a 21-pound box of ammunition in each hand, scanned obsessively for any sign of freshly turned dirt (indicating that the Japanese had planted a mine there) and walked on tiptoes. The man directly ahead of him exploded, and two more soon after. But there was no going back. Then it was Downey's turn: After stepping on a particularly well-hidden mine, he felt himself lifted skyward and hurled back to the ground, "breathless inside a clanging bell of concussion. He couldn't breathe. His lungs fought for air and it wouldn't come. He was conscious of the hot surge of blood rushing out of him." Downey was severely wounded but survived thanks to nearby medics.[3]

The next step was to call in the engineers for mine-clearing. As the Japanese used non-magnetic materials in their mines, they were invisible to mine detectors, so the job needed to be done by hand. Like many others, Howard McLaughlin learned to "crawl along the rows on your belly, probing the ground ahead of you very carefully with your bayonet." He slid it gingerly at a 45-degree angle into any suspicious area; if he met the slightest resistance, then he stopped pushing, for some Japanese mines were set to explode with as little as five pounds of pressure applied. The engineer then gently swept away as much of the sand covering the object as he could and planted a flag, either white (for possible mines) or red (for confirmed ones).[4] White meant that you could cross your fingers and take your chances walking there; red entailed death. If there was time to spare, he would unspool a length of cord with mini-charges attached so that it touched every flag. Ignited, the cord would destroy an entire minefield all at once.[5]

More often, however, engineers did not have time to spare. Mortars sometimes rained in, and slow-moving mineclearers always made tempting targets for snipers. They took shortcuts. "There's acid inside [a common type of mine], and when you break it, a battery is activated, and that sets off the charge," explained Al Abbatiello. "But you could grab them by the handle and set them to the side, so everybody could go around them."[6] In these cases, as they cleared the way through the field, the engineers would mark a narrow safe path with white tape to help the infantrymen following behind. When their squad moved up, Robert Maiden told Lonnie Corrazine, a new machine gunner from Texas, to do "double time across, [and] stay on the white tape. If you should receive fire, hit the deck on the tape." But when the Japanese opened up, Corrazine panicked and strayed outside. "All I saw after the explosion was the upper half of his body about twenty feet in the air," Maiden sadly recalled.[7] It was an iron rule: Stay on the tape. Transgressors would learn their lesson, as happened when Ernest Moreau and his squad were picking their way through a partially cleared minefield. A replacement, seeing an officer's body with a sword, wandered off to pick it up—a foolish thing to do even when one was not in the middle of a minefield—and promptly stepped on a mine. Despite the man's hollering for help, their sergeant ordered the rest of the squad to leave him there and walk on. A corpsman would (possibly) come along once engineers had checked out the mines.[8]

No rifleman liked minefields, but they were a relatively minor threat that engineers, once they had learned their location, could clear without too much trouble. Tanks and other vehicles, however, were particularly menaced by the Japanese practice of burying aerial bombs and torpedoes in places where armor was likeliest to pass. The explosions were often spectacular. Alvin Josephy saw a halftrack moving along a runway when "there was a burst of earth beneath [it], followed by a sharp crash. The vehicle rose slowly and turned over, settling in a cloud of dust and sand." Everyone nearby threw himself to the ground to avoid the flying debris. "Five burned bodies lay among the twisted wreckage."[9] When Robert Neiman's tank company ran into an antitank minefield, losses quickly mounted. "The third tank to my right blew up with a tremendous flash and cloud of dust," followed by at least two more tanks. From one of them, the entire "turret [flew] through the air, led by the flying figure of Gy.Sgt. Joe Bruno" (who miraculously survived).[10]

More dangerous still for their crews was when their advance faltered as they warily slowed or halted after mines had gone off. Their hesitation left them vulnerable to the Japanese antitank gunners hidden nearby. As Gerald Averill watched a Sherman "rising slowly, lazily into the air, turning on its side as it fell back, coming [to] rest, turret down" after it had rolled over a torpedo, the enemy was already "reaching for the [other] Shermans" with their "wicked 47mm antitank rounds." Mortars and artillery finished off any tankers who escaped their burning, shattered vehicles.[11]

While Shermans were impervious to mere bullets, a single Japanese armor-piercing antitank round could destroy them.[12] Sergeant T. Grady Gallant saw a round hit a Sherman's turret, leaving in its wake a hole "remarkably smooth, clean, and efficient, as if it had been made by a punch, but larger—about the circumference of a banana, and very straight." Inside, the round whirled around, bouncing off the sides, and after hitting the stack of high-explosive ammunition "acted like a beater in a mixing bowl of eggs, spinning and mixing the contents, splashing the wall of the bowl with whites and yolks until they are no longer recognizable as eggs at all, but are a jellied, liquefied mass blended into a viscoidal, sticky fluid." A few minutes later another Marine opened the hatch—the metal was still hot to the touch—and "looked at the floor of the tank, into the interior of the big machine, where the crew had been. And he vomited. Vomited over the places where the crew had sat."[13]

More often, the round would explode inside the turret, sending shrapnel flying within the tank's confined space. Pfc. Claude Livingston was a nineteen-year-old gunner in the 5th Tank Battalion whose groin was shredded by metal shards; the shrapnel also sliced through his bladder and colon and tore off his coccyx. Shortly afterward, a wounded Richard Wheeler was lying on the bottom bunk on a plane bound for Hawaii when he smelled something awful emanating from "the man whose body sagged the canvas stretcher bottom eight inches above my nose." It was Livingston. "They had him full of rubber tubes which dripped urine, fecal matter, and pus steadily into a glass jug beside me on the deck. He was in such agony that his face . . . was a twisted knot of pain. . . . A succession of sobs fought their way out through his clenched teeth." Even the morphine did not work. Against the odds (he'd been wounded on February 10), Livingston survived until July 17.[14]

The majority of tank hits occurred in the earlier weeks of the battle, when the Japanese had both substantial numbers of buried mines to create opportunities for the antitank gunners and sufficient antitank guns to take advantage of those opportunities. But as Marines learned on the job such opportunities became ever rarer. By the battle's later stages, tanks traveled in small groups of three or four at the most and were invariably preceded by teams of engineers to clear their way and flanked by infantry detailed with shooting suicidal "Satchel Charlies" before they came anywhere near. At the end, there was no defense left against the Shermans. As a flamethrower tank approached a cave, remembered Frank Caldwell, a group of its hapless defenders emerged and launched one final, impotent bid for glory. "One was an officer and he had his sword pulled, and he charged the tank at maximum range. The range of the flamethrower was about seventy-five feet. This tank guy didn't do a damn thing—he just sat there. That officer was pissed off; he charged this tank out of desperation. He had his sword up high, and . . . the tank gave him a blast with the flamethrower, hit the officer right in the crotch, and he jumped up high—still had his sword up high—and then he fell forward flaming, jamming his sword in the ground."[15]

14. Spider Traps and Snipers

"Spider traps" and snipers were other threats that diminished in direct proportion to the Americans' gradual accumulation of experience, territory, and expertise. A spider trap was a peculiarly Japanese innovation, generally consisting of a modified fifty-five-gallon metal barrel (once used to ship cement) that could fit—tightly—a soldier, a canteen, a gun, and a few rations. Buried, they became a one-man foxhole with a camouflaged steel lid.[1] The occupant could lift the lid to either take a shot or to emerge from hiding to stage an infiltration; when closed, it was as if he had simply vanished. Some spider traps were placed adjacent to a tunnel network, allowing the soldier to shoot from one, travel underground, and pop out somewhere else to shoot again.

As was typical on Iwo, the Japanese did not operate individually but instead covered each other. So, even when one was lucky enough to witness, as Bill Faulkner did, a Japanese opening the lid (and, being just as surprised as Faulkner, quickly dropping it and descending), one had to remain alert. When Faulkner ran over and was about to drop a grenade inside, Conrad Shanker stopped him so that he could explore what turned out to the entrance to a tunnel. A few minutes later, he emerged with blood dripping from his knife only to be shot in the head by a hidden sniper.[2]

Even if spider traps exacted relatively few deaths (at least compared to mortars), they were persistent irritants. In the very center of Gerald Averill's company there was one stay-behind lurking in a spider trap who "would raise his Nambu light machine gun over his head and, with the selector set on full automatic, would twist the gun in a half-circle over his head and then reverse it, filling the air with lead right at head and neck level as we squatted in the foxholes, keeping us ducking. Then he'd slip through a tunnel into another firing position. He was still putting on his act days later, when we were able to move out of position. No one ever saw him, just heard that gun whacking away, the rustle of its bullets passing close overhead."[3] According to Fred Haynes, other Japanese would take a single shot to poach a victim and then wait a few hours before firing again. That was plenty of time for the original unit to have moved out and an unsuspecting one to have moved up—and to lose another man.[4]

If the attritional rate was moderate, the ability of snipers to target individuals nonetheless magnified their impact. Being shot by one was never a pleasant experience, of course, and every Marine detested the feeling of being marked out specifically for attention. Dave Davenport was hit in the back "with paralyzing force. I was on the ground, knocked kicking. The pain was spreading over my torso in eddying whirlpools of agony. . . . I found I couldn't move. The intense pain was beginning to numb my lower body. There was absolutely no strength in my legs to push my body forward. . . . I did experience a noticeable stiffening of my body as I flinched, expecting momentarily another shot."[5]

It did not come, most likely because Davenport was actually serving as bait. It was common practice to wing a Marine and wait for the litter-bearers and corpsmen—the real targets of value; 827 corpsmen would be killed or wounded on Iwo—to arrive.[6] Alvin Josephy watched a four-man stretcher team carrying a wounded man as it came under sniper fire. One bearer was hit in the leg but the rest of the team managed to get under cover before they were killed. The wounded man died before they could get back to him.[7] Marked ambulances attracted many a sniper's eye, as did the medical personnel accompanying the wounded.

Marines tried a variety of ad hoc methods to flush out spider traps. Alfred Stone and a friend worked out one way when they were fired upon and Stone fell, pretending to be wounded. Fortunately, he had spotted the telltale muzzle flash and lay all but motionless for fifteen minutes as he surreptitiously sighted his rifle on the hole. Just after dark the star shells came out and the lid lifted. "The Jap put his head up and was looking at the rocky area where the Marines had gone. Then he began bringing his rifle out to fire, but as he did, I fired twice. Both of the rounds hit him in the head, which exploded. That took care of this problem."[8]

In this instance, Stone was successful, but success was costly in terms of time and effort. A better way eventually became standard practice. When a spider trap was discovered, the leader of a four-man fire team stayed back to provide covering fire if necessary while a rifleman sneaked up to within six yards. The two others moved to either side of the lid and waited. Then the first rifleman pulled the pin on a grenade and signaled for them to raise the lid about 45 degrees. The grenade was tossed in, the men dropped the lid, and it exploded before the surprised occupant had any chance of escaping or throwing the grenade back out.[9]

There was always grim satisfaction when a sniper was killed. After John Thurman and some buddies blew apart a long-troublesome one they took the time to go over and study their late antagonist. "His body was ripped and torn in half," said Thurman. "His head and chest were lying with his hips and legs about ten feet away. It was still very early in the morning and it was just getting light out . . . it was chilly. We could see steam coming off his insides. His heart was hanging just below the ribs of his chest in the sand—his heart was still beating."[10]

As time passed, that satisfaction became not quite so satisfying. Spider traps were rapidly diminishing in number and, perhaps more important, the snipers manning them were declining in expertise. A "sniper" at the beginning of the battle was far more skilled than one so designated by its end, when a sniper could be defined as anyone brandishing a rifle.

Thus, in the first several weeks there are many stories of their pinpoint accuracy, a large number involving shots to the head—the most difficult shots to make. As they were leaving the beach, especially, Marines were subjected to expert sharpshooting; there were many times, as Thomas Williams found, when one would jump into a shell hole and say hello to the other occupant, only to discover that he had already been precisely assassinated.[11] Gerald Averill later came across "a heavy machine gun team, the gunner, feet planted firmly in the sand on either side of the tripod, head low against the rear sight, aiming in on an unknown target. To his left, his assistant gunner lay alongside the gun, his hand on the half-empty belt, just short of the feedway. Both of them had been shot exactly between the eyes."[12] When Jay Rebstock dived into a foxhole the two men there stood up to make room. One was instantly shot in the middle of the forehead and the other had a bullet pierce his helmet and come out the other side. Obviously, snipers had been watching that hole closely.[13]

As U.S. forces advanced up the island, snipers began to miss more often, not only because the Japanese had lost their best-trained marksmen but because the Marines had grown wise to their tricks. For instance, Keith Neilson was running a telephone wire back to a command post when a bullet hit the sand twenty-five feet away. Instead of freezing, as a newbie would do, he immediately jumped into a shell hole. The sniper continued to take shots as he tried to get a bead on the Marine. His next bullet landed fifteen feet away, and the next, ten, and the next, five. Neilson saw that they were landing in a straight line—a rookie mistake—and followed their path with his eyes until he spotted the sniper's hiding spot. Knowing that the sniper now had him targeted, Neilson broke cover and ran off as the sniper vainly tried to hit him. Once a sniper's bolt-hole had been found like that, it was not long until a machine gun or tank eliminated it.[14]

15. Pillboxes, Bunkers, Blockhouses

Pillboxes, bunkers, and other emplacements like blockhouses were altogether a different story. (Marines often used the terms almost interchangeably. Technically speaking, a pillbox is a small concrete guard post equipped with apertures from which to fire a machine gun; a bunker is generally a larger structure, mostly underground; and a blockhouse is a thick-walled, aboveground variant of the bunker.) Even after the Marines had reached their highest level of lethal proficiency, every single one of these continued to form a dangerous obstacle.

In the face of scarcity, the Japanese were nothing if not enterprising. Volcanic sand was mixed with imported cement and seawater and reinforced with low-grade steel bars to form decent concrete—it was no-where near as good as American-made, as there were plenty of air pockets and visible seams, but it was sufficient nonetheless to ward off a limited number of direct hits with artillery and tank guns. Wooden ammunition crates were broken apart and their nails reused to provide additional fortification. Sandbags could be fashioned from the burlap or rice-straw bags used to hold food; a two-deep layer provided adequate protection against small-arms fire. Loose sand piled up and shaped around the walls and roof provided not only camouflage but absorbed projectiles and shell fragments.[1]

Incredibly, the Japanese managed to build at least fifteen hundred pillboxes on Iwo Jima. They tended to fit two or three men and had walls up to a foot thick. Robert Sherrod found a particularly well-protected one that had an additional ten feet of sand covering its sides.[2] Well hidden they were, too: Patrick Caruso received an unpleasant shock when he sat down to rest on a convenient ledge that turned out to be a (thankfully inactive) heavily disguised pillbox.[3] Owing to the inland pillboxes' prevalence and cunning placement, it was hard to knock them out with naval fire. Marines had to tackle each one—one by one.

In those situations, tanks were undoubtedly useful. When Mike Ladich's company was pinned down by a camouflaged pillbox, a tank rumbled up, the hatch opened, and its commander asked him to point out its location. A burst of machine-gun fire that ricocheted off the tank answered the question. The tank's machine gun poured fire into the pillbox's six-by-eighteen-inch aperture, followed by three or four rounds from its powerful 75mm gun. "When the shells exploded inside, the pillbox literally rose up from the ground and shuddered."[4]

Unfortunately, tanks also attracted unwelcome attention. Their presence could be counted on to prompt a rain of mortars and shells on any infantry nearby. Despite trying to help some beleaguered infantry, one commander was angrily told in no uncertain words to "park those fuckin' tanks someplace else" by some disgruntled recipients of his largesse.[5] Even absent any contribution from the enemy, tanks could be dangerous to be around in their own right. For many reasons, includ-

ing avoiding hours of deafness when a nearby tank opened fire, Marines quickly learned to stay well to their side or rear. "If the tank fired
the 75mm gun while a Marine was lying on the ground in front of the
tank, the muzzle blast could hurl a person five or ten feet through the
air," said Alfred Stone.[6]

Behind them they also left behind a trail of squashed corpses, unpleasant for everybody. Frank Walker was three feet away from a tank
that "chewed up a Marine just underneath the surface. . . . The blood
and body fluids sprayed onto me and I carried that on my clothes for
the remainder of the 36 days."[7] Jim Craig was trying to crawl back to a
command post when he came across a group of Japanese infiltrators
run over by tanks. "They had lain all day in the warm sun and some
were so badly crushed from the tank treads that their exposed intestines
lay like coiled snakes. Others were grossly bloated. A swarm of blue flies
buzzed in clusters in their gaping mouths and eyes."[8] If the corpses had
been there for some time, they deflated and rotted and looked "perfectly flat just like a paper doll."[9] But the smell was nauseating. Richard
Lowe accidentally sat on one while resting and soon "moved upwind
about 10 feet [and] faced the other way."[10] George Nations, meanwhile,
was trying to cook some rations but could "not enjoy my lunch" thanks
to the stench.[11]

Tanks, in any case, were of limited use against defensive structures
other than pillboxes. A fairly standard blockhouse, for instance, had
forty-inch-thick concrete walls, measured ten by twenty feet, and had a
five-foot ceiling. Inside were three rooms separated by foot-thick concrete walls, and the doorways between those rooms were narrow, to
contain blasts. Even a major explosion in one room would leave the
occupants of the other two unscathed and still fighting. Blockhouses,
too, were protected by a network of pillboxes and were designed to
deflect not merely tank guns but high-caliber naval fire. Even by Iwo
Jima standards, Kuribayashi's command blockhouse in the island's
north was gargantuan. About 150 feet long and 70 feet wide with
five-foot-thick walls and ten feet of reinforced concrete forming the
roof, engineers would need 8,500 pounds of explosives in five separate
charges to destroy it. Wes Plummer remembered that "when they blew

up that blockhouse, I thought the world had come to an end. I'd been in the midst of heavy fighting since D-Day and it was the loudest damned explosion I'd ever heard."[12]

Bunkers, because only their entrances were visible, were also almost impervious to tank fire or artillery. Direct hits with bazookas or a tank gun could blast off chunks of exposed concrete, but infantry needed to perform the "wet work" and the mopping up.[13] Early on, grenades were used plentifully. Throw enough in, and sooner or later the occupants would cease fighting. But they always proved stubborn—and dangerous, too, for the Japanese had their own supply of grenades. For every handful of grenades Captain LaVerne Wagner and his men tossed into one bunker, at least a dozen were thrown out. They persisted until none returned. When they finally entered the structure, they found parts of three corpses and seventy-five fresh grenades, neatly lined up.[14]

It was, in any case, quite simple for the Japanese to mitigate the effects of grenades, as Marines bitterly discovered. Adding a right angle to a rear-entrance passage and using small, slanted apertures hindered grenades from being tossed directly in; a drainpipe-sized ditch scooped in front caught them if they tried to roll them; interior walls reduced concussion and shrapnel; and a deep, narrow "well" at the defenders' feet allowed them to kick live grenades out of harm's way.[15]

The essential problem with using grenades or relying on tank fire was that not every defender was killed instantly. They took time to work, and in the interim if even one Japanese was left alive he was a threat. Outside one bunker, related Bill Faulkner, despite several large explosions, a shower of grenades emanated from the shaken defenders. Then some wounded Japanese charged out and made straight for the Marines, whose rifles had jammed. Fortunately, they "ran right into a machine gun we had set up to cover the attack. We moved around to the front of the bunker and found several Japs, all wounded but jabbering and trying to pull the pins of grenades. [Lieutenant Wesley] Bates tried his Japanese on them, asking them to surrender, but no luck." They had to shoot them one by one.[16]

A new alternative technique developed on Iwo to save time and effort was for a Marine to scramble to the top of a structure while his comrades diverted the defenders by firing into the apertures. Richard Wheeler watched one man scrape away the covering sand and plant an explosive charge directly on the roof. After he bounded to safety, there was a loud blast and a hole opened up in the concrete. Another accompanying Marine now thrust thermite grenades through the fissure to create enough heat and smoke to force the occupants outside. As they shoved open the steel door, Marines rushed forward and opened fire, emptying their magazines into the writhing bodies. Three Japanese managed to make it outside "and fell to the ground. One made a feeble attempt to rise, and Ruhl hurried forward to finish the job with his bayonet."[17]

Only one weapon was judged capable of annihilating Japanese with certainty, celerity, and economy: the flamethrower. The problem was that their operators were highly vulnerable to hostile fire. They had among the shortest life expectancies of any Marine, according to Robert Lanehart: The lifespan of "a flamethrower man [was counted] in seconds, twenty seconds or something like that, when you're in combat. Which I can believe. You make a good target. You can't duck too well with a flamethrower on your back."[18] Flamethrowers were always the largest men physically, as they needed to bear the seventy-two-pound heft of their equipment.[19] Husky or hulking replacements, proudly if innocently believing they were being selected for a signal honor, were often chosen to act as expendable operators by their grizzled, and suspiciously friendly, new comrades.[20] Whoever they were, they rarely lasted long. During a single attack on a pillbox, said Jay Rebstock, his platoon lost no fewer than three flamethrower men in quick succession.[21] Indeed, it was a rare thing to see, as Alvin Josephy did, a wounded one. As he was stretchered to the rear, this remarkably fortunate individual propped himself up on his elbows and giddily exclaimed to everyone he passed: "So long, everybody! I'm going back to the States. I been wounded. I'm saying goodbye to you all. I been wounded!"[22]

A lone flamethrower operator was a dead flamethrower operator. His weapon worked only at fairly close range and had a short duration (about eight seconds per tank), and so he needed sufficient protection to approach the target safely. Following guidelines set in mid-December 1944, Marines began to send escorts of several riflemen and BARmen along with their flamethrower operator; demolitions specialists also accompanied the team.[23]

On Iwo Jima, the Marines gradually evolved a three-stage process for destroying emplacements using these new units. First, the BARmen and riflemen would circle to either side of the structure to cover the flamethrower operator. They would fire into the aperture or apertures to give cover and to provide enough time for the flamethrower man to run up and shoot a stream of fuel inside before igniting it with "a metallic click, a whoosh, and a low-keyed roar" to annihilate the occupants.[24] It was hitting the aperture that required training and experience. According to Woody Williams, who knocked out seven pillboxes in a single day (killing twenty-one Japanese in the process), "if you fired the thing into the air and you had any air blowing toward you, it'd burn all the hair off your arms and eyebrows. It would kick back at you, so we fired it in two- or three-second bursts and rolled the flame on the ground. It would roll across the ground, twenty to twenty-five yards depending on terrain, and right into a pillbox."[25]

At which point began the second stage. Much of the twenty-foot-wide fireball would blow clear outside, "but a lot would penetrate the aperture," Williams added, giving the demolitions men "time to get up there and throw a satchel charge" inside to finish the job and help render the structure unusable.[26] Satchel charges weighed between eight and twenty pounds and contained C2 plastic explosive blocks. As their name indicates, they were canvas bags with a shoulder strap, which made their carriers look like overgrown schoolboys.[27]

Wise Marines stayed well back from the explosion, which sent chunks of concrete and metal fragments flying outward. Incredibly, too, there were some Japanese who had the presence of mind to hurl the satchel charge back outside. Sergeant Krywicki was covering a demolitions man who threw in the charge, only to have it land right back next to him. He vanished while Krywicki was spun around twice and knocked flat. All the buttons had been blown off his shirt, and he was deafened. (One ear would never regain much hearing.) His late colleague's scalp, "with all the hair still on it, flopped like a mop beside him," recalled Dan Levin.[28]

Finally, any survivors had to be killed. For obvious reasons, they were few and far between, as a flamethrower instantly turned a confined space into a super-heated furnace that sucked the oxygen out of the air and lungs. Those inside died of rapid and intense suffocation. (Some Japanese soldiers, ignorant that it was not the temperature but the lack of air that was lethal, hung blankets from the ceilings to reduce the heat.) For occupants not in the immediate vicinity (in the larger structures), their clothes and flesh would catch on fire; if they were able to make it outside, they would either die or be killed in short order. Near Kitano Point, for instance, a Japanese, aflame with napalm oozing over his skin, erupted from an exit holding a grenade in either hand. He threw them both, harmlessly, before expiring. Another time, a few soldiers emerged and "ran straight into the fire from my flamethrower," said Woody Williams. "As if in slow motion they just fell down."[29] The more veteran flamethrower men, like Williams, kept their igniters permanently lit to deal with the running-survivor problem. Thus, when two soldiers surprised Alfred Stone and began firing, he was fortunate to have a flamethrower man about twenty-five feet away who "calmly pulled the trigger on his flamethrower and covered them both with burning napalm. . . . The two Japanese were frozen in position when the burning napalm hit them and died instantly."[30]

While flamethrower operators rarely, if ever, saw the effects of their weapon on those Japanese trapped in pillboxes and bunkers (though they could hear screams and smell the seared flesh), the soldiers killed outside provided vivid evidence of their effectiveness.[31] It was particularly noticeable how men's heads glowed so brightly, like matches, after being deluged with fuel and set alight. It was their skins that blackened and split apart as liquefied fat burst through. A large fatty bubble often emerged from their rectums. As the flames diminished, the bubble did as well, but it never popped, prompting much curious commentary from passersby.[32] If anyone poked his head inside the structure, all he would see would be some "flamethrower-charred and bloodstained concrete walls," along with a few crispy bodies here and there.[33]

In Europe, prisoners were habitually taken before or after flame actions.[34] There, flamethrowers enjoyed a degree of psychological value in the sense that defenders would be frightened or demoralized into surrendering upon seeing them. In the Pacific, however, while Japanese soldiers were terrified by these fearsome weapons, they still did not surrender. They kept on fighting to the end, necessitating total annihilation.

So ruthlessly deadly was the combination flamethrower/demolition method that there appears to have been just a single prisoner taken on Iwo following its application, though this was more by accident than design. A captain once brought in to the Division Intelligence Section—which was desperately seeking prisoners to interrogate—a small, wiry Japanese who had been burned by a flamethrower. Said a surgeon, "His eyelids were swollen closed. The lips were also cracked and swollen and pouted outwards in a grotesque fashion. The upper teeth could just be seen deep in the tunnel of recently cooked flesh. Shreds of skin were peeling from the ears, nose, and cheeks. The man reeked with the pungent odor of burned flesh."[35] Even if little was gained from him, flame actions provided practical intelligence of a different nature. For Patrick Caruso, it was useful indeed to see the smoke billowing out from the emplacement's interconnected exits dozens and scores of yards away, now suddenly revealed. They would form the next targets—and so on and on until the Marines reached the caves of Iwo Jima.[36]

16. The Caves

Encountering cave defenses on Mount Suribachi in the first week of the battle, Marines had attacked them with grenades and flamethrowers in an ad hoc manner.[1] In those innocent days, some Marines had even entered cave systems to search for souvenirs. Howard Snyder and Chick Robeson actually dug their way into a cave that had been sealed a few days before. Inside, the "stench that met us was so foul we had to put on gas masks. We went in with a small flashlight and found the cave to have sections. Dead Japs lay all about, so thick we had to tread on some." The good news was that "we found souvenirs galore. I came out with several rifles, a canteen, and a bag full of smaller stuff, including a wristwatch. We also found some maps and other papers we turned over to Schrier. But we really caught hell for being so stupid, and the cave was blown shut a second time, so completely that no darned fools could try such a trick again."[2]

As they moved north, Marines found the Japanese defenders ever more firmly entrenched in ever more numerous, ever larger caves. Over the weeks of fighting, an eerie sound—"not unlike someone banging on the radiator in the apartment below," wrote Robert Sherrod—could be heard when shellfire died down and Marines placed their ears to the ground. It was the faint sound of metal pickaxes striking soft volcanic rocks as the Japanese burrowed deeper into the heart of the island.[3]

By that time, the process of killing Japanese had become wholly mechanical. For the smaller caves, Marines adapted the now-trusted pillbox method. Squad riflemen and BARmen circled left and right (avoiding the narrow fire lanes of cave-bound machine guns) and fired inside as best they could.[4] In the meantime, two demolitions men, having dispensed with their helmets, cartridge belts, and anything else that might clink or hinder them, would sneak to either side, dragging their satchel charges behind them with one hand grasping a .45 pistol (just in case) and a grenade or two in separate pockets. Once stationed on the cave entrance's lip, they set the thirty-second delay fuses, counted down, and tossed them in at the same moment. The thinking was that even if the defenders managed to throw one back, there would not be enough time to return the other.[5]

The resulting explosions shattered, disoriented, and shook those inside but did not generally bring down the roof or seal the cave's entrance with rubble and dirt. Finishing off the defenders was the task of the flamethrower man, who now rushed up and suffocated anyone still alive. Only then did the demolitions men place another charge above the cave entrance and direct its explosive force downward by piling heavy stones on top of it.[6] It was this step that finally plugged a cave. The last horrible thing that survivors—men toiling deeper down, away from the blasts and flames, as well as wounded men lying in lower chambers—saw before infinite darkness arrived was, in the flickering light of their lamps and candles, a wall of dirt and smashed rocks blocking their exit. A few might escape by groping their way to another undiscovered entrance, and some you could hear, according to Al Abbatiello, "digging at night, trying to get out," but most eventually committed suicide.[7] The muffled explosions Marines typically heard emanating afterward from sealed caves was the sound of Japanese soldiers holding grenades to their stomachs.[8] In one memorable instance, at exactly midnight a colossal explosion rocked an entire ridge, throwing up boulders, temporarily burying wondering Marines in their foxholes, and sending concrete blocks and dirt showering down. Inside a sealed cave system, the defenders had set off their supply of land mines and 125-pound aerial bombs to end their lives in spectacular fashion.[9]

Those trapped in the caves had long had a miserable existence. For weeks before their deaths they had been crammed inside what many suspected would become their charnel-house. The corpses they had dragged in to hide their true losses from the Marines had long since decayed, and the wounded's injuries were turning gangrenous. The air was filled with a sickening, fetid stench of pus, blood, and rot, the water reeked of sulfur, the temperature hit 120 degrees, and the humidity level rose to 98 percent. If any of the wounded "groaned with pain, they were told to shut up or strangled," said Saturo Omagari.[10] Men had fought for light and scraps of food as they succumbed to insanity and incoherence, overcome by fear of the coming flamethrowers and the prospect of being buried alive. Now that the nightmare had been rendered real by the Marine Corps, dying by grenade was their last, blessed choice, a final ray of rationality beaming through the murk of madness that had tormented them as they powerlessly awaited processing.

An archaeological team that opened and explored one such sealed cave in 2010 found that even after seventy years there was "a pervading odour of decomposition, a scent which clung to the team's clothes, skin, and hair." Lying scattered around were cooking utensils, rice cookers, opened food cans, mess kits, and bowls as well as personal items like wallets, spectacles, toothbrushes, and even hair pomade.

Bones were found embedded in the ceiling, implanted by the blast preceding the flames that had instantly boiled and steamed the contents of torn-apart water canteens. There was a gas mask—they were worn to try to filter the foul air—melted into the wall at head height.[11]

For the larger cave mouths, terrain permitting, tanks were used in place of infantry. Near the end, recalled Robert Maiden, two tanks armed with the standard 75mm gun were accompanied by a "Zippo tank" equipped with a flamethrower far more powerful than the portable versions. It could spew flame up to 150 yards for about a minute. Near Kitano Point, he added, there was a huge pit at the bottom of which were three caves with openings you could drive a truck through. The tanks descended until they could get a clear shot. Then two 75mm rounds were fired into each mouth followed by a "hot shot" from the Zippo tank.[12] In these instances, Japanese soldiers, all alight, would often bolt outside where the tanks' machine guns were waiting to cut them down. So automatic had become the Marines' actions by this stage of the battle that even this impressive sight was counted, said Bertrand Yaffe, as "merely a momentary diversion" by those already moving on to the next obstacle.[13]

There were exceptions to the rule, generally when tanks were unable to assist, a prisoner or two was available, or an experienced demolitions team was sufficiently confident to cut a few corners. Known as the most "cold-blooded, methodical, tobacco-chewing Jap annihilators" in the Pacific, a team comprising G. E. Barber and L. J. Byfield (ably assisted by S. Bencich and E. A. Bennett) "had a system that never failed," according to William Huie, a Seabee who saw them in action. Barber and Byfield, both Texans, were forty years old, veteran potash miners, and graduates of the Navy's Mine and Demolition School. Whenever they sallied forth to handle the big caves, they brought along a couple of prisoners. As they covered the entrance with their Tommy guns, a captive, waving a strip of toilet paper (white flags were in such short supply that each demolitions team was equipped with a roll of toilet paper for the purpose) was sent in to ask whether the defenders wished to surrender. If he did not emerge in ten minutes, they assumed he was dead and heaved a huge dynamite charge into the cave's mouth.

Any Japanese who then came running out were machine-gunned before Barber and his mates entered the cave to deal with the rest. In one, he said, "I never seen such a mess o' Japs. That blast had smashed their backbones, their jawbones, and some o' their skulls. One of 'em threw a grenade at me, so I finished killing 'em."

If the prisoner emerged, however, and reported no Japanese inside, they sealed the cave anyway—just in case he was lying. If, on the other hand, he said they refused to surrender Barber and Byfield sent in a second prisoner. "I like to give the little bastards two chances," the sporting Barber told Huie, "but it makes no difference whether they come out or not."

On the rare occasions when the defenders decided to come out peacefully, they were told to first remove their clothes, grab a piece of toilet paper, and walk out slowly with their hands up. Once outside, they had to turn around to show that nothing was being concealed. Then the original prisoner went in, retrieved the clothing, shook it out, and brought it all to Barber, who rechecked it. The prisoners could then get dressed and were escorted under heavy guard to a holding area.[14]

17. Surrendering and Prisoners

Barber and Byfield captured twenty or so prisoners—quite a haul for Iwo Jima—but their caution regarding surrenders was justified. There were many cases of Japanese ostensibly trying to surrender only to play murderous tricks on unwary Marines. Corpsman Jerry Cunningham was helping a Sergeant Holmes to coax Japanese out of a cave when two came running out next to each other. As Holmes shouted, "Hit the deck!" the pair suddenly parted ways, triggering a grenade tied between them on a string.[1] Another squad was approached by three Japanese with their hands raised. As they came closer, "the enemy soldier in the middle went down on all fours and became a human machine-gun tripod—a Nambu light machine gun had been strapped to his back, and one of his comrades fired off half a belt of ammunition, wounding several of the Marines before he was killed, along with his two comrades."[2] It became common practice to order potential captives to strip, even in chilly weather, to confirm that they were not concealing grenades.[3]

Just as often, Japanese committed suicide—the more public the better, in order to demonstrate the full measure of their commitment to the emperor. Once, a dozen Japanese walked out of a cave holding grenades to their heads. There was no attempt to kill the surprised Marines, only a defiant desire to take the honorable way out.[4] Near the end of the battle, Austin Montgomery and Dick Tilghman were awed to "see at least five of the enemy dive head first off the cliffs on the other side of the [Death] Valley, and down to their deaths on the rocks below."[5]

Even severely wounded Japanese proved hard to take prisoner. After exterminating a group who ignored their call to surrender, Marines found one still alive, injured and almost completely buried in the sand. A few inches from his right hand was a grenade. Detected, he hesitated as the Marines readied their guns and, thinking better of it, signaled instead for a cigarette before surrendering.[6] Marines habitually kept a close eye on "dead" soldiers lying with weapons suspiciously close to hand. Bill Faulkner and Robert Wells saw one such in a crater. They skirted the edge, watching him all the time. Suddenly Faulkner whirled and shot him. Asked why, he answered: "His eyes followed us around the crater."[7]

There were, however, times where Japanese soldiers did earnestly try to surrender. Master Sergeant Taizo Sakai, Kuribayashi's chief code clerk, was more than happy to put his hands up, asserting that he was not one of the "fanatics." He proved his worth by helping to induce others to surrender, warning when a banzai was likely to erupt from a cave, and providing much useful intelligence on enemy defenses.[8] John Lyttle was once startled by a Japanese shouting, in perfect English, "I don't go for this hari-kiri shit," and entreating him to accept his submission. It turned out he was from Chicago and had been visiting Japan before Pearl Harbor and found himself conscripted.[9]

But in a pattern replicated across the Pacific theater as a whole, such cases were isolated ones. Whereas in August 1944, some fifty thousand

German prisoners were arriving in the United States each month, just 1,990 Japanese had been captured since Pearl Harbor, two and a half years earlier. A year later, the war over, the U.S. Army held 1,538,837 German POWs and 24,138 Japanese.[10] Accordingly, of Iwo Jima's twenty-thousand-odd (estimates range from 18,060 to 25,000) defenders, every one but 216 died there. Of these, 59 were suborned Korean laborers expected to die with their masters but who had elected instead to disappoint them. Eleven of the prisoners died of their injuries, and 85 percent of the rest had been wounded by the time they fell into American hands.[11] Many of them had been unconscious when they were taken in, so they were hardly voluntary captives. So ashamed were they that when they awoke they gave false names and begged for their families not to be notified.[12]

When Japanese soldiers were captured, because they were indoctrinated to believe that the Americans tortured, beheaded, boiled in oil, and ate their prisoners, they were surprised to find themselves treated to cigarettes, perfunctory questioning, and medical treatment equal to that given to Americans.[13] One man, who asked Patrick Caruso not to torture him but to execute him immediately, was taken aback upon learning that neither would happen.[14] But that was only if they made it back to headquarters or a hospital ship; not all did. After two immobilized casualties were shot "while trying to escape" from a jeep ambulance by their Marine guards, Dr. James Vedder began ordering a corpsman to accompany POWs on their way to the rear to avoid similar incidents in future.[15]

By the final stages on Iwo Jima, however, it was easier, safer, faster, more practical, and more fulfilling to kill potential prisoners. One Japanese who had charged William Smith was wounded and lay at his feet. "So I finished him off. I don't think they could have done anything for him. Wasn't intentional or nothing, you know what I mean. We hardly took any prisoners, let's put it that way."[16] According to Ernest Moreau, after a lieutenant spent fifteen minutes coaxing the defenders from a cave by assuring them they would be treated decently and three Japanese emerged, they were immediately machine-gunned by a waiting Marine. No one but the lieutenant cared.[17]

Marines' responses to taking prisoners were a cross between calm matter-of-factness and vengeful anger. George Nations related an incident involving the latter:

As our tank maneuvered around a large boulder we saw a Jap sitting down with no clothes on, he appears to be blind and is crying. We fire a burst from the machine gun at him [but] just as we do our tank turns slightly to the right. The burst misses his chest and takes his left arm off at the elbow. His life's blood is now leaping out in great spurts and in rhythm with his heart beat. Our next burst hits him in the chest and his body slams back against the ground with a great invisible force. I'm not proud of this, but it happened forty years ago. We had a different outlook on these things. We had lost so many young Marines we couldn't let a Jap live even when trying to surrender. [18]

Rage at Japanese treatment of American captives helped provoke these harsh reactions. As no American voluntarily surrendered to the Japanese this late in the war, anyone who ended up in their hands had been taken while wounded or, as likely, kidnapped. Lieutenant Herbert Smith, for instance, had vanished without a trace one day as he walked back from battalion headquarters to his company. It is possible that infiltrators dragged him back to the caves. [19]

If so, his fate was unenviable. No Marine survived a Japanese interrogation. First Lieutenant Yamakazi Takeshi wrote that during a visit to regimental headquarters one day he noticed that a "Lieutenant Otani [killed in action shortly after] was then in the process of interrogating an American prisoner of war" and left it at that. As Takeshi was too circumspect to later mention, this POW was being tortured to death. [20]

Dean Winters knew a man who was captured "and pulled into a cave where they tortured him by splitting his finger webs up to his wrists. He was screaming uncontrollably. Our lieutenant got so angry he went in after him and was killed in the process." It is unlikely that the occupants of this cave were taken alive afterward. [21] Other Marines were found with all their fingers broken or their heads smashed open with rifle butts; one was discovered hanging nude by his ankles from the roof of a cave.[22] A pile of cigarette butts lay on the floor under his head. The skin all over his body was pitted by cigarette burns. Some were large, some small, some shallow, some deep.[23] (Regarding cigarettes, any Japanese caught carrying Lucky Strikes or the like was destined for the high jump. As Barber, the Texan demolitions man, put it: "It always makes me want to kill 'em when I find 'em with American cigarettes. I know that they got those cigarettes off'a dead Marines." He would not have been the only one to hold this view.)[24]

While brutal or callous or banal, these are not the words and actions of avowed racists but of men who had reached the end of their emotional and psychological tethers. Unstinting Japanese resistance and culturally shocking deceitfulness, weeks of unrelenting stress and anguish, rising casualty rolls and the loss of friends, the onset of dehumanization and the evolution of processing methods, the overwhelming desire to "just get it over with" and overpowering rage at Japanese atrocities, drove Marines onward to the very end.

18. After the Battle

Even after the virtual extinction of the Japanese garrison, the battle of Iwo Jima was not quite over. More survivors than anyone suspected still remained on the island. The official American tally was 2,469. Most of them (1,602) were quickly hunted down and liquidated. On April 19, for instance, when Marines discovered a group of 220 haggard Japanese in a cave, they squirted aviation fuel inside and ignited it with a flamethrower, killing 150 within minutes.

The rest (867) were taken prisoner one or two at a time. By early May, the Japanese were spending their days hiding in "the grass, near the bottom of trees, or in the crevices of rocks, and at night they became thieves and burglars, stealing from American supplies," said Lieutenant Musahino Kikuzo. Occasionally, a couple of fellow survivors would bump into one another and each would talk "about his own hard life" before setting out to "start again on his hopeless wandering." Musahino himself camped with a friend named Lieutenant Taki, and they knew these chance meetings were becoming ever rarer. After running into Lieutenant Soma and a companion—survival seemed to hinge on banding together in pairs—they never saw them again. Soma and the other fellow were buried alive in a cave soon after.

On the night of June 8–9, Taki and Musahino found a cave complex "filled with corpses. Hundreds of dead bodies still kept their shape, in a variety of poses." It had once been a field hospital, and everyone in it had been abandoned by their comrades. "So the wounded died of hunger right where they had been left. Black hair was still growing from some of the dead. . . . There were thousands of big black flies. Every time you drew a breath, several would fly into your mouth." Still, it was safe enough, so they stayed there for three days, but a machine gun eventually got Taki.

On June 12 Musahino made his way to the eastern coast to commit suicide by starvation—his sword was long gone, as were his grenades. He fainted and lay beneath a rock, waking a few days later with six or seven soldiers pointing rifles at him. They wrapped him in blankets and brought him to a hospital, where he was given nutritious food, injections, and medical treatment.[1]

There remained a few holdouts, who came in occasionally over the next several months. The very last survivors surrendered to a rather surprised pair of Air Force corporals driving a Jeep around the island on January 6, 1949—three and a half years after Japan's capitulation. According to their immediate superior, Sergeant Donald Cook, they had picked up two pedestrians standing by the side of the road "dressed in army fatigues and wearing army field jackets about two sizes larger than necessary." Originally mistaking them for visiting Chinese personnel (there were Chinese ships offshore removing wartime debris), they drove them to the motor pool and left them waiting while they went inside to the office. Upon the corporals' return, the hitchhikers had disappeared. Soon afterward, a staff sergeant found them gazing wonderingly at an American flag fluttering in the wind. He recognized them as Japanese and took them prisoner. Under questioning, they revealed the location of their hideout cave and solved the long-standing mysteries of the vanished canned ham that the Air Force men never got to eat the Christmas before and the ongoing disappearance of flashlight batteries. The two men, Matsudo Linsoki and Yamakage Kufuku, both machine gunners and former farmers, had learned, it seems, of the end of the war after stealing a copy of *Stars and Stripes* featuring a photo of General MacArthur and Emperor Hirohito standing together in Tokyo. As MacArthur was not bowing in the divine presence, they had begun to suspect that the war's outcome had developed not necessarily to Japan's advantage.[2]

In the meantime, the Americans had buried their dead. Unlike at Gettysburg, the procedure was by now well-established and -executed. The Marine Corps had stockpiled thousands of premade crosses and Stars of David, directed personnel to bury by unit rather than by date of death, and had already marked out the location of the planned cemeteries long before D-Day.[3] Five days after landing, with at least five hundred bodies collected, the first permanent internments began.

At the beginning of the process, a team harvested the dead's helmets, webbing, and weapons, which were driven to salvage depots to be either reissued or destroyed, and then three or four men sorted through the personal effects to establish identities and package whatever would be sent home to relatives. "There were some things that were taken out of the wallets, because we [understood] all the wallets were going back to the families," said Gage Hotaling, a chaplain. "So if we found some pornographic literature, that was immediately removed. . . . There were pictures of Marines with gook girls and so on, in all kinds of poses, and those were always removed."[4]

As at Gettysburg, most of the burial details were black units. Black Marines, the first of whom were recruited by the Marine Corps as late as mid-1942, were segregated from combat roles and otherwise restricted to unloading ammunition, operating transport vehicles, guard duty, road construction, lifting the wounded, and moving supplies. Nearly all, nonetheless, would come under fire, given that Iwo was a small island with a lot of artillery action and that they drove supply trucks to the frontline troops.[5] The details used bulldozers to plow trenches eight feet wide and between four and six feet deep. The bodies, enshrouded in ponchos, were interred two feet apart. As each was laid to rest, Graves Registration personnel removed one dog tag and left the other with the corpse.[6] Sometimes, there was just an unidentified arm or leg left to bury.[7]

A registrar then walked the length of each trench to confirm that the bodies were in the correct order. The burial men would call out the name, rank, and serial number of each corpse, and the registrar would repeat the details and write them down. A chaplain followed two bodies behind the registrar uttering the appropriate benediction for a Protestant, Catholic, or Jew. When all had reached the end of the trench, it would be filled in. A cross or star was planted and the dog tag removed earlier would be strung around it with the serial number, name, and service emblem stenciled on the headstone to allow careful cross-referencing later.[8] A body count of a hundred would have been registered as a light day, while March 2, with 247 burials, appears to have been the worst, according to Hotaling's records.[9]

A year later, relatives were given the choice whether to exhume a loved one and have him sent home for reburial or to leave him among his comrades. Most selected the latter. Unbeknownst to them, and kept a secret, the warm volcanic pumice had in the meantime wicked the moisture and fluids out of the bodies, leaving them as mummies.[10] The letters of condolence they received, as well, were models of discretion in certain matters.

Frank Caldwell, a company commander, devoted days to writing to the families of those killed, each letter comprising "three pages per casualty in longhand, in triplicate." His job was "to tell next of kin how we knew this fellow. Some of them I had to lie a little bit because I didn't know everybody or how they got killed."[11] Sometimes it was not good enough. A Captain Fields, having informed a boy's mother of his valorous death in the face of danger—he had stepped on a mine after disobeying instructions to stay within the safety zone—continued to receive querying letters from her for many months afterward. She refused to believe that her son was dead.[12] Other families angrily accused officers of causing their loved one's death through their incompetence and callousness. After Robert Neiman's tank company was hit by mortars and Sergeant Russell Lippert was killed, Neiman wrote to Lippert's wife describing the terrible magnitude of his loss to all his comrades. "She wrote a scathing reply," he recalled. "She was understandably upset, but she accused me of putting her husband in an untenable position and getting him killed." (The story has a curious postscript. When Joe Rosenthal, the photographer who shot the raising of the flag on Mount Suribachi, lost his helmet, some Marines told him to pick one from a pile collected from the dead. "He wrote that he had often wondered about the man whose helmet he had. The name written on it was Lippert.")[13]

There were, of course, enormous numbers of wounded and debilitated veterans of Iwo Jima. Whether a wounded man survived or not, or suffered more than he ought, largely depended on enjoying a modicum of good fortune in the hours after getting hit. The Marines' experience of the initial trauma period varied enormously. Thus, Richard Wheeler was shot in the neck and was incredibly lucky, first, that the bullet missed his carotid artery and jugular vein; second, that there was a fine surgeon in the next foxhole with the necessary clamps; third, that there was plasma immediately available; and fourth, that he was taken urgently to the beach and evacuated. Within two hours of being wounded he was lying in a clean bunk aboard a modern hospital ship, tended to by competent nurses and doctors.[14]

Not so fortunate was Lieutenant John Noe (who died in 1997). When a bullet collided with his lower jaw, it fractured his left mandible and passed out his right cheek. En route it shattered his right mandible, broke his right upper jaw, and ripped out most of the teeth on that side. Bone fragments and bullet shrapnel tore apart and gashed the cheeks up to his eyes. Bereft of a convenient corpsman, he had to walk to the rear holding the shattered parts of his face together while blood gushing into his throat came close to suffocating him. A hundred yards on, a Japanese sniper hit him in the right calf. Upon finally making it to the battalion aid station, where he was at last given morphine, it took several more hours for him to be evacuated to the beach. Even then, as a cold rain fell his litter was placed in the open hold of a landing craft with forty-five others. Their cries rebounded off the metal walls and, with no corpsman aboard, no drugs could be dispensed. Late at night the vessel clanged against the sides of a ship, and he heard shouting. But there was evidently no room, and they had to try several more times elsewhere before space could be found—nine and a half hours after his being wounded. By then, eight of the forty-six men aboard were dead, and another seven died soon after. Thus, fully a third of the casualties became fatalities on their way to what was not even a hospital ship but a transport ship hurriedly converted to emergency care. It took another six days for Noe to be flown out.[15]

The most serious casualties stayed in hospitals for months, or years, afterward. Keith Wheeler, who visited them in Hawaii, was sure that while Iwo Jima produced no instance of a "living basket case"—men who had lost all their limbs—there were plenty who had lost both of one set.[16] Wheeler had himself been wounded during the battle, and on the evacuation flight he met Chuck, who tossed and turned because he could not position his legs comfortably—despite their having been left somewhere on Iwo.[17] Among the worst cases, said a nurse, were those with gunshot and shrapnel wounds to the chest. Many others were paralyzed (and so lacked bladder and bowel control) by hits to the spine, and still more had lost much of their abdominal cavity, necessitating frequent colostomy dressings. Nearly all required oxygen, and casual observers to the ward could be forgiven for thinking that the men were held "together with rubber tubes" resembling "experiments à la Frankenstein."[18]

In the hospital visited by Wheeler, there was a place called the "quiet room" where there were no mirrors or reflective surfaces. Wheeler saw a youth lying in bed with no face from his nose downward; there was merely a flaring scarlet hole with his tongue lolling across his neck. He would die soon, everyone expected. Until then, it was considered advisable to hide the truth from him.[19]

Private Harold Lumbert, a former mechanic, was the most disfigured surviving veteran of Iwo. A piece of shrapnel had hit his face, and he had "lost the front of his skull from beneath his eyes down to the lower jaw. His lower jaw was fractured in five places. His nose was gone. There was a red gulch where it had been. Without bony support his whole face sagged and lost its human character. His lower eyelids were pulled down. The cheeks drooped. The unsupported upper lip hung like a rag. The broken jaw sagged so that his mouth lay open and drooled constantly." Surgeons sewed the remaining flaps of skin together, though when they burst open the wound "gapped open between sutures like a fat man's shirt." Cartilage was taken from a "recently killed human cadaver" (Wheeler is vague as to its former owner) and used to build a new nose. Surgeons then bolted an aluminum, face-shaped scaffolding to his skull and anchored with orthodontic bands to the two remaining molars on each side of his mouth a massive prosthetic plate to cover the face and replace his upper jaw and palate. That was just the beginning. After that, Lumbert endured an unending series of operations to tuck, fit, stitch, stretch, compress, and adjust his skin and fascia muscles, followed by years of rehabilitation. In late 1961, *Life* published Wheeler's follow-up story detailing a visit to see Lumbert. Wheeler described his return to civilian life and his succor in the arms of a loving family. It was lavishly replete with photographs— all shot from behind. Lumbert died a few years later, still in pain.[20]

Lumbert's long suffering is a reminder that Iwo left deep scars. Psychological, not just physical, trauma afflicted veterans for years afterward. A lot of men suffered from "the shakes" in the immediate aftermath of the battle. Alvin Josephy noticed that many soldiers' handwriting "looked like the jerky scrawl of a drunken man," and Victor Kleber went so far as to apologize to his family for his poor penmanship.[21] "I find it extremely difficult to sit down and write," he explained, "let alone concentrate my thoughts. This, I am told, is the normal reaction to sustained combat."[22]

Most of the time, as with combat fatigue, the shakes subsided after a few days of being away from the battlefield and a couple of good nights' sleep. Other men, especially if they had been grievously wounded, never quite recovered, and there were significant numbers of suicides after the war. These cases went unacknowledged, unrecognized, or unrecorded, but most Marines would have known, or known of, a comrade who had killed himself. One such was Lou Balog, a flamethrower man whose friend, Joe Czerniawski, was badly hit. He was "completely emasculated by shrapnel from that shell and was injured in one leg so it was shorter than the other. Later he went to California, where he committed suicide."[23]

Even after the initial shakes had gone, horrific visions and nightmares continued, though they could long lie dormant. For Dr. Thomas Brown, famed as the most composed man on Iwo, the first inkling that something was wrong came in the winter of 1949, following a long shift at the hospital. Stretched out on the sofa at home while his wife prepared dinner, he listened to a radio program called *Columbia Was There,* a documentary about the Normandy landings. He heard recordings of dive bombers, screeching shells, and bullets hissing by. All of a sudden, Brown "disintegrated emotionally," and began shivering and crying uncontrollably.[24]

Others, like Mike Vinich, were haunted by graphic memories of Japanese soldiers they had killed close-up. There was one youth in particular he had shot, that he "didn't think too much [of] then, but I've thought about it ever since. His face is in my eyes. I see him when I go to sleep at night."[25] The triggering incidents are unknown and unknowable. For Howard McLaughlin, writing only a couple of years ago, at least the visions are "not as bad at night now as it was when I first came home. It was especially bad on Helen when we were first married." Then she was the victim of

nightmares in which I was trying to get out of the way of a fired sniper round, or to reach some kind of cover as the mortar shells started dropping. In these—to me—very real happenings, my actions were brought on by reflexes learned in combat. In real time if you were lying down, you were always [in] a sort of a crouch, with one foot pulled up for leverage. Then when an emergency arose you were able to instantly jump or throw yourself up and over into another nearby hole for cover. Now, in the middle of the night, I would react to this dreamed threat in the same manner. If Helen was lucky, I went out of the bed on my side, onto the floor. But sometime I tried to jump towards her side of the bed. . . . At other times I would wildly throw an arm back for some reason and hit her in the face or chest. After all these years sometimes I still have these flashbacks, just as vivid to me as ever. They eventually stopped causing physical damage to Helen, but in some ways they're worse for me these days. Now they seem to run in a pattern in which I'm unable to do something either to help someone else or to save myself from some impending catastrophe. There is still terror in these dreams, but now much frustration also.[26]

Even on Iwo, psychiatric casualties could be divided between the "bulkhead stare" type of fatigue and patients suffering from genuine, terrified hysteria. The surgeon James Vedder was nonplussed when one such Marine was brought in to his aid station with no recognizable wounds. Neither was he obviously combat-fatigued, a condition familiar to Vedder since he saw it so often. Instead, the man's "eyes were rolled upward so only the white sclera were visible. The jaws were so tightly clenched that I could not examine his throat or tongue. Both his arms and legs were held in a rigidly extended position. The elbows could not be bent, and the fingers were so tightly doubled over that the nails were gouging the skin on both palms. His knees were held as stiffly as the elbows, there was no way I could flex them even slightly. In addition, the hips were held rigidly immobile. It was impossible to rotate them in any direction." Yet his breathing was normal and his bladder was functioning (there was an increasingly large wet spot). Overnight, said the corpsman who brought him, he had "stiffened out like a plank." Nothing had "happened" to him. Vedder immediately evacuated him.[27]

Other cases were often taken to base hospitals, their release dates uncertain. Their "disturbed wing," warned attending corpsmen, was a place where "you never dared turn your back on a patient. They'd climb you without warning." Hardly a day passed without their having to subdue somebody forcibly. The patients' symptoms generally conformed: strong and uncontrollable spastic tremors; shoulders, trunk, leg, hands, and neck jerking ceaselessly; anguished expressions on their faces owing, evidently, to physical and mental pain. When they spoke, if they could, they often repeated each word a dozen times, endlessly.

Otherwise, they seemed mute or deaf. Amnesia was common, not only of what happened on Iwo but of their lives before the battle. Each night was filled with terror, the victims quivering and cringing, eyes wide with fear, and they would often slip back into childlike poses.

A common treatment at the time was to administer heavy "hypnotic" doses of sodium amytal, a sedative that temporarily quieted the worst physical symptoms. During these periods of lucidity, a psychiatrist would attempt to tease out childhood events and psychological accelerants, with everything said being recorded by a stenographer. Afterward, a nurse would repeat to the patient all the things he had revealed under sedation. "Pounded long enough, insistently enough, with spoken evidence of his past," wrote a witness to these sessions, he would sometimes begin to recover his memory and speech. "Eventually, usually with surprise, he becomes aware of his strange surroundings" and calms down.

Three months before Iwo, a newer form of treatment for particularly disturbed patients was developed by Lieutenant Commander Ernst Schmidhofer. He hypnotized men until they ceased twitching and jerking, then, talking calmly and monotonously, he asked them to relax by closing their eyes, emptying their minds, focusing on their exhalation and inhalation. He directed them to repeat a line like, "My mind is a blank" or to repeat the letters of the alphabet. Essentially, Schmidhofer was teaching the men to meditate.

An initially skeptical Keith Wheeler watched him treat six patients: two Navy men and six Marines back from Iwo Jima and Okinawa. None had been treated previously, and when they were brought into the room they were trembling, yammering, and contorting so violently that they had to be lifted out of their stretchers. One slumped and cried, "Don't send me back; don't send me back." To Wheeler's surprise, Schmidhofer helped quiet them, but when he woke them up from the trance, their symptoms returned. "The six were like the writhing of the tentacles of an octopus," he said—but the writhing was less severe than it had been at the beginning. Each day they got a little better as they practiced exhalations and relaxation exercises until Schmidhofer announced that henceforth they could do it without his help.[28]

For them and many thousands of other veterans, the battle of Iwo Jima would never really end, but they could still take pride in what the Marine Corps had achieved as they sought to survive and thrive in the new world for which they had fought.

In 1968, the island was returned to Japan.

The Great Red God

I wrote this book to answer the seemingly straightforward question I posed in the introduction: What's it like being in battle? I thought it would be a lot easier, to tell you the truth, and this volume rather shorter. I've learned much over the course of researching the subject for the past X years—it's been such a long time I can't even remember when exactly I started working on *Men of War*, though my son, Edmund, is nearly six and I know that I was reading about Bunker Hill before he was born—but I remain stumped. Every time I think I've got a handle on the topic, that I have finally grasped the experience of combat, it slips infuriatingly away. Fortunately, I'm not the only one. Among old soldiers there exists the discombobulating sensation that war was simultaneously exhilarating and horrifying, terrifying and boring, cruel and kind, tragic and farcical. Mars demands much of his congregants.

Attempting to get to the heart of the problem, I've approached, or at least tried to approach, the subject from the perspective of that of an impartial historian; that is, I've dissected the combat experience from the perspective of an arbiter unweighted by preconceived notions and unhampered by any desire to hammer some political point home. I came, in other words, to the subject deliberately cold. Perhaps too cold, some might say. There are, I grant you, lengthy passages where I may seem detached and clinical—a particularly disturbing habit when discussing such sensitive and painful topics as dead sons, grievous trauma, and vicious suffering. My defense against the charge of hard-heartedness is that there are far too many books about war that sentimentalize, glamorize, or euphemize what happens during combat. If we are to seek the truth, as honest historians should, we must be determined to tell the truths that we find, no matter how discomfiting. But ultimately, I cleave with the poet Robert Southey (1774–1843) to an ironic sensibility on the subject of martial glory. In "The Battle of Blenheim," Southey cast a beady eye on the Duke of Marlborough's defeat of the French and Bavarians in 1704:

> They said it was a shocking sight
> After the field was won;
> For many thousand bodies here
> Lay rotting in the sun;
> But things like that, you know, must be
> After a famous victory.

I should add that my descriptions of the rotting bodies at Bunker Hill, Gettysburg, and Iwo Jima imply neither prescription nor proscription, though I shall admit that over the course of my research I've become somewhat more cautious when it comes to listening to drums beaten by amateurs rousing nations to war with one another. In this I follow Sir John Keegan, who, I recall reading, once observed that professional military historians—perhaps counterintuitively, considering their bloodthirsty interests—tend to be more pacific, if not pacifist, than the population at large because they keenly understand the costs, price, and tolls of war. In other words, they are more aware than most that embarking on war is like entering a dark room—one where monsters lurk and unexpected obstacles lie, where one can only stumble blindly about hoping for the best. In that dark room, even the simplest thing becomes very hard, and no matter what transpires or how incandescent the cause, men will be murdered, often mistakenly or accidentally, and sometimes pointlessly. In the end, no war has ever achieved what it set out to do. That does not mean that war is always unnecessary or never justified, but one must pick one's battles (so to speak) and be realistic as to balancing often incommensurate ends and means, knowns and unknowns.

Some might nevertheless cavil that a person cannot truly write of war until he or she has experienced its bite—which I haven't—but the flesh-witnessing of combat, while allowing an individual to be "blooded" in the mysteries of battle, to join the elite fraternity of veterans who have "seen the elephant" (as the Civil War phrase has it), comes fraught with an important but rarely discussed liability: One naturally tends to assume that one's own experience is automatically applicable to soldiers of times past. In this way, a Marine or army veteran of Fallujah during the latest Iraq War can define himself as the direct spiritual descendant of a Bunker Hill militiaman or perhaps even the latest embodiment in a long line of warriors representing what has been called the "Western way of war," a tradition that, some have argued, stretches back to the Greek hoplites who thwarted the ambitions of the eastern Persians. Hence the myth of the "universal soldier," the ultimately fallacious belief that the phenomenon of combat, and how it is experienced and conceived, is eternal and immutable.

On a superficial basis, this observation is accurate in the sense that men of war have shared certain experiences since the first glimmerings of recorded history. During the battle of Fallujah—regarded by some as a modern Gettysburg—American soldiers echoed their martial forebears in a variety of ways.[1] The sights, noted previously by General Burgoyne at Bunker Hill, were similarly spectacular: Lance Corporal Justin Boswood was in a firefight and "the whole house was shaking with 5.56mm rounds . . . SAWs going off with a two-hundred-round burst and the M-16s firing just as fast as you could pull the trigger. It was just awesome."[2] In place of drums sounding the advance, percussive heavy metal blared.[3] There was the habitual pre-combat accumulation and checking of equipment and weaponry, as documented repeatedly since the time of Homer. Whereas in the *Iliad*, we find loving lists of the helmets, greaves, armor, shields, swords, and spears borne by Greek and Trojan warriors alike, in Fallujah Sergeant David Bellavia's outfit "[threw] on our full battle rattle, which include[d]: ballistic-proof eye protection, smoke grenades for concealment, reinforced knee pads any skateboarder would envy, a five-quart CamelBak reservoir of water[,] thirty-five pound Interceptor Ballistic Armor fully loaded, two-and-a-half-pound Kevlar helmet, night vision, grenades, weapon, and ammunition."[4]

And, as ever, all were filthy. While George Orwell commented that "the men who fought at Verdun, at Waterloo, at Flodden, at Senlac, at Thermopylae—every one of them had lice crawling over his testicles," at Fallujah soldiers like Corporal Jason Howell "lathered Lamasil over their chafed waists, crotches, and feet. . . . Rubbed raw from the constant movement of combat, the young Marines used the cream to soothe the red splotches of peeling skin, blistering feet, and pus-stained sores that had developed on their bodies."[5] Near the end, everyone's uniforms, according to Bellavia, "were covered in dried gore, blood, grime, concrete dust, and smoke stains. All of us have brown slicks of diarrhea pasting our pants to our backsides. We're so sick that some of us can hardly walk. . . . We look like bedraggled castaways with whiskers and wild, red-rimmed eyes."[6]

Physiologically, too, the body's reactions to combat have not changed: Homer's heroes, God's Israelites, Caesar's Romans, Charlemagne's knights, all experienced the same dramatic increases in heart rate, loss of fine motor control, rising stress levels, and post-battle exhaustion following the typical adrenaline high that U.S. soldiers have in Iraq. King Henry V's words at Agincourt (at least as dramatized by Shakespeare) still splendidly describe every man of war's physical reaction to close-quarters combat:

> Then imitate the action of the tiger:
> Stiffen the sinews, summon up the blood,
> Disguise fair nature with hard-favored rage;
> Then lend the eye a terrible aspect: . . .
>
> Now set the teeth and stretch the nostril wide,
> Hold hard the breath and bend every spirit
> To his full height. (*Henry V,* act 3, scene 1, lines 6–17)

Despite these similarities, the assumption undergirding the "universal soldier" concept is fundamentally flawed. Its default position is that battle is statically isotropic: in other words, that the fighting experience has basically remained the same throughout history and can be viewed and understood from a single, unchanging perspective. But it is not. Combat, in fact, is dynamically anisotropic: War is felt, heard, tasted, seen, perceived, interpreted, in a shifting, subjective myriad of ways depending on context and culture. Rightly speaking, then, there is not one eternal experience of combat, but many *experiences* of combat that alter over time and space. Warfare, in short, has been typified not by stasis and continuity, but by diversity and variety, contradiction and change.

Even within the relatively compact American context, which extends only from 1775 until the present, there are gaping differences in how soldiers have understood war. Take, for example, the trope of the "Baptism of Fire," a staple of war literature. As Sergeant Bellavia remarks, "Combat distilled to its purest human form is a test of manhood [and] what a man finds there defines how he measures himself for the rest of his life. I embrace the battle. I welcome it into my soul."[7] To us, as moderns, it seems natural to assume that a person's time in combat is a momentous and life-altering event, and by extension the militiamen at Bunker Hill must have been transformed by their exposure to the British assault. But there is no evidence that they underwent any such form of self-realization. Instead, the older ones saw war as an inescapable part of everyday existence and combat as an interlude between day-to-day hardships, and so followed the biblical Job (7:1) in assuming that "the life of man upon earth is a warfare, and his days are like the days of a hireling." Youths may have been excited about being away from home and chores as they participated in their War Mitzvah (as it were), but their time with the colors was always temporary. During the Revolution, sixteen-year-old Peter Pond, for instance, was chafing under his parents' stricture that he should not leave despite his "Strong Desire to be a Solge" (as he wrote in his diary), but one evening at the tavern the drums and "Instraments of Musick were all Imployed to that Degrea that thay Charmed me" and Pond signed on along with "Miney lads of my Aquantans." Indulging in forbidden gingerbread and beer with his bounty, he completely forgot "that I had left my Parans who were Exceedingly trubled in Minde for my wellfair."[8] There was no more to it than having a lark before coming back to the farm.

It would not be for several more decades and the rise of the Romantic movement, with its focus on introspection, the self, and emotions, that soldiers would begin to believe that everything they had achieved in civilian life up until that moment, the challenges they had faced, and all their book-learning were worthless and empty when measured against a single instant of combat. An early example of this new outlook is provided by John Malcolm, a young, callow officer in 1813–14 who on the eve of his first battle was advised by his comrades that "in less than twenty-four hours hence, I might be wiser than all the sages and philosophers that ever wrote."[9] While Bellavia might certainly agree with that sentiment, such convictions are alien to the militiamen of Bunker Hill, and they must accordingly be understood on their own terms, not those of ours.

By the time of the Civil War, soldiers understood battle as a quest for self-fulfillment that could better the soul and were thus fascinated by their own feelings and passions toward the phenomenon of combat. To them, imagination, impulse, intuition, and the irrational were key to war. The dramatic was exalted, the intense celebrated, horror described, the sublime marveled at. In tones that would have been incomprehensible to those at Bunker Hill, John C. West, a Texas private, devoted no fewer than three letters (to his four-year-old son, his wife, and his brother) detailing at great length his own baptism of fire and what he had experienced at Gettysburg, a transcendent event.[10]

Much of this efflorescent enthusiasm would be killed off, quite literally, in the slaughterhouses of Antietam and the Wilderness. Certainly, by World War II there was little residue of the Romantic attitude that, as the Roman poet Horace had written, it was sweet and fitting to die for one's country. Whereas some very old veterans still saw their war through a gauzy veil of sentiment, few followed their example. In 1900, for instance, C. D. Westbrook, remembering his service with the 120th New York nearly forty years earlier, could assert that his Civil War comrades had "marched with unfaltering step . . . into the very jaws of death" to prove the Roman's maxim, but such a view was seen as noxiously anachronistic even before the end of the Great War.[11] (The poet

Wilfred Owen would devastatingly condemn Horace's famous line as "the old Lie.")

In its place was a regard for combat as a matter of managerial competency. The origins of this conception lay in the Victorian ideology of Positivism, a reaction against Romanticism that stressed a beetle-browed obsession with quantifying, standardizing, listing, and categorizing things, all things, from vertebrate species to human intelligence to economic statistics. Positivists devoured facts and figures, amassed tables and charts, because they believed that the path to illuminating empirical Truth lay in the systematic extrapolation of rational causes and effects from the chaos of the natural world. Charles Darwin, for instance, deduced the theory of evolution only after decades' worth of patient observation and the accumulation of vast amounts of data. In the military sphere, there was a new and keen interest in the science of ballistics, a compiling of intricate tables meticulously comparing the merits and flaws of different small arms, and a fascination with the historical typology of battles and their almost infinite complexity and splendor. Through the application of what was being called "military science," soldiers would fight their future battles based on rules and principles derived from primary facts and their painstaking application.[12]

The Marine Corps, generally seen as an exemplar of the blood-and-guts school of combat, was in fact a leader in this bloodless-and-brains field in the 1930s. At the time, an amphibious operation—the landing of a seaborne force on a defended hostile shore—was regarded among the global military intelligentsia as virtually impossible, a lethal folly.[13] Attacking troops were doomed in the face of beaches and bluffs hardened with machine guns and artillery, mines and barbed wire, entrenchments and emplacements. Proof of the pudding for all to see had been provided in World War I, during the campaign commonly abbreviated to "Gallipoli." In April 1915, the Mediterranean Expeditionary Force undertook a series of assaults against several beaches in the Dardanelles as part of an effort to knock the Turks out of the war. Losses were dreadful: At V Beach, just 21 of the first 200 men to disembark made it ashore; at W Beach, the Lancashire Fusiliers lost 600 out of 1,000 men before even hitting land.

In 1933, the Marines, alarmed at the likelihood of Japanese expansion into the Pacific and the consequent need to storm their conquered islands, took on the role of management consultants when they revisited the subject. The Marine Corps Schools (MCS) at Quantico—where the most promising officers were trained for high command—created an exclusive course in which each student was handed a copy of the official British history of Gallipoli and directed to dissect the operation ruthlessly to discover what had gone wrong. As they dug deeper into the mountain of reports, orders, and correspondence, they found that the Allied landings had collapsed owing not to the inherently risky nature of an amphibious assault but by ignorance, incompetence, bad luck, and gross underpreparation.[14]

With that analysis in hand, the Marine Corps later that year temporarily discontinued all other classes at the MCS so that the fifty-two students and their instructors could devote all their efforts to preparing a manual on amphibious warfare that would serve as the standard how-to guide to launching an assault on a defended Pacific island.[15] They eventually produced the *Tentative Manual for Landing Operations* (June 13, 1934), which would be continually revised until it provided an infallible step-by-step guide to success.[16] The Marines who landed at Iwo Jima (as well as other islands, and, of course, the Allied forces during the Normandy landings) would be its ultimate beneficiaries.

For our purposes, the *Tentative Manual* is most important for understanding the general perspective of the Marines of the Pacific theater. It exemplifies the managerial approach to combat and encapsulates the assumption that industrialized warfare was at heart a logistical issue based on colossal manufacturing capacity applied intelligently and according to "scientific" principles of efficiency. War should be run along business lines, in short.[17] A by-product of this ethos was the transformation of the combat experience into something little more than a technically proficient factory job: The Marines on Iwo Jima, for instance, considered themselves to be working on a lethal production line spewing out corpses. To apply their worldview to that of the Union and

Confederate men at Gettysburg, let alone their ancestors at Bunker Hill, would seem a major historical category error.

The same can be said of their descendants in Iraq and Afghanistan. Given the nature of the continuing shifts in American society and culture, the transformation of its armed forces from mass organizations into professional bodies of specialists, as well as the emphasis on technology and intelligence, perhaps in coming years future historians of combat experiences will similarly distinguish from even their most recent forebears the current generation of soldiers—men, and women, of war alike.

And here I end my investigation, more knowledgeable and maybe a little wiser. But even now, I still do not know for certain whether, at the supreme moment of crisis in combat, I would stand and fight alongside the grim-serried ranks of my comrades, or if I would flee. No one does—not until that dread moment arrives. Perhaps it's better that way.

Acknowledgments

Over the course of writing *Men of War,* I have accumulated a significant number of debts, and so I am glad to be able, at long last, to repay them—partially, at least.

For providing me with hard-to-find articles and essays, I thank John Heiser, historian at Gettysburg National Military Park; Erik Goldstein, curator of mechanical arts & numismatics at Colonial Williamsburg; Kathy O. Jackson of the Medical Society of Delaware; Col. Joseph H. Alexander, USMC (Ret.); and Alan Hawk of the National Museum of Health and Medicine. Matthew A. Boal and Scott N. Hendrix sent copies of their dissertations, both of which proved invaluable. Samuel Fore of the marvelous Harlan Crow Library in Dallas, Texas, very kindly supplied the unpublished transcript of Isaac Glynney's Bunker Hill diary.

I must also thank, profusely, Dr. Earl J. Hess of Lincoln Memorial University for reading an early and ungainly draft of the Bunker Hill chapter, as well as Richard Brookhiser and Michael Stephenson for braving the howling wilderness of the first-draft version of Gettysburg. Don N. Hagist, one of the foremost historians of the British Army during the War of Independence, dissected my arguments in the relevant sections of Bunker Hill and (tried to) set me right when I erred. It should go without saying, though I shall say it, that any remaining inaccuracies or misinterpretations are entirely my own.

The Frederick Lewis Allen Room at the New York Public Library is a haven for every writer, and I was fortunate indeed to benefit from its sanctuary for an unconscionably prolonged time owing to Jay Barksdale, its guardian. I'm also grateful to the librarians and staff of the Irma and Paul Milstein Division of United States History, Local History, and Genealogy for uncomplainingly hauling scores of heavy old books to my desk. Not only am I immensely thankful for the unparalleled resources of the grand old NYPL, but also for the wondrous holdings of the Butler Library at Columbia University: Time and time again they remind me that we all are beholden to the antiquarians, archivists, librarians, and scholars of ages past and present. Without their dedication and diligence, our preserved knowledge of history would be paltry indeed.

Producing and publishing a book requires an enormous investment of skill, time, money, persistence, and patience. Random House has neither stinted in its support nor swayed in its conviction that *Men of War* was a worthwhile project. For their aid and advice, I must thank my editors, Jonathan Jao and Will Murphy, as well as assistant editor Molly Turpin, who supervised the Herculean process of turning an idea into a book with seemingly effortless (though it wasn't) aplomb. Martin Schneider, the copy editor; Loren Noveck, my production editor; and Jenn Backe and Richard Elman, the production managers, devoted untold hours to making sure my prose was relatively coherent, my bibliography tidily arranged, and my pages neatly bound. David Lindroth did a splendid job of composing the maps armed with only the vaguest of instructions. My agent, Eric Lupfer of William Morris Endeavor, is a font of sound advice and shrewd judgment; it was he who so expertly midwifed, nurtured, and raised *Men of War* into the form it is today.

My father, Professor Paul Lawrence Rose, one of the finest and most penetrating of historians, died during my final stages of editing this book. He taught me an enormous amount about practicing history, and I think that he would have enjoyed reading (and commenting on) *Men of War,* as would my late grandfather, Professor Jack Rose (French Army, 1939–40, and the Queen's Own Royal West Kent Regiment until the war's end). My mother, Susan, as well as my siblings—Olivia, Zoë, and Ari—have been immoveable rocks of support throughout the writing process, as have Stephen and Craig. Accolades, too, must be bestowed upon Erna Olafson, David and Carolyn Hellerstein, Chad and Elizabeth, and Ben and Jamie. Mustn't forget, of course, Sabrina and Romy, and Kyla and Iliana.

And finally, I arrive at the dedicatees, my wife, Rebecca, and Edmund, our son. I cannot even begin to describe how wonderful they are, and how beloved. It was a long and difficult trek to finish *Men of War,* and they were unstintingly there every step of the way. To them, I owe everything still.

Notes

INTRODUCTION

1. Regarding the historiography of military history, see R. M. Citino's important essay, "Military Histories Old and New: A Reintroduction," *American Historical Review* 112, no. 4 (2007): 1070–90.
2. Quoted in H. H. Sargent, *Napoleon Bonaparte's First Campaign* (Chicago: A. C. Mc-Clurg and Co., 1895), 173.
3. B. Brecht, *Fragen eines lesenden Arbeiters* ("Questions from a worker who reads"), trans. M. Hamburger, in *Bertolt Brecht: Poems, 1913–1956,* ed. J. Willett and R. Manheim (London: Methuen, 1987), 252–53.
4. L. Tolstoy, "The Raid," trans. L. and A. Maude, in *Tales of Army Life* (London: Oxford University Press, 1932), 3.
5. On this issue, see my review, "How the Battle Was Won, If Not Yet the War," *Wall Street Journal,* July 16, 2011.
6. On the errors of the universal soldier thesis, see Lynn, *Battle: A History of Combat and Culture,* xiv–xvii.
7. Letter, Washington to John Augustine Washington, May 31, 1754, in *The Writings of George Washington,* ed. W. C. Ford (New York: G. P. Putnam's Sons, 1889–1893), 1:90.
8. As recorded by Horace Walpole, *Memoirs of the Reign of King George the Second,* 2nd ed. (London: Henry Colburn, 1847), 1:400.
9. See J. Glenn Gray, *The Warriors: Reflections on Men in Battle* (New York: Bison Books, 1998 edn.), 29–30; see also W. Broyles Jr., "Why Men Love War," in *The Vietnam Reader,* ed. W. Capps (New York: Routledge, 1991), 71.
10. Printed in Hatch, "New Hampshire at Bunker Hill," 218.

BUNKER HILL

1. Introduction

1. Paret, "The Relationship Between the American Revolutionary War and European Military Thought and Practice," in Paret, *Understanding War,* 37.
2. The entry may have been written by Edmund Burke. See *The Annual Register,* 83.
3. Letter, Feilding to Denbigh, July 18, 1775, in Balderston and Syrett (eds.), *The Lost War.* The Americans agreed, with Lieutenant Samuel Webb telling Silas Deane that "Major Bruce, who served two years in Portugal with General Lee, told my brother Joe

at the lines, that it was the hottest engagement he ever knew. Even, says he, the Battle of Minden did not equal it." Letter, Webb to Deane, July 11, 1775, in Webb (ed.), *Reminiscences of General Samuel B. Webb,* 11.

4. Letter, I. Seagrove to J. Blackburn, July 2, 1775, quoted in Flavell, "Government Interception of Letters from America and the Quest for Colonial Opinion in 1775," 414.

5. In the *Constitutional Gazette* of October 11, 1775, printed in Moore (ed.), *Diary of the American Revolution,* 1:116.

3. The Redoubt, Part One

1. A "large majority" of the New England militia, according to Dr. Thacher, arrived "carrying ordinary firearms, unprovided with bayonets, and habited in the style of country laborers." Thacher, *Military Journal,* 27. See also "An Account of the Battle of Bunker's Hill, by Major General Henry Dearborn, Published 1818," in which he claims that "not an officer or soldier of the continental troops engaged was in uniform, but were in the plain and ordinary dress of citizens." See Coffin (ed.), *Battle of Breed's Hill,* 23.

2. Swett, *History of Bunker Hill Battle,* 13.

3. Moore, *Life of General John Stark of New Hampshire,* 181. On the militiamen's occupations and wealth, see Fischer, *Paul Revere's Ride,* "Appendix O: The Lexington Militia: Quantitative Research," 319–20; tax list of Derryfield, December 24, 1775, printed in Potter, *History of Manchester,* 418–19.

4. Doddridge, *Notes on the Settlement and Indian Wars of the Western Parts of Virginia and Pennsylvania,* 91.

5. Kidder, *History of New Ipswich,* 95; Bolton, *Private Soldier under Washington,* 91–92; Fischer, *Paul Revere's Ride,* 159; Stephenson, *Patriot Battles,* 151.

6. Hagelin and Brown, "Connecticut Farmers at Bunker Hill."

7. According to G. E. Ellis, Prescott was wearing a linen coat; Swett agrees, calling it a "simple calico frock." R. Frothingham says that he wore a "blue coat and a three-cornered hat." Ellis, *Sketches of Bunker Hill Battle and Monument,* 29; Swett, *History of Bunker Hill Battle,* 19; Frothingham, *Siege of Boston,* 122.

8. Moore, *Life of General John Stark,* 134.

9. Kidder, *History of New Ipswich,* 95; see also Smith, *History of the Town of Peterborough,* 85.

10. Frothingham, "Address," 22.

11. Testimony of Nathaniel Rice, in Swett, *Notes to His Sketch,* 13.

12. Some authorities state 1742 as the oldest Besses in service, but G. Neumann notes that Long Land Pattern 1730s were stockpiled at the beginning of the war. See Stephenson, *Patriot Battles,* 121; Neumann, "Redcoats' Brown Bess." At the beginning of the Revolution, many active units were equipped with the superior—but still not gleamingly new—Pattern 1756 (.75-caliber, 46-inch-long barrel, 17-inch-long triangular socket bayonet, and steel ramrod), but over the course of the war a shortened version called the Short Land Musket Pattern 1769 was issued. See Bohy and Troiani, " 'We Meant to Be Free Always,' " 49–51, 58. On cost, see Bolton, *Private Soldier under Washington,* 107. According to Houlding, "It was . . . fairly common to find a regiment of foot armed with old and worn-out firearms." Houlding, *Fit for Service,* 146.

13. Churchill, "Gun Ownership in Early America," esp. 625 and table 1, "Extant Returns and Petitions Reporting Militia Armament, 1775–1776." On Colonel Little's regiment, see Wade and Lively, *This Glorious Cause,* 15.

14. There were, in short, more than enough guns to go around. So it was that Captain Charles Stuart, a Grenadiers officer, commented that General Gage was "foolish" to order that "no townsman [could] carry more than one firelock at a time." The New Englanders instead went to their illicit meetings armed with the single stipulated musket and then cheekily walked to and fro "eight or ten times a day, conveying each time [a different] one" until they had their stockpile. Letter, C. Stuart to Lord Bute, July 24, 1775, in Wortley (ed.), *Prime Minister and His Son,* 67.

15. Fischer, *Paul Revere's Ride,* 161.

16. Smith, *Peterborough, New Hampshire,* 85.

17. Entry for February 27, 1755, in Johnson (ed.), "Diary of Israel Litchfield," part 2, 255.

18. Potter, "Life and Remarkable Adventures," 15.

19. Kidder, *History of New Ipswich,* 95.

20. Fischer, *Paul Revere's Ride,* 161.

21. "Another Account of the Late Action at Bunker's Hill," *Rivington's Gazetteer,* August 3, 1775, printed in Dawson (ed.), "Bunker's Hill," 393.

22. Dearborn, "An Account of the Battle of Bunker's Hill," in Coffin (ed.), *Battle of Breed's Hill,* 19. One result of Bunker Hill was that when they returned home, the New Hampshire men lobbied fiercely for the issuing of bayonets. They told their Committee of Safety that it is "barbarous to let men be obliged to oppose bayonets with only gun barrels." *New Hampshire State Papers,* VI, 526, quoted in Elting, *Bunker's Hill,* 40.

23. Swett, *History of Bunker Hill Battle,* 20.

24. Isaac Glynney diary (unpublished), kindly provided by the Harlan Crow Library, Dallas, Texas.

25. On Gridley's background, see Huntoon, *History of the Town of Canton,* 360–79.

26. There is some debate on the length of the walls. The most authoritative accounts, however, concur that the redoubt was "about eight rods square." Provincial Congress of Massachusetts report, July 25, 1775, in Dawson (ed.), "Bunker's Hill," 388; P. Brown says it was about ten rods by eight. Brown, "Officer's Story of Bunker Hill."

27. Frothingham, *Siege of Boston,* 124.

28. The height of the walls is unclear. Henry Dearborn claimed they were "6 or 7 feet" high, but Lord Percy said the Americans were "intrenched up to their chins," or about four or five feet. Neither man saw the walls up close, with Dearborn fighting at the rail fence while Percy was stationed in Boston. Most accounts tend to support Dearborn, but if the men were standing on platforms it would have looked as if the walls came up only to their chins. Dearborn, "An Account of the Battle of Bunker's Hill," in Coffin (ed.), *Battle of Breed's Hill,* 16; Elting, *Bunker's Hill,* 23. On the platform, see Frothingham, *Siege of Boston,* 125.

29. As defined by Duffy, *Fire and Stone,* 225.

30. Quoted in Duffy, *Fire and Stone,* 72. A solid introduction to Vauban is H. Guerlac's essay, "Vauban: The Impact of Science on War," in *Makers of Modern Strategy,* ed. P. Paret, 64–90. J. Langins challenges Guerlac on several points; see Langins, "Eighteenth-Century French Fortification Theory after Vauban: The Case for Montalembert," in *The Heirs of Archimedes,* ed. B. D. Steele and T. Dorland, 333–59. On Americans' familiarity with Vauban's technical volumes, see Powers, "Studying the Art of War," 783.

31. Later that year, John Montrésor of the royal army composed a map of the area, "A survey of the peninsula of Charles Town shewing the three posts now garrison'd by His Majesty's troops for the winter," December 10, 1775; it is kept in the Henry Clinton Papers at the Clements Library at the University of Michigan. Its chief interest lies in

the new fortification built to cover the Neck from invasion, but Montrésor also shows a small fort on Breed's Hill, calling it the "redout on rebel hill." Its main defensive wall has been reoriented away from Boston toward the approach to the Neck from the mainland, as might be expected given British possession of the city. An online version can be seen at the online presentation of the "The Geometry of War: Fortification Plans from 18th-Century America" exhibition at the William L. Clements Library, University of Michigan, available at www.clements.umich.edu/exhibits/online/ geometry_of_war/geometry10.php, accessed February 7, 2014.

32. French, *First Year*, 216; Fisher, "Objective at Bunker Hill," 48.

33. Elting, *Bunker's Hill*, 21; Van Arsdale (ed.), *Discord And Civil Wars*, 17; letter, Barnard to an unidentified recipient, August 10, 1775, printed in Barnard, "Letter of Rev. Thomas Barnard," 35–41.

34. Hennell, *Gentleman Volunteer*, 91–92.

35. Leeke, *History of Lord Seaton's Regiment*, 1:32.

36. Quoted in Muir, *Tactics and the Experience of Battle*, 47.

37. Letter, Chester to Fish, July 22, 1775, in Dawson (ed.), "Bunker's Hill," 386.

38. Blaise de Lasseran-Massencôme, seigneur de Montluc, quoted in Nosworthy, *Anatomy of Victory*, 13. This almost benign view would change over the coming centuries. During the Second World War, analysts found that whereas just one in five new arrivals to the battlefront listed artillery as the most "fearful" weapon compared to one in two who believed that air attack was worse, with a month's hard combat under their belts these same men reversed their opinions exactly. Stouffer et al. (eds.), *American Soldier*, 2:236, Chart 8, "Ratings of the fearfulness of two enemy weapons in relation to length of time in combat."

39. Duffy, *Military Experience*, 245; Muir, *Tactics and the Experience of Battle*, 46.

40. On this distinction, see Dinter, *Hero or Coward*, 34–35.

41. Thacher, *Military Journal*, 30.

42. Testimony of John Dexter, in Swett, *Notes to His Sketch*, 6.

43. Testimony of William Low, in Swett, *Notes to His Sketch*, 12.

44. Testimony of Amos Foster, in Swett, *Notes to His Sketch*, 14.

45. Dearborn, "An Account of the Battle of Bunker's Hill," in Coffin (ed.), *Battle of Breed's Hill*, 19; Elting, *Bunker's Hill*, 27.

46. Powell, "Connecticut Soldier under Washington," 99.

47. B. P. Hughes, *Firepower*, 29.

48. Brown, "Officer's Story of Bunker Hill."

49. Powell, "Connecticut Soldier under Washington," 101.

50. Hughes, *Firepower*, 32–33.

51. Tielke, *Account of Some of the Most Remarkable Events*, 1:196. William Leeke observed, at Waterloo, that it was much easier to see round-shot from your own side soar overhead than it was to "catch sight of one coming through the air towards you." Leeke, *History of Lord Seaton's Regiment*, 32.

52. Longmore, *Treatise on Gunshot Wounds*, 38–39.

53. Diary entry, October 24, 1777, in Thacher, *Military Journal*, 113.

54. Bancroft's narrative, in Hill (ed.), *Bi-Centennial of Old Dunstable*, 59.

55. Murdock, *Bunker Hill*, 107. In his essay on Martin (99–117), Murdock is skeptical about some of his claims, but in my opinion, this one is very capable of being true.

56. Longmore, *Treatise on Gunshot Wounds*, 31; on the coins, see Longmore, *Gunshot Injuries*, 227–28.

57. Brown, *Beside Old Hearth-Stones,* 221.

58. Trumbull, *Autobiography, Reminiscences, and Letters,* 19. Edward Elley related that a cannonball "came bounding along the ground, and a youngster put his heel against it and was thrown into lockjaw and expired in a short time." Quoted in Dann, *Revolution Remembered,* 237. On "spent" cannon shot and amputated feet, see Longmore, *Treatise on Gunshot Wounds,* 24. Some English soldiers during the wars in Europe seventy years earlier took extraordinary risks by seeking their own side's expired cannonballs near the enemy so as to sell them back to their original owners. Travers, "Development of British Military Historical Writing and Thought from the Eighteenth Century to the Present," in *Military History and the Military Profession,* ed. D. A. Charters, M. Milner, and J. B. Wilson, 25. The error of placing one's feet in the way of a rolling cannonball was not confined to the eighteenth century: At Gettysburg in 1863, a Wisconsin soldier stuck out his heel to stop one such ball and had his leg torn off. He "cried like a child" to think that he had lost his limb in so inglorious a manner and mourned, "I shall always be ashamed to say how I lost it." Davis, Jr., *Three Years in the Army,* 226.

59. For the shot that killed Pollard, see diary entry of June 16 (*sic*) in Green (ed.), "Thomas Boynton's Journal," 255. For the anecdotes about Pollard's French and Indian War service as well as his final moments, see Brown, *Beside Old Hearth-Stones,* 329–33. James Stevens, an Andover man, heard that "they shot won of our men, won polerd of Bilrica." Entry of June 17, 1775, printed in Bailey, *Historical Sketches of Andover,* 336.

60. Letter, Amos Foster, August 3, 1825, printed in Sumner, "Reminiscences," 122. Brown notes that the shot took off his head. Brown, *Beside Old Hearth-Stones,* 332.

61. Holland, *History of Western Massachusetts,* 2:420.

62. Swett, *History of Bunker Hill Battle,* 22.

63. Testimony of William French, in Swett, *Notes to His Sketch,* 11.

64. On ordering the body thrown into the trench, see Dawson (ed.), "Bunker's Hill," 437n.; on the cleric, see Swett, *Notes to His Sketch,* 24 (note H); see also Swett, *History of Bunker Hill Battle,* 22; Frothingham, *Siege of Boston,* 126; "Prescott Manuscript," in Frothingham, *Battle-Field of Bunker Hill,* 19–20. C. Butler adds that Prescott consented to hold a burial after the battle. Butler, *History of the Town of Groton,* 338n5. On the next day's discovery of the grave, see Clarke, "Impartial and Authentic Narrative," 256.

65. Brown, "Officer's Story of Bunker Hill."

66. Brown, "Officer's Story of Bunker Hill"; Elting, *Bunker's Hill,* 25; Bancroft's narrative, in Hill (ed.), *Bi-Centennial of Old Dunstable,* 58. Interestingly, the granddaughter of Captain John Linzee of the *Falcon* later married Prescott's grandson. Brown, *Beside Old Hearth-Stones,* 27.

67. General Morning Orders, June 17, 1775, in Stevens (ed.), *General Sir William Howe's Orderly Book,* 1–2; French, *First Year,* 734–35 (appendix 15), 741 (appendix 20).

68. Spring, *With Zeal,* 60.

69. Cooper, *Practical Guide for the Light Infantry Officer,* xvi.

70. Heath, *Heath's Memoirs of the American War,* 28.

71. Bancroft's narrative, in Hill (ed.), *Bi-Centennial of Old Dunstable,* 59.

72. Winsor (ed.), *Memorial History of Boston,* 3:85n1. See also Bryant and Gay, *Popular History of the United States,* 3:403. A second instance: In June 1746, during the battle of Dettingen, Sir Andrew Agnew steeled his Scots Fusiliers for an oncoming onslaught of French cuirassiers by ordering them to open their ranks and let the cavalry pass through. "Dinna fire till ye can see the whites of their e'en," he cried, adding for good

measure, "If ye dinna kill them they'll kill you." ("So, Sir Andrew, I hear the cuirassiers rode through your regiment today," laconically observed King George II afterward. "Ou, ay, yer Majestee," replied this paragon of Highland sangfroid, "but they didna get oot again.") See Anderson, *Scottish Nation*, 2:679–80; and Agnew, "General Sir Andrew Agnew of Lochnaw," 37–38.

73. Winsor (ed.), *Memorial History of Boston*, 3:85n1.

74. Potter, "Life and Remarkable Adventures," 14.

75. Testimony of Jordan, printed in Swett, *Notes to His Sketch*, 15. Similarly, Isaac Bassett, stationed in the redoubt, "did not, myself, hear the order given; but it was often said by the soldiers of our regiment, that General Putnam ordered them 'not to fire on the enemy till they should see the color of their eyes, and then for every man to make sure of his mark.'" Testimony of Isaac Bassett, printed in Dawson (ed.), "Bunker's Hill," 429.

76. K. Yellin compiles a catalogue of the most common tropes. Yellin, *Battle Exhortation*, 71–72.

77. Quoted in Stanhope, *Notes of Conversations with the Duke of Wellington*, 13.

78. Hansen, "Battle Exhortation in Ancient Historiography," 169.

79. Quoted in Brown, *Beside Old Hearth-Stones*, 35.

80. Testimony of Simeon Noyes, in Swett, *Notes to His Sketch*, 13.

81. Testimony of Captain James Clark of Putnam's regiment, commanding 100 men, who arrived at the rail fence ten minutes after the firing began, in Swett, *Notes to His Sketch*, 7.

82. The deployments and precise numbers of some of the various companies and regiments are ambiguous, not helped by confusion among many writers as to the distinctions separating light infantry, grenadier, flank, and battalion/line troops. This summary is based on several sources, including Murdock, *Bunker Hill*, 14–18; Frothingham, *Siege of Boston*, 140–41; Morrissey, *Boston 1775*, 60; French, *First Year*, 232–34, 741 (appendix 20). Don N. Hagist helped enormously with figures and definitions in this respect.

83. The number of artillery pieces present is not entirely certain. Originally, Howe intended to bring four 6-pounders, four 12-pounders, and four 5.5-inch howitzers, but according to a letter to Lord Harvey, June 22 and June 24, 1775, he had "six field pieces, two light 12 pounders and two howitzers." Elting, *Bunker's Hill*, 23; Fortescue (ed.), *Correspondence of King George the Third*, 3:221.

84. "Letter from Boston, July 5th, 1775," printed in House of Commons, *The Detail and Conduct of the American War*, 14. After the battle, Cleaveland defended himself by testifying that he "sent 66 rounds to each gun, not more than half was fired," adding primly that "a commanding officer of artillery cannot be in every place." Disingenuously, Cleaveland omitted to state precisely which *caliber* these rounds were. Quoted in French, *First Year*, 749 (appendix 24).

85. F. Mackenzie's diary entry for April 22, 1775, notes that five sergeants, five corporals, and one hundred privates were "to do duty with the Royal Artillery." See French (ed.), *British Fusilier*, 73. Regarding the Lovells, who were on the pro-British side of the clan, see Jones, *Loyalists of Massachusetts*, 201–3. It is mentioned in an annotation to Washington's Revolutionary War Expense Accounts that James Lovell "was active in securing intelligence through spies; but how many and who were employed during the siege of Boston is not known." See note for July 15, 1775, in the George Washington Papers, Library of Congress.

4. The Beach

1. Wilkinson, "A Rapid Sketch of the Battle of Breed's Hill," in Coffin (ed.), *Battle of Breed's Hill,* 9–11 (James Wilkinson toured the site with Stark a year later); Moore, *Life of General John Stark,* 161; Potter, *History of Manchester,* 315, 433.

2. For contemporary descriptions of the Fusiliers, see Murdock, *Bunker Hill,* 137–39. Despite the Welch Fusiliers' storied reputation as, in the words of later American accounts, the "flower of the army" stationed in the Colonies, its Light component had been in a terrible mess for some time. At Lexington and Concord two months before, it had retreated in the face of the militia's shots and was only stopped when its officers scrambled to form a small line ahead of them "and presented their bayonets, and told the men that if they advanced they should die." On their performance at Lexington, see H. de Berniere, "General Gage's Instructions with a Curious Narrative of Occurrences" (1779), reprinted in Hudson, *History of the Town of Lexington,* 1:126–27n3; also informative is Urban, *Fusiliers,* 1–49.

3. Based on a compilation of muster-roll figures from WO 12 (National Archives, U.K.) by Don N. Hagist, "Bunker Hill Flank Company Casualties," which he sent to me on April 14, 2014. Another list, dated from about a week after the battle, differs in a few minor respects, and, it should be noted, includes both the 23rd's Light and Grenadier casualties but does not separate them. Thus, "Captain Blakeney, Lieutenant Beckwith, Lieutenant Cochrane, Lieutenant Lenthall, wounded; two sergeants, one drummer, eleven rank and file, killed; two sergeants, one drummer and fifer, thirty-five rank and file, wounded." See Gage, "Return of the Officers," printed in Force (ed.), *American Archives,* 4th ser., vol. 2, cols. 1098–99.

4. "Extracts of Letters Received in Philadelphia from a Gentleman in the Army, Dated Camp at Cambridge, June 27, 1775," printed in Force (ed.), *American Archives,* 4th ser., vol. 2, col. 1119.

5. Letter, Abigail Adams to John Adams, June 27, 1775, in Adams (ed.), *Familiar Letters of John Adams and His Wife Abigail Adams,* 71.

6. Quoted in Duffy, *Military Experience,* 253.

7. Colonel O. Williams, "A Narrative of the Campaign of 1780," Appendix B in Johnson, *Sketches of the Life and Correspondence of Nathanael Greene,* 1:496; Fischer, *Paul Revere's Ride,* 209.

8. Wolseley, *Story of a Soldier's Life,* 1:368–69. M. Hastings notes that "no U.S. or British regimental war diary that I have ever seen explicitly admits that soldiers fled in panic, as of course they sometimes do." Hastings, "Drawing the Wrong Lesson."

9. See Daddis, "Understanding Fear's Effect on Unit Effectiveness," 23.

10. "Rev. Peter Thacher's Narration," in Dawson (ed.), "Bunker's Hill," 383. See also J. Belknap's and E. Hazard's correspondence, August 8 to September 19, 1789, printed in Frothingham et al. (eds.), "Letter of Edward Everett," 96–99.

11. Hagist, "Shedding Light on Friendly Fire," 4–10. I am indebted to Mr. Hagist for kindly sending me the text of Abercrombie's letter to Sir Jeffrey Amherst, June 20, 1775. For surveys of this subject, see Shrader, "Friendly Fire: The Inevitable Price," 29–44; and Steinweg, "Dealing Realistically with Fratricide," 4–29.

12. "Combat stress" is the most common instigator of flight among veteran troops. Sir John Fortescue, historian of the British army, believed that "even the bravest man cannot endure to be under fire for more than a certain number of consecutive days, even if the fire be not very heavy." Letter, Fortescue to Lord Southborough, no date, printed

in *Report of the War Office Committee of Enquiry into "Shell-Shock," 9*. In the Second World War, army psychiatrists John Appel and Gilbert Beebe concluded that the average soldier reached his peak of fighting effectiveness in the first three months of combat and thereafter was gradually worn down until, at the 180-day mark, he was rendered almost useless until he was rotated to the rear for at least a few days' rest. "Just as an average truck wears out after a certain number of miles, it appears that the doughboy wore out, either developing an acute incapacitating neurosis or else becoming hypersensitive to shell fire, so overly cautious and jittery that he was ineffective and demoralizing to the newer men." See Appel and Beebe, "Preventive Psychiatry," 169–75; Wanke, "American Military Psychiatry," 133–34. The quotation regarding the "average truck" appears in Shephard, *War of Nerves*, 245.

13. For a discussion of this subject, see Stouffer et al. (eds.), *American Soldier*, 2:137–40, 118–27.

14. See L'Etang, "Some Thoughts on Panic in War," 278–85; and Ondishko, Jr., "View of Anxiety, Fear, and Panic," 58–60.

15. See, for instance, Thacher, *Military Journal*, 27. See also Samuel Drake's comment that "the regiments now serving in Boston were the choicest troops that army could muster." Drake (ed.), *Bunker Hill*, 13. Another nineteenth-century authority concurs by alleging that "every man preparing to attack the undisciplined provincials was a drilled soldier, and quite perfect in the art of war." Lossing, *Pictorial Field-Book*, 1:542. Henry Dearborn, a veteran of Bunker Hill, noted that at the battle General Howe "commanded a body of chosen troops, inured to discipline, and nearly double in number to his foe; possessed of artillery in abundance, prepared in the best manner; with an army at hand ready to re-inforce him, and led by officers, many of whom had seen service, all of whom had been bred to arms." "Reflections on the Campaigns of Sir William Howe . . . with an Incidental Account of the Battle of Bunker's Hill, Extracted from Major-General Henry Lee's *Memoirs of the War in the Southern Department of the United States*, Published 1812," printed in Coffin (ed.), *Battle of Breed's Hill*, 6–7.

16. On European averages, Fann, "On the Infantryman's Age," 165. On Henderson and others, see Palmer, "Longevity," 434–40. Henderson would die aged 105 in 1836.

17. Regarding the number of new recruits and length of service in America, I'm indebted to Don N. Hagist, who has analyzed the muster rolls for the 4th, 10th, 23rd, 35th, 38th, 43rd, 47th, 52nd, 59th, 63rd, and 64th Regiments, in WO 12 (Commissary General of Musters Office), National Archives (United Kingdom). Private communication, April 13, 2014.

18. Field, *Britain's Sea-Soldiers*, 1:153.

19. Ibid.

20. Houlding, *Fit for Service*, 160–62.

21. On drafting, see Houlding, *Fit for Service*, 120–25, and Hagist, *British Soldiers, American War*, 52–53; see also Spring, *With Zeal*, 105, 107.

22. An observation based on figures provided by Hagist, private communication, April 14, 2014.

23. Hagist, "Shedding Light on Friendly Fire," 7.

24. This section on the 18th/65th is based on the excellent article by Steven Baule and Don Hagist, "The Regimental Punishment Book of the Boston Detachments of the Royal Irish Regiment and 65th Regiment, 1774–1775," published in the *Journal of the Society for Army Research*. Mr. Hagist was kind enough to supply me with an advance copy.

25. Diary entry, June 25, 1775, printed in Van Arsdale (ed.), *Discord and Civil Wars*, 22.

26. Anderson, "People's Army: Provincial Military Service in Massachusetts," 505.

27. Fred Anderson's detailed estimates are used here. See Anderson, *People's Army,* 58–60, esp. n83.

28. Between 1755 and 1763, roughly 140 (but probably more) men signed up out of a total town population in 1760 of almost 760 people. That would mean there were about 380 white males living in Lexington, and we also find that 54 percent of them were older than 16. So let us say there were 205 eligible men. Even taking into account that some volunteers went more than once, that some came home early, and various other mitigating factors, it is hard to avoid concluding that between 50 percent and 60 percent of Lexington's eligible males went to war. See Hudson, *History of the Town of Lexington,* 1:413–16 (for rosters of volunteers) and 477 (for population).

29. Hawthorne, "Old News," in *Snow Image and Other Twice-Told Tales,* 130–31.

30. Data taken from Fischer, *Paul Revere's Ride,* Appendix O: "The Lexington Militia: Quantitative Research," 319–20.

31. Moore, *Life of General John Stark,* 181.

32. This list is based on Smith, *History of the Town of Peterborough,* 157–58, but supplemented by other sources. Some estimates of Peterborough's contribution range as low as sixteen and others, as high as forty or fifty, but twenty-six seems to be the most authoritative number. Resch, *Suffering Soldiers,* 23; Smith, *Peterborough, New Hampshire,* 92, 202–3, 370, 239–40, 176–78, 287, 264–70; Higginbotham, *War of American Independence,* 74.

33. Fischer, *Paul Revere's Ride,* Appendix O, "The Lexington Militia: Quantitative Research," 320.

34. Willcox, "Captain William Meacham at Bunker Hill," 203–7.

35. Roster, "Captain Benjamin Ames's Company (Presumably) at Bunker Hill," in Bailey, *Historical Sketches of Andover,* 319.

36. Gross, *Minutemen and Their World,* 71.

37. Fischer, *Paul Revere's Ride,* 158; Norton, "Marital Migration in Essex County, Massachusetts," 411; Waters, "Family, Inheritance, and Migration in Colonial New England," 65–66; Adams and Kasakoff, "Wealth and Migration in Massachusetts and Maine," 367.

38. See Quintal, Jr., *Patriots of Color,* and Alfred F. Young's preface, reproduced at http://www.nps.gov/archive/bost/patriotsofcolor/preface.htm. See also J. Lee Malcolm's article, "Slavery in Massachusetts and the American Revolution," *Journal of the Historical Society* 10, vol. (2010), 428.

39. Malcolm, "Slavery in Massachusetts," 417; on Boston's population, Greene and Harrington, *American Population,* 22.

40. The number of Americans ranged from 1,500 to 3,500 over the course of the day. If we take the average (2,500) and assume there were 33 blacks, we arrive at a figure of 1.32 percent representation, though there were almost certainly more than that bare minimum.

41. Malcolm, "Slavery in Massachusetts," 419–20, 427.

42. Bailey, *Historical Sketches of Andover,* 324.

43. Green, "Colonel William Prescott, 93.

44. Browne, *History of Hillsborough, New Hampshire,* 1:105–8, 111, esp. the list cataloguing Baldwin's company at Bunker Hill and the town's 1776 tax list. Whitcher, "Relation of New Hampshire Men to the Siege of Boston," 71.

45. Elting, *Bunker's Hill,* 11.

46. Lincoln (ed.), *Journals of Each Provincial Congress of Massachusetts,* entry of December 10, 1774, p. 71.

47. Fischer, *Paul Revere's Ride,* 155.

48. Johnson (ed.), "Diary of Israel Litchfield," 1:151.

49. Diary entry, November 14, 1774, in Johnson (ed.), "Diary of Israel Litchfield," 1:152.

50. Diary entry, April 13, 1775, in Johnson (ed.), "Diary of Israel Litchfield," 2:261.

51. Thus, on November 17, 1774, "in the afternoon 12 of us met . . . and exercised. We used what they call the Norfolk Exercise." Johnson (ed.), "Diary of Israel Litchfield," 1:152–3. See also Wright, "Some Notes on the Continental Army," 84–85.

52. Windham and Townshend, *Plan of Discipline*, iii, v–vi.

53. Anon., "Military Books of the Revolution," 60–61; Pickering, *Life of Timothy Pickering*, 1:18–19.

54. Letter, Adams to George Brinley, June 19, 1818, quoted in Dawson (ed.), "Bunker's Hill," 332n. An unwarrantedly long and mostly unwholesome controversy raged for decades in the nineteenth century over whether Putnam was even present at the battle. I shall spare readers the details, but the affair began with Henry Dearborn's somewhat meretricious accusations implying that Putnam was a grandstanding coward who had usurped Prescott's laurels. The general's defenders proved the case in Putnam's favor by producing dozens of eyewitness testimonies. The tale can be followed in, among other, Coffin (ed.), *Battle of Breed's Hill;* Swett, *Notes to His Sketch;* A. P. Putnam, *General Israel Putnam and the Battle of Bunker Hill: A Critique, Not a History* (Salem, MA: Putnam, 1901); Putnam, *Colonel Daniel Putnam's Letter Relative to the Battle of Bunker Hill and General Israel Putnam* (Hartford: Connecticut Historical Society, 1860); Drake, *General Israel Putnam: The Commander at Bunker Hill* (Boston: Nichols and Hall, 1875); F. J. Parker, *Colonel William Prescott, the Commander in the Battle of Bunker's Hill* (Boston: A. Williams, 1875).

55. Testimony of Dr. Snow, in Swett, *Notes to His Sketch,* 9. For a complaint about Stark's insurbordination, General Nathaniel Folsom's letter to the Committee of Safety, June 23, 1775, in Force (ed.), *American Archives,* 4th ser., vol. 2, col. 1069. See also Swett, *Notes to His Sketch,* 26 (note M). On Stark as part–New Englander, part–Scots-Irish, see Elting, *Bunker's Hill,* 12. A fuller narrative of the Stark-Hobart affair is given in Potter, *History of Manchester,* 435–36.

56. "Rank of the Regiments of Foot in the Service of the United Colonies," September 26, 1775, printed in Henshaw, "Orderly Book of Col. William Henshaw," 160.

57. Letter, Washington to Continental Congress, September 24, 1776. Washington Papers.

58. Letter, Greene to Nicholas Cooke, June 18, 1775, in R. K. Showman (ed.), *The Papers of General Nathanael Greene* (Chapel Hill: University of North Carolina Press, 13 vols., 1976–2005), 1:87; and letter, Greene to Samuel Ward, January 4, 1776, p. 176.

59. Quoted in Frothingham, *Siege of Boston,* 116.

60. Pickering, *Life of Thomas Pickering,* 1:19.

5. The Rail Fence

1. Letter, Chester to Fish, July 22, 1775, printed in Dawson (ed.), "Bunker's Hill," 386.

2. "Extract of a Letter From Boston to Gentleman in Scotland, Dated June 25, 1775," in Force (ed.), *American Archives,* 4th ser., vol. 2, cols. 1093–94; Butler, *History of the Town of Groton,* 339n6. On the color of the hay, Moore, *Life of General John Stark,* 159.

3. Letter, Chester to Fish, July 22, 1775, in Dawson (ed.), "Bunker's Hill," 386; Letter, Howe to Harvey, in Fortescue (ed.), *Correspondence of George the Third,* 3:221; "Extract of a Letter From Boston to Gentleman in Scotland, Dated June 25, 1775," in Force (ed.), *American Archives,* 4th ser., vol. 2, cols. 1093–94.

4. "Maynard's Account," in Temple, *History of Framingham*, 289.
5. This is based on a combination of two references: Gibbon, *Artillerist's Manual*, 227, and Griffiths, *Artillerist's Manual*, 371.
6. As noted in the narrative of the Committee of Safety, July 25, 1775, "Account of the Late Battle of Charlestown," in Force (ed.), *American Archives*, 4th ser., vol. 2, col. 1374; extract from letter, Robert Steele to William Sumner, July 10, 1825, in Scheer and Rankin, *Rebels and Redcoats*, 59; Heath, "An Account of the Battle of Bunker's or Breed's Hill," in Coffin (ed.), *Battle of Breed's Hill*, 3.
7. There are several slightly different definitions of these steps. I have used the version given in *Rules and Regulations for the Formations, Field Exercise, and Movements*, 1:11, 22–5, but see also Spring, *With Zeal*, 144–45.
8. Over time, the speed at which armies can move has greatly increased. Today's Marine Corps "normal" cadence is between 112 and 120 30-inch steps per minute, while "double time" consists of 180 36-inch paces. *Marine Corps Drill and Ceremonies Manual* (2003), Sections 1–8, 1–6.
9. Stone (ed.), *Journal of Captain Pausch*, 108.
10. Windham and Townsend, *Plan of Discipline*, 60.
11. Stedman, *History of the Origin, Progress, and Termination of the American War*, 1:128. For similar claims, see Moore, *Life of General John Stark*, 168; Ward, *War of the Revolution*, 1:89; Ketchum, *The Battle for Bunker Hill*, 96; French, *First Year*, 237.
12. See Elting, *Bunker's Hill*, 23. For the Foreign Legion and Chindit figures, see Terraine, *Smoke and the Fire*, 143–47; on what grunts tended to carry during the Fallujah battle, see Camp, *Operation Phantom Fury*, 390. The usual patrol weight "doubles when soldiers must be away from base for days in the unforgiving mountains, valleys and deserts of Afghanistan." T. Shanker, "Army Ends Delays on Lightweight Armor," *New York Times*, April 25, 2009. Thus, during the fighting in Marja in Afghanistan of February 2010, the Marines of Company K, Third Battalion, Sixth Marines, serving as vanguard, "had been told that ground reinforcements and fresh supplies might not reach them for three days. This meant they had to carry everything they would need during that time: water, ammunition, food, first-aid equipment, bedrolls, clothes and spare batteries for radios and night-vision devices. As they jogged forward, the men grunted and swore under their burdens, which in many cases weighed 100 pounds or more." C. J. Chivers, "Afghan Attack Gives Marines a Taste of War," *New York Times*, February 13, 2010.
13. Quoted in Kidder, *History of New Ipswich*, 77.
14. Spring, *With Zeal*, 139. See also Brumwell, *Redcoats*, 254–55. In 1750, during his first campaign, a young Howe was promoted to a captaincy in the 20th Foot, commanded by Lieutenant Colonel Wolfe. Eight years later, Howe gallantly led the 60th at the siege of Louisburg under the watchful eye of Wolfe, now a general. In a letter home, the latter praised "our old comrade" who "is at the head of the best-trained battalion in America, and his conduct in the campaign corresponded with the opinion we had formed of him." Given command of the Light Infantry, Howe distinguished himself at Quebec in 1759 by undertaking a dangerous mission, entrusted to him personally by Wolfe, to scale the Heights of Abraham with a small force and capture the French outpost at the top. Fisher, "Objective at Bunker Hill," 133. For Wolfe's advice, see "Instructions for the 20th Regiment (in Case the French Land) Given by Lieutenant-Colonel Wolfe at Canterbury," December 15, 1755, printed in Wolfe, *Instructions to Young Officers*, 51. The essay was well known in America at this time. See French, *First Year*, 235.

15. War Office, *Rules and Regulations*, 1:11.
16. D. J. Beattie, "The Adaptation of the British Army to Wilderness Warfare, 1755–1763," in *Adapting to Conditions*, ed. M. Ultee, 78. See also Russell, "Redcoats in the Wilderness," 629–52. Three ranks was common but not universal. France opted for four ranks in order to enhance their lines' shock value while the British by the time of Waterloo preferred two, to emphasize firepower. See Lynn, "Linear Warfare: Images and Ideals of Combat in the Age of Enlightenment," in his *Battle*, 120–21.
17. Spring, *With Zeal*, 140.
18. Quoted in Duffy, *Army of Frederick the Great*, 88.
19. General Howe to Lord Howe, June 22, 1775, printed in Fisher, "Objective at Bunker Hill," 120.
20. Letter, Clinton to William Phillips, December 5, 1775, quoted in French, *First Year*, 235. On the two-line formation, see Howe's letter to Lord Harvey, June 22 and 24, 1775, printed in Fortescue (ed.), *Correspondence of King George the Third*, 3:221.
21. Quoted in Duffy, *Army of Frederick the Great*, 88.
22. Letter, General Howe to Lord Howe, June 22, 1775, printed in Fisher, "Objective at Bunker Hill," 120.
23. Diary entry, June 17, 1775, in Van Arsdale (ed.), *Discord and Civil Wars*, 18.
24. Quoted in Spring, *With Zeal*, 140.
25. On the length of the fence, see Frothingham, *Battle-Field of Bunker Hill*, 10, and Moore, *Life of General John Stark*, 159. Howe, in his letter to Lord Harvey, June 22 and 24, 1775, says "this breastwork [was] about 300 yards in extent." Fortescue (ed.), *Correspondence of King George the Third*, 3:221.
26. See figures in Morrissey, *Boston 1775*, 61; and Murdock, *Bunker Hill*, 77n.
27. War Office, *Rules and Regulations*, 3:1. See *Marine Corps Drill and Ceremonies Manual* (May 5, 2003), Section 1–6.
28. Dearborn, "An Account of the Battle of Bunker's Hill," 15–23, published in Coffin (ed.), *Battle of Breed's Hill*, 17.
29. Dawson (ed.), "Bunker's Hill," 428–29.
30. Dearborn, "An Account of the Battle of Bunker's Hill," in Coffin (ed.), *Battle of Breed's Hill*, 23.
31. On this point, see Rose, *American Rifle*, esp. ch. 3.
32. Diary entries, November 16, 1774, February 14, 1775, March 10, March 11, in Johnson (ed.), "Diary of Israel Litchfield," 1:152, 2:253–54, 256–57.
33. Diary entries, March 20 and January 23, 1775, in Johnson (ed.), "Diary of Israel Litchfield," 2:257; 1:163.
34. Diary entry, March 21, 1775, in Johnson (ed.), "Diary of Israel Litchfield," 2:257–58.
35. See table in Harrington, "Roundball Ballistics in the Revolutionary War," 12.
36. Brumwell, *Redcoats*, 250.
37. Lamb, *Original and Authentic Journal of Occurrences*, 32. Dr. William Gordon, who described the battle in a missive from Roxbury (August 15, 1775), noted that the militia "have only common muskets, nor are these in general furnished with bayonets; but then they are almost all marksmen, being accustomed to sporting of one kind or other from their youth." Gordon, *History of the Rise, Progress, and Establishment*, 1:52.
38. Wilkinson, "A Rapid Sketch of the Battle of Breed's Hill," in Coffin (ed.), *Battle of Breed's Hill*, 11.
39. The *Chronicle*'s item of August 3, 1779, is reprinted in appendix 9 of Frothingham, *Siege of Boston*, 398–401. Israel Mauduit, in a hostile tract of 1781, uses identical lan-

guage. Clearly, he was the original author. Mauduit, *Three Letters to Lord Viscount Howe.*

40. This figure derived from Krenn, Kalaus, and Hall, "Material Culture and Military History," 103.

41. N. A. Roberts, J. W. Brown, B. Hammett, and P. D. F. Kingston, "A Detailed Study of the Effectiveness and Capabilities of 18th Century Musketry on the Battlefield," in *Bastions and Barbwire,* ed. T. Pollard and I. Banks, 1–21.

42. James, "Britain's Brown Bess."

43. "Maynard's Account," in Temple, *History of Framingham,* 290.

44. Krenn, Kalaus, and Hall, "Material Culture and Military History," 103.

45. Dearborn, "An Account of the Battle of Bunker's Hill," in Coffin (ed.), *Battle of Breed's Hill,* 20–21.

46. Letter, C. Stuart to Lord Bute, July 24, 1775, in Wortley (ed.), *Prime Minister and His Son,* 69.

47. The *London Chronicle* of January 11, 1776, quoted in Frothingham, *Siege of Boston,* 196n1.

48. Frothingham discovered this vignette in a contemporary British newspaper, which he left unnamed. *Siege of Boston,* 199.

49. Anon., "Observations on the Government's Account of the Late Action Near Charlestown," August 1, 1775, printed in Force (ed.), *American Archives,* 4th ser., vol. 2, col. 1099.

50. Donkin, *Military Collections and Remarks,* 223.

51. Letter, Chester to Fish, July 22, 1775, printed in Dawson (ed.), "Bunker's Hill," 386.

52. Bland, *Treatise of Military Discipline,* 134.

53. Letter, Percy to a "gentleman in London," September 4, 1776, printed in Force (ed.), *American Archives,* 5th ser., vol. 2, col. 168.

54. "Account of the Action of the 19th of April, by an Officer of One of the Flank Companies," printed in French (ed.), *British Fusilier,* 65–66.

55. Diary entry, April 19, 1775, in French (ed.), *British Fusilier,* 56.

56. Diary entry, June 25, 1775, in Van Arsdale (ed.), *Discord and Civil Wars,* 21–22.

57. Letter, Howe to Lord Harvey, June 22 and 24, 1775, printed in Fortescue (ed.), *Correspondence of King George the Third,* 3:221.

58. Dearborn, "An Account," printed in Coffin (ed.), *Battle of Breed's Hill,* 20–21.

59. "Maynard's Account," in Temple, *History of Framingham,* 290.

60. Entry of June 8, 1776, in Lamb, *Original and Authentic Journal of Occurrences,* 107.

61. Quoted in Muir, *Tactics and the Experience of Battle,* 25.

62. Diary entry, May 27, 1775, in Green (ed.), "Amos Farnsworth's Diary," 81. The same simile was recently used by an American sniper in Afghanistan who "noticed that the smaller rounds coming in were not snapping by his ears but buzzing like bumblebees as they passed—air resistance over distance having slowed them to less than the speed of sound." Cited in W. Langewiesche, "Distant Executioner," *Vanity Fair,* February 2010.

63. On the differences over time, see L. C. Haag's definitive article on the subject, "The Sound of Bullets."

64. Letter, Howe to Lord Harvey, June 22 and 24, 1775, printed in Fortescue (ed.), *Correspondence of King George the Third,* 3:221.

65. So rare, in fact, that French claims that Howe "never revealed any emotion or anxiety, even to his brother." *First Year,* 259.

66. On this subject, see Hendrix, *Spirit of the Corps,* 68–100. I am grateful to Dr. Hendrix for supplying me with a copy of his invaluable thesis.
67. Lamont, *Art of War,* 75–76.
68. Lamont, *Art of War,* 71.
69. Letter, Chester to Fish, July 22, 1775, printed in Dawson (ed.), "Bunker's Hill," 386.
70. "Letter from Boston, July 5th, 1775," printed in House of Commons, *Detail and Conduct of the American War,* 13–15. Howe would not be the only one blamed by his subordinates for the debacle. Thomas Gage, for marrying an American woman, was also despised. Conway, "British Army, 'Military Europe,' and the American War of Independence," 69–100, esp. note 15.
71. Quoted in Wilkinson, "Rapid Sketch of the Battle of Breed's Hill," printed in Coffin (ed.), *Battle of Breed's Hill,* 12n.
72. Drewe, *Case of Edward Drewe,* 85 (appendix); on Drewe's career, see 28–29.
73. Goldstein, "British Grenadier's Button," 70–78. I am indebted to Mr. Goldstein for sending me a copy of this important article. For the August tallies, see Gage's "Return of the Officers," printed in Force (ed.), *American Archives,* 4th ser., vol. 2, cols. 1098–99.
74. Gage, "Return of the Officers," printed in Force (ed.), *American Archives,* 4th ser., vol. 2, cols. 1098–99.
75. Longmore, *Gunshot Injuries,* 197–203.
76. J. Malcolm, "Reminiscences of a Campaign in the Pyrenees and South of France in 1814," in Anon. (ed.), *Memorials of the Late War,* 1:298.
77. "Extract of Letter From Doctor Grant, One of the Surgeons of the British Military Hospital in Boston, to a Friend in Westminster," June 23, 1775, printed in Dawson (ed.), "Bunker's Hill," 361.
78. Bancroft's narrative, in Hill (ed.), *Bi-Centennial of Old Dunstable,* 61; "Judge Prescott's Account of the Battle of Bunker Hill," printed in Frothingham, *Battle-Field of Bunker Hill,* 20.
79. On ricochets, see Gibbon, *Artillerist's Manual,* 254–56.
80. Quoted in D. M. Sivilich, "What the Musket Ball Can Tell: Monmouth Battlefield State Park, New Jersey," in *Fields of Conflict,* ed. D. Scott, L. Babits, and C. Haecker, 96.

6. The Redoubt, Part Two

1. Letter, Prescott to John Adams, August 25, 1775, printed in Dawson (ed.), "Bunker's Hill," 390–91.
2. Letter, Stuart to Lord Bute, July 24, 1775, in Wortley (ed.), *Prime Minister and His Son,* 69.
3. On this point, see the Address of Major Edwin B. Wight, printed in Curtis, *History of the Twenty-Fourth Michigan of the Iron Brigade,* 424. An extremely valuable contribution is Reardon, "Writing Battle History," 252–63.
4. See Murdock, *Bunker Hill,* 71–72n; Dearborn, "An Account of the Battle of Bunker's Hill," in Coffin (ed.), *Battle of Breed's Hill,* 18; Swett, *Notes to His Sketch,* 22 (note E); Paul Lunt's diary entry of June 17, printed in Green (ed.), "Paul Lunt's Book," 194; "Extract of a Letter From Boston to Gentleman in Scotland, Dated June 25, 1775," in Force (ed.), *American Archives,* 4th ser., vol. 2, col. 1093; "Rev. Peter Thacher's Narrative," June 1775, printed in Dawson (ed.), "Bunker's Hill," 384; Anon. (ed.), "Journals of Lieut.-Col. Stephen Kemble," entry of June 12, 1775, 44.
5. This material is based on Artwohl, "Perceptual and Memory Distortion," 18–24; Klinger, *Police Responses.*

6. Klinger, *Police Responses,* 19.
7. "The Thirty-fifth, Royal Sussex, Infantry," extracted from *Case of Edward Drewe,* published in Dawson (ed.), "Bunker's Hill," 368–69.
8. Quoted in Dann, *Revolution Remembered,* 25.
9. Quoted in Dann, *Revolution Remembered,* 91.
10. Fontenot, "Fear God and Dreadnought," 23.
11. Grossman, *On Combat,* 31. For the research into performance deficits, see Lieberman et al., "Fog of War," section II, C7–C14.
12. See "Account of the Late Battle of Charlestown," Committee of Safety Report, July 25, 1775, in Force (ed.), *American Archives,* 4th ser., vol. 2, col. 1374.
13. Printed in Dawson (ed.), "Bunker's Hill," 371.
14. "Statement Prepared by Order of the Provincial Congress of Massachusetts, for Transmission to Great Britain," July 25, 1775, in Force (ed.), *American Archives,* 4th ser., vol. 2, cols. 1373–76. Thacher's influential narrative of the battle, upon which the Committee of Safety drew, had also outlined the two-attack scheme. See "Rev. Peter Thacher's Narration," June 1775, printed in Dawson (ed.), "Bunker's Hill," 383.
15. Diary entry, June 16 [*sic*], 1775, in Green (ed.), "Thomas Boynton's Journal," 255.
16. Letter, Prescott to Adams, August 25, 1775, in Dawson (ed.), "Bunker's Hill," 391.
17. Letter, Stuart to Lord Bute, July 24, 1775, in Wortley (ed.), *Prime Minister and His Son,* 69. Emphasis added.
18. Scudder, "Battle of Bunker Hill," 88.
19. Letter, J. Waller to unidentified recipient, June 21, 1775, held by the Massachusetts Historical Society.
20. "Judge Prescott's Account of the Battle of Bunker Hill," printed in Frothingham et al. (eds.), "Letter of Edward Everett," 70.
21. Isaac Glynney diary (unpublished).
22. Page's map remarks that the breastwork "was first forced by Grenadiers and regiments immediately opposite to it, which had for some time before formed one line in order to return the enemy's fire." Quoted in French, *First Year,* 242n29.
23. Gage, "Return of the Officers" (see figures for the Royal Regiment of Artillery), in Force (ed.), *American Archives,* 4th ser., vol. 2, col. 1098; French, *First Year,* 241.
24. Quoted in Webster, "Account of the Battle of Bunker Hill," 20.
25. Dearborn, "An Account of the Battle of Bunker's Hill," in Coffin (ed.), *Battle of Breed's Hill,* 13.
26. Quoted in French, *First Year,* 242–43.
27. Isaac Glynney diary (unpublished).
28. "Judge Prescott's Account of the Battle of Bunker Hill," in Frothingham et al. (eds.), "Letter of Edward Everett," 71.
29. "Another Account of the Late Action at Bunker's Hill," printed in *Rivington's Gazeteer,* August 3, 1775, in Dawson (ed.), "Bunker's Hill," 389–90.
30. "Judge Prescott's Account of the Battle of Bunker Hill," in Frothingham et al. (eds.), "Letter of Edward Everett," 71.
31. Letter, Prescott to Adams, August 25, 1775, in Dawson (ed.), "Bunker's Hill," 391. Peter Brown thought that at about 2:30 P.M. there had been as many as 700 men in the redoubt. Brown, "Officer's Story of Bunker Hill."
32. Diary entry, June 17, 1775, in Green (ed.), "Amos Farnsworth's Diary," 83.
33. Letter, Chester to Fish, July 22, 1775, printed in Dawson (ed.), "Bunker's Hill," 386–87.
34. Frothingham, *Centennial,* 56.
35. Letter, Chester to Fish, July 22, 1775, printed in Dawson (ed.), "Bunker's Hill," 386–87.

36. Bancroft's narrative, in Hill (ed.), *Bi-Centennial of Old Dunstable*, 60. Bancroft's emphasis.

37. Frothingham, *Centennial*, 57. "Maynard's Account," in Temple, *History of Framingham*, 291.

38. Bancroft's narrative, in Hill (ed.), *Bi-Centennial of Old Dunstable*, 61. Emphasis in original.

39. Frothingham (ed.), "Judge Prescott's Account of the Battle of Bunker Hill," in *Proceedings of the Massachusetts Historical Society*, 71. For Farnsworth, see his diary entry of June 17, 1775, in Green (ed.), "Amos Farnsworth's Diary," 83.

40. "A Letter From Abel Parker, Esq., Judge of Probate," May 27, 1818, printed in Dawson (ed.), "Bunker's Hill," 421; Bancroft's narrative, in Hill (ed.), *Bi-Centennial of Old Dunstable*, 61.

41. Letter, J. Waller to unidentified recipient, June 21, 1775, held by the Massachusetts Historical Society.

42. Entry of August 24, 1787, "A Groton Man Shot Pitcairn," in Green (ed.), *Collection of Papers*, 259–60, originally published as "Extracts from Dr. Belknap's Note-books," *Proceedings of the Massachusetts Historical Society*, 93. See also Murphy, " 'We Have All Lost a Father,' " 20–24.

43. Quoted in Frothingham, *Centennial*, 111.

44. J. L. Bell, "Who Killed Major John Pitcairn?" in Andrlik, Harrington, and Hagist (eds.), *Journal of the American Revolution*, 38–43.

45. On Tupper, see Murdock, *Bunker Hill*, 19n; on Gage's report confirming same, see Frothingham, *Siege of Boston*, 195n3.

46. Letter, John Waller to Jacob Waller, June 22, 1775, printed in Drake (ed.), *Bunker Hill*, 29–30.

47. M. Hunter, *The Journal of General Sir Martin Hunter* (Edinburgh, 1894), quoted in French, *First Year*, 248; Gage, "Return of the Officers," in Force (ed.), *American Archives*, 4th ser., vol. 2, col. 1098.

48. Lushington, *Life and Services of General Lord Harris*, 42.

49. Letters, Rawdon to the Earl of Huntingdon, June 20 and August 3, 1775, in Bickley (ed.), *Historical Manuscripts Commission*, 3:155, 157.

50. Letter from a Rhode Island gentleman to a friend in New York, June 29, 1775, *Rivington's Gazetteer*, printed in Moore (ed.), *Diary of the American Revolution*, 1:99n1.

51. Frothingham, *Siege of Boston*, 150n1; Clarke, "Impartial and Authentic Narrative," 22. Neither source has impeccable authority.

52. Letter, John Waller to Jacob Waller, June 22, 1775, printed in Drake (ed.), *Bunker Hill*, 29–30. For the names of Waller's friends, see letter, J. Waller to unidentified recipient, June 21, 1775, held by the Massachusetts Historical Society. For the probable captains, see Clarke, "Impartial and Authentic Narrative" and "General Gage's Despatch to the Home Government," printed in Dawson (ed.), "Bunker's Hill," 260, 361–63.

53. Noyes, *History of Norway*, 44.

54. Report of Ensign Studholme Brownrigg, June 21, 1775, to Lt-Gen Hodgson, in Hart, "Echoes of Bunker Hill," 39.

55. "Extract of a Letter From an Officer of the Army, in Boston, to His Friend in England," June 25, 1775, in Force (ed.), *American Archives*, 4th ser., vol. 2, cols. 1092–93.

56. Peter Brown letter, "Officer's Story of Bunker Hill."

57. "Maynard's Account," in Temple, *History of Framingham*, 291. Isaac Glynney, in his

unpublished diary, confirmed that in the final moments he threw stones. Bancroft's narrative, in Hill (ed.), *Bi-Centennial of Old Dunstable*, 61–62.

58. Butler, *History of the Town of Groton*, 340.

59. A letter from Charles Chauncy to Richard Price, July 18, 1775, observes that the Americans "came out well stocked with" ammunition. Printed in Ashburner (ed.), "Richard Price Letters," 299.

60. Some months before the battle, the Americans had made valiant, if unsuccessful, efforts to secure a plentiful reserve of ammunition for the war to come. On March 18, British lieutenant Mackenzie noted in his diary that a "country man was stopped at the lines, going out of town [Boston] with 19,000 ball cartridges, which were taken from him. When liberated, he had the insolence to go to headquarters to demand the redelivery of them. When asked who they were for, he said they were for his own use." They were not returned. French (ed.), *British Fusilier*, 42. This story was confirmed by Lieutenant Williams of the 23rd Regiment, in Van Arsdale (ed.), *Discord and Civil Wars*, 9.

61. Wilkinson (having heard it from one of the American colonels present), "Rapid Sketch of the Battle of Breed's Hill," printed in Coffin (ed.), *Battle of Breed's Hill*, 11n.

62. Entry for June 14, "Extracts From an Orderly Book, Supposed to Be Capt. Chester's," printed in Frothingham, *Battle-Field of Bunker Hill*, 39; Grosvenor quoted in Webster, "Account of the Battle of Bunker Hill."

63. "Maynard's Account," in Temple, *History of Framingham*, 284.

64. Hatch, "New Hampshire at Bunker Hill," 215; Smith, *Peterborough, New Hampshire*, 325.

65. As told to Ward, *History of the Town of Shrewsbury*, 56.

66. See his letter to Continental Congress, January 30, 1776, in George Washington Papers, Library of Congress.

67. Letter, Jesse Lukens, September 1775, quoted in Frothingham, *Siege of Boston*, 192, with further details cited in Bolton, *Private Soldier Under Washington*, 121; testimonies of Josiah Cleaveland and Nathaniel Rice, in Swett, *Notes to His Sketch*, 13; Frothingham, *Siege of Boston*, 192. On British estimates of their ammunition needs, see Washington's letter to Continental Congress, January 30, 1776, in George Washington Papers.

68. Letter, Chauncy to Price, July 18, 1775, in Ashburner (ed.), "Richard Price Letters," 299.

69. Brumwell, *Redcoats*, 246.

70. Hadden, *Hadden's Journal and Orderly Books*, 74.

71. *New Hampshire State Papers* VI, 526, quoted in Elting, *Bunker's Hill*, 40.

72. "Maynard's Account," in Temple, *History of Framingham*, 291.

73. Letter, Samuel Webb to Silas Deane, July 11, 1775, in Frothingham et al. (eds.), "Letter of Edward Everett," 83.

74. Letter, Waller to Waller, June 22, 1775, in Drake (ed.), *Bunker Hill*, 28.

75. Brown, "Officer's Story of Bunker Hill"; Chase and Dawson (eds.), *Diary of David How*, ix.

76. "Another Account of the Late Action at Bunker's Hill," *Rivington's Gazeteer*, August 3, 1775, printed in Dawson (ed.), "Bunker's Hill," 389–90.

77. Lossing, *Pictorial Field-Book*, 546.

78. Potter, "Life and Remarkable Adventures," 15.

79. Bancroft's narrative, in Hill (ed.), *Bi-Centennial of Old Dunstable*, 62.

80. Letter, J. Waller to unidentified recipient, June 21, 1775, held by the Massachusetts Historical Society.

81. Dearborn, "An Account of the Battle of Bunker's Hill," in Coffin (ed.), *Battle of Breed's Hill,* 19.
82. "Nasty, Brutish and Not That Short," *The Economist,* December 16, 2010. I'm grateful to Mark Lee for this reference.
83. Quoted in Frothingham, *Siege of Boston,* 150; Elting, *Bunker's Hill,* 35.
84. Potter, "Life and Remarkable Adventures," 15.
85. Elting, *Bunker's Hill,* 36; Letter, Chester to Fish, July 22, 1775, in Dawson (ed.), "Bunker's Hill," 387; Letter, Chester and Webb to Webb, June 19, 1775, in Frothingham, *Siege of Boston,* 416.
86. French, *First Year,* 251.
87. French, *First Year,* 252.
88. Letter, Rawdon to the Earl of Huntingdon, June 20, 1775, in Bickley (ed.), *Historical Manuscripts Commission,* 3:155.
89. Letter, Burgoyne to Lord Rochfort, in Fonblanque, *Political and Military Episodes,* 147.
90. Wade and Lively, *This Glorious Cause,* 21.
91. Letter, Steele to W. Sumner, July 10, 1825, printed in Scheer and Rankin, *Rebels and Redcoats,* 59–60.
92. Smith, *Peterborough, New Hampshire,* 232–35.
93. Quoted in Bailey, *Historical Sketches of Andover,* 323.
94. As reported by the *Essex Gazette,* June 1829, printed in Bailey, *Historical Sketches of Andover,* 327.
95. Swett, *Notes to His Sketch,* 25 (note L).
96. Smith, *Peterborough, New Hampshire,* 323–25; Resch, *Suffering Soldiers,* 23.
97. On the number of prisoners taken, their experiences, and survivors, see French, *First Year,* 252; Leach, "Journal Kept by John Leach," 255–63; Green, "American Prisoners Taken at the Battle of Bunker Hill," 168–69. Also, *Rivington's Gazetteer,* July 13, 1775, reported a similar number; see Moore, *Diary of the American Revolution,* 1:103.
98. Clarke, "Impartial and Authentic Narrative," 255–56.
99. Quoted in French, *First Year,* 253–54. Clinton's emphasis.
100. Letter, Burgoyne to Lord Rochfort, in Fonblanque, *Political and Military Episodes,* 147.
101. Lieutenant Archelaus Fuller, Joseph Nichols, and John Cleaveland, quoted in Anderson, *People's Army,* 143–44.
102. Klinger, "Police Responses," 92 (table 10); Grossman, *On Combat,* 14–16.
103. Quoted in French, *First Year,* 255.
104. Trumbull, *Autobiography, Reminiscences, and Letters,* 22.

7. The Wounded and the Dead

1. Norwood, "Medicine in the Era of the American Revolution," 395; Gilman, "Medical Surgery," 493.
2. Allen, "Medicine in the American Revolution," 426. On the breakdown of doctors attached to the American troops, see Estes, " 'Disagreeable and Dangerous Employment,' " 290.
3. Stephenson, *Patriot Battles,* 164.
4. Dann, *Revolution Remembered,* 81.
5. Manring et al., "Treatment of War Wounds," 2176.
6. "Return of the Killed, Wounded, and Missing in the Action of the 19th of April, 1775," printed in French (ed.), *British Fusilier,* 61. On Hawkstone, letter from Joseph Thaxter, November 30, 1824, *The United States Literary Gazette* 1 (1824–1825), 264.

7. On triage, see Manring et al., "Treatment of War Wounds," 2169.

8. Neale, *Letters From Portugal and Spain,* 17.

9. Wooden, "Wounds and Weapons of the Revolutionary War," 61. I am indebted to Kathy O. Jackson of the Medical Society of Delaware for supplying me with a copy of this article. See also Cantlie, *History of the Army Medical Department,* 344. On conservative approaches, see Manring et al., "Treatment of War Wounds," 2177.

10. Phalen, "Surgeon James Mann's Observations on Battlefield Amputations," 463–66; diary of Dr. Charles Gilman, quoted in Gilman, "Medical Surgery," 493–94. On Dr. Guthrie, famed as the man who could amputate in five minutes, see Cantlie, *History of the Army Medical Department,* 344.

11. Grattan, *Adventures with the Connaught Rangers,* 77.

12. Diary entry, October 24, 1777, in Thacher, *Military Journal,* 113.

13. See, for instance, Balingall, *Introductory Lectures to a Course of Military Surgery,* Lecture 1, p. 35. In the words of a group of modern researchers, amputation "transformed a complex wound into a simple wound with a better chance of recovery." Manring et al., "Treatment of War Wounds," 2176.

14. Appendix, "Official Account of General Gage, Published in the *London Gazette,*" compiled June 25, 1775, supplemented by the "Return of the Officers," in Force (ed.), *American Archives,* 4th ser., vol. 2, cols. 1098–99.

15. I have used the detailed tables in Longmore, *Gunshot Injuries,* 700–2.

16. On the mid-thigh mortality rate, see Gillett, *Army Medical Department,* 18.

17. Letter, J. Hall to Elbridge Gerry, June 27, 1775, published in Henkels (ed.), *Letters and Papers of Elbridge Gerry,* 86.

18. Pruitt, Jr., "Combat Casualty Care and Surgical Progress," 715–18.

19. Diary entry, August 17, 1775, in "Extracts from President Stiles's Diary," in Dawson (ed.), "Bunker's Hill," 397–98.

20. Based on muster-roll information provided by Don N. Hagist, "Bunker Hill Flank Company Casualties," private communication, April 14, 2014.

21. *London Chronicle,* January 11, 1776, quoted in Frothingham, *Siege of Boston,* 196n1. On Page's leg, see French, *First Year,* 747–48 (appendix 23).

22. Letter, Washington to John Augustine Washington, July 27, 1775, in Washington Papers. There are several other tallies, which do not significantly alter these numbers. See Frothingham, *Siege of Boston,* 193; Seybolt, "Note on the Casualties of April 19, and June 17, 1775," 525–28; Murdock, *Bunker Hill,* 75.

23. Potter, "Life and Remarkable Adventures," 15–16.

24. Diary entry, June 17, 1775, in Green (ed.), "Diary of Amos Farnsworth," 83–84.

25. Smith, *History of the Town of Peterborough,* 157; Smith, *Peterborough, New Hampshire,* 199–200, 205–7.

26. Frothingham, *Siege of Boston,* 194. The doctors' names were Thomas Kittredge, William Eustis, Walter Hastings, Thomas Walsh, Isaac Foster, Col. Bricket, David Townsend, and John Hart.

27. Cantlie, *History of the Army Medical Department,* 139. On the takeover of the almshouse and poorhouse, letter dated July 22, 1775, from Chauncy to Richard Price, printed in Ashburner (ed.), "Richard Price Letters," 298; see also Frothingham, *Siege of Boston,* 194.

28. Potter, "Life and Remarkable Adventures," 15–16.

29. Goldstein, "British Grenadier's Button," 70–78.

30. Stephenson, *Patriot Battles,* 167; Clarke, "Impartial and Authentic Narrative," 264.

31. Letter, Laurie to J. Roebuck, June 23, 1775, quoted in Conway, "British Army Officers and the American War for Independence," 271.

32. Orders of July 17, printed in Stevens (ed.), *General Sir William Howe's Orderly Book*, 44.
33. "A Narrative of the Life and Character of William Crawford," reprinted in Hagist, *British Soldiers, American War*, 67. Crawford, aged seventy-three and a cantankerous alcoholic, would be hanged in 1823 for murdering his son.
34. Orders of July 17, printed in Stevens (ed.), *General Sir William Howe's Orderly Book*, 44. Looting has a long history.
35. Muir, *Tactics and the Experience of Battle*, 251–52.
36. Muir, *Tactics and the Experience of Battle*, 221–22.
37. Gage, in letter to Lord Barrington, June 25, 1775, mentions that he is submitting a list of men recommended for promotion "occasioned by the loss of officers on the 17th instant." Carter (ed.), *Correspondence of General Thomas Gage*, 2:685.
38. Letter, Gordon to Dorothea, Lady Fife, July 9, 1775, quoted in Conway, "British Army Officers and the American War for Independence," 276. Some, for political reasons, received still more accelerated promotions. Lieutenant William Pitcairn, whose father, the major, was killed in the battle, had been commissioned on March 2, 1773, making him 109th in seniority among first lieutenants in the Marines. Yet he was elevated to captain lieutenant on July 27, thereby vaulting him over the heads of 108 of his peers, some of whom (such as William Feilding, commissioned January 22, 1764, and ranked 58th) had more than a decade's worth of experience over him. Lieutenant Pitcairn had fought bravely at Bunker Hill, but there was a "sympathy" vote additionally weighing in his favor that led to much envy among those not so fortunate as to lose a famous father. Lord Sandwich comforted Feilding, who was "not a little mortif[ied]" at hearing of Pitcairn's meteoric rise, that the latter's case "is not to be looked upon as a precedent." See letters, Lord Denbigh to Feilding, August 8, 1775, and Feilding to Denbigh, October 8, 1775, in Balderston and Syrett (eds.), *Lost War*, 35–36, 45–47.
39. R. Brown, "Psychology," in *An Oxford Companion to the Romantic Age: British Culture, 1776–1832*, ed. I. McCalman, 361–69; Vidal, "Psychology in the 18th Century," 89–119.
40. Letter, Amos Foster, August 3, 1825, printed in Sumner, "Reminiscences," 122.
41. Hagist, *British Soldiers, American War*, x–xi.
42. Quoted in Paret, *Imagined Battles*, 48.
43. Quoted in Erffa and Staley, *Paintings of Benjamin West*, 222.
44. Barker, *British in Boston*, 64; Letter, Feilding to Denbigh, October 8, 1775, in Balderston and Syrett (eds.), *Lost War*, 45–47. See also "Organization of the Royal Marines, 1775," printed in Drake (ed.), *Bunker Hill*, 74.
45. On the resignations, see Lt. Gordon's letter of July 7, 1775, cited in Conway, "British Army Officers and the American War for Independence," 267.
46. Trumbull, *Autobiography, Reminiscences, and Letters*, 22.
47. Quoted in Bailey, *Historical Sketches of Andover*, 328–29.

8. Aftermath

1. Letter, Rawdon to the Earl of Huntingdon, August 3, 1775, in Bickley (ed.), *Historical Manuscripts Commission*, 3:159.
2. Quoted in French, "General Haldimand in Boston," 94.
3. G. Raudzens, "In Search of Better Quantification for War History," 1–30. I have used Raudzens's compilations for the battles of Lobositz, Leuthen, Prague, Plassy, Kolin, Rossbach, Hochkirch, Zorndorf, the Plains of Abraham, Kunersdorf, Minden, Liegnitz, and Torgau.

4. Letter, Thomas Gage to Dartmouth, June 25, 1775, in Carter (ed.), *Correspondence of General Thomas Gage*, 1:407.
5. "Extract of a Letter From an Officer on Board One of the King's Ships at Boston, to His Friend in London," June 23, 1775, in Force (ed.), *American Archives*, 4th ser., vol. 2, cols. 1067–68.
6. Letter, Anon. to Francis Downman, June 18, 1775, printed in Whinyates (ed.), *Services of Lieut.-Colonel Francis Downman*, 23.
7. Colonel W. Grayson to General Weedon, June 26, 1781, printed in Reed, *Life and Correspondence of Joseph Reed*, 2:355.

GETTYSBURG

1. Introduction

1. Based on the report by MacDonald, "Gettysburg Holds Greatest Fourth."
2. According to Drew Gilpin Faust, for instance, the Civil War "attained a scale that shocks and horrifies—a scale of drama and scale of death that prefigured the slaughter of the century that followed." Indeed, the charnel-houses of Antietam and Chicka-mauga, Chancellorsville and Gettysburg would "presage the slaughter of World War I's Western Front and the global carnage of the twentieth century." Her lecture, originally given to the National Endowment for the Humanities and titled "The Civil War and the Meaning of Life," was published as "Telling War Stories," 19–25; quotation 20; Faust, "Civil War Soldier and the Art of Dying," 3. For a critical view of the 1865–1945 master narrative, see Chickering, "Total War," in *Anticipating Total War*, 13–28.
3. See Ferro, *Great War*, 199. On interwar Franco-British views, Strachan, "On Total War and Modern War," 348; Baumann and Segesser, "Shadows of Total War," in *Shadows of Total War*, ed. R. Chickering and S. Förster. For German interpretations, see Jünger, "Total Mobilization," in *Heidegger Controversy*, ed. R. Wolin; Ludendorff, *Nation at War*, 169. H. Speier's 1941 essay, "Ludendorff: The German Concept of Total War," in *Makers of Modern Strategy*, ed. E. M. Earle, is a sound source on the general's thoughts, such as they were. See also Kutz, "Fantasy, Reality, and Modes of Perception," in Chick-ering, Förster, and Grenier (eds.), *World at Total War*, 189–206. On postwar American revisionism, see Walters, "General William T. Sherman and Total War," 447–80; Wal-ters, *Merchant of Terror*, xiii, xviii. This book reproduces and enlarges upon his 1948 argument but was written in the shadow of the My Lai massacre in Vietnam—the consequence, says Walter, of "Sherman's philosophy." R. F. Weigley felt that Lincoln's orders for Sherman to attack Southern resources "held the germ of the total wars of the twentieth century, and of the bomb at Hiroshima." Weigley, *Towards an American Army*, 86–87.
4. A recent example of this modernist view is provided by White, "Born in the USA."

2. Combat in the Civil War

1. This figure excludes shots taken by the cavalry, skirmishers, sharpshooters, or the more excitable soldiers, which would skew the results, and treats only soldiers in attack for-mation or behind entrenchments. Trinque, "Rifle-Musket in the Civil War," 62–64. Trinque based his finding on some 386 reports in which yardage was mentioned.
2. It is today a commonplace to declare that the new generation of rifle-muskets "changed

the course of the war" owing to their ability to shoot at long range. This technologically teleological view is severely flawed in that it does not take into account real-world battle factors, nor does it include the difference between theoretical capabilities and actual use. The idea seems to have originated with A. L. Wagner's influential book *Organization and Tactics,* in which he says that the new rifles' 1,000-yard range made "infantry fire . . . so deadly as to effect marked changes in tactical formations" and practice. For works based on this theory, see for instance, Linderman, *Embattled Courage,* 135–36; and Catton, *Reflections on the Civil War,* 126–31.

3. These statements are based on painstaking detective work in the official records; see Griffith, *Battle Tactics,* 146–50; Hess, *Rifle Musket in Civil War Combat,* 108, 109–13, table 4.3.

4. Oliver, Hicks, and Carr, *History of Company E,* 23.

5. Anon. (eds.), *Union Army,* 2:148.

6. M. de Saxe, *My Reveries Upon the Art of War,* 298.

7. For background, see M. A. Bonura, "A French Army in America: The U.S. Army's Adoption of a French Way of Warfare From 1814 to 1835," a paper pre-circulated as part of the Transatlantic Currents in Military Theory Session, held at the Society for Military History Annual Meeting, May 2012.

8. E. S. Riley (ed.), *"Stonewall Jackson": A Thesaurus of Anecdotes and Incidents in the Life of Lieut.-General Thomas Jonathan Jackson, C.S.A.* (Annapolis: E. S. Riley, 1920), 101.

9. A. Ducaunnès-Duval (ed.), *Notes inédites de l'Empereur Napoléon Ier sur les mémoires militaires du Général Lloyd* (Bordeaux: G. Gounouilhou, 1901). On Lloyd, see P. J. Speelman, *Henry Lloyd and the Military Enlightenment of Eighteenth-Century Europe* (Westport, CT: Greenwood Press, 2002); and T. Travers, "The Development of British Military Historical Writing and Thought From the Eighteenth Century to the Present," in *Military History and the Military Profession,* ed. D. A. Charters, M. Milner, and J. B. Wilson (Westport, CT: Praeger, 1992), 25–27.

10. Bousquet, *Scientific Way of Warfare,* esp. ch. three, "Thermodynamic Warfare and the Science of Energy."

11. A. H. Jomini (trans. O. F. Winship and E. E. McLean), *Summary of the Art of War, or, a New Analytical Compend of the Principal Combinations of Strategy, of Grand Tactics and of Military Policy* (New York: G. P. Putnam and Co., 1854), 101. D. Chandler discusses Napoleon's tricks in more detail in "Napoleon: Classical Military Theory and the Jominian Legacy," in his *On the Napoleonic Wars,* 245–46. According to R. Von Caemmerer, for Jomini, as for Napoleon, "annihilation of the hostile army in battle and pursuit is the only guiding star for all his military thinking." R. Von Caemmerer (trans. K. Von Donat), *The Development of Strategical Science During the Nineteenth Century* (London: Hugh Rees, 1905), 28; see also 109.

12. To Isaac Trimble, quoted in Freeman, *R. E. Lee: A Biography* (New York: Charles Scribner's Sons, 4 vols., 1934–35), 3:58.

13. L. A. Coolidge, *Ulysses S. Grant* (Boston: Houghton Mifflin, 2 vols., 1924), 54.

14. Fully one in five French men (some claim four in ten) born between 1790 and 1795 died in Napoleon's wars. J. Lynn, "The Sun of Austerlitz: Romantic Visions of Decisive Battle in Nineteenth-Century Europe," in his *Battle,* 397n56, citing J. Houdaille, "Pertes de l'armeé de terre sous le Prémier Empire," *Population,* January–February 1972. Being conscripted in 1812 proved the shortest straw: 70 percent of French youths aged twenty were killed. See J. France, *Perilous Glory: The Rise of Western Military Power* (New Haven: Yale University Press, 2011), 213.

15. Durkin (ed.), *John Dooley, Confederate Soldier,* 104–5.

16. The British military theorist J. F. C. Fuller believed that the bayonet in the Civil War was as obsolete as the pike, a weapon last seen sometime in the seventeenth or early eighteenth century. Fuller, *Grant and Lee,* 47.

17. J. Buechler, " 'Give 'Em the Bayonet,' " in J. T. Hubbell (ed.), *Battles Lost and Won,* 135. (Buechler is one of the critics.)

18. "Consolidated Statement of Wounds, &C., for the Battles Around Spotsylvania Court-House, Va., From May 8, 1864 to May 21, 1864," *The War of the Rebellion,* 1st ser., 36, pt. 1, p. 237. Hereafter *Official Records.*

19. Letter, O. Ladley to mother and sisters, July 6, 1863, printed in Becker and Thomas (eds.), *Hearth and Knapsack,* 143. Oscar Jackson wrote that the death of a Confederate by Corporal Selby's bayonet was "a remarkable thing in a battle and was spoken of in the official report." Jackson (ed.), *Colonel's Diary,* 74. On the 75th's casualties, see Busey and Martin (eds.), *Regimental Strengths and Losses at Gettysburg,* 253.

20. General Orders No. 128, May 25, 1862, in *Official Records,* 1st ser., 11, 3:192.

21. *Scientific American,* June 14, 1862, 371.

22. McWhiney and Jamieson, *Attack and Die,* 161; Letter, Jackson to S. Bassett French, March 31, 1862, in *Official Records,* 1st ser., 12, 3:842.

23. Bierce, "Crime at Pickett's Mill," in *Devil's Dictionary, Tales, and Memoirs,* 691.

24. Diary entry, August 31, 1862, in Wainwright (ed.), *Philadelphia Perspective,* 436.

25. Borcke, *Memoirs of the Confederate War for Independence,* 44.

26. Byrne and Weaver (eds.), *Haskell of Gettysburg,* 162.

27. Anon., *Reunions of the Nineteenth Maine Regiment Association,* 13.

28. Excerpt from Urban, "Dreaming on the Conestoga," printed in Felton (ed.), "In Their Words," 95.

29. "Report of Colonel Wheelock G. Veazey, Sixteenth Vermont Infantry," July 17, 1863, in *Official Records,* 1st ser., 27, 1:1042.

30. Castel, "Mars and the Reverend Longstreet," 103–14.

31. Nosworthy, *Bloody Crucible of Courage,* 411–12.

32. Quoted in McWhiney and Jamieson, *Attack and Die,* 153.

3. The Machine Breaks Down: The Reality of Combat

1. Nosworthy, *Bloody Crucible of Courage,* 412–14.

2. Weygant, *History of the One Hundred and Twenty-Fourth Regiment,* 17, 29.

3. Pula, "Fifth German Rifles at Gettysburg," 53.

4. Chamberlain, *Passing of the Armies,* 98.

5. Guelzo, "Unturned Corners of the Battle of Gettysburg," 109n10, citing Cole, *Command and Communications Frictions,* 80.

6. "Report of Brig. Gen. J. B. Kershaw, C.S. Army," October 1, 1863, *Official Records,* 1st ser., 27, 2:368; J. B. Kershaw, "Kershaw's Brigade at Gettysburg," in *Battles and Leaders of the Civil War,* ed. R. U. Johnson and C. C. Buell, 3:335–36; Coxe, "Battle of Gettysburg," 433–36, on 434.

7. In fact, said adjutant Theodore Dodge, the only people who knew "the why and the wherefore, the cause and the effect of the marchings and countermarchings of a large army" were those at Army headquarters. Everyone else was completely at sea. Dodge, "Left Wounded," 317.

8. "Report of Brig. Gen. John W. Geary, U.S. Army, Commanding Second Division," July 29, 1863, *Official Records,* 1st ser., 27, 1:826.

9. Letter, A. S. Williams to J. B. Bachelder, November 10, 1885, in Ladd and Ladd (eds.), *Bachelder Papers,* 1:216.
10. Durkin (ed.), *John Dooley, Confederate Soldier,* 102–3.
11. Quoted in Hutchinson, "To Gettysburg and Beyond," 88.
12. Evans, " 'All Was Complete Chaos,' " 37.
13. D. L. Thompson, "With Burnside at Antietam," in *Battles and Leaders,* ed. Johnson and Buell, 2:660.
14. Colonel Adrian Root, 94th New York, was one of the few who succeeded in rebooting a stalled attack. During the assault against the Confederate positions on Marye's Heights at Fredericksburg on December 13, 1862, "the fire of the enemy became so incessant and galling and so many of my men fell killed or wounded that the front line of the brigade slackened its pace, and the men, without orders, commenced firing. A halt seemed imminent, and a halt in the face of the terrific fire to which the brigade was exposed would have been death; or worse, a disastrous repulse." Root requested that Colonel Bates, leading the 12th Massachusetts, unite his regiment with the brigade and mount a joint bayonet charge. "By the strenuous exertions of the regimental commanders and other officers, the firing was nearly discontinued. The brigade resumed its advance, and as the men recognized the enemy their movement increased in rapidity until, with a shout and a run, the brigade leaped the ditches, charged across the railway, and occupied the wood beyond, driving the enemy from their position, killing a number with the bayonet, and capturing upwards of 200 prisoners." See "Report of Col. Adrian R. Root, Ninety-Fourth New York Infantry, Commanding First Brigade," December 23, 1862, *Official Records,* 1st ser., 21, p. 487.

5. Marching to Gettysburg

1. Grandchamp, "2nd Rhode Island Volunteers," 73, 77.
2. Ward, " 'Sedgwick's Foot Cavalry,' " 58.
3. Longstreet, *From Manassas to Appomattox,* 365.
4. Benedict, *Vermont at Gettysburg,* 14. Charles Benton, 150th New York, suggested an alternative reason: "Heavy cannonading has a tendency to produce sleepiness in some persons." A friend of his "casually remarked, 'That always makes me sleepy. Wake me up if my regiment starts, will you?' and despite the fact that shells were dropping and exploding here and there in our immediate vicinity, or ripping through the trees above us, he was soon sleeping soundly on the grass." Benton, *As Seen From the Ranks,* 39–40.
5. Oates, *War Between the Union and the Confederacy,* 212.
6. Letter, "Suggestions From an Old Soldier," *New York Times,* April 24, 1861, 2. Some of his other advice was actually rather sound and sensible.
7. R. Carter, "Reminiscences of the Campaign and Battle of Gettysburg," in *The Gettysburg Papers,* ed. K. Bandy and F. Freeland, 2:707.
8. Laney, "Wasted Gallantry," 30.
9. Elmore, "Meteorological and Astronomical Chronology of the Gettysburg Campaign," 19.
10. Sword, "Capt. Mckee's Revolver and Capt. Sellers' Sword," 50.
11. For an example, see Elmore, "Meteorological and Astronomical Chronology of the Gettysburg Campaign," 12–13.
12. Anon., "Gettysburg Weather Reports," 23.
13. Elmore, "Meteorological and Astronomical Chronology of the Gettysburg Campaign," 10.

14. Letter, July 30, 1903, printed in Sauers (ed.), *Fighting Them Over,* 448.
15. Bigelow, *Peach Orchard,* 54.
16. Herdegen, "Old Soldiers and War Talk," 17.
17. Quoted in Wheeler, *Witness to Gettysburg,* 221.
18. Doyle, Smith, and McMurry (eds.), *This Wilderness of War,* 10–11.
19. Diary entry, April 6, 1862, in Boyd, *Civil War Diary,* 29.
20. Campbell, " 'Remember Harper's Ferry,' " 65.
21. Meinhard, "First Minnesota at Gettysburg," 80–81.
22. Address by A. Cowan, in New York Monuments Commission, *In Memoriam, Alexander Stewart Webb, 1835–1911,* 67.

6. Skirmishing

1. Benedict, *Vermont at Gettysburg,* 8–9; Oates, *War Between the Union and the Confederacy,* 211; Smith, *History of the Nineteenth Regiment,* 79.
2. Winschel, "Heavy Was Their Loss," 8.
3. Patterson, "Death of Iverson's Brigade," 15.
4. Stevens, *Souvenir of Excursion to Battlefields,* 16.
5. Culp, *25th Ohio Veteran Volunteer Infantry,* 78; and New York State Monuments Commission (ed.), *Final Report on the Battlefield of Gettysburg,* 2:932.
6. Letter, C. A. Richardson to J. B. Bachelder, August 18, 1869, in Ladd and Ladd (eds.), *Bachelder Papers,* 1:314–15; "Reports of Lieut. Col. James M. Bull, 126th New York Infantry, Commanding Third Brigade," July 8, 1863, *Official Records,* 1st ser., 27, 1:472.
7. There was an occasional exception, such as John De Forest, who wrote that "skirmishing is not nearly so trying as charging or line fighting. In the first place, you generally have cover; in the second, if you are shot at you can also shoot." Even so, De Forest later changed his mind when he spent more than a month on skirmishing duty and fifty or sixty of his regiment were killed. De Forest, *Volunteer's Adventures,* 111, 116.
8. Wert, *Gettysburg,* 155.
9. Quoted in Hartwig, "Unwilling Witness," 46.
10. See R. Carter, "Reminiscences of the Campaign and Battle of Gettysburg," in *Gettysburg Papers,* ed. K. Bandy and F. Freeland, 2:726; Livermore, *Days and Events,* 67. For the musician's comment, Hunter, "High Private's Sketch of Sharpsburg," 16.
11. Page, *History of the Fourteenth Regiment,* 142–43.
12. Page, *History of the Fourteenth Regiment,* 143.
13. Yee, "Sharpshooting at Gettysburg," 45.
14. Diary entry, July 2, 1863, in Jones (ed.), *Civil War Memoirs of Captain William J. Seymour,* 73.
15. Norton, *Attack and Defense of Little Round Top,* 301.
16. Norton, *Attack and Defense of Little Round Top,* 73.
17. Excerpt from Urban, "Dreaming on the Conestoga," printed in Felton (ed.), "In Their Words," 98.
18. Woodward, *Our Campaigns,* 271.
19. Stevens, *Berdan's United States Sharpshooters,* 340.
20. Urban, "Dreaming on the Conestoga," printed in Felton (ed.), "In Their Words," 98.
21. Dunaway, *Reminiscences of a Rebel,* 87.
22. Parker, *Henry Wilson's Regiment,* 340–41.
23. Stearns, *Three Years with Company K,* 207, 325.

24. R. Thompson, "A Scrap of Gettysburg," in *Gettysburg Papers*, ed. K. Bandy and F. Freeland, 2:955–56. Thompson claims that the Union marksmen were from Berdan's unit, but they were in fact from 1st Company, Massachusetts Sharpshooters (1st Andrew Sharpshooters).
25. Elmore, "Skirmishers," 11.
26. Wade, "Untold History Recited at a Meeting of the Regiment," 1.
27. Stevens, *Souvenir of Excursion to Battlefields*, 15; Galwey, *Valiant Hours*, 107.
28. Galwey, *Valiant Hours*, 110–11.
29. Stevens, *Souvenir of Excursion to Battlefields*, 11.
30. Stevens, *Souvenir of Excursion to Battlefields*, 16.
31. Quoted in Adelman, "Hazlett's Battery at Gettysburg," 69.

7. Artillery Versus Artillery

1. Smith, *Famous Battery and Its Campaigns*, 102.
2. Scribner, *How Soldiers Were Made*, 294.
3. Letter, July 4, 1863, printed in Benedict, *Army Life in Virginia*, 166.
4. Murray, "Artillery Duel in the Peach Orchard," 79.
5. Nosworthy, *Bloody Crucible of Courage*, 421–22; Gibbon, *Artillerist's Manual*, 357.
6. "Report of Lieut. Col. Freeman McGilvery, First Main Light Artillery, Commanding First Volunteer Brigade," no date, *Official Records*, 1st ser., 27, 1:881.
7. Nevins (ed.), *Diary of Battle*, 242–43.
8. Gibbon, *Artillerist's Manual*, 358.
9. Baker, *History of the Ninth Mass. Battery*, 59.
10. Campbell, "Baptism of Fire," 59n53.
11. Alexander, *Military Memoirs of a Confederate*, 421.
12. Murray, "Artillery Duel in the Peach Orchard," 83.
13. Anon., "Visit to the Gettysburg Battlefield," 2.
14. Andrews (ed.), *History of Marietta and Washington County*, 626.
15. Elmore, "Grand Cannonade," 107.
16. Letter, William Johnston to Smith, no date, printed in Smith, *Famous Battery and Its Campaigns*, 143.
17. Bigelow, *Peach Orchard*, 55.
18. Fuger, "Cushing's Battery at Gettysburg," 407.
19. Address by Smith, 136th New York, read May 3, 1894, in Bandy and Freeland (eds.), *Gettysburg Papers*, 1:345.
20. Campbell, "Baptism of Fire," 59n52.
21. Elmore, "Grand Cannonade," 105n15; Meyer, "Pioneer's Story," in Muffly (ed.), *Story of Our Regiment*, 467.
22. Address by Smith, in Bandy and Freeland (eds.), *Gettysburg Papers*, 1:345.
23. Address by Smith, in Bandy and Freeland (eds.), *Gettysburg Papers*, 1:345–46.
24. Stevens, *Souvenir of Excursion to Battlefields*, 25.
25. Diary of Lieutenant Parsons, printed in Washburn, *Complete Military History and Record of the 108th Regiment N.Y. Vols.*, 49–51; Busey and Martin (eds.), *Regimental Strengths and Losses at Gettysburg*, 244.
26. On relative infantry and artillery casualties, Glatthaar, *Soldiering in the Army of Northern Virginia*, 54. On artillery casualties specifically, E. P. Alexander stated that his command of twenty-six guns sustained losses of 147 men and 116 horses; four-fifths of the

human casualties were caused by artillery. Letter, E. P. Alexander, "Causes of Lee's Defeat at Gettysburg," 106; see also Griffith, *Battle Tactics,* 174.

27. Stiles, *Four Years Under Marse Robert,* 217–18.

28. The Vermonter was an anonymous man of the 13th Vermont, whose letter was printed in the *National Tribune,* August 30, 1894, in Sauers (ed.), *Fighting Them Over,* 435; Nelson, *Battles of Chancellorsville and Gettysburg,* 163–64; for the sergeant, see Meinhard, "First Minnesota at Gettysburg," 85. During the artillery fighting on July 2 when Early's guns opened up on Cemetery Hill, Captain William Seymour wrote that "ever and anon an ammunition chest would explode, sending a bright column of smoke far up towards the heavens." See Jones (ed.), *Civil War Memoirs of William J. Seymour,* 74.

29. Letter, July 4, 1863, printed in Benedict, *Army Life in Virginia,* 176.

30. Lecture by James Stewart, "Battery B, Fourth U.S. Artillery at Gettysburg," read April 5, 1893, in Bandy and Freeland (eds.), *Gettysburg Papers,* 1:375.

31. Benedict, *Vermont at Gettysburg,* 10.

32. Nevins (ed.), *Diary of Battle,* 242–43.

33. Elmore, "Grand Cannonade," 102.

34. J. Bigelow, "Account of the Engagement of the 9th Mass. Battery by Capt. Bigelow," no date, printed in Ladd and Ladd (eds.), *Bachelder Papers,* 1:178.

35. Diary entry, April 7, 1862, in Boyd, *Civil War Diary,* 37.

36. Barnes, Otis, and Huntington (eds.), *Medical and Surgical History of the War of the Rebellion,* Part 3, 2:704.

37. On Beary, see Long, "Surgeon's Handiwork," 83–84. On Gage, Dr. Joseph Holt's memoirs, printed in Brown, *University Greys,* 38.

38. Quoted in Hess, *Union Soldier in Battle,* 28–29.

39. Hitchcock, *War from the Inside,* 60.

40. Patriot Daughters of Lancaster, *Hospital Scenes,* 11. On Cushing's battery, see Benedict, *Vermont at Gettysburg,* 15.

41. Stiles, *Four Years Under Marse Robert,* 218.

42. Excerpt from Urban, "Dreaming on the Conestoga," printed in Felton (ed.), "In Their Words," 89–90.

8. Artillery Versus Infantry

1. Campbell, "Baptism of Fire," 59.

2. Letter, J. W. Hand, July 24, 1890, printed in Sauers (ed.), *Fighting Them Over,* 221–22.

3. Campbell, "'Remember Harper's Ferry,'" 104.

4. Nosworthy, "Rifle Musket and Associated Tactics," 35.

5. Crumb (ed.), *Eleventh Corps Artillery at Gettysburg,* 76, 77.

6. Sawyer, *Military History of the 8th Regiment Ohio Vol. Inf'y,* 131.

7. Hartwig, "'I Have Never Been in a Hotter Place,'" 67.

8. Kieffer, *Recollections of a Drummer-Boy,* 112. See Busey and Martin (eds.), *Regimental Strengths and Losses at Gettysburg,* 241.

9. Elmore, "Effects of Artillery Fire on Infantry at Gettysburg," 117.

10. Letter, July 14, 1863, printed in Benedict, *Army Life in Virginia,* 186.

11. Winschel, "Gettysburg Diary of Lieutenant William Peel," 105, quoted in Long, "Confederate Prisoners of Gettysburg," 103.

12. Shultz, "Benner's Hill," 80.

13. On the 55th Ohio, Howard, *Autobiography of Oliver Otis Howard,* 1:436; on the 16th

Georgia, Jorgensen, "Wofford Sweeps the Wheatfield," 37. J. Bigelow reports General Humphries saying that thirty out of thirty-five men in a single company were killed and disabled by a lone shell. Bigelow, *Peach Orchard*, 55.

14. Gottfried, "'Friendly' Fire at Gettysburg," 78–84; Elmore, "Effects of Artillery Fire on Infantry at Gettysburg," 117–22.

15. Letter, Robert Cruikshanks to Mary, July 3, 1863, at "Civil War Letters 1863," available at http://www.salem-ny.com/1863letters.html, accessed September 21, 2011.

16. "'The Iron Brigade' 7th Wisconsin Infantry at Gettysburg, Pa.: report by Lt. Col. John Callis," in Ladd and Ladd (eds.), *Bachelder Papers*, 1:142.

17. "Report of E. Livingston Price, One Hundred and Forty-Fifth New York Infantry," July 23, 1863, *Official Records*, 1st ser., 27, 1:801. The offending officer claimed that Price had been overexcited and that defective shells and improper fuses had been at fault. "Report of Col. Archibald L. MacDougall, One Hundred and Twenty-Third New York Infantry, Commanding First Brigade," July 26, 1863, *Official Records*, 1st ser., 27, 1:784.

18. Letter, Robert Cruikshanks to Mary, July 3, 1863, at "Civil War Letters 1863," available at http://www.salem-ny.com/1863letters.html, accessed September 21, 2011.

19. Talk by Winfield Scott, "Pickett's Charge as Seen From the Front Line," read February 8, 1888, in Bandy and Freeland (eds.), *Gettysburg Papers*, 2:905; Bowen, "From Round Top to Richmond," 2; Wyckoff, "Kershaw's Brigade at Gettysburg," 41.

20. Dougherty, "Wartime Amputations," 756.

21. Barnes, Otis, and Huntington (eds.), *Medical and Surgical History of the War of the Rebellion*, Part 3, 2:707n3.

22. Holstein, *Three Years in the Field Hospitals*, 42.

23. Letter, Hubbard, March 15, 1915, printed in Sauers (ed.), *Fighting Them Over*, 360.

24. Letter, Goldstein, July 19, 1906, printed in Sauers (ed.), *Fighting Them Over*, 412.

25. Address by Bowen, November 11, 1888, in Nicholson (ed.), *Pennsylvania at Gettysburg*, 2:605.

9. Infantry Versus Infantry—The Attack

1. Elmore, "Casualty Analysis of the Gettysburg Battle," 98–99.

2. Martin et al. (eds.), *History of the Fifty-Seventh Regiment*, 88.

3. Diary entry, July 2, 1863, in Jones (ed.), *Civil War Memoirs of Captain William J. Seymour*, 75.

4. Winschel, "Posey's Brigade at Gettysburg," 92. Regarding various reactions, a man of the 14th Connecticut observed his fellows awaiting the Confederate assault on their line: "It was, indeed, an anxious moment. One you can see is looking at the far off home he will never see again. Another is looking at his little ones. . . . Others are communing with Him before whom so many will shortly have to appear." Page, *History of the Fourteenth Regiment*, 152.

5. Campbell, "'Remember Harper's Ferry,'" 1:60.

6. Hess, *Union Soldier in Battle*, 147.

7. Barber, *Army Memoirs*, 52–53.

8. Barrett (ed.), *Yankee Rebel*, 19.

9. Durkin (ed.), *John Dooley, Confederate Soldier*, 99.

10. Small, *Road to Richmond*, 185.

11. Benedict, *Vermont at Gettysburg*, 14. Emphasis added.

12. Sword, "Union Sgt. Isaac W. Barnes," 127.

13. Quoted in Rollins (ed.), *Pickett's Charge,* 131.

14. Glatthaar, *Soldiering in the Army of Northern Virginia,* 174; Fox, *Regimental Losses,* 38; Glatthaar, *General Lee's Army,* 282.

15. Letter, O. Ladley to mother and sisters, July 16, 1863, in Becker and Thomas (eds.), *Hearth and Knapsack,* 147.

16. Marbaker, *History of the Eleventh New Jersey Volunteers,* 98–99, 104.

17. Quoted in Davis, "Music and Gallantry in Combat During the American Civil War," 149.

18. Cheek and Pointon, *History of the Sauk County Riflemen,* 39.

19. Morgan, *Personal Reminiscences of the War of 1861–1865,* 70.

20. Parker, *Henry Wilson's Regiment,* 334. The phrase "womanlike scream" was used by Daniel Chisholm, 116th Pennsylvania, at a later date: See his diary entry of August 25, 1864, in Menke and Shimrak (eds.), *Civil War Notebook of Daniel Chisholm,* 35.

21. Toombs, *New Jersey Troops in the Gettysburg Campaign,* 223–25; Busey and Martin (eds.), *Regimental Strengths and Losses at Gettysburg,* 247.

22. Storch and Storch, " 'What a Deadly Trap We Were in,' " 20.

23. Bauer (ed.), *Soldiering,* 117; Watkins, *"Co. Aytch,"* 34.

24. Goss, *Recollections of a Private,* 39.

25. Letter, Andrew Humphreys to friend, December 1862, in Humphreys, *Andrew Atkinson Humphreys,* 180.

26. Anon., *Reunions of the Nineteenth Maine Regiment Association,* 13.

27. Watkins, *"Co. Aytch,"* 34.

28. Stanley, *Autobiography,* 189–90.

29. Quoted in Hess, *Union Soldier in Battle,* 92.

30. Benton, *As Seen From the Ranks,* 47–48.

31. Nevins (ed.), *Diary of Battle,* 56.

32. Diary entry, September 20, 1862, in Grimsley and Miller (eds.), *Union Must Stand,* 60.

33. Meinhard, "First Minnesota at Gettysburg," 82.

34. Stevens, *Reminiscences of the Civil War,* 114.

35. Nosworthy, *Bloody Crucible of Courage,* 63.

36. On double-quick time, see Pula, "26th Wisconsin Volunteer Infantry at Gettysburg," 78. The 1st Minnesota, a first-class veteran unit, advanced at this pace on July 2. See Meinhard, "First Minnesota at Gettysburg," 82.

37. Coxe, "Battle of Gettysburg," 434.

38. Hartwig, " 'I Have Never Been in a Hotter Place,' " 67.

39. Quoted in Coco, "Rawley W. Martin Story," 34.

40. Nosworthy, *Bloody Crucible of Courage,* 138.

41. Benton, *As Seen From the Ranks,* 161.

42. Wing, *Soldier's Story,* 69. In general, see Davis, "Music and Gallantry in Combat During the American Civil War," 141–72.

43. Sword, "Pye's Sword at the Rail Cut," 29–32.

44. Letter, O. Ladley to mother and sisters, July 16, 1863, in Becker and Thomas (eds.), *Hearth and Knapsack,* 147.

45. "Report of Lieut. Col. P. A. Work, First Texas Infantry," July 9, 1863, *Official Records,* 1st ser., 27, 2:410.

46. See O'Brien, " 'Hold Them with the Bayonet,' " 74; on Davis, see Winschel, "Heavy Was Their Loss," 5–10.

47. Byrne and Weaver (eds.), *Haskell of Gettysburg,* 162.

48. Paper by R. Dawes, "With the Sixth Wisconsin at Gettysburg," (1890), in Bandy and Freeland (eds.), *Gettysburg Papers,* 1:219.

49. Address by J. V. Pierce, 147th New York, July 1, 1888, in New York Monuments Commission, *Final Report on the Battlefield of Gettysburg,* 3:992.

10. Infantry Versus Infantry—The Defense

1. O'Brien, " 'Perfect Roar of Musketry,' " 90.
2. Nosworthy, *Bloody Crucible of Courage,* 256.
3. Letter, J. L. Brady to J. B. Bachelder, May 24, 1886, in Ladd and Ladd (eds.), *Bachelder Papers,* 3:1398.
4. Letter, David Shields to J. B. Bachelder, August 27, 1884, in Ladd and Ladd (eds.), *Bachelder Papers,* 2:1068. To the suggestion that the rear rank loaded and passed up rifles to the front rank, Shields retorted that "it sounds very militia like to me."
5. Bowen, "Diary of Captain George D. Bowen," 133.
6. Adkin, *Gettysburg Companion,* 109.
7. Lader, "Personal Journey of Pvt. David Ballinger," 94; Toombs, *New Jersey Troops in the Gettysburg Campaign,* 290; Carter, *Four Brothers in Blue,* 308. See also Bowen, "From Round Top to Richmond," 3.
8. Address by W. Scott, 126th New York, "Pickett's Charge as Seen From the Front Line," read February 8, 1888, in Bandy and Freeland (eds.), *Gettysburg Papers,* 2:906–7.
9. Letter, E. Southard, August 19, 1897, printed in Sauers (ed.), *Fighting Them Over,* 231.
10. Jackson (ed.), *Colonel's Diary,* 71.
11. Olney, "Battle of Shiloh," 577–89, on 583.
12. Lader, "Personal Journey of Pvt. David Ballinger," 91.
13. Hill, *Our Boys,* 306.
14. Diary entry, August 25, 1864, in Menke and Shimrak (eds.), *Civil War Notebook of Daniel Chisholm,* 36.
15. Saxton, *Regiment Remembered,* 82.
16. Vautier, *History of the 88th Pennsylvania Volunteers,* 106–7.
17. Stevens, *Souvenir of Excursion to Battlefields,* 29.
18. Anon., *Reunions of the Nineteenth Maine Regiment Association,* 11.
19. Anon., "How They Fire in Battle," 279.
20. Stillwell, *Story of a Common Soldier,* 44.
21. Gibbon, *Artillerist's Manual,* 356; Nosworthy, *Bloody Crucible of Courage,* 306, 432.
22. Hess finds two minutes, but Adkin suggests every thirty seconds. I've averaged it out for illustrative purposes. Hess, *Rifle Musket in Civil War Combat,* 100–4; Adkin, *Gettysburg Companion,* 97.
23. Hess, *Rifle Musket in Civil War Combat,* 100–4.
24. Warren, *Declaration of Independence and War History,* 30.
25. Weygant, *History of the One Hundred and Twenty-Fourth Regiment,* 179–80.
26. On the accuracy at Bunker Hill, see Rose, "Marksmanship in 1775," 44–47, 70.
27. See Rose, *American Rifle,* 190–91. On wartime training, or the lack of it, Bilby, *Small Arms at Gettysburg,* 76–80.
28. Marvin, *Fifth Regiment Connecticut Volunteers,* 16.
29. Stillwell, *Story of a Common Soldier,* 55–56.
30. Carter, *Four Brothers in Blue,* 309; Joseph Cogswell noticed the same thing. Cogswell, "The Battle of Gettysburg," in *The 'Dutchess County Regiment' in the Civil War,* ed. S. G. Cook and C. E. Benton, 32.
31. Neese, *Three Years in the Confederate Horse Artillery,* 35–36.
32. Quoted in Nosworthy, *Roll Call to Destiny,* 83.

33. Sergeant Silas Adams, cited in Smith, *History of the Nineteenth Regiment,* 71.
34. Preston, *History of the Tenth Regiment of Cavalry, New York State Volunteers,* 112.
35. Memoir by George Grant, read May 10, 1898, in Bandy and Freeland (eds.), *Gettysburg Papers,* 1:261.
36. Byrne and Weaver (eds.), *Haskell of Gettysburg,* 159.
37. On shins, see letter, W. S. Rosecrans to General McNeil, September 27, 1864, *Official Records,* 1st ser., 41, 3:412; on knees, see Orders of Major General T. C. Hindman, Trans-Mississippi Army; December 4, 1862, 1st ser., 22, 1:83. Report of Lieut. Col. Walton Dwight, September 12, 1863, in *Official Records,* 1st ser., 27, 1:342.
38. Excerpt from Urban, "Dreaming on the Conestoga," printed in Felton (ed.), "In Their Words," 95.
39. Vautier, *History of the 88th Pennsylvania Volunteers,* 106; see also the recollections of Lieutenant Colonel A. J. Sellers (90th Pennsylvania), in Nicholson (ed.), *Pennsylvania at Gettysburg,* 1:484.
40. Diary entry, July 2, 1863, in Runge (ed.), *Four Years in the Confederate Artillery,* 50.
41. Diary entry, June 28, 1862, in Barrett (ed.), *Yankee Rebel,* 32.
42. Bowen, "From Round Top to Richmond," 3.
43. Stanley, *Autobiography,* 190; letter, C. L. Harris to father, July 4, 1863, in Washburn, *Complete Military History and Record of the 108th Regiment N.Y. Vols.,* 52.
44. Nosworthy, *Bloody Crucible of Courage,* 230; Blackford, *War Years with Jeb Stuart,* 123–24.
45. Judson, *History of the Eighty-Third Regiment Pennsylvania Volunteers,* 67, 69–70.
46. For an outline, Adkin, *Gettysburg Companion,* 108.
47. O'Brien, "'Perfect Roar of Musketry,'" 90.
48. Hardee, *Rifle and Light Infantry Tactics,* 58; Bowen, "Diary of Captain George D. Bowen," 133.
49. Quoted in Hess, *Union Soldier in Battle,* 112.
50. Dodge, "Left Wounded," 321.
51. Ward, *History of the Second Pennsylvania Veteran Heavy Artillery,* 66; Meyer, "Private's Story and Story of Company A," in Muffly (ed.), *Story of Our Regiment,* 537.

11. The Attack Continues

1. See Appendix, in Lader, "7th New Jersey in the Gettysburg Campaign," 65–67. In Union regiments the designated company was usually Company K, and a breakdown of the 7th New Jersey's numbers finds that whereas the average number of casualties per company (excluding killed) was about ten, Company K suffered seventeen.
2. Winschel, "Heavy Was Their Loss," 11, 170; Winschel, "Colors Are Shrouded in Mystery," 79–80.
3. Underwood, *History of the Twenty-Sixth Regiment of the North Carolina Troops,* 50–52, 72; Hadden, "Deadly Embrace," 20, 27–33. On casualties, see Smith, Jr., *For the Good of the Old North State,* 4.
4. Letter, P. Welsh to M. Welsh, March 31, 1863, in Kohl and Richard (eds.), *Irish Green and Union Blue,* 81.
5. Dreese, "Ordeal in the Lutheran Theological Seminary," 104.
6. Letter, P. Welsh to M. Welsh, March 31, 1863, in Kohl and Richard (eds.), *Irish Green and Union Blue,* 82, 156–57.
7. Underwood, *History of the Twenty-Sixth Regiment of the North Carolina Troops,* 99.
8. Keller, "Pennsylvania's German-Americans," in *Damn Dutch,* ed. D. L. Valuska and C. B. Keller, 138.

9. Evans, "Cries of the Wounded Were Piercing and Horrible," 35.
10. Quoted in Hess, *Union Soldier in Battle,* 28.
11. Dunkelman, "Additional Notes on the 154th New York at Gettysburg," 74.
12. Jorgensen, "John Haley's Personal Recollection of the Battle of the Wheatfield," 75.
13. This section is based on accounts by Lee, "Reminiscences of the Gettysburg Battle," 54–60, on 56; Isham, "Story of a Gunshot Wound," in Chamberlin, *Sketches of War History, 1861–1865,* 4:430; Farlow and Barry (eds.), "Vincent B. Osborne's Civil War Experiences," 108–33, on 120; (Douglas) Letter, August 5, 1863, in Long, "Confederate Prisoners of Gettysburg," 98; Ward, "Incidents and Personal Experiences on the Battlefield at Gettysburg," 345–49, on 347.
14. Hill, *Our Boys,* 306.
15. Wing, *Soldier's Story,* 69.
16. Carter, *Four Brothers in Blue,* 234.
17. Anon. (ed.), *Biographical and Historical Memoirs,* 337–38.

12. The Critical Moment

1. Scribner, *How Soldiers Were Made,* 273–74.
2. Benton, *As Seen From the Ranks,* 35.
3. Lecture by Dawes, "With the Sixth Wisconsin at Gettysburg," in Bandy and Freeland (eds.), *Gettysburg Papers,* 1:219.
4. Bierce, "Crime at Pickett's Mill," in *Devil's Dictionary,* 690–91.
5. Scribner, *How Soldiers Were Made,* 259.
6. Benson (ed.), *Berry Benson's Civil War Book,* 22.
7. Meinhard, "First Minnesota at Gettysburg," 80–81.
8. Dunkelman and Winey, "Hardtack Regiment in the Brickyard Fight," 22.
9. Galwey, *Valiant Hours,* 118.
10. Diary entry, in Tomasak (ed.), *One Hundred Forty-Third Pennsylvania Volunteer Regiment,* 64–65.
11. Bowen, "Diary of Captain George D. Bowen," 129.
12. Quoted in Hartwig, "11th Army Corps," 33–49.
13. Talk by Stewart, "Battery B, Fourth U.S. Artillery at Gettysburg," in *Gettysburg Papers,* ed. Bandy and Freeland, 1:370–71; Tomasak, "143rd Pennsylvania Volunteer Regiment," 53.
14. Address by Pierce, in New York Monuments Commission, *Final Report on the Battlefield of Gettysburg,* 3:992.
15. Letter, April 2, 1891, in Sauers (ed.), *Fighting Them Over,* 282.
16. Dunkelman, " 'We Were Compelled to Cut Our Way Through Them,' " 34–56. See also the important analysis of Costa, "Scarring and Mortality Selection Among Civil War POWs." On Confederate prisoners and their fates, see Mulligan, "Death of a Secessionist Regiment," 94–110.

13. Holding the Line

1. Benton, *As Seen From the Ranks,* 35. So green had been the regiment that when the first shell screeched over their heads, recalled Thomas Vassar, it provoked "an exhibition of fluttering coat-tails" as scared men sprinted in all directions. T. Vassar, "Reminiscences," in Cook and Benton (eds.), *'Dutchess County Regiment' in the Civil War,* 190.
2. Quoted in Dreese, "151st Pennsylvania Volunteers at Gettysburg," 60.

3. Tompkins and Tompkins, *Company K,* 20.
4. Nosworthy, *Bloody Crucible of Courage,* 436; Gibbon, *Artillerist's Manual,* 359.
5. Fuger, "Cushing's Battery at Gettysburg," 408; Cooksey, "Union Artillery at Gettysburg on July 3," 101.
6. Address by John Bigelow, printed in Baker, *History of the Ninth Mass. Battery,* 214–15.
7. Bigelow, "Account of the Engagement," in Ladd and Ladd (eds.), *Bachelder Papers,* 1:177: "Usually in an engagement a few rounds of canister will repel a charge."
8. Wyckoff, "Kershaw's Brigade at Gettysburg," 42; Coxe, "Battle of Gettysburg," 434.
9. Quoted in Campbell, "Voices of Gettysburg," 19.
10. Miller, "Perrin's Brigade on July 1, 1863," 27.
11. Carter, *Four Brothers in Blue,* 325.
12. Davis, "Death and Burials of General Richard Brooke Garnett," 112–13.
13. Coxe, "Battle of Gettysburg," 434.

14. At Close Quarters

1. Marbaker, *History of the Eleventh New Jersey Volunteers,* 175; see also Dodge, "Left Wounded," 321.
2. Laidley, "Breech-Loading Musket," 67. The official tally is "Report by Lieut. John R. Edie, Acting Chief Ordnance Officer, Army of the Potomac," no date, in *Official Records,* 1st ser., 27, 1:225–26, which differs in minor respects. The total number is close enough to make no difference. The number of guns left behind has been remarked upon several times, generally owing to the misapprehension that the high proportion of overloaded pieces proves that soldiers were reluctant to fire their weapons at the enemy. This is an argument evidently based on S. L. A. Marshall's influential—if now discredited—contention in his *Men Against Fire: The Problem of Battle Command,* that not more than 15 percent of American combat soldiers fired their weapons in World War II. On Marshall's controversial assertion, see Rose, *American Rifle,* 339–41; on replacement arms, see Haines, *History of the Fifteenth Regiment New Jersey Volunteers,* 94.
3. Hohenlohe-Ingelflingen, *Letters on Infantry,* 34.
4. Simon Hubler account, "Just the Plain, Unvarnished Story," 4.
5. Stillwell, *Story of a Common Soldier,* 252.
6. Meinhard, "First Minnesota at Gettysburg," 82, 84.
7. Polley, *Hood's Texas Brigade,* 169.
8. Watkins, *"Co. Aytch,"* 34.
9. Meinhard, "First Minnesota at Gettysburg," 87.
10. Smith, *History of the Nineteenth Regiment,* 82.
11. "Address of Col. Edward Hill," in Trowbridge and Farnsworth (eds.), *Michigan at Gettysburg,* 108–9.
12. Coffman, "Vital Unit," 44.
13. Fuger, "Cushing's Battery at Gettysburg," 409.
14. Address by W. O. Beauchamp, 1st New York Light Artillery, July 3, 1888, in New York Monuments Commission, *Final Report on the Battlefield of Gettysburg,* 3:1184.
15. Baker, *History of the Ninth Mass. Battery,* 81.
16. Smith, *Famous Battery and Its Campaigns,* 104.
17. Nosworthy, *Bloody Crucible of Courage,* 446–47.
18. Winschel, "Heavy Was Their Loss," 11.
19. Campbell, "Baptism of Fire," 74.

20. Gilmor, *Four Years in the Saddle,* 99. One wonders whence this tradition derived. Possibly, it could be Irish in origin. The Louisiana Brigade was heavily Irish, and a year earlier Richard Taylor had seen the same brigade's Irishmen going "mad with cheering," among them a "huge fellow, with one eye closed and half his whiskers burned by powder" who was "riding cock-horse on a gun" at Port Republic. Taylor, *Destruction and Reconstruction,* 93.

15. Surrender

1. Dawes, *Service with the Sixth Wisconsin Volunteers,* 168–69.
2. Campbell, " 'Remember Harper's Ferry,' " 2:106.
3. Letter, December 10, 1909, printed in Sauers (ed.), *Fighting Them Over,* 414.
4. Excerpt from Urban, "Dreaming on the Conestoga," printed in Felton (ed.), "In Their Words," 101.
5. Dougherty, " 'We Have Come to Stay!,' " 53.
6. Small, *Road to Richmond,* 68.
7. Pula (ed.), *Memoirs of Wladimir Krzyżanowski,* 49.
8. Diary entry, June 28, 1862, in Barrett (ed.), *Yankee Rebel,* 34.
9. Redwood, "Confederate in the Field," in *Photographic History of the Civil War,* 8:174; Anon., "Fighting," 339.
10. Byrne and Weaver (eds.), *Haskell of Gettysburg,* 189.

16. The Return to Normal

1. Quoted in Hess, *Union Soldier in Battle,* 1.
2. Talk by Dawes, "With the Sixth Wisconsin at Gettysburg," in Bandy and Freeland (eds.), *Gettysburg Papers,* 1:234.
3. Alexander (ed. G. W. Gallagher), *Fighting for the Confederacy,* 208.
4. Oration by C. D. MacDougall, 111th New York, in New York Monuments Commission, *Final Report on the Battlefield of Gettysburg,* 2:800–1.
5. Eby (ed.), *Virginia Yankee in the Civil War,* 113.
6. Excerpt from Urban, "Dreaming on the Conestoga," in Felton (ed.), "In Their Words," 89.
7. Anonymous Union soldier at Shiloh, quoted in Moore (ed.), *Civil War in Song and Story, 1860–1865,* 64–65.
8. Quoted in Campbell, "Voices of Gettysburg," 16.
9. Lader, "Personal Journey of Pvt. David Ballinger," 88–89.
10. Diary entry, April 8, 1862, in Boyd, *Civil War Diary,* 42.

17. Sights, Sounds, Smells

1. Carter, *Four Brothers in Blue,* 324.
2. Patriot Daughters of Lancaster, *Hospital Scenes,* 11.
3. In the Army of Northern Virginia, one in eight men was killed in action during the war; about the same died of disease. Adding in other causes of noncombat fatalities (e.g., executions, accidents), brings the total to one in four dying while in military service. Another 25 percent were wounded at least once. By adding together the figures of killed, wounded, captured, died of disease, and discharged for disability, three out of every four soldiers who served under Lee became victims. Glatthaar, *Soldiering in the Army of Northern Virginia,* 16–17. A typical unit that fought at Gettysburg, Company

E of the 20th North Carolina, began its war on April 16, 1861, with 107 men. Over the next four years, twenty-six of these would be killed or mortally wounded in battle and fourteen would die of disease, leaving sixty-seven living at war's end. Of the survivors, fifteen were permanently disabled with wounds and sixteen had been wounded but recovered fully, so leaving thirty-six unharmed (or one-third of the original recruits). Nineteen of these, however, had never been in combat as they were detailed for other duties, so really only seventeen (16 percent) emerged from the war unscathed.

4. Adkin, *Gettysburg Companion,* 508.
5. Cited in Lash, "'Pathetic Story,'" 77.
6. Campbell, "Voices of Gettysburg," 16.
7. Busey and Martin (eds.), *Regimental Strengths and Losses at Gettysburg,* 242 (chart 6.1, "Union Regimental Losses").
8. Busey and Martin (eds.), *Regimental Strengths and Losses at Gettysburg,* 262–63 (chart 6.2, "Union Regiments with Losses Greater Than Fifty Percent"), 298 (chart 7.2, "Confederate Regiments with Losses Greater Than Fifty Percent"), 230 (chart 5.1, "Average Regimental Engaged Strengths").
9. Carter, *Four Brothers in Blue,* 325.
10. Quoted in Coco, *Strange and Blighted Land,* 56.
11. Bucklin, *In Hospital and Camp,* 188.
12. Quoted in Hess, *Union Soldier in Battle,* 38.
13. Stiles, *Four Years Under Marse Robert,* 220.
14. Diary entry, July 2, 1863, in Runge (ed.), *Four Years in the Confederate Artillery,* 50–51.
15. Quoted in Pfanz, *Gettysburg,* 369.
16. Quoted in Hess, *Union Soldier in Battle,* 22.
17. Hess, *Union Soldier in Battle,* 22.
18. Survivors' Association, *History of the 118th Pennsylvania Volunteers,* 249.
19. Musgrove, *Autobiography,* 94, 92. According to John Wert, "swine were found revelling in the remains [of a corpse] in a manner horrible to contemplate." See Wert, *Complete Hand-Book,* 163.
20. Craft, *History of the Hundred Forty-First Regiment,* 128.
21. Anon., "Scenes and Incidents at Gettysburg," 39.
22. Meyer, "Pioneer's Story," in Muffly (ed.), *Story of Our Regiment,* 465; see also Marbaker, *History of the Eleventh New Jersey Volunteers,* 109.
23. Letter, July 14, 1863, printed in Benedict, *Army Life in Virginia,* 190.
24. Brown, *Twenty-Seventh Indiana Volunteer Infantry,* 394.
25. Stiles, *Four Years Under Marse Robert,* 220.
26. Haines, *History of the Fifteenth Regiment New Jersey Volunteers,* 96.
27. Campbell, "Aftermath and Recovery of Gettysburg," 110.
28. Stevens, *Three Years in the Sixth Corps,* 254.
29. Coco, *Strange and Blighted Land,* 51.
30. Meyer, "Pioneer's Story," in Muffly (ed.), *Story of Our Regiment,* 466.
31. Stiles, *Four Years Under Marse Robert,* 220.

18. The Dead

1. Musto, "Treatment of the Wounded at Gettysburg," 123.
2. Letter, A. M. Eby to J. B. Bachelder, October 20, 1885, in Ladd and Ladd (eds.), *Bachelder Papers,* 2:1131. This story is reproduced with a few contrasting details in J. A. Moore's address, in Nicholson (ed.), *Pennsylvania at Gettysburg,* 2:706. According to

Moore (707), the soldier had only been shot in the leg, "by no means fatally," possibly making the reason for his suicide a fear of being captured, but Eby was adamant that his abdominal injury "would beyond doubt have proved mortal."

3. Fulks, "Another Irony of Gettysburg," 62.
4. Bowen, "Diary of Captain George D. Bowen," 135–36.
5. Meyer, "Pioneer's Story," in Muffly (ed.), *Story of Our Regiment,* 465.
6. Letter, July 14, 1863, in Benedict, *Army Life in Virginia,* 190.
7. Wadding, "Story of Company I," in Muffly (ed.), *Story of Our Regiment,* 780.
8. Quoted in Coco, *Strange and Blighted Land,* 50.
9. Elmore, "Less Than Brave," 127.
10. Letter, O. C. Brown to A. Dunham, July 6, 1863, printed in Nash, *History of the Forty-Fourth New York Regiment Volunteer Infantry,* 295; Hutchinson, "Bringing Home a Fallen Son," 68.
11. "Report of Lt. Col. Charles H. Morgan," in Ladd and Ladd (eds.), *Bachelder Papers,* 3:1367.
12. Coco, *Strange and Blighted Land,* 76, and his *On the Bloodstained Field,* 41; Lamb, *History of the United States Army Medical Museum,* 19, 146.
13. Conklin, "Long March to Stevens Run," 54–55.
14. On identification and tags, see Gross, "Grave Situation," 119–23; Stahl, "Pvt. George Matthews," 98–99; Stahl, "Pvt. John Wright," 56–58. In 1906 the War Department approved General Order Number 204 authorizing the universal issuing of dog tags.
15. Byrne and Weaver (eds.), *Haskell of Gettysburg,* 195.
16. Letter, W. Hays to S. Williams, July 17, 1863, in *Official Records,* 1st ser., 27, 1:378, remarking that "one female (private) in rebel uniform" was buried. There was at least one woman captured at Gettysburg. The hospitalized Thomas Read of 5th Michigan excitedly notified his parents that "i must tel you we have got a female secesh here, she was wounded at gettiburg but our doctors soon found her out. i have not seen her but the[y] say she is very good looking. the poor girl [h]as lost a leg; it is a great pity she did not stay at home with her mother." Quoted in Coco, *Strange and Blighted Land,* 152. These enigmatic women may have sneaked into the army to accompany their husbands or fiancés. At Chickamauga, a captured Northern female was purportedly sent back to her lines under a flag of truce and "a message to the effect that, 'As the Confederates do not use women in war, this woman, wounded in battle, is returned to you.'" The original source for this anecdote appears to be Young, *Women and the Crisis,* 97. It has been widely quoted, but generally without the important qualifier "to the effect."
17. Carter, *Four Brothers in Blue,* 325.
18. Jordan, Jr., "Gettysburg and the Seventeenth Maine," 52.
19. Quoted in Johnson, *Battleground Adventures,* 174–75.
20. Parker, *Henry Wilson's Regiment,* 345.
21. Diary entry, April 8, 1862, printed in Boyd, *Civil War Diary,* 41.
22. Bowen, "Diary of Captain George D. Bowen," 135.
23. Foster, "Four Days at Gettysburg," 382. On rotting, see McLean, "Days of Terror in 1863," 2.
24. Adkin, *Gettysburg Companion,* 186.

19. The Wounded

1. Keen, "Military Surgery in 1861 and in 1918," printed in *Rehabilitation of the Wounded,* 11–22 (on 14).

2. Coco, *Strange and Blighted Land,* 154–55.

3. At the end of 1861 the Sanitary Commission had surveyed the medical personnel of 200 regiments and concluded that 2 percent were incompetent and another 13 percent were of doubtful competence. Nevertheless, two-thirds were performing their duties "with creditable energy and earnestness," and the number would rise over the course of the war. Hall, "Lessons of the War Between the States," 412. On Bailey, see Miller, "Perrin's Brigade on July 1, 1863," 31.

4. Letters, July 6, 9, and 10, 1863, in Garrison, *John Shaw Billings,* 64–66.

5. Hall, "Lessons of the War Between the States," 419.

6. "Report of Surg. Jonathan Letterman, U.S. Army, Medical Director, Army of the Potomac," October 3, 1863, in *Official Records,* 1st ser., 27, 1:196.

7. Fuller, *Personal Recollections,* 102.

8. Letter, July 24, 1890, in Sauers (ed.), *Fighting Them Over,* 221.

9. Barziza, *Adventures of a Prisoner of War,* 54.

10. Davis, *Escape of a Confederate Officer From Prison,* 5–6.

11. Peltz, "Two Brass Buttons," 1.

12. See Holt's memoir, in Brown, *University Greys,* 39.

13. Quoted in Adkin, *Gettysburg Companion,* 233.

14. Benton, *As Seen From the Ranks,* 31.

15. Vautier, *History of the 88th Pennsylvania Volunteers,* 109.

16. Campbell, "Aftermath and Recovery of Gettysburg," 114.

17. Durkin (ed.), *John Dooley, Confederate Soldier,* 111, 114.

18. Weygant, *History of the One Hundred and Twenty-Fourth Regiment,* 183.

19. Buehler, *Recollections of the Rebel Invasion,* 26.

20. Barziza, *Adventures of a Prisoner of War,* 54.

21. Muffly, "Adjutant's Story," in Muffly (ed.), *Story of Our Regiment,* 245.

22. Martz, "It Was Not a Happy Time," 121.

23. Dougherty, "Wartime Amputations," 755–63; Diffenbaugh, "Military Surgery in the Civil War," 492; Manring et al., "Treatment of War Wounds," 2177.

24. E. Foner, *Reconstruction,* 125; A. J. Bollet, "Amputations in the Civil War," in *Years of Change and Suffering,* ed. J. M. Schmidt and G. R. Hasegawa, 57–67.

25. Albin, "Use of Anesthetics During the Civil War," 99–100, 106; Connor, "Chloroform and the Civil War."

26. Quoted in Coco, *On the Bloodstained Field,* 7.

27. On deaths, see Albin, "Use of Anesthetics During the Civil War, 1861–1865," 111.

28. Stevens, *Berdan's United States Sharpshooter,* 521–23.

29. Chisolm, *Manual of Military Surgery for the Use of Surgeons in the Confederate Army,* 380–81.

30. Daniel, *Recollections of a Rebel Surgeon,* 205.

31. Fuller, *Personal Recollections,* 101–2.

32. Dunkelman and Winey, "The Hardtack Regiment in the Brickyard Fight," 27–28.

33. Casey (ed.), "Ordeal of Adoniram Judson Warner," 234.

34. Spisak, "62nd Pennsylvania Volunteer Infantry," 92.

35. Barnes, Otis, and Huntington (eds.), *Medical and Surgical History of the War of the Rebellion,* Part 3, 2:707–8.

36. Quinones, "Drug Abuse During the Civil War," 1007–20.

37. For a cautious explanation, see Hyman, Wignall, and Roswell, "War Syndromes and Their Evaluation," 398–99.

38. Quoted in Campbell, "Voices of Gettysburg," 16.

39. A selection is reproduced at http://home.comcast.net/~9thmassbattery/AHesse.html. Accessed September 21, 2014.

40. These letters are quoted in Campbell, "Voices of Gettysburg," 19.

41. Quoted in Dougherty, "History of the McPherson Farm at Gettysburg," 28. On cowardice, see Gordon, "'I Never Was a Coward.'"

42. Lader, "7th New Jersey in the Gettysburg Campaign," 65.

43. Quoted in Hess, *Pickett's Charge*, 338.

44. On Thompson's career, see his obituary in the *Orange County Times-Press*, December 3, 1918, p. 6; and entry for "Thirty-Second Colored Troops Regiment," in *History of Pennsylvania Volunteers, 1861–5*, ed. S. P. Bates, 5:1047–48.

45. Letter, November 20, 1862, in Scott (ed.), *Fallen Leaves*, 143.

46. The officer in question was Oliver Wendell Holmes. See "The Soldier's Faith," May 30, 1895, in Holmes (ed.), *Speeches by Oliver Wendell Holmes*, 65.

47. Bruce, *Twentieth Regiment of Massachusetts Volunteer Infantry*, 177–79.

48. Dean, Jr., "'We Will All Be Lost and Destroyed,'" 150–51.

49. Pizarro, Silver, and Prause, "Physical and Mental Health Costs," 193–200. See also J. Andersen, "'Haunted Minds': The Impact of Combat Exposure on the Mental and Physical Health of Civil War Veterans," in *Years of Change and Suffering*, ed. Schmidt and Hasegawa, 143–58.

IWO JIMA

1. Introduction

1. Clifford, *Progress and Purpose*, 22; Moy, *War Machines*, 126–28; Isely and Crowl, *U.S. Marines and Amphibious War*, 34; Gordon, "Thomas Holcomb," in Millett and Shulimson (eds.), *Commandants of the Marine Corps*, 255.

2. See, for instance, Burrell, "Breaking the Cycle of Iwo Jima Mythology," 1143–86.

3. The Strategy

1. On the long evolution of this strategy, see Cosmas and Shulimson, "Culebra Maneuver," 121–32; Shulimson and Cosmas, "Teddy Roosevelt and the Corps' Sea-Going Mission," in *Crucibles*, ed. R. S. Burrell, 97–107; Turk, "United States Navy and the 'Taking' of Panama, 1901–03," 92–96; Grenville and Young, *Politics, Strategy, and American Diplomacy*, 305–7; and Herwig and Trask, "Naval Operations Plans Between Germany and the U.S.A., 1898–1913," 56–58; Lorelli, *To Foreign Shores*, 10; Ellis, "Advanced Base Operations in Micronesia," esp. 1, 5, 15–16, 18–23; Ballendorf and Bartlett, *Pete Ellis*; J. J. Reber, "Pete Ellis: Amphibious Warfare Prophet," in *Crucibles*, ed. R. S. Burrell, 175–89. For a comparative view, A. R. Millett, "Assault From the Sea: The Development of Amphibious Warfare Between the Wars: The American, British, and Japanese Experiences," in *Military Innovation in the Interwar Period*, ed. W. Murray and Millett, 72. An excellent survey is Smith, *Development of Amphibious Tactics in the U.S. Navy*, 19.

5. The Landing

1. Recollections of Sgt. Frank Juszli, in Kessler and Bart (eds.), *Never in Doubt*, 121.
2. Recollections of Pfc. Fred Schribert, in Kessler and Bart (eds.), *Never in Doubt*, 40.
3. Averill, *Mustang*, 121.
4. Cockrel, "How It Was on Iwo," in O'Sheel and Cook (eds.), *Semper Fidelis*, 100.
5. Dyer, *Amphibians Came to Conquer*, 2:1005.
6. Carter, *Beans, Bullets, and Black Oil*, 289, 291. On cigarette supplies, see "Death Valley, Iwo Jima, February 25, 1945: Pfc. Jay Rebstock, USMC (E Co., 2nd Bn., 27th Marines)," in Drez (ed.), *Twenty-Five Yards of War*, 228.
7. McMillan, *Old Breed*, 342–43.
8. On Japanese supplies and expectations, see Eldridge and Tatum (eds.), *Fighting Spirit*, 88.
9. Alexander, *Storm Landings*, 146.
10. Matthews, *Assault*, 25–26; Levin, *From the Battlefield*, 64.
11. Yaffe, *Fragments of War*, 82, 83.
12. Josephy, *Long and the Short and the Tall*, 160.
13. Quoted in Haynes and Warren, *Lions of Iwo Jima*, 64.
14. Matthews, *Assault*, 26–27.
15. Price and Knecht, "Peleliu 1944," 21.
16. Recollections of Miller, in McLaughlin and Miller, *From the Volcano to the Gorge*, 274–75.
17. Vedder, *Surgeon on Iwo*, 23.
18. Richard Newcomb, "Invasion," in Smith (ed.), *United States Marine Corps in World War II*, 717; Stone, *Marine Remembers Iwo Jima*, 22; Vedder, *Surgeon on Iwo*, 28. Equipped with a fifty-pound bag filled with medical instruments and supplies, Vedder had to drag it up a 70-degree embankment twelve feet high by attaching a rope, climbing to the top, and then pulling the bag after him while under fire.
19. Interview, Rebstock, in Drez (ed.), *Twenty-Five Yards of War*, 230.
20. Averill, *Mustang*, 123.
21. Interview, Rebstock, in Drez (ed.), *Twenty-Five Yards of War*, 234.
22. Matthews, *Assault*, 20.
23. Wheeler, " 'Those Sons-of-Bitches Killed My Buddy!,' " in Smith (ed.), *United States Marine Corps in World War II*, 755.
24. McLaughlin and Miller, *From the Volcano to the Gorge*, 100–2, 183.
25. McLaughlin, in McLaughlin and Miller, *From the Volcano to the Gorge*, 119.
26. McLaughlin, in McLaughlin and Miller, *From the Volcano to the Gorge*, 165.
27. On the development and employment of LVTs, see Roan, "Roebling's Amphibian"; Bailey, *Alligators, Buffaloes, and Bushmasters*, 34–41; Hough, Ludwig, and Shaw, *Pearl Harbor to Guadalcanal*, 1:32–33; Anon., "Roebling's 'Alligator' for Florida Rescues."
28. Wheeler, *Iwo*, 73; interview, Rebstock, in Drez (ed.), *Twenty-Five Yards of War*, 231.
29. Matthews, *Assault*, 29.
30. On the LCVP, Heitmann, "Man Who Won the War," 35–50; Mountcastle, "From Bayou to Beachhead," 20–29.
31. Interview, Williams, in Smith (ed.), *Iwo Jima*, 65.
32. Vedder, *Surgeon on Iwo*, 7.
33. Weaver, "D Day," in O'Sheel and Cook (eds.), *Semper Fidelis*, 106.
34. Kuzuhara, "Operations on Iwo Jima," 35.
35. Interview, Hathaway, in Smith (ed.), *Iwo Jima*, 35.
36. Marquand, "Iwo Jima Before H-hour," 495.

37. Weller, "Development of Naval Gunfire Support in World War Two," in *Assault From the Sea*, ed. M. L. Bartlett, 279–81; Haynes and Warren, *Lions of Iwo Jima*, 65.
38. Sherrod, *On to Westward*, 169.
39. Marquand, "Iwo Jima Before H-hour," 499.
40. Gallant, *Friendly Dead*, 28–30.
41. Rottman and Dennis, *U.S. World War II Amphibious Tactics*, 52.
42. Caruso, *Nightmare on Iwo*, 27–28.
43. Toyn, *Quiet Hero*, 79.
44. Levin, *From the Battlefield*, 64–67.
45. Thurman, *We Were in the First Waves*, loc. 254.
46. Interview, D'Amico, in Kessler and Bart (eds.), *Never in Doubt*, 187.
47. Lofgren (ed.), "Diary of First Lieutenant Sugihara Kinryu," 124.
48. Wheeler, *Iwo*, 40.
49. Josephy, *Long and the Short and the Tall*, 156–57.
50. Levin, *From the Battlefield*, 64–67.
51. Quoted in Huie, *From Omaha to Okinawa*, 46.

6. The Beach

1. Averill, *Mustang*, 123–24.
2. Quoted in O'Donnell, *Into the Rising Sun*, 228.
3. McConnell, "How One Squad Fared."
4. Gallant, *Friendly Dead*, 31–33.
5. Levin, *From the Battlefield*, 66–67, 73.
6. Gallant, *Friendly Dead*, 35.
7. Rottman and Dennis, *U.S. World War II Amphibious Tactics*, 53.
8. R. Henri, "Logistics Afloat," in Smith (ed.), *United States Marine Corps in World War II*, 769–71.
9. Matthews, *Assault*, 36.
10. Neiman and Estes, *Tanks on the Beaches*, 121–22.
11. Cockrel, "How It Was on Iwo," in O'Sheel and Cook (eds.), *Semper Fidelis*, 101.
12. Gallant, *Friendly Dead*, 13.
13. Brown, *Battle Wounds of Iwo Jima*, 26; Report by Intelligence Staffs of CINCPAC-CINCPOA, Fleet Marine Force, V Amphibious Corps, 3rd, 4th, and 5th Marine Divisions, *Defense Installations on Iwo Jima*, Bulletin 136–45, June 10, 1945, p. 5.
14. Wheeler, *We Are the Wounded*, 207.
15. Shiveley, *Last Lieutenant*, 49.
16. Sherrod, *On to Westward*, 180.
17. Wheeler, *Iwo*, 196.
18. Shiveley, *Last Lieutenant*, 53.
19. Sherrod, *On to Westward*, 180.
20. Walker and White, *Preparing for the Rain on Iwo Jima Isle*, 104.
21. Levin, *From the Battlefield*, 94.
22. "Patrick Mooney and the Graves: Deputy Director, Combat Veterans of Iwo Jima; Director, National Museum of the Marine Corps, Docent and Visitors' Services," in Smith (ed.), *Iwo Jima*, 308.
23. Shiveley, *Last Lieutenant*, 63.
24. Vedder, *Surgeon on Iwo*, 35.

25. Caruso, *Nightmare on Iwo*, 29.
26. Wheeler, *Iwo*, 195–96.
27. McLaughlin and Miller, *From the Volcano to the Gorge*, 46.
28. Interview, Baxter, in O'Donnell, *Into the Rising Sun*, 248.
29. Matthews, *Assault*, 139.
30. Vedder, *Surgeon on Iwo*, 36–37.
31. McLaughlin and Miller, *From the Volcano to the Gorge*, 45.
32. Brown, *Battle Wounds of Iwo Jima*, 119.
33. Brown, *Battle Wounds of Iwo Jima*, 125–26.
34. Berry (ed.), *Semper Fi, Mac*, 309.
35. Levin, *From the Battlefield*, 77; Josephy, *Long and the Short and the Tall*, 158.
36. Sherrod, *On to Westward*, 178.
37. Interview, Sergeant William Smith, in Kessler and Bart (eds.), *Never in Doubt*, 47.
38. Kelly, *Battlefire!*, 202; Matthews, *Assault*, 36, 40.
39. Yaffe, *Fragments of War*, 96.
40. Yaffe, *Fragments of War*, 96.
41. McLaughlin and Miller, *From the Volcano to the Gorge*, 25.
42. Sherrod, *On to Westward*, 171, 173.
43. Gallant, *Friendly Dead*, 57.
44. Lorelli, *To Foreign Shores*, 283.
45. Bartley, *Iwo Jima*, 68, also note 24.
46. Norton and Maffioli, *Grown Gray in War*, 43.
47. Brown, *Battle Wounds of Iwo Jima*, 57.
48. Quoted in Haynes and Warren, *Lions of Iwo Jima*, 73.
49. Cockrel, "How It Was on Iwo," in O'Sheel and Cook (eds.), *Semper Fidelis*, 102. In keeping with his mythic reputation, when Liversedge came down with stomach pains and was quietly sedated, Williams discreetly took over until his superior was feeling better. The changeover had to be kept secret, otherwise it "would have been a cataclysmic blow to morale." Haynes and Warren, *Lions of Iwo Jima*, 170.
50. On this subject, Hamner, *Enduring Battle*, 15–16. See also my review, "Where They Got Their Grit," *Wall Street Journal*, May 14, 2011.
51. Sherrod, *On to Westward*, 179.
52. Brown, *Battle Wounds of Iwo Jima*, 57–58.
53. J. Lardner, "A Correspondent at the Battle," in Smith (ed.), *United States Marine Corps in World War II*, 726.
54. Yaffe, *Fragments of War*, 96.
55. Gallant, *On Valor's Side*, 335.
56. McLaughlin and Miller, *From the Volcano to the Gorge*, 226.
57. Haynes and Warren, *Lions of Iwo Jima*, 73–74.
58. Leader, "Killing Fields of Sulfur Island."
59. Shiveley, *Last Lieutenant*, 50.
60. Gallant, *Friendly Dead*, 18.
61. Interview, Rebstock, in Drez (ed.), *Twenty-Five Yards of War*, 233–34.
62. Levin, *From the Battlefield*, 68.
63. Interview, Rebstock, in Drez (ed.), *Twenty-Five Yards of War*, 235.
64. McLaughlin and Miller, *From the Volcano to the Gorge*, 135.
65. Rowe, "Memories."
66. Interview, Nummer, in Smith (ed.), *Iwo Jima*, 10.

67. Shiveley, *Last Lieutenant*, 53.
68. Toyn, *Quiet Hero*, 99.
69. Alexander, *Closing In*, 31.
70. Levin, *From the Battlefield*, 97.
71. Wheeler, *Iwo*, 185.
72. Interview, Moreau, in Kessler and Bart (eds.), *Never in Doubt*, 100.
73. Interview, Bryan, in *Iwo Jima—36 Days of Hell*.
74. Thurman, *We Were in the First Waves*, loc. 794.
75. Berry (ed.), *Semper Fi, Mac*, 92.
76. Thurman, *We Were in the First Waves*, loc. 932–47.
77. Haynes and Warren, *Lions of Iwo Jima*, 95.
78. Norton and Maffioli, *Grown Gray in War*, 46.
79. Quoted in Haynes and Warren, *Lions of Iwo Jima*, 144–45.
80. Interview, Nummer, in Smith, *Iwo Jima*, 10.
81. Crowder, *Iwo Jima Corpsman!*, 86. A similar story is mentioned in Henri et al., *U.S. Marines on Iwo Jima*, 297.
82. For Kuribayashi's bulletin, see Eldridge and Tatum (eds.), *Fighting Spirit*, 92.
83. Leader, "Killing Fields of Sulfur Island."
84. McLaughlin and Miller, *From the Volcano to the Gorge*, 129.
85. Nations, "Iwo Jima—One Man Remembers."

7. The Nights

1. Wheeler, *Iwo*, 136.
2. Y. Horie, "Explanation of Japanese Defense Plan and the Battle of Iwo Jima, Chichi Jima, January 25, 1946," appendix 2, in Eldridge and Tatum (eds.), *Fighting Spirit*, 187.
3. Haynes and Warren, *Lions of Iwo Jima*, 109.
4. Quoted in Haynes and Warren, *Lions of Iwo Jima*, 142–43.
5. Stone, *Marine Remembers Iwo Jima*, 125.
6. Matthews, *Assault*, 173.
7. O'Donnell, *Into the Rising Sun*, 250–51.
8. Toyn, *Quiet Hero*, 85.
9. Interview, Buzzard, in Smith (ed.), *Iwo Jima*, 83.
10. Matthews, *Assault*, 122.
11. McLaughlin and Miller, *From the Volcano to the Gorge*, 109.
12. Eldridge and Tatum (eds.), *Fighting Spirit*, 112; Sherrod, *On to Westward*, 197.
13. Matthews, *Assault*, 67.
14. Davenport, *D-Plus Forever*, 61–62.
15. Wheeler, *Iwo*, 126.
16. Walker and White, *Preparing for the Rain on Iwo Jima Isle*, 97.
17. McLaughlin and Miller, *From the Volcano to the Gorge*, 122.
18. McLaughlin and Miller, *From the Volcano to the Gorge*, 112, 245.
19. Stone, *Marine Remembers Iwo Jima*, 61.
20. Simpson, "Iwo Jima: A Surgeon's Story."
21. McLaughlin and Miller, *From the Volcano to the Gorge*, 240; Matthews, *Assault*, 121.
22. McLaughlin and Miller, *From the Volcano to the Gorge*, 259–60; see also Stone, *Marine Remembers Iwo Jima*, 61, for the bowel-moving benefits of pineapple juice.

23. McLaughlin and Miller, *From the Volcano to the Gorge*, 119–21.
24. Shiveley, *Last Lieutenant*, 65.
25. Averill, *Mustang*, 132.
26. Matthews, *Assault*, 142–43.
27. Torok, *Stepping Stones Across the Pacific*, 70.
28. Dashiell, "Words They Spoke," in O'Sheel and Cook (eds.), *Semper Fidelis*, 217–18.
29. Matthews, *Assault*, 68.
30. Davenport, *D-Plus Forever*, 163.
31. Davenport, *D-Plus Forever*, 164.
32. Caruso, *Nightmare on Iwo*, 68–69.
33. Matthews, *Assault*, 70.
34. McConnell, "How One Squad Fared."
35. Matthews, *Assault*, 124.
36. McLaughlin, and Miller, *From the Volcano to the Gorge*, 66.
37. Vedder, *Surgeon on Iwo*, 38–60.
38. Wheeler, "'Those Sons-of-Bitches Killed My Buddy!,'" in Smith (ed.), *United States Marine Corps in World War II*, 762, 765.
39. Interview, Nummer, in Smith, *Iwo Jima*, 10–11.
40. Huie, *From Omaha to Okinawa*, 48–49.
41. Maiden, *Return to Iwo Jima + 50*, 55.
42. Haynes and Warren, *Lions of Iwo Jima*, 171.
43. Caruso, *Nightmare on Iwo*, 156.
44. McLaughlin and Miller, *From the Volcano to the Gorge*, 65.
45. Interview, Abbatiello, in Smith (ed.), *Iwo Jima*, 150.
46. McLaughlin and Miller, *From the Volcano to the Gorge*, 65.
47. Daugherty, *Fighting Techniques of a Japanese Infantryman*, 32.
48. Matthews, *Assault*, 137; interview, Abbatiello, in Smith (ed.), *Iwo Jima*, 151.
49. McLaughlin and Miller, *From the Volcano to the Gorge*, 86.
50. Thurman, *We Were in the First Waves*, loc. 975.
51. Interview, Dobbins, in Kessler and Bart (eds.), *Never in Doubt*, 33–34.
52. Interview, Simms, in Kelly, *Battlefire!*, 201.
53. Caruso, *Nightmare on Iwo*, 53.
54. Yaffe, *Fragments of War*, 48.
55. Henri et al., *U.S. Marines on Iwo Jima*, 100.
56. Matthews, *Assault*, 75, 88.
57. See, for instance, Matthews, *Assault*, 91.
58. In Berry (ed.), *Semper Fi, Mac*, 306.
59. Lucas with Drum, *Indestructible*, 99–103.
60. Haynes and Warren, *Lions of Iwo Jima*, 214.
61. McLaughlin and Miller, *From the Volcano to the Gorge*, 89–90.
62. Torok, *Stepping Stones Across the Pacific*, 30.
63. Brown's book contains three independent accounts—which differ from each other in several fairly unimportant respects—of a deadly scuffle in a foxhole, an illustration of the degree of confusion attending these occurrences. Brown, *Battle Wounds of Iwo Jima*, 71.
64. Haynes and Warren, *Lions of Iwo Jima*, 180.
65. Wheeler, *Iwo*, 149.
66. Stone, *Marine Remembers Iwo Jima*, 66–67.
67. See Daugherty, *Fighting Techniques of a U.S. Marine*, 69.

68. Daugherty, *Fighting Techniques of a Japanese Infantryman,* 29.
69. Wheeler, *We Are the Wounded,* 120–23, 208; Haynes and Warren, *Lions of Iwo Jima,* 187.
70. Brown, *Battle Wounds of Iwo Jima,* 71. I've integrated a few accounts that differ in minor ways.
71. Caruso, *Nightmare on Iwo,* 79.

8. The Madness in the Method

1. Josephy, *Long and the Short and the Tall,* 179.
2. Seebohm, "On the Birds of the Volcano Islands," 189–92.
3. J. Lardner, "A Correspondent at the Battle," in Smith (ed.), *United States Marine Corps in World War II,* 728.
4. Davenport, *D-Plus Forever,* 175.
5. Yaffe, *Fragments of War,* 96–97.
6. See, for example, Josephy, *Long and the Short and the Tall,* 190; O'Donnell, *Into the Rising Sun,* 247; Maiden, *Return to Iwo Jima + 50,* 46; Renzi and Roehrs, *Never Look Back,* 167.
7. Walker and White, *Preparing for the Rain on Iwo Jima Isle,* 104.
8. Thurman, *We Were in the First Waves,* loc. 863.
9. Interview, Gentile, in Kessler and Bart (eds.), *Never in Doubt,* 97.
10. Haynes and Warren, *Lions of Iwo Jima,* 220.
11. McLaughlin and Miller, *From the Volcano to the Gorge,* 32.
12. Interview, Moreau, in Kessler and Bart (eds.), *Never in Doubt,* 102.
13. McLaughlin and Miller, *From the Volcano to the Gorge,* 75.
14. Vedder, *Surgeon on Iwo,* 77.
15. Stone, *Marine Remembers Iwo Jima,* 50, 123.
16. Crowder, *Iwo Jima Corpsman!,* 23.
17. Thurman, *We Were in the First Waves,* loc. 477.
18. Interview, Schribert, in Kessler and Bart (eds.), *Never in Doubt,* 44.
19. Interview, Pvt. Liberato G. Riccio, in Kessler and Bart (eds.), *Never in Doubt,* 20.
20. Vedder, *Surgeon on Iwo,* 119.
21. Matthews, *Assault,* 2–3.
22. Torok, *Stepping Stones Across the Pacific,* 43–44.
23. One wounded man who was accidentally left behind overnight said that Japanese soldiers searched nearby bodies for food, though his watch was also taken. See Crowder, *Iwo Jima Corpsman!,* 79–80.
24. Lucas with Drum, *Indestructible,* 96.
25. Interview, Pfc. Domenick Tutalo, in Smith (ed.), *Iwo Jima,* 107.
26. Interview, Copeland, in *Iwo Jima—36 Days of Hell.*
27. Interview, Moreau, in Kessler and Bart (eds.), *Never in Doubt,* 102.
28. The most infamous case of skull-taking was publicized in *Life* magazine (May 22, 1944), which reproduced a photograph of a twenty-year-old "war worker" in Phoenix, Arizona, admiring a skull her beau had sent. Revealingly, the boyfriend was a "big, handsome Navy lieutenant" who had "picked [it] up on the New Guinea beach." The officer in question would be reprimanded after the outcry, but we should bear in mind that he was hardly a frontline combat soldier. It seems not unduly unrealistic to speculate that this officer had purchased it from someone on the beach and had not simply stumbled across a cleanly boiled skull. On this case, see Weingartner, "Trophies of War," 53–67.

29. Nations, "Iwo Jima—One Man Remembers." For additional background, see S. Harrison, "Skull Trophies of the Pacific War," 817–36.

30. Interview, Peters, in *Iwo Jima: Red Blood, Black Sand*. An article reporting on Peters's talk to a school class noted that "Peters kept mementos of his time on Iwo Jima that he shared with the class—a small Japanese flag he found in an abandoned sniper's [lair], a money bag from a fallen soldier and a sword surrendered by a Japanese officer." There was no mention of the gold teeth. Faller, "War Memories Still Fresh." Mr. Peters died peacefully on May 27, 2013.

31. Interview, Gentile, in Kessler and Bart (eds.), *Never in Doubt*, 97.

32. Haynes and Warren, *Lions of Iwo Jima*, 86.

33. Brown, *Battle Wounds of Iwo Jima*, 66.

34. Interview, Buzzard, in Smith, *Iwo Jima*, 88–89.

35. Price and Knecht, "Peleliu 1944," 12. The term "Asiatic stare" evolved from a prewar phrase used to "describe the eccentric pattern of behavior characteristic of those who had been too long in Far East stations." See McMillan, *Old Breed*, 230.

36. Vedder, *Surgeon on Iwo*, 113–14; Gallant, *On Valor's Side*, 349–51.

37. McLaughlin and Miller, *From the Volcano to the Gorge*, 190.

38. Jones, *Gyrene*, 217.

39. Josephy, *Long and the Short and the Tall*, 177.

40. Interview, Baxter, in O'Donnell, *Into the Rising Sun*, 249.

41. O'Donnell, *Into the Rising Sun*, 249.

42. Berry (ed.), *Semper Fi, Mac*, 215.

43. Gallant, *On Valor's Side*, 349–50.

44. Allen, *First Battalion of the 28th Marines*, 180.

45. Interview, Mik, in Kessler and Bart (eds.), *Never in Doubt*, 158.

46. Allen, *First Battalion of the 28th Marines*, 165n10.

47. Vedder, *Surgeon on Iwo*, 75–76.

48. Interview, Doran, in Kessler and Bart (eds.), *Never in Doubt*, 175.

49. Interview, Boyle, in Kessler and Bart (eds.), *Never in Doubt*, 117.

50. Jones, *Gyrene*, 209–10.

51. Toyn, *Quiet Hero*, 114.

52. Crowder, *Iwo Jima Corpsman!*, 25.

53. Stouffer et al. (eds.), *American Soldier*, 2:443, Table 12, "Incidence of Anxiety Symptoms Among Overseas Troops, Europe and Pacific Compared."

54. Josephy, *Long and the Short and the Tall*, 178.

55. Josephy, *Long and the Short and the Tall*, 169.

56. Wheeler, *Iwo*, 173.

57. Cameron, *American Samurai*, 157, 159, 162.

58. Goudreau, "Nursing at an Advance Naval Base Hospital," 885–86.

59. For instance, Nations, "Iwo Jima—One Man Remembers."

60. Torok, *Stepping Stones Across the Pacific*, 76.

61. See, for instance, Walker and White, *Preparing for the Rain on Iwo Jima Isle*, 100; and Thurman, *We Were in the First Waves*, loc. 546.

62. Interview, Moreau, in Kessler and Bart (eds.), *Never in Doubt*, 101.

63. Quoted in Eldridge and Tatum (eds.), *Fighting Spirit*, 135.

64. McLaughlin and Miller, *From the Volcano to the Gorge*, 70–72.

65. Walker and White, *Preparing for the Rain on Iwo Jima Isle*, 97.

66. O'Donnell, *Into the Rising Sun*, 231–32.

67. Henri et al., *U.S. Marines on Iwo Jima*, 209.

68. Averill, *Mustang,* 132.
69. McLaughlin and Miller, *From the Volcano to the Gorge,* 23.
70. Interview, Riccio, in Kessler and Bart (eds.), *Never in Doubt,* 19.
71. Berry (ed.), *Semper Fi, Mac,* 309.
72. Davenport, *D-Plus Forever,* 82.
73. Matthews, *Assault,* 33.
74. Berry (ed.), *Semper Fi, Mac,* 309.
75. Interview, McDiarmid, in *Iwo Jima—36 Days of Hell.*
76. Wheeler, *Iwo,* 227.
77. Walker and White, *Preparing for the Rain on Iwo Jima Isle,* 105.
78. Quoted in Cockrel, "How It Was on Iwo," in O'Sheel and Cook (eds.), *Semper Fidelis,* 105.
79. Wheeler, *Iwo,* 227.
80. Averill, *Mustang,* 137, 144.
81. Interviews, Caldwell and Baxter, in O'Donnell, *Into the Rising Sun,* 243–44, 247; Maiden, *Return to Iwo Jima + 50,* 51; Caruso, *Nightmare on Iwo,* 25. See also Alexander, *Closing In,* 47.
82. Interview, Williams, in Smith (ed.), *Iwo Jima,* 66.
83. Josephy, *Long and the Short and the Tall,* 193.
84. Allen, *First Battalion of the 28th Marines,* appendix II, "Unit Rolls for 19 February 1945," esp. 267–68.
85. Interview, Neilson, in *Iwo Jima—36 Days of Hell;* interview, Severance, in O'Donnell, *Into the Rising Sun,* 253.
86. Wheeler, *We Are the Wounded,* 52.
87. Lowe, "Assault on Iwo Jima."
88. Caruso, *Nightmare on Iwo,* 35, 46–47, 96, 123.
89. McConnell, "How One Squad Fared."
90. Kessler and Bart (eds.), *Never in Doubt,* 9–10.
91. Matthews, *Assault,* 70.
92. Caruso, *Nightmare on Iwo,* 103.
93. Haynes and Warren, *Lions of Iwo Jima,* 198–99.
94. Berry (ed.), *Semper Fi, Mac,* 266.
95. Interview, Dobbins, in Kessler and Bart (eds.), *Never in Doubt,* 38.
96. Lowe, "Assault on Iwo Jima."
97. McLaughlin, in McLaughlin and Miller, *From the Volcano to the Gorge,* 86. See, for example, the identical sentiments—"Please make it a wound when it comes, not my death"—expressed by Thompson in Berry (ed.), *Semper Fi, Mac,* 309.
98. McLaughlin and Miller, *From the Volcano to the Gorge,* 96.
99. Interview, Berry (ed.), *Semper Fi, Mac,* 264.
100. Quoted in Hess, *Union Soldier in Battle,* 94.
101. Letter, J. W. Hand, 136th New York, July 24, 1890, printed in in Sauers (ed.), *Fighting Them Over,* 222.
102. Interview, Doran, in Kessler and Bart (eds.), *Never in Doubt,* 174–75.
103. Haynes and Warren, *Lions of Iwo Jima,* 122–23.
104. Interview, Buzzard, in Smith, *Iwo Jima,* 91–92.
105. Interview, Leman, in *Iwo Jima—36 Days of Hell.*
106. Interview, Barrett, in *Iwo Jima—36 Days of Hell.* On Haley, see Jorgensen, "John Haley's Personal Recollection of the Battle of the Wheatfield," 65.

107. Interview, Rebstock, in Drez (ed.), *Twenty-Five Yards of War*, 234; Josephy, *Long and the Short and the Tall*, 176; and Maiden, *Return to Iwo Jima + 50*, 38.
108. Matthews, *Assault*, 52–53.
109. McLaughlin and Miller, *From the Volcano to the Gorge*, 147.
110. Yaffe, *Fragments of War*, 98–99.
111. Interview, Dobbins, in Kessler and Bart (eds.), *Never in Doubt*, 35.
112. Interview, Schribert, in Kessler and Bart (eds.), *Never in Doubt*, 42.
113. Matthews, *Assault*, 202; Wheeler, *Iwo*, 183.
114. Interview, Caldwell, in O'Donnell, *Into the Rising Sun*, 244.
115. Transcript, interview with Wornham 88 (Marine Corps Oral History Program, Columbia University ORHO).
116. On "infantillery," see Cameron, *American Samurai*, 86.
117. Haynes and Warren, *Lions of Iwo Jima*, 202.
118. Cameron, *American Samurai*, 87n105.
119. McLaughlin and Miller, *From the Volcano to the Gorge*, 93.
120. Sherrod, *On to Westward*, 212.
121. Alphabetical selection was common. Replacement rifleman Russell Werts, for instance, was placed with "Wade, Wegman, Wenzel, Westmoreland and White" and ordered to go into combat with a squad, "half of whom I had never met." Vedder, *Surgeon on Iwo*, 5–6, 112. On Werts, see Jones, *Gyrene*, 63.
122. Caruso, *Nightmare on Iwo*, 59.
123. Interview, Dobbins, in Kessler and Bart (eds.), *Never in Doubt*, 34.
124. Shiveley, *Last Lieutenant*, 62; interview, Chandler, in *Iwo Jima—36 Days of Hell*.
125. This insignia system was first tried out on Iwo. Each man had a four-digit identifier: The first number clarified rank (1 for private, up to 9 for general, so anyone higher than 4 was an officer), the second regiment, the third battalion, and the fourth company. They were also color-coded (blue for infantry, yellow for engineers, red for artillery, tanks, and mortars) and surmounted by a division symbol (a rectangle for the 5th, a half-moon for the 4th, and a triangle for the 3rd). For explanations, see Torok, *Stepping Stones Across the Pacific*, 29; interview, Abbatiello, in Smith, *Iwo Jima*, 150; and McLaughlin, in McLaughlin and Miller, *From the Volcano to the Gorge*, 28, 98–99.
126. Transcript, interview with Wornham, 87 (Marine Corps Oral History Program, Columbia University ORHO).
127. Caruso, *Nightmare on Iwo*, 83.
128. Interview, Salisbury, in *Iwo Jima: Red Blood, Black Sand*.
129. Vedder, *Surgeon on Iwo*, 62.
130. Rowe, "Memories." On distance, see also Crowder, *Iwo Jima Corpsman!*, 22.
131. Interview, Gentile, in Kessler and Bart (eds.), *Never in Doubt*, 92–96.
132. Maiden, *Return to Iwo Jima + 50*, 60.
133. Transcript, interview with Karch, 30–31 (Marine Corps Oral History Program, Columbia University ORHO).
134. McMillan, *Old Breed*, 407.
135. Interview, Gentile, in Kessler and Bart (eds.), *Never in Doubt*, 92.
136. Davenport, *D-Plus Forever*, 178.
137. McLaughlin and Miller, *From the Volcano to the Gorge*, 95.

9. Understanding Hearts and Minds

1. Matthews, *Assault,* 18–19.
2. Cockrel, "How It Was on Iwo," in O'Sheel and Cook (eds.), *Semper Fidelis,* 102.
3. Quoted in Zurlinden, Josephy, Dempsey, Levin, and Smith, "Iwo: The Red-Hot Rock," in O'Sheel and Cook (eds.), *Semper Fidelis,* 90.
4. Matthews, *Assault,* 161.
5. Interview, Rebstock, in Drez (ed.), *Twenty-Five Yards of War,* 242.
6. Yaffe, *Fragments of War,* 113; Shiveley, *Last Lieutenant,* 62.
7. Averill, *Mustang,* 127.
8. Averill, *Mustang,* 133.
9. Matthews, *Assault,* 161.
10. Interview, Doran, in Kessler and Bart (eds.), *Never in Doubt,* 243.
11. Interview, Williams, in Smith (ed.), *Iwo Jima,* 66.
12. Interview, Chandler, in *Iwo Jima—36 Days of Hell.*
13. Cockrel, "How It Was on Iwo," in O'Sheel and Cook (eds.), *Semper Fidelis,* 102.
14. Haynes and Warren, *Lions of Iwo Jima,* 91.
15. Interview, Tutalo, in Smith, *Iwo Jima,* 106.
16. Interview, Abbatiello, in Smith, *Iwo Jima,* 154.
17. Haynes and Warren, *Lions of Iwo Jima,* 91.
18. Interview, Kropf, in Kessler and Bart (eds.), *Never in Doubt,* 244.
19. Cockrel, "How It Was on Iwo," in O'Sheel and Cook (eds.), *Semper Fidelis,* 104.
20. Quoted in O'Donnell, *Into the Rising Sun,* 253.
21. Interview, Doran, in Kessler and Bart (eds.), *Never in Doubt,* 171.
22. Caruso, *Nightmare on Iwo,* 66–67.
23. Interview, Kropf, in Kessler and Bart (eds.), *Never in Doubt,* 244.
24. Quoted in O'Donnell, *Into the Rising Sun,* 241.
25. Quoted in O'Donnell, *Into the Rising Sun,* 236–37.
26. Quoted in O'Donnell, *Into the Rising Sun,* 247.
27. On this matter, see Dower's innovative *War Without Mercy,* 9, 11.
28. Ford, "'Best Equipped Army in Asia?,'" 88, 96, 99–101.
29. Coox, "Effectiveness of the Japanese Military Establishment in the Second World War," in Millett and Murray (eds.), *Military Effectiveness,* 2.
30. See, for example, Kennedy, *Military Side of Japanese Life,* 81.
31. H. Tsuyoshi, review of "Nomonhan: Japan against Russia, 1939, by Alvin D. Coox," 481, 485; for an in-depth analysis of Japanese performance, see Drea, "Nomonhan"; and Goldman, *Nomonhan 1939.*
32. Ford, "'Best Equipped Army in Asia?,'" 104.
33. Thompson, "Behind the Fog of War: A Glance at the History and Organization of the Jap Army," quoting Robert Leurquin, in Thompson et al., (eds.), *How the Jap Army Fights,* 23–24.
34. Coox, "Effectiveness of the Japanese Military Establishment in the Second World War," in Millett and Murray (eds.), *Military Effectiveness,* 1.
35. Coox, "Effectiveness of the Japanese Military Establishment in the Second World War," in Millett and Murray (eds.), *Military Effectiveness,* 6; on U.S. figures, see "U.S. Automobile Production Figures," Wikipedia.com, available at http://en.wikipedia.org/wiki/U.S._Automobile_Production_Figures, accessed September 16, 2014.
36. Trefalt, "Fanaticism, Japanese Soldiers, and the Pacific War, 1937–45," in *Fanaticism and Conflict in the Modern Age,* ed. M. Hughes and G. Johnson, 39–40; Young, "Ide-

ologies of Difference and the Turn to Atrocity: Japan's War on China," in *World at Total War,* ed. R. Chickering, S. Förster, and B. Greiner, 349–50. On Japanese barracks, discipline, and indoctrination as well as the history of surrendering and treatment of POWs, see Drea, "Trained in the Hardest School," in his *In the Service of the Emperor,* 75–90; and Drea, *Japan's Imperial Army.* On POWs, see also Linderman, *World Within War,* 144–46.

37. Ford, "Dismantling the 'Lesser Men' and 'Supermen' Myths," 544–45; Clifford, *Progress and Purpose,* 269.

38. Ford, "U.S. Assessments of Japanese Ground Warfare Tactics," 325.

39. Ford, "U.S. Perceptions of Military Culture," 77. On passing on documents, which otherwise would have made "very good souvenir[s]," see Crowder, *Iwo Jima Corpsman!,* 61.

40. On the release and impact of these items of news, see Dower, *War Without Mercy,* 48–52. On Siffleet, see "Leonard Siffleet," Wikipedia.com, available at http://en.wikipedia.org/wiki/Leonard_Siffleet, accessed September 16, 2014.

41. Ford, "Dismantling the 'Lesser Men' and 'Supermen' Myths," 547, 553; Ford, "U.S. Assessments of Japanese Ground Warfare Tactics," 326, 329; Ford, "U.S. Perceptions of Military Culture," 90.

42. Ford, "U.S. Assessments of Japanese Ground Warfare Tactics," 344–46.

43. Ford, "Dismantling the 'Lesser Men' and 'Supermen' Myths," 570.

44. Ford, "U.S. Assessments of Japanese Ground Warfare Tactics," 355, 347–50.

45. Alexander, *Storm Landings,* 100–1. The Iwo battalion commander is quoted in McKinney, *Portable Flame Thrower Operations in World War II,* 225.

46. See McKinney, *Portable Flame Thrower Operations in World War II,* 8–16, 34–36, 46–47, 158.

47. Showalter, "War to the Knife," 98. Dower disagrees, remarking that Allies and Japanese dehumanized each other. Dower, *War Without Mercy,* 11.

48. Bergerud, "No Quarter: The Pacific Battlefield," 5, 8–9.

49. Cameron, "Fanaticism and the Barbarisation of the Pacific War, 1941–5," in *Fanaticism and Conflict in the Modern Age,* ed. Hughes and Johnson, 52.

50. This section drawn from Jones, *Gyrene,* 13, 15, 19, 20–21, 26, 40; Cameron, *American Samurai,* 52–57, 60–62 (Table 2, "Monthly Inductions Into the Marine Corps, Volunteer and Selective Service, February 1941–July 1945"); and Millett, *Semper Fidelis,* 373–75.

51. Stouffer et al. (eds.), *American Soldier,* I, Table 4, "Proportion of Men Saying They Are 'Not So Clear' or 'Not Clear at All' About Why We Are Fighting This War, Classified by Their Evaluation of the Importance of Such Understanding and Their Knowledge of the Four Freedoms," 439–40 (and see footnote 2, 433–34), and Table 3, "Topics Chosen by Enlisted Men as Those They Would Most Like to Know More About," 438.

52. On production, see Coox, "Effectiveness of the Japanese Military Establishment in the Second World War," in Millett and Murray (eds.), *Military Effectiveness,* 21; on Sadakaji, see Drea, "Nomonhan," 90.

10. The Method in the Madness

1. Stone, *Marine Remembers Iwo Jima,* 4–5; Interview, Oullette, in *Never in Doubt,* ed. Kessler and Bart, 10. On Marine organizational reforms, see Gordon, "Thomas Holcomb," in *Commandants of the Marine Corps,* ed. Millett and Shulimson, 266.

2. Kelly, *Battlefire!,* 198.

3. Haynes and Warren, *Lions of Iwo Jima,* 217–18.

4. Davenport, *D-Plus Forever,* 75.
5. Interview, Gentile, in Kessler and Bart (eds.), *Never in Doubt,* 96; Maiden, *Return to Iwo Jima + 50,* 53.
6. Interview, Dobbins, in Kessler and Bart (eds.), *Never in Doubt,* 33.
7. Interview, Voight, in O'Donnell, *Into the Rising Sun,* 242.
8. Stone, *Marine Remembers Iwo Jima,* 5.
9. Interview, Dobbins, in Kessler and Bart (eds.), *Never in Doubt,* 37.
10. Davenport, *D-Plus Forever,* 184.
11. Maiden, *Return to Iwo Jima + 50,* 37; interview, Caldwell, in O'Donnell, *Into the Rising Sun,* 250; Wheeler, *Iwo,* 220.
12. Sherrod, *On to Westward,* 215.
13. Davenport, *D-Plus Forever,* 184.
14. Boal, "Field Expedient Armor Modifications to U.S. Armored Vehicles," 21–25.
15. Neiman and Estes, *Tanks on the Beaches,* 94, 119.
16. About two other threats, tankers could do nothing. For the first several days, Japanese artillery fire scored deadly hits and their bottom hulls, always a weak spot, were vulnerable to huge naval and torpedo mines buried in the sand. Nevertheless, as the fighting continued and the Japanese lost ground and equipment, these twin dangers declined.
17. Eldridge and Tatum (eds.), *Fighting Spirit,* 135.
18. Haynes and Warren, *Lions of Iwo Jima,* 144–45.

11. The Japanese Defensive System

1. Gatchel, *At the Water's Edge,* 122–24, 128.
2. Gatchel, *At the Water's Edge,* 131.
3. On the factional politics at Imperial Headquarters, see, for instance, Kuzuhara, "Operations on Iwo Jima," 34.
4. Alexander, *Storm Landings,* 110; Hayashi, *Kogun,* 115–16; Kuzuhara, "Operations on Iwo Jima," 28–29.
5. It is important to realize that the evolutionary process of Japanese defensive strategy was neither predetermined nor upwardly unidirectional. The U.S. Army, for example, had encountered at Attu Island as early as May 1943 a deserted beach while 2,500 defenders under Colonel Yasuyo Yamasaki hid in the hills. As the army advanced inland, fire erupted from three sides of the valley surrounding them. There would be just 29 Japanese taken alive, but the defenders would inflict 1,750 casualties out of a force of 15,000. Likewise, at Biak Island in May 1944, Colonel Naoyuki Kuzume's garrison of 11,400 abandoned the beach and retreated to a spider's web of fortified positions, foxholes, pillboxes, tunnels, AA guns, observation posts, and bunkers located in the caves and along ridgelines. It took the 41st Infantry Division nearly a month to take the island. Denfield, *Japanese World War II Fortifications,* 10–12.
6. Kuzuhara, "Operations on Iwo Jima," 37.
7. Marquand, "Iwo Jima Before H-hour," 498.
8. Transcript, interview with Rogers, 84–85 (Marine Corps Oral History Program, Columbia University ORHO). On the pillboxes, Alexander, *Storm Landings,* 132.

12. Adapt or Die

1. Isely and Crowl, *U.S. Marines and Amphibious War,* 485–86.
2. Henri et al., *U.S. Marines on Iwo Jima,* 275.

3. Transcript, interview with Wornham, 82 (Marine Corps Oral History Program, Columbia University ORHO).
4. Report, "Defense Installations on Iwo Jima," 3–4.
5. Interview, Williams, in *Iwo Jima—36 Days of Hell;* Leader, "Killing Fields of Sulfur Island."
6. Gallant, *Friendly Dead,* 85–86.
7. See frontispiece in Gallant, *Friendly Dead.* Author's calculation.
8. "Iwo Jima operation, February–March 1945," prepared for Joint Intelligence Center, Pacific Ocean Area (JICPOA), Map NH-104136, available at www.history.navy.mil/photos/events/wwii-pac/iwojima/iwo-0.htm, accessed January 29, 2014.
9. Interview, Abbatiello, in Smith, *Iwo Jima,* 156.
10. Rodriguez, "Battle for Iwo Jima."
11. Interview, Salisbury, in *Iwo Jima: Red Blood, Black Sand.*
12. Transcript, interview with Hogaboom, 226 (Marine Corps Oral History Program, Columbia University ORHO).
13. Hoffman, "Legacy and Lessons of Iwo Jima," 75–76.
14. Henri et al., *U.S. Marines on Iwo Jima,* 146–47.
15. Interview, Bain, in Kessler and Bart (eds.), *Never in Doubt,* 26n.
16. Crowder, *Iwo Jima Corpsman!,* 67–68.
17. McConnell, "How One Squad Fared."
18. See the reports in Maiden, *Return to Iwo Jima + 50,* 54–65.
19. Eldridge and Tatum (eds.), *Fighting Spirit,* 85–86.
20. Diary entry, February 21, 1945, in Lofgren (ed.), "Diary of First Lieutenant Sugihara Kinryu," 126–27.
21. Eldridge and Tatum (eds.), *Fighting Spirit,* 113.
22. Cited in Alexander, *Storm Landings,* 140.
23. Diary entry, February 23, 1945, in Lofgren (ed.), "Diary of First Lieutenant Sugihara Kinryu," 130.

13. Minefields and Antitank Weapons

1. Thurman, *We Were in the First Waves,* loc. 588.
2. Brown, *Battle Wounds of Iwo Jima,* 61.
3. Wheeler, *We Are the Wounded,* 113–15.
4. McLaughlin and Miller, *From the Volcano to the Gorge,* 74–75.
5. McLaughlin and Miller, *From the Volcano to the Gorge,* 74–75.
6. Interview, Abbatiello, in Smith (ed.), *Iwo Jima,* 151.
7. Interview, Maiden, in O'Donnell, *Into the Rising Sun,* 245–46.
8. Interview, Moreau, in Kessler and Bart (eds.), *Never in Doubt,* 103.
9. Josephy, *Long and the Short and the Tall,* 174.
10. Neiman and Estes, *Tanks on the Beaches,* 127–29.
11. Averill, *Mustang,* 133.
12. Stone, *Marine Remembers Iwo Jima,* 121.
13. Gallant, *Friendly Dead,* 81–82.
14. Wheeler, *We Are the Wounded,* 91, 171–75.
15. Interview, Caldwell, in O'Donnell, *Into the Rising Sun,* 249–50. The phrase "Satchel Charlies" comes from McLaughlin and Miller, *From the Volcano to the Gorge,* 63.

14. Spider Traps and Snipers

1. Shiveley, *Last Lieutenant,* 66; Toyn, *Quiet Hero,* 95.
2. Wheeler, *Iwo,* 89–90.
3. Averill, *Mustang,* 132–33.
4. Haynes and Warren, *Lions of Iwo Jima,* 200.
5. Davenport, *D-Plus Forever,* 227–28.
6. On corpsmen casualties, see Alexander, *Closing In,* 38–39.
7. Josephy, *Long and the Short and the Tall,* 183.
8. Stone, *Marine Remembers Iwo Jima,* 113.
9. Stone, *Marine Remembers Iwo Jima,* 18–19.
10. Thurman, *We Were in the First Waves,* loc. 1018.
11. Interview, Williams, in *Iwo Jima—36 Days of Hell.* See also interviews with Herb Hammond and Craig Leman.
12. Averill, *Mustang,* 135.
13. Interview, Rebstock, in Drez (ed.), *Twenty-Five Yards of War,* 242.
14. Brown, *Battle Wounds of Iwo Jima,* 29.

15. Pillboxes, Bunkers, Blockhouses

1. Rottman and Palmer, *Japanese Pacific Island Defenses,* 25–26, 30.
2. Sherrod, *On to Westward,* 193.
3. Caruso, *Nightmare on Iwo,* 74.
4. Brown, *Battle Wounds of Iwo Jima,* 25–26.
5. Yaffe, *Fragments of War,* 99–100.
6. Stone, *Marine Remembers Iwo Jima,* 6; see also Pfc. Jack Russell in Toyn, *Quiet Hero,* 131.
7. Walker and White, *Preparing for the Rain on Iwo Jima Isle,* 93.
8. Shiveley, *Last Lieutenant,* 83.
9. Nations, "Iwo Jima—One Man Remembers."
10. Lowe, "Assault on Iwo Jima."
11. Nations, "Iwo Jima—One Man Remembers."
12. Haynes and Warren, *Lions of Iwo Jima,* 223.
13. Wheeler, *Iwo,* 142. According to artillery officer William Buchanan, "At the time we didn't have an effective method of either destroying or neutralizing the defenders in a very restricted area so that it fell to the job of the thin green line to get in there and dig them out in hand to hand combat." See transcript of interview with Buchanan, 81 (Marine Corps Oral History Program, Columbia University ORHO).
14. Wheeler, *Iwo,* 102.
15. Rottman and Palmer, *Japanese Pacific Island Defenses, 1941–45,* 25.
16. Wheeler, Iwo, 126.
17. Wheeler, " 'Those Sons-of-Bitches Killed My Buddy!,' " in Smith (ed.), *United States Marine Corps in World War II,* 760.
18. Interview, Lanehart, in Kessler and Bart (eds.), *Never in Doubt,* 83.
19. See Pfc. Bernard Link, in Haynes and Warren, *Lions of Iwo Jima,* 118; and Thompson, in Berry (ed.), *Semper Fi, Mac,* 302.
20. Gallant, *Friendly Dead,* 76.
21. Interview, Rebstock, in Drez (ed.), *Twenty-Five Yards of War,* 241.
22. Josephy, *Long and the Short and the Tall,* 194.

23. See McKinney, *Portable Flame Thrower Operations in World War II*, appendix 17, Training Order, 3rd Marine Division HQ, "Tactical Employment of Flame Throwers," 19 December 1944, 307–11.
24. On the description of a flamethrower's sound, Wheeler, *Iwo*, 148–49.
25. Interview, Williams, in Smith (ed.), *Iwo Jima*, 67–69.
26. Interview, Williams, in Smith (ed.), *Iwo Jima*, 67–69; see also interview with Luther Crabtree, a demolitions man, in O'Donnell, *Into the Rising Sun*, 239–40.
27. Shiveley, *Last Lieutenant*, 68; interview, Williams, in Smith (ed.), *Iwo Jima*, 70.
28. Levin, *From the Battlefield*, 102.
29. Interview, Williams, in Smith (ed.), *Iwo Jima*, 67–69; interview, Lindberg, in O'Donnell, *Into the Rising Sun*, 236–37; Wheeler, *Iwo*, 192, 216.
30. Stone, *Marine Remembers Iwo Jima*, 82.
31. Interview, Lanehart, in Kessler and Bart (eds.), *Never in Doubt*, 84; interview, Lindberg, in O'Donnell, *Into the Rising Sun*, 236–37.
32. Gallant, *Friendly Dead*, 75.
33. Yaffe, *Fragments of War*, 112.
34. McKinney, *Portable Flame Thrower Operations in World War II*, 223–24.
35. Vedder, *Surgeon on Iwo*, 87–88.
36. Caruso, *Nightmare on Iwo*, 94–95.

16. The Caves

1. Wheeler, *Iwo*, 143.
2. Wheeler, *Iwo*, 177.
3. Sherrod, *On to Westward*, 183; Vedder, *Surgeon on Iwo*, 133.
4. Shiveley, *Last Lieutenant*, 70.
5. McLaughlin and Miller, *From the Volcano to the Gorge*, 79.
6. McLaughlin and Miller, *From the Volcano to the Gorge*, 105.
7. Interview, Abbatiello, in Smith (ed.), *Iwo Jima*, 151.
8. Wheeler, *Iwo*, 167.
9. Josephy, *Long and the Short and the Tall*, 187; Stone, *Marine Remembers Iwo Jima*, 98; Crowder, *Iwo Jima Corpsman!*, 53, all referring to the same incident.
10. Haynes and Warren, *Lions of Iwo Jima*, 144–45.
11. Price and Knecht, "Peleliu 1944," 33–34.
12. Interview, Maiden, in O'Donnell, *Into the Rising Sun*, 252.
13. Yaffe, *Fragments of War*, 139.
14. Huie, *From Omaha to Okinawa*, 53–55.

17. Surrendering and Prisoners

1. Brown, *Battle Wounds of Iwo Jima*, 60.
2. Haynes and Warren, *Lions of Iwo Jima*, 147.
3. Vedder, *Surgeon on Iwo*, 191.
4. Shiveley, *Last Lieutenant*, 91–92.
5. Brown, *Battle Wounds of Iwo Jima*, 34.
6. Wheeler, *Iwo*, 150.
7. Wheeler, *Iwo*, 150.
8. Haynes and Warren, *Lions of Iwo Jima*, 224.
9. Haynes and Warren, *Lions of Iwo Jima*, 226.

10. Laurie, "Ultimate Dilemma of Psychological Warfare in the Pacific," 117, 120 (appendix, "Place of Custody of Enemy POWs").
11. Gallant, *Friendly Dead*, 92.
12. Renzi and Roehrs, *Never Look Back*, 97.
13. Laurie, "Ultimate Dilemma of Psychological Warfare in the Pacific," 109.
14. Caruso, *Nightmare on Iwo*, 87.
15. Vedder, *Surgeon on Iwo*, 217.
16. Interview, Smith, in Kessler and Bart (eds.), *Never in Doubt*, 48.
17. Interview, Moreau, in Kessler and Bart (eds.), *Never in Doubt*, 103.
18. Nations, "Iwo Jima—One Man Remembers."
19. Caruso, *Nightmare on Iwo*, 92–93.
20. Quoted in Eldridge and Tatum (eds.), *Fighting Spirit*, 122.
21. Interview, Winters, in O'Donnell, *Into the Rising Sun*, 238–39.
22. Haynes and Warren, *Lions of Iwo Jima*, 146.
23. Brown, *Battle Wounds of Iwo Jima*, 151–52.
24. Huie, *From Omaha to Okinawa*, 53–55.

18. After the Battle

1. His story is included in Eldridge and Tatum (eds.), *Fighting Spirit*, 113–20. See also Straus, *Anguish of Surrender*, 57–59.
2. See "Matsudo Linsoki," available at www.wanpela.com/holdouts/profiles/linsoki.html, accessed February 5, 2014; see also the brief AP story in *New York Times*, January 9, 1949, 22; and Smith (ed.), *Iwo Jima*, xxi.
3. "Patrick Mooney and the Graves," in Smith (ed.), *Iwo Jima*, 308–9.
4. Interview, Hotaling, in Kessler and Bart (eds.), *Never in Doubt*, 112–13.
5. See Willie, *African American Voices from Iwo Jima*, esp. chapter 5, "Taking the Island."
6. "Patrick Mooney and the Graves," in Smith (ed.), *Iwo Jima*, 309–10.
7. According to Rebstock, in Drez (ed.), *Twenty-Five Yards of War*, 245.
8. "Patrick Mooney and the Graves," in Smith (ed.), *Iwo Jima*, 311–12.
9. Interview, Hotaling, in Kessler and Bart (eds.), *Never in Doubt*, 113.
10. "Patrick Mooney and the Graves," in Smith (ed.), *Iwo Jima*, 312–13.
11. Interview, Caldwell, in O'Donnell, *Into the Rising Sun*, 244.
12. Interview, Maiden, in O'Donnell, *Into the Rising Sun*, 45–46.
13. Neiman and Estes, *Tanks on the Beaches*, 131.
14. Wheeler, *We Are the Wounded*, 38.
15. Wheeler, *We Are the Wounded*, 39–42.
16. Wheeler, *We Are the Wounded*, 110.
17. Wheeler, *We Are the Wounded*, 92.
18. Goudreau, "Nursing at an Advance Naval Base Hospital," 886.
19. Wheeler, *We Are the Wounded*, 203.
20. Wheeler, *We Are the Wounded*, 193; Wheeler, "The Story of a Man's Face," 90–115.
21. Josephy, *Long and the Short and the Tall*, 174–75.
22. Haynes and Warren, *Lions of Iwo Jima*, 235–36.
23. Brown, *Battle Wounds of Iwo Jima*, 36.
24. Brown, *Battle Wounds of Iwo Jima*, 157–58.
25. Interview, Vinich, in O'Donnell, *Into the Rising Sun*, 238.
26. McLaughlin and Miller, *From the Volcano to the Gorge*, 196–98.

27. Vedder, *Surgeon on Iwo,* 65.
28. Wheeler, *We Are the Wounded,* 140–53.

The Great Red God

1. Thus, the colonel of the 2nd Brigade, 10th Mountain Division: "Fallujah will be the Gettysburg of this war." Quoted in P. K. O'Donnell, *We Were One: Shoulder to Shoulder with the Marines Who Took Fallujah* (Philadelphia: Da Capo Press, 2006), 221.
2. Quoted in D. Camp, *Operation Phantom Fury: The Assault and Capture of Fallujah, Iraq* (Minneapolis: Zenith Press, 2009), 267.
3. D. Bellavia and J. R. Bruning, *House to House: A Soldier's Memoir* (New York: Free Press, 2008), 69. For an extended examination, see J. Pieslak, *Sound Targets: American Soldiers and Music in the Iraq War* (Bloomington: University of Indiana Press, 2009).
4. Bellavia and Bruning, *House to House,* 71.
5. G. Orwell, *Homage to Catalonia* (New York: Harcourt, 1980 [1938]), 76; D. J. Danelo, *Blood Stripes: The Grunt's View of the War in Iraq* (Mechanicsburg, PA: Stackpole Books, 2006), 149. J. C. McManus observes that "the skin of the grunts was peppered with nicks and cuts. Their eyes were rimmed with dark circles. They stank of dust, cordite, stale MRE crumbs, body odor, and soiled underwear. The sweaty T-shirts that hugged their irritated skin had given many of them prickly heat." McManus, *Grunts: Inside the American Infantry Combat Experience, World War II Through Iraq* (New York: NAL Caliber, 2010), 379.
6. Bellavia, *House to House,* 273.
7. Bellavia, *House to House,* 112–13.
8. N. G. Pond (ed.), "Experiences in Early Wars in America: Life Story of an Ambitious American Youth Who at Sixteen Years of Age Was Fired with the Spirit of Patriotism and Against the Will of His Parents Marched to the Battle-Line in Defense of His Country," *Journal of American History* 1 (1907): 89–93.
9. J. Malcolm, "Reminiscences of a Campaign in the Pyrenees and South of France in 1814," in *Memorials of the Late War,* ed. Anon. (Edinburgh: Constable & Co., 1831), 1:247–48.
10. See Letters No. 8, July 8, 1863; No. 9, July 9; and No. 10, July 27, in J. C. West, *A Texan in Search of a Fight: Being the Diary and Letters of a Private Soldier in Hood's Texas Brigade* (Waco, TX: J. S. Hill and Co., 1901), 84–97.
11. Letter, Westbrook, September 20, 1900, printed in R. A. Sauers (ed.), *Fighting Them Over: How the Veterans Remembered Gettysburg in the Pages of the National Tribune* (Baltimore: Butternut and Blue, 1998), 316.
12. For instance, E. B. Hamley, *The Operations of War Explained and Illustrated* (Edinburgh and London: William Blackwood and Sons, 1878), 472.
13. See, for depressing summaries of the situation, H. W. Wilson, *Battleships in Action* (Boston: Little Brown, and Company, 1926), 2:286; and B. Liddell Hart, *The Defence of Britain* (New York: Random House, 1939), 130.
14. See J. A. Isely and P. A. Crowl, *The U.S. Marines and Amphibious War: Its Theory, and Its Practice in the Pacific* (Princeton, NJ: Princeton University Press, 1951), 18–20; H. M. Smith, *The Development of Amphibious Tactics in the U.S. Navy* (Washington, DC: History and Museums Division Headquarters, U.S. Marine Corps, 1992), 19; T. A. Gibson, "Gallipoli, 1915," and D. M. Weller, "The Development of Naval Gunfire Support in World War Two," in *Assault From the Sea: Essays on the History of Am-*

phibious Warfare, ed. M. L. Bartlett (Annapolis, MD: Naval Institute Press, 1983), 142–53, 262–64.

15. K. J. Clifford, *Progress and Purpose: A Developmental History of the United States Marine Corps, 1900–1970* (Washington, DC: History and Museums Division Headquarters, United States Marine Corps, 1973), 139–40 (appendix F, "Outline of the Development of the Landing Operations Manual"), 141–42 (appendix G, "Students and Instructors Who Were Assigned to MCS During Preparation of *Tentative Landing Operations Manual*—November 1933 Through May 1934").

16. T. Moy, *War Machines: Transforming Technologies in the U.S. Military, 1920–1940* (College Station: Texas A&M University Press, 2001), 134–37; Clifford, *Progress and Purpose*, 45–46.

17. On this subject, see Rose, *American Rifle* (New York: Delacorte Press, 2008), ch. 8, "Roosevelt's Rifle."

Bibliography

BUNKER HILL

Adams, C. F. (ed.). *Familiar Letters of John Adams and His Wife Abigail Adams, During the Revolution.* New York: Hurd and Houghton, 1876.

Adams, J. W., and A. B. Kasakoff. "Wealth and Migration in Massachusetts and Maine, 1771–1798." *Journal of Economic History* 45 (1985).

Agnew, C. "General Sir Andrew Agnew of Lochnaw, Bt—28 Years a Fusilier." *Journal of the Royal Highland Fusiliers* 24, no. 2 (2000).

Allen, V. "Medicine in the American Revolution." Part 2. *Journal of the Oklahoma State Medical Association* 63, no. 11 (1970).

Anderson, F. *A People's Army: Massachusetts Soldiers and Society in the Seven Years' War.* Chapel Hill: Institute of Early American History and Culture/University of North Carolina Press, 1984.

———. "A People's Army: Provincial Military Service in Massachusetts During the Seven Years' War." *William and Mary Quarterly* 40, no. 4 (1983).

Anderson, W. *The Scottish Nation: Or, the Surnames, Families, Literature, Honours, and Biographical History of the People of Scotland.* 3 vols. Edinburgh: A. Fullarton and Co., 1864.

Andrlik, T., H. T. Harrington, and D. N. Hagist (eds.). *Journal of the American Revolution.* Yellow Springs, OH: Ertel Publishing, 2013.

Anon. *The Annual Register, or a View of the History, Politics, and Literature for the Year 1781.* London: J. Dodsley, 1782.

Anon. (ed.). "Journals of Lieut.-Col. Stephen Kemble, 1773–1789." *Collections of the New-York Historical Society* 16 (1883).

Anon. (ed.). *Memorials of the Late War.* 2 vols. Edinburgh: Constable and Co., 1831.

Anon. "Military Books of the Revolution." *The Historical Magazine and Notes and Queries Concerning the Antiquities, History, and Biography of America,* vol. 1 (1857).

Appel, J. W., and G. W. Beebe. "Preventive Psychiatry: An Epidemiologic Approach." *Journal of the American Medical Association* 131 (1946). August 13.

Artwohl, A. "Perceptual and Memory Distortion During Officer-Involved Shootings." *FBI Law Enforcement Bulletin* 71, no. 10 (2002).

Ashburner, W. (ed.). "Richard Price Letters, 1767–1790." *Proceedings of the Massachusetts Historical Society* 17 (1903).

Bailey, S. L. *Historical Sketches of Andover (Comprising the Present Towns of North Andover and Andover), Massachusetts.* Boston: Houghton, Mifflin and Company, 1880.

Balderston, M., and D. Syrett (eds.). *The Lost War: Letters From British Officers During the American Revolution.* New York: Horizon Press, 1975.

Balingall, G. *Introductory Lectures to a Course of Military Surgery, Delivered in the University of Edinburgh.* Edinburgh: Adam Black, 1830.

Barker, J. *The British in Boston: Being the Diary of Lieutenant John Barker of the King's Own Regiment From November 15, 1774 to May 31, 1776.* Edited by E. E. Dana. Cambridge, MA: Harvard University Press, 1924.

Barnard, T. "Letter of Rev. Thomas Barnard." *Proceedings of the Bunker Hill Monument Association,* 1902.

Bickley, F. (ed.). *Historical Manuscripts Commission: Report on the Manuscripts of the Late Reginald Rawdon Hastings, Esq., of the Manor House, Ashby de la Zouch.* 4 vols. London: His Majesty's Stationery Office, 1928–47.

Bland, H. *A Treatise of Military Discipline; in Which Is Laid Down and Explained the Duty of the Officer and Soldier, Through the Several Branches of the Service.* 6th ed. London: J. and P. Knapton, S. Birt, T. Longman, and T. Shewell, 1746.

Bohy, J., and D. Troiani. "'We Meant to Be Free Always': The Guns of April 19, 1775." *American Rifleman,* July 2010.

Bolton, C. K. *The Private Soldier Under Washington.* New York: Charles Scribner's Sons, 1902.

Brown, A. E. *Beside Old Hearth-Stones.* Boston: Lee and Shepard, 1897.

Brown, P. "Officer's Story of Bunker Hill." *New York Times,* June 21, 1896.

Browne, G. W. *The History of Hillsborough, New Hampshire, 1735–1921.* 2 vols. Manchester, NH: John B. Clarke Company, 1921.

Brumwell, S. *Redcoats: The British Soldier and War in the Americas, 1755–1763.* Cambridge, U.K.: Cambridge University Press, 2002.

Bryant, W. B., and S. H. Gay. *A Popular History of the United States, From the First Discovery of the Western Hemisphere by the Northmen, to the End of the Civil War.* 5 vols. New York: Charles Scribner's Sons, 1896.

Butler, C. *History of the Town of Groton, Including Pepperell and Shirley, From the First Grant of Groton Plantation in 1655.* Boston: T. R. Marvin, 1848.

Camp, D. *Operation Phantom Fury: The Assault and Capture of Fallujah, Iraq.* Minneapolis: Zenith Press, 2009.

Cantlie, N. *The History of the Army Medical Department.* 2 vols. London: Churchill Livingstone, 1974.

Carter, C. E. (ed.). *The Correspondence of General Thomas Gage, 1763–1775.* 2 vols. New Haven: Yale University Press, 1931–33.

Charters, D. A., M. Milner, and J. B. Wilson (eds.). *Military History and the Military Profession.* Westport, CT: Praeger, 1992.

Chase, G. W., and H. B. Dawson (eds.). *Diary of David How, a Private in Colonel Paul Dudley Sargent's Regiment of the Massachusetts Line, in the Army of the American Revolution.* New York: Morrisania, 1865.

Churchill, R. H. "Gun Ownership in Early America: A Survey of Manuscript Militia Returns." *William and Mary Quarterly* 60, no. 3 (2003).

Clarke, J. "An Impartial and Authentic Narrative of the Battle Fought on the 17th of June, 1775, Between His Britannic Majesty's Troops and the American Provincial Army on Bunker's Hill Near Charles Town in New England." *Magazine of History with Notes and Queries, Extra Numbers 5–8* (1909).

Coffin, C. (ed.). *History of the Battle of Breed's Hill.* Portland, ME: D.C. Colesworthy, 1835.

Conway, S. "The British Army, 'Military Europe,' and the American War of Independence." *William and Mary Quarterly* 67, no. 1 (2010).

————. "British Army Officers and the American War for Independence." *William and Mary Quarterly* 41, no. 2 (1984).

Cooper, T. H. *A Practical Guide for the Light Infantry Officer: Comprising Valuable Extracts From All the Most Popular Works on the Subject, with Further Valuable Information.* London: Robert Wilks, 1806.

Curtis, O. B. *History of the Twenty-Fourth Michigan of the Iron Brigade, Known as the Detroit and Wayne County Regiment.* Detroit: Winn and Hammond, 1891.

Daddis, G. A. "Understanding Fear's Effect on Unit Effectiveness." *Military Review* 84, no. 4 (2004).

Dann, J. C. (ed.), *The Revolution Remembered: Eyewitness Accounts of the War for Independence.* Chicago: University of Chicago, 1980.

Davis, Jr., C. E. *Three Years in the Army: The Story of the 13th Massachusetts Volunteers From July 16, 1861 to August 1, 1864.* Boston: Rockwell and Churchill, 1893.

Dawson, C. B. (ed.). "Bunker's Hill." *Historical Magazine* 3, no. 6 (1868).

Dinter, E. *Hero or Coward: Pressures Facing the Soldier in Battle.* London: Frank Cass, 1985.

Doddridge, J. *Notes on the Settlement and Indian Wars of the Western Parts of Virginia and Pennsylvania From 1763 to 1783, Inclusive, Together with a Review of the State of Society and Manners of the First Settlers of the Western Country.* Pittsburgh: J. S. Ritenour and W. T. Lindsey, 1912 [1824].

Donkin, R. *Military Collections and Remarks.* New York: H. Gaine, 1777.

Drake, S. A. (ed.). *Bunker Hill: The Story Told in Letters From the Battlefield by British Officers Engaged.* Boston: Nichols and Hall, 1875.

Drewe, E. *The Case of Edward Drewe, Late Major of the Thirty-Fifth Regiment of Foot.* Exeter, U.K.: B. Thorn and Son, 1782.

Duffy, C. *The Army of Frederick the Great.* Newton Abbot, U.K.: David and Charles, 1974.

————. *Fire and Stone: The Science of Fortress Warfare, 1660–1860.* 2nd ed. Mechanicsburg, PA: Stackpole Books, 1996.

————. *Military Experience in the Age of Reason.* London: Routledge and Kegan Paul, 1987.

Ellis, G. E. *Sketches of Bunker Hill Battle and Monument: With Illustrative Documents.* Charlestown, MA: C. P. Emmons, 1851.

Elting, J. *Battle of Bunker's Hill.* Monmouth Beach, NJ: Phillip Freneau Press, 1975.

Erffa, H. von, and A. Staley. *The Paintings of Benjamin West.* New Haven and London: Yale University Press, 1986.

Estes, J. W. " 'A Disagreeable and Dangerous Employment': Medical Letters From the Siege of Boston, 1775." *Journal of the History of Medicine and Allied Sciences* 31 (1976).

Fann, W. R. "On the Infantryman's Age in Eighteenth-Century Prussia." *Military Affairs* 41, no. 4 (1977).

Field, C. *Britain's Sea-Soldiers: A History of the Royal Marines and Their Predecessors and of Their Services in Action, Ashore and Afloat.* 2 vols. Liverpool: Lyceum Press, 1924.

Fischer, D. H. *Paul Revere's Ride.* New York: Oxford University Press, 1994.

Fisher, H. "The Objective at Bunker Hill." *Proceedings of the Bunker Hill Memorial Association* (1907).

Flavell, J. M. "Government Interception of Letters From America and the Quest for Colonial Opinion in 1775." *William and Mary Quarterly* 58, no. 2 (2001).

Fonblanque, E. B. *Political and Military Episodes in the Latter Half of the Eighteenth Century Derived From the Life and Correspondence of the Right Hon. J. Burgoyne, General, Statesman, Dramatist.* 2 vols. London: Macmillan and Co., 1876.

Fontenot, G. "Fear God and Dreadnought: Preparing a Unit for Confronting Fear." *Military Review* 75, no. 4 (1995).

Force, P. (ed.). *American Archives: Consisting of a Collection of Authentick Records, State Papers, Debates, and Letters and Other Notices of Publick Affairs, the Whole Forming a Documentary History of the Origin and Progress of the North American Colonies; of the Causes and Accomplishment of the American Revolution; and of the Constitution of the Government of the United States.* 9 vols. Washington, DC: M. St. Claire Clarke and P. Force, 1837–53.

Fortescue, J. (ed.). *The Correspondence of King George the Third.* 6 vols. London: Macmillan and Co., 1927–28.

French, A. (ed.). *A British Fusilier in Revolutionary Boston; Being the Diary of Lieutenant Frederick Mackenzie, Adjutant of the Royal Welch Fusiliers, January 5–April 30, 1775, with a Letter Describing His Voyage to America.* Cambridge, MA: Harvard University Press, 1926.

———. *The First Year of the American Revolution.* New York: Houghton Mifflin, 1934.

———. "General Haldimand in Boston, 1774–1775." *Proceedings of the Massachusetts Historical Society* 66 (1936–1941).

Frothingham, R. "Address." *Proceedings of the Bunker Hill Monument Association,* 1876.

———. *The Battle-Field of Bunker Hill: With a Relation of the Action by William Prescott, and Illustrative Documents.* Boston: R. Frothingham, 1876.

———. *The Centennial: Battle of Bunker Hill, with a View of Charlestown in 1775, Page's Plan of the Action, Romans's Exact View of the Battle, and Other Illustrations.* Boston: Little, Brown, and Co., 1875.

———. *History of the Siege of Boston, and of the Battles of Lexington, Concord, and Bunker Hill, Also, an Account of the Bunker Hill Monument, with Illustrative Documents.* 6th ed. Boston: Little, Brown, and Co., 1903.

Frothingham, R., M. Tuttle, T. C. Amory, D. Hoppin, M. Foote, and S. A. Green. "Letter of Edward Everett; Account of the Battle of Bunker Hill; Letter of James Warren; Letter of Samuel B. Webb; Diary of Lieutenant-Colonel Storrs; Extracts From an Orderly Book; Letter of Brigadier-General Jones; Note-Books of Jeremy Belknap." *Proceedings of the Massachusetts Historical Society* 14 (1875).

Gibbon, J. *The Artillerist's Manual, Compiled From Various Sources, and Adapted to the Service of the United States.* 2nd ed. New York: D. Van Nostrand, 1863.

Gillett, M. C. *The Army Medical Department, 1775–1918.* Washington, DC: Center of Military History, 1981.

Gilman, C. M. "Medical Surgery in the American Revolution." *Journal of the Medical Society of New Jersey* 57, no. 8 (1960).

Glynney, I. *Diary* (unpublished). Harlan Crow Library, Dallas, TX.

Goldstein, E. "A British Grenadier's Button From a Bunker Hill Grave." *Military Collector and Historian* 60, no. 1 (2008).

Gordon, W. *The History of the Rise, Progress, and Establishment of the Independence of the United States of America: Including an Account of the Late War and of the Thirteen Colonies, From Their Origin to That Period.* 3 vols. New York: Samuel Campbell, 1794.

Grattan, W. *Adventures with the Connaught Rangers, 1809–1814.* Edited by C. Oman. London: Edward Arnold, 1902 [1847].

Green, S. A. "American Prisoners Taken at the Battle of Bunker Hill." *New England Historical and Genealogical Register* 42 (1888).

———. (ed.). "Amos Farnsworth's Diary." *Proceedings of the Massachusetts Historical Society* 12 (1897–99).

———. (ed.). *A Collection of Papers Relating to the History of the Town of Groton, Massachusetts.* Cambridge, MA: John Wilson and Son, 1899.

———. "Colonel William Prescott, and Groton Soldiers at the Battle of Bunker Hill." *Proceedings of the Massachusetts Historical Society* 43 (1909–1910).

———. (ed.). "Paul Lunt's Book." *Proceedings of the Massachusetts Historical Society* 12 (1871–73).

———. (ed.). "Thomas Boynton's Journal." *Proceedings of the Massachusetts Historical Society* 15 (1876–77).

Greene, E. B., and V. D. Harrington. *American Population Before the Federal Census of 1790.* New York: Columbia University Press, 1932.

Griffiths, F. A. *The Artillerist's Manual, and British Soldier's Compendium.* 9th ed. London: Parker and Son, 1862.

Gross, R. A. *The Minutemen and Their World.* New York: Hill and Wang, 1976.

Grossman, D. *On Combat: The Psychology and Physiology of Deadly Conflict in War and in Peace.* 3rd ed. Millstadt, IL: Warrior Science Publications, 2008.

Haag, L. C. "The Sound of Bullets." *AFTE Journal* 34 (2002).

Hadden, J. M. *Hadden's Journal and Orderly Books: A Journal Kept in Canada and Upon Burgoyne's Campaign in 1776 and 1777.* Albany, NY: Joel Munsell's Sons, 1884.

Hagelin, W., and R. A. Brown. "Connecticut Farmers at Bunker Hill: The Diary of Colonel Experience Storrs." *New England Quarterly* 28, no. 1 (1955).

Hagist, D. N. *British Soldiers, American War: Voices of the American Revolution.* Yardley, PA: Westholme Publishing, 2012.

———. "Shedding Light on Friendly Fire at Bunker Hill." *American Revolution* 1, no. 3 (2009).

Hansen, M. H. "Battle Exhortation in Ancient Historiography: Fact or Fiction?" *Historia* 42, no. 2 (1993).

Harrington, H. T. "Roundball Ballistics in the Revolutionary War: What Caused Rifle Shots to Go Over the Heads of the Enemy." *Southern Campaigns of the American Revolution* 3, no. 5 (2006).

Hart, A. B. "Echoes of Bunker Hill." *Proceedings of the Bunker Hill Monument Association* (1911).

Hastings, M. "Drawing the Wrong Lesson." *New York Review of Books,* March 11, 2010.

Hatch, R. M. "New Hampshire at Bunker Hill." *Historic New Hampshire* 30, no. 4 (1975).

Hawthorne, N. *The Snow Image and Other Twice-Told Tales.* New York: Thomas Y. Crowell and Co., 1902.

Heath, W. *Heath's Memoirs of the American War.* New York: A. Wessels Co., 1904.

Hendrix, S. *The Spirit of the Corps: The British Army and the Pre-National Pan-European Military World and the Origins of American Martial Culture, 1754–1783.* PhD. diss., University of Pittsburgh, 2005.

Henkels, S. V. (ed.). *The Letters and Papers of Elbridge Gerry, Catalogue No. 1005 for an Auction Held December 6, 1909* (1909).

Hennell, G. *A Gentleman Volunteer: The Letters of George Hennell From the Peninsular War, 1812–13.* Edited by M. Glover. London: Heinemann, 1979.

Henshaw, W. "Orderly Book of Col. William Henshaw." *Proceedings of the Massachusetts Historical Society* 15 (1876–77).

Higginbotham, D. *The War of American Independence: Military Attitudes, Policies, and Politics, 1763–1789.* New York: Macmillan, 1971.

Hill, J. B. (ed.). *Bi-Centennial of Old Dunstable, Address by Hon. S. T. Worcester, October 27, 1873, Also Colonel Bancroft's Personal Narrative of the Battle of Bunker Hill.* Nashua, NH: E. H. Spalding, 1878.

Holland, J. G. *History of Western Massachusetts: The Counties of Hampden, Hampshire, Franklin, and Berkshire.* 2 vols. Springfield, MA: Samuel Bowles and Co., 1855.

Houlding, J. A. *Fit for Service: The Training of the British Army, 1715–1795.* Oxford, U.K.: Oxford University Press, 1981.

House of Commons. *The Detail and Conduct of the American War, Under Generals Gage, Howe, Burgoyne, and Vice Admiral Lord Howe: With a Very Full and Correct State of the Whole of the Evidence, as Given Before a Committee of the House of Commons; and the Celebrated Fugitive Pieces, Which Are Said to Have Given Rise to That Important Enquiry, the Whole Exhibiting a Circumstantial, Connected, and Complete History of the Real Causes, Rise, Progress, and Present State of the American Rebellion.* 3rd ed. London: Richardson and Urquhart, 1780.

Hudson, C. *History of the Town of Lexington, Middlesex County, Massachusetts, From Its First Settlement to 1868.* 2 vols. New York and Boston: Houghton Mifflin, 1913.

Hughes, B. P. *Firepower: Weapons Effectiveness on the Battlefield, 1630–1850.* New York: Sarpedon, 1997.

Huntoon, D. T. V. *History of the Town of Canton, Norfolk County, Massachusetts.* Cambridge, MA: John Wilson and Son, 1893.

James, G. "Britain's Brown Bess." *Petersen's Rifle Shooter,* September 23, 2010. Available at www.rifleshootermag.com/rifles/featured_rifles_bess_092407/, accessed September 15, 2014.

Johnson, R. B. (ed.). "Diary of Israel Litchfield." Parts 1 and 2. *New England Historical and Genealogical Register* 129 (1975).

Johnson, W. *Sketches of the Life and Correspondence of Nathanael Greene, Major General of the Armies of the United States, in the War of the Revolution.* 2 vols. Charleston, SC: A. E. Miller, 1822.

Jones, E. A. *The Loyalists of Massachusetts: Their Memorials, Petitions, and Claims.* London: St. Catherine Press, 1930.

Ketchum, R. M. *The Battle for Bunker Hill.* New York: Doubleday, 1962.

Kidder, F. *The History of New Ipswich: From Its First Grant in 1736, to the Present Time: with Genealogical Notices of the Principal Families, and Also the Proceedings of the Centennial Celebration, September 11, 1850.* Boston: Gould and Lincoln, 1852.

Klinger, D. *Police Responses to Officer-Involved Shootings.* Department of Justice report, NCJ 192286 (2006).

Krenn, P., P. Kalaus, and B. Hall. "Material Culture and Military History: Test-Firing Early Modern Small Arms." *Material History Review* 42 (1995).

Lamb, R. *An Original and Authentic Journal of Occurrences During the Late American War From Its Commencement to the Year 1783.* Dublin: Wilkinson & Courtney, 1809.

Lamont, M. de. *The Art of War, Containing the Duties of All Military Officers in Actual Service; Including Necessary Instructions, in Many Capital Matters, by the Knowledge of Which, a Man May Soon Become an Ornament to the Profession of Arms.* Philadelphia: Robert Bell, 1776.

Leach, J. "A Journal Kept by John Leach, During His Confinement by the British, in Boston Gaol, in 1775." *New England Historical and Genealogical Register* 19, no. 3 (1865).

Lee Malcolm, J. "Slavery in Massachusetts and the American Revolution." *Journal of the Historical Society* 10, no. 4 (2010).

Leeke, W. *The History of Lord Seaton's Regiment (the 52nd Light Infantry) at the Battle of Waterloo.* 2 vols. London: Hatchard and Co., 1866.

L'Etang, H. "Some Thoughts on Panic in War." *Brassey's Annual* 77 (1966).

Lieberman, H. R., G. P. Bathalon, C. M. Falco, C. A. Morgan III, P. J. Niro, and W. J. Tharion. "The Fog of War: Decrements in Cognitive Performance and Mood Associated with Combat-Like Stress." Section 2. *Aviation, Space, and Environmental Medicine* 76, no. 7 (2005).

Lincoln, W. (ed.). *The Journals of Each Provincial Congress of Massachusetts in 1774 and 1775, and of the Committee of Safety.* Boston: Dutton and Wentworth, 1838.

Longmore, T. *Gunshot Injuries: Their History, Characteristic Features, Complications, and General Treatment, with Statistics Concerning Them as They Have Been Met with in Warfare.* 2nd ed. London: Longmans, Green and Co., 1895.

———. *A Treatise on Gunshot Wounds.* Philadelphia: J. B. Lippincott and Co., 1862.

Lossing, B. J. *The Pictorial Field-Book of the Revolution.* 2 vols. New York: Harper and Brothers, 1851.

Lushington, S. R. *The Life and Services of General Lord Harris, G. C. B. During His Campaigns in America, the West Indies, and India.* 2nd ed. London: J. W. Parker, 1845.

Lynn, J. A. *Battle: A History of Combat and Culture.* Cambridge, MA: Westview, 2003.

Manring, M. M., A. Hawk, J. H. Calhoun, and R. C. Andersen. "Treatment of War Wounds: A Historical Review." *Clinical Orthopaedics and Related Research* 467 (2009).

Mauduit, I. *Three Letters to Lord Viscount Howe, with Remarks on the Attack at Bunker's Hill, to Which Is Added, a Comparative View of the Conduct of Lord Cornwallis and General Howe.* London: G. Wilkie, 1781.

McCalman, I. *An Oxford Companion to the Romantic Age: British Culture, 1776–1832.* Oxford: Oxford University Press, 1999.

Moore, F. (ed.). *Diary of the American Revolution: From Newspapers and Original Documents.* 2 vols. New York: Charles Scribner, 1860.

Moore, H. P. *A Life of General John Stark of New Hampshire.* New York: No publisher, 1949.

Morrissey, B. *Boston 1775: The Shot Heard Around the World.* London: Osprey, 1995.

Muir, R. *Tactics and the Experience of Battle in the Age of Napoleon.* New Haven and London: Yale University Press, 2000 edn.

Murdock, H. *Bunker Hill: Notes and Queries on a Famous Battle.* Boston: Houghton Mifflin, 1927.

Murphy, J. F. "We Have All Lost a Father." *Naval History* 16, no. 5 (2002).

Neale, A. *Letters From Portugal and Spain; Comprising the Account of the Operations of the Armies Under Their Excellences Sir Arthur Wellesley and Sir John Moore, From the Landing of the Troops at Mondego Bay to the Battle at Corunna.* London: Richard Phillips, 1809.

Neumann, G. "The Redcoats' Brown Bess." *American Rifleman,* December 9, 2009. Available at www.americanrifleman.org/article.php?id=14722&cat=3&sub=11, accessed September 15, 2014.

Norton, S. L. "Marital Migration in Essex County, Massachusetts, in the Colonial and Early Federal Periods." *Journal of Marriage and the Family* 35, no. 3 (1973).

Norwood, W. F. "Medicine in the Era of the American Revolution." Part 2. *International Record of Medicine* 171, no. 7 (1958).

Nosworthy, B. *The Anatomy of Victory: Battle Tactics, 1689–1763.* New York: Hippocrene Books, 1990.

Noyes, D. *The History of Norway: Comprising a Minute Account of Its First Settlement, Town Officers, the Annual Expenditures of the Town, with Other Statistical Matters; Interspersed with Historical Sketches, Narrative and Anecdote, and Occasional Remarks of the Author.* Norway, ME: D. Noyes, 1852.

Ondishko, Jr., J. J. "A View of Anxiety, Fear, and Panic." *Military Affairs* 36, no. 2 (1972).

Palmer, J. "Longevity." *Proceedings of the Massachusetts Historical Society* 8 (1866).

Paret, P. *Imagined Battles: Reflections of War in European Art*. Chapel Hill: University of North Carolina Press, 1997.

————. (ed.). *Makers of Modern Strategy: From Machiavelli to the Nuclear Age*. Princeton, NJ: Princeton University Press, 1986.

————. *Understanding War: Essays on Clausewitz and the History of Military Power*. Princeton, NJ: Princeton University Press, 1992.

Phalen, J. "Surgeon James Mann's Observations on Battlefield Amputations." *Military Surgeon* 87 (1940).

Pickering, O. *The Life of Timothy Pickering*. 4 vols. Boston: Little, Brown, and Co., 1867–73.

Pollard, T., and I. Banks (eds.). *Bastions and Barbwire*. Leiden, The Netherlands: Brill, 2008.

Potter, C. E. *The History of Manchester, Formerly Derryfield, in New Hampshire; Including That of Ancient Amoskeag, of the Middle Merrimack Valley*. Manchester, NH: C. E. Potter, 1856.

Potter, I. R. "The Life and Remarkable Adventures of Israel Ralph Potter." *Magazine of History with Notes and Queries, Extra Numbers 13–16* (1911).

Powell, W. S. "A Connecticut Soldier Under Washington: Elisha Bostwick's Memoirs of the First Years of the Revolution." *William and Mary Quarterly* 6, no. 1 (1949).

Powers, S. L. "Studying the Art of War: Military Books Known to American Officers and Their French Counterparts During the Second Half of the Eighteenth Century." *Journal of Military History* 70, no. 3 (2006).

Pruitt, Jr., B. A. "Combat Casualty Care and Surgical Progress." *Annals of Surgery* 243, no. 6 (2006).

Quintal, Jr., G. *Patriots of Color: 'A Peculiar Beauty and Merit;' African Americans and Native Americans at Battle Road and Bunker Hill*. Boston: National Historical Park, 2002.

Raudzens, G. "In Search of Better Quantification for War History: Numerical Superiority and Casualty Rates in Early Modern Europe." *War and Society* 15, no. 1 (1997).

Reardon, C. "Writing Battle History: The Challenge of Memory." *Civil War History* 53, no. 3 (2007).

Reed, W. B. *The Life and Correspondence of Joseph Reed*. 2 vols. Philadelphia: Lindsay and Blakiston, 1847.

Report of the War Office Committee of Enquiry into 'Shell-Shock.' London: Imperial War Museum, 2004 [1922].

Resch, J. P. *Suffering Soldiers: Revolutionary War Veterans, Moral Sentiment, and Political Culture in the Early Republic*. Amherst: University of Massachusetts Press, 1999.

Rose, A. *American Rifle: A Biography*. New York: Delacorte Press, 2008.

Russell, P. E. "Redcoats in the Wilderness: British Officers and Irregular Warfare in Europe and America, 1740 to 1760." *William and Mary Quarterly* 35, no. 4 (1978).

Scheer, G. F., and H. F. Rankin. *Rebels and Redcoats: The American Revolution Through the Eyes of Those Who Fought and Lived It*. New York: World Publishing Company, 1957.

Scott, D., L. Babits, and C. Haecker (eds.). *Fields of Conflict: Battlefield Archaeology from the Roman Empire to the Korean War*. Washington, DC: Potomac Books, 2009.

Scudder, H. N. "The Battle of Bunker Hill." *Atlantic Monthly* 36 (1875).

Seybolt, R. F. "Note on the Casualties of April 19, and June 17, 1775." *New England Quarterly* 4, no. 3 (1931).

Shephard, B. *A War of Nerves: Soldiers and Psychiatrists in the Twentieth Century*. Cambridge, MA: Harvard University Press, 2003.

Showman, R. K. (ed.). *The Papers of General Nathanael Greene*. 13 vols. Chapel Hill: University of North Carolina Press, 1976–2005.

Shrader, C. R. "Friendly Fire: The Inevitable Price." *Parameters* 22 (1992).

Smith, A. *History of the Town of Peterborough, Hillsborough County, New Hampshire: With the Report of the Proceedings at the Centennial Celebration in 1839; an Appendix Containing the Records of the Original Proprietors; and a Genealogical and Historical Register.* Boston: George H. Ellis Co., 1876.

Smith, J. *Peterborough, New Hampshire, in the American Revolution.* Peterborough, NH: Peterborough Historical Society, 1913.

Spring, M. *With Zeal and with Bayonets Only: The British Army on Campaign in North America, 1775–1783.* Norman: University of Oklahoma Press, 2008.

Stanhope, P. H. *Notes of Conversations with the Duke of Wellington, 1831–1851.* New York: Longmans, Green, and Co., 1888.

Stedman, C. *The History of the Origin, Progress, and Termination of the American War.* 2 vols. London: C. Stedman, 1794.

Steele, B. D., and T. Dorland (eds.). *The Heirs of Archimedes: Science and the Art of War Through the Age of Enlightenment.* Cambridge, MA: MIT Press, 2005.

Steinweg, K. K. "Dealing Realistically with Fratricide." *Parameters* 25 (1995).

Stephenson, M. *Patriot Battles: How the War of Independence Was Fought.* New York: HarperCollins, 2007.

Stevens, B. F. (ed.). *General Sir William Howe's Orderly Book at Charlestown, Boston, and Halifax, June 17, 1775 to May 26, 1776.* London: Benjamin Franklin Stevens, 1890.

Stone, W. L. (ed.). *Journal of Captain Pausch, Chief of the Hanau Artillery During the Burgoyne Campaign.* Albany, NY: Joel Munsell's Sons, 1886.

Stouffer, R., A. A. Lumsdaine, M. H. Lumsdaine, R. M. Williams, Jr., M. B. Smith, I. L. Janis, S. A. Star, and L. S. Cottrell, Jr. (eds.). *The American Soldier: Studies in Social Psychology in World War II.* 4 vols. Princeton, NJ: Princeton University Press, 1949–50.

Sumner, W. H. "Reminiscences Relating to General Warren and Bunker Hill." *New England Genealogical and Historical Register* 12 (1858).

Swett, S. *History of Bunker Hill Battle: With a Plan.* Boston: Munroe and Francis, 1826.

———. *Notes to His Sketch of Bunker Hill Battle.* Boston: Munroe and Francis, 1825.

Temple, J. H. *History of Framingham, Massachusetts, Early Known as Danforth's Farms, 1640–1880, with a Genealogical Register.* Framingham, MA: Town of Framingham, 1887.

Terraine, J. *The Smoke and the Fire: Myths and Anti-Myths of War, 1861–1945.* London: Sidgwick & Jackson, 1980.

Thacher, J. *A Military Journal During the American Revolution, from the Commencement to the Disbanding of the American Army.* Hartford, CT: Hurlbut, Williams, and Co., 1862.

Tielke, J. G. von (trans. C. and R. Craufurd). *An Account of Some of the Most Remarkable Events of the War Between the Prussians, Austrians, and Russians, From 1756 to 1763; and a Treatise on Several Branches of the Military Art.* 2 vols. London: C. and R. Craufurd, 1787–88.

Trumbull, J. *Autobiography, Reminiscences, and Letters of John Trumbull, from 1756 to 1841.* New York: Wiley and Putnam, 1841.

Ultee, M. (ed.). *Adapting to Conditions: War and Society in the Eighteenth Century.* Tuscaloosa: University of Alabama Press, 1986.

Urban, M. *Fusiliers: The Saga of a British Redcoat Regiment in the American Revolution.* New York: Walker and Co., 2007.

Van Arsdale, J. (ed.). *Discord and Civil Wars, Being a Portion of the Journal Kept by Lieutenant Williams of His Majesty's Twenty-Third Regiment While Stationed in British North America During the Time of the Revolution.* Buffalo, NY: Salisbury Club, 1954.

Vidal, F. "Psychology in the 18th Century: A View from Encyclopedias." *History of the Human Sciences* 6, no. 1 (1993).

Wade, H. T., and R. A. Lively. *This Glorious Cause: The Adventures of Two Company Officers in Washington's Army.* Princeton, NJ: Princeton University Press, 1958.

Wanke, P. "American Military Psychiatry and Its Role Among Ground Forces in World War II." *Journal of Military History* 63, no. 1 (1999).

War Office. *Rules and Regulations for the Formations, Field Exercise, and Movements of His Majesty's Forces.* London: J. Walter for the War Office, 1792.

Ward, A. H. *History of the Town of Shrewsbury, Massachusetts: From Its Settlement in 1717 to 1829, with Other Matter Relating Thereto Before Not Published, Including an Extensive Family Register.* Shrewsbury: S. G. Drake, 1847.

Ward, C. *The War of the Revolution.* 2 vols. New York: Macmillan, 1952.

Waters, J. J. "Family, Inheritance, and Migration in Colonial New England: The Evidence from Guilford, Connecticut." *William and Mary Quarterly* 39, no. 1 (1982).

Webb, J. W. (ed.). *Reminiscences of General Samuel B. Webb of the Revolutionary Army.* New York: Globe Stationery and Printing Co., 1882.

Webster, D. "An Account of the Battle of Bunker Hill." *North American Review* 7 (1818).

Whinyates, F. A. (ed.). *The Services of Lieut.-Colonel Francis Downman, R.A., in France, North America, and the West Indies, Between the Years 1758 and 1784.* Woolwich, U.K.: Royal Artillery Institution, 1898.

Whitcher, W. "The Relation of New Hampshire Men to the Siege of Boston." *Magazine of History with Notes and Queries* 6 (1907).

Willcox, E. S. "Captain William Meacham at Bunker Hill." *New England Historical and Genealogical Register* 49 (1895).

Windham, W., and G. Townshend. *A Plan of Discipline Composed for the Use of the Militia of the County of Norfolk.* London: J. Shuckburgh, 1760.

Winsor, J. (ed.). *The Memorial History of Boston, Including Suffolk County, Massachusetts, 1630–1880.* 4 vols. Boston: James R. Osgood and Co., 1882.

Wolfe, J. *Instructions to Young Officers.* 2nd ed. Edinburgh, 1780.

Wolseley, G. J. *The Story of a Soldier's Life.* 2 vols. New York: Charles Scribner's Sons, 1904.

Wooden, A. C. "The Wounds and Weapons of the Revolutionary War from 1775 to 1783." *Delaware Medical Journal* 44, no. 3 (1972).

Wortley, J. (ed.). *A Prime Minister and His Son: From the Correspondence of the 3rd Earl of Bute and of Lt.-General the Hon. Sir Charles Stuart, K.B.* London: John Murray, 1925.

Wright, J. W. "Some Notes on the Continental Army." *William and Mary Quarterly* 11, no. 2 (1931).

Yellin, K. *Battle Exhortation: The Rhetoric of Combat Leadership.* Columbia: University of South Carolina Press, 2008.

GETTYSBURG

Adelman, G. E. "Hazlett's Battery at Gettysburg." *Gettysburg Magazine* 21 (1999).

Adkin, M. *The Gettysburg Companion: The Complete Guide to America's Most Famous Battle.* Mechanicsburg, PA: Stackpole Books, 2008.

Albin, M. A. "The Use of Anesthetics During the Civil War, 1861–1865." *Pharmacy in History* 42, nos. 3 and 4 (2000).

Alexander, E. P. "Causes of Lee's Defeat at Gettysburg." *Southern Historical Society Papers* 4, no. 3 (1877).

———. *Fighting for the Confederacy: The Personal Recollections of General Edward Porter Alexander.* Edited by G. W. Gallagher. Chapel Hill: University of North Carolina Press, 1989.

————. *Military Memoirs of a Confederate: A Critical Narrative.* New York: Charles Scribner's Sons, 1907.

Andrews, M. R. (ed.). *History of Marietta and Washington County, Ohio and Representative Citizens.* Chicago: Biographical Publishing Company, 1902.

Anon. (ed.). *Biographical and Historical Memoirs of Pulaski, Jefferson, Lonoke, Faulkner, Grant, Saline, Perry, Garland, and Hot Spring Counties, Arkansas.* Chicago: Goodspeed Publishing Company, 1889.

Anon. "Fighting." *Scientific American 7*, no. 22, Nov. 29, 1862.

Anon. "Gettysburg Weather Reports." *Blue and Gray Magazine 5*, no. 2 (1987).

Anon. "How They Fire in Battle." *Scientific American 7*, no. 18, Nov. 1, 1862.

Anon. *Reunions of the Nineteenth Maine Regiment Association, at Portland, Bath, Belfast, Augusta and Richmond.* Augusta, ME: Sprague, Owen, and Nash, 1878.

Anon. "Scenes and Incidents at Gettysburg." *Harper's Weekly 8*, no. 368, Jan. 16, 1864.

Anon. "Suggestions From an Old Soldier." *New York Times*, April 24, 1861.

Anon. (eds.). *The Union Army: A History of Military Affairs in the Loyal States, 1861–1865—Records of the Regiments in the Union Army—Cyclopedia of Battles—Memoirs of Commanders and Soldiers.* 8 vols. Madison, WI: Federal Publishing Co., 1908.

Anon. "A Visit to the Gettysburg Battlefield." *Brooklyn Daily Eagle*, August 1, 1863.

Baker, L. W. *History of the Ninth Mass. Battery: Recruited July, 1862; Mustered in Aug. 10, 1862; Mustered Out June 9, 1865, at the Close of the Rebellion.* South Framingham, MA: Lakeview Press, 1888.

Bandy, K., and F. Freeland (eds.). *The Gettysburg Papers.* 2 vols. Dayton, OH: Morningside Press, 1978.

Barber, L. W. *Army Memoirs.* Chicago: J. M. W. Jones Stationery and Printing Co., 1894.

Barnes, J. K., G. A. Otis, and D. L. Huntington (eds.). *The Medical and Surgical History of the War of the Rebellion.* Washington, DC: Government Printing Office, 1883.

Barrett, J. G. (ed.). *Yankee Rebel: The Civil War Journal of Edmund Dewitt Patterson.* Knoxville: University of Tennessee Press, 2004.

Barziza, D. et U. *The Adventures of a Prisoner of War, 1863–1864.* Edited by R. H. Shuffler. Austin: University of Texas Press, 1964.

Bates, S. P. (ed.). *History of Pennsylvania Volunteers, 1861–5: Prepared in Compliance with Acts of the Legislature.* 5 vols. Harrisburg, PA: B. Singerly, 1869–1871.

Bauer, K. J. (ed.). *Soldiering: The Civil War Diary of Rice C. Bull, 123rd New York Volunteer Infantry.* San Rafael, CA: Presidio Press, 1977.

Baumann, T., and D. M. Segesser. "Shadows of Total War in French and British Military Journals, 1918–1939." In *The Shadows of Total War: Europe, East Asia, and the United States, 1919–1939*, edited by R. Chickering and S. Förster. New York: Cambridge University Press, 2003.

Becker, C. M., and R. Thomas (eds.). *Hearth and Knapsack: The Ladley Letters, 1857–1880.* Athens: Ohio University Press, 1988.

Benedict, G. G. *Army Life in Virginia: Letters From the Twelfth Vermont Regiment and Personal Experiences of Volunteer Service in the War for the Union, 1862–63.* Burlington, VT: Free Press Association, 1895.

————. *Vermont at Gettysburg: A Sketch of the Part Taken by the Vermont Troops in the Battle for Gettysburgh.* Burlington, VT: Free Press Association, 1870.

Benson, S. W. (ed.). *Berry Benson's Civil War Book: Memoirs of a Confederate Scout and Sharpshooter.* Athens: University of Georgia Press, 2007.

Benton, C. E. *As Seen From the Ranks: A Boy in the Civil War.* New York: G. P. Putnam's Sons, 1902.

Bierce, A. "The Crime at Pickett's Mill." In *The Devil's Dictionary, Tales, and Memoirs,* edited by S. T. Joshi. New York: Library of America, 2011.

Bigelow, J. *The Peach Orchard: Gettysburg, July 2, 1863.* Minneapolis: Kimball-Storer Co., 1910.

Bilby, J. G. *Small Arms at Gettysburg: Infantry and Cavalry Weapons in America's Greatest Battle.* Yardley, PA: Westholme, 2008.

Blackford, W. W. *War Years with Jeb Stuart.* New York: Charles Scribner's Sons, 1946.

Blake, H. N. *Three Years in the Army of the Potomac.* Boston: Lee and Shepard, 1865.

Borcke, H. von. *Memoirs of the Confederate War for Independence.* Philadelphia: J. B. Lippincott and Co., 1867.

Bousquet, A. *The Scientific Way of Warfare: Order and Chaos on the Battlefields of Modernity.* New York: Columbia University Press, 2009.

Bowen, G. A. "The Diary of Captain George D. Bowen, 12th Regiment New Jersey Volunteers." *Valley Forge Journal* 2, no. 2 (1984).

Bowen, R. E. "From Round Top to Richmond." *The Old Guard* 4, no. 1 (1889).

Boyd, C. F. (ed. M. Throne). *The Civil War Diary of Cyrus R. Boyd, Fifteenth Iowa Infantry, 1861–1863.* Baton Rouge: Louisiana State University Press, 1998.

Brown, E. *The Twenty-Seventh Indiana Volunteer Infantry in the War of the Rebellion, 1861 to 1865: First Division, 12th and 20th Corps: a History of Its Recruiting, Organization, Camp Life, Marches, and Battles.* Monticello, IN: R. E. Brown, 1899.

Brown, M. M. *The University Greys: Company A, Eleventh Mississippi Regiment, Army of Northern Virginia, 1861–1865.* Richmond, VA: Garrett and Massie, 1940.

Browne, Jr., E. C. "Battery H, 1st Ohio Light Artillery: Controversy in the Cemetery." *Gettysburg Magazine* 26 (2002).

Bruce, G. A. *The Twentieth Regiment of Massachusetts Volunteer Infantry, 1861–1865.* Boston and New York: Houghton, Mifflin, and Co., 1906.

Bucklin, S. *In Hospital and Camp: A Woman's Record of Thrilling Incidents Among the Wounded in the Late War.* Philadelphia: John E. Potter and Co., 1869.

Buechler, J. " 'Give 'Em the Bayonet'—a Note on Civil War Mythology." In *Battles Lost and Won: Essays From Civil War History,* edited by J. T. Hubbell. Westport, CT: Greenwood Press, 1975.

Buehler, F. J. *Recollections of the Rebel Invasion and One Woman's Experience During the Battle of Gettysburg.* Gettysburg, PA: Star and Sentinel Printing, 1900.

Busey, J. P., and D. G. Martin (eds.). *Regimental Strengths and Losses at Gettysburg.* Hightstown, NJ: Longstreet House, 1994.

Byrne, F. L., and A. T. Weaver (eds.). *Haskell of Gettysburg: His Life and Civil War Papers.* Kent, OH: Kent State University Press, 1989.

Campbell, E. "The Aftermath and Recovery of Gettysburg." Part 1. *Gettysburg Magazine* 11 (1994).

———. "Baptism of Fire: The Ninth Massachusetts Battery at Gettysburg, July 2, 1863." *Gettysburg Magazine* 5 (1991).

———. " 'Remember Harper's Ferry': The Degradation, Humiliation, and Redemption of Col. George L. Willard's Brigade, Part 1." *Gettysburg Magazine* 7 (1992).

———. " 'Remember Harper's Ferry': The Degradation, Humiliation, and Redemption of Col. George L. Willard's Brigade, Part 2." *Gettysburg Magazine* 8 (1993).

———. "Voices of Gettysburg: How the Army of the Potomac Viewed the Campaign." *North and South* 7 (2004).

Carter, R. G. *Four Brothers in Blue, or Sunshine and Shadows of the War of the Rebellion: A Story of the Great Civil War From Bull Run to Appomattox.* Washington, DC: Gibson Bros., 1913.

Casey, J. B. (ed.). "The Ordeal of Adoniram Judson Warner: His Minutes of South Mountain and Antietam." *Civil War History* 28, no. 3 (1982).

Castel, A. "Mars and the Reverend Longstreet: Or, Attacking and Dying in the Civil War." *Civil War History* 33, no. 2 (1987).

Catton, B. *Reflections on the Civil War.* Edited by J. Leekley. Garden City, NY: Doubleday & Co., 1981.

Chamberlain, J. L. *The Passing of the Armies: An Account of the Final Campaign of the Army of the Potomac, Based Upon Personal Remininscences of the Fifth Army Corps.* New York: G. P. Putnam's Sons, 1915.

Chandler, D. G. *On the Napoleonic Wars: Collected Essays.* Mechanicsburg, PA: Stackpole Books, 1999 edn.

Cheek, P., and M. Pointon. *History of the Sauk County Riflemen, Known as Company 'A,' Sixth Wisconsin Veteran Volunteer Infantry, 1861–1865.* Madison, WI: Democrat Printing Company, 1909.

Chickering, R. "Total War: The Use and Abuse of a Concept." In *Anticipating Total War: The German and American Experiences, 1871–1914,* edited by M. F. Boemeke, R. Chickering, and S. Förster. Cambridge, U.K.: Cambridge University Press, 1999.

Chisolm, J. J. *Manual of Military Surgery for the Use of Surgeons in the Confederate Army; with an Appendix of the Rules and Regulations of the Medical Department of the Confederate Army.* Charleston, SC: Evans and Cogswell, 1861.

Coco, G. A. *On the Bloodstained Field: 130 Human Interest Stories of the Campaign and Battle of Gettysburg.* Gettysburg, PA: Thomas Publications, 1987.

———. "The Rawley W. Martin Story." *Gettysburg Magazine* 33 (2005).

———. *A Strange and Blighted Land: Gettysburg: the Aftermath of a Battle.* Gettysburg, PA: Thomas Publications, 1995.

Coffman, R. "A Vital Unit." *Civil War Times Illustrated* 20 (June 1982).

Cole, P. M. *Command and Communications Frictions in the Gettysburg Campaign.* Orrtanna, PA: Colecraft Industries, 2006.

Conklin, G. W. "The Long March to Stevens Run: The 134th New York Volunteer Infantry at Gettysburg." *Gettysburg Magazine* 21 (1999).

Connor, J. T. H. "Chloroform and the Civil War." *Military Medicine* 169 (Feb. 2004).

Cook, S. G., and C. E. Benton (eds.). *The 'Dutchess County Regiment' in the Civil War: Its Story as Told by Its Members.* Danbury, CT: Danbury Medical Printing Co., 1907.

Cooksey, P. C. "The Union Artillery at Gettysburg on July 3." *Gettysburg Magazine* 38 (2008).

Costa, D. L. "Scarring and Mortality Selection Among Civil War Pows: A Long-Term Mortality, Morbidity, and Socioeconomic Follow-Up." California Center for Population Research On-Line Working Paper Series PWP-CCPR-2010–035, November 29, 2010.

Coxe, J. "The Battle of Gettysburg." *Confederate Veteran* 21, no. 9 (September 1913).

Craft, D. *History of the Hundred Forty-First Regiment, Pennsylvania Volunteers, 1862–1865.* Towanda, PA: Reporter-Journal Printing Company, 1885.

Crumb, H. S. (ed.). *The Eleventh Corps Artillery at Gettysburg: The Papers of Major Thomas Ward Osborn, Chief of Artillery.* Hamilton, NY: Edmonston Publishing, Inc., 1991.

Culp, E. C. *The 25th Ohio Veteran Volunteer Infantry in the War of the Union.* Topeka, KS: George W. Crane & Co., 1885.

Daniel, F. E. *Recollections of a Rebel Surgeon (and Other Sketches), or, in the Doctor's Sappy Days.* Chicago: Clinic Publishing Co., 1901.

Davis, J. A. "Music and Gallantry in Combat During the American Civil War." *American Music* 28, no. 2 (2010).

Davis, S. "The Death and Burials of General Richard Brooke Garnett." *Gettysburg Magazine* 5 (1991).

Davis, S. B. *Escape of a Confederate Officer From Prison: What He Saw at Andersonville: How He Was Sentenced to Death and Saved by the Interposition of Abraham Lincoln.* Norfolk, VA: Landmark Publishing Company, 1892.

Dawes, R. R. *Service with the Sixth Wisconsin Volunteers.* Marietta, OH: E. R. Alderman, 1890.

Dean, Jr., E. T. "'We Will All Be Lost and Destroyed': Post-Traumatic Stress Disorder and the Civil War." *Civil War History* 37 (1991).

De Forest, J. *A Volunteer's Adventures: A Union Captain's Record of the Civil War.* Edited by J. H. Croushore. New Haven: Yale University Press, 1946.

De Saxe, M. "My Reveries upon the Art of War." In *Roots of Strategy: A Collection of Military Classics.* Edited by Maj. T. R. Philips. Mechanicsburg, PA: Stackpole Books, 2002.

Diffenbaugh, W. G. "Military Surgery in the Civil War." *Military Medicine* 130 (May 1965).

Dodge, T. A. "Left Wounded on the Field." *Putnam's Monthly Magazine* 14, no. 21 (September 1869).

Dougherty, J. J. "A History of the Mcpherson Farm at Gettysburg." *Gettysburg Magazine* 26 (2002).

———. "'We Have Come to Stay!': The 143rd Regiment Pennsylvania Volunteer Infantry and the Fight for Mcpherson's Ridge, July 1, 1863." *Gettysburg Magazine* 24 (2001).

Dougherty, P. J. "Wartime Amputations." *Military Medicine* 158 (December 1993).

Doyle, J. A., J. D. Smith, and R. M. McMurry (eds.). *This Wilderness of War: The Civil War Letters of George W. Squier, Hoosier Volunteer.* Knoxville: University of Tennessee Press, 1998.

Dreese, M. A. "The 151st Pennsylvania Volunteers at Gettysburg: July 1, 1863." *Gettysburg Magazine* 23 (2000).

———. "Ordeal in the Lutheran Theological Seminary: The Recollections of First Lt. Jeremiah Hoffman, 142nd Pennsylvania Volunteers." *Gettysburg Magazine* 23 (2000).

Dunaway, W. F. *Reminiscences of a Rebel.* New York: Neale Publishing Company, 1913.

———. "Additional Notes on the 154th New York at Gettysburg." *Gettysburg Magazine* 29 (2003).

Dunkelman, M. H. "'We Were Compelled to Cut Our Way Through Them, and in Doing So Our Losses Were Heavy': Gettysburg Casualties of the 154th New York Volunteers." *Gettysburg Magazine* 18 (1998).

Dunkelman, M. H., and M. J. Winey. "The Hardtack Regiment in the Brickyard Fight." *Gettysburg Magazine* 8 (1993).

Durkin, J. T. (ed.). *John Dooley, Confederate Soldier: His War Journal.* Washington, DC: Georgetown University Press, 1945.

Eby, C. D. (ed.). *A Virginia Yankee in the Civil War: The Diaries of David Hunter Strother.* Chapel Hill: University of North Carolina Press, 1961.

Elmore, T. L. "Casualty Analysis of the Gettysburg Battle." *Gettysburg Magazine* 35 (2006).

———. "The Effects of Artillery Fire on Infantry at Gettysburg." *Gettysburg Magazine* 5 (1991).

———. "The Grand Cannonade: A Confederate Perspective." *Gettysburg Magazine* 19 (1999).

———. "Less Than Brave: Shirkers, Stragglers, and Scavengers in the Army of Northern Virginia." *Gettysburg Magazine* 31 (2004).

———. "A Meteorological and Astronomical Chronology of the Gettysburg Campaign." *Gettysburg Magazine* 13 (1995).

———. "Skirmishers." *Gettysburg Magazine* 6 (1992).

Evans, T. "'All Was Complete Chaos': As a Federal Regular Saw Second Manassas." *Civil War Times Illustrated* 6, no. 9 (January 1968).

———. "The Cries of the Wounded Were Piercing and Horrible." *Civil War Times Illustrated* 7, no. 4 (July 1968).

Farlow, J., and L. Barry (eds.). "Vincent B. Osborne's Civil War Experiences." *Kansas Historical Quarterly* 20 (May 1952).

Faust, D. G. "The Civil War Soldier and the Art of Dying." *Journal of Southern History* 67, no. 1 (2001).

———. "Telling War Stories." *New Republic,* June 30, 2011.

Ferro, M. *The Great War, 1914–1918.* London: Routledge, 1991 [1969].

Foner, E. *Reconstruction: America's Unfinished Revolution, 1863–1877.* New York: Harper Perennial, 2002.

Foster, J. Y. "Four Days at Gettysburg." *Harper's New Monthly Magazine* 28, no. 165 (Feb. 1864).

Fox, W. F. *Regimental Losses in the American Civil War, 1861–1865.* 4th ed. Albany, NY: Albany Publishing Company, 1898.

Fuger, F. "Cushing's Battery at Gettysburg." *Journal of the Military Service Institution of the United States* 41 (1907).

Fulks, S. "Another Irony of Gettysburg." *Gettysburg Magazine* 44 (2011).

Fuller, C. A. *Personal Recollections of the War of 1861 as Private, Sergeant, and Lieutenant in the Sixty-First Regiment, New York Volunteer Infantry.* Sherburne, NY: News Job Publishing House, 1906.

Fuller, J. F. C. *Grant and Lee: A Study in Personality and Generalship.* Bloomington: Indiana University Press, 1957.

Galwey, T. F. *The Valiant Hours: Narrative of 'Captain Brevet,' an Irish-American in the Army of the Potomac.* Edited by W. S. Nye. Harrisburg, PA: Stackpole Company, 1961.

Garrison, F. H. *John Shaw Billings: A Memoir.* New York: G. P. Putnam's Sons, 1915.

Gibbon, J. *The Artillerist's Manual, Compiled From Various Sources, and Adapted to the Service of the United States.* 2nd ed. New York: D. Van Nostrand, 1863.

Gilmor, H. *Four Years in the Saddle.* New York: Harper and Brothers, 1866.

Glatthaar, J. T. *General Lee's Army: From Victory to Collapse.* New York: Free Press, 2008.

———. *Soldiering in the Army of Northern Virginia: A Statistical Portrait of the Troops Who Served Under Robert E. Lee.* Chapel Hill: University of North Carolina Press, 2011.

Gordon, L. J. "'I Never Was a Coward': Questions of Bravery in a Civil War Regiment." Frank L. Klement Lecture No. 14. Milwaukee: Marquette University Press, 2005.

Goss, W. L. *Recollections of a Private: A Story of the Army of the Potomac.* New York: Thomas Y. Crowell and Co., 1890.

Gottfried, B. M. "'Friendly' Fire at Gettysburg." *Gettysburg Magazine* 27 (2002).

Grandchamp, R. "The 2nd Rhode Island Volunteers in the Gettysburg Campaign." *Gettysburg Magazine* 42 (2010).

Griffith, P. *Battle Tactics in the Civil War.* New Haven: Yale University Press, 2001.

Grimsley, M., and T. D. Miller (eds.). *The Union Must Stand: The Civil War Diary of John Quincy Adams Campbell, Fifth Iowa Volunteer Infantry.* Knoxville: University of Tennessee Press, 2000.

Gross, J. "A Grave Situation: Privately Purchased Identification Devices with Gettysburg Association." *Gettysburg Magazine* 42 (2010).

Guelzo, A. C. "The Unturned Corners of the Battle of Gettysburg: Tactics, Geography, and Politics." *Gettysburg Magazine* 45 (2011).

Hadden, R. L. "The Deadly Embrace: The Meeting of the Twenty-Fourth Regiment, Michigan Infantry and the Twenty-Sixth Regiment of North Carolina Troops at Mcpherson's Woods, Gettysburg, Pennsylvania, July 1, 1863." *Gettysburg Magazine* 5 (1991).

Haines, A. *History of the Fifteenth Regiment New Jersey Volunteers.* New York: Jenkins and Thomas, 1883.

Hall, C. R. "The Lessons of the War Between the States." *International Record of Medicine* 171, no. 7 (July 1958).

Hardee, W. J. *Rifle and Light Infantry Tactics; for the Exercise and Manoeuvres of Troops When Acting as Light Infantry or Riflemen.* Philadelphia: Lippincott, Grambo, and Co., 1855.

Hartwig, D. S. "The 11th Army Corps on July 1, 1863." *Gettysburg Magazine* 2 (1990).

———. "'I Have Never Been in a Hotter Place': Brigade Command at Gettysburg." *Gettysburg Magazine* 25 (2001).

———. "Unwilling Witness to the Rage of Gettysburg." In *The Most Shocking Battle I Have Ever Witnessed: The Second Day at Gettysburg.* Papers of the 2006 Gettysburg National Military Park Seminar. National Park Service, 2008.

Herdegen, L. J. "Old Soldiers and War Talk: The Controversy Over the Opening Infantry Fight at Gettysburg." *Gettysburg Magazine* 2 (1990).

Hess, E. J. *Pickett's Charge: The Last Attack at Gettysburg.* Chapel Hill and London: University of North Carolina Press, 2001.

———. *The Rifle Musket in Civil War Combat: Reality and Myth.* Lawrence: University Press of Kansas, 2008.

———. *The Union Soldier in Battle: Enduring the Ordeal of Combat.* Lawrence: University Press of Kansas, 1997.

Hill, A. F. *Our Boys: The Personal Experiences of a Soldier in the Army of the Potomac.* Philadelphia: John E. Potter, 1864.

Hitchcock, F. L. *War from the Inside, or Personal Experiences, Impressions, and Reminiscences of One of the 'Boys' in the War of the Rebellion.* Philadelphia: J. B. Lippincott, 1904.

Hohenlohe-Ingelflingen, K. zu. *Letters on Infantry.* Translated by N. L. Walford. 2nd ed. London: Edward Stanford, 1892.

Holmes, O. W. (ed.). *Speeches by Oliver Wendell Holmes.* Boston: Little, Brown, and Co., 1900.

Holstein, A. M. E. *Three Years in the Field Hospitals of the Army of the Potomac.* Philadelphia: J. B. Lippincott, 1867.

Howard, O. O. *Autobiography of Oliver Otis Howard.* 2 vols. New York: Baker and Taylor Co., 1907.

Hubler, S. "Just the Plain, Unvarnished Story of a Soldier in the Ranks." *New York Times,* June 29, 1913.

Humphreys, H. H. *Andrew Atkinson Humphreys: A Biography.* Philadelphia: John C. Winston Co., 1924.

Hunter, A. "A High Private's Sketch of Sharpsburg." *Southern Historical Society Papers* 11 (1883).

Hutchinson, M. W. "Bringing Home a Fallen Son: The Story of Lt. Willis G. Babcock, 64th New York Volunteer Infantry." *Gettysburg Magazine* 30 (2004).

———. "To Gettysburg and Beyond: A Vermont Captain's Letters to His Wife." *Gettysburg Magazine* 25 (2001).

Hyman, K. C., S. Wignall, and R. Roswell, "War Syndromes and Their Evaluation: From the U.S. Civil War to the Persian Gulf War." *Annals of Internal Medicine* 125, no. 5 (1996).

Isham, A. B. "The Story of a Gunshot Wound." In *Sketches of War History, 1861–1865: Papers Prepared for the Ohio Commandery of the Military Order of the Loyal Legion of the*

United States, 1890–1896. Edited by W. H. Chamberlin. Cincinnati: Robert Clarke Company, 1896.

Jackson, D. P. (ed.). *The Colonel's Diary: Journals Kept Before and During the Civil War by the Late Colonel Oscar L. Jackson of New Castle, Pennsylvania, Sometime Commander of the 63rd Regiment O.V.I.* Sharon, PA: David P. Jackson, 1922.

Johnson, C. *Battleground Adventures: The Stories of Dwellers on the Scenes of Conflict in Some of the Most Notable Battles of the Civil War.* Boston: Houghton Mifflin, 1915.

Johnson, R. U., and C. C. Buell (eds.). *Battles and Leaders of the Civil War.* 4 vols. New York: Century Company, 1884–88.

Jones, T. L. (ed.). *The Civil War Memoirs of Captain William J. Seymour: Reminiscences of a Louisiana Tiger.* Baton Rouge: Louisiana State University Press, 1991.

Jordan, Jr., W. B. "Gettysburg and the Seventeenth Maine." *Gettysburg Magazine* 8 (1993).

Jorgensen, J. "John Haley's Personal Recollection of the Battle of the Wheatfield." *Gettysburg Magazine* 27 (2002).

———. "Wofford Sweeps the Wheatfield." *Gettysburg Magazine* 22 (2000).

Judson, A. M. *History of the Eighty-Third Regiment Pennsylvania Volunteers.* Erie, PA: B. F. H. Lynn, 1865.

Jünger, E. "Total Mobilization." In *The Heidegger Controversy: A Critical Reader,* edited by R. Wolin, translated by J. Golb and R. Wolin. New York: Columbia University Press, 1991.

Keen, W. W. "Military Surgery in 1861 and in 1918." *Rehabilitation of the Wounded: Annals of the American Academy of Political and Social Science* 80 (1918).

Keller, C. B. "Pennsylvania's German-Americans, a Popular Myth, and the Importance of Perception." In *Damn Dutch: Pennsylvania Germans at Gettysburg,* edited by D. L. Valuska and C. B. Keller. Mechanicsburg, PA: Stackpole Books, 2004.

Kernek, C. B. "Civil War Surgery: Gettysburg, Summer of 1863." *Indiana Medicine* 84, no. 12 (Dec. 1991).

Kieffer, H. M. *The Recollections of a Drummer-Boy.* 6th ed. Boston: Ticknor and Co., 1889.

Kohl, L. F., and M. C. Richard (eds.). *Irish Green and Union Blue: The Civil War Letters of Peter Welsh, Color Sergeant, 28th Regiment Massachusetts Volunteers.* New York: Fordham University Press, 1986.

Kutz, M. "Fantasy, Reality, and Modes of Perception in Ludendorff's and Goebbels's Concepts of 'Total War.'" In *A World at Total War: Global Conflict and the Politics of Destruction, 1937–1945,* edited by R. Chickering, S. Förster, and B. Grenier. Cambridge, U.K.: Cambridge University Press, 2005.

Ladd, D. L., and A. J. Ladd (eds.). *The Bachelder Papers: Gettysburg in Their Own Words.* 3 vols. Dayton, OH: Morningside Press, 1994.

Lader, P. J. "The 7th New Jersey in the Gettysburg Campaign." *Gettysburg Magazine* 16 (1997).

———. "The Personal Journey of Pvt. David Ballinger, Company H, 12th New Jersey Volunteers." *Gettysburg Magazine* 24 (2001).

Laidley, T. T. S. "Breech-Loading Musket." *United States Service Magazine* 3 (1865).

Lamb, D. A. *A History of the United States Army Medical Museum, 1862–1917, Compiled From the Official Records.* Unpublished manuscript, 1917.

Laney, D. M. "Wasted Gallantry: Hood's Texas Brigade at Gettysburg." *Gettysburg Magazine* 16 (1997).

Lash, G. G. "'A Pathetic Story': The 141st Pennsylvania (Graham's Brigade) at Gettysburg." *Gettysburg Magazine* 14 (1996).

Lee, A. "Reminiscences of the Gettysburg Battle." *Lippincott's Magazine of Popular Literature and Science* 6 (1883).

Linderman, G. F. *Embattled Courage: The Experience of Combat in the American Civil War.* New York: Free Press, 1989.

Linn, J. B. "A Tourist at Gettysburg." *Civil War Times Illustrated* 29, no. 4 (Sept./Oct. 1990).

Livermore, T. L. *Days and Events, 1860–1866.* Boston: Houghton Mifflin, 1920.

Long, R. "The Confederate Prisoners of Gettysburg." *Gettysburg Magazine* 2 (1990).

———. "A Gettysburg Encounter." *Gettysburg Magazine* 7 (1992).

———. "A Surgeon's Handiwork." *Gettysburg Magazine* 12 (1995).

Longstreet, J. *From Manassas to Appomattox: Memoirs of the Civil War in America.* Philadelphia: J. B. Lippincott, 1896.

Ludendorff, E. *The Nation at War.* Translated by A. S. Rappoport. London: Hutchinson and Co., 1936.

Lynn, J. A. *Battle: A History of Combat and Culture.* Cambridge, MA: Westview, 2003.

MacDonald, W. A. "Gettysburg Holds Greatest Fourth." *New York Times,* July 5, 1938.

Manring, M. M., A. Hawk, J. H. Calhoun, and R. C. Andersen, "Treatment of War Wounds: A Historical Review." *Clinical Orthopaedics and Related Research* 467 (2009).

Marbaker, T. D. *History of the Eleventh New Jersey Volunteers From Its Organization to Appomattox, to Which Is Added Experiences of Prison Life and Sketches of Individual Members.* Trenton, NJ: MacCrellish and Quigley, 1898.

Marshall, S. L. A. *Men Against Fire: The Problem of Battle Command.* Norman: University of Oklahoma Press, 2000 [1947].

Martin, J. M., E. C. Strouss, R. G. Madge, R. I. Campbell, and M. C. Zahniser (eds.). *History of the Fifty-Seventh Regiment, Pennsylvania Veteran Volunteer Infantry.* Meadville, PA: McCoy and Calvin, 1904.

Martz, J. A. "It Was Not a Happy Time: What the Civilians of Gettysburg Saw and Heard During the Battle." *Gettysburg Magazine* 18 (1998).

Marvin, E. E. *The Fifth Regiment Connecticut Volunteers: A History Compiled From Diaries and Official Reports.* Hartford, CT: Wiley, Waterman, and Eaton, 1889.

McLean, W. "The Days of Terror in 1863." *Gettysburg Compiler,* July 1, 1908.

McWhiney, G., and P. D. Jamieson. *Attack and Die: Civil War Military Tactics and the Southern Heritage.* Tuscaloosa: University of Alabama Press, 1982.

Meinhard, R. W. "The First Minnesota at Gettysburg." *Gettysburg Magazine* 5 (1991).

Menke, W. S., and J. A. Shimrak (eds.). *The Civil War Notebook of Daniel Chisholm: A Chronicle of Daily Life in the Union Army, 1864–1865.* New York: Orion Books, 1989.

Miller, J. M. "Perrin's Brigade on July 1, 1863." *Gettysburg Magazine* 13 (1995).

Moore, F. (ed.). *The Civil War in Song and Story, 1860–1865.* New York: P. F. Collier, 1889.

Morgan, W. H. *Personal Reminiscences of the War of 1861–1865.* Lynchburg, VA: J. P. Bell Co., 1911.

Muffly, J. W. (ed.). *The Story of Our Regiment: A History of the 148th Pennsylvania Vols., Written by the Comrades.* Des Moines, IA: Kenyon Printing and Manufacturing Company, 1904.

Mulligan, T. P. "Death of a Secessionist Regiment: The Losses of the 1st Tennessee at Gettysburg." *Gettysburg Magazine* 40 (2009).

Murray, R. L. "The Artillery Duel in the Peach Orchard, July 2, 1863." *Gettysburg Magazine* 36 (2007).

Musgrove, R. W. *Autobiography of Captain Richard W. Musgrove.* 1921.

Musto, R. J. "The Treatment of the Wounded at Gettysburg: Jonathan Letterman: the Father of Modern Battlefield Medicine." *Gettysburg Magazine* 37 (2007).

Nash, E. A. *A History of the Forty-Fourth New York Regiment Volunteer Infantry in the Civil War, 1861–1865.* Chicago: R. R. Donnelley and Sons, 1911.

Neese, G. M. *Three Years in the Confederate Horse Artillery*. New York: Neale Publishing Company, 1911.

Nelson, A. H. *The Battles of Chancellorsville and Gettysburg*. Minneapolis: A. H. Nelson, 1899.

Nevins, A. (ed.). *A Diary of Battle: The Personal Journals of Colonel Charles S. Wainwright, 1861–1865*. New York: Da Capo Press, 1998.

New York Monuments Commission (ed.). *In Memoriam, Alexander Stewart Webb, 1835–1911*. Albany: J. B. Lyon, 1916.

New York State Monuments Commission (ed.). *Final Report on the Battlefield of Gettysburg*. 3 vols. Albany, NY: J. B. Lyon, 1900.

Nicholson, J. P. (ed.). *Pennsylvania at Gettysburg: Ceremonies at the Dedication of the Monuments Erected by the Commonwealth of Pennsylvania to Mark the Positions of the Pennsylvania Commands Engaged in the Battle*. 2 vols. Harrisburg, PA: E. K. Meyers, 1893.

Norton, O. W. *The Attack and Defense of Little Round Top, Gettysburg, July 2, 1863*. New York: Neale Publishing Company, 1913.

Nosworthy, B. *The Bloody Crucible of Courage: Fighting Methods and Combat Experience of the Civil War*. New York: Carroll and Graf, 2003.

———. "The Rifle Musket and Associated Tactics." *North and South* 7, no. 1 (2004).

———. *Roll Call to Destiny: The Soldier's Eye View of Civil War Battles*. New York: Carroll and Graf, 2008.

Oates, W. C. *The War Between the Union and the Confederacy and Its Lost Opportunities, with a History of the 15th Alabama Regiment and the Forty-Eight Battles in Which It Was Engaged*. New York and Washington, DC: Neale Publishing Company, 1905.

O'Brien, K. E. "'A Perfect Roar of Musketry': Candy's Brigade in the Fight for Culp's Hill." *Gettysburg Magazine* 9 (1993).

———. "'To Unflinchingly Face Danger and Death': Carr's Brigade Defends Emmitsburg Road." *Gettysburg Magazine* 12 (1995).

———. "'Hold Them with the Bayonet': De Trobriand's Brigade Defends the Wheatfield." *Gettysburg Magazine* 21 (1999).

Olds, F. A. "Brave Carolinian Who Fell at Gettysburg: How Colonel Henry King Burgwyn Lost His Life." *Southern Historical Society Papers* 36 (1908).

Oliver, J. B., E. F. Hicks, and B. B. Carr. *History of Company E, 20th N.C. Regiment, 1861-'65*. Goldsboro, NC: Nash Brothers, 1905.

Olney, W. "The Battle of Shiloh, with Some Personal Reminiscences." *Overland Monthly* 5 (1885).

Page, C. D. *History of the Fourteenth Regiment, Connecticut Volunteer Infantry*. Meriden, CT: Horton Printing Company, 1906.

Parker, J. L. *Henry Wilson's Regiment: The History of the Twenty-Second Massachusetts Infantry, the Second Company Sharpshooters, and the Third Light Battery, in the War of the Rebellion*. Boston: Regimental Association, 1887.

Patriot Daughters of Lancaster. *Hospital Scenes After the Battle of Gettysburg, July 1863*. Lancaster, PA: Daily Inquirer Steam Job Print, 1864.

Patterson, G. A. "The Death of Iverson's Brigade." *Gettysburg Magazine* 5 (1991).

Peltz, H. S. "Two Brass Buttons." *Gettysburg Compiler*, March 15, 1887.

Pfanz, H. *Gettysburg: Culp's Hill and Cemetery Hill*. Chapel Hill: University of North Carolina Press, 1993.

Pizarro, J., R. C. Silver, and J. Prause. "Physical and Mental Health Costs of Traumatic War Experiences Among Civil War Veterans." *Archives of General Psychiatry* 63 (2006).

Polley, J. B. *Hood's Texas Brigade: Its Marches, Its Battles, Its Achievements*. New York: Neale Publishing Company, 1910.

Preston, N. D. *History of the Tenth Regiment of Cavalry, New York State Volunteers: August, 1861, to August, 1865*. New York: D. Appleton and Co., 1892.

Pula, J. S. "The 26th Wisconsin Volunteer Infantry at Gettysburg." *Gettysburg Magazine* 23 (2000).

———. "The Fifth German Rifles at Gettysburg." *Gettysburg Magazine* 37 (2007).

———. (ed.). *The Memoirs of Wladimir Krzyżanowski*. San Francisco: R & E Research Associates, 1978.

Quinones, M. A. "Drug Abuse During the Civil War (1861–1865)." *International Journal of the Addictions* 10, no. 6 (1975).

Redwood, A. C. "The Confederate in the Field." In *The Photographic History of the Civil War*. 10 vols. New York: Review of Reviews Co., 1911.

Rollins, R. (ed.). *Pickett's Charge: Eyewitness Accounts at the Battle of Gettysburg*. Mechanicsburg, PA: Stackpole Books, 2005.

Rose, A. *American Rifle: A Biography*. New York: Delacorte Press, 2008.

———. "Marksmanship in 1775: Myth or Reality?" *American Rifleman*, July 2010.

Runge, W. H. (ed.). *Four Years in the Confederate Artillery: The Diary of Private Henry Robinson Berkeley*. Chapel Hill: University of North Carolina Press, 1961.

Sauers, R. A. (ed.). *Fighting Them Over: How the Veterans Remembered Gettysburg in the Pages of the National Tribune*. Baltimore: Butternut and Blue, 1998.

Sawyer, F. *A Military History of the 8th Regiment Ohio Vol. Inf'y: Its Battles, Marches, and Army Movements*. Cleveland: Fairbanks and Co., 1881.

Saxton, W. *A Regiment Remembered: The 157th New York Volunteers: From the Diary of Capt. William Saxton*. Cortland, NY: Cortland County Historical Society, 1996.

Schmidt, J. M., and G. R. Hasegawa (eds.). *Years of Change and Suffering: Modern Perspectives on Civil War Medicine*. Roseville, MN: Edinborough Press, 2009.

Scott, R. G. (ed.). *Fallen Leaves: The Civil War Letters of Major Henry Livermore Abbott*. Kent, OH: Kent State University Press, 1991.

Scribner, B. F. *How Soldiers Were Made, or, the War as I Saw It Under Buell, Rosecrans, Thomas, Grant and Sherman*. New Albany, IN: Donohoe and Henneberry, 1887.

Shotwell, M., and C. G. Samito. "An Irish-American at Gettysburg: Capt. James F. McGunnigle and the Ninth Massachusetts Volunteer Infantry." *Gettysburg Magazine* 21 (1999).

Shultz, D. "Benner's Hill: What Value? Andrews' Artillery Battalion and the Heights East of Town." *Gettysburg Magazine* 44 (2011).

Small, A. R. *The Road to Richmond: The Civil War Letters of Major Abner R. Small of the Sixteenth Maine Volunteers*. Edited by H. A. Small. New York: Fordham University Press, 2000.

Smith, J. D. *The History of the Nineteenth Regiment of Maine Volunteer Infantry, 1862–1865*. Minneapolis: Great Western Printing Co., 1909.

Smith, J. E. *A Famous Battery and Its Campaigns, 1861–'64*. Washington, DC: W. H. Lowdermilk and Co., 1892.

Smith, Jr., L. W. *For the Good of the Old North State: A Statistical Study of North Carolina and Army of Northern Virginia at the Battle of Gettysburg*. Society for the Preservation of the 26th Regiment North Carolina Troops, 2005.

Speier, H. "Ludendorff: The German Concept of Total War." In *Makers of Modern Strategy: Military Thought From Machiavelli to Hitler*, edited by E. M. Earle. New York: Atheneum, 1966.

Spisak, E. D. "The 62nd Pennsylvania Volunteer Infantry: A Forgotten Regiment of Distinction." *Gettysburg Magazine* 26 (2002).

Stahl, J. "Pvt. George Matthews of the 87th and 40th New York State Volunteers." *Gettysburg Magazine* 33 (2005).

———. "Pvt. John Wright of the 61st Ohio Infantry." *Gettysburg Magazine* 38 (2008).

Stanley, H. M. *The Autobiography of Sir Henry Morton Stanley*. New York: Houghton Mifflin, 1909.

Stearns, A. C. *Three Years with Company K*. Edited by A. A. Kent. Cranbury, NJ: Associated University Presses, 1976.

Stevens, C. M. *Berdan's United States Sharpshooters in the Army of the Potomac, 1861–1865*. St. Paul, MN: Price-McGill Company, 1892.

Stevens, G. T. *Three Years in the Sixth Corps: A Concise Narrative of Events in the Army of the Potomac, From 1861 to the Close of the Rebellion, April, 1865*. Albany, NY: S. R. Gray, 1866.

Stevens, H. S. *Souvenir of Excursion to Battlefields by the Society of the Fourteenth Connecticut Regiment and Reunion at Antietam, September 1891*. Washington, DC: Gibson, 1893.

Stevens, J. W. *Reminiscences of the Civil War: A Soldier in Hood's Texas Brigade, Army of Northern Virginia*. Hillsboro, TX: Hillsboro Mirror Print, 1902.

Stiles, R. *Four Years Under Marse Robert*. New York: Neale Publishing Co., 1910.

Stillwell, L. *The Story of a Common Soldier, or, Army Life in the Civil War, 1861–1865*. 2nd ed. Kansas City, MO: Franklin Hudson Publishing Co., 1920.

Storch, M., and B. Storch. " 'What a Deadly Trap We Were in': Archer's Brigade on July 1, 1863." *Gettysburg Magazine* 6 (1992).

Strachan, H. "On Total War and Modern War." *International History Review* 22, no. 2 (2000).

Survivors' Association. *History of the 118th Pennsylvania Volunteers (Corn Exchange Regiment), From Their First Engagement at Antietam to Appomattox*. Philadelphia: J. L. Smith, 1905.

Sword, W. "Capt. Mckee's Revolver and Capt. Sellers' Sword with Weed's Brigade on Little Round Top." *Gettysburg Magazine* 9 (1993).

———. "An Iron Brigade Captain's Revolver in the Fight on Mcpherson's Ridge." *Gettysburg Magazine* 7 (1992).

———. "Pye's Sword at the Rail Cut." *Gettysburg Magazine* 6 (1992).

———. "Roll of the Dice: Two 24th Michigan Officers Test Their Luck in the Gettysburg Campaign." *Gettysburg Magazine* 21 (1999).

———. "Union Sgt. Isaac W. Barnes: Company E, 125th New York Volunteer Infantry Describes in Vivid Detail the Fighting at Plum Run on July 2, and 'Pickett's Charge' on July 3." *Gettysburg Magazine* 29 (2003).

Taylor, R. *Destruction and Reconstruction: Personal Experiences of the Late War in the United States*. Edinburgh and London: William Blackwood and Sons, 1879.

Taylor, W. H. "Some Experiences of a Confederate Assistant Surgeon." *Transactions of the College of Physicians of Philadelphia* 28 (1906).

Tomasak, P. (ed.). *One Hundred Forty-Three Pennsylvania Volunteer Regiment: Avery Harris Civil War Journal*. Luzerne, PA: Luzerne National Bank, 2000.

———. "The 143rd Pennsylvania Volunteer Regiment in Hell's Firestorm on July 1 at Gettysburg." *Gettysburg Magazine* 38 (2008).

Tompkins, D. A., and A. S. Tompkins, *Company K, Fourteenth South Carolina Volunteers*. Charlotte, NC: Observer Printing and Publishing House, 1897.

Toombs, S. *New Jersey Troops in the Gettysburg Campaign, June 5 to July 31, 1863*. Orange, NJ: Evening Mail Publishing House, 1888.

Trinque, B. "The Rifle-Musket in the Civil War." *North and South* 11, no. 3 (2009).

Trowbridge, L. S., and F. E. Farnsworth (eds.). *Michigan at Gettysburg: Proceedings Incident to the Dedication of the Michigan Monuments Upon the Battlefield of Gettysburg, June 12th, 1889, Together with a Full Report of the Monument Commission*. Detroit: Winn & Hammond, 1889.

Underwood, G. C. *History of the Twenty-Sixth Regiment of the North Carolina Troops, in the Great War, 1861–'65*. Wilmington, NC: Broadfoot Publishing Company, 1999 [1901].

Urban, B. F. W. "Dreaming on the Conestoga." In "In Their Words: Dreaming on the Conestoga," edited by S. Felton. *Gettysburg Magazine* 37 (2007).

Vautier, J. D. *History of the 88th Pennsylvania Volunteers in the War for the Union, 1861–1865*. Philadelphia: J. B. Lippincott, 1894.

Wade, P. "Untold History Recited at a Meeting of the Regiment in Bridgeport, Conn." *Gettysburg Compiler*, September 22, 1896.

Wagner, A. L. *Organization and Tactics*. 2nd ed. Kansas City, MO: Hudson-Kimberly, 1897.

Wainwright, N. B. (ed.). *A Philadelphia Perspective: The Diary of Sidney George Fisher Covering the Years 1834–1871*. Philadelphia: Historical Society of Pennsylvania, 1967.

Walters, J. B. "General William T. Sherman and Total War." *Journal of Southern History* 14, no. 3 (1948).

———. *Merchant of Terror: General Sherman and Total War*. New York: Bobbs-Merrill Co., 1973.

The War of the Rebellion: A Compilation of the Official Records of the Union and Confederate Armies. 70 vols. in 128 parts. Washington, DC: Government Printing Office, 1880–1901.

Ward, D. A. " 'Sedgwick's Foot Cavalry': The March of the Sixth Corps to Gettysburg." *Gettysburg Magazine* 22 (2000).

Ward, G. W. *History of the Second Pennsylvania Veteran Heavy Artillery (112th Regiment Pennsylvania Volunteers), from 1861 to 1866, including the Provisional Second Penn'a Heavy Artillery*. 2nd ed. Philadelphia: Geo. W. Ward, 1904.

Ward, W. C. "Incidents and Personal Experiences on the Battlefield at Gettysburg." *Confederate Veteran* 8, no. 8 (August 1900).

Warren, H. N. *The Declaration of Independence and War History: Bull Run to the Appomattox*. Buffalo, NY: Courier Co., 1894.

Washburn, G. H. *A Complete Military History and Record of the 108th Regiment N.Y. Vols. From 1862 to 1864, Together with Roster, Letters, Rebel Oaths of Allegiance, Rebel Passes, Reminiscences, Life Sketches, Photographs, Etc., Etc*. Rochester, NY: No publisher, 1894.

Watkins, S. R. *"Co. Aytch," Maury Grays, First Tennessee Regiment; or, a Side Show of the Big Show*. Nashville: Cumberland Presbyterian Publishing House, 1882.

Weigley, R. F. *Towards an American Army: Military Thought From Washington to Marshall*. New York: Columbia University Press, 1962.

Wert, J. D. *Gettysburg: Day Three*. New York: Simon and Schuster, 2001.

Wert, J. H. *A Complete Hand-Book of the Monuments and Indications and Guide to the Positions on the Gettysburg Battlefield*. Harrisburg, PA: R. M. Sturgeon, 1886.

Weygant, C. H. *History of the One Hundred and Twenty-Fourth Regiment, N.Y.S.V.* Newburgh, NY: Journal Printing House, 1877.

Wheeler, R. *Witness to Gettysburg: Inside the Battle That Changed the Course of the Civil War*. Mechanicsburg, PA: Stackpole Books, 2006.

White, D. "Born in the USA: A New World of War." *History Today* 60, no. 6 (June 2010).

Wing, S. *The Soldier's Story: A Personal Narrative of the Life, Army Experiences, and Marvelous Sufferings Since the War of Samuel B. Wing.* Phillips, ME: Phonograph Steam Book and Job Printing, 1898.

Winschel, T. J. "The Colors Are Shrowded in Mystery." *Gettysburg Magazine* 6 (1992).

———. "The Gettysburg Diary of Lieutenant William Peel." *Gettysburg Magazine* 9 (1993).

———. "Heavy Was Their Loss: Joe Davis's Brigade at Gettysburg." *Gettysburg Magazine* 2 (1990).

———. "Posey's Brigade at Gettysburg." *Gettysburg Magazine* 5 (1991).

Woodward, E. M. *Our Campaigns; or, the Marches, Bivouacs, Battles, Incidents of Camp Life and History of Our Regiment During Its Three Years Term of Service.* Philadelphia: John E. Potter, 1865.

Wyckoff, M. "Kershaw's Brigade at Gettysburg." *Gettysburg Magazine* 5 (1991).

Yee, G. "Sharpshooting at Gettysburg." *Gettysburg Magazine* 39 (2008).

Young, A. *The Women and the Crisis: Women of the North in the Civil War.* New York: McDowell, Obolensky, 1959.

IWO JIMA

Alexander, J. H. *Closing In: Marines in the Seizure of Iwo Jima.* Washington, DC: Marine Corps Historical Center, 1994.

———. *Storm Landings: Epic Amphibious Battles in the Central Pacific.* Annapolis, MD: Naval Institute Press, 1997.

Allen, R. E. *The First Battalion of the 28th Marines on Iwo Jima: A Day-by-Day History From Personal Accounts and Official Reports, with Complete Muster Rolls.* Jefferson, NC: McFarland & Co., 1999.

Anon. "Roebling's 'Alligator' for Florida Rescues." *Life,* October 4, 1937.

Averill, G. P. *Mustang: A Combat Marine.* Novato, CA: Presidio Press, 1987.

Bailey, A. W. *Alligators, Buffaloes, and Bushmasters: The History of the Development of the LVT Through World War II.* Washington, DC: History and Museums Division, Headquarters, U.S. Marine Corps, 1986.

Ballendorf, D. A., and M. L. Bartlett. *Pete Ellis: An Amphibious Warfare Prophet, 1880–1923.* Annapolis, MD: Naval Institute Press, 1997.

Bartlett, M. L. (ed.). *Assault From the Sea: Essays on the History of Amphibious Warfare.* Annapolis, MD: Naval Institute Press, 1983.

Bartley, W. S. *Iwo Jima: Amphibious Epic.* Historical Section, Division of Public Information Headquarters, U.S. Marine Corps, 1954.

Bergerud, E. "No Quarter: The Pacific Battlefield." *Historically Speaking* 3, no. 5 (2002).

Berry, H. (ed.). *Semper Fi, Mac: Living Memories of the U.S. Marines in World War II.* New York: Arbor House, 1982.

Boal, M. A. "Field Expedient Armor Modifications to U.S. Armored Vehicles." Unpublished MA thesis. U.S. Army Command and General Staff College, Fort Leavenworth, Kansas, 2006.

Brown, T. M. *Battle Wounds of Iwo Jima.* New York: Vantage Press, 2002.

Burrell, R. S. "Breaking the Cycle of Iwo Jima Mythology: A Strategic Study of Operation Detachment." *Journal of Military History* 68, no. 4 (2004).

———. (ed.). *Crucibles: Selected Readings in U.S. Marine Corps History.* 2nd ed. Bel Air, MD: Academx Publishing Services, 2004.

Cameron, C. M. *American Samurai: Myth, Imagination, and the Conduct of Battle in the First Marine Division, 1941–1951.* Cambridge, U.K.: Cambridge University Press, 1994.

Carter, W. R. *Beans, Bullets, and Black Oil: The Story of Fleet Logistics Afloat in the Pacific During World War II.* Newport, RI: Naval War College Press, 1998 [1953].

Caruso, P. F. *Nightmare on Iwo.* Annapolis, MD: Naval Institute Press, 2001.

Chickering, R., S. Förster, and B. Greiner (eds.). *A World at Total War: Global Conflict and the Politics of Destruction, 1937–1945.* Cambridge, U.K.: Cambridge University Press, 2005.

Clifford, K. J. *Progress and Purpose: A Developmental History of the United States Marine Corps, 1900–1970.* Washington, DC: History and Museums Division Headquarters, United States Marine Corps, 1973.

Cosmas, G. A., and J. Shulimson. "The Culebra Maneuver and the Formation of the U.S. Marine Corps' Advance Base Force, 1913–14." In *Assault From the Sea: Essays on the History of Amphibious Warfare,* edited by M. L. Bartlett. Annapolis, MD: Naval Institute Press, 1983.

Crowder, R. *Iwo Jima Corpsman!: The Bloodiest Battle of the Marine Corps, Written by a Navy Corpsman Attached to the Third Marine Division, 1945.* Tuscaloosa, AL: SEVGO Press, 1988.

Daugherty III, L. J. *Fighting Techniques of a Japanese Infantryman, 1941–1945: Training, Techniques, and Weapons.* St. Paul, MN: MBI Publishing Co., 2002.

———. *Fighting Techniques of a U.S. Marine, 1941–1945: Training, Techniques, and Weapons.* Osceola, WI: MBI Publishing Co., 2000.

Davenport, D. *D-Plus Forever.* New York: Rivercross Publishing, 1993.

Denfield, D. C. *Japanese World War II Fortifications and Other Military Structures in the Central Pacific.* Edited by S. Russell. 3rd ed. Saipan: Northern Mariana Islands Division of Historic Preservation, 2002.

Dower, J. *War Without Mercy: Race and Power in the Pacific War.* New York: Pantheon Books, 1986.

Drea, E. J. *In the Service of the Emperor: Essays on the Imperial Japanese Army.* Lincoln: University of Nebraska, 1998.

———. *Japan's Imperial Army: Its Rise and Fall, 1853–1945.* Lincoln: University of Nebraska, 2009.

———. "Nomonhan: Japanese-Soviet Tactical Combat, 1939." Leavenworth Papers No. 2, Combat Studies Institute, U.S. Army Command and General Staff College, Fort Leavenworth, Kansas, January 1981.

Drez, R. J. (ed.). *Twenty-Five Yards of War: The Extraordinary Courage of Ordinary Men in World War II.* New York: Hyperion, 2001.

Dyer, G. C. *The Amphibians Came to Conquer: The Story of Admiral Richmond Kelly Turner.* 2 vols. Washington, DC: U.S. Government Printing Office, 1972.

Eldridge, R. E., and C. W. Tatum (eds.). *Fighting Spirit: The Memoirs of Major Yoshitaka Horie and the Battle of Iwo Jima.* Annapolis, MD: Naval Institute Press, 2011.

Ellis, E. H. "Advanced Base Operations in Micronesia." Report 712J, Intelligence Section, Division of Operations and Training, U.S. Marine Corps, 1921.

Faller, A. "War Memories Still Fresh." *Effingham Daily News,* March 27, 2009.

Ford, D. " 'The Best Equipped Army in Asia?': U.S. Military Intelligence and the Imperial Japanese Army Before the Pacific War, 1919–41." *International Journal of Intelligence and CounterIntelligence* 21, no. 1 (2007).

———. "Dismantling the 'Lesser Men' and 'Supermen' Myths: U.S. Intelligence on the Imperial Japanese Army After the Fall of the Philippines, Winter 1942 to Spring 1943." *International Journal of Intelligence and CounterIntelligence* 24, no. 4 (2009).

———. "U.S. Assessments of Japanese Ground Warfare Tactics and the Army's Campaigns in the Pacific Theatres, 1943–1945: Lessons Learned and Methods Applied." *War in History* 16, no. 3 (2009).

———. "U.S. Perceptions of Military Culture and the Japanese Army's Performance During the Pacific War." *War and Society* 29, no. 1 (2010).

Gallant, T. G. *The Friendly Dead.* Garden City, NY: Doubleday & Co., 1964.

———. *On Valor's Side.* Garden City, NY: Doubleday & Co., 1963.

Gatchel, T. L. *At the Water's Edge: Defending Against the Modern Amphibious Assault.* Annapolis, MD: Naval Institute Press, 1996.

Goldman, S. D. *Nomonhan 1939: The Red Army's Victory That Shaped World War II.* Annapolis, MD: Naval Institute Press, 2012.

Gordon, J. W. "Thomas Holcomb." In *Commandants of the Marine Corps,* edited by A. R. Millett and J. Shulimson. Annapolis, MD: Naval Institute Press, 2004.

Goudreau, A. A. "Nursing at an Advance Naval Base Hospital During the Iwo Jima Campaign." *American Journal of Nursing* 45, no. 11 (1945).

Grenville, J. A. S., and G. B. Young. *Politics, Strategy, and American Diplomacy: Studies in Foreign Policy, 1873–1917.* New Haven: Yale University Press, 1966.

Hamner, C. H. *Enduring Battle: American Soldiers in Three Wars, 1776–1945.* Lawrence: Kansas University Press, 2011.

Harrison, S. "Skull Trophies of the Pacific War: Transgressive Objects of Remembrance." *Journal of the Royal Anthropological Institute* 12 (2006).

Hayashi, S. *Kogun: The Japanese Army in the Pacific War.* Edited by A. D. Coox. Quantico, VA: Marine Corps Association, 1959 [1951].

Haynes, F., and J. A. Warren, *The Lions of Iwo Jima.* New York: Henry Holt and Co., 2008.

Heitmann, J. A. "The Man Who Won the War: Andrew Jackson Higgins." *Louisiana History* 34, no. 1 (1993).

Henri, R., J. G. Lucas, W. Keyes Breech, D. K. Dempsey, and A. M. Josephy, Jr. *The U.S. Marines on Iwo Jima: By Five Official Marine Combat Writers.* Washington, DC: Infantry Journal, 1945.

Herwig, H. H., and D. F. Trask. "Naval Operations Plans Between Germany and the U.S.A., 1898–1913." In *The War Plans of the Great Powers, 1880–1914,* edited by P. Kennedy. Boston: Allen & Unwin, 1985.

Hess, E. J. *The Union Soldier in Battle: Enduring the Ordeal of Combat.* Lawrence: University Press of Kansas, 1997.

Hoffman, J. T. "The Legacy and Lessons of Iwo Jima." *Marine Corps Gazette* 79, no. 2 (1995).

Hough, F. O., V. E. Ludwig, and H. I. Shaw, Jr. *Pearl Harbor to Guadalcanal: History of U.S. Marine Corps Operations in World War II.* Historical Branch, G-3 Division, U.S. Marine Corps, Washington, DC, 1958.

Hughes, M., and G. Johnson (eds.). *Fanaticism and Conflict in the Modern Age.* New York and London: Frank Cass, 2005.

Huie, W. B. *From Omaha to Okinawa: The Story of the Seabees.* New York: E. P. Dutton & Co., 1945.

Isely, J. A., and P. A. Crowl, *The U.S. Marines and Amphibious War: Its Theory, and Its Practice in the Pacific.* Princeton, NJ: Princeton University Press, 1951.

Jones, Jr., W. D. *Gyrene: The World War II United States Marine.* Shippensburg, PA: White Mane Books, 1998.

Jorgenson, J. "John Haley's Personal Recollection of the Battle of the Wheatfield." *Gettysburg Magazine* 27 (2002).

Josephy, Jr., A. M. *The Long and the Short and the Tall.* Short Hills, NJ: Burford Books, 2000 [1946].

Kelly, A. L. *Battlefire! Combat Stories From World War II*. Lexington: University Press of Kentucky, 1997.

Kennedy, A. D. *The Military Side of Japanese Life*. London, 1924.

Kennedy, P. (ed.). *The War Plans of the Great Powers, 1880–1914*. Boston: Allen & Unwin, 1985.

Kessler, L. S., and E. B. Bart (eds.). *Never in Doubt: Remembering Iwo Jima*. Annapolis, MD: Naval Institute Press, 1999.

Kuzuhara, K. "Operations on Iwo Jima: Utility of Combat Lessons Learned." Paper presented to USA-Japanese Ground Self-Defense Force Military History Exchange, U.S. Army Command and General Staff College, Fort Leavenworth, September 1990.

Laurie, C. D. "The Ultimate Dilemma of Psychological Warfare in the Pacific: Enemies Who Don't Surrender, and GIs Who Don't Take Prisoners." *War and Society* 14, no. 1 (1996).

Leader, R. A. "The Killing Fields of Sulfur Island." *Notre Dame Magazine,* Winter 2002–03.

Levin, D. *From the Battlefield: Dispatches of a World War II Marine*. Annapolis, MD: Naval Institute Press, 1995.

Linderman, G. F. *The World Within War: America's Combat Experience in World War II*. New York: Free Press, 1997.

Lofgren, J. F., (ed.). "Diary of First Lieutenant Sugihara Kinryu: Iwo Jima, January–February 1945." *Journal of Military History* 59, no. 1 (1995).

Lorelli, J. A. *To Foreign Shores: U.S. Amphibious Operations in World War II*. Annapolis, MD: Naval Institute Press, 1995.

Lowe, R. "The Assault on Iwo Jima: Memories." "Company C, 1st Battalion, 23rd Marines" website. Available at www.c123rd.com/our-wwii-marines/lowe-richard/memories, accessed September 14, 2014.

Lucas, J. F., with D. K. Drum. *Indestructible: The Unforgettable Story of a Marine Hero at the Battle of Iwo Jima*. New York: Da Capo Press, 2006.

Maiden, R. F. *Return to Iwo Jima + 50*. Xlibris, 2000.

Marquand, J. P. "Iwo Jima Before H-hour." *Harper's Magazine,* May 1945.

Matthews, A. R. *The Assault*. New York: Simon and Schuster, 1947.

McConnell, W. W. "How One Squad Fared on Iwo Jima." *Marine Corps Gazette* 93, no. 2 (Feb. 2009). Online version.

McKinney, L. L. *Portable Flame Thrower Operations in World War II*. Washington, DC: Historical Office, Chemical Corps, 1949.

McLaughlin, Jr., H. N., and R. C. Miller. *From the Volcano to the Gorge: Getting the Job Done on Iwo Jima*. Kindle edition. Standish, ME: Tower Publishing, 2010.

McMillan, G. *The Old Breed: A History of the First Marine Division in World War II*. Washington, DC: Infantry Journal Press, 1949.

Millett, A. R. *Semper Fidelis: The History of the United States Marine Corps*. New York: Free Press, 1991.

Millett, A. R., and W. Murray (eds.). *Military Effectiveness: The Second World War*. Cambridge, U.K.: Cambridge University Press, 2010.

Millett, A. R., and J. Shulimson (eds.). *Commandants of the Marine Corps*. Annapolis, MD: Naval Institute Press, 2004.

Mountcastle, J. W. "From Bayou to Beachhead: The Marines and Mr. Higgins." *Military Review* 60, no. 3 (1980).

Moy, T. *War Machines: Transforming Technologies in the U.S. Military, 1920–1940*. College Station: Texas A&M University Press, 2001.

Murray, W., and A. R. Millett (eds.). *Military Innovation in the Interwar Period*. Cambridge, U.K.: Cambridge University Press, 1996.

Nations, G. W. "Iwo Jima—One Man Remembers." Available at www.iwojima-onemanremembers .com/Iwo_Jima-One_Man_Remembers.htm, accessed September 16, 2015.

Neiman, R. M., and K. W. Estes. *Tanks on the Beaches: A Marine Tanker in the Pacific War*. College Station: Texas A&M University Press, 2003.

Norton, B. N., and L. Maffioli. *Grown Gray in War: The Len Maffioli Story*. Annapolis, MD: Naval Institute Press, 1997.

O'Donnell, P. K. *Into the Rising Sun: In Their Own Words, World War II's Pacific Veterans Reveal the Heart of Combat*. New York: Free Press, 2002.

O'Sheel, P., and G. Cook (eds.). *Semper Fidelis: The U.S. Marines in the Pacific, 1942–1945*. New York: William Sloane Associates, 1947.

Price, N., and R. Knecht. "Peleliu 1944: The Archaeology of a South Pacific D-Day." *Journal of Conflict Archaeology* 7, no. 1 (2012).

Renzi, W. A., and M. D. Roehrs. *Never Look Back: A History of World War II in the Pacific*. Armonk, NY: M. E. Sharpe, 1991.

Report by Intelligence Staffs of CINCPAC-CINCPOA, Fleet Marine Force, V Amphibious Corps, 3rd, 4th, and 5th Marine Divisions. *Defense Installations on Iwo Jima*. Bulletin 136–45, June 10, 1945.

Report by Joint Intelligence Center, Pacific Ocean Area. "Iwo Jima Operation, February–March 1945." Map NH-104136, March 1945.

Roan, R. W. "Roebling's Amphibian: The Origin of the Assault Amphibian." Command and Staff College Education Center, Marine Corps Development and Education Command, Quantico, VA, 1987.

Rodriguez, A. W. "The Battle for Iwo Jima." "Company C, 1st Battalion, 23rd Marines" website. Available at www.c123rd.com/our-wwii-marines/rodriguez-arthur-w-rod/the -battle-for-iwo-jima, accessed September 14, 2014.

Rottman, G. L., and P. Dennis. *U.S. World War II Amphibious Tactics: Army and Marine Corps, Pacific Theater*. New York: Osprey Publishing, 2004.

Rottman, G. L., and I. Palmer. *Japanese Pacific Island Defenses, 1941–45*. Oxford, U.K.: Osprey Publishing, 2003.

Rowe, G. "Memories." "Company C, 1st Battalion, 23rd Marines" website. Available at www .c123rd.com/our-wwii-marines/rowe-guy/memories, accessed September 14, 2014.

Sauers, K. A. (ed.) *Fighting Them Over: How the Veterans Remembered Gettysburg in the Pages of the National Tribune*. Baltimore: Butternut and Blue, 1998.

Seebohm, H. "On the Birds of the Volcano Islands." *The Ibis* 3, no. 10 (1891).

Sherrod, R. *On to Westward: War in the Central Pacific*. New York: Duell, Sloan, and Pearce, 1945.

Shiveley, J. C. *The Last Lieutenant: A Foxhole View of the Epic Battle for Iwo Jima*. Bloomington and Indianapolis: Indiana University Press, 2006.

Showalter, D. "War to the Knife: The U.S. in the Pacific, 1941–1945." Address to the National Institute for Defense Studies, Tenth Forum, "The Pacific War as Total War," 2011.

Shulimson, J., and G. A. Cosmas. "Teddy Roosevelt and the Corps' Sea-Going Mission." In *Crucibles: Selected Readings in U.S. Marine Corps History*, edited by R. S. Burrell. 2nd ed. Bel Air, MD: Academx Publishing Services, 2004.

Simpson, R. W. "Iwo Jima: A Surgeon's Story." *Leatherneck*, February 1990. Online version.

Smith, H. M. *The Development of Amphibious Tactics in the U.S. Navy*. History and Museums Division Headquarters, U.S. Marine Corps, Washington, DC, 1992.

Smith, L. (ed.). *Iwo Jima: World War II Veterans Remember the Greatest Battle of the Pacific.* New York: W. W. Norton & Co., 2008.

Smith, S. E. (ed.). *The United States Marine Corps in World War II: The One-Volume History, From Wake to Tsingtao—by the Men Who Fought in the Pacific, and by Distinguished Marine Experts, Authors, and Newspapermen.* New York: Random House, 1969.

Stone, A. R. *A Marine Remembers Iwo Jima: Dog Company, 2nd Battalion, 27th Marines, Fifth Marine Division.* Austin, TX: Eakin Press, 2000.

Stouffer, R. A., A. A. Lumsdaine, M. H. Lumsdaine, R. M. Williams, Jr., M. B. Smith, I. L. Janis, S. A. Star, and L. S. Cottrell, Jr. (eds.). *The American Soldier: Studies in Social Psychology in World War II.* 4 vols. Princeton, NJ: Princeton University Press, 1949–50.

Straus, U. *The Anguish of Surrender: Japanese POWs of World War II.* Seattle: University of Washington Press, 2003.

Thompson, P. W., H. Doud, J. Scofield, and M. A. Hill (eds.). *How the Jap Army Fights.* New York and London: Penguin Books, 1942.

Thurman, J. R. *We Were in the First Waves of Steel Amtracs Who Landed on Iwo Jima.* Kindle edition. Bloomington, IN: AuthorHouse, 2009.

Torok, T. *Stepping Stones Across the Pacific: A Collection of Short Stories from the Pacific War.* CreateSpace, 1999; no pub., 2011 edition.

Toyn, G. W. *The Quiet Hero: The Untold Medal of Honor Story of George E. Wahlen at the Battle for Iwo Jima.* Clearfield, UT: American Legacy Media, 2006.

Tsuyoshi, H. Review of "Nomonhan: Japan Against Russia, 1939, by Alvin D. Coox." *Journal of Japanese Studies* 13, no. 2 (1987).

Turk, R. W. "The United States Navy and the 'Taking' of Panama, 1901–03." *Military Affairs* 38, no. 3 (1974).

Vedder, J. S. *Surgeon on Iwo: Up Front with the 27th Marines.* Novato, CA: Presidio Press, 1984.

Walker, M. F., and B. White. *Preparing for the Rain on Iwo Jima Isle: The True Story of the Battle of Iwo Jima Survivor, Marion Frank Walker, Corporal, United States Marine Corps.* Kindle edition. Bloomington, IN: AuthorHouse, 2009.

Weingartner, J. J. "Trophies of War: U.S. Troops and the Mutilation of Japanese War Dead, 1941–1945." *Pacific Historical Review* 61, no. 1 (1992).

Wheeler, K. "The Story of a Man's Face." *Life,* December 8, 1961.

———. *We Are the Wounded.* New York: E. P. Dutton & Co., 1945.

Wheeler, R. *Iwo.* New York: Lippincott & Crowell, 1980.

Willie, C. E. *African American Voices from Iwo Jima.* Jefferson, NC: McFarland & Co., 2010.

Yaffe, B. A. *Fragments of War: A Marine's Personal Journey.* Annapolis, MD: Naval Institute Press, 1999.

Video

Iwo Jima: Red Blood, Black Sand. Spectrum Films, 1995.

Iwo Jima—36 Days of Hell. Timeless Media Group Production, 2006.

Transcripts

Interview with Brigadier General W. W. Buchanan, by B. M. Frank, June 11 and 16, 1969.

Interview with General R. E. Hogaboom, by B. M. Frank, April 1–3 and 8, 1970, no. 813.

Interview with Brigadier General F. Karch, by J. Ringler, January 15, 1972, no. 1072.

Interview with Brigadier General W. W. Rogers, by L. E. Tatem, June 15, 22, and 24, 1969, no. 740.

Interview with Lieut. General T. Wornham, by B. M. Frank, February 23, 1967 and April 2, 1968, no. 717.

All transcripts available at the Marine Corps Oral History Program, Columbia University Oral History Research Office (ORHO), Columbia University, New York City.

Index

ABOUT THE AUTHOR

Alexander Rose is the author of *Washington's Spies: The Story of America's First Spy Ring*, upon which the AMC drama series *Turn* is based, as well as *American Rifle: A Biography*.

www.alexrose.com
www.facebook.com/Alex.Rose.Writer

About the Type

This book was set in Garamond, a typeface originally designed by the Parisian type cutter Claude Garamond (c. 1500–61). This version of Garamond was modeled on a 1592 specimen sheet from the Egenolff-Berner foundry, which was produced from types assumed to have been brought to Frankfurt by the punch cutter Jacques Sabon (c. 1520–80).

Claude Garamond's distinguished romans and italics first appeared in *Opera Ciceronis* in 1543–44. The Garamond types are clear, open, and elegant.